ROYAL FEUD

Michael Thornton was born in 1941 at Pinkneys Green, near Maidenhead in Berkshire, the son of an English bomb disposal officer and a Welsh mother, at whose family home at Denbigh, in the Vale of Clwyd, he spent his early childhood. He studied modern history at King's College, London University, and made his publishing debut at nineteen when he joined Sir John Betjeman, Sir Compton Mackenzie and others as the youngest contributor to the book, *Gilbert Harding by his Friends*. At twenty-three he became film and drama critic of the *Sunday Express*, writing many memorable features in the 1970s, including revealing profiles of Queen Elizabeth the Queen Mother, the Duchess of Windsor, John Profumo and Margaret Thatcher. His international bestseller, *Jessie Matthews*, a biography of the great British musical star, was described by Sir John Gielgud as 'one of the most vivid and absorbing theatre books ever written'. In 1982 his moving series for the *Daily Express* on Ingrid Bergman's long battle against cancer was widely praised within the medical profession for its accuracy and insight. He lives on the Mediterranean island of Menorca, where he is currently studying Catalan.

Also by Michael Thornton
JESSIE MATTHEWS

Michael Thornton

ROYAL FEUD
The Queen Mother and the Duchess of Windsor

Pan Books London and Sydney

First published in Great Britain 1985 by Michael Joseph Ltd
This edition published 1986 by Pan Books Ltd,
Cavaye Place, London SW 10 9PG
9 8 7 6 5 4 3 2 1
© Michael Thornton 1985
ISBN 0 330 29505 5
Printed and bound in Great Britain by
Richard Clay (The Chaucer Press) Ltd, Bungay, Suffolk

To my sister
JEAN THORNTON WHEELER
who helped in this as in all things
with my love

CONTENTS

LIST OF ILLUSTRATIONS

THE BRITISH ROYAL FAMILY SINCE QUEEN VICTORIA

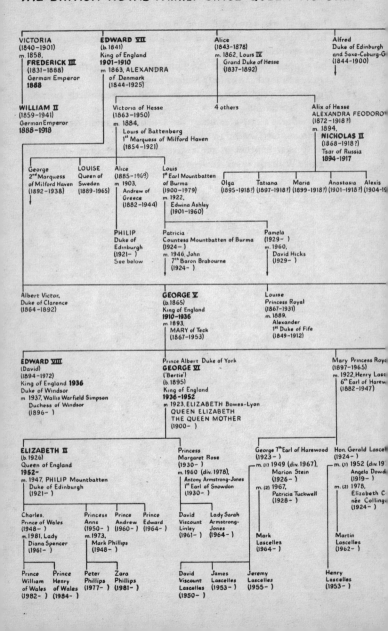

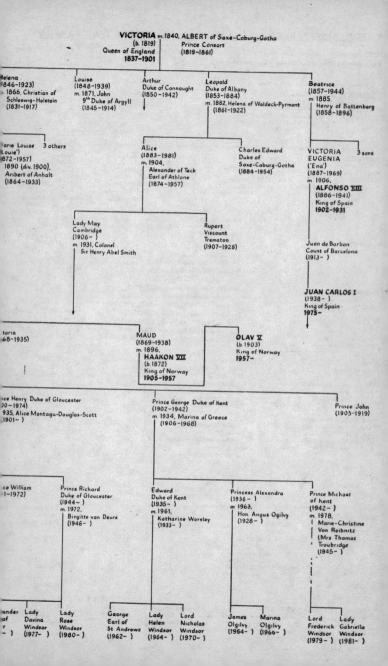

VICTORIA m.1840, **ALBERT** of Saxe-Coburg-Gotha
(b. 1819)   Prince Consort
Queen of England   (1819-1861)
1837-1901

Helena   Louise   Arthur   Leopold   Beatrice
(1846-1923)   (1848-1939)   Duke of Connaught   Duke of Albany   (1857-1944)
m. 1866, Christian of m. 1871, John   (1850-1942)   (1853-1884)   m 1885,
Schleswig-Holstein   9th Duke of Argyll   m 1882, Helena of Waldeck-Pyrmont   Henry of Battenberg
(1831-1917)   (1845-1914)   (1861-1922)   (1858-1896)

Marie Louise   3 others   Alice   Charles Edward   VICTORIA   3 sons
('Louie')   (1883-1981)   Duke of   EUGENIA
(1872-1957)   m. 1904,   Saxe-Coburg-Gotha   ('Ena')
1890 (div. 1900),   Alexander of Teck   (1884-1954)   (1887-1969)
Aribert of Anhalt   Earl of Athlone   m 1906,
(1864-1933)   (1874-1957)   **ALFONSO XIII**
                                                                                        (1886-1941)
                                                                                        King of Spain
                                                                                        1902-1931

                      Lady May   Rupert   Juan de Borbon
                      Cambridge   Viscount   Count of Barcelona
                      (1906-)   Trematon   (1913-)
                      m 1931, Colonel   (1907-1928)
                      Sir Henry Abel Smith
                                                                                         JUAN CARLOS I
                                                                                         (1938-)
                                                                                         King of Spain
                                                                                         1975-

...toria   MAUD   OLAV V
(...68-1935)   (1869-1938)   (b. 1903)
                      m. 1896,   King of Norway
                      HAAKON VII   **1957-**
                      (b. 1872)
                      King of Norway
                      1905-1957

...ce Henry Duke of Gloucester   Prince George Duke of Kent   Prince John
(...0-1974)   (1902-1942)   (1905-1919)
...935, Alice Montagu-Douglas-Scott m 1934, Marina of Greece
(...1901-)   (1906-1968)

...ce William   Prince Richard   Edward   Princess Alexandra   Prince Michael
(...1-1972)   Duke of Gloucester   Duke of Kent   (1936-)   of Kent
                 (1944-)   (1935-)   m 1963,   (1942-)
                 m. 1972,   m. 1961,   Hon. Angus Ogilvy   m 1978,
                 Birgitte van Deurs   Katharine Worsley   (1928-)   Marie-Christine
                 (1946-)   (1933-)   Von Reibnitz
                                                                                       (Mrs Thomas
                                                                                       Troubridge
                                                                                       (1945-)

...ander   Lady   Lady   George   Lady   Lord   James   Marina   Lord   Lady
of   Davina   Rose   Earl of   Helen   Nicholas   Olgilvy   Olgilvy   Frederick   Gabriella
...)   Windsor   Windsor   St Andrews   Windsor   Windsor   (1964-)   (1966-)   Windsor   Windsor
           (1977-)   (1980-)   (1962-)   (1964-)   (1970-)   (1979-)   (1981-)

MORGANATIC MARRIAGE IN THE BRITISH ROYAL FAMILY

MM denotes a morganatic marriage with the wife holding rank and status unequal to that of her husband

*m denotes a secret, unconstitutional or unapproved marriage

==== denotes illegitimate children

GEORGE III (b.1738) King of England **1760-1820**
*m (1) 1759, Hannah Lightfoot (b.1730) — 3 children?
m.(2) 1761, CHARLOTTE of Mecklenburg-Strelitz (1744-1818)

Edward Duke of York (1739-1767)

GEORGE IV (b.1762) King of England **1820-1830**
*m (1) 1785, Maria Fitzherbert (1756-1837)
m.(2) 1795, CAROLINE of Brunswick (1768-1821)

Frederick Duke of York (1763-1827) m.1790, Frederica of Prussia (1767-1840)

WILLIAM IV (b.1765) King of England **1830-1837** m.1818, ADELAIDE of Saxe-Meiningen (1792-1849)

Edward Duke of Kent (1767-1820)
*m (1) ? Mlle. Julie de St. Laurent sons?
m.(2) 1818 Victoria of Saxe Coburg-Saalfeld (1786-1861)

Charlotte (1796-1817)

by Dorothea Bland Mrs Jordan (1761-1816)

Charlotte (b. and d.1819)

Elizabeth (1820-1821)

==== George FitzClarence 1st Earl of Munster (1794-1842)
==== Lord Henry FitzClarence (1795-1817)
==== Lady Sophia FitzClarence (1796-1837)
==== Lady Mary FitzClarence (1798-1864)
==== Lord Frederick FitzClarence (1799-1854)
==== Lady Elizabeth FitzClarence (1801-1856)
==== Lord Adolphus FitzClarence (1802-1856)
==== Lady Augusta FitzClarence (1803-1858)
==== Lord Augustus FitzClarence (1805-1854)
==== Lady Amelia FitzClarence (1807-1858)

Alexander Prince of Hesse (1823-1888) **MM** 1851, *Julia*, Countess of Hauke created Princess of Battenberg (1825-1895)

Marie of Hesse (MARIA FEODOROVNA) (1824-1880) m. **ALEXANDER II** (b.1818) Tsar of Russia **1855-1881**

Charles of Hesse (1809-1877) m. Elizabeth of Prussia (1815-1855)

VICTORIA (b.1819) Queen of England **1837-1901** m.1840, ALBERT of Saxe-Coburg-Gotha Prince Consort (1819-1861)

Louis. Prince of Battenberg 1st Marquess of Milford Haven (1854-1921) m 1884, Victoria of Hesse (1863-1950)

Grand Duke Vladimir (1847-1909) m. Marie of Mecklenburg-Schwerin (1854-1920)

Louis IV m.1862, Alice (1843-1878)
Grand Duke of Hesse (1837-1892)

Grand Duke Andrew (1879-1956) **MM** 1921, Mathilde Kschessinska (1872-1971)

George 2nd Marquess of Milford Haven (1892-1938)

LOUISE (1889-1965) m.(2nd wife) 1923, **GUSTAV VI** (b.1882) King of Sweden **1950-1973**, who m.(1)1905, Princess Margaret of Connaught (1882-1920)

Alice of Battenberg (1885-1967) m.1903, Andrew of Greece (1882-1944)

Louis 1st Earl Mountbatten of Burma (1900-1979)

Prince Bertil of Sweden (1912-) m.1976, Lilian Craig, née Davies created H.R.H. Princess Lilian (1915-)

PHILIP m.1947, **ELIZABETH II** Mountbatten Duke of Edinburgh (1921-) | (b.1926) Queen of England **1952-**

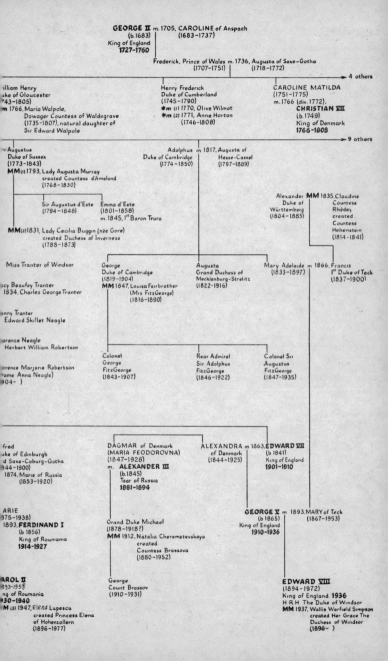

GEORGE II m.1705, CAROLINE of Anspach
(b.1683)
King of England
1727-1760
(1683-1737)

Frederick, Prince of Wales m.1736, Augusta of Saxe-Gotha
(1707-1751)   (1718-1772)

→ 4 others

William Henry
Duke of Gloucester
(1743-1805)
m 1766, Maria Walpole,
Dowager Countess of Waldegrave
(1735-1807), natural daughter of
Sir Edward Walpole

Henry Frederick
Duke of Cumberland
(1745-1790)
*m (1) 1770, Olive Wilmot
*m (2) 1771, Anne Horton
(1746-1808)

CAROLINE MATILDA
(1751-1775)
m.1766 (div. 1772),
CHRISTIAN VII
(b.1749)
King of Denmark
1766-1808

→ 9 others

=Augustus
Duke of Sussex
(1773-1843)
MM(1)1793, Lady Augusta Murray
created Countess d'Ameland
(1768-1830)

Adolphus m 1817, Augusta of
Duke of Cambridge   Hesse-Cassel
(1774-1850)   (1797-1889)

Sir Augustus d'Este   Emma d'Este
(1794-1848)   (1801-1858)
m.1845, 1st Baron Truro

Alexander MM 1835, Claudine
Duke of Württemberg   Countess Rhédey
(1804-1885)   created Countess Hohenstein
(1814-1841)

MM(2)1831, Lady Cecilia Buggin (née Gore)
created Duchess of Inverness
(1788-1873)

Miss Tranter of Windsor

George
Duke of Cambridge
(1819-1904)
MM 1847, Louisa Fairbrother
(Mrs FitzGeorge)
(1816-1890)

Augusta
Grand Duchess of
Mecklenburg-Strelitz
(1822-1916)

Mary Adelaide m 1866, Francis
(1833-1897)   1st Duke of Teck
(1837-1900)

...cy Beaufoy Tranter
1834, Charles George Tranter

...nny Tranter
...Edward Skillet Neagle

...orence Neagle
...Herbert William Robertson

...orence Marjorie Robertson
...ame Anna Neagle)
1904-)

Colonel
George
FitzGeorge
(1843-1907)

Rear Admiral
Sir Adolphus
FitzGeorge
(1846-1922)

Colonel Sir
Augustus
FitzGeorge
(1847-1935)

...fred
...uke of Edinburgh
...d Saxe-Coburg-Gotha
...844-1900)
1874, Marie of Russia
(1853-1920)

DAGMAR of Denmark
(MARIA FEODOROVNA)
(1847-1928)
m. ALEXANDER III
(b.1845)
Tsar of Russia
1881-1894

ALEXANDRA m 1863, EDWARD VII
of Denmark   (b 1841)
(1844-1925)   King of England
1901-1910

...ARIE
...875-1938)
1893, FERDINAND I
(b 1856)
King of Roumania
1914-1927

Grand Duke Michael
(1878-1918?)
MM 1912, Natalia Cheremetevskaya
created
Countess Brassova
(1880-1952)

GEORGE V m 1893, MARY of Teck
(b.1865)   (1867-1953)
King of England
1910-1936

...AROL II
...893-1953)
...ng of Roumania
...930-1940
...M (3) 1947, Elena Lupescu
created Princess Elena
of Hohenzollern
(1896-1977)

George
Count Brassov
(1910-1931)

EDWARD VIII
(1894-1972)
King of England 1936
H R H The Duke of Windsor
MM 1937, Wallis Warfield Simpson
created Her Grace The
Duchess of Windsor
(1896-)

I

A MEETING
AFTER THIRTY YEARS

WEDNESDAY, JUNE 7, 1967, was Derby Day in Britain, and for once, in spite of the vagaries of the English summer, it had dawned with perfect racing weather. Under almost cloudless blue skies, Epsom Downs lay bathed in brilliant sunshine. It flooded the grandstand and the parade ring, highlighted Tattenham Corner, and dappled the course along which the Queen and her family would drive that afternoon in the traditional royal motorcade to the winning post.

In terms of atmosphere, the Derby is hard to upstage, but this year some of its thunder had been unexpectedly stolen. Three hours before the great classic of the turf was due to start, fifteen miles away in the centre of London, another royal occasion was taking place which had captured the public imagination with its dramatic possibilities.

In the shade of the tall spreading plane trees in the Mall, a crowd of more than five thousand, only one hundred of them officially invited, had assembled to watch Queen Elizabeth II unveil a plaque on the wall of Marlborough House to mark the centenary of the birth of her grandmother.

Queen Mary, that magnificent matriarch of the British monarchy, dimly remembered in the public mind for her inimitable toques and superbly upright deportment, had been dead for fourteen years, and it is doubtful that the occasion would have generated such intense interest but for one factor.

Her errant eldest son, the Duke of Windsor, who had abdicated as King Edward VIII in 1936, was attending the unveiling, his first official public appearance in Britain with other members of the Royal Family since his mother's funeral. And – of still greater interest to the jostling onlookers – his twice-divorced American wife, the former Mrs Wallis Simpson, for the first time in their thirty years of marriage, had been formally invited by Buckingham Palace to accompany him.

To many this development seemed the final irony in the long saga of the Windsors. In life, Queen Mary had regarded her eldest son's wife with undisguised horror. A reserved woman, never given to overstatement, she had once written the name of Mrs Simpson in her diary and followed it with a salvo of five exclamation marks.[1] She had consistently refused to receive her, and, when asked by her son to explain the reason, she had replied uncompromisingly, 'because she is an adventuress'.[2] Now, in death, the old queen had become the catalyst for an Establishment olive branch to the daughter-in-law she herself had never known.

It had been widely stated that the unveiling would mark the first official recognition of the Duchess of Windsor by the British sovereign. But Elizabeth II had already met her American aunt-in-law privately two years earlier when she had made a much-publicized visit to the London Clinic following the Duke of Windsor's eye operation.

To royalty watchers, courtiers, and friends of the Royal Family, the real piquancy of this occasion lay not in the reaction of the Queen – a mere child of ten at the time of the Abdication – but in the attitude of her influential and immensely popular mother. The point had been accurately caught the day before by one of the London gossip columns: 'The poignancy of the Duchess's meeting with the members of her husband's family will be heightened by her encounter, for the first time since 1936, with her sister-in-law, the Queen Mother.'[3]

Even Queen Mary, although she had never consented to receive the Duchess of Windsor, had relented sufficiently six years after the Abdication to write, in a letter to her eldest son, 'I send a kind message to your wife.'[4] And in 1951, when Wallis was taken ill in New York, the old lady had actually gone so far as to enquire solicitously after her health.[5]

But the attitude of Queen Elizabeth the Queen Mother towards her American sister-in-law had remained consistent for a third of a century. It was one of icy and unwavering hostility. Enmity had flared between the two women at their earliest encounter in 1934, two years before the Abdication. The Duchess of York, as she then was, took an instant dislike to the sleek, chic, epigrammatic Mrs Simpson. And Wallis, quickly aware of the coolness of this influential member of the Royal Family, unwisely took to mimicking Elizabeth's mannerisms and to deriding her ultra-feminine, sometimes *baroque* style in fashion. 'The Dowdy Duchess' was how Wallis liked to describe her.[6]

During the 326-day reign of King Edward VIII, the Duchess of York, as wife of the heir to the throne, had found herself obliged to meet her brother-in-law's favourite on several occasions. Unexpectedly forced into the position of having to receive Wallis Simpson in her own home, Elizabeth succeeded, without overt discourtesy, in conveying 'a distinct impression'[7] to the intruder that she was 'not sold'[8] on the King's American friend.

Later, at one of Edward VIII's dinner parties in London, the Yorks were again confronted by Mrs Simpson, minus Mr Simpson, and Elizabeth was noticeably remote, royally squashing Winston Churchill's mischievous attempt to raise the matter of George IV's clandestine marriage with Mrs Fitzherbert.[9]

But it was at Balmoral two months later that the Duchess of York openly showed her antipathy towards 'the lady with two husbands living'.[10] Invited to the castle to dine with the King, Elizabeth was visibly angered when Wallis Simpson, casting herself in the role of official hostess, walked forward to receive her. The public snub that was delivered by Elizabeth to Wallis on that September evening in 1936 reverberated throughout international society. It also marked the last meeting between the two women for more than thirty years.

In less than three months, the Duchess of York was to become the new Queen-Empress, and shortly after that Wallis Simpson would become her sister-in-law, but the relationship signified nothing to Elizabeth.

One week before the Windsor wedding, George VI had exercised his prerogative as the fountain of honour and deprived Wallis of royal status. The ex-King was to be His Royal Highness for his lifetime. Wallis was to be merely Her Grace the Duchess of Windsor. As such, she was not entitled to be addressed as 'Ma'am', like the other ladies of the Royal Family. Officially speaking, women would not curtsey to her, and men would not bow, although in the event many did. For the sister-in-law of a reigning sovereign, it was an unparalleled public insult, and for the rest of their lives both the Windsors believed that Queen Elizabeth's personal influence had been responsible for the King's action.

Time did nothing to heal the intense mutual antagonism. Two years after the Abdication, one of the new Queen's ladies-in-waiting was shaken by the uncharacteristic sharpness and implacable anger with which Elizabeth announced that, even if the Duchess of Windsor were to return to Britain, she would not receive her.[11]

The acrimony between the two women haunted the corridors of power. British prime ministers, American presidents, cabinet ministers, ambassadors and even foreign dictators found themselves caught up in it.

'A feud' was how the Duchess of Windsor herself described it,[12] and the motive she attributed to Elizabeth's opposition was jealousy – 'a woman's jealousy'.[13] Some took this to mean jealousy of the Duke of Windsor, whose looks, charm and personality might eclipse the hesitant, stammering figure of Elizabeth's husband, the new King. But later the Windsors would confide to friends that they believed Queen Elizabeth's hostility to be of a more personal kind; that it was not so much jealousy of the Duke, as of the Duchess, for having married him.[14]

The ending of a world war in no way curtailed the smaller war between the sisters-in-law. And when, in 1952, George VI died suddenly at the early age of fifty-six, his health broken by the burden of kingship his brother had bequeathed him, the widowed Queen's bitterness intensified. Thereafter, on the few occasions when anyone had the temerity to mention the Duchess of Windsor in her presence, Elizabeth would refer to her sister-in-law as 'the woman who killed my husband'.[15]

The early widowhood of her antagonist did nothing to soften Wallis's fierce resentment of the long years of ostracism. Queen Mary's official biographer, visiting the Windsors in France as late as January 1958, considered that the Duchess's 'facial contortion',[16] when speaking of the Queen Mother, seemed 'akin to frenzy'.[17]

And now, eight years later, in the warm June sunshine filtering through the spreading plane trees in the Mall, the stage was set at last for an historic reunion between two charismatic and remarkable women who had detested each other for more than three decades. The band of the Coldstream Guards was playing 'The Skye Boat Song', which struck some onlookers as a strangely appropriate prelude to the return of the man whom a handful of diehard romantics had continued to toast, after his abdication, as 'the King over the Water'.

As on all their joint visits to Britain in the previous thirty years, the Windsors were not accommodated at any of the royal residences and were staying, as usual, at Claridge's. But on this occasion, for the first and last time during their marriage, they drove together in a royal limousine as part of the official procession travelling the short distance, a mere one hundred yards, from St James's Palace to Marlborough House.

The moment their car came into view, they were clapped and cheered by the waiting crowds, and one woman shouted 'Edward' – 'as if she had waited thirty years to do so'.[18] The Windsors took their places at the end of the front line of guests, and closest to the plaque soon to be unveiled. They were followed by the Duke's younger brother, Prince Henry, Duke of Gloucester – now using a walking stick after suffering a slight stroke – and his quiet, self-effacing duchess, Alice.

Wallis Windsor, dressed in a deep blue shantung coat, with a knee-length hemline noticeably higher than any other woman present, a tiny matching blue straw pillbox hat crowning her elaborately upswept dark hair, and a white mink muffler elegantly draped over each shoulder, at once presented an image startlingly different from the other royal ladies – 'like the denizen of another planet', as one observer described it.[19] Beside her, the Duke of Windsor, in morning dress, fiddled with his tie, looking strained and somewhat nervous.

There was a momentary pause and an atmosphere of intense anticipation before the cheers rang out again as a maroon Rolls Royce drove slowly into view, its occupant instantly recognized and gesturing in inimitable style to the applauding onlookers. The door was held open, and with a vivid flash of colour, out stepped Queen Elizabeth the Queen Mother, dressed in a pale lilac coat, the familiar three strands of pearls, and one of her characteristically ornate hats in a deeper lilac. She was accompanied by her Woman of the Bedchamber, the Hon. Mrs John Mulholland, and by the Comptroller of her Household, Lord Adam Gordon.

Only six months earlier, ironically on the thirtieth anniversary of the Abdication that made her Queen, Elizabeth had undergone a major abdominal operation that was regarded as serious – cancer had been widely rumoured at the time. She had then had a lengthy period of convalescence away from public view, and the unveiling was her first official public appearance since her illness.

In the previous year, Leonard M. Harris had produced a public opinion survey on the leading members of the British Royal Family. From questions to the public about the Queen Mother, Mr Harris had completed 'a picture whose only negative touches are a suggestion of artificiality ("too much smiling") and a hint of dominance ("she tells them where they get off", "I've heard she's a tartar in her own household") . . . In the main,' he concluded, 'the aura is positive and favourable, with only occasional hints that public and private face may not be identical.'[20]

But if Elizabeth on this occasion privately felt any sense of ordeal or distaste over her obligatory encounter with her brother-in-law and his wife, she gave no public indication of it. Smiling and composed as always, and moving gracefully on peeptoe high-heeled shoes, she walked slowly but confidently towards where the Windsors stood.

She greeted the Duke first. Windsor, in exile, had had harsh words to say about the sister-in-law who had so long ignored and ostracized his wife. But as the Queen Mother stretched out a pale-gloved hand towards him, a certain innate chivalry came to the fore, and he bowed his head with courtly grace to kiss her hand. As if in response to this courtesy, Elizabeth averted her head slightly in order that the Duke might also kiss her cheek, a feat which he accomplished with a certain difficulty on account of her veil.

The Queen Mother then turned towards the Duchess of Windsor, who had meantime been watching her with a pleasant, smiling but neutral expression on her face.

'How nice to see you again,' Elizabeth could be heard saying,[21] in the clear, bell-like tones so characteristic of members of her family, the Bowes-Lyons. Again she stretched out her hand, and the Duchess took it. There would be no kisses between these two. The handshake seemed to be maintained for several seconds while the cameras recorded what was clearly an historic moment.

A crowned and anointed queen, and the last Empress of India, the Queen Mother is entitled to a bow or a curtsey from every member of the Royal Family with the exception of the reigning Queen and her husband. Even Prince Philip invariably bows his head to kiss his mother-in-law's hand. But the Duchess of Windsor did not curtsey to her sister-in-law.

Elizabeth gave no sign of having noticed the omission. Appearing to be entirely at ease, she continued to talk to the Duchess for several minutes, moving her head in an animated way from one side to another, recalling the acid sentence which Wallis Windsor had used in her memoirs about a meeting with the Duchess of York in 1936. 'Her justly famous charm was highly evident.'[22]

None of the Queen Mother's subsequent remarks was overheard, but the Duchess was seen to answer what her sister-in-law was saying, although newsreel coverage of the occasion shows her replies to have been somewhat monosyllabic.

Wallis's failure to curtsey to the Queen Mother was re-emphasized a few moments later when the Queen and Prince Philip arrived on the scene. As the reigning monarch walked past her uncle and aunt-in-law, giving them both a somewhat perfunctory nod, the Duchess of Windsor was seen to bob a brief but unmistakable curtsey.[23]

The Duke bowed his head deeply as his niece, the Queen, passed him. In that moment, the Queen Mother looked across the Gloucesters to the Windsors and Wallis returned her glance. It was as if there was awareness between the two adversaries that Wallis had been prepared to curtsey to the daughter but not to the mother.

There followed a short and solemn service, conducted by Dr Robert Stopford, Bishop of London, in thanksgiving for 'the life and example of Thy servant Queen Mary'. Then the Queen walked over and parted the blue curtains covering the plaque – a head of Queen Mary in bronze.

Once the service was over, the Queen and her mother moved around chatting with guests. The Queen Mother went up to the Windsors and was seen to say something which caused them both to smile broadly. For a brief moment, the tension of the occasion was broken.

Then, ahead of her daughter, the Queen Mother said goodbye to the Windsors. The Duke once more went through the process of kissing her hand and cheek. The Duchess shook hands but once again did not curtsey. A moment later, the Queen reached the Duchess and this time Wallis did curtsey.

The Queen, Prince Philip, the Queen Mother and the Duchess of Gloucester departed to Epsom for the Derby. The Windsors had not been invited to join them there in the Royal Box. Instead they drove off to Kensington Palace for a small private luncheon given for them by the Duke's widowed sister-in-law, Princess Marina, Duchess of Kent. The entire ceremony had lasted a mere quarter of an hour – 'fifteen emotionally charged minutes', as one observer described it the following day.[24]

In that brief space of time, what had once seemed unthinkable in royal circles had finally come to pass. Wallis Warfield Spencer Simpson Windsor had at last taken her place publicly among her husband's family. And for the first time in more than thirty years she had come face to face with the sister-in-law whose animosity had frozen her out of British life and society.

The bitterness between the two women had lasted too long, and gone too deep, to be ended by the mere shaking of hands and a display of superficial politeness. Their feud – certainly the longest and the strangest in the history of Britain's royal house – was to smoulder on for another nine years until time and circumstances dictated an honourable truce.

2

ELIZABETH OF GLAMIS
AND BESSIEWALLIS OF BALTIMORE

ON THE FACE OF IT, and to their respective partizans, the two protagonists who met in the Mall on that June morning in 1967, after an estrangement of three decades, seemed to be the complete antithesis of each other.

Elizabeth Bowes-Lyon, the 'smiling Duchess' of the 'twenties and 'thirties, the wartime Queen of England who refused to leave London during the blitz, or to allow her daughters to be sent out of the country, had become the most active and beloved dowager queen in British history.

As a public figure she has been almost universally popular, seeming to embody the ideals of devotion to duty, service to her country, and impeccable public behaviour.

Diehard republicans – not excluding the Soviet Communist variety – have been known to warm to her immense personal charm. Even the IRA, in recognition of her unique hold on public affection, suspended demonstrations and all other activities during one of her visits to Canada, only to resume them promptly, on her departure, in time for the arrival of her daughter, Princess Margaret.

Wallis Simpson, on the other hand, the archetypal *femme fatale*, who induced a king-emperor to relinquish throne and empire, never achieved popularity with the public. In the general estimation she is condemned – both for causing a king to abandon his duty, and later for sharing with him what some considered to be a shallow and frivolous lifestyle.

Many of her fellow Americans, especially women, disapprove of her for having caused a major constitutional upheaval in another country. And the British, despite the evidence of Edward VIII's chronic unsuitability for kingship, never forgave her for the Abdication, or for proving that a national idol had feet of the commonest clay.

Even in her eighties, in widowhood and rapidly disintegrating health, the Duchess of Windsor still attracted anger, hostility and criticism in Britain.

The Queen Mother's mode of life always contrasted sharply with the café society existence of the Windsors. The most prolific royal patron of the arts in Britain since George IV, Elizabeth has counted the Sitwells, Benjamin Britten, Augustus John and Noël Coward among her close friends. She speaks French like a Frenchwoman. Wallis, whose principal reading was an occasional detective novel, spoke execrable French, even after living in France for more than forty years.

As Duchess of Windsor, Wallis became a leader of fashion and topped the lists of the world's best-dressed women. Elizabeth, as Queen and Queen Mother, never made the lists once, serenely ignoring each passing trend and wearing only what she believed would suit her comfortable figure.

On the surface, therefore, there was sufficient divergence of taste and personality to explain why Elizabeth of York did not take to Wallis Simpson when they first met in 1934.

But dislike grew into abhorrence on both sides, and it was something far deeper than superficial differences that caused this to happen. Was it perhaps more a question of unsuspected affinities? For beneath the surface, the wistfully charming Duchess of York and the brashly wisecracking Mrs Simpson had rather too much in common for comfort.

Both were women of strong and determined character. Both dominated their royal husbands but were at pains to conceal the fact. The complete dependence of George VI and of the Duke of Windsor upon the women they married was expressed by different observers some years apart in almost identical words.

In 1922, the future Viscount Davidson became aware of Lady Elizabeth Bowes-Lyon's reluctance to marry the King's second son and to assume the responsibilities of life as a member of the Royal Family. Of his friend, the Duke of York, Davidson wrote: 'The question was, what was he to do? He could not live without her, and certainly he would never marry anyone else.'[1]

Later, after their marriage, Sir Henry Channon – the ubiquitous 'Chips' – was to say of the Yorks: 'He had few friends and was almost entirely dependent on her (the Duchess of York), whom he worshipped. She was his will power, his all.'[2]

At a luncheon in the spring of 1948, Winston Churchill sat next to Queen Mary's close friend and lady-in-waiting, Mabell, Countess of Airlie, and they discussed the Windsors.

'The Duke's love for her is one of the great loves of history', said Churchill. 'I saw him when she had gone away for a fortnight. He was miserable – haggard, dejected, not knowing what to do. Then I saw him when she had been back for a day or two, and he was a different man – gay, debonair, self-confident. Make no mistake, he can't live without her.'[3]

Such was the totalitarian nature of the love inspired by these outwardly contrasting women whose husbands could not live without them and who became sworn enemies.

Neither wished their power to be apparent, at the time or in retrospect. In May 1958, John Wheeler-Bennett came to the end of five and a half years of work on his official life of King George VI. 'When he had finished the book,' records Harold Nicolson's biographer, 'Wheeler-Bennett sensed that the Queen Mother was not pleased with the dominant role he had assigned to her.'[4]

Five years later, in 1963, the Duchess of Windsor gave a rare interview in Paris to the British journalist, Susan Barnes, later Mrs Anthony Crosland. 'I'm quite aware' said the Duchess trenchantly, 'that some people assume I'm the boss.' And she proceeded with vigour to refute the idea.[5] Her arguments lacked conviction. Every one close to the Windsors knew that she *was* the boss, and that the Duke deferred to her wishes happily until the day he died.

The similarities multiply. Both Elizabeth and Wallis would become renowned for creating a distinctive individual style – in their appearances, and in the houses in which they lived. Lady Airlie, visiting the new Queen at Buckingham Palace only a few weeks after the Abdication, found that that gloomy royal mausoleum 'was already beginning to show the traces of her own personality – the little feminine touches which I had always associated with her. "It looks homelike already," I said spontaneously. The King who had come in for a few minutes smiled proudly . . . "Elizabeth could make a home anywhere." '[6]

More than forty years later, Prince Charles would echo this opinion, writing of his grandmother's 'exquisite taste in so many things', and of her 'making any house she lives in a unique haven of cosiness and character'.[7]

Wallis's skill as a *châtelaine* both rivalled and resembled that of her sister-in-law. One of the most accomplished of French hostesses, the Comtesse René de Chambrun, said of the Duchess of Windsor: '*Elle donnait toujours à ses maisons un air de fête*.'[8] And Lady Mosley, a frequent visitor to the Windsors' Paris house in the Bois de Boulogne, would remember with nostalgia 'the rich and beautiful table of the Duchess, with its talk that was always amusing and sometimes brilliant, fantastic food and sumptuous wines'.[9]

Both women developed over the years a strangely similar repartee, based on an offbeat, self-mocking style of humour.

'Can you remember the first thing [the Duke] said to you?', Kenneth Harris asked the Duchess in a television interview in October 1969. The timing of her reply was that of a practised *comedienne*: 'No. I don't remember the last things he said to me.'[10]

The Queen Mother, warned by a lady-in-waiting that the reception rooms of a certain public building were a great distance from the entrance, responded: 'I shall arrive at 3.30 and proceed by roller skate.'[11]

Both sisters-in-law were vital, energetic and fun-seeking. Neither loved anything better than a party, or the excuse for one. The Queen Mother, even in her eighties, has displayed a social energy that has frequently exhausted her staff. From her remote Scottish retreat, the Castle of Mey, there came reports in 1981 of her 'leaving house-guests and family members worn out by her late-evening high-jinks. After presiding over impromptu fun until two or three in the morning, she herself has been trotting off to bed as fresh as a daisy. The post-dinner programme has included energetic Scottish dancing, charades and a game of cards called Racing Demon – a violent business which can easily lead to broken fingers.'[12]

Wallis's taste for parties was also legendary. 'She loved anything to do with a party,' said John Utter, the Duke's private secretary. 'She had to make sure she never missed one.'[13]

In her sixties, she did the Twist in public in Paris. In her seventies, she was photographed dancing the Hully Gully and the Jerk in a mini-skirt. Even in widowhood, and after fracturing a hip, the Duchess still retained her appetite for night life. 'Why don't we go somewhere tonight?' she urged a friend at Cap Ferrat in 1973. 'I haven't been anywhere. How about Monte Carlo?'[14]

Throughout their lives both women would have a special affinity with homosexual men. In the 'thirties in London, one of Wallis Simpson's most favoured friends was the homosexual playboy, Johnnie McMullen, who predicted hopefully, 'mark my words, she will become the power behind the throne'.[15]

Johnnie was similarly devoted to Somerset Maugham's divorced wife, Syrie. After learning that McMullen was spending the summer in

Syrie's London house, Maugham confessed to 'a strong hope that at the end of the season when debutantes settle these matters she will make an honest woman of him.'[16]

Wallis's later and closer relationship with a far richer homosexual, the Woolworth heir James Paul Donahue Jr, achieved such notoriety in terms of publicity that for a time the Windsor marriage appeared to be under serious strain.

Elizabeth also attracted and enjoyed the company of homosexual men. For a time, she was even a sort of homosexual sex symbol. In the late 'twenties and early 'thirties, at an annual London drag event known as Lady Malcolm's Ball, the Duchess of York was the subject of an uncannily accurate impersonation by one of London's leading transvestites. After Elizabeth's elevation to the throne, the same man continued his impersonation annually with increasingly regal overtones. From a chauffeur-driven Daimler would step a smiling, tiara'd and crinolined figure who appeared instantly recognizable. As passers-by burst into loyal applause, the guest-of-honour would adjust a white mink stole, gesture in familiar style with a delicately gloved hand, incline a gracious head and then sweep on up the steps. Spectators often went home without suspecting that they had been watching a drag queen instead of the real thing.

When she was eventually informed of this bizarre tribute, Elizabeth was greatly amused. The nuances of homosexual humour were familiar to her. A large number of the male friends she drew around her over the years – Harold Nicolson, Cecil Beaton, Benjamin Britten, Oliver Messel, Terence Rattigan, James Pope-Hennessy – were homosexual. She has a civilized understanding of men whose relationships with women are only platonic. A number of her senior courtiers have been lifelong bachelors. She has often referred to them affectionately as 'my knitting brigade'.

To Noël Coward, perhaps her closest homosexual friend, she was 'the darling QM'.[17] In 1964, Sir Noël recorded: 'I have a feeling I might become a bore about the Queen Mother. I have always liked her since we first met in the 'twenties, and of late years I have come to adore her. She has irrepressible humour, divine manners and a kind heart. My affection for her has gone far beyond royal *snobisme*. She is also, I am proud and happy to say, genuinely fond of me.'[18]

Elizabeth and Wallis were both always cheerfully fond of alcohol, and circulars dispatched to those expecting the Queen Mother as guest of honour at a function discreetly advised that Her Majesty would 'appreciate the offer of a drink'. A favourite tipple was helpfully specified: one part gin and two parts Dubonnet. On two occasions in December 1982, the mixture was graciously accepted – at around 10.15 in the morning. At the races, Elizabeth finds pink gin equally acceptable. And when one of her horses wins, she likes green and yellow Chartreuse to celebrate.[19]

While the stimulation of alcohol seems to add extra zest to the Queen Mother's sparkling public performance, it appeared to have the reverse effect on the Windsors. 'The Duke would never touch a drop of drink before seven in the evening,' said John Utter, 'but that is no guarantee of what can be drunk after seven, and sometimes the sound of their drunken bickering was unbearable.'[20]

After the Duke of Windsor's death in 1972, Wallis became increasingly reluctant to eat and heavily reliant on alcohol to combat her loneliness. When the Duchess's health began to decline, one of her oldest friends, Kitty Miller, widow of the American impresario Gilbert Miller, confided, 'For a long time she kept going on just a nip of Scotch or vodka, but now she's not allowed it.'[21]

The feuding sisters-in-law, such vividly contrasting personalities on the surface, had indeed many unsuspected affinities of character and temperament. Beyond this, their lives were linked by a series of strange and almost eerie coincidences.

Each of them traces her ancestry – Wallis through her mother, Elizabeth through her father – to the same North American State of Virginia. Both families emigrated from England and settled there within only thirty years of each other.

Wallis's ancestor, eighteen-year-old Peter Montague of Bovency, Buckinghamshire, was the first to arrive in 1621.[22] He married the daughter of the Governor of Virginia, represented his county in the Colonial assembly, the House of Burgesses, and became a prosperous planter of tobacco, wheat and barley.

Elizabeth's ancestor, Augustine Warner I, born in England or Wales in 1611, arrived in Virginia in 1650, when he was 39.[23] He built a splendid mansion called Warner Hall on an arm of the Severn, that flows into the York River and then into Chesapeake Bay, where the first English emigrants had sailed in 1607 to found the tragic settlement of Jamestown. Warner quickly prospered. He became a Colonel of the Militia, a Justice, and – like Wallis's forbear, Peter Montague, who was only eight years his senior – a Burgess in the General Assembly.

The next to arrive, in 1662, from his English home in Berkshire, was Wallis's paternal ancestor, Richard Warfield, who settled in the neighbouring State of Maryland. Richard's ancestor, Pagan de Warfield, had come from France with William the Conqueror, had fought for him at the Battle of Hastings, and had been rewarded by the victorious invader with an estate called Warfield's Walk, one of sixteen areas of land that divided Windsor Forest.

Almost a thousand years later, Pagan de Warfield's descendant would come to know Windsor very well indeed and would bear the name of that town in her own title, after failing in her bid to become *châtelaine* of Windsor Castle.

'A part of me remains in the vicinity . . .', she would write, 'and history is herewith given fair warning that one day a pale and anonymous phantom may be observed in the shadows along the Cedar Walk that is such a distinctive feature of [Fort Belvedere], perhaps even after Herne the Hunter has tired of his hunting.'[24]

Both Elizabeth Bowes-Lyon and Wallis Warfield can claim descent from three kings: Elizabeth from Robert II of Scotland, from the eleventh-century King of Ireland, Brian Boru, and from the first Tudor sovereign of England, Henry VII; Wallis from Edward III of England, from Simon de Montacute, King of the Isle of Man in the fourteenth century, and from the great Indian Chief, King Powhatan, whose daughter, Pocahontas, married one of Virginia's first English colonists, John Rolfe. Both women have a British dukedom in the ancestry of their mothers – Wallis, the dukedom of Manchester; Elizabeth, the dukedom of Portland. The two dukedoms – Portland created in 1716, and Manchester three years later – rank next to each other in the precedence of the British peerage.

More than a century and a half before they first came face to face, the lives of these two women had a tangible link. Elizabeth Bowes-Lyon's most celebrated American forbear was George Washington, who became the first President of the United States in 1789. But he would never have lived to hold that office without the timely intervention of Wallis's ancestor. For during the War of Independence twenty years earlier, it was a Montague who saved Washington's life by stepping in front of him to take the sabre cut of a British soldier.[25] Washington's twentieth century kinswoman was never to return the favour to her contemporary, Montague's descendant.

With an ancestry that was undeniably aristocratic, and wholly British in its origins on both sides of her family, Wallis was understandably irritated by the suggestions – 'the wild canards',[26] as she called them – that she was a *petite bourgeoise* who 'had come from the wrong side of the tracks in Baltimore'.[27]

This view is still occasionally advanced even today. The journalist and critic, Alastair Forbes, a noted authority on British royalty in the twentieth century, prefaces his discussion of the Duchess of Windsor's origins with the words: 'For those who are prepared to accept that there can be class distinctions of any kind in the United States . . .'[28]

Woodrow Wyatt, Chairman of the Horserace Totalisator Board and a friend of the Queen Mother, echoes patronizingly: 'In so far as it is possible for there to be grand families in Baltimore the Warfields were one of them.'[29]

But Mr Forbes, the son of a Bostonian, knows better than Woodrow Wyatt, and continues: '. . . she [Wallis] can be said to come from a far higher stratum than, say, Princess Grace of Monaco, Jacqueline Bouvier or the Jerome or Vanderbilt ladies of the nineteenth century. By present English standards of birth she might rank rather below two recent royal duchesses, and rather above two others.'[30]

American genealogists need no such assurances. The Maryland Historical Society classified the Warfields as 'old, old Baltimore', and the Montagues as one of 'the first families of Virginia'.[31]

In the American Civil War, thirty years before her birth, Wallis's family were on the same side as Elizabeth Bowes-Lyon's forbears. All four of Wallis's grandparents were staunch Southern sympathizers, supporting the Confederate cause against Abraham Lincoln. The Warfields and the Montagues were pro-British and anti-Yankee.

Unlike Virginia, Maryland did not secede from the Union, but Wallis's grandfather, Henry Mactier Warfield, was one of the first Baltimoreans to demand secession. In April 1861, with the declaration of war between the States, Warfield was arrested by Lincoln's men and imprisoned with his friend, Severn Teackle Wallis – after whom Wallis Windsor's father was named – at nearby Fort McHenry, the successful defence of which, in 1812, against a long-range night bombardment by the British Fleet, had provided the inspiration for Francis Scott Key's 'The Star-spangled Banner'.

Elizabeth Bowes-Lyon's other celebrated American ancestor was General Robert E. Lee, leader of the Confederate cause which Wallis's grandparents ardently supported.

While Lee fought his heroic campaign against mounting odds, Warfield obstinately refused, throughout fourteen months of imprisonment, to take the oath of allegiance to the Union in return for his freedom. He coldly informed Secretary of War Edwin Stanton, 'Sir, as I am confined without charges, I renew my claim to be discharged without conditions.'[32] In the end; unable to break his resolve, the Federal Government gave up and Warfield was released without taking the oath.

On April 9, 1865, Lee, an elegant figure with his jewelled sword, surrendered his army at Appomattox to General Ulysses S. Grant, a sombre contrast in his plain private's dress.

Thirty-one years later, by the strangest coincidence of all, Wallis Warfield was born in the same building that once had been the Confederate headquarters of Elizabeth Bowes-Lyon's ancestor, Robert E. Lee.[33] Even at the moment of Wallis's birth there existed a link with the woman she would come to regard as her greatest enemy.

On September 28, 1853, Frances Dora Smith of Blendon Hall, near Bexley in Kent, a descendant of Elizabeth's first American ancestor Augustine Warner I, married the Hon. Claude Lyon Bowes – the family name was shortly afterwards reversed and hyphenated – who twelve years later succeeded his brother as the thirteenth Earl of Strathmore.

His eldest son, Claude George Bowes-Lyon, born on March 14, 1855, was a quiet, serious and handsome boy. At the age of ten he assumed the courtesy title of Lord Glamis when his father succeeded to the earldom. 'Claudie' joined his father's old regiment, the second Life Guards, and found himself, at twenty-five, on duty at Windsor Castle. There he formed a lifelong disenchantment for the *milieu* of the Court. The habitual drunkenness and heavy gambling in the officers' mess, and the leering gossip about the extra-marital adventures of Queen Victoria's heir, Edward Prince of Wales, repelled him.

The royal governess, Marion Crawford, remembered him as 'a most gentle and humorous person. He was a countryman through and through. He timed all his movements by country things – the coming of the migrants, the wild geese on the river, the rising of the sap . . . He always made his cocoa for breakfast himself, ate plum pudding for lunch every day of his life, and always had beside him at meals a small jug of water with which he diluted his wine.'[34]

A family sadness shortly enabled Lord Glamis to return to the country existence which he loved. On January 19, 1881, his grand-mother, Charlotte Grimstead, the Dowager Lady Glamis, died. Charlotte had been the central figure in a rumoured tragedy that has become the most tantalizing of all the Strathmore family legends. Married on December 21, 1820, to the eleventh Earl's heir, Thomas Lord Glamis, Charlotte gave birth ten months later to a son – recorded in Douglas' *Scots Peerage* as 'born and died, October 21, 1821'.[35]

But the legend insists that the child did not die. So hideously deformed at birth that he could never inherit the title or estates, he had been baptized as a Christian and was therefore kept alive, although he was officially recorded as having died. A year later, on September 28, 1822, Charlotte bore a second son, Thomas George, who was entirely normal and eventually became the twelfth Earl.

But Charlotte's tragic first-born lived on and on, allegedly confined at the family's Scottish stronghold, Glamis Castle, in a secret room ten feet wide by fifteen long, hidden deep in the immensely thick walls.[36] There the family 'monster' – 'his chest an enormous barrel, hairy as a doormat . . . his head ran straight into his shoulders and his arms and legs were toy-like'[37] – survived into horrifying old age, fed through an iron grille by one trusted keeper, and unseen by any one else in the family except each incumbent earl and his heir, the latter reputedly initiated into the grim secret on his twenty-first birthday.

During the 1870s, a workman at Glamis 'came upon a door opening up a long passage'. Exploring the passage, the man 'became alarmed'. He told the Clerk of the Works who ordered all repairs to be abandoned and sent a telegram to the thirteenth Earl – Elizabeth's grandfather – in London, and another to the Strathmore lawyer in Edinburgh. Both came at once to Glamis and interrogated the workman as to what he had seen. The result was that the man and his family 'were subsidized and induced to emigrate'.[38]

No one knows for certain exactly when the deformed heir died, but the workman episode certainly suggests that he was still very much alive in his fifties.

Elizabeth Bowes-Lyon's mother, the Countess of Strathmore, once tried to get the Glamis factor, Andrew Ralston, to tell her the truth about the family secret. 'He looked at her gravely and slowly shook his head. He said: "Lady Strathmore, it is fortunate you do not know it and will never know it, for if you did you would never be happy." '[39]

The real truth of the matter almost certainly died with the tragic mother, Charlotte Grimstead, in 1881, but more than seventy years later the legend of 'the Monster of Glamis' was to provide fresh ammunition in the bitter personal war between the Queen Mother and the Duchess of Windsor.

Claudie – Lord Glamis – had been Charlotte Grimstead's favourite
grandson, and in her will she left him an eventual inheritance of 'my
public house known as the Strathmore Arms at St Paul's Walden, the
beer house known as the Woodman at Whitewell with the paddock
adjoining and all my other real estate in the parish of St Paul's Walden
or any adjoining parish referred to as my Walden property'. Since 'all
my other real estate' included the splendid Queen Anne mansion and
park of St Paul's Walden Bury, and many hundreds of acres of the
finest farming land in Hertfordshire, Glamis was potentially a rich
man. The estate was valued at £40,000 in 1882.

Although the inheritance devolved initially upon Claudie's father
for his lifetime, the thirteenth Earl, already the owner of some 24,700
acres, at once decided that his son should have both the tenancy and
the income of St Paul's Walden Bury to enjoy immediately.

Now comfortably off at the age of twenty-five, Lord Glamis
within a month had proposed marriage to Nina Cecilia Cavendish-
Bentinck, the first cousin of the Duke of Portland, and great-grand-
daughter of the third Duke who had twice been George III's prime
minister.

'Celia', a slim, russet-haired beauty of eighteen, accepted him. They
were married at Petersham parish church on July 16, 1881, with her
seventeen-year-old twin sisters, Anne and Hyacinth, as bridesmaids,
and her twenty-three-year old cousin, William, the sixth Duke of
Portland, to give her away. The clergyman who married them, the
Reverend Robert Liddell, was a cousin of that beguiling child, Alice
Liddell, who had served as the model for Lewis Carroll's heroine in
Alice in Wonderland.

Claudie and Celia settled down happily within the honeysuckle and
magnolia-covered red walls of St Paul's Walden Bury, and nine
months and one day later, on April 17, 1882, the new Lady Glamis
gave birth to their first child, the Hon. Violet Bowes-Lyon. A second
daughter, Mary, later Lady Elphinstone, followed in 1883; a male
heir, Patrick, the Master of Glamis, in 1884; three more sons, John in
1886, Alexander in 1887, and Fergus in 1889; a third daughter, Rose,
later the Countess Granville, in 1890; and a fifth son, Michael, in
1893.

But only sixteen days after Michael's birth, their eldest child, Violet,
died from diphtheria at the age of eleven.[40] This sudden grief for the
young parents seems to have put an end to Celia's almost yearly
childbearing. Lord Glamis was now thirty-eight and his wife was

thirty-one. They already had seven living children and there were no plans to enlarge their family any further.

Two years later, in Baltimore, the staid and sober Warfields of Maryland faced a family crisis. The head of the clan, old Henry Mactier Warfield, had died in 1884, having fathered five sons.

The eldest, Daniel, died young. The second, Solomon Davies Warfield – Uncle Sol – who was now head of the family, was a rich and successful banker and President of the Continental Trust Company, where his office was humorously known as Solomon's Temple. The third brother, Richard Emory Warfield, was said to be deeply religious, and lived with his wife in Philadelphia, where he was prominent in the insurance business. The fourth, Henry Warfield – Uncle Harry – was always known as 'General', through having once been adjutant general of Maryland. He had married a Baltimore girl, Rebecca Denison, and had a farm at Timonium in Baltimore County.

All three surviving elder brothers were rich and successful. It was only the youngest, Teackle Wallis Warfield – named by his father after the friend, Severn Teackle Wallis, imprisoned with him in 1861 – who had failed to inherit the old man's flair for making money.

On the strength of his family name, T. Wallis, as he preferred to be known – he hated the name Teackle – was a member of the exclusive Bachelors' Cotillion in Baltimore. Yet at the age of twenty-six he was earning a pittance as a clerk. His health was frail through the early taint of tuberculosis, and he was still living at 34 East Preston Street, the Baltimore house of his widowed mother and his eldest brother Sol.

For all his handicaps, however, T. Wallis had an undoubted attraction for women. The few photographs of him that survive show a pale, lean, rather poetic face, large and appealing eyes, and a sensitive mouth lightly fringed by a small but handsome moustache. The entire Warfield family was united in shock and disapproval when T. Wallis suddenly announced, in the summer of 1895, that he wished to marry Alice Montague, a high-spirited but penniless Virginian almost the same age as himself, and frequently described by the Baltimore newspapers as 'one of the two beautiful Montague sisters'.[41]

T. Wallis's mother, Mrs Henry Warfield, was opposed to the match partly on account of disquieting rumours to the effect that Alice was flighty, but chiefly because she suspected that the girl was merely using her son as a means of marrying into a wealthy family.

Uncle Sol, a cold, reserved and puritanical man who never married, also disapproved, and went to see the Montagues to impress upon them the seriousness of T. Wallis's tuberculosis, and the improbability that he would ever fully recover from the disease. To Sol's surprise, Alice's family seemed quite as dismayed as he was. The Montagues saw themselves as 'old line' and privately considered the Warfields *parvenus*, raised out of their station by 'new' money. Like everyone else in Maryland and Virginia, they had also heard the persistent but unfounded rumour that the Warfields were really Jewish and that their name had been changed from something else. Why otherwise would a family name a son Solomon?

The opposition of both families failed to dissuade the young pair. When the Montagues refused Alice the money for a trousseau, she borrowed fifty dollars from a Baltimore lawyer, Isaac Straus, and went with T. Wallis to a pawnshop to buy the ring.

In her memoirs, perhaps significantly, the Duchess of Windsor gives the date of her parents' marriage as June 1895,[42] but she has brought the event forward by as much as five months. It was on November 19, 1895, that Dr C. Ernest Smith, Rector of the Church of St Michael and All Angels in Baltimore, 'was called upon to officiate at a quiet marriage which attracted little attention at the time. On that day Teackle Wallis Warfield took as his bride Miss Alice M. Montague, a communicant of the parish. The ceremony took place in the rectory, at 1929 St Paul Street, in the presence of several friends.'[43]

'In the presence of several friends' sounds rather as if both families stayed away. This factor, coupled with lack of funds, may have dictated the quieter location of the rectory, in preference to a public ceremony in church. The other alternative, which can scarcely be overlooked, is that Alice may have realized she was pregnant, although it would hardly have been apparent so early.

Exactly seven months later to the day, on June 19, 1896, in an unpretentious wooden building known as Square Cottage at the Monterey Inn, Blue Ridge Summit, Pennsylvania, a daughter was born – 'somewhat in advance of calculations and in an atmosphere of crisis' explains the Duchess of Windsor.[44]

There is certainly evidence of the 'crisis', for Lewis Miles Allen, a twenty-two-year-old doctor just out of medical college and then on the staff of the University of Maryland Hospital, received an emergency summons to the Monterey Inn. There, in Alice's hotel bedroom, he delivered the eight-pound child.

'Doctor, is the baby all right?' the mother asked, according to the account of Wallis's cousin. 'Has she all her fingers and all her toes?'

And Allen is alleged to have answered, 'She's perfect in every way. In fact, she's fit for a king!'[45]

The child was named Bessiewallis – Bessie after her mother's sister, and also after her cousin and godmother, Bessie Montague Brown; Wallis after her father.

For more than eighty years afterwards, speculation would continue about the circumstances of this birth. It was not then a legal necessity to register births in Pennsylvania. If the Warfields did make a registration, no record of it survives today. Curiously, although the movements of her parents are faithfully chronicled, there was no mention of the child in any newspaper – in Maryland, Virginia or Pennsylvania.

At intervals over the years attempts were made by the American and British press to dispute the official date of birth, especially after a slip of the tongue by her aunt, Mrs Bessie Merryman, suggested that Wallis was really seven years older than she admitted. Four days after her eightieth birthday in 1976, it was reported that 'genealogists are still in hot dispute over whether that is in fact her age'.[46] Queen Mary's official biographer, the late James Pope-Hennessy, used to tell friends privately that Queen Mary had ordered an investigation into the Duchess of Windsor's origins and had received evidence that the official date of birth was incorrect.[47]

Even Wallis herself seemed in doubt. 'Years before, out of curiosity, I had once asked my mother ... and she had answered impatiently that she had been far too busy at the time to consult the calendar, let alone the clock'.[48]

But such evidence as there is supports the official date. It has been confirmed by Baltimore contemporaries who knew her in her pram and at school. There is also the factor than an earlier date of birth would raise the question of legitimacy – something which would scarcely have escaped attention in Baltimore, where contemporaries later proved eager to discuss every aspect of her life among them.

It is yet another of the many strange coincidences between the two women that four years later the birth of Elizabeth Bowes-Lyon would create a similar mystery and a continuing dispute.

If the birth of Bessiewallis Warfield somehow passed unnoticed in the summer of 1896, the rapidly failing health of her father did not. The principal reason for the young Warfields' stay in the summer resort of Blue Ridge Summit was the faint hope that the mountain air might help to arrest T. Wallis's now rampant tuberculosis.

Only two days after Bessiewallis's birth, a Baltimore newspaper noted that Alice's mother-in-law, Mrs Henry Warfield, was also staying at the Monterey Inn.[49] But there was no mention of the child. Two weeks later, another Baltimore newspaper noted that Alice's sister, Bessie, and her husband, D. Buchanan Merryman, were at a nearby hotel.[50] The day before, there had been a faint note of hope. 'Mr Wallis Warfield, who has been very ill, is slightly improved.'[51] And on September 28: 'Mr and Mrs Wallace (sic) Warfield have returned to Baltimore after spending the summer in the Blue Ridge Mountains.'[52] Once again, there was no reference to their one piece of good news.

By now T. Wallis was in a wheelchair, a wasted figure in the final stages of tuberculosis. Soon Alice dared not even take the baby to his bedside for fear of infection. But she did, at his request, have Bessie-wallis photographed for the first time on November 12 and she brought the results to show him.

'I'm afraid, Alice, she has the Warfield look,' he murmured quietly. 'Let us hope that in spirit she'll be like you – a Montague.'[53]

Three days later, on November 15, 1896, Teackle Wallis Warfield died. He was almost twenty-seven years old.

Next day's Baltimore paper recorded the news without surprise. 'Mr Warfield has been in failing health for about a year, and his death was not unexpected.'[54]

Alice Warfield, a penniless widow with an orphaned child, did the only thing she could. She accepted the charity of her husband's family, and took Bessiewallis to live with her mother-in-law and Uncle Sol at the well-staffed Baltimore house on fashionable East Preston Street. It was to be their home for the next five years.

In London, in the last foggy December of the old century, more than six years after the birth of her last child, Lady Glamis found to her astonishment that she was pregnant – at the age of thirty-seven.

It was a shock, certainly, and entirely unplanned, but Claudie Glamis seemed delighted by the news, and Celia herself began to look forward to another baby, for now only the youngest two – Rose, nine, and Michael, seven – were still around the house.

The newcomer, they thought, was due in late August, and Lady Glamis agreed with her husband that after eight pregnancies, and a long interval since her last child, it might be as well to arrange a nursing home on this occasion. Plans were duly laid, and the beginning of August 1900 found Celia Glamis staying at the London flat of her parents-in-law, the Earl and Countess of Strathmore, in Belgrave

Mansions, Grosvenor Gardens, almost opposite Victoria Station.[55]

Her husband had travelled north to Glamis Castle, where Lord and Lady Strathmore were about to arrive for a three-month visit from their other ancestral home, Streatlam Castle in County Durham.[56] August 4 was a hot Bank Holiday Saturday. London seemed strangely deserted. Almost every one in society had left for Cowes, for Scotland or for the continent.

That morning at Osborne House on the Isle of Wight, Queen Victoria, eighty-one and in failing health, presided sadly over the memorial service for her second son, Prince Alfred, Duke of Edinburgh and Saxe-Coburg, who had died from cancer at the age of fifty-six. In the Mall, the blinds were drawn across the windows of his London home, Clarence House.

And while the old Queen-Empress knelt in prayer for her 'poor darling Affie', the child who would become the last Queen-Empress began her life – like Bessiewallis Warfield, precipitately and ahead of time – only three hundred yards from Buckingham Palace, where she would reign as Queen of England for fifteen years, and not much further from 'darling Affie's' residence, Clarence House, which would one day be her London home.

It is still in some doubt whether the Hon. Elizabeth Bowes-Lyon[57] entered the world at Belgrave Mansions, in the back of a London ambulance, or at the maternity home to which Lady Glamis was rushed. In the year of her eightieth birthday, when the subject of her birthplace became a topic of some controversy, the Queen Mother is alleged to have told one of her biographers, Helen Cathcart, that she was born in the ambulance.[58]

As in the case of Bessiewallis Warfield – but far stranger for one of the British peerage's best-known families – no mention of Elizabeth's arrival was made in any newspaper, in London, Hertfordshire or Scotland. There was not even the conventional birth notice in The Times.

A telegram was dispatched to Glamis Castle to inform Celia's husband of her safe delivery, but Claudie, occupied by the traditional summer pursuits of cricket and shooting, did not return south. Instead he was busy leading his team to a resounding victory over the Strathmore XI at Glamis, where he made nine runs out of his side's total of 303 for nine declared, and took three wickets when the opposition was bowled out for only 80.[59]

It is not surprising to discover that it took seven weeks before Lord

Glamis found the time to register the birth of his ninth child, and only then when her christening was a mere forty-eight hours away. On Friday, September 21, now back in Hertfordshire, he went into Hitchin, paid a fine of seven shillings and six pence for failing to report the birth within the statutory period of six weeks,[60] and informed the local registrar, Mr C. H. Baylis, that his daughter had been born on August 4 at St Paul's Walden Bury.

By this deception, Lord Glamis risked conviction as a felon and penal servitude for life under the Forgery Act of 1861, but it is easy to understand why he did it. He was at 'The Bury' for the weekend, the christening was imminent, and telling the truth would entail a long and tiresome journey to London to the appropriate registration district. Besides these practical considerations, it was then, as Helen Cathcart observes, 'a convention to be born in the family home . . . and to be registered there, as Lord Glamis contrived'.[61]

Two days later, after the morning service on Sunday, September 23, the seven-week-old child was christened Elizabeth Angela Marguerite at the fourteenth-century font of All Saints' Church, St Paul's Walden, by the Vicar, the Reverend Tristram Valentine. Twelve years earlier, as Chaplain of the London Hospital in Whitechapel, he had had the less pleasant task of conducting the funeral services for several of the victims of Jack the Ripper.

Belgrave Mansions and the London ambulance had now, at the stroke of a pen, been deleted from the life history of Britain's future queen.

Shortly after her coronation in 1937, Elizabeth, almost certainly knowing the truth, but loyally adhering to her father's declaration on her birth certificate, unveiled a plaque in the Wedgwood green and cream chancel of All Saints' Church. The wording on it is as follows: 'The organ and this tablet were placed in this church by a parishioner to the glory of God and in memory of the coronation of Their Majesties King George VI and Queen Elizabeth, May 12, 1937. Her Majesty Queen Elizabeth was born in this parish August 4, 1900, baptised in this church, September 23, 1900, and here worshipped.'

Every biography for the next forty-three years, including Sir John Wheeler-Bennett's official life of King George VI, maintained this fiction.[62]

The author Dorothy Laird, beginning work in 1959 on a biography personally approved by the Queen Mother,[63] was astonished to learn from her brother, Sir David Bowes-Lyon, that she had *not* been born at

St Paul's Walden Bury. He 'indicated that the legend that she was born at St Paul's Walden was harmless . . . the whole event of birth and registration – a younger member of a large family – was considered unimportant at the time.'[64] Miss Laird, a straightforward Scot, could not help becoming aware that the Queen Mother herself wished the official version of her birthplace to be maintained, and in her final text the author compromised by giving the date of her birth but not the place.

There the matter rested until the Queen Mother's eightieth birthday celebrations in the summer of 1980, when rumours in the parish of St Paul's Walden – that she had not been born there after all – reached the ears of a *Sunday Times* reporter, Alison Miller. Challenged by Miss Miller, a Clarence House spokesman admitted that the Queen Mother had been born in London, but refused to say where. Defensively he added, 'It really doesn't matter where she was born, or if there were inaccuracies. The Queen Mother was born one of millions of ordinary people. When she married at the age of twenty-three, she became fairly important. When she was thirty-six, she became a very important person. And since then she has become more and more special in every sense. So does it matter why something happened long ago? Strathmore did the evil deed, and he is dead. If he did wrong, it didn't show.'[65]

St Paul's Walden did not willingly surrender its most illustrious native. The plaque remains in All Saints' Church, and the present Vicar, the Reverend Dendle French, writes: 'There are no plans to have the wording changed . . . The tradition here among the elderly in fact is that Queen Elizabeth *was* born in this parish! . . . I have yet to be convinced that Queen Elizabeth was *not* born here! . . . I had a conversation in 1980 with the surviving daughter of my predecessor, the Rev. H. T. Valentine, who baptized Elizabeth Bowes-Lyon in 1900. Miss Valentine was eleven at the time and remembered the day that Lady Glamis gave birth to a daughter. Two quite independent sources have named a *local* doctor who was present at the birth.'[66]

While the dispute continues, the Queen Mother herself remains silent – even, apparently, to her own entourage. One harassed member of her staff at Clarence House, Mrs Lucy Murphy, apologized for the confusion. 'I am sorry I cannot be more helpful – I know how difficult it is to answer questions without answers!'[67]

'The mystery', says Helen Cathcart, 'is simply that she likes to keep a little to herself, to tease us.'[68]

Dorothy Laird agrees. 'She is a very Highland person: some things are very private and secret. She dislikes all things being known about her at all times, and will keep little inconsequential matters to herself, even from her own Household.'[69]

One thing seems indisputable. Bessiewallis Warfield and Elizabeth Bowes-Lyon, born in different continents and in greatly contrasting circumstances, yet both 'one of millions of ordinary people', were to become, as personalities and historical figures, very far from ordinary.

The British astrologer Roger Elliot thinks that 'the real cause of antipathy between them is the Queen Mother's Mars being very close to Wallis's Venus and Sun (so lots of anger) and even more important, her Saturn being right opposite Wallis's Sun, causing an outraged sense of discipline and decorum'.[70]

For those who believe in astrology, the conflict between the two women was inevitable, thirty-four years before they even met. It was ordained in the moment each of them was born.

3

THE GIRL
WHO MIGHT HAVE BEEN QUEEN

'IS OUR FATE IN OUR STARS or does it lie within ourselves?' asked the Duchess of Windsor at the beginning of her memoirs.[1]

In her case the question is understandable. However little one may incline towards a belief in predestination, any study of the Duchess's life, and of the lives that were changed so dramatically because of her, makes it hard to escape the conclusion that the forces of destiny were working overtime, and that Wallis Simpson, almost in spite of herself, was their chosen catalyst.

New evidence will reveal that had it not been for the intransigence of the man who later was most vehemently opposed to Wallis – King George V – the Prince of Wales would have made a suitable and possibly happy marriage to an eminently respectable British beauty fifteen years before Mrs Simpson arrived on the royal scene. But the King, for the most trivial of reasons, vetoed the Prince's first choice for a bride, and in doing so opened the way to all that he most feared and later deplored in the life of his eldest son.

Like that of the girl from Baltimore, the early progress of Elizabeth Bowes-Lyon also seems to have about it the curiously strong aura of an inevitable destiny.

In 1902, in her fortieth year, Lady Glamis gave birth to her tenth and last child, the Hon. David Bowes-Lyon, and in the following year, Katharine, Duchess of Atholl, visited Celia at the flat in Belgrave Mansions, Victoria.

'I was very impressed by the charm and dignity of a little daughter, two or three years old, who came into the room,' recorded the Duchess, '. . . as if a little princess had stepped out of an eighteenth-century picture.'[2]

At about the same time that the regal attributes of the future Queen Elizabeth were first being discerned in London, the attractions of the future Duchess of Windsor became apparent to her cousin Elizabeth in Baltimore.

'. . . while rambling up Charles Street one sunny afternoon, I noticed in a go-cart a very attractive child dressed in white with a large pink bow on her cap. When asked who she was, the nurse replied, "This is Wallis, Mrs Warfield's little girl."

'It was not that she was so pretty but she had individuality and charm, and she possessed, even then, the most entrancing little glance out of the corner of her eye, with head tilted to one side. I had hardly gone a block when I met her mother. "Alice," I said, "I've just seen your little girl; I feel that some day she will do something wonderful; she already has so much personality." '³

She also had an early strength of will. She detested the name, Bessiewallis – a product of the Baltimore tradition of giving children two names and joining them together – and soon insisted upon discarding Bessie, which she associated with cows, in favour of Wallis alone.

From the beginning, her power to attract attention was constantly noted. Dr Lewis Allen, who had brought her into the world, saw her several times as a child and later recalled her as 'quite pretty, with long hair and exceptionally magnetic in her personality'.⁴ Cleveland Amory, a one-time friend of the Duchess of Windsor, who later fell out with her when he abandoned the task of ghost-writing her memoirs, quotes an 'elderly Baltimorean who knew her well' as saying that her first words were not 'ma-ma' but 'me-me'.⁵ If this seems suspiciously ill-natured, it is perhaps easier to accept his further contention that her first dolls were named Mrs Astor and Mrs Vanderbilt.⁶

Amory cites this as an indication of early social aspirations, but there is a more plausible explanation. Her childhood was haunted by the spectre of insecurity. Her memory of it would affect her later decisions profoundly. Almost every day of her young life she was made sharply aware of the power which money conferred and of the humiliations and dangers that came from being without it.

While her first cousins, the children of General Harry and Uncle Emory Warfield, lived on large farms in the country, in Southern-style mansions with spacious rooms and impressive verandahs, waited on by negro servants, with horses in the stables and cattle grazing as far as the eye could see, Wallis and her mother were poor relations, dependent upon the charity of Uncle Sol, a 'reserved, unbending, silent'⁷ man of whom Wallis was 'always a little afraid'.⁸

Her widowed grandmother, an austere Episcopalian in her sixties, wore only black and was a fanatical Southerner in her views. 'Never marry a Yankee,' she warned her granddaughter,[9] and added, 'Never allow a man to kiss your hand. If you do, he'll never ask you to marry him.'[10]

When old Mrs Warfield heard gossip in Baltimore that her son Sol had fallen in love with his widowed sister-in-law, she promptly ordered Alice and her daughter out of the house. So, at the age of five, Wallis found herself sharing her mother's small room in the cheap, seedy Brexton Hotel. Alice got a job making children's clothes for the Women's Exchange, and for a time mother and daughter went to live at the Baltimore home of Aunt Bessie Merryman, before finding rooms of their own at the Preston Apartment House on Preston Street.

There, to make ends meet, Alice started taking paying guests for dinner, and possibly renting rooms also. A young medical student, Charles F. Bove, who later became a well-known surgeon in France, referred to Wallis as 'my landlady's' child,[11] adding, 'I was particularly fascinated by the young girl who helped her mother serve the meals I took with the family. She was an exuberant child . . . hair parted in braids, high cheekbones and a prominent nose that made one think of an Indian squaw.'[12]

Later Alice rented a three-storey brownstone at 212 East Biddle Street, Baltimore, where she continued to let rooms, but chiefly to relations and friends. Wallis resented and always vigorously denied subsequent suggestions that her mother 'had run a boarding house'.[13]

The Hon. Elizabeth Bowes-Lyon had been born in circumstances very far removed from the penury and insecurity in which Wallis Warfield spent her childhood.

On February 16, 1904, when Elizabeth's grandfather, the thirteenth Earl of Strathmore, died at the age of seventy-nine, she acquired the courtesy title of Lady Elizabeth. Her parents, the new Earl and Countess of Strathmore, were now a peer and peeress of the realm, with the imposing prefix, The Right Honourable, before their names.

They were also the owners of some 65,000 acres and of three ancestral homes: St Paul's Walden Bury, Streatlam Castle in County Durham,[14] and Glamis, a vast, battlemented fortress just north of Dundee, in the Glen of Strathmore, with its cluster of pointed grey turrets rising like witches' hats into the skies above the distant Grampian hills.

There a King of Scotland, Malcolm II, was brutally murdered in 1034, his bleeding body carried up the huge circular stone staircase to die in the room still called after him from the wounds inflicted on Hunter's Hill. From here the beautiful widow of the sixth Lord Glamis was taken to imprisonment in Edinburgh Castle, there to be burned alive in 1537 as a witch through 'the hatred which the King [James V] carried to her brothers'.

James's daughter, Mary Queen of Scots, stayed at Glamis in August 1562 on her journey north to crush the Earl of Huntly's rebellion. And Shakespeare, the most famous alleged visitor of all, is said to have conceived his play, *Macbeth*, while staying there, setting King Duncan I's murder by Macbeth, the Thane of Glamis, in the old guardroom of the castle, still known as Duncan's Hall.

There is no firm evidence that Shakespeare really stayed at Glamis,[15] but Bonnie Prince Charlie certainly did, and so did Sir Walter Scott, who wrote of his first visit there in 1793: 'Peter Proctor, seneschal of the Castle, conducted me to my apartments in a distant part of the building. I must own that when I heard door after door shut, after my conductor had retired, I began to consider myself as too far from the living, and somewhat too near the dead.'[16]

The castle's grim legacy included not only the secret of the family 'monster', but also at least nine accredited and highly active ghosts. Among them were the Grey Lady, the Tongueless Woman, the Mad Earl, Jack the Runner, the Negro Boy and Earl Beardie, who was still heard occasionally rattling his dice as he gambled with the Devil.

'From ghoulies and ghosties and long-leggety beasties and things that go bump in the night, Good Lord, deliver us!' If Lady Elizabeth Bowes-Lyon ever felt constrained to invoke that ancient Scottish prayer, her fear was never apparent, although her elder sister, Rose, the Countess Granville, once admitted: 'When ... the Queen Mother and I were children, we would sometimes be sent down-stairs to fetch something. We always raced through Duncan's Hall and the Banqueting Room. As for King Malcolm's Room, where Malcolm was murdered, there was a bloodstain on the floor that would *never* wash out. So my mother had the whole floor boarded over.'[17]

In the summer of 1905, a few weeks before her fifth birthday, Lady Elizabeth went with her three-year-old brother, David Bowes-Lyon, to a party given by the Duchess of Buccleuch[18] for her grandchildren at Montagu House in Whitehall.

The Duchess, born Lady Louisa Hamilton, third daughter of the first Duke of Abercorn, was Mistress of the Robes to Queen Alexandra and had held the same position under Queen Victoria. An imposing figure, she had been one of the great hostesses of the Victorian age. Montagu House, where she still entertained lavishly, was one of London's last ducal palaces, standing opposite the entrance into Horse Guards Parade, with impressive gates, a porter's lodge, and a tree-lined drive fronting onto Whitehall. The gardens behind the house extended all the way to the Thames Embankment.[19]

Wearing a long blue and white dress with a velvet wrap, her dark hair adorned with a large blue bow, Elizabeth clutched her brother's hand protectively as they walked from the Strathmore coach past the liveried footmen into the magnificent white marble hall of Montagu House. There they were confronted by dozens of children of their own age and background. One of the youngest present, at three and a half, was the Duchess of Buccleuch's little granddaughter, Lady Alice Scott, who would one day be Elizabeth's sister-in-law, the Duchess of Gloucester.

There was a conjurer, a magic lantern, and a great deal of noise. Pride of place in the *mêlée* went to three royal children: Prince Edward of Wales, eleven, who was introduced to everyone present as David; Prince Albert of Wales, nine, who was simply Bertie; and their sister, Princess Mary, just eight, but taller than both her brothers.

The extrovert David was quickly the life and soul of the party, but Prince Bertie, already afflicted by a chronic speech impediment, was silent and withdrawn, standing awkwardly to one side and watching the dancing and the games with a solemn, unsmiling expression. At tea he found himself next to the pretty girl with the blue bow in her dark hair and his shyness began to melt a little in the warmth of her smile. For a long time afterwards, so the legend goes, he would remember her gesture in prising the crystallized cherries off her sugar cake and transferring them to his plate.[20]

Bertie and Elizabeth would have no way of knowing, then or later, that their first meeting had taken place in a house originally built and owned by an ancestor of the woman who would cause them to become King and Queen – Wallis Warfield.[21]

While Elizabeth was attracting attention with her large blue bow at Montagu House, Wallis was refusing to wear the same colour at her own first children's party in Baltimore. 'On that occasion,' she admitted later, 'I am supposed to have persuaded my mother, after a foot-stamping scene, to substitute for the blue sash she wanted me to wear with my white dress a bright red one. "I remember exactly what you said," my aunt now insists. "You told your mother you wanted a red sash so the boys would notice you." '22

At the age of six she had gone to a kindergarten school in Baltimore, Miss O'Donnell's, named after its founder Ada O'Donnell, and four years later, with the financial assistance of Uncle Sol, she enrolled at one of Baltimore's best private girls' schools, Arundell, on St Paul Street, not far from the rectory where her parents had married.

In 1908, when Wallis was twelve, Alice Warfield remarried. Her second husband was John Freeman Rasin – 'Young Free' – the son of a prosperous but not entirely reputable Baltimore politician. Through his money – he had inherited a comfortable income from a trust fund – the fortunes of Wallis and her mother rapidly improved, but socially the match was *mal vu* in Baltimore, where it was widely rumoured that Rasin had been Alice's lover for some time before the marriage. Rasin's own lifestyle did nothing to redeem Alice's now *déclassé* image locally. According to Wallis, her stepfather spent most of his time in bed, reading newspapers, chain-smoking, and drinking rather more than was good for him at the corner saloon.

One of her contemporaries who wrote Wallis's name down on a list of girls she wished to invite to her party, found it crossed out. Upon enquiring why, her parents explained that while Wallis herself might be welcome in their home, the visit could under no circumstances be returned.

Uncle Sol, aghast at the damage he foresaw to his niece's social standing, now proposed to remove Wallis from her mother's care and to raise her in his own household. Had she agreed, her future, in material terms, would have been assured, and she would almost certainly have become sole heiress to her uncle's considerable fortune. But the condition was that she should sever all relations with Alice. It says a great deal for Wallis Warfield that she firmly rejected the offer and chose to remain with her mother.

In this she showed discernment as well as loyalty. For all her problems, Alice was a woman of admirable personality and intelligence.

'I was a happy child, I really was,' her daughter remembered sixty-five years later. 'My mother was always so gay, and what a great sense of humour she had.'23 A sample of the 'trigger wit' that Wallis would inherit occurred when her mother tripped and tumbled down the stairs of a five-and-ten-cent store. To a worried clerk who rushed up to ask if he could help her, Alice replied, 'Yes, just take me at once to the five-and-ten-cent coffin counter.'[24]

Although much divided them in terms of wealth, privilege and social status, Alice Montague Warfield Rasin shared many qualities of character with Celia Strathmore.

It was from their mothers that Elizabeth and Wallis derived not merely their humour, but also their lively interest in the world around them. 'If you find a person a bore, the fault lies in you',[25] Celia taught her children, and Alice would have agreed with her.

There was also a certain imperturbability which the two mothers had in common. A friend, sitting with Lady Strathmore in the drawing room at St Paul's Walden Bury, found it impossible to ignore the water that was steadily streaming down one wall from some unknown plumbing disaster. Eventually she could no longer resist the temptation to mention it to her hostess. 'Oh dear,' murmured Lady Strathmore rather absently, 'we must move that sofa.'[26]

The butler at Glamis was frequently the worse for drink, and 'seemed always to be falling about and pouring wine down people's backs, but . . . Lady Strathmore coped quite unruffled'.[27]

Perhaps the one aspect in which Alice Warfield Rasin and Celia Strathmore differed was in the degree of religious knowledge they instilled into their children's lives. Gay, light-hearted, witty and charming as she clearly was, Alice hardly emerges as a devout woman, but Celia certainly was one.

At Glamis, the chapel was used for prayers daily, and all the women in the family, as well as each female guest, wore little white caps made of thick crochet lace. On Sundays, Celia Strathmore, with the white lace cap on her head, sat at the harmonium and played accompaniments to the hymns. At St Paul's Walden Bury the family said morning prayers together every day, and in London they attended church every Sunday, all of them taking seriously the Strathmore motto, 'In thou, my God, I place my trust without change to the end'.

'At the age of six and seven,' David Bowes-Lyon recalled, 'we could each have written a fairly detailed account of all the Bible stories. This knowledge was entirely due to our mother's teaching. She also taught us the rudiments of music, dancing and drawing, at all of which my sister became fairly proficient.'[28]

In 1908, Elizabeth and David became pupils for two terms at the London school of a Froebel-trained teacher in her twenties, Constance Goff, at 25 Marylebone High Street.

Joan Woollcombe, a fellow pupil there, recalled more than sixty years later: 'The boys learned boxing and we girls fencing and we all slid easily into languages through plays in French and German, and took happily to geometry.

'Elizabeth and David . . . were pleasant children, tidy in their tussore smocks . . . I watched her change her after-lunch banana for David's bad one at school. To us children this seemed a tremendous sacrifice.

'Looking back it is easy to see now that, with Elizabeth, it was already there – the little girl who would have to cope with situations all her life seemed able to take them, even then, in her stride.

'Lady Strathmore asked Miss Goff to tea in their London home in St James's Square. When she arrived she found that her hostess had been delayed, but she was received by Elizabeth who rang for tea, poured it out, and made conversation until her mother arrived.'[29]

In the same year, on November 21, 1908, the eight-year-old Lady Elizabeth made the first in a lifetime of public appearances when, in a dress of white muslin and lace, and carrying a bouquet of pale pink roses, she appeared as a bridesmaid at the Guards' Chapel, Wellington Barracks, at the wedding of her eldest brother, Patrick, Lord Glamis, to Lady Dorothy Osborne, the third daughter of the Duke of Leeds.

The regal qualities first noted six years earlier by the Duchess of Atholl were becoming more widely recognized. Also in 1908 there appeared Mrs Andrew Lang's *The Book of Princes and Princesses*, the fly-leaf of which bore the words, 'Dedicated to Elizabeth Angela Margaret (sic) Bowes-Lyon by the Authoress'.

In the following summer of 1909, the Reverend Dr John Stirton, Minister of Glamis – who later, as Minister of Crathie and Chaplain to King Edward VIII at Balmoral, would figure in Elizabeth's life during one of the most dramatic occasions leading up to the Abdication – was invited to the castle by Lady Strathmore.

In the Glamis drawing room he found the family assembled, and old Mr Neal, the Scottish dance teacher from Forfar, with his fiddle at the ready beneath his long white beard. Seated on the floor were the nine-year-old Lady Elizabeth, in a long dress of rose-pink and silver in the style of James I's daughter, the future Winter Queen of Bohemia; and seven-year-old David Bowes-Lyon, in a jester costume with cap and bells.

'. . . the Countess sat down at the piano', recalled Dr Stirton, 'and played a few bars of a quaint old minuet. Suddenly, as if by a magician's touch, two little figures seemed to rise from the floor and dance, with admirable precision and grace . . .

'For one brief, yet supreme, half-hour the seventeenth and twentieth centuries were one . . . suddenly the music stopped and the little dancers, making a low bow and curtsey, clapped their hands with delight, and in this way brought the minds of all back to present-day reality . . . Lady Elizabeth, on being asked . . . the name of the character she had adopted, said with great *empressement*: "I call myself the Princess Elizabeth".'[30]

To the third Lord Gorell,[31] sixteen years her senior, Elizabeth appeared 'small for her age, responsive as a harp, wistful and appealing one moment, bright-eyed and eager the next, with a flashing smile of appreciative delight, an elfin creature swift of movement'.[32]

A contemporary, Lord David Cecil, just eight months her junior, met her amid 'the slim Adam columns and pale plastered drawing-rooms of Lansdowne House' and remembered the 'grave, enchanting smile . . . the drowsy caressing voice . . . the delicious gurgle of laughter . . . sitting demurely at the tea-table; or best of all, at a fancy-dress party dressed as a Vandyck child, with high square bodice and stiff satin skirts, surrounded by a bevy of adorers'.[33]

It was at a Glamis garden party in the summer of 1910 that Elizabeth met the palmist. 'The woman with the witch-hair and onyx eyes took the tiny hand . . . She looked piercingly into the eager little face . . . The gypsy woman spoke with sudden, intense fierceness. A touch of awe. "You will live to be a queen – and the mother of a queen." '[34]

Her French governess, Mademoiselle Lang, asked her if she had had her hand read.

' "Yes, I did. But she was silly. She says I'm going to be a queen when I grow up."

' "That you can't be, unless they change the laws of England for you," said the practical Mademoiselle.

'Elizabeth tossed her hat on a chair. "Who wants to be a queen anyway?" Dancing round the room she began to sing the old French nursery rhyme which she had just learned, "*S'il fleurisse je serai reine.*" '[35]

In 1911, at the age of fifteen, Wallis Warfield attended the fashionable girls' summer camp, Burrlands, a mile and a half from Middleburg, Virginia, located at the country estate of Charlotte Noland, who taught athletics at Wallis's school, Arundell. There she developed an intense but unrequited crush on Charlotte's brother, Philip Noland, who was thirty-five, and also acquired her first boyfriend, seventeen-year-old Lloyd Tabb, who found her far more sophisticated and advanced than other girls of her age. He also detected 'a touch of pathos and sweetness bordering on wistfulness . . . Her ability to see the amusing side of things was very pronounced'.[36]

She seems not to have impressed Miss Noland overmuch, who would later say of her, 'I have never known anyone who could so consistently for so many years so successfully evade the truth.'[37]

She graduated from Arundell in June 1912, and went on to an exclusive boarding school, Oldfields, at Glencoe in Maryland, where her mother and aunt had been pupils before her. Over each room in the dormitory was a sign that read, 'Gentleness and Courtesy are expected of the Girls at all Times'.

At sixteen she was already developing an independent and notice-ably offbeat style of her own. She was the first Baltimore girl to have her hair bobbed. She wore the first black beauty patch and the first hobble skirt seen in the city. Sometimes her chosen image was start-lingly mannish – a close-fitting shirtwaister, an Eton collar, a bow tie at her throat, a wide patent leather belt drawn very tight to reveal the astonishingly small waist, and the overall effect crowned by the droll addition of a monocle.

It was hardly surprising that the opposite sex began to gravitate towards her very early, or that she earned the reputation among her female contemporaries in Baltimore of being 'fast' where men were concerned. 'She was a honey pot,' her cousin, Basil Gordon, said later. 'She attracted men the way molasses attracts flies.'[38]

She was still at Oldfields when she learned, in April 1913, that her mother had found her stepfather dead in bed – from Bright's disease. Rasin's income died with him and Alice and her daughter were poor again.

The programme for the fourteen girls in Wallis's graduation class at Oldfields was 'Debut, travel, marriage'.[39] Marriage, she herself would say, was 'the only thing that we had to look forward to . . . the condition of marriage had been made to seem to us the only state desirable for a woman – and the sooner the better'.[40]

At seventeen, she wrote in a friend's birthday book the words of Benedick in Shakespeare's *Much Ado About Nothing*: 'I do much wonder that one man, seeing how much another man is a fool when he dedicates his behaviours to love, will, after he hath laughed at such shallow follies in others, become the argument of his own scorn by falling in love.'[41]

And at her farewell dance at Oldfields in 1914, the girls were asked to sign their names and write their comments on life. Most of the comments were trite. 'It's the little things in life that count' . . . 'Three cheers for English History' . . . 'Hey down there, turn off the water'. In the middle of the list, in a strong and confident hand that dominated all the rest both in size and boldness, came the inscription: Wallis Warfield, Baltimore, March 3rd. 'All is Love'.[42]

August 4, 1914, was Lady Elizabeth Bowes-Lyon's fourteenth birthday. In celebration of the event, the Strathmores had taken a box that evening at the London Coliseum for the weekly variety programme. In the first half, they watched Lipinski's Dog Comedians 'in their remarkable Canine Play, "Every Day Life in a German Town" ', and Roshanara 'in selections from her repertoire of Indian and Burmese dances, including the Snake Dance'.[43]

During the intermission, it was announced from the stage that as from 11 p.m. Britain would be at war with the Kaiser's Germany. From the family box, an incredulous Elizabeth watched as the audience erupted in a frenzy of patriotic fervour. In the second half, when Alexandra Fedorowa, the ballerina from the Imperial Opera House, St Petersburg, appeared and danced Saint-Saëns' The Dying Swan – which seemed a poignant elegy for the last, fluttering hours of peace in Europe – she was given a thunderous ovation, for it was already understood that Czarist Russia would be Britain's ally in the conflict.

The Strathmore family drove home to 20 St James's Square through streets already thronged with Union Jacks and singing crowds

Four of Elizabeth's brothers, Patrick, John, Fergus and Michael,[44] at once left to join their regiments. Potential marriages were accelerated. On September 17, Fergus married the Earl of Portarlington's daughter, Lady Christian Dawson-Damer, and twelve days later, John married the Hon. Fenella Hepburn-Stuart-Forbes-Trefusis, the daughter of Lord Clinton.

Elizabeth, meanwhile, travelled north with her parents to Glamis, to begin work on turning the castle into a military hospital.

The first shots of what became World War I were fired in France on August 22 at the Battle of Mons, which ended with sixteen hundred dead or wounded. At Le Cateau four days later, the casualties numbered three thousand.

In America, which would not enter the war for almost three years,

Uncle Sol issued a statement to the Baltimore press that autumn. 'The report that I will give a large ball for my debutante niece, Miss Wallis Warfield, is without foundation in that I do not consider the present a proper time for such festivities, when thousands of men are being slaughtered in Europe.'[45]

If it came as a blow to Wallis that she would not have a coming-out dance of her own, her disappointment soon faded with the arrival of a letter to say that she had been selected as one of the forty-seven Baltimore debutantes invited to be presented at the coveted opening ball of the Bachelors' Cotillion (always spelled locally without the second 'i') on December 7, 1914. There, at eighteen, in a gown of white satin and chiffon, embroidered with pearls – copied from a ballroom dress in which Irene Castle was then dancing to spectacular success on Broadway – she made her official debut.

Her twenty-seven-year-old cousin, Henry Warfield Jr, who escorted her to the ball in white tie and tails, promised, 'Kiddo, I can assure you that you will be the most enchanting, most ravishing, most exquisite creature at the Cotillion.'[46] And at the Lyric Theatre, Baltimore, when her cousin-by-marriage, Major-General George Barnett, in the full dress uniform of the Marine Corps, led her onto the dance floor, Henry's prediction proved correct. Wallis Warfield was what she had always longed to be: the belle of the ball.

While Wallis was dancing at her debut in Baltimore, the first wounded soldiers were arriving at Glamis Castle. With Mary long since married, and Rose away training at a London hospital, Elizabeth was now the last of the Bowes-Lyon daughters left at home.[47] She and her mother had been working hard.

'We were so busy knitting, knitting, knitting,' she later remembered, 'and making shirts for the local battalion, the fifth Black Watch. My chief occupation was crumpling up tissue paper until it was so soft that it no longer crackled, to put into the lining of sleeping bags.'[48]

As each of the wounded arrived at Glamis, Lady Strathmore met them at the main door and settled them into one of the sixteen beds arranged round the panelled walls of the vast dining-room. For the next five years, not one of those beds was to be empty.

In due course, Lady Rose returned from her hospital training and took over the supervision of the nursing. Elizabeth, at fourteen, was judged too young to join her in this. Instead she served meals and tea to the soldiers, made sure they were supplied with cigarettes and tobacco, and took photographs of them to send to their families. As Dorothy

Laird was to say: '. . . she teased and charmed them into good spirits
. . . she played and sang for them, wrote letters for those unfit to write
and generally helped to restore them to normality, because some of the
men were badly shattered in body and spirit. She then had her early
lessons in complete, selfless control, in the iron discipline and sense of
duty that lie under her smile.'[49]

In September 1915, Fergus, a captain in the Black Watch regiment,
came home on leave to spend his first wedding anniversary with his
wife at Glamis, and to see their two-month-old baby daughter,
Rosemary, for the first time. After just three days with his family,
Fergus left Glamis again to return to France. One week later a telegram
arrived at the castle to say that he had been killed in action at the Battle
of Loos on September 27.

An unnatural silence descended upon Glamis. The invalided soldiers
turned off their gramophone, refrained from playing the piano, and
avoided walking in the grounds. As soon as she realized this, Lady
Strathmore sent them a message that they were to carry on as usual
since they were the family's guests.

Death also came to the Warfields, though less unexpectedly. Wallis's grandmother, old Mrs Henry Mactier Warfield, fell and broke her
hip, developed pneumonia, and died in December 1915. The family
went into mourning for three months, after which Wallis accepted an
invitation to visit her cousin, Corinne, and her husband, Captain
Henry Mustin of the United States Navy, at Pensacola Air Station in
Florida, of which Mustin had recently been appointed commandant.

On the day after she arrived there, in April 1916, Wallis was
introduced to a naval pilot, Lieutenant (junior grade) Earl Winfield
Spencer, Jr.

'Win' Spencer, then twenty-seven – eight years Wallis's senior – had
been born in Kansas, the son of a British mother from Jersey, in the
Channel Islands, and an American father, who was a leading member
of the Chicago Stock Exchange. Virile, confident, and aggressively
masculine in his personality, Spencer attracted Wallis so rapidly that
that evening she began a letter to her mother with the words, 'I have
just met the world's most fascinating aviator'.[50]

On the evening of Saturday, September 16, 1916, while Lord
Strathmore and David Bowes-Lyon were out shooting in the hills near
Glamis, a spark ignited a joist in one of the chimneys of the castle, and
burning soot fell onto the snow boards on the roof, starting a rapid
blaze in the ninety-foot-high keep.[51] While panic erupted among the

servants, Lady Elizabeth calmly took control, summoning the Glamis
and Forfar fire brigades, only to discover that their hoses were not long
enough to draw water from the River Dean, a few hundred yards
away. Realizing that Glamis was now in danger of being destroyed,
she quickly telephoned the larger Dundee fire service and urged them
to come immediately.

Meanwhile, forming a chain of thirty people, 'Lady Elizabeth . . . at
once set to work to remove the tapestries and other articles of antique
and historic value from the rooms which were threatened.'[52] Armed
with brooms, she and her helpers also swept down the circular
staircase, and away from the drawing-room, hundreds of gallons of
cascading water from a vast lead tank on the roof that had burst owing
to the intense heat.

Later, when the Dundee brigade had at last arrived and got the fire
under control, a spectator, unaware of her identity, plagued her with
questions about how it had started. ' "I've no time to make conversation!" Lady Elizabeth exclaimed. Unwonted asperity was in her voice
and the lounger withdrew discomfited. "Who's yon prood lassie?" he
ruefully enquired.'[53]

On the same day that Elizabeth became the heroine of the Glamis
fire, Wallis Warfield announced her engagement to Win Spencer. The
news was considered by the Baltimore press to be 'of unusual interest
to Society in Maryland, as well as in Virginia', since Wallis was 'one of
the most popular girls in Society' and 'has been a belle ever since she
made her debut two years ago'.[54]

They were married on November 8, 1916, at the Christ Protestant
Episcopal Church in Baltimore, where she had been confirmed. Uncle
Sol gave her away, and she left for a short honeymoon with Spencer in
White Sulphur Springs, West Virginia, before returning with him, via
New York, to Pensacola.

Wallis, at twenty, had married in haste – 'out of curiosity', according to her cousin, Lelia Barnett[55] – and she hardly needed leisure to
repent. She, who had then never touched alcohol in her life, soon
discovered that Win drank heavily, and that when he did, he became
aggressive, neurotic, obsessively jealous, and occasionally violent.

The United States declaration of war on April 6, 1917, brought
Spencer promotion to full lieutenant, and in June he was assigned
command of the Naval Air Station at Squantum, near Boston.

The Armistice in November 1918 found Wallis in San Diego, where
Win was lieutenant-commander of the air station on North Island, but

by this time the marriage was hanging together by the finest of threads. Spencer's treatment of his wife had taken a sadistic turn. One afternoon he locked her into the bathroom and left her there for many hours, far into the night.

The first summer of peace in 1919 brought Lady Elizabeth Bowes-Lyon a belated coming-out into British society. At the beginning of April, she went to stay at Althorp, the ancestral home of the sixth Earl Spencer – whose granddaughter, Lady Diana, would become Princess of Wales sixty-two years later – to be bridesmaid at the wedding of her close friend, Lady Lavinia Spencer, to the Hon. Luke White.[56]

Lord David Cecil has described Elizabeth as 'a noticeable debutante', partly because – as Wallis Simpson was to point out, far less kindly – she dressed 'picturesquely, unfashionably'.[57] Lady Airlie remembered her as 'very unlike the cocktail-drinking, chain-smoking girls who came to be regarded as typical of the nineteen-twenties. Her radiant vitality and a blending of gaiety, kindness and sincerity made her irresistible to men'.[58]

Elizabeth often returned from dances to 20 St James's Square in a brougham with a coachman and one old horse. 'In the middle of the street, in the early hours of the morning, the horse would suddenly stop. The Lady Elizabeth would put her head through the window and ask the coachman, "Is everything all right?"

' "It's quite all right, Milady," he would reply. "The horse has just stopped for a little sleep." '[59]

At Ascot in June 1919, Elizabeth received a second prophecy concerning her future. As she walked towards the Royal Enclosure with a friend, the Hon. Mrs Donald Forbes, a clairvoyant known as Gypsy Lee stopped her and made the same prediction as the palmist at Glamis nine years earlier: 'One day you will be Queen – and the mother of a queen.'[60]

Wallis Warfield Spencer, soon to be separated from her alcoholic husband, would also be the subject of a clairvoyant's prediction in New York. The woman told her that she would have two more marriages, and that in middle life, between the ages of forty and fifty, she would exercise 'considerable power of some kind . . . You will become a famous woman . . . The power that is to come to you will be related to a man.'[61]

Without knowing it, Wallis was on the point of her first meeting with the man who was to be the source of that power.

On April 7, 1920, HMS *Renown*, carrying the heir to the British throne, the Prince of Wales, and his cousin, Lord Louis Mountbatten, en route to a tour of New Zealand and Australia, put in to San Diego. That afternoon, the acting Commander-in-Chief of the US Pacific Fleet, Vice-Admiral Clarence Williams, gave a reception on board his flagship, USS *New Mexico*, in honour of the Prince and his cousin. Among those presented were Lieutenant-Commander and Mrs Earl Winfield Spencer Jr.

Wallis and her husband shook hands with the twenty-five-year-old prince, whose golden hair, blue eyes and boyish looks had already inspired such epithets in the American press as 'Prince Charming of the World', 'the salesman of the British Empire', and 'The Most Eligible Bachelor Yet Uncaught'. After a few words of perfunctory greeting the Spencers also shook hands with Lord Louis Mountbatten, and the royal cousins moved on down the reception line.

The Duke of Windsor makes no reference to this first meeting in his memoirs, and neither he nor Mountbatten remembered the occasion later. The Duchess, in her own memoirs,[62] claimed that the meeting never took place, but for years afterwards she chided both the Duke and Mountbatten for their failure to recall so momentous an encounter.[63]

His Royal Highness Prince Edward Albert Christian George Andrew Patrick David, great-grandson of Queen Victoria, grandson of Edward VII, and eldest son of George V, had also been the subject of prophecy. Shortly after his birth on June 23, 1894, at White Lodge, Richmond Park, the Scottish socialist leader, Kier Hardie, had said in the House of Commons: 'From his childhood onwards this boy will be surrounded by sycophants and flatterers by the score and will be taught to believe himself as of a superior creation. A line will be drawn between him and the people he is to be called upon some day to reign over. In due course, following the precedent which has already been set he will be sent on a tour round the world, and probably rumours of a morganatic alliance will follow and the end of it all will be the country will be called upon to pay the bill.'[64]

Some years later, the celebrated astrologer, Count Louis Hamon – 'Cheiro' – would write that the Prince of Wales's birth chart 'shows influences . . . that . . . point to changes . . . greatly affecting the Throne of England . . . [He] was born under peculiar astrological circumstances which make his character a difficult one to understand . . . [He] is determined not to "settle down" until he feels a *grande passion* but, it is well within the range of possibility . . . that he will fall a victim to a devastating love affair. If he does, I predict that the Prince will give up everything, even the chance of being crowned, rather than lose the object of his affection.'[65]

The earliest object of his affection in a romantic sense was a married woman twelve years his senior, Viscountess Coke, the daughter-in-law of the third Earl of Leicester, whom he first met early in 1915, during one of his leaves from active service with the Grenadier Guards in France. The Leicesters, whose Norfolk estate, Holkham, was close to Sandringham, had long been friends as well as neighbours of the British Royal Family.[66]

It was to the sympathetic Marion Coke that the young prince, then twenty, poured out some of the frustrations of his exalted position. 'The Grenadiers have had thirty-five officers killed; isn't it too ghastly to think of . . . ?', he wrote to her in March 1915. 'But, of course I never went near the fighting; [I was] kept right away as usual!!'[67]

Lady Coke had called her younger son – born at the end of 1915 – David, the name by which the Prince of Wales was known to his intimate friends and within the Royal Family. The Prince stood as sponsor for the child at the christening.

'It is *too* nice of you to suggest a little dancing for me tomorrow night,' he wrote to Marion in March 1917 from Buckingham Palace. 'It will be my only chance of getting out at all in the evening from this *most* depressing of places!'[68] And two months later, there was no mistaking the strength of this first attachment when he wrote to the Viscountess: 'You have been too angelically kind to me for words and have absolutely changed my life.'[69]

The Prince's devotion to Lady Coke might be classified as 'puppy love'. There was, of course, no question of the lady abandoning a secure and happy marriage to the heir to an earldom, or of the Prince of Wales marrying her even if she did.

Until this time it had been the invariable rule for the heir to the British throne to marry foreign royalty. George V had married his dead brother's fiancée, Princess May of Teck. Edward VII had married Princess Alexandra of Denmark. And Queen Victoria had married Prince Albert of Saxe-Coburg-Gotha.

But the war against the Kaiser's Germany, and the increasing insularity of British public opinion, had caused George V to revise his once inflexible views in this respect. After a Privy Council meeting on July 17, 1917, at which the King relinquished all his German titles and proclaimed the establishment of the House of Windsor, George V noted in his diary: 'I also informed the Council that May and I had decided some time ago that our children would be allowed to marry into British families. It was quite a historical occasion.'[70]

Citing the eventual marriage of the King's daughter, Princess Mary, to Viscount Lascelles, and of his second son, the Duke of York, to Lady Elizabeth Bowes-Lyon, George V's most recent biographer, Kenneth Rose, says: 'Had the Prince of Wales produced a bride of similar background, there is no reason to believe that the King would have withheld his consent.'[71]

Yet within only six months of the Privy Council meeting in July 1917, the Prince of Wales produced a potential British bride of the most impeccable background imaginable – a duke's daughter no less – and George V *did* emphatically refuse his consent to the match.

Of the girl in question, Lady Rosemary Leveson-Gower, the younger daughter of the Duke of Sutherland, Kenneth Rose has written, '. . . it was never a serious romance'.[72]

The evidence proves Mr Rose mistaken. The Dowager Lady Hardinge of Penshurst, whose husband was at that time Assistant Private Secretary to George V, and subsequently Private Secretary to both Edward VIII and George VI, wrote, of the Prince's attitude to Lady Rosemary: '. . . he wished to marry . . . but there was opposition to the match . . . One can wonder forever how the history of our Monarchy in the twentieth century and after would have turned out, if the Prince of Wales had had his way in those early days.'[73]

In fact, as we shall see, the Prince proposed marriage, and would almost certainly have been accepted had Lady Rosemary not learned of the King's opposition to his son's choice.

Lady Rosemary Millicent Leveson-Gower was born on August 9, 1893, which made her almost a year older than the Prince of Wales. Her father, 'Strath', the fourth Duke of Sutherland, had been a Liberal Member of Parliament, and her mother, formerly Lady Millicent St Clair-Erskine, daughter of the fourth Earl of Rosslyn, was one of the outstanding beauties of the Victorian age – 'a woman of pellucid beauty', as one writer has described her.[74]

Rosemary inherited her mother's smile, much of her beauty, and something of her charm. Sir James Barrie based the character of his ageless heroine in the play, *Mary Rose*, on Rosemary. Her son, the present Earl of Dudley, explains: 'Barrie was a great friend of my mother and his play was inspired by her when she was a girl . . . the title, *Mary Rose*, was an inversion of her name, Rosemary.'[75]

Humour seems to have been the predominant quality in her character. When she was young, Barrie often took her to the theatre. 'I used to take her to the play,' he wrote later, 'and lead her away in the middle thereof until she came to of her mirth. She was fond of fishing in the North in those days, but her laugh established such a relationship between her and her intended victims that I don't remember her landing many fish.'[76]

She met the Prince of Wales in 1917 while she was working as a Red Cross nurse in France. In her hospital there was one wounded soldier suffering so badly from shell-shock that he was unable to speak at all. The doctors believed that if only one word could be induced, others would follow. Rosemary sat for hours in front of this man, telling funny stories and pausing before familiar words in the hope that he would supply the blanks. When this failed, she resorted to cajolery, coaxing, even flirtation. Finally, with the Prince of Wales looking on, the soldier pointed at her and with tremendous effort stammered out one word: 'Darling'. The Prince was delighted and also very moved.[77]

By February 1918, they were both back in England – he to spend some weeks making a tour of the defence plants – and by now it was evident to their friends that the Prince was in love with her.

At that time we find Lady Cynthia Asquith reporting: 'Pamela Lytton . . . told us of the wild excitement fluttering all the girls over the Prince of Wales who, "unbeknownst" to the King, has taken to going to all the dances. So far, he dances most with Rosemary and also motors with her in the day time. No girl is allowed to leave London during the three weeks of his leave and every mother's heart beats high.'[78]

But even before Lady Cynthia had penned this diary entry, the Prince had decided that Lady Rosemary was the girl he wished to become Princess of Wales. He asked her to marry him and informed his father.

For Rosemary's reaction, and that of the King, we must now depend on the late Lady Victor Paget.[79] Her account deserves attention. She was one of Rosemary's closest friends and contemporaries, being eighteen months her senior, and, as the Hon. Bridget Colebrooke, was to be one of her bridesmaids. In addition to this, Bridget was herself briefly the mistress of the Prince of Wales, and after Rosemary's death, she also became the mistress of Rosemary's husband, Viscount Ednam.[80]

In 1972, in the week after the Duke of Windsor's death, Lady Victor remembered: 'Rosemary was extraordinarily beautiful – about five feet six inches tall, with very blonde hair and magnificent blue eyes. She had a slightly turned up nose, a very distinctive husky voice, and the most enchanting personality of anyone I ever knew.

'After a while, it was obvious to us all – but not, I think, to her – that the Prince of Wales was in love with her.

'One day she came to see me and told me that the Prince had asked her to marry him. To begin with she was absolutely against the idea, and said, "I couldn't possibly."

'She was a very independent person. As a duke's daughter, she had an income of her own of about £5,000 a year – a lot of money then – so, you see, she had no need of ambition. In any case the thought of becoming Queen simply appalled her.

'But the Prince asked her over and over again, and very gradually she began to come round to the idea. She admitted, "I'm very fond of him." And the next time I saw her, she said, "I've been thinking about it very hard. He's like a child, weak and very irresponsible, but you know, I think I could make something of him.' At that point, we thought there would be an announcement at any moment, and if it hadn't been for the King I think there would have been.'[81]

George V did not disapprove of Rosemary personally. He considered her a charming, moral and respectable girl. But he had reservations about her mother, Millicent Duchess of Sutherland. 'Strath', the fourth Duke, had died five years earlier, and Millicent had startled society by remarrying, at the age of forty-seven, little more than a year later. Her second marriage – to Brigadier-General Percy Desmond FitzGerald – was a rapid failure, and within five years they were divorced. Millicent immediately married for the third time, at the age of fifty-two, to Lt-Colonel George Ernest Hawes, who was a known homosexual. Another divorce followed.

In 1918, at the time that the Prince of Wales wanted to marry Rosemary, Millicent was separated from her second husband, and the King felt it undesirable for the daughter of a woman liable to be divorced to become Princess of Wales and the future Queen of England.

Millicent, however, was not finally the deciding factor. The clincher was the record of Millicent's brother, the fifth Earl of Rosslyn. Before his father's death in 1890, Harry Rosslyn had had a meagre allowance of £250 a year. On inheriting the earldom, his annual income escalated to £17,000. He went on an amazing gambling spree that lasted for 36 years and inspired the popular song, 'The Man Who Broke the Bank of Monte Carlo'. In 1897 came his first bankruptcy. In 1920 he lost £6,000 in one night at the casino in Monte Carlo. By the time of his third bankruptcy in 1926, it was estimated that he had gambled away at least a quarter of a million pounds. When he published his auto-biography in 1928, he called it, *My Gamble with Life*. It was his gambling that led to his first divorce in 1902. A second divorce – from an American actress given to drugs and drink – followed in 1907, but his third marriage, in 1908, produced a devoted and long-suffering wife – 'Tommy' – who bore him two sons and a daughter, and tolerated his infidelities as well as his improvidence. By 1918, Harry Rosslyn had been twice divorced, twice bankrupt, and was drinking so heavily that he was usually encountered leaving public places feet first.

George V was hyper-sensitive on the subject of intemperance. For many years he himself had been plagued by rumours that he was addicted to drink. In reality he drank sparingly, but the legend of the drunkard king was possibly encouraged by his florid complexion and loud quarter-deck voice.

It would be bad enough, the King thought, to have a daughter-in-law whose uncle's gambling and divorces might be spread in columns across the popular press. But to have a Princess of Wales and a future Queen with a close relation who might be seen keeling over on public occasions was a prospect he could not bring himself to face. There was already one member of the Royal Family, Princess Marie Louise – Cousin Louie – whose taste for alcohol sometimes caused her to be seen in 'an unfortunate condition' at Court functions.

The King told his son that, charming as Rosemary was, the match was ill-advised. It was a decision he must have regretted many times in the last eighteen months of his life, when Wallis Simpson's supremacy became apparent.

'As soon as she found out about the King's disapproval, Rosemary's attitude changed completely,' said Lady Victor Paget. 'From that moment on, she always gave the impression that she had never intended to marry the Prince of Wales. I don't think it was, in any sense, a question of saving her own face. She was not an ambitious woman, but she minded very much that her family – after all, one of the oldest in our history – should be thought not good enough. As for the Prince, he was bitter and furious. I don't think he ever forgave his father. I also felt that from that time on, he made up his mind that he would *never* make what might be called a suitable marriage, to please his family.'[82]

A year later, on March 8, 1919, Lady Rosemary Leveson-Gower married the Prince of Wales's best friend, Eric, Viscount Ednam, heir to the earldom of Dudley.[83] The Prince of Wales attended their wedding at St Margaret's Westminster, with his grandmother, Queen Alexandra, and his aunts, Princess Victoria and Princess Alice, Countess of Athlone. As a wedding present, the Prince gave Rosemary a sapphire and diamond brooch.

In her first letter as Viscountess Ednam, written to her mother from Witley Court, Worcester, on the day after the wedding, Rosemary is clearly still at pains to spare the feelings of her family: 'What a good thing I never contemplated marrying the Prince of Wales merely for the sake of the glamour as [I] got all that as well as Eric. Cheering crowds for ten miles. Torchlights by the hundred, and at every corner odd explosions which we shall never know whether they were rockets for our welcome or pistol shots badly aimed at the car by enraged Bolshevists.'[84]

The Prince of Wales stood as sponsor for Rosemary's first son, born ten months later.[85] She was to bear two further sons, [86] the elder of whom, Jeremy, was to be tragically killed at the age of seven in 1929 when his cycle ran off the pavement and was hit by a lorry.

Lady Ednam lovingly planned a special garden in remembrance of Jeremy in the grounds of the Ednams' home, Himley Hall. Seven months later, Rosemary was in Le Touquet, where Eric Ednam was ill at Chalet du Bois, the villa belonging to his stepmother, the Countess of Dudley – the former musical comedy star Gertie Millar.

Rosemary had to fly back alone to England for a meeting at Himley with the architect who was helping her to create the garden in memory of Jeremy. She had already booked her flight when, by chance, a seat fell vacant on an earlier plane and she took it in order to have more time to keep her appointment. The third Marquess of Dufferin and Ava, Speaker of the Northern Ireland Senate, the baronet Sir Edward Ward, and a Mayfair socialite, Mrs Henrik Loeffler, were her three travelling companions in the small Junker monoplane on its flight to Croydon.

But the plane was never to reach Croydon. At about three o'clock on that Monday afternoon, July 21, 1930, it disintegrated in mid-air and crashed near the village green of Meopham in Kent. All four passengers and both pilots were killed. The body of the beautiful Viscountess

Ednam, who might so easily have become Queen of England, was found in a nearby orchard. She was identified only by the pearls she had been wearing.

The Prince of Wales, stunned by the news of her death, at once sent a personal message to Lord Ednam, and a large and beautiful wreath to Rosemary's funeral four days later at Himley Hall, where she was buried in the Garden of Memory that she had planned for her son.

After attending Rosemary's funeral, Alfred Duff Cooper wrote a poem which Millicent Sutherland framed and always kept on her dressing table. The last verse ran:

> *If years be given us which were denied you,*
> *Age may dim eyes that today are blind with tears,*
> *Yet we shall see that smile and hear that laughter,*
> *Echoing for ever through the empty years.*[87]

A year later, the Prince, who had never forgotten his first sight of her as a nurse in France, opened the Rosemary Ednam Memorial Extension at the Royal Northern Hospital at Stoke on Trent.

Only a matter of days after his father had vetoed his proposed engagement to Lady Rosemary Leveson-Gower in March 1918, the Prince of Wales attended a party in London at 31 Belgrave Square. By yet another of the weird coincidences which punctuate this story, the hostess was Maud Kerr-Smiley, the sister of Ernest Simpson, and the woman who would introduce Wallis Simpson to London society ten years later.

Outside, a young married woman, Freda Dudley Ward, and her Latin American escort for the evening, 'Buster' Dominguez, were just crossing Belgrave Square when the maroons went off, signalling a Zeppelin raid. Dominguez drew Freda into the lighted portico of number 31, and asked the butler who was standing inside, 'May we wait here until the raid is over?' At that moment, Mrs Kerr-Smiley and her guests, including the Prince of Wales, came down the staircase to shelter in the basement of the house. They invited Freda and Dominguez to join them.

The Prince became engrossed in conversation with Freda, and when the 'all-clear' sounded half an hour later, Dominguez vanished into the night leaving them to dance together until three in the morning.[88] It was the beginning of a love affair that was to dominate the Prince's life for the next sixteen years.

Just five weeks younger than the heir to the throne, Freda was born

Winifred May Birkin, granddaughter of a baronet, and daughter of a wealthy Nottingham lace manufacturer, Colonel Charles Birkin, and his American wife, Claire Howe of New York.[89] She had been married for five years to William Dudley Ward, the Liberal Member of Parliament for Southampton and the Vice-Chamberlain of the Royal Household. He was sixteen years her senior. They had two young daughters, aged four and two, but by the time of Freda's first encounter with the Prince of Wales, the Ward marriage was merely a polite arrangement, a front maintained in public, behind which both went their separate ways.

Shortly, Lady Cynthia Asquith would note: 'Saw the Prince of Wales dancing round with Mrs Dudley Ward, a pretty little fluff with whom he is said to be rather in love.'[90]

The Prince was certainly in love, and Freda was certainly pretty – tiny, delicately made, with a thin, high, but unusually charming voice, and a delightfully droll sense of humour. A 'little fluff', however, she emphatically was not. She was a woman of taste, discernment, powerful intellect and considerable strength of character.

Her influence on the Prince of Wales was exemplary. He frequently asked her to marry him and she just as frequently told him, with great firmness, that it was out of the question. She would have to get a divorce, and the heir to the throne could *never* marry a divorced woman.

Although their relationship was common knowledge throughout society, it was conducted with absolute discretion and there was never publicity nor any hint of scandal. For the next sixteen years Freda displayed the same quality of self-effacing dignity that had been shown by Maria Fitzherbert in the life of George IV and Alice Keppel in the life of Edward VII.

In periodic outbursts against his son's waywardness, George V would refer to Freda disparagingly as 'the lacemaker's daughter' or 'the South American whore', but the rest of the Royal Family acknowledged her good influence, and even the King later conceded, after Wallis Simpson's emergence, that 'at least Mrs Dudley Ward came of a much better class and had an established position'.[91]

Six weeks after the Prince of Wales first encountered Wallis Warfield Spencer and her husband in San Diego, on his way to New Zealand, Lady Elizabeth Bowes-Lyon was invited to a ball given at 7 Grosvenor Square on May 20, 1920, by one of George V's closest friends, Lord Farquhar. There she met again – probably for the first time since the children's party at Montagu House in 1905, certainly for the first time as an adult[92] – the King's second son, Prince Albert, who two weeks later was to be created Duke of York.

Bertie is alleged to have said to his equerry, Captain the Hon. James Stuart, 'That's a lovely girl you've been dancing with. Who is she?'[93] He was very soon dancing with her himself, and Lady Airlie was to record: 'The Duke told me long afterwards that he had fallen in love that evening, although he did not realize it until later.'[94]

The following August, when the Royal Family went to Balmoral, Princess Mary, who was staying with the Airlies at Cortachy Castle, visited Glamis while reviewing the Forfarshire Girl Guides, and began a warm friendship with Elizabeth. The Duke of York, who was shooting with Lord and Lady Ancaster at Drummond Castle, also came to Glamis that month for the first time.

It was not long after this visit that Queen Mary observed to Lady Airlie: 'I have discovered that [Bertie] is very much attracted to Lady Elizabeth Bowes-Lyon. He's always talking about her. She seems a charming girl but I don't know her very well.'[95] This was certainly not news to Lady Airlie, who already realized that the Duke 'was deeply in love'.[96]

In the spring of 1921, the Duke of York informed his parents that he intended to propose marriage. 'You'll be a lucky fellow if she accepts you' said the King.[97]

Elizabeth did not accept him. 'She was frankly doubtful,' explained Lady Airlie, 'uncertain of her feelings, and afraid of the public life which would lie ahead of her as the King's daughter-in-law.'[98]

York seemed inconsolable and Lady Strathmore was deeply sorry for him. 'I do hope he will find a nice wife who will make him happy,' she wrote to Lady Airlie. 'I like him so much and he is a man who will be made or marred by his wife.'[99]

In the summer of 1921, Queen Mary decided to join the Duke of York on a visit to Glamis. 'I always felt that the visit . . . was inspired by her desire to help him,' wrote Lady Airlie, 'although she was much too tactful to let it be apparent'.[100]

The Queen and her son arrived to find Lady Strathmore seriously ill in bed and Lady Elizabeth as *châtelaine* of Glamis in her place. Queen Mary, whose standards were exacting, was impressed by the calm efficiency with which a girl of only twenty-one succeeded in combining the responsibilities of nursing her mother, running a large castle, and acting as hostess to royalty.

As the Queen left the castle, she drew Elizabeth towards her and kissed her affectionately on both cheeks. Afterwards she told Lady Airlie that she was more than ever convinced that this was 'the one girl who could make Bertie happy'.[101]

York persisted in his courtship. 'It is delightful here and Elizabeth is very kind to me,' he wrote to his mother from Glamis. 'The more I see of her the more I like her.'[102]

But Elizabeth Bowes-Lyon was not the easiest girl to court. Her habitual unpunctuality – never as pronounced as that of Queen Alexandra, but nevertheless a permanent feature of her life – was in evidence even then. '. . . once when [the Duke] arrived for dinner,' remembered Lady Hardinge, 'I and the other girls staying in the castle were still assembled in Lady Elizabeth's room, as she had not quite finished dressing. A message from Lady Strathmore came, saying that the Duke had arrived – but I'm afraid we kept him waiting a little.'[103]

At Bisham Abbey on the Thames, Lady Nina Balfour invited the young couple out on boating expeditions. The Duke would stretch out his hand and take Elizabeth's, and she, gently but firmly, would pull her hand away.[104]

On February 28, 1922, another link with the Royal Family was forged when Elizabeth was bridesmaid at the wedding in Westminster Abbey of the King's daughter, Princess Mary, to Viscount Lascelles.

By the middle of the year, however, Bertie had still not overcome Elizabeth's reluctance. He also learned to his consternation that she had received proposals of marriage from no fewer than five other men, several of them highly eligible.

To his friend, the future Viscount Davidson, he poured out his unhappiness. 'He declared that he was desperately in love, but that he was in despair for it seemed quite certain that he had lost the only woman he would ever marry . . . The King's son cannot propose to the girl he loves, since custom requires that he must not put himself in the position of being refused, and to that ancient custom the King, his father, firmly adhered. Worse still, I gathered that an emissary had already been sent to ascertain whether the girl was prepared to marry him, and that it had failed . . . I suggested that in the Year of Grace 1922 no high-spirited girl of character was likely to accept a proposal made at second hand; if she was as fond of him as he thought she was, he must propose himself . . .'[105]

At the end of the year, the Prince of Wales, also a friend of Elizabeth by now, urged her to accept Bertie. He told her 'she had better go ahead and marry him, and eventually "go to Buck House" '.[106] From this advice it would seem that eight years before he met Wallis Simpson, and fourteen years before he abdicated, the thought had occurred to him that he might somehow escape kingship and that his brother might reign in his place at that 'most depressing of places', Buckingham Palace.

But in the first week of 1923, rumours – all without genuine foundation – that the King and Queen had once considered Elizabeth Bowes-Lyon as a possible bride for the heir to the throne, found their way into print. On January 5, the London morning newspaper, the *Daily News*, headlined its front page with the words, SCOTTISH BRIDE FOR PRINCE OF WALES.

Elizabeth was not named, but her identity was obvious. 'The future Queen of England is the daughter of a well-known Scottish peer, who is the owner of castles both north and south of the Tweed.' She was also described as 'one of the closest friends of Princess Mary'.[107]

The same evening, *The Star* also splashed the story on its front page under the headline, LOVE MATCH FOR THE PRINCE.[108]

That weekend, Chips Channon was a fellow guest of Lady Elizabeth at Lord Gage's house in Sussex. 'The evening papers have announced her engagement to the Prince of Wales', he wrote in his diary. 'So we all bowed and bobbed and teased her, calling her "Ma'am": I am not sure that she enjoyed it. It couldn't be true, but how delighted everyone would be! She certainly has something on her mind . . . she is more gentle, lovely and exquisite than any woman alive, but this evening I thought her unhappy and distraite . . . Poor Gage is desperately fond of her – in vain, but he is far too heavy, too Tudor and squirearchal for so rare and patrician a creature as Elizabeth.'[109]

Next day, Buckingham Palace issued an official denial on behalf of the Prince of Wales. 'This report is as devoid of foundation as was the previous very definite statement of His Royal Highness's engagement to a foreign princess.'[110]

The following Saturday, January 13, the Duke of York drove down to St Paul's Walden Bury. There, walking alone with Elizabeth through the winter trees of the wood where she had played as a child, and which she had once described as 'the haunt of fairies, with its anemones and ponds, and moss-grown statues',[111] he proposed yet again – and was accepted. That afternoon, by prearranged code, the words, 'All right. Bertie', were telegraphed to Sandringham to give the good news to the King and Queen.

On the Monday, January 15, the King wrote in his diary, 'Bertie and Greig[112] arrived after tea and informed us that he was engaged to Elizabeth Bowes-Lyon, to which we gladly gave our consent. I trust they will be very happy.' Queen Mary added: 'We are delighted and he looks beaming.'[113]

'I am very very happy and I can only hope that Elizabeth feels the same as I do', wrote the Duke to his mother. 'I know I am very lucky to have won her over at last.'[114]

On January 16, when the Court Circular officially announced the engagement, Chips Channon noted: '. . . we had begun to despair that she would ever accept him . . He is the luckiest of men, and there's not a man in England today that doesn't envy him. The clubs are in gloom.'[115]

Meanwhile, at 17 Bruton Street, the Strathmores' new London house, Elizabeth was showing surprising aplomb and also a trace of imperiousness in dealing with the press.

'Mother, leave this gentleman to *me*,' she told Lady Strathmore on the arrival of a reporter from *The Star*, Harry Cozens-Hardy.

' "I suppose you have come to congratulate me? How very kind of you. I am *so* happy, as you can see for yourself". A pause, and then: "You ask where is the Duke? Well, Bertie – you know everybody calls him Prince Bertie – has gone out hunting and he won't be back until this evening, when, I've no doubt (*smiling*), I shall see him." '[116]

Shortly afterwards, an equerry was sent round to Bruton Street with instructions from the King. Royal ladies did not give statements to reporters. There were to be no further interviews.

On January 20, Elizabeth, with Lord and Lady Strathmore, went to Sandringham to meet the King and Queen and also Queen Alexandra, now seventy-eight and totally deaf. It was a daunting ordeal, but the bride-to-be sailed through it with flying colours. 'Elizabeth is with us now,' wrote Queen Mary, 'perfectly charming, so well brought up and will be a great addition to the family.'[117]

The King was no less enthusiastic. 'She is a pretty and charming girl and Bertie is a very lucky fellow.'[118]

On that first visit to Sandringham, King George even waived for her his strict rule of punctuality. One evening she came into dinner with the Duke two minutes late and apologized charmingly to the King. Had it been anyone else there would have been a stern reprimand. To her he said, 'You are not late my dear, I think we must have sat down two minutes too early.'[119]

Lady Hardinge recorded: '. . . one or two of the older members of Queen Mary's entourage . . . said that it was thought wise that Lady Elizabeth should not see "too much" of her old friends after her marriage . . . The older ladies were afraid that we would not treat her with enough dignity. And I was so anxious to be courteous and to behave properly towards her, that I became very formal and decorous – so that it took the Duchess of York some time after her marriage to come to terms with all our conventional efforts to treat her correctly.'[120]

Three months later, on April 26, 1923, Lady Elizabeth Bowes-Lyon left 17 Bruton Street on her father's arm for the last time as a commoner. On her drive to Westminster Abbey she had only a police escort, and the troops along the route did not present arms. She left the Abbey as Her Royal Highness the Duchess of York, a princess of the United Kingdom, and the fourth lady in the land, ranking directly after Queen Mary, Queen Alexandra and the King's daughter, Princess Mary.

From the beginning, George V – who had once said, of daughters-in-law, 'I must say I dread the idea and always have'[121] – capitulated entirely to her charm. In the first autumn of the marriage, the King wrote to his son from Balmoral: 'The better I know and the more I see of your dear little wife, the more charming I think she is and everyone falls in love with her here.'[122]

When a senior courtier mentioned to the King that the Duchess of York was sometimes unpunctual, George replied: 'Ah, but if she weren't late, she would be perfect, and how horrible that would be.'[123]

The King's enthusiasm was swiftly shared by both the public and the press, by whom she was dubbed the 'Smiling Duchess'.

Soon, however, Elizabeth began to suffer from the same sort of publicity backlash that Lady Diana Spencer was to experience sixty years later, after her marriage to Prince Charles. Was the 'Smiling Duchess' perhaps just a little too good to be true?

This term, as the former Chester Herald, James Frere, has noted, 'was not always applied to her in the kindest way, people averring that it was impossible for her to be so permanently good-natured as she would lead them to believe by her everlasting smile, which must surely be put on for the benefit of the public, and that when she got home it fell from her like a mask, to be replaced by a perfectly vile temper, and the unkindest behaviour to all around her. Her pink and white complexion was also made the target for unkind remarks by those who remembered Queen Alexandra's enamelled face, and also by those whose own complexions were the result of many hours of work and a great expenditure of money.'[124]

While the Duchess of York experienced the fickleness of public popularity, Wallis Warfield Spencer had survived several separations from her alcoholic husband.

During one of these, in 1921, in Washington, where her mother, Alice Rasin, had now gone to work as a hostess at the Chevy Chase Country Club, Wallis met an attractive man with whom she was to have a relationship for two years: Don Felipe Espil, the six-foot-tall, thirty-five-year-old First Secretary at the Argentine Embassy. 'He was intelligent, ambitious, subtle, gracious', she would say of him, 'in many respects the most fascinating man I have ever met . . . he acted as both teacher and model in the art of living.'[125]

In 1924, after her relationship with Espil had ended, Wallis made her final attempt at a reconciliation with Win Spencer. He was now stationed in Hong Kong, and he wrote to ask her to join him there. But on arrival she found Spencer's drinking as bad as ever and the reconciliation was short-lived. She moved out of his apartment and never lived with him as his wife again. She went to stay in Peking with an old friend, Katherine Moore Bigelow, and her new husband, Herman Rogers.

Wallis was to remain in China for almost two years. It was to be the most mysterious and controversial period in her life, and was later to form the subject of a strange dossier compiled on the orders of King George V.

Back in Washington in 1926, she found that her mother, at the age of fifty-six, had married a third husband, Charles Gordon Allen. In a cousin's visitors' book on the fourth of July, Alice had written, characteristically, 'Here on the fourth with my third'. And on a photograph of her sitting on her new husband's knee, she wrote: 'Alice on her last lap'.

Wallis had now decided to divorce Spencer, but she met with immediate opposition from both sides of her family. 'The Montague women do not get divorced', her aunt, Bessie Merryman, told her uncompromisingly.[126] Her Uncle Sol, whose family, the Warfields, had never had a divorce in their entire annals since 1662, vowed: 'I won't let you bring this disgrace upon us. What will the people of Baltimore think?'[127]

Whatever they thought, Wallis went ahead with the case. While it was pending, Uncle Sol died. The bulk of his estimated five million dollars went towards establishing a home for aged and indigent gentlewomen in Baltimore. All Wallis got was a $15,000 trust fund and the guarantee of a room in the old ladies' home should she ever need it. Uncle Sol, clearly, did not estimate his niece's prospects very highly.

Her divorce from Spencer came through on December 10, 1927. A year earlier, Wallis had met Ernest Simpson in Washington.

'Reserved in manner,' she would later write, 'yet with a gift of quiet wit, always well dressed, a good dancer, fond of the theatre, and obviously well read, he impressed me as an unusually well-balanced man. I had acquired a taste for cosmopolitan minds, and Ernest obviously had one. I was attracted to him and he to me . . .'[128]

Eleven months younger than herself, Ernest Aldrich Simpson had been born and brought up in New York, the son of an American mother and of an English father who was the head of the ship brokers, Simpson, Spence and Young, for whom Ernest worked. After graduating from Harvard, Ernest had gone to England, served in the Household Brigade and Coldstream Guards, and had married, in 1923, a divorcee from Massachusetts, Dorothea Parsons Dechert, by whom he had a baby daughter, Audrey.

Dorothea would later say of Wallis that she had 'enough of "what it takes" to steal a man. Mr Simpson walked out on me while I was ill in a hospital in Paris.'[129] And later Dorothea would add: 'From the moment I met her, I never liked her at all . . . she moved in and helped herself to my house and my clothes and, finally, to everything.'[130]

Within months of Wallis's divorce, the Simpsons were also divorced. Ernest transferred to his firm's British office, and at the end of May 1928, Wallis arrived in London, taking a small apartment in Stanmore Court. On July 21 she married Simpson at Chelsea Register Office.

With the help of his sister, Maud Kerr-Smiley – in whose home the Prince of Wales had met Freda Dudley Ward ten years earlier – they found a furnished house at 12 Upper Berkeley Street, which they rented from Lady Chesham for a year.

London had two reigning idols at this time. One was the Duke and Duchess of York's baby daughter, Princess Elizabeth, who had been born on April 21, 1926, and whose every outing in her pram was faithfully chronicled by a fascinated press.

The other was the Prince of Wales, whose continuing mystique as the eternally eligible bachelor had just inspired a popular song by Herbert Farjeon and Harold Scott, which began:

> *I've danced with a man*
> *Who's danced with a girl*
> *Who's danced with the Prince of Wales . . .*

That winter, George V came close to death from a streptococcal infection, and Wallis got her second look at the heir to the throne.

'On a rainy afternoon, as I was driving past St James's Palace on the way to the City to pick up Ernest at his office, I saw the scarlet-coated sentries at the entrance suddenly stiffen to attention and present arms. A black motor emerged into St James's Street. As it passed my car, I caught a fleeting glimpse through the side window of a delicate boyish face staring straight ahead, the whole expression suggesting the gravity of a deep inward concern . . . The chauffeur turned round, to say in awed tones, "Madam, that was the Prince of Wales." '[131]

By the following year, Freda Dudley Ward's monopoly of the Prince was no longer absolute. In the summer of 1929, at Leicester Fair, he met the American beauty, Viscountess Furness, and promptly invited her to dine alone with him at York House, St James's Palace.

Thelma Furness and her twin sister Gloria – known as 'the magnificent Morgans' – were born in Lucerne, where their father, Harry Hays Morgan, was the American Consul.[132] At sixteen Thelma had eloped and married a man twice her age, James Vail ('Junior') Converse, grandson of the founder of the Bell Telephone Company, and a black sheep relation of the Croesus-like J. P. Morgan. Their wedding reception was held in Washington at the Chevy Chase Country Club where Wallis's mother was then a hostess. Meanwhile, Thelma's sister Gloria had married Reginald Claypoole Vanderbilt, heir to the railroad billions, and been left a widow at the age of twenty-one.

In 1926, following her divorce from Converse, Thelma married another man twice her age, the widowed Viscount Furness, head of the Furness shipping lines. Their son, Tony, had been born just four months before she met the Prince of Wales, but the Furness marriage was already precarious.

At twenty-five, Thelma's attractions tended towards the voluptuous. Cecil Beaton found her and her twin 'as alike as two magnolias and with their marble complexions, raven tresses and flowing dresses, with their slight lisps and foreign accents, they diffuse an Ouida atmosphere of hothouse elegance and lacy femininity'.[133]

The affair, which was to last five years, progressed swiftly. It would not exclude Freda Dudley Ward from the Prince's life, but from this point on she and Thelma would share him.

Within six months of their meeting, Thelma was on safari with the Prince in Nairobi, of which she would write: 'This was our Eden, and we were alone in it. His arms about me were the only reality; his words of love my only bridge to life. Borne along on the mounting tide of his ardour, I felt myself being inexorably swept from the accustomed moorings of caution. Each night I felt more completely possessed by our love, carried ever more swiftly into uncharted seas of feeling, content to let the Prince chart the course, heedless of where the voyage would end.'[134]

In the meantime, Wallis Simpson had rushed to Washington on learning that her mother was seriously ill with cancer. Alice was already in a coma when her daughter arrived, and died three days later, on November 2, 1929.

On her return to London, Wallis at last found a permanent London home for Ernest and herself – a three-bedroomed apartment at 5 Bryanston Court – and Somerset Maugham's ex-wife, Syrie, advised her on decoration and furniture.

With the help of Ernest's sister, Maud Kerr-Smiley, Wallis was beginning to make friends in London society. One of them was Consuelo Thaw, whose husband, Benny, was First Secretary at the American Embassy. She was also the elder sister of Thelma Furness.[135] Not long after Thelma's return from her romantic safari with the Prince of Wales, she received a telephone call from Consuelo, asking if she might bring a friend to cocktails at Thelma's house at 21 Grosvenor Square.

'Mrs Simpson is fun,' Consuelo assured her sister. 'You will like her'.[136]

Thelma did like her – so much, in fact, that when, a few months later, Consuelo had to drop out of a weekend party Thelma was planning for the Prince of Wales at Burrough Court, the Furness hunting lodge at Melton Mowbray, she asked the Simpsons to take her place. On a Friday afternoon in November 1930,[137] nursing a heavy cold and nervously practising her curtsey on the train, Wallis travelled up to Melton Mowbray with Ernest.

There, in the drawing-room at Burrough Court, Thelma Furness introduced her to the Prince of Wales. Wallis made her curtsey successfully and then another to his brother, Prince George.

Studying the elder brother carefully, she took in 'the slightly wind-rumpled golden hair, the turned-up nose, and a strange, wistful, almost sad look about the eyes when his expression was in repose'.[138]

Just four months after the tragic death of Rosemary Ednam, the English beauty he had once chosen as his future queen, the Prince had been introduced to the woman who was to be the means of his escape from the birthright that oppressed him.

At thirty-four, Wallis Warfield Spencer Simpson had entered the private and privileged world of the British royal family. The stage was now set for her first encounter with Her Royal Highness the Duchess of York.

Read faster!

4

'THAT WOMAN'

ON THE SECOND DAY of the weekend party at Burrough Court in November 1930, Wallis Simpson was placed next to the Prince of Wales at luncheon.

Over the telephone the day before, her sister-in-law, Maud Kerr-Smiley, had warned her that Royalty must always be allowed to lead in any conversation and that Wallis must neither introduce new topics nor discuss politics or matters of a controversial nature. Describing their conversation some twenty years later with the assistance of a ghost writer, the Duke of Windsor claimed that he raised the subject of central heating.

'But . . . a verbal chasm opened under my feet. Mrs Simpson did not miss the great boon that her country has conferred upon the world. On the contrary, she liked our cold houses. A mocking look came into her eyes. "I am sorry, Sir," she said, "but you have disappointed me."

' "In what way?"

' "Every American woman who comes to your country is always asked the same question. I had hoped for something more original from the Prince of Wales." '[1]

The Duchess, in her own memoirs, could not 'imagine how the subject ever came up',[2] and their hostess on that occasion, Lady Furness, dismissed the alleged exchange as "fiction . . . it would have been not only bad taste but bad manners. At that moment Wallis Simpson was as nervous and as impressed as any woman would have been on first meeting the Prince of Wales.'[3] The Duchess seems to agree with her. 'The truth is that I was petrified . . .'[4]

One thing is certain. When Wallis Simpson left Burrough Court on the following day, no devastating *rapport* had been established between her and the Prince, and she admitted, 'I had already dismissed from mind the possibility of our ever meeting again.'[5]

It was almost six months before they did meet again and then he appeared to remember her only vaguely. On his return from his South American tour, Thelma Furness gave an afternoon reception for him at 21 Grosvenor Square. The Simpsons were present. 'As he passed close by his glance happened to fall on me. He then nudged Thelma, who was standing beside him, and seemed to be asking her in a whisper, "Haven't I met that lady before?" In any event he presently came over to where Ernest and I were standing to say, "How nice to see you again. I remember our meeting at Melton." '6

Six weeks later, on June 10, 1931, Wallis Simpson was presented at Court by an American friend, Mildred Anderson, who had married an Englishman. Although once divorced, Wallis – like Lady Furness before her – was eligible for presentation once she had established with the Lord Chamberlain's office that she had been the innocent party.

In a dress lent to her by Consuelo Thaw, with a train, feathers and fan provided by Thelma Furness, she entered the throne room at Buckingham Palace and curtsied to King George V and Queen Mary, who were flanked by the Prince of Wales and Queen Victoria's only surviving son, the eighty-one-year-old Duke of Connaught.

In his memoirs, the Duke of Windsor claimed to have noticed her out of the long line of women being presented. '. . . I was struck by the grace of her carriage and the natural dignity of her movements.'7

The Duchess, more realistically, reports that as the Royal Family later walked in procession through the State apartments, she overheard the Prince of Wales saying to the Duke of Connaught, 'Uncle Arthur, something ought to be done about the lights. They make all the women look ghastly.'8

Afterwards, at a cocktail party at Thelma Furness's house, the Prince admired Wallis's presentation gown and she chided him sardonically.

' "But, sir," I responded with a straight face, "I understood that you thought we all looked ghastly."

'He was startled. Then he smiled. "I had no idea my voice carried so far." '9

When the Simpsons left the party, they found the Prince outside, standing by his car, deep in conversation with his equerry, Brigadier-General Gerald ('G') Trotter. Catching sight of them, the Prince offered them a lift home, which they gratefully accepted.

On arrival at Bryanston Court, Wallis asked if the Prince and General Trotter would care to come in for a nightcap. The Prince politely declined. ' "I'd like very much to see your flat one day," he said. "I'm told it's charming . . . But I have to be up so early. Still, if you would be so kind as to invite me again, I'd like to do so." '10

Seven months passed before the next contact between them, which came in the middle of January 1932, in the form of a note from the Prince, asking the Simpsons to spend the last weekend of the month with him at Fort Belvedere, his private retreat at Sunningdale on the edge of Windsor Great Park.

A strange castellated conglomeration of mock-Gothic towers and battlements in beige-coloured stone, Fort Belvedere was a 'Grace and Favour' house that belonged to the Crown. Built originally in the eighteenth century by George II's third son, William, Duke of Cumberland, as a real fort – against a possible attack by the Young Pretender, Prince Charles Edward Stuart – it had been embellished by Sir Jeffry Wyatville in the reign of George IV, and had been neglected for many years when the Prince of Wales and Freda Dudley Ward first found it in April 1930.

When the Prince asked his father if he might live there, the King was surprised. ' "What could you possibly want that queer old place for? Those damn week-ends I suppose." But then he smiled, "Well, if you want it, you can have it." '[11]

It was, said Lady Diana Cooper, 'a child's idea of a fort . . . it had battlements and cannon and cannon-balls and little furnishings of war. It stood high on a hill, and the sentries, one thought, must be of tin . . . The house is an enchanting folly and only needs fifty red soldiers stood between the battlements to make it into a Walt Disney coloured symphony toy.'[12]

During that first weekend at the Fort, Wallis found the private life of the Prince of Wales 'a model of sedateness'.[13] She discovered, with incredulity, that he did needle point. Ernest helped his host to cut down overgrown laurel bushes, and Thelma Furness presided as hostess. Once again the Simpsons departed without any deep personal link having been forged, and it was a further eight months before they were invited back – once for tea, and once for the weekend.

In the first three months of 1933, however, Wallis and Ernest spent four weekends at the Fort, and when, at the end of March, they sailed on the *Mauretania* for New York, there was a *bon voyage* message for them, signed Edward P. News of this brought them deferential treatment from other passengers, which Wallis found flattering.

The first pointedly personal attention the Prince showed to Wallis alone came on June 19, her thirty-seventh birthday, when he gave a dinner party for her at Quaglino's and presented her with an orchid plant.

Two weeks later, on July 4, the Simpsons returned the hospitality by giving an American-style dinner for the Prince at Bryanston Court, consisting of black bean soup, grilled lobster, fried chicken Maryland and a cold raspberry soufflé.

Although Wallis was 'never quite certain about the durability of his interest in either Ernest or me', they nevertheless found themselves 'becoming permanent fixtures at the Fort weekends. The association imperceptibly but swiftly passed from an acquaintanceship to a friendship.'[14]

Thelma Furness was divorced that year from her husband, just as Freda Dudley Ward had been divorced finally in 1931, but in neither case had the change in marital status affected their relationship with the Prince.

At the beginning of 1934, Thelma decided to join her twin, Gloria Vanderbilt, on a trip to California. She broke the news of her departure to the Prince on January 12, and when he heard that she would be away for five or six weeks, 'his face took on a look of resignation, as if to imply that although this was not to his liking, he would say nothing that might interfere with my pleasure'.[15]

Four days later, Lady Furness lunched at the Ritz with Wallis Simpson, who observed: 'Oh, Thelma, the little man is going to be so lonely.'

'Well, dear,' she answered, 'you look after him for me while I'm away. See that he does not get into any mischief.'[16]

After a farewell dinner with the Prince at the Fort, Thelma sailed on January 20. The following Friday, soon after she docked, the Prince called her in New York. It was raining in London, he told her, and the Simpsons were at the Fort for the weekend.

Three days later he went to dine with them at Bryanston Court, and a few days after that he telephoned Wallis – the first time he had ever called in person. He was giving a dinner at the Dorchester on the following Tuesday, January 30, and he wanted the Simpsons to be there.

That evening was perhaps the turning point. While the others were away from the table dancing, the Prince began to talk to Wallis about his work and his hopes for the monarchy in the future. Suddenly he stopped. 'But I am boring you,' he apologized. 'On the contrary,' she replied, 'I couldn't be more interested. Please, please go on.'

He looked at her questioningly and then said, 'Wallis, you're the only woman who's ever been interested in my job.'[17]

This remark represented the grossest possible ingratitude to Freda

Dudley Ward, who for sixteen years had shown the most detailed interest in every aspect of his public work. Only months earlier she had helped him to found the Feathers Club Association – named after his personal emblem – to aid the unemployed. The truth was that the ill-advised departure of Thelma Furness had opened up a temporary vacuum in the life of a lonely and inadequate personality, and Wallis was the woman immediately on hand to fill that vacuum.

The very next afternoon he was at Bryanston Court for cocktails and stayed on, an unexpected guest, for dinner. The following weekend, the Simpsons were again at the Fort. Three days later, the Prince dined at Bryanston Court and took them to a nightclub. Two days after that he dined alone with Wallis in a restaurant, and on the following day the Simpsons were back at the Fort for yet another weekend.

So it continued until Thelma Furness returned to London. In New York, and on the liner, *Bremen*, bringing her back to Southampton, Thelma had been ardently pursued by the twenty-three-year-old Prince Aly Khan, elder son of the Aga Khan. Aly, with his black hair, dark skin and glittering brown eyes, was irresistibly attractive to women. There had been several great beauties in his life already. They included the outstanding British debutante of her era, Margaret Whigham, later the Duchess of Argyll; and Peggy Harmsworth, wife of the Hon. Esmond Harmsworth, later Viscount Rothermere.

Aly had bombarded Thelma with invitations and notes, and had filled her cabin with red roses from floor to ceiling. Word of this had evidently filtered through to Fort Belvedere. When Thelma was reunited with the Prince of Wales over dinner at her house in Regent's Park on Thursday, March 22, 1934, there was an undoubted coolness in the air. 'I hear Aly Khan has been very attentive to you,' he said suddenly. 'Are you jealous, darling?' she asked.[18] The Prince did not reply. They sat in awkward silence, but before leaving he invited her down to the Fort for the weekend.

There she found that the Prince, 'although formally cordial, was personally distant. He seemed to want to avoid me. I knew that something was wrong. But what? What had happened in those short weeks while I was away?'[19]

She took the problem to her friend, Wallis Simpson, at Bryanston Court. 'But the only answer I got to my questions was the saccharine assurance, "Darling, you know the little man loves you very much. The little man was just lost without you."'[20]

While they were talking, Wallis's maid came into the room. 'Wallis was irritated. "I told you," she said, "I did not want to be disturbed . . ."

'. . . "But, Madam," [the maid] said hesitantly, half in a whisper, "it's His Royal Highness."

'Wallis looked at me strangely. "Excuse me," she said, and left the room. The door was left open. I heard Wallis in the next room saying to the Prince, "Thelma is here", and I half rose from my chair, expecting to be called to the telephone. There was no summons, however, and when Wallis returned, she made no reference to the conversation.'[21]

The Duchess of Windsor's version of Thelma's visit is rather different. '. . . she asked me point-blank if the Prince was interested in me – "keen" was the word she used.

'This was a question I had expected and I was glad to be able to give her a straight answer. "Thelma," I said, "I think he likes me. He may be fond of me. But, if you mean by keen that he is in love with me, the answer is definitely no." '[22]

But was it? The following weekend, on Good Friday, March 30, Thelma drove the Simpsons down to Fort Belvedere. On the Saturday evening, at dinner, she noticed that the Prince and Wallis 'seemed to have little private jokes. Once he picked up a piece of salad with his fingers; Wallis playfully slapped his hand. I, so over-protective of heaven knows what, caught her eye and shook my head at her. She knew as well as everybody else that the Prince could be very friendly, but no matter how friendly, he never permitted familiarity.

'Wallis looked straight back at me. And then and there I knew the "reason" was Wallis . . . I knew then that she had looked after him exceedingly well. That one cold, defiant glance had told me the entire story.'[23]

Thelma went to bed early without saying good night to anyone. She had a bad cold. Later the Prince came up to her room to ask if there was anything she would like sent up.

' "Darling," I asked bluntly, "is it Wallis?"

'The Prince's features froze. "Don't be silly!" he said crisply. Then he walked out of the room, closing the door quietly behind him. I knew better. I left the Fort the following morning.'[24]

Thelma Furness was never to return to Fort Belvedere and she was never to see or hear from the Prince of Wales again. Her name is not mentioned once in the memoirs of the Duke of Windsor, in spite of the fact that it was she who introduced him to his future wife.

His devoted equerry, Brigadier-General 'G' Trotter, was eventually to lose his position in the royal household through his obstinate loyalty to Lady Furness. When it was made plain to him that he was expected to drop the discarded favourite as summarily as his master had done, he reportedly replied, 'Sir, I made friends with Thelma at your request. I don't sack my friends.'[25]

One month after Thelma's exit, it was the turn of Freda Dudley Ward to be expunged from the Prince's life. After some weeks of complete silence from him, during which her elder daughter, Penelope, had been seriously ill, Mrs Dudley Ward put through a call to St James's Palace. The Prince's switchboard operator, who had known and admired Freda for many years, told her in great distress: 'I have something so terrible to tell you that I don't know how to say it.' Urged by Freda to continue, the operator admitted, 'I have orders not to put you through.'[26]

Freda's younger daughter, Angela – to her and her sister the heir to the throne had been known affectionately as 'Little Prince' – also tried to reach him urgently when she feared that a police charge brought against her for careless driving might endanger the future career of her fiancé, Lieutenant Robert Laycock, who had been in the car with her at the time. To every one of her telephone calls, the Prince's butler, Osborne, replied that his master was 'not at home', and a letter from Angela pleading for the Prince's help and advice went unanswered. Seven months later an invitation to Angela's wedding to Bob Laycock was similarly ignored.

Freda Dudley Ward was also not mentioned in the Duke of Windsor's memoirs. Her sixteen years of devotion to him were stricken from the record of his life.

Mrs Dudley Ward behaved with greater dignity and loyalty than he deserved. She remained the active chairman of the Feathers Club Association for thirty years. She gave no interviews about her role in the life of the Prince of Wales. Unlike Lady Furness, she wrote no memoirs. And, alas for history, before her death in 1983, she destroyed her entire correspondence, including all the Prince's love letters. 'Her daughter told me that she saw her burn the lot,' Lady Donaldson said later.[27]

Members of the Royal Family respected Freda Dudley Ward's discretion. 'George [the Duke of Kent] remained my friend to the last,' she once said.[28] And Lord Mountbatten said of her, 'There was something religious, almost holy, about his love for her. She was the only woman he ever loved that way. She deserved it. She was sweet and good, a good influence on him. None of the others were. Wallis's influence was fatal.'[29]

People blamed Wallis Simpson for the Prince's callous behaviour to Thelma and Freda, but the astrologer, Count Louis Hamon – 'Cheiro' – cited another possible reason: 'Persons born under such peculiar astrological conditions [as he] exhibit remarkable fluctuations of feeling – they pass from ardour to indifference in a few seconds, and they are very liable to be charged with inconstancy'.[30]

His strange capriciousness of character was also noted by Noël Coward. '... having kept Noël up to all hours to supply piano accompaniment to the Prince's ukelele, he cut him dead next day in Hawes & Curtis, where all the smart young men of the time went for their famous backless evening waistcoats and haberdashery in general. When, on Noël's next visit there, he saw the Duke of York he pretended not to notice, but the Duke, in marked contrast, came over to him and was as friendly as could be ...'[31]

There was no mistaking the ascendancy of Wallis in the Prince's life in the summer of 1934. In June she was at Fort Belvedere for ten days, spending her birthday and his there. In August, chaperoned by her aunt, Bessie Merryman – since Ernest was in America on business – she was with him throughout the entire month at a house he had rented in Biarritz. During September, after Aunt Bessie's departure for Italy, Wallis and the Prince went on a Mediterranean cruise in Lord Moyne's yacht, the *Rosaura*.

Among the Prince's party that summer were Lieutenant-Commander Colin Buist and his wife, Gladys, who were close friends of the Duke and Duchess of York. Colin Buist had been a fellow naval cadet and term-mate of the Duke of York at Osborne and Dartmouth, and was later his equerry for four years. News of the Prince's strong attachment to Wallis Simpson, therefore, soon reached the Yorks and the rest of the Royal Family, of whom, at this point, Wallis had met only one member – the Prince's youngest brother, Prince George, shortly to be created Duke of Kent.

The Duke and Duchess of York had been steadily gaining public popularity since their marriage eleven years earlier. Their second daughter, Princess Margaret Rose, had been born at Glamis Castle on August 21, 1930, and by 1934, the 'little Princesses' were attracting press interest and public adulation rivalled only by Hollywood's child wonder, Shirley Temple.

The Duchess of York, George V's only daughter-in-law for more than a decade, was on good terms with her brother-in-law, the Prince of Wales, until Wallis Simpson arrived on the scene. As Duke of Windsor, he would say that Elizabeth 'had brought into the family a lively and refreshing spirit'.[32]

To Lady Diana Cooper, the Prince of Wales admitted that his new sister-in-law had been a boon to the Royal Family. 'He described the gloom of Buckingham Palace; how he himself and all of them "froze up" whenever they got inside it; how bad-tempered his father was; how the Duchess of York was the one bright spot there. They all love her and the King is in a good temper whenever she is there.'[33]

The Prince became a frequent visitor to the Yorks' London home, 145 Piccadilly. There he would join in the evening session of nursery games with his nieces, Elizabeth and Margaret. There was one original and favourite game called Winnie-the-Pooh. Sitting in front of the fire, the Duchess of York would read from a story book. When she had finished, her daughters and their uncle would have to mime the characters in the story. One evening, as he left the house, the Prince of Wales turned to his sister-in-law and said: 'You make family life so much fun.'[34]

Elizabeth had greatly improved the Duke of York. In adolescence he had developed serious gastric problems, a direct consequence of his being badly fed by his nurse in infancy. His acute stammer was probably the result of his father's instructions to his tutor that he should be broken of his left-handedness, and all his life he was subject to sudden outbursts of temper, fits of introspective gloom and deep melancholy.

It was Elizabeth who persuaded him to see the celebrated therapist Lionel Logue, who did much to reduce the chronic hesitation in the Duke's public speaking. Elizabeth accompanied him to Logue's Harley Street clinic and often seemed to give him the will to get through his speeches. As the King's official biographer, Sir John Wheeler-Bennett, would later say: 'Hers was the ability to sustain or reward him by a single smile or gesture in the public battles which he waged with his stammer; hers the capacity to calm with a word that passionate temper which ever and anon would burst its bounds.'[35]

Sometimes Elizabeth was peremptory in her firmness with her husband. Laura, Duchess of Marlborough recalled. 'The Yorks had to attend an evening public function in Leicester, and for fear of fog a special Pullman train was laid on to take us all there from Grantham.

We boarded the train in evening dress at Grantham, where a considerable crowd had gathered. The Duke was very shy and rushed along the carriage, pulling down the blinds. I was very impressed by the way that the Duchess snapped them up again immediately, saying to her husband, "Bertie, you must wave." '[36]

Their marriage was transparently a love match. 'They are such a sweet little couple and so fond of each other,' Duff Cooper wrote to Lady Diana after seeing the Yorks at a theatre in 1926. 'They reminded me of us, sitting together in the box having private jokes, and in the interval when we were all sitting in the room behind the box they slipped out, and I found them standing together in a dark corner of the passage talking happily as we might. She affects no shadow of airs or graces.'[37]

Three years later, at an Edgar Wallace play, Virginia Woolf saw the Duchess of York as 'a simple, chattering, sweet-hearted, little round-faced young woman in pink . . . her wrists twinkling with diamonds, her dress held on the shoulder with diamonds.'[38]

But the sweet-heartedness and chatter camouflaged a formidable intellect. When the Yorks stayed at the British Embassy in Berlin in 1929 on their way back from the Crown Prince of Norway's wedding to Princess Märtha of Sweden in Oslo,[39] Harold Nicolson, then Chargé d'Affaires at the Embassy, motored them to the Golf Club for luncheon.

'He found the Duchess delightful, incredibly gay and simple. It was a tragedy that she should be royal. She was clever. She talked to Harold perceptively about Some People,[40] whereas the Duke had only read the Arketall story and got it wrong.'[41]

'. . . she and Cyril Connolly are the only two people who have spoken intelligently about the "landscape" element in Some People,' Nicolson wrote to his wife, Vita Sackville-West. 'She said, "You choose your colours so carefully; that bit about the Palace in Madrid was done in grey and chalk-white; the Constantinople bits in blue and green; the desert bits in blue and orange." '[42] Nicolson 'could not exaggerate her charm. It was overwhelming. The Duke's was less evident.'[43]

But charm and intelligence was not the whole story in the case of the Duchess of York. Elizabeth's turbulent Scottish ancestry had instilled a vein of steel into her character. She was nobody's fool and no one trifled with her. Marion Crawford, who joined the Yorks' household as governess in April 1932, perceived the strength of the Duchess's personality very quickly, and was to write, of their initial interview, '. . . for the first time I met that long cool stare'.[44]

There was a streak of stubbornness in Elizabeth's psychology. When she had made up her mind about something, nothing and no one could change it. The education of her daughters was a case in point. The princesses were taught according to 'a clearly conceived plan, which was framed by their mother. By comparison with the curricula of the leading girls' schools of that day or this, the plan would be considered somewhat old-fashioned; indeed Queen Mary, who was by temperament more inclined than her daughter-in-law to put a high value on strictly intellectual discipline, sometimes expressed her misgivings. But the Duchess of York had a definite idea of the sort of training she wished her daughters to receive, and pursued her course untroubled by other people's doubts . . . When, for example, it became apparent that Princess Elizabeth would never progress beyond the simplest elements of mathematics, it did not worry the Duchess at all.'[45]

The Yorks were resolutely unfashionable. They did not grace the *salons* of the great hostesses of the day like Lady Cunard and Lady Colefax, who both hastened to adopt Wallis Simpson. Emerald Cunard, indeed, was inhibited from inviting the Yorks by the knowledge that some of her more *outré* conversational gambits – such as 'Christmas is only for servants'[46] – would not have impressed Elizabeth favourably, and might have provoked 'that long cool stare' Marion Crawford had already encountered.

The Yorks, it is true, were prized friends of one of Emerald's rival hostesses, the Hon. Mrs Ronald Greville, but on the whole they disregarded smart society. They had no need of it. The great landed families of the British establishment – the Cecils, the Howards, the Airlies, the Beauforts, the Buccleuchs and the Pembrokes – were all close friends of them both.

Chips Channon found the Duke of York 'good, dull, dutiful and good-natured', and the Duchess 'well-bred, kind, gentle and slack . . . always charming, always gay, pleasant and smiling . . . mildly flirtatious in a very proper romantic old-fashioned Valentine sort of way . . . She makes every man feel chivalrous and gallant towards her.'[47]

If the Yorks were conservative, however, they were not straitlaced. They had both liked Thelma Furness, feeling the same about her as one of their closest friends, Helen Hardinge, who described Thelma as 'a gay, but kindly woman'.[48]

During the five years of Thelma's ascendancy, the Yorks were often at Fort Belvedere, and one winter weekend the Duchess had even gone skating with Thelma on an ice-covered Virginia Water, both of them clinging on to kitchen chairs for support. Thelma later remembered: 'She found the sight of the two of us thus equipped terribly funny and we were both soon off in gales of laughter. The lovely face of the Duchess, her superb colouring heightened by the cold, her eyes wrinkled with the sense of fun that was never far below the surface, made a picture I shall never forget. All her charm, good humour and character were so evident then as always . . . I remember thinking at the time that if I ever had to live in a bungalow in a small town, this is the woman I would most like to have as a next-door neighbour to gossip with while hanging out the washing in our backyards.'[49]

The Yorks deprecated the callous manner in which Thelma had been discarded by the Prince of Wales. Twelve years later, when she went to Buckingham Palace with her son, Viscount Furness – who was to receive the Victoria Cross awarded posthumously to his elder brother – Thelma was touched that the King spoke to her personally, with great kindness, and gave her a message from the Queen.[50]

On August 28, 1934, while the Prince of Wales was still in Biarritz with Mrs Simpson, the Court Circular announced the engagement of his youngest surviving brother, Prince George, to the beautiful Princess Marina of Greece.[51] On September 16, Princess Marina landed at Folkestone, and after a drive through cheering London crowds, left with Prince George for Balmoral, to find the Duke and Duchess of York and the eight-year-old Princess Elizabeth waiting to greet her at Ballater station. Later the Duchess of York drove over from Birkhall to teach Marina how to dance Highland reels.

On October 12, Prince George was created Duke of Kent, the date of the wedding was set for November 29, and invitations were sent out to eight hundred guests for a dinner and reception to be held at Buckingham Palace two days earlier.

That prolific diarist, Marie Belloc Lowndes, informs us: 'I heard . . . that when King George and Queen Mary were shown the final list of invitations – and that the Prince [of Wales] had put in the Simpsons' name among the list of those he wished included, the King had drawn a line through the name. The Prince hearing of this went to his parents and said that if he were not allowed to invite these friends of his, he would not go to the ball. He pointed out that the Simpsons were remarkably nice Americans, that it was important England and America should be on cordial terms, and that he himself had been most kindly entertained in the States. His parents gave way and the Simpsons duly came to the ball' – but only, adds Lady Hardinge, 'after a certain amount of hesitation.'[53]

At Buckingham Palace, on the evening of Tuesday, November 27, 1934, therefore, the Royal Family, joined by the King and Queen of Denmark, the King and Queen of Norway, and a gathering of lesser European royalty, had their first sight of the new woman in the life of the Prince of Wales.

She could hardly have made a more vivid first impression. While the bride-to-be, Princess Marina, wore a simply-cut white evening gown, and Queen Mary was her usual regal self in silver brocade with ice-blue *paillettes*, Wallis Simpson rivetted attention in a dramatic dress of violet *lamé* highlighted by a brilliant green sash. 'Mrs Simpson, there is no question about it,' said Princess Marina's brother-in-law, Prince Paul, Regent of Yugoslavia, 'you are wearing the most striking gown in the room.'[54] From the bracelet on her wrist glittered the first jewel the Prince of Wales had given her that summer – a diamond and emerald charm.

It soon became apparent that the Prince wished her to be the centre of attention. Ernest Simpson was repeatedly left standing alone while the heir to the throne took Wallis over to meet friends and relations.

Prince Christopher of Greece later recalled: '. . . he laid a hand on my arm in his impulsive way: "Christo, come with me. I want you to meet Mrs Simpson . . ." "Mrs Simpson, who is she?" I asked. "An American," then he smiled. "She's wonderful," he added. The two words told me everything. It was as though he had said: "She is the only woman in the world." '[55]

The Prince also took Wallis – alone, without Ernest – over to where the King and Queen were standing. 'I want to introduce a great friend of mine,' he told his parents.[56] King George and Queen Mary were aware by now of her presence in their son's life, but not of the extent of her influence or the seriousness of the relationship. Wallis curtsied to them both, and Queen Mary later told Lady Airlie that she 'had shaken hands with her without thinking much about it'.[57]

To Wallis, however, the moment – the only occasion on which she would meet her future husband's parents – was 'truly memorable . . . It was the briefest of encounters – a few words of perfunctory greeting, an exchange of meaningless pleasantries, and we moved away. But I was impressed with Their Majesties' great gift for making everyone they met, however casually, feel at ease in their presence.'[58]

The Prince of Wales then took his new friend to meet the Duke and Duchess of York. There could hardly have been a greater contrast in visual terms between the two women: Wallis vivid in violet; Elizabeth the essence of understated femininity in soft orchid pink. Wallis curtsied. For the first time she encountered what she later described as 'the almost startling blueness'[59] of the Duchess of York's eyes, and felt that cool, appraising glance sweep over her.

The Yorks were gravely polite, but in Elizabeth there was an attitude of almost tangible reserve. Mrs Simpson would never see the laughter and friendliness that the Duchess had shown Lady Furness. Without a word having been spoken to indicate it, the Prince's sister-in-law and his American lady were opponents.

Elizabeth's close friend, Helen Hardinge, who also saw Mrs Simpson for the first time on this occasion, commented: 'Everyone *wanted* to like her.'[60] But Lady Hardinge did not like her, and neither did the Duchess of York.

Forty years later, the Dowager Lady Hardinge of Penshurst remembered that occasion clearly. 'I am afraid Mrs Simpson went down badly with the Duchess from the word go. It may have been the rather ostentatious dress, or the fact that she allowed the Prince of Wales to push her forward in what seemed an inappropriate manner. The Duchess of York was never discourteous in my experience, but those of us who knew her very well could always tell when she did not care for something or someone, and it was very apparent to me that she did not care for Mrs Simpson at all.'[61]

Two days after the Palace reception, the Simpsons were at Westminster Abbey for the Kent wedding. The Prince of Wales had provided them with prominent places on a side aisle, from which they had an uninterrupted view of the altar.

With Prince George now married, Lord Louis Mountbatten was the only member of the Prince of Wales's family who remained a constant guest at Fort Belvedere. The Yorks had never been frequent visitors to the Fort. Even when they came there, the Duchess was always conscious of her position. One photograph, taken during Lady Furness's reign as hostess at the Fort, shows a group of eight around the pool, seven of them relaxing in swimming costumes. The Duchess of York alone sits resplendent in a dress, hat and pearls.

It was during one of the Yorks' rare visits to the Fort early in 1935 that the antipathy between Elizabeth and Wallis Simpson first came into the open. After a year as the object of the Prince of Wales's emotional interest, Wallis had become increasingly confident of her ascendancy over him. Ernest Simpson was fading further and further into the background of her life.

Aware of the Duchess of York's tacit disapproval of her, Wallis took to deriding Elizabeth's fussy style of dressing, privately dubbing her 'the Dowdy Duchess'.[62] On occasion, Wallis would entertain guests at the Fort with a satirical impression of Elizabeth's voice, mannerisms and facial expressions. One such guest, Ella Hogg, the wife of Brigadier Oliver Hogg,[63] later told friends that 'Mrs Simpson considered the Duchess of York's too goody-goodiness to be false and artificial and it was that sort of imitation.'[64]

During the Yorks' visit to the Fort early in 1935, Elizabeth walked into the drawing-room just as Wallis was in the middle of one of her imitations. Mrs Hogg, who was present on that occasion, was later to say that 'from the moment of overhearing, the Duchess of York became her implacable enemy. Mrs Simpson said she had no sense of humour.'[65]

This incident requires interpretation. The Duchess of York was seldom accused, either then or later, of lacking a sense of humour. Peter Townsend, writing of Elizabeth as Queen of England, was to say that she 'had a delicious and highly imaginative sense of the ridiculous.'[66]

There is ample evidence that Elizabeth by no means took all the activities of royalty entirely seriously. To her daughters, she would speak of 'zoo teas'[67] – occasions when she would be required to eat in public, and a crowd of spectators would stand and watch her just as they would watch an animal's feeding time at the zoo. Above all, Elizabeth was herself a dedicated mimic and unlikely to be offended by mimicry. Princess Margaret would say of her mother: 'She could convulse us all with her imitations. There was that play, *Crown Matrimonial*, about the Abdication. I shall never forget her imitation of the actress imitating her.'[68]

If Elizabeth's dislike of Mrs Simpson intensified after the Fort Belvedere incident, it is likely to have been due less to mimicry than to Wallis's blatant indiscretion. In ridiculing the King's daughter-in-law in front of guests of the Prince of Wales, Wallis Simpson demonstrated that, unlike Freda Dudley Ward and Thelma Furness, she had no idea of how to behave in royal circles, or of the obligations imposed by friendship with the heir to the throne.

On February 4, Wallis and the Prince left for a ski-ing holiday in

Kitzbühl. Ernest Simpson had declined an invitation to join them,
allegedly having urgent business in New York. Among the party was
the Prince's former equerry, the Hon. Bruce Ogilvy, second son of
Lady Airlie and a lifelong friend of the Duchess of York. Ogilvy, also,
did not like Wallis Simpson, regarding her as 'the interloper who
changed and spoilt everything'.[69]

The Kitzbühl visit was not a great success. Wallis made no attempt
to learn to ski, and the party went on to Vienna and Budapest.

After their return at the end of February, Wallis found her husband
more distant than ever, and also became aware 'of a rising curiosity
concerning me, of new doors opening, and a heightened interest even
in my casual remarks. I was stimulated; I was excited; I felt as if I were
borne upon a rising wave that seemed to be carrying me ever more
rapidly and even higher. Now I began to savour the true brilliance and
sophistication of the life of London.'[70]

It was at this point that Lady Cunard and Lady Colefax became
particularly active in entertaining Wallis. And on April 5, Chips
Channon recorded: 'We had a luncheon party here, and the plot was to
do a "politesse" to Mrs Simpson. She is a jolly, plain, intelligent, quiet,
unpretentious and unprepossessing little woman, but as I wrote to
Paul of Yugoslavia today, she has already the air of a personage who
walks into a room as though she almost expected to be curtsied to. At
least, she wouldn't be too surprised. She has complete power over the
Prince of Wales, who is trying to launch her socially . . .'[71]

A month later, on May 6, it was George V's Silver Jubilee. It was
evident that by now even members of the public were beginning to
wonder whether the forty-year-old still-unmarried Prince of Wales
would ever become King, or would remain so even if he did.

As the Duke and Duchess of York, with the two princesses, drove
out of Buckingham Palace in a State landau drawn by four bay horses,
one man's voice rose above the cheers that greeted them. 'There goes
the hope of England.'[72]

Wallis Simpson watched the royal processions from a most unexpected vantage point. The day before, the telephone had rung at the
house in St James's Palace occupied by the King's Assistant Private
Secretary, Major the Hon. Alexander Hardinge, and his wife. Helen
Hardinge recorded: '. . . a senior servant on the Prince of Wales' staff
came through with a message from HRH. As none of the windows
of his own residence, York House, overlooked the processional
route, HRH had to find accommodation for his servants elsewhere.

Unfortunately, said the servant, "one or two scullery maids" had been left out of the plans, and could I please help?

'I was slightly surprised, because the Prince had never asked me to help him in this way before, although there had been many processions in the past. I also did not understand why a window at Buckingham Palace would not do – these would have had a fine view of the procession. But I saw no reason to turn down HRH's seemingly innocent request on behalf of one or two of his humbler servants, so I said that I would be delighted if they came. I went back to my window plan and placed one of the best views – that from the window in my bedroom – at their disposal . . .

'. . . sometime after we returned home, having attended the Thanksgiving Service, I learned the identity of the "one or two scullery maids". "They" were Mrs Simpson and one of her friends. It all became clear: the Prince of Wales could not have sent Mrs Simpson to see the procession from Buckingham Palace, because his father would not have sanctioned it. Yet if he had not arranged for her to see it somewhere, she would have been bitterly disappointed with him.

'We met the Prince of Wales at a party that evening, and he greeted me much more effusively than usual, thanking me enthusiastically for this hospitality. I suddenly realized that he had not played a trick on me deliberately, but thought I had known from the start whom I was inviting into my home. Perhaps "scullery maid" was the codename used by the Prince's staff? I never enquired. Alec said that the incident did not matter and was very much amused by the whole thing.'[73]

When the incident was related to the Duchess of York, she neither laughed nor commented. She was silent and looked pensive. She may have been wondering what sort of woman it was who felt able to enter the Hardinges' house with no invitation and without even the knowledge of her hosts.

Eight days later, on May 14, Mr and Mrs Ernest Simpson appeared together at the Silver Jubilee State Ball at Buckingham Palace. The moment the dancing began, the Prince of Wales led Wallis on to the floor. This time, however, the presence of the King and Queen, seated on the dais, did not cause Wallis to feel at ease. 'As David and I danced past,' she remembered, 'I thought I felt the King's eyes rest searchingly on me. Something in his look made me feel that all this graciousness and pageantry were but the glittering tip of an iceberg that extended down into unseen depths I could never plumb, depths filled with an icy menace for such as me. Also through the panoply of pomp I discerned that here was a frail old man.'[74]

But George V was not too frail for an outburst of fury over Wallis Simpson's second appearance at the palace. The King considered her 'unsuitable as a friend, disreputable as a mistress, unthinkable as Queen of England'.[75]

To his cousin, Count Albert Mensdorff, the former Austrian ambassador, King George protested that Wallis had been invited to the palace against his wishes and without his knowledge. 'That woman in my own house!' he raged.[76]

Of his son, the King said scathingly: 'He has not a single friend who is a gentleman. He does not see any decent society. And he is forty-one.' Mensdorff countered that the Prince had many excellent qualities, especially charm. 'Yes, certainly,' the King agreed. 'That is the pity. If he were a fool, we would not mind. I hardly ever see him and don't know what he is doing.'[77]

Two weeks later, on May 31, Chips Channon noted a scene in Lady Cunard's box at the opera. 'I was interested to see what an extraordinary hold Mrs Simpson has over the Prince. In the interval she told him to hurry away as he would be late in joining the Queen at the LCC Ball – and she made him take a cigar from out of his breast pocket. "It doesn't look very pretty," she said. He went, but was back in half an hour.'[78]

Society was beginning to speculate over the nature of this 'extraordinary hold' one hitherto little-known American woman now exercised over the most coveted male in the British Empire. The majority verdict was that the source of her power must be sexual. After their relationship ended, Thelma Furness had confided to friends that the Prince of Wales was a most unsatisfactory lover. He achieved orgasm so rapidly that his partner was left in a state of sexual frustration.

The Prince was not over-generously endowed sexually. One male friend who knew him well and went swimming with him often, admitted: 'To put it bluntly, he had the smallest pecker I have ever seen. Can you imagine what this did to him? Here are all these beautiful women all over the world, all ready and willing to go to bed with the Prince Charming of the world, all of them expecting the most eventful romantic night of their lives. And the ones who made it with him, can you imagine their disappointment? And can you imagine how he felt?'[79]

Wallis Simpson was rumoured to be the first woman who was able to cure the Prince's sexual deficiencies. The means by which she was supposed to have done this were usually attributed to her stay in China, where she was said to have visited the 'singsong houses' in which specialized sexual techniques were practised, particularly with regard to impotence and other male sexual dysfunction. King George V had ordered a dossier to be compiled on Wallis Simpson's 'China phase', and its content was reportedly one of the principal factors in the King's hostility towards her.

There was every kind of inspired guesswork about the relationship. John McMullen considered the Prince of Wales ' "God's gift to women" because he adores them and simply has no interest whatever in any man.'[80]

There were those who questioned this. The Prince supposedly disliked homosexuals, yet rumours of a latent homosexual streak in his character persisted throughout his life, and those who felt inclined to credit them, pointed to the masculinity of Wallis Simpson's personality: the thin, angular body; the large hands; the huge head with its strong, determined jaw; the ability to dominate.

Indeed, her domination of the heir to the throne was becoming more and more disturbingly evident. In August 1935, while Wallis — once again minus her husband — was cruising with the Prince in the Mediterranean on yachts belonging to the Duke of Westminster and Daisy Fellowes, the Archbishop of Canterbury, Cosmo Gordon Lang, was at Balmoral having a 'long and intimate talk'[81] with the King about his son's unsuitable liaison. Lang confided to Lady Airlie that the King 'believes that this affair is much more serious than the others. That is what worries him'.[82]

In early October, Lady Diana Cooper dined at Fort Belvedere and reported to Chips Channon that 'Mrs Simpson was glittering, and dripped in new jewels and clothes'.[83] People were bemused by the transformation of Wallis. Ronald Tree, meeting her for the first time soon after her arrival in London, had found her 'metallic elegance' unattractive.[84]

Cecil Beaton, who saw her first in 1930, found her then 'somewhat brawny and raw-boned . . . Her voice had a high nasal twang'. Five years later, however, he 'liked her immensely . . . found her bright and witty, improved in looks and chic'.[85]

And the beautiful Mrs Charles Sweeny, formerly Margaret Whigham and later Duchess of Argyll, considered Wallis 'not out-

standing in any way, nor well dressed' when she met her first in 1933 at
a luncheon party given by Margaret's mother-in-law, Mrs Robert
Sweeny. 'Her hair was parted down the middle, arranged in "ear-
phones", and her voice was harsh. My impression was of quite a plain
woman with a noticeably square jaw, and not particularly amusing. . .
I cannot help marvelling how she changed . . .'[86]

On November 6, 1935, the King's third son, Prince Henry, Duke of
Gloucester, married the Duke of Buccleuch's daughter, Lady Alice
Scott. 'Now all the children are married except David,' wrote the King
in his diary.[87]

The new Duchess of Gloucester found it 'rather a sad Christmas,
with the King ill and [the Prince of Wales] away ski-ing in St Anton
with Mrs Simpson. This was another reason why Prince Henry and I
were discouraged from going abroad, because we had also had the idea
of going ski-ing and there could have been the embarrassment of a
meeting.'[88]

Also absent from Sandringham was the Duchess of York, who was
confined to bed at 145 Piccadilly with pneumonia. 'Elizabeth is
progressing,' the King wrote to the Duchess of Gloucester, 'but very
slowly and it may be some days before she can come here, as she is still
so weak.'[89]

The Simpsons, meanwhile, were invited as guests to Trent Park, the
home of Sir Philip Sassoon, a close friend of the Royal Family. Marie
Belloc Lowndes, a fellow guest on that occasion, noted the deference
with which Wallis was now being treated. Before dinner on the first
evening there had been a protracted debate as to whether Sassoon
ought to place Wallis on his right. In the end he treated her as an
ordinary guest and the Duchess of Rutland took precedence.

The same respect was not accorded to Ernest. Mrs Lowndes 'felt
that the unfortunate Mr Simpson was regarded with a considerable
measure of contempt by all the men there. He was obviously regarded
as *un mari complaisant*. That, I am convinced he was not.'[90]

When the Simpsons left, the other guests asked Marie Belloc
Lowndes what she thought of Wallis. 'I said that what had struck me
most were her perfect clothes and that I had been surprised, considering that she dressed so simply, to see that she wore such a mass of
dressmakers' jewels. At that they all screamed with laughter, explaining that all the jewels were real, that the Prince of Wales had given her
fifty thousand pounds' worth at Christmas, following it up with sixty
thousand pounds' worth of jewels a week later at the New Year. They

explained that his latest gift was a marvellous necklace which he had bought from a Paris jeweller.'[91]

Marie Belloc Lowndes was incredulous, and later asked the American critic, Alexander Woollcott, if he thought the Prince of Wales was really in love with Mrs Simpson. 'Yes,' said Woollcott, 'she has him like *that*.'[92]

From Trent Park, the Simpsons continued their royal progress to Denham Place, the nearby home of Sir Robert Vansittart, then Permanent Under-Secretary of State for Foreign Affairs. The Vansittarts, who were only casual acquaintances, had rather surprisingly asked the Simpsons to stop off for an extra night in their house. Wallis felt herself under close scrutiny. By now the British security services, alerted by American press speculation about her friendship with the Prince of Wales, and also by the flattering attentions paid to her by the German Embassy,[93] were keeping a careful watch on her and on some of her friends. Of Vansittart, she wrote: '. . . something in the atmosphere made me nervous . . . It did not take me long to realize why I was under his roof. He was looking me over, dissecting me, no doubt, in the light of what he had been reading about me in his Foreign Office digest of the overseas press.'[94]

In the second week of 1936, Harold Nicolson, the friend and admirer of the Duchess of York, encountered Wallis and the Prince of Wales as fellow guests of Sibyl Colefax at the first night of Noël Coward's *Tonight at Eight-Thirty*. 'Mrs Simpson', he recorded in his diary, 'is bejewelled, eyebrow-plucked, virtuous and wise. I was impressed by the fact that she forbade the Prince to smoke during the *entr'acte* in the theatre itself. She is clearly out to help him.' Nicolson, however, confessed to 'an uneasy feeling that Mrs Simpson, in spite of her good intentions, is getting him out of touch with the type of person with whom he ought to associate. Go home pondering on all these things and a trifle sad. Why am I sad? Because I think Sibyl is a clever old bean who ought to concentrate upon intellectual and not social guests. Because I think Mrs Simpson is a nice woman who has flaunted suddenly into this absurd position. Because I think the P. of W. is in a mess. And because I do not feel at ease in such company.'[95]

George V would have been the first to agree. In the last weeks of his life, the King exclaimed passionately to Lady Algernon Gordon-Lennox: 'I pray to God that my eldest son will never marry and have children, and that nothing will come between Bertie and Lilibet and the throne.'[96]

To his Prime Minister, Stanley Baldwin, the despairing monarch predicted: 'After I am dead the boy will ruin himself in twelve months.'[97]

The old King's health had been rapidly failing since the early autumn. On December 3, the death of his favourite sister, Princess Victoria – loathed by the Prince of Wales, who considered her 'a bitch of the first order'[98] – plunged him into a melancholy from which he never emerged. He cancelled his attendance at the State opening of Parliament, and did not appear in public again.[99]

On the afternoon of Thursday, January 16, while he was shooting in Windsor Great Park, a note was brought to the Prince of Wales from Queen Mary. It told him that the royal physician, Lord Dawson of Penn, was 'not too pleased with Papa's state at the present moment', and suggested that he should 'propose' himself for the coming weekend at Sandringham, but in a casual manner so as not to alarm the King.[100]

Wallis was at the Fort and he handed her Queen Mary's note to read. The following morning, the Prince flew to Sandringham in his private aeroplane. That evening he telephoned Wallis in London to tell her that the King was obviously dying and could not survive more than two or three days. On the Sunday, the Prince drove down to London to alert the Prime Minister. He then flew back to Sandringham with the Duke of York, but without the Duchess, who was still not well enough to travel.

On the evening of Monday, January 20, Wallis Simpson was at a London cinema for a charity gala organized by her friends, Betty and Ormonde Lawson-Johnston. During the film, Lord Dawson's final bulletin informed the audience: 'The King's life is moving peacefully to its close.'

At five minutes to midnight, George V died peacefully in the presence of his wife and sons. Queen Mary's first act as a widow was to kiss the hand of her eldest son, the new sovereign. The first act of Edward VIII's reign was for the King to telephone Wallis Simpson with the news.

John McMullen, who was with her when the call came through from Sandringham, recorded: 'Everybody cried a little, but Wallis was really very wonderful. And, mark my words, she will become the power behind the throne.'[101]

Marie Belloc Lowndes noted that the new King 'insisted on flying to London the day following his father's death, the real reason being that

Mr and Mrs Simpson were on the point of starting for America. My view ... was that Mrs Simpson, supposing that everything would be so altered that her royal friendship would come to an end, felt that the most dignified thing to do would be for her to leave England for a while. Long after I learnt that the new King had arranged to meet her at the Ritz. She was ten minutes late and Lord Charles Montagu whom I met shortly after saw him stamping up and down the long corridor, looking angry and anxious till she came in and joined him.'[102]

Sir Alan Lascelles, the Assistant Private Secretary to the late King, 'actually believed that Edward and Mrs Simpson had laid plans to run away together in February, and that only King George V's death prevented it'.[103]

'Tommy' Lascelles was not an admirer of the new King. Seven years his senior and a diehard establishmentarian, he had resigned from the Prince's household in 1929 because of his disapproval of the heir's behaviour. Lascelles 'once told Edward exactly what he thought of him. "Yes," was the reply, "I was not made to be Prince of Wales." '[104]

The question now was whether he was made to be King. On January 22, he startled courtiers by appearing as a spectator – in defiance of royal tradition – at his own proclamation as sovereign. Standing beside him was the ubiquitous Wallis.

Chips Channon recorded: 'Afterwards I saw a large black car (the King's) drive away, with the blinds pulled half down. The crowd bowed, thinking that it contained the Duchess of Kent, but I saw Mrs Simpson ...

'We are all rivetted by the position of Mrs Simpson. No man has ever been so in love as the present King; but can she be another Mrs Fitzherbert? If he drops her she will fall – fall – into the nothingness from whence she came, but I hope he will not, for she is a good, kindly woman, who has had an excellent influence on the young Monarch.'[105]

On the same day that Wallis Simpson was assuming her regal role at the proclamation ceremony, the Duchess of York was travelling to Sandringham to comfort the widowed Queen Mary.

Six days later, Mrs Simpson, now the friend of the King and no longer needing the subterfuge of 'scullery maid', watched George V's funeral procession from St James's Palace. As the cortège rounded the corner of Marlborough House, there, in the Glass Coach, sitting with Queen Mary, the Queen of Norway and the Princess Royal,[106] was the woman Wallis had already recognized as her arch-antagonist – the Duchess of York.

Between the King's senior sister-in-law and the American woman expected to be 'the power behind the throne', the battle was already joined.

To Wallis, Elizabeth, even as Queen and Queen Mother, would always be 'the Dowdy Duchess'.

A friend of Wallis, who was the owner of a cosmetic shop on Worth Avenue, once sent her a box of a new powder called 'Duchess of York'. In an acid reply, Wallis thanked her friend for the powder, adding: 'And you know where I'll put it.'[107]

5

MRS SIMPSON DROPS IN
AT ROYAL LODGE

THE ACCESSION OF EDWARD VIII made the Duke of York Heir Presumptive to the Throne. The Duchess of York now superseded in rank the King's sister, the Princess Royal, and became the second lady in the land.

By Order in Council, the words, 'Our Gracious Queen Mary, the Duke of York and the Duchess of York', were inserted into all prayers, liturgies and collects for the Sovereign and the Royal Family.

The Loyal Toasts also had a new form. The first was 'The King'; the second, 'Queen Mary, the Duke and Duchess of York and other members of the Royal Family'. Ambassadors now came to pay their respects to the Yorks at 145 Piccadilly after they had presented their credentials to the King. Only when King Edward married, and a Queen Consort reigned beside him, would the Duchess of York be ousted from her new position of official eminence.

Elizabeth had been greatly debilitated by the attack of pneumonia before Christmas, and her doctors recommended a period of convalescence by the sea. On March 4, therefore, the Yorks and their daughters left London by car for one of the Duke of Devonshire's estates, Compton Place, Eastbourne, where they were to spend a month.

From there, on March 9, the Duchess of York wrote to the royal physician, Lord Dawson of Penn, about the old King. 'I miss him dreadfully,' she confessed. 'Unlike his own children I was never afraid of him, and in all the twelve years of having me as a daughter-in-law he never spoke one unkind or abrupt word to me . . . He was so kind, and so *dependable*.'[1]

Was this perhaps an oblique or subconscious way of saying that her mercurial brother-in-law was *not* to be depended on? The theme seemed to be developed further in the rest of her letter.

'I am really very well now, and, I think, am now only suffering from the effects of a family break-up – which always happens when the head of a family goes. Though outwardly one's life goes on the same, yet everything is different – especially spiritually, and mentally. I don't know if it is the result of being ill but I mind things that I don't like more than before.'[2]

It is natural to wonder what exactly were the things the Duchess of York did not like and minded more than before. Perhaps she minded hearing about an unbecoming witticism made by the King's American friend only three weeks after the old King's death.

On February 12, Chips Channon had recorded: 'Honor and I went to tea with the Brownlows. There we found assembled the "new Court", Mrs Simpson very charming and gay and vivacious. She said she had not worn black stockings since she gave up the Can-Can . . .'[3]

Elizabeth may also have minded hearing that the King had held 'a successful "do"' at Fort Belvedere, just twenty days after his father's funeral, and that 'he donned his wee bonnet and marched round the table, his stalwart piper behind him, playing "Over the Sea to Skye" and also a composition of his own'.[4]

If the Duchess of York heard about this, she would also have heard that the King's subservience to Mrs Simpson was greater than ever. Lady Diana Cooper, a guest at the 'successful "do"', found the King 'unchanged in manners and love. Wallis tore her nail and said "Oh!" and forgot about it, but he needs must disappear and arrive back in two minutes, panting, with two little emery-boards for her to file the offending nail.'[5]

Wallis had progressed beyond removing cigars from the royal pocket and forbidding the royal person to smoke in theatres. She now lectured the monarch on his duties in front of his guests. 'Wallis must not get too bossy,' wrote Diana Cooper. 'I had rather she had not said to him at dinner that she wanted to encourage his *reading* his papers and documents, that he was inclined to have them read to him – but that it was essential he should learn to master the points in them. She is right of course, as he made haste to say. "Wallis is quite right. She always is. I shall learn it quite soon." '[6]

The Yorks, dismayed by reports of the King's abject behaviour towards his American lady, were now conspicuous by their absence from Fort Belvedere.

The Duke of Gloucester and his new bride, Alice, were occasional visitors. '. . . they sometimes invited us over to dinner,' Princess Alice remembered. 'This was awkward, as we were as unhappy with the liaison as the rest of the family, but as a brother Prince Henry felt obliged to go.'[7]

The Duke of Kent had seen much of Wallis Simpson at the Fort before his marriage, and to please her husband, Princess Marina occasionally invited the King and Wallis to tea at Coppins or to dinner at their London house, 3 Belgrave Square.

Queen Mary, aware of all the rumours, maintained a dignified silence. In February, she confided to her friend and lady-in-waiting, Mabell Airlie: 'I have not liked to talk to David about this affair with Mrs Simpson, in the first place because I don't want to give the impression of interfering with his private life, and also because he is the most obstinate of all my sons. To oppose him over doing anything is only to make him more determined to do it. At present he is utterly infatuated, but my great hope is that violent infatuations usually wear off.'[8]

The Yorks were further dismayed when they learned that the King intended to make drastic cuts and economies in the various Royal staffs. Lady Hardinge later commented: '. . . he would refer to Mrs Simpson for advice on all such matters. The Civil List provided the King with ample money at this time, and such economies were unnecessary . . . the probable result – that Royal servants with long records as good, honest and loyal workers would be thrown onto the rapidly rising heap of the British unemployed – was shocking. (They were saved from this fate only by the efforts of the Royal Family, with help from the Royal Household.) It might have been slightly less surprising if King Edward had not, as Prince of Wales, shown such great concern for the lot of the jobless. But while continuing to show outward concern, he did not think of his own staff in the same light – although he could well afford their wages.'[9]

It was predictable that the King's first assault should be on 'dear Sandringham', as George V had called it. To Edward VIII, however, it was 'this voracious "white elephant"' where his father's 'private war with the twentieth century had ended in the almost complete repulse of the latter'.[10]

At the King's request, the Duke of York went up to Norfolk, taking with him a friend, Lord Radnor,[11] who was an experienced landowner, and the two of them spent a fortnight surveying the Sandringham estate. The Duke prepared a clear and concise report of sound economies that could be made. The King read it, considered it entirely too moderate and went ahead with his own cuts, ordering

the dismissal of various people, and only telling his brother and the
rest of the family after it had been done. The Duke of York was
distressed, and the Duchess was angry that her husband's work and
recommendations had been ignored.

At his accession, King Edward had wanted Sir Godfrey Thomas, his
own secretary for seventeen years, to accept the key post of Principal
Private Secretary to the Sovereign. Thomas, a modest and realistic
man, declined on the grounds that he was insufficiently qualified for
the job. It was then offered to Major the Hon. Alexander Hardinge,
son of the former Viceroy of India, Lord Hardinge of Penshurst, and
Assistant Private Secretary to King George V since 1920.

Alec Hardinge, who accepted the post, was the new King's contemporary, being just one month his elder. Beyond this, however, they had
nothing in common. Hardinge was an establishment man whose views
and habits were ultra-conservative. He and his wife – a Cecil by birth –
were close friends of the Duke and Duchess of York, the Duchess
having been one of Helen Hardinge's bridesmaids. And like the Yorks,
the Hardinges both took an unfavourable view of Wallis Simpson,
Helen Hardinge later noting, 'we did not *seek* her company, ourselves'.[12]

Friends of the Hardinges, and those who were not dependent on the
King's favour, came close to ostracizing his American lady.

'Some of our friends who were obliged by common politeness to
meet her on social occasions felt the same,' wrote Lady Hardinge. 'I
had one friend who absolutely refused to shake hands with her. "What
did you do?" I asked her, after they had been introduced at a party.
"Oh," she replied, "it was quite easy. I dropped my handbag just as she
got to me, so I had to stoop down to find it."

'Others – particularly the group that came to be known as the "Ritz
Bar set" – felt differently. To them, Mrs Simpson seemed to provide a
heaven-sent opportunity to enter Royal society ... Diplomats –
especially German diplomats – sought her company. In many rich,
rather than aristocratic, households, she was made welcome ...'[13]

Undoubtedly the Dowager Lady Hardinge of Penshurst believed
this when she wrote it, in retrospect, in 1967, but the reality was very
different. Many aristocratic households had welcomed Wallis Simpson since her arrival in London. Lord and Lady Sackville invited her to
Knole even before she had entered the life of the Prince of Wales. Later,
in the years of her ascendancy, the Duke and Duchess of Marlborough
had her to stay at Blenheim, and, as we have seen, Sir Philip Sassoon, a

close friend of the Royal Family, invited her to Trent Park. The Earl of Dudley, the Earl and Countess of Portarlington and the Earl of Granard were among many other aristocrats who invited her to be their guest. As Cecil Beaton noted in 1936: 'Even the old Edwardians receive her, if she happens to be free to accept their invitations.'[14] British society, later so anxious to disown its interest in Wallis Simpson, was hedging its bets.

Helen Hardinge was in fact one of the first to take seriously the possibility that the King intended to marry the lady. She recalled that before his accession, 'members of the Prince of Wales' own Household tended to regard Mrs Simpson's frequent visits with some amusement . . . and I once told one of them: "You all think this is a great joke, but I'm not so sure it is." '[15]

Before the end of March 1936, Helen Hardinge was to be 'disturbed by my own conviction – which nobody else seemed to share – that King Edward was not satisfied just with having Mrs Simpson as his constant companion, but that he was set on marrying her, whatever the constitutional consequences'.[16]

Concern began to grow among courtiers over the King's erratic working hours and his steadily declining interest in official business. 'It was scarcely realized at this early stage', wrote Alec Hardinge later, 'how overwhelming and inexorable was the influence exerted on the King by the lady of the moment. As time went on it became clearer that every decision, big or small, was subordinated to her will . . . It was she who filled his thought at all times, she alone who mattered, before her the affairs of state sank into insignificance.'[17]

On March 10, Alec Hardinge was late for a luncheon party that included the Chancellor of the Exchequer, Neville Chamberlain, 'as usual, owing to the new King's strange hours', noted his wife.[18] The next day she added: 'Alec worried about his work',[19] and two days later: 'Nothing but a ghastly conversation in the evening [with two older members of the Royal Household] about how awful the new King is.'[20] And on March 27: 'Confusion in the King's affairs because he's so unpractical.'[21]

It was at a party the King gave at Windsor Castle on March 28 that Helen Hardinge 'first thought that he had reached the point of no return'.[22]

The King had invited the Hardinges to be his guests as well as Lord Wigram, George V's Private Secretary, and Lady Wigram. Nora Wigram was among those who had strong feelings about Mrs

Simpson, and knowing that Wallis would be present, Lady Wigram tried to refuse to go, but her husband, 'Wig', insisted that she should.

The Hardinges and the Wigrams were waiting at the Sovereign's Entrance to the castle when the King arrived from Fort Belvedere with his guests. They included both the Simpsons, the Yorks' friends, Colin and Gladys Buist, and an American woman called Buttercup Kennedy, whom no one seemed to have heard of before, although she would be heard of again, in very dramatic circumstances, before the year was over. 'The King and Mrs Simpson were in a teasing mood,' records Lady Hardinge, 'and they made some apparently joking references to "matching" Buttercup Kennedy with Mr Simpson.'[23]

The King and his guests went into the White Drawing Room, where a cinema projector had been installed, and they all sat and watched a newsreel of the Grand National, followed by an Eddie Cantor film. When the films were over, the party walked and talked in the Grand Corridor of the castle. 'Mrs Simpson was very agreeable to everyone', noted Lady Hardinge, 'and she admired the Victorian settings of my jewellery.'[24]

Some of the finest portraits in the Grand Corridor were of King George IV, a monarch whose private life had often been the subject of scandal and concern.

At the age of twenty-one, and while still Prince of Wales, George IV met a twice-widowed Roman Catholic, Maria Fitzherbert, six years his senior. Overwhelmed by her beauty, the Prince threatened – and even attempted – suicide as a means of extorting from her a promise of marriage. She went abroad to avoid him, but he pestered her through the mails, his pursuit culminating in a thirty-five page letter of proposal.

She returned to London, and on December 15, 1785, they were secretly married in her drawing-room in Park Street, Mayfair, in defiance of the Act of Settlement of 1701, which forbade any member of the Royal Family to become a Roman Catholic, or to marry one; and also of the Royal Marriages Act of 1772, by which the Prince of Wales required his father's consent to marry. Although an open secret in society, the Prince at once denied the marriage to his close friend, the Whig politician, Charles James Fox.

In the summer of 1794, the Prince brusquely abandoned Mrs Fitzherbert for the charms of an Irish bishop's daughter, Frances, Countess of Jersey, and in the following year, in order to get his massive debts paid, the Prince agreed to marry his first cousin, Princess

Caroline of Brunswick. Appalled by the sight of his gauche, coarse and unwashed bride, the Prince gasped, 'I am not well; pray get me a glass of brandy.'[25]

He went through the wedding ceremony drunk, weeping, and supported by male guests standing on either side of him. A daughter, Princess Charlotte, was born in 1796, after which the Prince and Princess of Wales separated. In 1800, he returned to live with Mrs Fitzherbert, who only took him back after the Queen had written to beg her to do so, and Pope Pius VII had given his sanction. After some nine years of happy domesticity, the Prince abandoned her again in favour of the middle-aged Marchioness of Hertford.

In 1811, George III's precarious mental health finally collapsed, and the Prince of Wales became Regent until his father's death in 1820.

George IV's promiscuous and mentally-unstable wife, Caroline, hastened back to England to claim her rights as Queen, and while the King proceeded against her for divorce in the House of Lords – an action which failed – Mrs Fitzherbert, with scrupulous loyalty, remained abroad with the evidence of the secret first marriage which could have prejudiced the trial and shaken the throne. On July 19, 1821, both the King's wives were excluded from his coronation in Westminster Abbey. But when George IV died in 1830, he left instructions 'that my constant companion, the Picture of my beloved wife, my Maria Fitzherbert, may be interred with me, suspended round my neck by a Ribbon as I used to wear it when I lived, and placed right upon my Heart'.[26]

His brother, William IV, at once offered Mrs Fitzherbert the title of duchess and the right to use the Royal liveries for her servants, but she gracefully declined. When, later, she dined at the Royal Pavilion, the King himself received her and helped her from her carriage.

She died in 1837 in Brighton, and was buried there in the Church of St John the Baptist, where she had made her confession every week at a time when the church was closed, seen only by a young charwoman, who was instructed by the priest to drop a deep curtsey to the heavily veiled lady, 'for maybe it was the Queen of England, and maybe not'.[27]

This chapter of British royal history must have been in the minds of Edward VIII and Mrs Simpson on the evening in March 1936 when they walked in the Grand Corridor at Windsor Castle.

'Gradually, from desultory talk,' records Lady Hardinge, 'the story of George IV and Mrs Fitzherbert seemed to detach itself and as a theme made its way into the conversation. And as we wandered among the paintings that night, perhaps because of the hints and talk about them, their presence became very real, and George IV and Mrs Fitzherbert seemed to emerge and join us. They seemed more solid, less brittle, than ourselves. Our little group bristled with unspoken confidences about the present, as we discussed the personal affairs of George IV.'[28]

Helen Hardinge went home and noted in her diary: 'Too many ghosts at this party.'[29] She was now convinced that the King was bent on marriage.

The Royal Marriages Act did not apply to the Sovereign personally, only to his family. As far as the Act of Settlement was concerned, Wallis Simpson was not a Roman Catholic. If she chose to divorce her second husband, there was nothing in the British Constitution to prevent the King from marrying her.

Helen Hardinge urged that Walter Monckton, a distinguished constitutional lawyer long known to her husband, ought to be consulted. 'But Walter Monckton turned out to be in India, and the handful of people in this country to whom I could mention my conclusion thought it was too wild to even be considered. The general feeling was that so long as Mr Simpson's presence gave the relationship at least the outward aspect of a threesome, there would be no danger.'[30]

This was still the opinion of the Duke and Duchess of York. Much as both of them disliked Wallis Simpson, and disapproved of her influence, neither could believe that the King really intended to marry her. As a possibility, it was unthinkable, largely because of the repercussions it would entail in their own lives.

Helen Hardinge began to wonder if she was mistaken. Yet in the lengthy discussions that took place at this time concerning the new Civil List, the King concerned himself most with the provision to be made for a Queen. When the Civil List was announced in April 1936, a clause provided £40,000 a year for a Queen Consort, if the King should marry, to be increased to £70,000 if she survived the King.

On March 31, Helen Hardinge noted in her diary: 'Alec very much depressed by HM's irresponsibility.'[31] Hardinge was disturbed by the King's open and blatant disagreement with his own government over the conduct of British foreign policy. Far from seeing Hitler and Mussolini as threats to Britain, Edward VIII made no secret of his admiration for the Fascist dictators. The record of Edward's dealings with his cousin, the Duke of Saxe-Coburg, a member of the Nazi Party, who was imprisoned after the war by the Americans, leaves no room for doubt about the King's sympathies.

Wallis Simpson was also suspected, though with less cause, of having pro-German leanings, largely because of the flattering attentions paid to her by Hitler's envoy, Ribbentrop, and by the German Embassy in London.

At the beginning of his reign, King Edward had initialled every piece of paper he read. This proved to be a mistake. Within weeks of his accession, the absence of the royal initials demonstrated just how little official reading he was doing. As his obsession with Wallis Simpson grew, the King stopped reading State papers completely, leaving the task to Alec Hardinge.

Shocked alarm was manifested in Whitehall when documents containing official secrets were returned not merely unread, but stained with the rings of wet glass bottoms, and after protracted delays. When Stanley Baldwin discovered from Hardinge that crucial Cabinet documents were being left lying around at Fort Belvedere while Wallis Simpson's friends came and went, the Prime Minister, for the first and – to date – last time in British history, restricted the documents made available to the King to those requiring the royal signature. This was a direct breach of the Constitution, since the monarch is entitled to see everything, but it is the measure of the distrust Edward VIII inspired in his own government. It is also the measure of the King's complete preoccupation that he never realized this form of censorship was taking place.

On April 2, Harold Nicolson noted: 'I dine with Mrs Simpson to meet the King. Black tie; black waistcoat. A taxi to Bryanston Court; an apartment dwelling; a lift; butler and maid at door; drawing room; many orchids and white arums. The guests consist of Lady Oxford, Lady Cunard, Lady Colefax, Kenneth Lindsay, the Counsellor of the US Embassy at Buenos Aires plus wife, and Alexander Woollcott. Mr Ernest Simpson enters bringing in the King. We all bow and curtsey . . . It is evident that Lady Cunard is incensed by the presence of Lady Colefax, and that Lady Colefax is furious that Lady Cunard should also have been asked. Lady Oxford appears astonished to find either of them at what was to have been a quite intimate party . . . something snobbish in me is rather saddened by all this. Mrs Simpson is a perfectly harmless type of American, but the whole setting is slightly second-rate. I do not wonder that the Sutherlands and the Stanleys are sniffy about it all.'[32]

April also brought Wallis Simpson another encounter with the
Duchess of York. This time the cause was the King's purchase of an
American station wagon, a type of vehicle then virtually unknown in
Britain. The Duchess of Windsor has recorded: 'One afternoon, David
said, "Let's drive over to Royal Lodge. I want to show Bertie the car."
There were three other guests staying at the Fort that weekend, and
they went along with us.'[33]

Turning into the entrance of Royal Lodge, the King proudly swung
his new station wagon around the circular driveway and drew up with
a flourish outside the front door, where the Duke and Duchess of York
were waiting, having received a telephone call to say he would be
coming. While the King took the Duke for a drive to show off the
virtues of his new acquisition, Wallis once again found herself face to
face with the Duchess.

On this occasion, possibly due to the presence of the other three
guests, Elizabeth clearly made an effort not to allow her dislike of the
American visitor to be apparent. And in a memorably acid phrase that
was to reverberate down the years, Wallis later recorded: 'Her justly
famous charm was highly evident.'[34] Wallis was also to recall 'the
beauty of her complexion and the almost startling blueness of her eyes.
Our conversation, I remember, was largely a discussion on the merits
of the garden at the Fort and that at Royal Lodge.'[35]

This seems a natural enough topic since they were standing in one of
the two gardens under discussion, but clearly, in what was an unexpected and also an uninvited confrontation, Elizabeth was restricting
conversation to subjects of a strictly impersonal nature.

In a few minutes, the King and the Duke of York returned in the
station wagon, and the party walked through the garden and into the
house. Once again the ghost of Maria Fitzherbert must have been
hovering, for Wallis Simpson entered the forty-foot-long green-
panelled saloon designed by Jeffry Wyatville for Maria's royal husband, and sat down to have tea at a table directly beneath a portrait of
George IV.

In a few moments the ten-year-old Princess Elizabeth and the
five-year-old Princess Margaret Rose – 'both', in Wallis's recollection,
'so blonde, so beautifully mannered, so brightly scrubbed that they
might have stepped straight from the pages of a picture book'[36] – came
into the room with their governess, Marion Crawford.

Miss Crawford had already heard much about Mrs Simpson, and
while her charges helped themselves to orange juice from the table, the

Scottish governess took shrewd note of the visitor. 'She was a smart, attractive woman, already middle-aged, but with that immediate friendliness American women have. She appeared to be entirely at her ease; if anything, rather too much so.'[37]

Miss Crawford, besides recognizing Wallis's assurance, was not slow to discern her domination of Edward. 'She had a distinctly proprietary way of speaking to the new King. I remember she drew him to the window and suggested how certain trees might be moved, and a part of a hill taken away to improve the view.'[38]

From an uninvited guest, and the friend of the King, by whose 'grace and favour' Royal Lodge continued to be leased to the Yorks, this behaviour seems so blatant that one must assume it was deliberate. Had something in the conversation about the two gardens stung Wallis into making an oblique criticism of the Yorks' landscaping? The trees and rhododendrons at Royal Lodge were the Duke's pride and joy and he had recreated the garden personally out of an over-grown wilderness. Or was Wallis's remark a deliberate warning signal from the woman whose friend believed she would become 'the power behind the throne'?

If it was the latter, then the message was clear: I, Wallis Simpson, now rule the man to whom you owe this house. You may not like me, but I have the power to control your lives and even to change your garden if I wish. Was this what the King's friend wanted 'the Dowdy Duchess' to understand?

'I have never admired the Duke and Duchess more than on that afternoon,' wrote Marion Crawford. 'With quiet and charming dignity they made the best of this awkward occasion and gave no sign whatever of their feelings. But the atmosphere was not a comfortable one . . .'[39]

Perhaps in awareness of this, the Duchess of York said to the governess: 'Crawfie, would you like to take Lilibet and Margaret into the woods for a while?'

As they left the house, Princess Elizabeth asked uneasily, 'Crawfie, who is she?'[40]

Besides observing Mrs Simpson, the governess had also observed the King. '. . . it was impossible not to notice the change in Uncle David. He had been so youthful and gay. Now he looked haggard and distraught. He fumbled incessantly with his tie, and seemed not to be listening to what was said to him. He made plans with the children, and then forgot them.'[41]

The visit lasted an hour. 'David and his sister-in-law carried on the conversation', Wallis remembered, 'with his brother throwing in only an occasional word.'[42]

By the time the guests departed, the King had converted his brother to enthusiasm for the American station wagon. But Wallis 'left with a distinct impression that . . . the Duchess was not sold on David's other American interest'.[43]

Marion Crawford realized how unwelcome Mrs Simpson's appearance at Royal Lodge had been by the frozen silence which prevailed concerning it. 'No one alluded to that visit when we met again later in the evening . . . nothing whatever was said, though I suppose most of us had the subject in our minds. Maybe the general hope was still that, if nothing was said, the whole business would blow over.'[44]

'Crawfie' was not the only one to notice Wallis's complete sovereignty over the sovereign. On May 10, we find Chips Channon recording: 'It appears that the King is Mrs Simpson's absolute slave, and will go nowhere where she is not invited.'[45]

By now, she would later claim, Wallis had discovered – by means of a love letter intended for her husband, and wrongly addressed to her – that Ernest Simpson had found someone else. This was Mary Kirk Raffray, Wallis's closest school friend at Oldfields and one of her bridesmaids when she married Win Spencer.

A little earlier, Bernard Rickatson-Hatt, editor-in-chief of Reuters and an old friend of the Simpsons, had been at York House with the King and Ernest. When Rickatson-Hatt got up to leave, Simpson had asked him to remain, and turning to the King had made a dramatic statement. Wallis, he said, would have to chose between them. What did the King intend doing about it? Did he intend to marry her? The King then rose from his seat and said: 'Do you really think that I would be crowned without Wallis by my side?'[46]

One day in May, while they were talking in the garden at the Fort, the King told Wallis that he was inviting the Prime Minister to dinner at York House and wanted her to be present. 'Then he paused, and after a moment, with his most Prince Charming smile, added, "It's got to be done. Sooner or later my Prime Minister must meet my future wife."

'"David," I exclaimed, "you mustn't talk that way. The idea is impossible. They'd never let you!"

'"I'm well aware of all that," he said almost gaily, "but rest assured, I will manage it somehow." '[47]

The York House dinner took place on May 27. Wallis helped the King to plan both the menu and the table decorations, and the guests, besides the Baldwins, were the Mountbattens; Duff and Diana Cooper; Lord and Lady Wigram; Emerald Cunard; the King's equerry, Lieut-Colonel the Hon. Piers ('Joey') Legh and his wife, Sarah; Admiral of the Fleet Sir Ernle Chatfield and Lady Chatfield; and the American aviator, Colonel Charles Lindbergh and his wife, Anne.

Helen Hardinge, who was not present on this occasion, alleges: 'In the seating arrangements for the dinner . . . Mrs Simpson was given precedence over the Prime Minister's wife.'[48]

This was not the case. Mrs Baldwin sat on the King's right at dinner, and was therefore given precedence over the eight other women present. In his diary, Baldwin commented: 'My wife was well-placed, but I own it surprised me to see Mrs Simpson at one end of the table and Lady Cunard at the other.'[49]

Baldwin 'did recognize that Mrs Simpson's influence on the King was not without its good side'.[50]

Lord Davidson, the friend of the Duke of York, adds: 'SB discounted the wilder tales. The relationship between the King and Mrs Simpson might be intimate, but his personal impression of her was not unfavourable and he was not disposed to interfere . . . I did not share SB's favourable impression of Mrs Simpson.'[51]

Lucy Baldwin had once electrified a fashionable gathering by asking who Mrs Simpson was. When she found out, 'Mrs Baldwin's comments, then and after, were less bland. For her, and for women like her throughout the Empire, Mrs Simpson had stolen the Fairy Prince.'[52]

Helen Hardinge heard that Wallis 'was very pleasant and active in looking after the guests. She was not nonplussed by their barely-concealed and not entirely friendly curiosity.'[53]

Wallis's own recollection of the dinner was that 'the Baldwins were pleasant but distant. As so often before in the company of those of power and influence, I was conscious of the assaying glance, the unspoken, probing question beneath the polite surface of the conversation.'[54]

That evening was the last occasion on which the Simpsons would be seen together in public, and when, on the following morning, the list of the King's guests was published in the Court Circular,[55] their names achieved an extra prominence by coming last. The words, 'and Mr and Mrs Ernest Simpson', stood out from the others like the neon billing of stars in a Broadway musical.

Lady Hardinge comments: 'It was ironic that the Press which had steadfastly restrained itself from linking HM's name with Mrs Simpson was now obliged to do so at his insistence. Great efforts were made to stop the King from doing this, by those members of his staff who were trying to protect him. But the two persons concerned apparently believed that the appearance of her name alongside those of a lot of distinguished people, most of whom would have been a lot happier if she had not been there, would somehow smooth their path towards marriage . . . If Mayfair society had shown any self-restraint before in speculating about King Edward's private life, it had no cause to do so now.'[56]

A troubled Queen Mary showed the Court Circular notice to Lady Airlie. ' "He gives Mrs Simpson the most beautiful jewels". After a long pause she added, "I am so afraid that he may ask me to receive her."

'Bright spots of crimson were burning on her cheek bones. It was easy to imagine what such a demand would represent to her all-pervading loyalty to the Monarchy.'[57]

Wallis now informed her husband that she was starting divorce proceedings. Ernest Simpson moved out of Bryanston Court and into the Guards Club. The King arranged for Wallis to see his own solicitor, George Allen, who was under no illusion about the eventual purpose of the case. 'Are you quite sure, Mrs Simpson, that you want a divorce?' he asked her.[58] When she assured him that she did, he undertook to find her legal representation, since his own firm, Allen and Overy, were not divorce solicitors.

The first firm approached, Charles Russell & Co., refused to take the case on the grounds that it was liable to cause publicity damaging to the King. Walter Monckton eventually introduced Wallis to Theodore Goddard, who agreed to act for her, and unwisely retained the services of the most celebrated and publicized advocate of his day, Norman Birkett KC.

On May 29, Edward VIII's Coronation was officially proclaimed for May 12, 1937, and the King was already concerned with arrangements for Wallis's attendance. He had 'taken steps to see that the Earl Marshal's Office were making allowances for her to be present at the ceremony, whether or not she was to be crowned Queen, and had ordered that she should have a prominent position not unlike the Royal Box at other coronations – this enclosure was promptly named, and afterwards referred to, by the staff of the Earl Marshal's Office as "the Loose Box"!'[59]

By now, even junior members of the Royal Family were having reservations about being in Mrs Simpson's company. On May 31, Wallis's American friend, 'Mike' Scanlon, recorded in his diary: 'Another weekend at the Fort. Wallis there, but not Ernest. The Rex Bensons, the Duke and Duchess of Gloucester, the Duchess most nervous and fidgety.'[60]

At the beginning of June, Wallis went off to Paris with Scanlon's wife, Gladys, to buy new hats, and the King, his nerves clearly on edge in her absence, had a row with the highest-ranking member of his court, Lord Cromer, the Lord Chamberlain of the Household.

Wallis was back in time for Ascot, which the King did not attend on account of Court mourning, but Wallis went in regal style, and shortly afterwards, Ramsay MacDonald, the former Prime Minister, 'spoke . . . of what he described as the King's appalling obstinacy in sending his mistress to Ascot in a royal carriage . . . He contended that if she were a widow it would not matter. "The people of this country do not mind fornication," he said, "but they loathe adultery." '[61]

Criticism was steadily mounting. Sir Alan Lascelles, never an admirer of Edward VIII, 'said the King was like the child in the fairy story who was given every gift except a soul . . . He had no real friends for whom he cared a straw. His private secretaries had a devil of a time. He would disappear every Thursday to Tuesday to the Fort where none of them was allowed to follow. Despatch boxes were actually lost when not attended to. Even when in London he shut himself up in Buckingham Palace giggling with Mrs Simpson for hours on end, while the royal footmen would say to the waiting secretaries, "The lady is still there." '[62]

Even Chips Channon noted with dismay on July 7: 'The Simpson scandal is growing, and she, poor Wallis, looks unhappy. The world is closing in around her, the flatterers, the sycophants, and the malice. It is a curious social juxtaposition that casts me in the role of Defender of the King. But I do, and very strongly in society, not for loyalty so much as for admiration and affection for Wallis, and in indignation against those who attack her.'[63]

On July 9, the King gave a second dinner party at York House, once again organized by Wallis. The occasion provided her with a further opportunity to win over the Duke and Duchess of York, who ranked highest of those invited. The other guests were the Marquess of Willingdon, a recent Viceroy of India, and the Marchioness; Lady Diana Duff Cooper, wife of the Secretary of State for War; the Earl

Stanhope, Parliamentary Under-Secretary of State for Foreign Affairs, and the Countess Stanhope; Margot Asquith (the Countess of Oxford and Asquith), widow of the Liberal Prime Minister; Winston and Clementine Churchill; Alec and Helen Hardinge; Sir Samuel Hoare, First Lord of the Admiralty, and Lady Maud Hoare; Sir Philip Sassoon, Under-Secretary of State for Air; Captain David Margesson, the Government Chief Whip; Sir Edward Peacock, a Director of the Bank of England and Receiver-General of the Duchy of Cornwall, and Lady Peacock; and Lady Colefax. The Duchess of York sat on the King's right at dinner, and Wallis Simpson was once again at the head of the table, with Sir Samuel Hoare on her right, and Lady Colefax at the opposite end of the table.

The Yorks had returned that afternoon from a public engagement at the Hertfordshire Agricultural Society's Show at Hatfield Park, where, by a coincidence of some irony, the royal couple had been attended by the Duke's equerry, the Hon. Thomas Coke, elder son of the first woman in the life of Edward VIII, Viscountess Coke.[64]

That evening at York House, Helen Hardinge saw signs of Wallis 'enthusiastically moving into the regal role into which she had cast herself',[65] and Sir Samuel Hoare, later Lord Templewood, remembered 'not only her sparkling talk, but also her sparkling jewels in very up-to-date Cartier settings'. He considered her 'very attractive and intelligent, very American with little or no knowledge of English life'.[66]

Wallis herself recalled: 'As I had before at the dinner for Mr Baldwin, I felt the same well-bred, but not so well-concealed, curiosity'.[67]

Forty-seven years after the York House dinner, one of the guests, Lady Diana Cooper, a society legend at the age of ninety-one, remembered clearly the Duchess of York's attitude towards Mrs Simpson on that evening. 'She was cool and remote from first to last, both from disapproval of paraded illicit love, and also from dread of possibly finding herself a queen.'[68]

Yet again the saga of a King of England's clandestine romance and marriage entered the conversation. 'After dinner', records Lady Hardinge, 'Mr Churchill sat with the Duchess of York and made an excellent historical speech. The topic he chose was an embarrassingly loaded one: King George IV and Mrs Fitzherbert. The Duchess heard him out, and then commented rather absently, "Well, that was a *long* time ago."'[69]

Forty years later, Lady Hardinge admitted: 'The Duchess had a sort of warning expression on her face that would have deterred anyone less obsessed by his own powers of oratory than Churchill.'[70]

But if Churchill was aware of the royal displeasure, he did not heed it. Astonishingly, he moved on to an even more dangerous discourse on the wars between the Red Rose of Lancaster and the White Rose of York. The point was certainly not lost on the Duchess of York. The King was shortly embarking on a Balkan cruise under the alias of one of his subsidiary titles, the Duke of Lancaster. It had already been privately mooted in Royal circles that if Mrs Simpson were to marry the King, she need not take the title of Queen, but might conceivably be Duchess of Lancaster.

With an even colder and still more knowing look, Elizabeth once again heard Churchill out, and then, reports Lady Hardinge, 'she said – rather more emphatically – "That was a very, *very* long time ago." '[71]

Not long before her death, Lady Hardinge enlarged on this account. 'When I wrote my book in 1967, I had to employ some measure of tact, since so many of the people concerned were still living.

'The Duchess of York's second answer to Churchill was very emphatic, verging on sharpness, which was quite unlike her. Even Churchill could not mistake her meaning. He had somewhat overstepped the line. It was very much a royal dismissal, as if to say, "I have heard enough." She was not prepared at that time, or at any time to my knowledge, to hear anything, however oblique, in favour of Mrs Simpson.'[72]

On the following morning, the Court Circular again published the list of the King's guests, and this time Wallis's name not only had the prominence of coming last but also of being alone, unaccompanied by that of her husband: '. . . and Mrs Ernest Simpson'.[73]

The second Court Circular announcement fuelled a campaign against Wallis that had been simmering all summer on the part of her fellow American, Viscountess Astor,[74] Britain's first woman Member of Parliament. The coincidences that Wallis and Nancy both belonged to Virginian families and had both been divorced in no way inhibited Lady Astor's trenchant criticism.

On May 28, the day of the first Court Circular announcement, Harold Nicolson had recorded: 'Nancy Astor is terribly indignant at the King for having invited to his first official dinner Lady Cunard and Mr and Mrs Simpson. She says that the effect in Canada and America will be deplorable. She considers Lady Cunard and Chips Channon as "disintegrating influences", and she deplores the fact that any but the best Virginian families should be received at Court . . . In any case, she is determined to tell the King that although Mrs Simpson may appear at Court, she must not appear in the Court Circular. I suggest to her that any such intimation would be regarded by HM as a gross impertinence. She says that when the dignity of the United States and the British Empire is involved, it is her duty to make such sacrifices.'[75]

Nancy was clearly unaware that the Montagues were considered one of 'the first families of Virginia',[76] and after the second Court Circular announcement her indignation became more shrill.

On July 20, one of the 'disintegrating influences' she abhorred, Chips Channon, was 'at the Kemsleys' ball at Chandos House, a grandiose, high season affair with "all London" present . . . Honor sat with Wallis Simpson, who was in a rage, as she had just received a letter from an MP signed by a well-known name, which she was clever enough not to reveal, in which he warned Mrs Simpson against Lady Astor and her campaign. Wallis asked Honor for her advice, and soon Honor had spilt the beans about Nancy Astor's various attacks on me in regard to Wallis at the House of Commons. I fear that there may be a proper scandal and "bust up" as Wallis will, and in fact, already has, told the King.'[77]

The news spread rapidly, for a week later Sir Robert Bruce Lockhart can be found noting: 'Emerald (Cunard) told me . . . that Lady Astor has been attacking Mrs Simpson very violently – and by implication the King – in the House of Commons and elsewhere and that a Member of Parliament had written to Mrs Simpson and Mrs Simpson had shown the letter to the King.'[78]

It is not without significance that Nancy Astor was a dedicated admirer of the Duchess of York. In the following year, when Elizabeth and her husband were crowned King and Queen, Nancy was one of several critics of Wallis Simpson to receive official recognition. She was made a Companion of Honour.

It was hardly surprising that a campaign was now building up against Wallis. All discretion and sense of propriety had vanished from the behaviour of the King and herself.

On July 27, at supper at Emerald Cunard's, Chips Channon saw her 'literally smothered in rubies'.[79]

In recent years, the Duchess of Windsor's apologists have made much of their contention – impossible to prove and difficult to sustain

– that she was never the King's mistress before she married him. This dubious argument avoids the central question of taste. Whether the relationship was physically consummated or not prior to marriage is hardly the point. By constantly appearing in public covered in costly jewels bought for her by the adoring King, Wallis Simpson proclaimed herself *maîtresse en titre* to society at large. It was on the grounds of vulgar display, rather than alleged immorality, that the criticism of her, and of him, was justified.

The criticism was by no means confined to the upper classes. A footman, asked why he had left the employment of King Edward VIII at Fort Belvedere, replied, to a prospective employer in London: 'Well, Madam, the butler, Mr Osborne, sent me down to the swimming pool with two drinks. When I got there what did I see but His Majesty painting Mrs Simpson's toenails. My Sovereign painting a woman's toenails. It was a bit much, Madam. I gave notice at once.'[80]

The King, meanwhile, had chartered Lady Yule's palatial yacht, the *Nahlin*, which awaited him at anchor at Sibenik on the Yugoslavian coast. Crates and cases addressed to 'the Duke of Lancaster' were carried on board, and under his ducal alias the King left England with Wallis on August 8 in an aircraft of the King's Flight. That evening in Paris they boarded a private coach attached to the Orient Express.

They had embarked on possibly the most disastrous public relations exercise in modern history. Only one week later, a London weekly magazine broke the otherwise general British press embargo on the King's romance by publishing a front-page photograph of him with his American lady. The caption read, 'The Duke of Lancaster and a Guest'.[81]

The 'Duchess of Lancaster' – the unnamed subject of Winston Churchill's mischief at the York House dinner one month earlier – would be dubbed 'Queen Wallis' by the American press before the *Nahlin* cruise was over. Indeed, in the months ahead, even the highest-ranking official of the British Court, the Lord Chamberlain of the Royal Household, would defer to her as if he fully expected her to become Queen of England. 'Mrs Simpson's invitations', it would be said, 'came to rank as commands.'[82]

The *Nahlin*'s captain once replied to a curious reporter, 'We have come from nowhere. We are going nowhere.'[83] His words were true of Edward VIII and Wallis Simpson. The cruise of the *Nahlin* was to be a voyage into oblivion for them both.

While Wallis, the unofficial red rose of Lancaster, sailed

unknowingly into the sunset of her brief reign, Elizabeth, the white rose of York, travelled north with her husband to their Scottish home, Birkhall, on Deeside, for a traditional royal summer holiday. If there was one person in Britain who would never defer to Queen Wallis in any circumstances, even if that title somehow became a reality, it was the Duchess of York.

P.S. Hurry up

6

THE DUCHESS OF YORK
REJECTS QUEEN WALLIS

EDWARD VIII's BALKAN ADVENTURE started to go badly wrong before he and Wallis Simpson had even set foot on board the *Nahlin*. On August 9, when the Orient Express paused at Salzburg, the King and Wallis unwisely strolled together along the platform, only to be ambushed by a stealthy pack of photographers. Within hours, the pictures of them together were being wired around the world. When British newspapers published them, the figure of Mrs Simpson was dutifully painted out, showing the King apparently alone. Elsewhere, however, they appeared side by side, and bundles of foreign press cuttings began to arrive in Whitehall, as well as on Queen Mary's writing desk at Buckingham Palace.

After a further brief stop at Krainburg to have tea with the Regent of Yugoslavia, Prince Paul, and his wife, Princess Olga – sister of Princess Marina, Duchess of Kent – the King and Wallis arrived on the quay at Sibenik at breakfast-time on August 10 to find the *Nahlin*, gleaming white from stem to stern, surrounded by twenty thousand excited peasants in Yugoslav national costume, scores of reporters, and a veritable army of press photographers. The fragile alias of the Duke of Lancaster crumbled for ever amid roars of 'Long live the King'.

On board, occupying the eight luxurious staterooms, were the Duff Coopers; Lord Sefton; Mrs Josephine ('Foxie') Gwynne;[1] Lord Beaverbrook's sister-in-law, Helen Fitzgerald; Colin and Gladys Buist; Lord and Lady Brownlow; the Duke of Kent's equerry, Humphrey Butler, and his wife 'Poots'; the King's favourite golfer, Archie Compston; and Wallis's old friends from Peking days, Herman and Katherine Rogers. Completing the party were two of the King's secretaries, Godfrey Thomas and Tommy Lascelles, and his equerry, Major John Aird.

The *Nahlin*, closely shadowed by two Royal Navy destroyers, *Grafton* and *Glowworm*, made her leisurely way down the Yugoslav coast, putting into various Adriatic ports, in every one of which – due to the press publicity – it appeared to be common knowledge that a royal romance was in progress. When the *Nahlin* lay at anchor off a small fishing village below Cetinje, thousands of peasants appeared with flaming torches and sang folk songs from the shore.

Wallis recorded the King's reaction. ' "I suppose," David said, "you think this is for me."

' "Of course," I answered, unwarily. "Who else would it be for?"

' "You're wrong," he said, half mockingly. "It's all for you – because these simple people believe a king is in love with you."

' "This is madness," I expostulated. "If you're not more discreet, you'll have everybody else knowing that."

' "Discretion," he said, almost proudly, "is a quality which, though useful, I have never particularly admired." '2

This soon became all too evident. In Trogir, he walked hand in hand with Wallis through the streets, surrounded by hundreds of curious students. In Dubrovnik, they were swept along by a surging mob chanting, *'Zivila Ljubav'* – 'Long live love'. And in Ragusa, Diana Cooper saw an entire village lining the streets, 'cheering their lungs out with looks of ecstasy on their faces'.3

Lady Diana remembered: '. . . [the King] slept at one end of the yacht with Mrs Simpson and we slept at the other. We all knew it was a love affair, but we didn't suspect a divorce, or marriage, or abdication. She was still married to Ernest Simpson, and he would write to her quite often. She would throw an envelope across the table [to the King] and say: "Ernest has sent you these stamps."

' "Oh, how good of Ernest," he would say. He was a stamp collector, you see.'4

At Corfu, the party dined with King George II of Greece, only recently restored to his throne from exile, and his mistress, Mrs Britten-Jones, 'an exceedingly good-looking Englishwoman, whose soldier husband had just divorced her, or been divorced by her'.5

On arriving back on board the *Nahlin*, there was trouble. 'The King was fussing proudly over Mrs Simpson, and went down on his hands and knees to pull her dress from under the chair feet. She stared at him as one might at a freak: "Well, that's the *maust* extraordinary performance I've ever seen"; and then she started to criticize his manner, the way he had talked to Mrs Jones, his attitude to the other king. Edward VIII began to look irritated and sad . . .'6

Diana Cooper felt that 'the sooner the trip ends for us, the better. It's impossible to enjoy antiquities with people who won't land for them and who call Delphi Delhi. Wallis is wearing very very badly. Her commonness and Becky Sharpishness irritate ... The truth is she's bored stiff by him, and her picking on him and her coldness towards him, far from policy, are irritation and boredom.'[7]

Wherever the yacht sailed, cameras were trained upon it, and one particular photograph was to have world-wide publication and impact. It shows Wallis Simpson standing close to the King and resting the slim long fingers of her right hand on his left arm. She is looking at him with an expression of knowing and smiling intimacy. The King is looking down at her hand, his face the very image of a man totally infatuated.

On August 25, when the *Nahlin* passed through the narrow Corinth Canal, the King stood half-naked on the bridge in full view of thousands of goggling spectators. Diana Cooper and Jack Aird were horrified by this exhibition. 'Diana turned to me and said, "Wallis, look at all these people. Do you think you could possibly get the King to at least put his shirt on until we get out of sight of the Greeks?"

' "After you, my dear Diana," I said. "If this were my President, I might. But you have had more experience in dealing with kings." '[8]

In the end, no one remonstrated with the King, who remained shirtless. When the yacht reached Athens, there was further friction. Jack Aird asked Wallis to use her influence to dissuade Edward from dining ashore with the Earl of Dudley in a small café. 'Jack turned with ill-concealed anger. "It's undignified. Can't you understand that? You must use your influence." '[9]

Wallis tried, but the King waved aside the objection. That evening he and Wallis dined with Eric Dudley at the café, and the disapproving Aird dined alone on the yacht.

In Istanbul, the Turkish dictator, Mustafa Kemâl Atatürk, treated Wallis as if she were already Edward's queen, seating her beside the King in the parade, and on his, Atatürk's, right at dinner.

The King and Wallis now left the *Nahlin* and proceeded in Atatürk's private train to Budapest and Vienna. Czar Boris III personally drove the train for them across Bulgaria, allowing the King to blow the steam whistle from time to time.

At the Hotel Ritz in Budapest, King Edward amused himself by teaching the barmaid how to mix cocktails. And in Vienna, he visited a public bath house and wandered round the steam-room naked, to the astonishment of the ultra-conservative Austrians present. It must have been the most bizarre royal odyssey since the Prince Regent's wife, Caroline of Brunswick, cavorted through Europe with her Italian chamberlain, Bartolomeo Bergami.

It ended on September 14 in Zurich, where the King left Wallis to go on alone to Paris for shopping, while he flew back to London.

That evening he dined with Queen Mary at Buckingham Palace. Preoccupied as she was with her impending move to Marlborough House, she had read every one of the foreign newspaper reports sent to her and therefore knew the full extent of her son's indiscretion. Yet such was the inhibition and reserve of her relationship with him that the only personal question she ventured was on the level of innocuous small talk. 'Didn't you find it terribly warm in the Adriatic?'[10]

She was encouraged by the news that the King planned to spend the last two weeks of the month at Balmoral, continuing the tradition of his father. But she would have been less happy had she known that Edward did not intend to invite the same establishment figures King George had welcomed year after year. In the words of his future wife, he felt that the 'grouping would be improved by a leaven of less exalted but none the less stimulating people such as he had entertained on the *Nahlin*'.[11]

The most conspicuous absentee would be the seventy-one-year-old Primate of all England, Cosmo Gordon Lang, Archbishop of Canterbury, who had been at Balmoral the previous summer to commiserate with George V about the Prince of Wales's liaison with Mrs Simpson. Lang believed that the old King's death had been hastened by his son's infatuation.

An open divergence now appeared between the new King and the Duke and Duchess of York. On learning that Dr Lang had not been invited to Balmoral, the Duchess hastened to ask him to stay with them instead. 'The kind Yorks bade me come to them at Birkhall,' he wrote. 'It was a delightful visit. They were kindness itself. The old house is full of charm and the Duchess has done much with the garden . . . It was strange to think of the destiny which may be awaiting the little Elizabeth, at present second from the Throne! She and her lively little sister are certainly most entrancing children.'[12]

Helen Hardinge noted that the Duchess of York gave the Archbishop a cocktail before dinner 'and pointed out half-apologetically that there was "a little gin in it". The Archbishop took it, commenting, "I'm sure *you* would not give me anything that was bad for me." '[13]

When the time came for Lang to leave Birkhall, he was told that he must come again, 'so that the links with Balmoral may not be wholly broken'.[14] The Yorks were increasingly becoming the guardians of tradition and continuity in the monarchy.

On the Sunday before Edward VIII arrived at Balmoral, the Duke and Duchess of York were present at Crathie Church to hear the King's Domestic Chaplain, Dr John Stirton – formerly the Minister at Glamis, whom a nine-year-old child had once told, 'I call myself the Princess Elizabeth' – preach a sermon of great dramatic impact about Nero, the Roman emperor who committed suicide during a rebellion.

Edward VIII was also an emperor. He too would shortly face a rebellion of sorts. The difference, in terms of kingship, was that Edward was already in the process of committing suicide, before his throne was actually threatened.

At the outset, however, he came to Balmoral in a blaze of personal popularity. 'GREAT ENTHUSIASM MARKS ARRIVAL OF THE KING', proclaimed the front page headline of the Aberdeen evening newspaper on the day he went into residence at the castle.[15]

It took only four days for the enthusiasm to fade. Several months earlier, the King had been asked by the Lord Provost of Aberdeen to open the new Royal Infirmary buildings in the city. He had declined on the grounds of Court mourning for his father, although full mourning had officially ended on July 20, more than two months earlier. Instead, the King deputed the Duke of York to perform the ceremony on his behalf, which puzzled many people, for what applied to one brother surely applied equally to the other.

On the afternoon of Wednesday, September 23, at the same time that the Duke and Duchess of York were being greeted in Aberdeen by the Lord Provost, Edward Watt, and were receiving 'a stirring welcome'[16] from huge crowds, the King, who had said that he could not appear in the city on that day, was seen driving in his private car to meet Wallis Simpson's train.

It is frequently said, incorrectly, that the King met Wallis at Ballater Station, which is only a few miles from Balmoral.[17] He did not. Two days earlier, the Duke and Duchess of Kent had been photographed at Aberdeen Station waiting for the Ballater train.[18] But what was good enough for royalty was not good enough for Wallis. The King could not bear to think of her having to wait to change trains. Instead he drove himself sixty miles to Aberdeen, into the centre of a city he had said he could not visit on that day, and where his brother and sister-in-law were at that very moment carrying out a public engagement on his behalf.

Marie Belloc Lowndes records: 'The train was late, and he had to wait some time in the station. Though he wore motoring goggles, which he apparently thought would conceal his identity, of course everyone there recognized him, except one policeman, who "told him off" for leaving his car in the wrong part of the station yard. He took this good-humouredly and moved his car.'[19]

The train eventually arrived, and Wallis, accompanied by Katherine and Herman Rogers, found the royal chauffeur waiting for them. The King put the Rogers into the back seat, Wallis into the seat beside him, and drove off, but by this time still more people had seen and recognized him.

Later that day, the full disaster of the episode became apparent. On the front page of the Aberdeen evening newspaper, side by side with a photograph of the Duke and Duchess of York opening the new Infirmary buildings, there was a headline: 'HIS MAJESTY IN ABERDEEN – SURPRISE VISIT IN CAR TO MEET GUESTS'. 'The King made an unexpected visit to Aberdeen today to welcome some of his guests who travelled from London by train . . . His Majesty did not enter the Station but received his guests at the entrance. Only a few people, mostly railway employees, were at the station entrance at the time but they immediately recognized His Majesty as he stepped from his car. They doffed their hats and caps and their greeting was acknowledged by a salute from the King who was in Highland dress. He again saluted as the car drove off.'[20]

The effect of this was one of profound disillusion locally. 'Aberdeen will never forgive him,' noted Chips Channon.[21]

It was not only Aberdeen. Within hours, the story was known all over Scotland. In addition, someone had shown the newspaper to the Duchess of York, who was furious. She knew, without being told, whom it was the King had gone to meet, and that made her even angrier. A friend close to the Royal Family remembered: 'It was one of the very few occasions when she was *really* angry. She was indignant on behalf of the local people. She said it was irresponsible and absurd of the King to go in person to meet the train. There were any number of people who could have gone on his behalf without causing such a hurtful impression and such damaging publicity. She felt that the Duke of York and herself had been made to look thoroughly foolish, deputizing for a king who had enough free time to drive all that way to meet friends, but not to take on a job of work.'[22]

On the following morning, Wallis took precedence over the Duke and Duchess of York in the Court Circular. The announcement read as follows: 'Balmoral Castle, September 23. Mrs Ernest A. Simpson and Mr and Mrs Herman L. Rogers have arrived at the Castle.

'The Duke of York, who was accompanied by the Duchess of York, today on His Majesty's behalf opened the New Buildings of the Royal Infirmary, Aberdeen. The Lady Helen Graham and the Hon. Thomas Coke were in attendance.'[23]

With the Aberdeen incident, the King had caused widespread offence locally and had alienated the Scottish middle classes. The Court Circular announcement now completed the damage by infuriating the landed families. As for the Duchess of York, the juxtaposition of Wallis Simpson's name with that of her husband and herself, coming on top of the events of the day before, caused deep and implacable resentment. Friends noticed that any mention of Mrs Simpson now brought a steely look into Elizabeth's blue eyes and produced an ominous tightening of her mouth.

'In the castle,' Marie Belloc Lowndes recorded, 'Mrs Simpson was given the rooms which had been in turn inhabited by Queen Victoria, Queen Alexandra and Queen Mary. From these she used to issue forth late each morning, in shorts. She and the King, both wearing shorts, would go about the village of Crathie, exciting horror and disapproval by their appearance.'[24]

Wallis certainly occupied Queen Mary's bedroom, but the rest seems doubtful. Photographs taken during her week at Balmoral show Wallis looking almost *over*dressed for the Highlands. Mary, Duchess of Buccleuch, who was a guest at the castle for three of the seven days Wallis was in residence, says: 'I am not aware that the King and Mrs Simpson ever wore shorts in Scotland, and should think, like you, it most unlikely. In fact, the King was always in a kilt, except for stalking.'[25]

What is beyond dispute is that Wallis's brash American personality grated at Balmoral. When the King took her to see the beach by Loch Muick, she commented tactlessly, in front of the staff, 'Just like Dubrovnik!' – 'a comparison', observed Helen Hardinge, 'which did not go down any better than the casual, careless way of referring to a voyage which had not been popular in many respects'.[26]

In the hope of avoiding further *faux pas*, various members of the

Royal household had had quiet talks with Mrs Simpson, 'to try to explain how certain things would not be acceptable', noted Helen Hardinge. 'She had been told that it was simply impossible for her to succeed Queen Mary as Queen. But such warnings did not seem to penetrate her mind. For *anyone* to step into Queen Mary's shoes was really a very difficult exercise; for her, it was an impossibility.'[27]

On the evening of Saturday, September 26, the King gave a dinner and reception at Balmoral, to which the Duke and Duchess of York were invited. Elizabeth, still angry inside over recent events, did not want to go, but the Duke of York felt obliged to support his brother and insisted that they should. An added factor was that the Duke and Duchess of Kent were staying at the castle, and Princess Marina was already six months pregnant with her second child, the future Princess Alexandra.[28] The Yorks did not want Marina to be distressed in any way by family friction.

Most of the King's dinner guests that evening – the Kents, the Duke and Duchess of Sutherland, the Earl and Countess of Rosebery, the Herman Rogers and others – were staying in the castle, and were therefore already assembled when the Yorks arrived. Mary, Duchess of Buccleuch, who had left the castle with her husband earlier that day, 'saw no signs of Mrs Simpson acting as official hostess' during her stay at Balmoral,[29] but the occasion of the Yorks' arrival was evidently an exception.

As Elizabeth preceded her husband into the drawing-room of the castle, Wallis Simpson walked forward confidently to receive her.

There were some eighteen other people present in the room at the time, including the King's equerry, Colonel the Hon. Piers ('Joey') Legh, and Wallis's gesture struck observers in different ways. Some considered it a mistaken act of politeness; others an attempt to ingratiate herself with the Yorks. The majority opinion was closer to the view of one person present who regarded it as 'a deliberate and calculated display of power'.[30]

If there was uncertainty over Wallis's motive, there could be none regarding Elizabeth's reaction. All accounts agree with the laconic statement of Baldwin's biographers: 'The Duchess of York openly showed her resentment at being received by Mrs Simpson.'[31]

But what form did this resentment take? Years later, Peter Townsend, writing of Elizabeth as Queen, would say: 'Only rarely did she betray anger – and then it was in her eyes, which blazed, bluer than ever.'[32] And her lifelong friend, Lord David Cecil, would add: 'For someone so unaggressive she has a very strong personality . . . She *could* be formidable. I have never seen it.'[33]

That evening at Balmoral, Wallis Simpson *did* see it. Within seconds she, and every one else in the room, was made aware just how formidable the Duchess of York could be when displeased. With a 'freezing expression', Elizabeth, devoid of her usual smile, walked straight past Mrs Simpson, ignoring her attempted welcome, and said, 'as if to no one in particular, "I came to dine with the King."

'The Duke of York seemed embarrassed and very nervous, and the King, looking rather startled, abruptly broke off his conversation with a group of guests and came forward to greet his brother and sister-in-law.'[34]

For Elizabeth, the comedy was at an end. She had overheard herself ridiculed; been forced into receiving the lady, uninvited, in her own home; listened to her garden being rearranged; and done the King's work in order that his friend should not be kept waiting at a railway station. Now an American divorcee was sleeping in Queen Mary's bed and play-acting at being Queen in her place. It had all gone a great deal too far. That evening, in front of the King's guests, household and servants, Wallis's ill-judged presumption rebounded on her publicly.

The Duchess of York took precedence at dinner, sitting on the King's right, with the Duchess of Sutherland on his left. The Duke of York sat opposite the Duchess of Sutherland, with the Duchess of Kent on his right and the Countess of Rosebery on his left. Wallis once again sat at the head of the table, but it was Elizabeth who led the ladies from dinner, without so much as a glance in the direction of the American visitor.

A number of other guests arrived after dinner, including Alec and Helen Hardinge and the Minister of Crathie, Dr John Stirton, whom the King had invested earlier that day as a Commander of the Royal Victorian Order. Everyone congregated in the ballroom where the King had arranged a screening of the latest Fred Astaire-Ginger Rogers musical, *Swing Time*. It was a light-hearted film, but not even Jerome Kern's lilting songs – 'A Fine Romance', 'It's Not in the Cards', 'Pick Yourself Up' – succeeded in imparting gaiety to an evening that had begun badly.

The Yorks left early. Outwardly, Elizabeth had recovered her good humour, but everyone present had been made to realize that she would never accept Wallis Simpson in any capacity. Of the reasons for her early departure from Balmoral that evening, we are told by Professor

Robert Sencourt, in a book which makes 'humble acknowledgement to . . . Queen Elizabeth the Queen Mother, of whom I saw much when the guest of her parents at Glamis Castle', that when 'The Duchess of York . . . a very religious woman . . . found that Mrs Simpson received her . . . She left as soon as she conveniently could'.[35]

Despite heavy rain showers, hundreds of people gathered outside Crathie Church the following morning to watch the Royal Family arriving for the Sunday service. King Edward drove up in a car with the Duke of Kent. The Duke of York was also there, with the two princesses, Elizabeth and Margaret. The Duchess of York was conspicuous by her absence. No statement was issued to the effect that she was indisposed, and it was one of the very rare occasions in her life when she did not go to church on a Sunday.

Was it that she anticipated a further confrontation with Mrs Simpson? Or had the events of the evening before left her with insufficient repose of mind for an act of spiritual worship?

Helen Hardinge, who was present at the service, wrote of it, in her diary: 'Church — the King and Duke of Kent talk all the time, which makes a bad impression. Alec and Joey [Legh] not much better.'[36] Certainly there was plenty to talk about.

On the following morning, the Court Circular merely noted, of the previous Saturday: 'The Duke and Duchess of York dined with The King this evening.'[37] It was one of the few understatements of an amazing year.

On Wednesday, September 30, the King and Wallis departed from Balmoral never to return, leaving behind them a sorry trail of back-stairs gossip and resentment. One of Wallis's innovations — the introduction of the three-decker toasted sandwich — had not endeared her to the castle staff, any more than the King's summary dismissal of old and loyal retainers, carried out on her advice during their re-organization of Balmoral.

The King's axe-wielding caused distress to the Duke of York, who had not been consulted, even though he was near at hand at Birkhall. 'David only told me what he had done after it was over,' wrote the Duke to Queen Mary from Glamis Castle, 'which I might say made me rather sad. He arranged it all with the official people up there. I never saw him alone for an instant . . .'[38]

Of the general impression left behind by Edward VIII's visit, Marie Belloc Lowndes wrote: 'The bitterest feeling is in Scotland, where the fact Mrs Simpson was at Balmoral, Queen Victoria's cherished home, so enrages them, that a number of Scotch peers and peeresses don't mean to attend the Coronation. They say in Scotland that if the King marries Mrs Simpson it will simply be "an open adulterous connection". I myself am astonished at the strength of the feeling. It is amazing.'[39]

The King was also losing ground rapidly in London, where the effect of the world-wide publicity from the *Nahlin* cruise was now making itself felt. Harold Nicolson was shortly confessing to irritation that 'that silly little man *en somme* should destroy a great monarchy by giggling into a flirtation with a third-rate American'.[40]

On October 14, the Hardinges, doubtless bearing in mind the Duchess of York's experience at Balmoral, talked to a member of Queen Mary's household – she had now moved to Marlborough House – ' "re caution needed over which invitations the Queen should accept at Buckingham Palace". For we knew that if she were exposed to an "accidental" meeting with Mrs Simpson, it would cause her already trying position to become even more painful.'[41]

The very next day, October 15, the constitutional crisis so long feared and anticipated, came into being. The London news agency, The Press Association, telephoned Alec Hardinge with the explosive information that Wallis Simpson's divorce petition was to be heard at Ipswich Assizes on October 27. She had already taken a cottage nearby – Beech House, Felixstowe – in order to establish residence in the area.

Hardinge realized that the situation was now critical. He at once wrote to the Prime Minister, begging Baldwin 'to see the King and ask if these proceedings could not be stopped, for the danger in which they placed him (HM) was becoming every day greater'.[42]

Baldwin was reluctant to intervene even at this stage, but eventually agreed to seek an audience with the King, which took place at Fort Belvedere on Tuesday, October 20. After an hour's discussion, during which little progress was made, Baldwin asked bluntly, 'Must the case really go on?'

The King replied: 'I have no right to interfere with the affairs of an individual. It would be wrong were I to attempt to influence Mrs Simpson just because she happens to be a friend of the King's.'[43]

It was following this abortive interview that Hardinge called on the Duke and Duchess of York at 145 Piccadilly, and for the first time officially warned them both that the possibility of abdication, and of their succeeding to the throne, could no longer be ignored.

The Duchess was incredulous; the Duke aghast. Looking at her husband's ashen face, Elizabeth's anger intensified.

The King, meanwhile, through his friendship with Britain's two most powerful newspaper magnates – Lord Beaverbrook and the Hon. Esmond Harmsworth – had managed to secure a gentleman's agreement that the divorce would be reported only briefly by the British press and without sensation.

The agreement did not inhibit the American press, however, which was now in full cry. On the day before Wallis's petition was heard, the New York *Daily Mirror* ran a gigantic headline that occupied three-quarters of its front page: 'KING TO MARRY "WALLY". WEDDING NEXT JUNE'.[44] Unknown to them, the King was planning an even earlier wedding. Wallis's divorce would become final on April 27, and it was the King's intention to marry her in time for her to be crowned with him on May 12.

Marie Belloc Lowndes arrived in America on the day of the hearing. 'There were an unusual number of reporters to meet the boat at New York, and eight of these gentlemen came up to me and asked simultaneously: "What do you think of your new American Queen?" '[45]

Meanwhile, at 2.17 on the afternoon of Tuesday, October 27, the case of *Simpson W.* v. *Simpson E. A.* came before Sir John Hawke at Ipswich Assizes in circumstances that were without precedent in British legal history. The court was surrounded by police, who prevented photographers from taking pictures and smashed two press cameras in the process.

When Wallis entered the witness-box, a chair was provided for her, although it was the normal custom for a woman to stand while testifying in her own divorce case. Afterwards, when she and her solicitor, Theodore Goddard, left the court-room, the doors were slammed and locked behind her to prevent reporters from following.

The evidence revealed that on July 28 of that year, Ernest Simpson had spent the night in bedroom number four of the Hotel de Paris at Bray with a 'Mrs Simpson' who was not his wife. The judge, already irritated by the fascist-style police operation outside, commented testily, 'Well, I suppose I must come to the conclusion that there was adultery in this case.'

Wallis's counsel, Norman Birkett, ventured smoothly, 'I assume what your Lordship has in mind.'

Sir John Hawke replied angrily, 'How do you know what is in my mind? What is it that I have in my mind, Mr Birkett?'

Birkett answered, 'I think with great deference that your Lordship may have in mind what is known as "ordinary hotel evidence" where the name of the lady is not disclosed. With respect, I thought that might have been in your Lordship's mind.'

With a faint trace of sarcasm, the judge responded: 'That is what it must have been, Mr Birkett. I am glad of your help.'

Birkett continued: 'That lady's name, my Lord, was mentioned in the petition . . .'

It was indeed, and it was to be of special interest to Alec and Helen Hardinge. The lady was a Mrs E. H. Kennedy – the same Buttercup Kennedy to whom they had been introduced at Windsor Castle on March 28, when the King and Wallis had made jokes together about 'matching' Buttercup with Ernest Simpson.[46]

Wallis was given her decree nisi, and the costs were awarded against Ernest. 'They could scarcely have been otherwise', comments Helen Hardinge, 'for the evidence of his adultery, albeit on a single occasion, appeared to be overwhelming.'[47]

Lady Hardinge's obvious scepticism concerning Buttercup Kennedy was quickly to be shared by the Duke and Duchess of York, Queen Mary, and the rest of the Royal Family. A subsequent investigation by Thomas Barnes, the King's Proctor, and Sir Donald Somervell, the Attorney General, found that 'the divorce – even if it had some collusive fact – e.g. the willingness of Mrs S. that her husband should be unfaithful – was not a collusive divorce in the ordinary or any provable sense'.[48]

Despite this, to the Yorks, Queen Mary and the Hardinges, Wallis's second divorce would always be 'a put-up job', made possible by Ernest Simpson's cooperation in smoothing his wife's path to marriage with the King.

Faithful to the gentleman's agreement, the British press reported the hearing in brief, discreet paragraphs. Elsewhere in the world there were lurid headlines: 'KING'S MOLL RENO'D IN WOLSEY'S HOME TOWN' . . . and 'L'AMOUR DU ROI VA BIEN!'

Now more and more stories of Wallis Simpson's regal aspirations began to circulate. An American friend of Marie Belloc Lowndes 'had seen a letter by [Wallis] to a lady in New York, who had been kind to her in her youth, and in the letter she said: "Strange as it may seem, I am going to be Queen of England." '[49]

There were reports that she had tried to order a London department store to embroider the royal cypher on her underwear,[50] and that in a ladies' powder room, she had pushed another woman aside as she was about to sit down at the mirror, saying she was in a hurry. When the other woman remonstrated and accused her of rudeness, Wallis Simpson is said to have replied, 'You won't talk to me like that when I'm Queen of England.'[51]

On the day after the divorce, Harold Nicolson was noting: '... there are very serious rumours that the King will make her Duchess of Edinburgh and marry. The point is whether he is so infatuated as to insist on her becoming Queen or whether the marriage will be purely morganatic. The Duchess of Rutland is very sensible about the whole thing, and does not believe that he would do anything so foolish. Nonetheless I gather from other people that there is considerable danger.'[52]

Wallis herself was at pains to refute the rumours. When Cecil Beaton went to photograph her at 16 Cumberland Terrace, her new rented house in Regent's Park, he suggested a background of scrolls of ermine pinned on a white cloth. 'She immediately responded with, "Don't do anything connected with the Coronation for me. I want none of that now." And again, when I asked her to lower her chin, "as though bowing", the unfortunate simile caused her to look sharply at me.'[53]

Outwardly there was still no appearance of crisis. On November 3, the King put on a good performance at his first and last State opening of Parliament, but only three days later, Helen Hardinge was writing in her diary: 'Government are not prepared to carry on.'[54]

Chips Channon believed that the King 'certainly wants to marry Wallis, but she is probably too canny to allow it, yet what a temptation it must be for a Baltimore girl. One could not blame her if she did. If he married her, both Honor and Jean [Norton] argued, he would have to abdicate immediately, as if he did not, we would have unrest, a Socialist agitation, and a "Yorkist" party.'[55]

If a 'Yorkist' party materialized, it would be without help from the Yorks. At this time, the Duke was writing gloomily to Queen Mary: 'I have been meaning to come and see you but I wanted to see David first. He is very difficult to see and when one does he wants to talk about others matters.

'It is all so worrying and I feel we all live a life of conjecture; never knowing what will happen tomorrow, and then the unexpected comes ...'[56]

On the day the Duke wrote those words, Chips Channon encountered Wallis at the opera, 'in a simple black dress with a green bodice and dripping with emeralds – her collection of jewels is the talk of London'.[57]

Alas for Lady Hardinge's contention that Mrs Simpson 'never met any of King George V's people',[58] that night at the opera Wallis was introduced to Lord Cromer, one of the old King's most trusted friends and still Lord Chamberlain of the Royal Household, the senior official of the Court. 'The Cromers, suave aristocrats, were obsequious', recorded Channon, 'and Honor remarked that they did everything except curtsey. Poor Wallis, the cynosure of all eyes, she can do no right. All her tact, sweetness and charm – are they enough?'[59]

But faint praise for Wallis did come from a most unexpected quarter. Sir Robert Bruce Lockhart revealed: 'Queen [Mary] is supposed to have said, "I don't like it, but the one thing that I have always feared for David is drink. I was afraid it would ruin him or make him a laughing-stock. And she [Mrs Simpson] has been a sane influence in that respect. And this is important." '[60]

On November 11, the King performed his last public engagement in London by laying a wreath at the Cenotaph, and left for Portland to spend two days with the Home Fleet.

On his return to Fort Belvedere on the evening of November 13, he found waiting for him the famous letter from his Private Secretary, Alec Hardinge, warning him that 'the silence of the British Press on the subject of Your Majesty's friendship with Mrs Simpson is not going to be maintained'.

The King reacted angrily to the letter and to Hardinge's plea 'for Mrs Simpson to go abroad *without further delay*'.[61]

Wallis, alarmed to learn that the resignation of the Government was now a possibility, later claimed she had agreed with Hardinge that she ought to leave, but that the King had replied peremptorily, 'You'll do no such thing. I won't have it. This letter is an impertinence.'[62]

Cole Lesley, the biographer of Noël Coward, remembered: 'Feelings ran high . . . the dearest of friends quarrelled violently; when Winston Churchill at luncheon asked why the King shouldn't be allowed to marry his cutie, Noël – summing it up for most people – said, "Because England doesn't wish for a Queen Cutie." '[63] Even that avowed Simpsonite, Chips Channon, was forced to concede that 'the country, or much of it, would not accept Queen Wallis, with two live husbands scattered about . . .'[64]

Yet still she was treated in London with the deference due to a royal

personage. At a charity concert at the Yugoslav Legation, attended by
Prince and Princess Paul, the Duke of Kent and the Infanta Beatrix, the
hostess, Madame Grouitch 'became quite maddening; while leading
the royalties down to supper, she suddenly spied Mrs Simpson, and
seizing her, dragged her, in spite of her protests, before the photographers, and then pushed her into the Royal supper room. It is this
sort of behaviour which causes Wallis such trouble and she, poor
woman, was indignant.'[65]

But there were indications in her own behaviour that she anticipated
some form of regal status. Lord Beaverbrook, meeting her at about this
time, noted: 'I was greatly interested by the way the other women
greeted her. There were about six women who were present at the
dinner or who came in afterwards. All but one of them greeted Mrs
Simpson with a kiss. She received it with appropriate dignity, but in no
case did she return it.'[66]

Advised now by Walter Monckton, the King met the Prime Minister
at Buckingham Palace on November 16. Baldwin 'pointed out to him
that the position of the King's wife was different from the position of
any other citizen in the country; it was part of the price which the King
has to pay. His wife becomes Queen; the Queen becomes the Queen of
the country; and therefore, in the choice of a Queen, the voice of the
people must be heard . . .'[67]

The King said, 'I want you to be the first to know that I have made up
my mind and nothing will alter it – I have looked at it from all sides –
and I mean to abdicate to marry Mrs Simpson.'[68]

Baldwin returned in a state of shock to 10 Downing Street and told
his Chief Whip, Captain David Margesson: 'I have heard such things
from my King tonight as I never thought to hear. I am going to bed.'[69]

That evening the King went to Marlborough House to see Queen
Mary and his sister, the Princess Royal. With them he found his
newly-married sister-in-law, Alice, the Duchess of Gloucester, who
was almost a stranger to him. 'He was in a great state of agitation',
remembered Princess Alice, 'and asked his mother if I could leave the
room as he had a very serious family matter to discuss. Queen Mary
was discernibly angered by this request, but with many apologies she
asked me to go, which of course I did.'[70]

In her absence, the King told his mother and sister of his determination to marry Wallis Simpson, and asked Queen Mary to receive her.
She refused. Pressed by him for the reason, she replied coldly, 'Because
she is an adventuress!'[71]

On the following day, November 17, the King told an appalled Duke of York of his intention to abdicate, and Queen Mary, bemused by her son's intended marriage to 'a lady with two husbands living',[72] exclaimed to the Prime Minister, 'Well, Mr Baldwin! *This* is a pretty kettle of fish!'[73]

That evening, the King left London for the last official engagement of his reign – a tour of the depressed areas of South Wales – and at 'a pompous, manqué dinner' given by Lady Cunard, Chips Channon sat with Prince and Princess Paul and Mrs Simpson, 'who looked very well tonight, like a Vermeer, in a Dutch way. The conversation got on to tiaras, and Princess Olga said hers gave her a headache. Wallis Simpson laughingly added, "Well, anyway, a tiara is one of the things I shall never have …" There was an embarrassed pause, Diana [Cooper] is convinced that Wallis and the King will marry in secret, immediately after the Coronation. I half hope so, half believe it is fated.'[74]

Wallis was still refuting marriage rumours, however, as well as aspirations of queenship. Harold Nicolson reported that Lady Colefax had had a heart-to-heart with her 'and found her really miserable. All sorts of people had come to her reminding her of her duty and begging her to leave the country. "They do not understand", she said, "that if I did so, the King would come after me regardless of anything. They would then get their scandal in a far worse form than they are getting it now." Sibyl then asked her whether the King had ever suggested marriage. She seemed surprised, and said, "Of course not." '[75]

The King was telling a different story. On the evening of his return from South Wales, he sent for his brother, the Duke of Kent, and told him that he was going to marry Wallis.

'The Duke of Kent gasped, "What will she call herself?" "Call herself?" the King echoed. "What do you think – Queen of England of course." "She is going to be Queen?" "Yes and Empress of India, the whole bag of tricks." '[76]

Kent, flabbergasted, rushed home to dress and tell his wife and Princess Olga. Not surprisingly, they were all late arriving at Chips Channon's dinner party that evening, which the King and his queen-designate attended.

Two days later, Wallis lunched at Claridge's with Esmond Harmsworth, who urged upon her the compromise of a morganatic marriage – by which she would become the king's wife but not Queen. A suitable title, he thought, would be Duchess of Lancaster – the very possibility at which Churchill had hinted mischievously to the Duchess of York that summer.

But queenship was still in the air. 'The King is insane about Wallis, insane,' wrote Chips Channon on the following day. '. . . Someone at Cartiers foolishly told Bertie Abdy that they are re-setting magnificent, indeed fabulous jewels for Wallis, and for what purpose if she is not to be Queen? And the Duke of Kent's mysterious remark to Kitty Brownlow here at dinner that "in a month or six weeks time something terrific will happen. I wish I could tell you now." '[77]

The King's first reaction to Harmsworth's morganatic solution had been one of distaste, but his options were diminishing daily. On November 25, he asked the Prime Minister to submit the morganatic proposal to the British Cabinet and also to the Dominion governments. Baldwin was reluctant. 'Do you really wish that, Sir?' he asked. The King said that he did.

On the same day, the Duke of York was writing to Sir Godfrey Thomas: 'If the worst happens and I have to take over, you can be assured that I will do my best to clear up the inevitable mess, if the whole fabric does not crumble under the shock and strain of it all.'[78]

Chips Channon saw Wallis once more, at a dinner party in Belgrave Square. 'She was wearing new jewels – the King must give her new ones every day . . . We talked of houses, and I suggested that she should move to Belgravia and she didn't reply. It is these occasional lapses which are mysterious. Why not say "I'll look about" or something casual instead of leaving one with the feeling that she won't want a house in May as she'll be living in Buckingham Palace. I personally think that he'll marry her, and soon.'[79]

After the blistering snub delivered by the Duchess of York to Wallis at Balmoral, the two women had not met again, and would not do so for more than thirty years, but Wallis had become increasingly aware that Elizabeth was the major obstacle to her ambitions.

The last occasion on which the King and Wallis were seen in public together prior to the Abdication was at Sir Philip Sassoon's house in Park Lane, where they went to watch a newsreel film of the King's tour of South Wales. That evening they encountered Sassoon's cousin, Mrs Hannah Gubbay, one of Elizabeth's staunchest friends and supporters, who had consistently refused to receive Wallis, in spite of determined efforts by the King to persuade her to do so.

Marie Belloc Lowndes recorded: 'Hannah, of course, was there and Mrs S. was really rude to her, speaking coldly of Hannah's friendship with the Duchess of York.'[80]

Elizabeth's contempt for Wallis was now submerged in her efforts to keep her husband calm in the face of mounting anxiety. Her own composure appeared absolute. Helen Hardinge noted on November 27: 'Go out to see the Duchess of York who is an angel as usual. Much cheered by those delicious children who came in from the swimming baths with terrific accounts of their own exploits.'[81]

That day, the Cabinet met to discuss the morganatic proposal, and opinion against it was virtually unanimous, Neville Chamberlain believing that it 'would only be a prelude to the further step of making Mrs S. Queen with full rights'.[82]

Nevertheless telegrams were sent to all the Dominion governments asking them to choose one of three possible courses: (1) The King should marry Mrs Simpson and she should be recognized as Queen. (2) The King should marry her and she should not become Queen (the morganatic proposal). (3) The King should abdicate in favour of the Duke of York.

The same day, the Channons were to have been guests at Wallis's dinner party for the King, but at four-thirty in the afternoon a note was brought to them to say that Mrs Simpson was indisposed and that the dinner was postponed. As dusk fell that evening, a Royal Daimler whisked Wallis and Aunt Bessie from Cumberland Terrace to the security of Fort Belvedere. Although the British press, astonishingly, had *still* not broken its silence on the crisis, the role of Mrs Simpson in Edward VIII's life was becoming uncomfortably well known to the public.

While Sir Oswald Mosley had been marching his blackshirts through the East End of London in a demonstration of support for the King, rival extremists had painted crude slogans — 'Down with the American whore' — on walls and railway bridges. She had received menacing anonymous letters, and there had been threats to blow up her house. Two well-dressed women, posing as personal friends, had obtained access to Wallis and had then violently abused her. A man in the street had tried to throw vitriol at her face, and bricks were hurled through the windows of neighbouring houses.[83]

Her flight from Cumberland Terrace marked the end of Wallis Simpson's reign over London society. From the security of the Fort, she dispatched 'a charming note' to the Channons 'to say that she had a sort of breakdown yesterday, and must be kept quite quiet and away from visitors and the telephone for a week'.[84]

A day later, Channon was noting: 'There is no hope for the King, none, and it looks almost certainly as if the Yorks will succeed . . . Honor and I will be out of the royal racket having backed the wrong horse, but I don't much mind.'[85]

On the same day, Ramsay MacDonald said of the King: 'That man has done more to harm his country than any man in history',[86] and Harold Nicolson wrote: '. . . he imagines that the country, the great warm heart of the people, are with him. I do not think so. The upper classes mind her being an American more than they mind her being divorced. The lower classes do not mind her being an American but loathe the idea that she has had two husbands already.'[87]

On the evening of November 29, the Duke and Duchess of York left London to fulfil public engagements in Edinburgh. 'I hate going to Scotland to do what I have to do as I am so worried over this whole matter,' wrote the Duke. 'I feel like the proverbial "sheep being led to the slaughter", which is not a comfortable feeling.'[88]

The following afternoon, the Duke was installed as Grand Master Mason of Scotland, and next morning the Duchess of York received the Freedom of Edinburgh, addressed by the Lord Provost as 'Beloved Duchess, daughter of our northern land, gracious servant of the State, ambassadress of Empire.'[89] After the national anthem had been played, the entire audience rose and sang – 'with unusual fervour' – 'Will Ye No' Come Back Again?' That evening, when the Yorks attended a charity performance at the Empire Theatre, Edinburgh, they were welcomed 'with a prolonged expression of loyalty and affection, and the popular Duchess, smiling with all her characteristic charm, waved several times as she faced the crowded tiers.'[90]

While Chips Channon in London was noting that 'things are moving in favour of the Yorks',[91] the Bishop of Bradford, Dr Walter Blunt, addressing his Diocesan Conference, was commending the King to God's grace, 'which he will so abundantly need – for the King is a man like any other – if he is to do his duty properly. We hope that he is aware of this need. Some of us wish that he gave more positive signs of such awareness.'

These words, intended as a lament for the King's lack of regular churchgoing, rather than as a reference to his relationship with Mrs Simpson, appeared the following morning in provincial newspapers in Leeds, Manchester, Edinburgh and other major cities.

The 'blunt instrument' – as it became mockingly known – dealt a death blow to the gentleman's agreement among the national newspaper proprietors. While the King was learning from Baldwin that the Cabinet and the Dominion governments had turned down the idea of Wallis Simpson either as Queen or as morganatic wife, the London dailies prepared to break their long silence on what H. L. Mencken was to describe as 'the greatest news story since the Resurrection'.[92]

At 7.25 the following morning – Thursday, December 3 – as the Duke and Duchess of York stepped from their train at Euston Station, they were confronted by a phalanx of photographers and a wall of newspaper placards announcing, in giant black letters, THE KING'S MARRIAGE.

Elizabeth, her famous smile for once invisible, clutched her husband's arm, and they hastened to see an exasperated Queen Mary, whose comment on the situation was suitably expressive: 'Really! this might be Roumania!'[93]

Both the Yorks had engagements in London that day – the Duke at Wandsworth Technical School and at the London Hospital dinner at Claridge's; the Duchess at the Mothercraft Training Society in Highgate. All were cancelled. Elizabeth told Helen Hardinge that they 'felt so miserable that they did not think they should undertake public engagements if they could help it'.[94]

There was also depression at Fort Belvedere. The King and Wallis were both unnerved by the morning newspapers – Edward by his first experience of serious criticism in forty-two years of cossetted royal life; Wallis by the massive concentration on her personal role in the crisis.

The blaze of publicity at last brought them to the decision that Alec Hardinge had urged upon them three weeks earlier. Wallis would leave the country immediately. That evening, as she set out on the first stage of her journey to France in the company of Lord Brownlow, and while her house in Cumberland Terrace 'was surrounded . . . by a booing, stone-throwing mob',[95] the King went to Marlborough House to visit his mother. There he found the Duke and Duchess of York, and his sister, the Princess Royal.

A coolness had developed between the Duchess of York and her brother-in-law. Elizabeth was appalled by the way the King had treated his family during the crisis. Queen Mary, in her seventieth year, had suffered profound distress, sleepless nights and loss of weight through anxiety – all within months of her husband's death. Yet her eldest son had ignored her for ten days, and was only there now at her urgent request.

The Yorks, who had the most at stake if it came to abdication, were also left out of the King's counsels and confidence. 'Everyone knows more than we do,' Elizabeth had complained bitterly. 'We know nothing. Nothing!'[96]

Elizabeth pointedly declined to take part in the family conference. The Duke of York recorded: '. . . later (in Mary's and my presence) David said to Queen Mary that he could not live alone as King and must marry Mrs —'[97] He could not even bring himself to write the surname Simpson, which had come to represent the total disruption of his life, and the lives of his family.

'When David left after making this dreadful announcement to his mother,' wrote the Duke, 'he told me to come and see him at the Fort the next morning.'[98]

The Duke of York telephoned his brother the following morning – Friday, December 4 – but was put off until Saturday. On Saturday, the King told him to come and see him on Sunday. On Sunday he telephoned the Fort again, to be told that the King was in conference and would speak to him later. The King did not telephone. All through Monday, December 7 – the day on which the King's principal supporter, Winston Churchill, was howled down in the House of Commons – the Duke of York and his wife waited at Royal Lodge for news.

Finally it came. 'My brother rang me up at ten minutes to seven p.m. to say "Come and see me after dinner." I said "No, I will come and see you at once." I was with him at seven p.m. The awful and ghastly suspense of waiting was over. I found him pacing up and down the room, and he told me his decision that he would go.'[99]

Elizabeth never forgot those four nightmarish days when her husband was left in humiliating silence. The memory of them coloured her attitude towards her brother-in-law for ever after.

She also never forgot the rumours of what had been going on during those days. There is official evidence not yet available to the public that serious consideration was given, on account of his speech defect and doubts about his capacity for kingship, to the possibility of bypassing the Duke of York in the order of succession, in favour of one of his brothers.[100]

The Duke of Gloucester was a stolid, uninspiring figure with a taste for alcohol that was growing steadily more pronounced. He seemed an even less likely candidate for the throne than York.

The Duke of Kent, on the other hand, was good-looking, debonair, married to a beautiful European princess, and the only one of the brothers who already had a son to succeed him. But there had been a streak of wildness in Prince George's youth. He had experimented with drugs and was known to be bisexual. Black women and white men had figured in his pre-marital and extra-marital sexual adventures. One of his earliest male lovers had been Noël Coward.[101] This background made him a questionable candidate to restore confidence in the stability of the British monarchy.

The Prime Minister considered all these factors, as well as the characters and personalities of the respective wives. The Duchess of York was not only the most experienced of the three, but also the most popular, and her two children were national idols.

There would be no change in the order of succession. 'The Yorks', Baldwin decided, 'will do it very well.'[102]

Wallis, meanwhile, pursued across France by the bloodhounds of the press, had finally reached sanctuary with Katherine and Herman Rogers at the Villa Lou Viei at Cannes. She had arrived there in the early hours of December 6, crouched on the floor of the car with a rug over her head.[103]

Even at this late stage, she at once began a series of impassioned telephone calls to Fort Belvedere to urge the King not to abdicate. Owing to the structure of the Fort, a voice raised in any room on the ground floor could be heard clearly all over the house. It was unfortunate for Wallis that the King's side of these anguished conversations was overheard and remembered by the Royal Family's principal financial adviser, Sir Edward Peacock, who noted 'the insistence over the telephone of the lady that he should fight for his rights. She kept up that line until near the end, maintaining that he was King and his popularity would carry everything . . .'[104]

Having listened to further exchanges, Peacock was profoundly unimpressed when Wallis issued her famous statement to the effect that she was 'willing, if such action would solve the problem, to withdraw from a situation that has been rendered both unhappy and untenable'.[105]

Peacock's estimate of this was cynical. 'She apparently began to think of her own unpopularity, and a statement was suggested, which she issued from Cannes. The King approved, well realizing that this would to some extent divert criticism from her to him, the very thing he wanted.'[106]

When the statement was published on December 8, it was hailed by the credulous as the end of the crisis. By that stage, however, the process of abdication was already in motion, and the Royal Family – particularly the Duchess of York and Queen Mary – regarded Wallis's offer to withdraw as a piece of face-saving sham. The claim, in her statement, that she had 'invariably wished to avoid any action or proposal which would hurt or damage His Majesty or the Throne', infuriated them. Did this woman not realize the damage she had already done? Only two days later, the Independent Labour Member of Parliament, James Maxton, would tell the House of Commons that 'the monarchical institution has now outlived its usefulness' and that 'the peace and prosperity of the people require a more stable and dignified form of government of a republican kind . . .'

At a party given by Lady Cunard, Chips Channon met the Duchess of Marlborough, 'who asked me in her frank breezy way, did I not think that all the while Wallis had been playing a double game?'.[107] The Royal Family thought exactly this, and most especially the Duchess of York, who agreed entirely with Queen Mary's assessment of Wallis as 'an adventuress'. Even the Kents, George and Marina, who had been the most favourably disposed to Wallis of all the family, had sharply changed their attitude when the crisis began. The Duke of Kent, the King's favourite brother, had exploded in fury at one point: 'He is besotted on the woman. One can't get a word of sense out of him.'[108] Stanley Baldwin had added that the King 'seemed bewitched . . .'.[109]

The view within the Royal Family was that Wallis had brainwashed a man whose mind was temporarily unhinged by an obsession. They believed she had played covertly for high stakes, always aiming at the Queen's crown, although consistently denying this. When the highest ambition proved beyond her reach, she settled for morganatic marriage to the King. When that also eluded her, she still held out for marriage, even though it meant the King abandoning his throne, because she knew that without marriage there would be no security against suffering the same fate as Freda Dudley Ward and Thelma Furness.

This, right or wrong, was the interpretation of Wallis's behaviour by the Royal Family. They did not believe for one moment that she ever truly intended to withdraw from the life of the King, either on the throne or off. It was this that would count against her afterwards: the image of a cold and calculating schemer; a woman in whom the

Duchess of York's friend, Helen Hardinge, could find 'little to admire
. . . except her apparently infinite tenacity'.[110]

The Duchess of York had returned to London with the Duke from
Royal Lodge on the evening of December 7. Elizabeth's apparently
imperturbable manner had concealed, even from close friends, the fact
that the crisis, and the alarming prospect it presented to the Yorks and
their children, had undermined her almost as much as her husband.
Only a few days earlier, during a shooting party at Wilton House,
Salisbury, which the royal couple briefly attended, the Countess of
Pembroke told Loelia, Duchess of Westminster that 'she thought the
Duchess of York very depressed'.[111]

Weeks of suppressed anxiety and her efforts to keep her husband
calm now took their toll, and Elizabeth succumbed to an attack of
influenza. She was therefore lying in her sickbed when her husband
witnessed the King's signing of the Abdication papers at Fort Belvedere at ten o'clock on the morning of Thursday, December 10.

The Yorks were together later when '. . . the London mob came to
its senses, and with the rush and roar of a mighty wave poured in the
direction of Hyde Park Corner, where it converged on 145 Piccadilly.
So great and unexpected was the noise that the Duchess of York . . .
felt obliged to get up in order to see what it was all about. On telling
her husband . . . and suggesting that he ought to show himself to the
people, he said in his usual shy and diffident manner, "But what on
earth am I to say to them?" '[112]

It was also in her sickroom at three o'clock that afternoon that
Elizabeth received a visit from her mother-in-law, Queen Mary. The
Yorks' governess, Marion Crawford, waiting outside the door, recorded: 'Queen Mary came out and tears were streaming down her
face. The Duchess was lying propped up among pillows. I thought
that she too had been crying. She held out her hand to me. "I'm
afraid there are going to be great changes in our lives, Crawfie,"
she said. "We must take what is coming to us and make the best
of it." '[113]

That afternoon, after Baldwin had completed his historic account to
the Commons of the Abdication crisis, Lady Astor 'sang out' to Chips
Channon: 'People who have been licking Mrs Simpson's boots ought
to be shot.'[114]

Baldwin himself spoke to Harold Nicolson of the King: ' "You see,
Nicolson, the man is mad. MAD . . . He could see nothing but that
woman. He did not realize that any other considerations avail. He

lacks religion . . . He doesn't realize that there is anything beyond. I told his mother so. The Duke of York has always been bothered about it. I love the man. But he must go." '[115]

And while Edward VII's mistress, the Hon. Mrs George Keppel, voiced the view that 'the King has shown neither decency, nor wisdom, nor regard for tradition',[116] Tommy Lascelles was taking much the same line as Baldwin: ' "He was without a soul" [Lascelles kept on repeating] and this has made him a trifle mad . . . he never cared for England or the English . . . He rather hated this country . . . and did not like being reminded of his duties. The new King will be first-class – no doubt about it." '[117]

At 1.52 p.m. on the following day – Friday, December 11, 1936 – His Majesty's Declaration of Abdication Act received Edward VIII's own Royal Assent in the House of Lords. In that moment, Elizabeth, propped up against her pillows at 145 Piccadilly, ceased to be Her Royal Highness the Duchess of York and became Her Majesty The Queen, consort of King George VI, and Empress of India.

That evening the ex-King dined at Royal Lodge with the new King, Queen Mary, the Duke of Gloucester, the Duke of Kent, the Princess Royal, the Earl of Athlone and Princess Alice, Countess of Athlone. 'That last family dinner party was too awful,' Elizabeth told a friend years later. 'Thank goodness I had flu and couldn't go.'[118] She did, however, send a short note to her brother-in-law wishing him well in the uncertain future that now lay before him.

In his broadcast to the nation that night, the ex-King – introduced on the orders of his successor as 'His Royal Highness Prince Edward' – spoke of his brother's 'fine qualities . . . And he has one matchless blessing, enjoyed by so many of you and not bestowed on me – a happy home with his wife and children.'[119]

Wallis Simpson listened to those words at the Villa Lou Viei in Cannes, lying on a sofa with her hands over her eyes, weeping.

The Duke of Kent also wept, exclaiming, 'It isn't possible! It isn't happening!', as he watched Edward take leave of his family at Royal Lodge and bow to his brother, the new King.[120] At two o'clock on the morning of December 12, the Royal Navy destroyer, HMS *Fury*, moved silently and unescorted out of Portsmouth Harbour, carrying the former sovereign on the first stage of an exile that only death would end.

'There will be, I would say, millions of people with aching hearts,' Colonel Josiah Wedgwood had declared in the House of Commons during the Abdication debate. 'They will carry on for England. They will take that oath because he wished it, and if they sometimes raise their glass to a King over the water, who shall blame them?'[121]

Nine hours after his brother's departure, the new King George VI, 'pale and haggard, yet with an innate dignity and integrity which compelled the respect and reverence, as well as the protective instinct of his hearers . . . in a low, clear voice, but with many hesitations',[122] addressed his Accession Council at St James's Palace: '. . . With my wife and helpmeet by my side, I take up the heavy task which lies before me. In it I look for the support of all my peoples.

'Furthermore, my first act on succeeding my brother will be to confer on him a Dukedom and he will henceforth be known as His Royal Highness the Duke of Windsor.'[123]

Queen Mary, commending the new King to the nation, added: 'With him I commend my dear daughter-in-law, who will be his Queen. May she receive the same unfailing affection and trust which you have given me for six and twenty years.'[124]

That afternoon, the new Duke of Windsor telegraphed through the Admiralty: 'Have had good crossing. Glad to hear this morning's ceremony went off so well. Hope Elizabeth better. Best love and best of luck to you both. David.'[125]

On the following day, a Sunday, prayers were offered throughout the Empire for 'our most gracious Sovereign Lord King George . . . our gracious Queen Elizabeth'.

Elizabeth would almost always be gracious. There would only ever be one exception to the rule, and that would be in her dealings with the woman who had caused the whole traumatic upheaval to come about; the woman she would find it impossible to forgive for almost forty years: Wallis Simpson.

I don't blame her!
How would you feel?

7

THE QUEEN-EMPRESS
AND THE NON-ROYAL DUCHESS

ON THE DAY THAT GEORGE VI recognized the inevitability of his accession as King and Emperor, he went in despair to his mother at Marlborough House. '... when I told her what had happened,' he recorded afterwards, 'I broke down and sobbed like a child'.[1]

Queen Mary was later to describe her second son as 'appalled' by the prospect of kingship. 'He was devoted to his brother', she told Harold Nicolson, 'and the whole abdication crisis made him miserable. He sobbed on my shoulder for a whole hour – there, upon that sofa.'[2]

But the reluctant King had unsuspected reserves of fortitude. Twenty years earlier he had expressed his personal philosophy in words of unflinching stoicism. 'You must live according to the best you know – you can't do more. There can be no running away. You must face what is coming to you and take what comes.'[3]

A few days before the Abdication, Chips Channon had noted: 'The Yorks are staggered and behaving well.'[4] Yet it was only deep religious faith on the part of both which enabled them to control their sense of horrified incredulity, occasionally bordering on panic. The Duchess's Scottish maid, Catherine Mclean, found her reading her Bible, and afterwards noted that the place-mark was at St John, chapter 14, beginning, 'Let not your heart be troubled . . .'

This deep initial disquiet gave way quite quickly to a feeling of calm resignation. On the day after her accession, the new Queen-Empress Elizabeth felt able to write: 'I can hardly now believe that we have been called to this tremendous task and . . . the curious thing is that we are not afraid. I feel that God has enabled us to face the situation calmly.'[5]

The former King, meanwhile, had not even arrived at his first temporary refuge – Schloss Enzesfeld, the home near Vienna of Baron and Baroness Eugene de Rothschild – before a savage reaction began in British society against Wallis Simpson and himself.

The opening salvo of what Osbert Sitwell called *Rat Week*[6] came on December 13 in an unpleasantly sanctimonious broadcast by the Archbishop of Canterbury. 'From God he had received a high and sacred trust,' said Lang of Edward VIII. 'Yet by his own will he has abdicated – he has surrendered the trust. With characteristic frankness he has told us his motive. It was a craving for private happiness. Strange and sad it must be that for such a motive, however strongly it pressed upon his heart, he should have disappointed hopes so high and abandoned a trust so great. Even more strange and sad it is that he should have sought his happiness in a manner inconsistent with the Christian principles of marriage, and within a social circle whose standards and ways of life are alien to all the best instincts and traditions of his people. Let those who belong to this circle know that to-day they stand rebuked by the judgment of the nation which had loved King Edward.'[7]

Blanche Dugdale noted in her diary: '. . . Sibyl Colefax wept at hearing Archbishop's broadcast strictures on The Hostesses. Lady Cunard said "Ridiculous – I hardly know Mrs Simpson."'[8] Poor Emerald's frivolous disavowal availed her nothing. She was never to regain royal favour. The new Queen and Queen Mary had already marked her as *persona non grata*.

'. . . the other day in my presence,' Queen Mary would shortly write to Prince Paul, the Regent of Yugoslavia, 'Bertie told George he wished him and Marina never to see Lady Cunard again and George said he would not do so. I fear she has *done David a great deal of harm* as there is no doubt she was great friends with Mrs S. at one time and gave parties for her. Under the circumstances I feel none of us, in fact people in society, should meet her. I am sure you will agree one should not meet her again after what has happened and I am hoping that George and Marina will no longer see certain people who alas were friends of Mrs S. and Lady Cunard's and also David's . . . As you may imagine I feel very strongly on the matter but several people have mentioned to me what harm she has done.'[9]

The Duke of Kent may not have needed the new King's strictures regarding Lady Cunard. The abdication of his favourite brother had rocked Kent's fragile stability and transformed his attitude towards Wallis Simpson. Rumours began to circulate of a possible divorce between himself and Princess Marina, and Sir Robert Bruce Lockhart would shortly describe Kent as 'A nervous wreck . . . Capable of doing anything. Wants to kill Mrs Simpson.'[10]

Queen Mary's feelings were almost as violent. The Marquess of Salisbury, visiting her a few days after the Abdication, found her 'not weeping, as he had feared, but furious and outraged. "The person who needs most sympathy is my second son," she reminded him indignantly. "He is the one who is making the sacrifice." '[11]

Almost four months later, the old Queen remained intransigent and unrelenting towards her eldest son. 'HM is still angry with the Duke,' wrote an old friend, Lady Bertha Dawkins, at the end of March, 'and I really think that helps her to bear what she called "the humiliation" of it all.'[12]

Queen Mary's attitude towards her future daughter-in-law was even more extreme. Chips Channon noted that 'certainly she and the Court group hate Wallis Simpson to the point of hysteria, and are taking up the wrong attitude: why persecute her now that all is over? Why not let the Duke of Windsor, who has given up so much, be happy? They would be better advised to be civil if it is beyond their courage to be cordial.'[13]

But the British national sport of putting in the boot after a scandal – so pronounced after the imprisonment of Oscar Wilde, and still unpleasantly evident decades later following the resignation of John Profumo, the Argyll divorce case, and the trial of Jeremy Thorpe – was in full cry in the months immediately after the Abdication.

Even Wallis Simpson's most innocuous friend, the American gossip John McMullen, found himself ostracized. 'When it was all over, poor little Johnnie was left, a forlorn bit of flotsam, as the tide went out. Those who knew that he had known Mrs Simpson eyed him reproachfully . . .'[14]

McMullen was bemused by the social backwash. 'Why, do you know,' he said, 'one hears quite charming, intelligent people make quite revolting statements about her . . . I am terribly sorry for them both and fearful of what life may hold for them. It is a terrible position for her to be in and I should hate to be hated the way she is in London since the abdication.'[15]

In the whole of British society, only one hostess could be found who admitted to any regard for Mrs Simpson, or even to receiving her as a house guest. That was the Duchess of Marlborough, who cheerfully confessed: 'We had her to stay at Blenheim; I liked her.'[16]

Elsewhere, as Osbert Sitwell gleefully recorded in Rat Week, 'the sickened cock crew thrice'. In February 1937, the Winston Churchills were present at a dinner party given by Chips Channon. Clementine

Churchill had disagreed profoundly with her husband about the Abdication, feeling that Edward VIII should have put his duty before his private happiness. But she viewed with scorn those friends of the ex-King and of Wallis Simpson who had turned their coats after the crisis.

During the course of the dinner, Channon noted, 'Lord Granard tactlessly attacked the late King and Mrs Simpson to his neighbour, Clemmie Churchill, who turned on him and asked crushingly, "If you feel that way, why did you invite Mrs Simpson to your house and put her on your right?" A long embarrassed pause followed . . .'[17]

Ernest Simpson was also getting the cold shoulder in London. Various business acquaintances had become pointedly distant. When he walked into the bar of the Guards Club, several of the members turned their backs on him, and there was even talk of asking him to resign from one of his other clubs. Some of this antagonism ceased a few months later when Simpson fought and won a slander action against a society woman who had alleged that he had been paid not to defend the divorce – a belief widely held in London, but for which there appeared to be no definite proof.

Even in literary circles, controversy raged. Winston Churchill and Compton Mackenzie both publicly attacked Hector Bolitho, the author of *King Edward VIII, His Life and Reign*, the first biography of the former sovereign, which appeared in March 1937. In his native New Zealand, at the age of twenty-two, Bolitho had been attached to the Prince of Wales's suite when HMS *Renown* brought Edward to Auckland in 1920, and had made his *début* in literature with an admiring book called *With the Prince in New Zealand*.

But the Abdication had brought a sharp change in Bolitho's attitude. Compton Mackenzie charged him with altering his biography from its polite serial form – published in the magazine, *Leisure*, halfway through the King's reign in 1936 – to a markedly less complimentary version in the post-Abdication book, which depicted Windsor as 'increasingly stubborn and conceited over his popularity';[18] spoke of 'his fantastic vanity',[19] and described him as 'a distraught, unreasonable man',[20] who 'had no friends',[21] and 'who came to disaster through the slow disintegration of his character'.[22]

Compton Mackenzie referred to the book contemptuously as 'that tarnished weathercock of a narrative',[23] and congratulated Bolitho on 'the thoroughness of the *volte face*: it has . . . the acrobatic precision of a perfect somersault[24] . . Strange metamorphoses are recorded of humanity, but none so strange of literature as this metamorphosis of a toothless serial into a sharp-fanged book'.[25]

Like many other Abdication feuds, this one was never mended. Thirty-five years later, in his ninetieth year, Sir Compton Mackenzie was still critical of Hector Bolitho, then seventy-five and in failing health in a Brighton nursing home. 'He ratted,' said Sir Compton scornfully.[26] Bolitho himself always defended his biography of Edward VIII. 'Of course I changed my view of him,' he agreed once. '*He* changed.'[27]

While Wallis Simpson's personal prestige plummetted in London, that of the new Queen-Empress soared. Three days after her accession, on George VI's forty-first birthday, the King had conferred the Order of the Garter on his wife. The same distinction was soon afterwards given to her father, the Earl of Strathmore, who also had a United Kingdom earldom granted to him in addition to his Scottish titles.

Elizabeth's position of influence was soon officially emphasized. The Regency Act of 1937 named her as the first Queen Consort in British history to be eligible to serve as a Counsellor of State and to transact royal business in the absence of the sovereign. The King's confidence in his wife was further demonstrated by his insistence that she should precede him on all but the most formal of public occasions. As the Queen, with smiling self-possession, swept regally from the royal car to acknowledge the cheers of the crowd, followed at a distance by the diffident, hesitant figure of the King, it seemed for all the world as if it was Elizabeth who was the sovereign and George her dutiful and self-effacing consort.

Critics of Edward VIII and Mrs Simpson were suddenly conspicuous for the public honours bestowed upon them. Friends of Edward and Wallis were equally conspicuous for the lack of official recognition accorded them. One of these was the Earl of Dudley, whose son comments: '. . . my father was of course one of the Duke of Windsor's closest friends for most of his life, but never received any public recognition for his services as Regional Commissioner in the Midlands during the War. And I personally was always given to understand that the failure of the Government to give him any form of award was because of his friendship with the Duke.'[28]

At the time of George VI's accession, his private secretary, as Duke of York, had been Sir Eric Miéville. But it was Edward VIII's foremost critic, Major Alexander Hardinge – an adherent of the new Queen, and the husband of one of her closest friends – who was chosen to continue in the crucial role of Principal Private Secretary to the sovereign. He received a knighthood two months later. Alan Lascelles, the other arch-antagonist of the ex-King, also retained his position as Assistant Private Secretary, and six years later succeeded Hardinge in the senior post.

The second Assistant Private Secretary, Sir Godfrey Thomas, known for his loyalty and sympathy towards the Duke of Windsor, whom he had served devotedly for eighteen years, was swiftly eased out of the Palace secretariat and transferred to a post without influence – as private secretary to the Duke of Gloucester.

Eleven days after the Abdication, there was further internal evidence at Buckingham Palace of the extent to which the former reign and régime was being repudiated.

Lord Brownlow, who, on the direct orders of King Edward, had escorted Wallis Simpson on her journey to France, was a Lord-in-Waiting. He had been due to go into Waiting at Buckingham Palace on December 21, the day on which George VI received the Archbishop of Canterbury, whom Brownlow had threatened to sue for slander as a result of his condemnatory broadcast castigating the ex-King's 'social circle'. Brownlow's threat had extracted a grudging private apology from Lang. On the following day, December 22, Perry Brownlow saw in the Court Circular that the Marquess of Dufferin and Ava had succeeded as Lord-in-Waiting in his place. Brownlow telephoned Buckingham Palace and was curtly informed that his name could never appear in the Court Circular again.

He demanded to speak to the Lord Chamberlain, Lord Cromer – that same Lord Cromer who had shown such obsequious deference to Mrs Simpson less than two months earlier. Cromer informed him that his resignation had been accepted, although he had never actually resigned.

'Am I to be turned away, like a dishonest servant with no notice, no warning, no thanks, when all I did was to obey my Master, the late King?' said Brownlow.

'Yes,' replied Cromer.[29]

Brownlow's offences were manifold in the eyes of Hardinge, Lascelles, and especially Queen Elizabeth. He had accompanied 'that woman' to Cannes in circumstances that had attracted world-wide publicity. He had helped her to compose, and had personally issued, her statement offering to withdraw, which was regarded by the Royal Family as a piece of theatrical public relations. He had gone from

Cannes to Schloss Enzesfeld to become the first British visitor received in exile by the ex-King. On his return to London, he had unwisely offered an account of his experiences to Queen Mary, who was in no mood to hear them, and brusquely declined to receive him. And finally, he had threatened the venerable Primate, Archbishop Lang, who was held in affection and esteem by the new King and Queen. But it was his escort duty across France that constituted Brownlow's principal offence. Any public association with Wallis Simpson was fatal to a career at the new Court.

'Are we all on the "Black List"?' Chips Channon wondered in his diary. 'Are the Sutherlands, the Marlboroughs, the Stanleys? I cannot believe that it is Queen Elizabeth's doing. She is not so foolish . . .'[30] But the possibility had obviously occurred to him.

On January 21, the Duke of Windsor's stay at Schloss Enzesfeld was enlivened by the arrival of one of his oldest friends, Major Edward Metcalfe, popularly known as 'Fruity'. Metcalfe had been ski-ing at Kitzbühl, and knowing that the Duke must be lonely and bored – forbidden as he was to meet Wallis until the divorce decree became absolute in April – he offered to join him for a short visit.

At the time of Metcalfe's arrival, Windsor was involved in a series of long and tortuous telephone conversations with his brother, the King, over the financial arrangements agreed between them at the time of the Abdication. Edward had agreed to sell his life tenancy of Sandringham and Balmoral for a capital sum in the region of £1,000,000, plus an income of £21,000 a year from the Privy Purse. Owing to a dispute between the solicitors acting for the two brothers, there had been some delay in implementing the financial settlement, and a certain amount of friction had developed.[31]

Metcalfe quickly recognized that Windsor had not yet reconciled himself to the diminished status of a former king and sometimes forgot the augmented status of his younger brother, the new King. On the evening of his arrival, Metcalfe wrote to his wife: 'Tonight he [Windsor] was told at dinner that HM wanted to talk on the phone to him. He said he couldn't take the call but asked it to be put through at 10 p.m. The answer to this was that HM said *he would talk at 6:45 p.m. tomorrow* as he was *too busy to talk any other time.* It was pathetic to see HRH's face. He couldn't believe it! He's been so used to having everything done as he wishes. I'm afraid he's going to have many more shocks like this.'[32]

Windsor's telephone calls to the King were not only about money.

The Duke, possibly with the mistaken notion that he was helping a new and inexperienced monarch, had taken it upon himself to advise his brother about political matters and foreign affairs.

'This advice', noted Walter Monckton, 'often ran counter to the advice which the King was getting from his responsible ministers in the government. This caused him trouble which no one would understand who did not know the extent to which before the Abdication the Duke of Windsor's brothers admired and looked up to him'.[33]

Hardinge and Lascelles strongly disapproved of Windsor's repeated interference, and Queen Elizabeth watched with sharp resentment the unsettling effect which his brother's telephone calls had on the King.

'The Duke', wrote Monckton, 'was particularly quick in understanding and decision, and good on the telephone, whereas George VI had not the same quickness and was troubled by the impediment in his speech.'[34]

The King's nerves, in that first anxious year of his reign, were often frayed, and there were occasional outbursts of temper – 'gnashes', as his household privately referred to them. It was noted that these frequently occurred following one of Windsor's long-distance calls, particularly if reference had been made to Wallis Simpson. The Duke was now constantly urging his brother to prepare to welcome Wallis into the Royal Family – a suggestion that was deeply disturbing to the King, who already knew that both his wife and his mother had made up their minds never to receive her.[35]

Queen Elizabeth, observing her husband's growing exasperation, was insistent that the telephone conversations should cease, a viewpoint entirely welcome to Hardinge and Lascelles, who wanted the Duke of Windsor's influence eliminated permanently.[36]

Urged on by his wife, the King at last put his foot down. 'I'm afraid, David, that I can't go on telephoning to you anymore,' he told his brother. 'Are you serious?' asked Windsor incredulously. 'Yes, I'm sorry to say that I am. The reason must be clear to you.'[37]

The only reason the Duke could see was the hostility towards him of the new King's advisers, chiefly Hardinge and Lascelles – 'that staid, tightly linked aristocratic bureaucracy which had hedged in the Monarchy since Queen Victoria's time'.[38] This section of the Court, wrote Windsor thirty years later, wished to be rid of him, and he thought that 'those closest' to his brother were not displeased that this should be so.[39]

'Those closest' was a significant phrase. There could have been no clearer reference to the person the Duke believed was responsible for his gradual freezing-out – his sister-in-law, Queen Elizabeth.

The void in which he increasingly found himself began to have its effect on Windsor. On February 2, when his only sister, Mary, the Princess Royal, and her husband, the Earl of Harewood, arrived to visit him – the first members of the Royal Family to do so since his abdication – he was visibly on the verge of tears when he met them on the railway station platform in Vienna.

Three weeks later, they were followed by Windsor's favourite brother, Prince George, the Duke of Kent, who arrived for a five-day visit without his wife, Princess Marina, who had given birth to their second child, Princess Alexandra, just two months earlier.

In the middle of March, the Duke's cousin, Lord Louis Mountbatten, arrived for three days to offer himself, with the new King's blessing, as best man at the Windsor wedding. The Duke, as Prince of Wales, had been best man at Mountbatten's own wedding to the Hon. Edwina Ashley in 1922, and now wished to return the compliment. But Windsor was still tragically unaware of the extent of his estrangement from the Royal Family and declined his cousin's offer. 'This will be a royal wedding,' he explained. 'My two younger brothers will come over as supporters.'[40]

Just how unlikely a prospect this was is borne out by a conversation which George VI had at this time with the former Liberal prime minister, David Lloyd George, whose wife recorded in her diary: 'HM is most anxious that the Duke should not return to this country, but D. told him that he did not take that view and thought HM would be wiser not to oppose it.

' "She would never dare to come back here," said HM.

' "There you are wrong," replied D.

' "She would have no friends," said HM.

'D. did not agree.

' "But not you or me?" said the King anxiously.'[41]

In the three months since the Abdication, Wallis Simpson had also become a prey to anxiety and insecurity. Still holed up with the patient Herman Rogers at the Villa Lou Viei in Cannes – which had been deluged with sackloads of 'hate mail' from all over the world – she spoke to her future husband daily on the telephone to Vienna.

'Of course he's on the line for hours & hours every day to Cannes,' reported Fruity Metcalfe to his wife. 'I somehow don't think these talks go so well sometimes. It's only after one of them he ever seems a bit worried and nervous. She seems to be always picking on him and complaining about something that she thinks he hasn't done or ought to do . . .'[42]

It seems clear that even now Wallis was fearful that she might in some way lose the security of marriage. One of the things that had made her apprehensive was the fact that Baroness Kitty de Rothschild had remained on at Schloss Enzesfeld, without her husband, for seven weeks after Windsor's arrival there.

After the Baroness's departure, Metcalfe reported: 'Kitty is *out* completely – all due to W who apparently was very jealous of her. Isn't it staggering?'[43] Wallis's jealousy – if that is what it was – seems not to have been motivated by fierce possessive love so much as by fear of losing her strategic hold over the ex-King.

In mid-March, Lord Louis Mountbatten, who occupied Metcalfe's room adjacent to the Duke's, overheard another example of this curious insecurity.

'Darling,' began Windsor, over the telephone to Wallis, 'I've just spent the happiest day of my exile. Dickie's here!' There was a pause and then: 'Oh, no, *no*, darling! I could never be *really* happy with *you* not here, but this was the nearest thing to not being *un*-happy!'[44]

While Mountbatten was in Vienna, observing with dismay the Duke of Windsor's total subservience to his future wife, Harold Nicolson was at Buckingham Palace, watching the new Queen-Empress's performance at a dinner-party.

'She wears upon her face a faint smile indicative of how she would have liked her dinner-party were it not for the fact that she was Queen of England. Nothing could exceed the charm or dignity which she displays, and I cannot help feeling what a mess poor Mrs Simpson would have made of such an occasion. It demonstrated to us more than anything else how wholly impossible that marriage would have been . . . Thereafter, the Queen drops us a deep curtsey which is answered by all the ladies present'.[45]

In April, the Duff Coopers – virtually the only leading members of society to survive unscathed from their association with Edward VIII and Wallis Simpson – were invited to Windsor Castle for the weekend. 'So much for the black list, anyway,'[46] wrote Lady Diana, to whom Elizabeth appeared a 'spell-binding Queen . . . in gloss of satin, a lily and rose in one'.[47]

After the King and all the other guests, including a piqued Diana, had gone to bed, the Queen sat up drinking tea with Duff Cooper for an hour. 'She put her feet up on a sofa and talked of Kingship and "the intolerable honour" but not of the crisis.'[48]

Lady Diana told Chips Channon that the atmosphere at Windsor under the new régime had been very different from Edward VIII's entertainments at Fort Belvedere. 'That was an operetta,' she said, 'this an institution.'[49]

Wallis, meanwhile, no longer hemmed in by the press in Cannes, was at last able to emerge from the Villa Lou Viei on a number of sightseeing excursions in quest of somewhere suitable to be married. Her own choice was a handsome white villa called the Château de la Cröe at Cap d'Antibes, only five miles from Cannes. At about the same time, however, Herman Rogers received an offer from a slight acquaintance of his, a French-born naturalized American named Charles Eugène Bedaux, to use his sixteenth-century turreted grey stone castle, the Château de Candé in the village of Monts, near Tours, in central France. Nothing much was known about Bedaux, except that he had amassed a vast personal fortune through a system of industrial efficiency.

The choice of the two possible locations was referred to the King, who opted firmly for Candé rather than La Cröe on the Riviera, which had the image of a playground for the idle rich.

The King's choice was to prove deeply unfortunate for the Windsors, for the influence of Bedaux was to lead them into disastrous misjudgements, and he himself was to commit suicide in a Miami jail cell seven years later, after being charged with treason as a Nazi collaborator.

It was at Candé, therefore, on May 3, that Wallis received a telephone call from London to say that her divorce decree had at last been made absolute. She at once called the Duke in Austria. He caught the Orient Express from Salzburg that afternoon and arrived at Candé at lunchtime on the following day. After a separation of five months the lovers were reunited.

With the Coronation of the King and Queen now only a week away, they decided to delay their wedding until June. On May 8, Wallis legally changed her name by deed poll to Mrs Wallis Warfield, a somewhat futile attempt to erase the track record of two previous husbands, and, in particular, the notoriety of the name, Mrs Simpson.

In London, Emerald Cunard told Sir Robert Bruce Lockhart that she felt 'sure that the Duke of Windsor has not yet lived with Mrs Simpson, and that he worships her as a virginal saint'. Lockhart understandably noted in his diary, 'I doubt this.'[50]

Lady Cunard's belief tallied, however, with something Wallis herself had once said to Jack Aird during the *Nahlin* cruise: 'I have had two husbands, and I never went to bed with either of them.'[51]

Both statements put a heavy strain on credulity. Win Spencer and Ernest Simpson were both highly-sexed, virile men. Both had four wives and both were noted for their ardent womanizing. It seems highly improbable that either would have been content to live for eight years – the span of Wallis's time with each of them – with any woman on a purely platonic basis. Wallis's remark to Aird, if it was ever made, was clearly an attempt to improve her image as a potential consort in the eyes of the King's friends. As to Lady Cunard's belief, the photographs taken on-shore during the *Nahlin* cruise alone – some of them showing the King with his arms hungrily locked around Wallis – make it more than doubtful that he had ever 'worshipped her as a virginal saint'.

On the same day that Wallis went through the public relations exercise of reverting to her maiden name, the following statement was issued to press reporters by Herman Rogers:

'His Royal Highness the Duke of Windsor announces that his marriage to Mrs Wallis Warfield, daughter of the late Mr and Mrs Teackle Warfield, of Maryland, will take place at the Château de Candé, Monts, on Thursday, June 3. Invitations to the wedding of the Duke of Windsor and Mrs Warfield will be confined to those who have been with them during the past months. There will be no member of the royal family present.' Not only had Wallis's two previous husbands been expunged from the record, but – in this statement – so had her mother's second and third marriages.

'David longed to have his sister and his brothers, and most of all his mother, near him at his marriage,' wrote Wallis later. 'As is his habit, he kept his feelings to himself in that regard; a Royal upbringing, whatever else it may do to the heart and mind, confers a kind of unbreakable pride. But I knew without his ever saying so how deep was his disappointment. The unspoken order had gone out: Buckingham Palace would ignore our wedding. There would be no reconciliation, no gesture of recognition. That also meant that many of the friends with whom David had made his life would find it "awkward" to come to Candé. It was as if a glacial current had begun to flow between us and our accustomed associations.'[52]

On May 12, King George VI and Queen Elizabeth rode through the streets of London in their golden State Coach to be crowned at Westminster Abbey.

At Candé, Wallis listened to the radio broadcast of the ceremony. It must have been a bitter moment for her when she heard the Archbishop of Canterbury speak the words, 'Receive the Crown of glory, honour, and joy', as he placed the Queen Consort's diadem – blazing with the world's most famous diamond, the fabulous Koh-i-Noor – on the head of her arch-enemy, Elizabeth Bowes-Lyon.

Wallis had not merely lost a crown. She had lost it to the woman she most disliked in the whole world; the hated 'Dowdy Duchess' who had come between her and the realization of her regal aspirations. 'The words of the service rolled over me like an engulfing wave,' she later admitted. 'I fought to suppress every thought, but all the while the mental image of what might have been and should have been kept forming, disintegrating, and re-forming in my mind.'[53]

What should have been, in her view, was only too clear. She, Wallis Warfield of Baltimore, should have been sitting there in Elizabeth's place, on the consort's Throne, wearing the Queen's crown, and receiving the homage of the British Empire.

But the Coronation finally dispelled that illusion for ever – even in the mind of the staunchest of all Edward VIII's supporters, Winston Churchill. 'At the moment when Queen Elizabeth was crowned as Consort, after making vows of the utmost solemnity, and receiving tokens of grace for her special task, Winston turned to Clementine and, his eyes full of tears, said: "You were right; I see now that the 'other one' wouldn't have done." '[54]

When the official Coronation photographs were published, the diminutive figure of the new Queen-Empress, wearing the consort's crown and decked in the purple and ermine trappings of queenship, seemed suddenly to have acquired a formidable new regality that boded ill for Wallis. Majesty had swathed the 'Smiling Duchess'.

Six days later, the newly-crowned King and Queen attended a ball given by the Duke and Duchess of Sutherland at Hampden House in Mayfair. Vast crowds gathered outside to cheer them on their arrival and departure. One of those invited, however, kept a very low profile. Lady Cunard, who had dreamed of becoming Mistress of the Robes to Queen Wallis, wisely delayed her arrival until after the royal party had left. Like others in the preceding months, and many more in the years to come, Emerald took the matter of Queen Elizabeth's displeasure very seriously.

Realizing now that his family would remain obdurate in their determination to ignore his wedding, and that neither Gloucester nor Kent would come as 'supporters', the Duke of Windsor was forced to find a best man after all.

The offer made by his cousin, Dickie Mountbatten, in mid-March, suddenly no longer stood. Just before the Abdication, Mountbatten had written to the King to assure him that he could rely on his continued support as 'a friend of Wallis'.[55] Three months later, Mountbatten had not only offered himself as best man – allegedly with George VI's blessing – but had led Windsor to believe that he could persuade the King, the Duke of Gloucester and the Duke of Kent to attend the wedding also.

Mountbatten was playing a curious double game, for there was never the remotest possibility of the King's attendance. He had even suggested to Windsor the date ultimately selected for the wedding – June 3 – a choice that was hardly likely to commend itself to Queen Mary, since it was also the birthday of her late husband, King George V, to whom Wallis Simpson had been anathema.

Whatever Mountbatten's motives, he quickly had cause to regret his cavalier assurances. At the beginning of the year he had been appointed Personal Naval ADC to the new King and was invested as a Knight Grand Cross of the Royal Victorian Order. It was clearly in his interests to support the new régime, which was dominated by a Queen who had always watched the flamboyant lifestyle of the Mountbattens with cool reservations. Elizabeth's attitude had sharpened into overt suspicion since their involvement with Wallis Simpson at the Fort Belvedere weekends, the York House dinner for the Baldwins, and the Balmoral houseparty.

The Queen's uncompromising attitude towards her brother-in-law and his future wife sent a new and icy wind blowing through the corridors of Buckingham Palace, and Mountbatten, fly helmsman that he was, trimmed his sails accordingly. On May 5 he wrote to the Duke of Windsor regretfully declining an invitation to the wedding and explaining that 'while "Bertie" and "Georgie" had been willing to come, other people had stepped in to create a situation which made all the Duke's friends most unhappy'.[56]

There were no prizes for guessing who the 'other people' were. It was the Queen, backed by Queen Mary, Alec Hardinge and Tommy Lascelles. It seems improbable that the King, as Defender of the Faith, would ever have considered attending the third marriage of a twice-divorced woman, but there is some evidence to show that the Duke of Kent had been prepared to go – though without his wife.[57]

In the event, Kent was dissuaded, and so was one of the few leading courtiers still sympathetic to Windsor, Sir Ulick Alexander, Keeper of the Privy Purse, who was bluntly informed that he could not expect to retain his post if he attended his former master's wedding.[58]

Faced with a steadily growing line of turned backs, Windsor wrote on May 17 to ask the faithful Fruity Metcalfe to be best man. Metcalfe at once accepted, thereby completing a curious circle. Windsor had been Mountbatten's best man in 1922. Mountbatten was Metcalfe's best man in 1925, when he married Lady Alexandra Curzon. And Metcalfe was now to be Windsor's best man.

All this while, however, unknown to the ex-King, urgent consultations had been going on in London which were designed to cast a far darker shadow over the forthcoming marriage than the mere absence of royal supporters.

At Fort Belvedere on December 9, the day before the Abdication, Edward VIII had extracted a promise from his brother, the Duke of York, that Wallis Simpson would be raised to royal rank upon their marriage.

How implicitly the departing King believed his successor's assurance on this point was made clear by Windsor's utter incredulity when the undertaking was eventually broken. 'My brother *promised* me there would be no trouble over the title!' he said. 'He *promised* me!'[59]

The difficulty was that George VI, in a moment of considerable nervous strain and emotion, had given the promise without consulting his wife, his mother, or any of his advisers. When they learned what he had done, there was general consternation. Hardinge and Lascelles, both bitter opponents of Mrs Simpson, felt it would create a disastrous impression to confer royal rank upon a twice-divorced woman, who had been instrumental in the former King abandoning his throne, and who was at that time almost universally unpopular.

Queen Mary, who had promised her husband, King George V, that she would never receive Wallis under any circumstances, was aghast at the idea.

The fiercest opposition of all came from the Queen. Elizabeth made it clear to her husband that his brother's marriage would not alter her attitude in any respect. If the King chose to receive his American sister-in-law, he would do so alone. The Queen felt that the Royal Family had already been seriously damaged by the Abdication crisis, and that any form of recognition of the Duke of Windsor's marriage, and of his future wife, would compromise the new reign, and the position of the King and herself.[60]

George VI was now torn between conflicting emotions. While he shrank from inflicting a public wound on his exiled brother in the shape of an official slur on his wife, he also recoiled from the prospect of elevating to royal status a woman his own wife and mother refused to meet. In view of the attitude of the Queen and Queen Mary, the King seriously doubted whether many ladies in British society would be prepared to show Wallis the courtesy due to royal rank, even if it were conferred on her.

In Queen Elizabeth's mind, there existed one other, far more practical consideration. How could she or the King be sure that the marriage would last? The lady had already divorced two husbands. Why not a third? If the future Duchess of Windsor was recognized as Her Royal Highness, she would remain royal for life, even if her marriage to the Duke ended, for 'as King George VI reminded Baldwin at the time, once a person has become a Royal Highness there is no means of depriving him or her of the title'.[61]

The Queen, in particular, doubted that the marriage would last.[62] Even the Duke of Windsor's ally, Churchill, agreed with her. 'He falls constantly in and out of love,' he said of the Duke. 'His present attachment will follow the course of all the others.'[63] And Stanley Baldwin had echoed this conviction: 'His family are all wondering what will become of him when at last he opens his eyes and sees the sort she really is.'[64]

Once this train of thought had entered the minds of the King and Queen, the unfortunate possibilities multiplied. If the marriage ended in divorce, and the Duchess remarried, might the world be presented with the prospect of Her Royal Highness Mrs Smith, for example? And if the Duke remarried, the precedent of having created his first wife a Royal Highness, would mean that his second wife would have to become one also. Faced with this line of reasoning, the King recognized that he would be forced to go back on his over-hasty promise to his brother.

But how to do it? George VI and his advisers were now on extremely delicate and uncertain ground. Because there was no precedent in history for the *voluntary* abdication of a British sovereign,[65] constitutional experts were initially in a quandary as to the precise status of Edward VIII once he had ceased to be King.

On the day of his accession, December 11, 1936, George VI noted: 'Lord Wigram & Sir Claud Schuster (as representative of the Lord Chancellor) came to see me ... to ask me what my brother King Edward VIII was going to be known as after his abdication. The question was an urgent one, as Sir John Reith (Director of the BBC) was going to introduce him on the air that night as Mr Edward Windsor. I replied – That is quite wrong. Before going any further I would ask what has he given up on his abdication? S. [Schuster] said I am not sure. I said, It would be quite a good thing to find out before coming to me. Now as to his name. I suggest HRH D of W [indsor]. He cannot be Mr E.W. as he was born the son of a Duke. That makes him Ld E.W. anyhow. If he ever comes back to this country, he can stand & be elected to the H of C. Would you like that? S. replied No.

'As D of W he can sit & vote in the H of L. Would you like that? S. replied No. Well if he becomes a Royal Duke he cannot speak or vote in the H of L & he is not being deprived of his rank in the Navy, Army or R. Air Force. This gave Schuster a new lease of life and he went off quite happy.'[66]

On the orders of the new King, therefore, the ex-King was introduced that evening by Sir John Reith as 'His Royal Highness Prince Edward', and on the following morning, George VI, at his Accession Council at St James's Palace, announced that his brother 'will henceforth be known as His Royal Highness the Duke of Windsor'.[67]

It is also significant that on March 8, 1937, the Letters Patent creating the Dukedom of Windsor, bore the superscription, 'HRH Prince Edward, Duke'.[68]

In spite of this clear evidence of the new King, as 'the fount of all honours', having confirmed his brother's continued right to the title of Royal Highness after the Abdication and *before* the actual creation of the Dukedom of Windsor, it would later be argued – for reasons which will become obvious – that George VI had *re*-created his brother a Royal Highness.

In fact, as every constitutional expert in recent years has agreed – except those writers whose brief it is to justify the Court's attitude towards the Duchess of Windsor – Edward had never lost the title of Royal Highness. In abdicating, Edward VIII had relinquished the throne and the titles adhering to his position as King and Emperor. It was a legal and constitutional impossibility to renounce his royal birth and the titles which flowed from that.

As Philip M. Thomas correctly stated in *Burke's Peerage*: 'The position is that immediately upon his abdication and without any special act of the Prerogative, the former sovereign became, as son of a sovereign and pursuant to Letters Patent of November 30, 1917, a Prince of the United Kingdom of Great Britain and Northern Ireland, with the qualification of Royal Highness . . .'[69]

In addition to these Letters Patent of King George V's reign, Edward's continuing royal and princely rank is doubly emphasized by what Queen Victoria decreed in Letters Patent of February 5, 1864: '. . . that besides the children of Sovereigns of these Realms, the children of the sons of any Sovereign of Great Britain and Ireland shall have *and at all times hold and enjoy* [italics added] the title, style and attribute of "Royal Highness", with their titular dignity of Prince or Princess prefixed to their respective Christian names . . .'

Since Edward was the eldest son of a sovereign, and also the eldest son of the eldest surviving son of a sovereign, it follows that he had never forfeited the rank of Prince or the title of Royal Highness. It was to be the cornerstone of the argument justifying the Duchess of Windsor's exclusion from royal rank that he had, by abdication, forfeited both privileges.

If Queen Elizabeth II were to abdicate in favour of her heir, the Prince of Wales, she would automatically become Her Royal Highness the Princess Elizabeth, Duchess of Edinburgh – unless King Charles III exercised his Royal Prerogative, or an Act of Parliament was passed, enabling her to bear some higher title.[70] Failing this, British Common Law – with which not even the Royal Prerogative can interfere – would apply, and the Queen's title after abdication would be compounded of the rank with which she was born, and the rank she acquired through marriage.

In 1937, therefore, the former King was legally His Royal Highness Prince Edward, soon to be confirmed as Duke of Windsor. Upon marriage, his wife would share his titles and royal status unless some legal loophole could be found to prevent her from doing so.

That otherwise scrupulous royal biographer, the Countess of Longford, has twice stated – in two recent books[71] – that the Duchess of Windsor 'had no automatic right to her husband's title. If she received it [the HRH], it would have to be deliberately conferred on her by letters patent from the King himself.'[72]

This statement, which Lady Longford says[73] she 'was finally given . . . (roughly) by the Windsor Archives', is entirely without foundation.

Letters Patent – an open letter from the sovereign conferring some right or grant – are certainly employed in the creation of a title, such as a peerage or a Royal dukedom, for example. But there are no Letters Patent, known to British law, regulating the status or rank of the wife of a Royal duke, peer, or title-holder. The status of all wives in Britain is determined by one thing only – Common Law – with which the sovereign, even by use of the Royal Prerogative, is powerless to interfere.

It is through Common Law that Lady Longford herself, as the wife of a peer, is, *ipso facto*, a peeress and of noble rank. It was Common Law which dictated the announcement in the *London Gazette* in April 1923, when the Duke of York married Lady Elizabeth Bowes-Lyon, that the bride would take 'the title, style or attribute of Royal Highness in accordance with the settled general rule that a wife takes the status of her husband'.

There was no necessity for such an announcement in 1934 at the time of the Duke of Kent's marriage, since his bride, Princess Marina, was already a Royal Highness by virtue of her birth as a member of the Royal Family of Greece. In November 1935, however, a similar announcement – confirming the royal status of the bride – was made when the Duke of Gloucester married Lady Alice Montagu-Douglas-Scott. Both Elizabeth Bowes-Lyon and Alice Scott had automatically become, on marriage, Royal Highnesses and Princesses of the United Kingdom.

The same rule applied in the case of four further commoners who were to marry British princes: Katharine Worsley, who married the present Duke of Kent in 1961; Birgitte van Deurs, who married Prince Richard (now Duke) of Gloucester in 1972; Marie Christine von Reibnitz, formerly Mrs Tom Troubridge, who married Prince Michael of Kent in 1978; and Lady Diana Spencer, who married the Prince of Wales in 1981.

All four automatically became a Royal Highness and a Princess, even though one of them, Princess Michael, had been divorced from her first husband, and was also a Roman Catholic, thereby causing her second husband, Prince Michael – under the terms of the Act of Settlement of 1701 – to forfeit his place in the order of succession to the throne.

If Common Law and 'the settled general rule' prevailed, Mrs Wallis Warfield, on June 3, 1937, would also become, *ipso facto*, a Princess and Her Royal Highness the Duchess of Windsor. But George VI, at the insistence of his wife and mother[74], now deemed it expedient to deprive Wallis of royal rank, and grounds had to be found to give an appearance of legality to an action that has since been judged to be illegal under the constitution.

The three leading law officers of the Crown – the Home Secretary, Sir John Simon; the Lord Chancellor, Lord Hailsham; and the Attorney General, Sir Donald Somervell – faced immediate problems on the grounds of inconsistency.

As King, Edward VIII had proposed that he might marry Mrs Simpson without her becoming Queen. The compromise suggested was that she should become Her Highness (not Her Royal Highness) the Duchess of Lancaster, ranking below Queen Mary, the Duchess of York, Princess Elizabeth, Princess Margaret, the Duchess of Gloucester, the Duchess of Kent, and Princess Alice, Countess of Athlone.[75] This proposal was rejected by the Government, in the persons of the same three law officers who were now considering Wallis's future title.

And on December 4, Prime Minister Baldwin had said, in the House of Commons: 'Suggestions have appeared in certain organs of the press yesterday, and again today, that, if the King decided to marry, his wife need not become Queen. These ideas are without foundation. There is no such thing as what is called morganatic marriage known to our law.'

But in the five months since those words had been spoken, morganatic marriage had miraculously *become* 'known to our law'. For if His Royal Highness the Duke of Windsor, who had been denied such a marriage as King, married a lady whom the British Government intended should be known only as Her Grace the Duchess of Windsor, a morganatic marriage was indisputably what he was getting after all.

Morganatic marriage – derived from the medieval Latin, *matrimonium ad morganaticum*, meaning 'marriage on the morning-gift'; and also from the German, *Morgengabe*, implying that the morning-gift, or dowry, was all that the bride need expect – is defined legally as 'the lawful and inseparable conjunction of a man of noble or illustrious birth with a woman of inferior station, upon condition that neither the wife nor her children shall partake of the titles, arms, or dignity of the husband, or succeed to his inheritance, but be contented with a certain allowed rank assigned to them by the morganatic contract'.[76]

There had been a number of notable morganatic marriages within foreign royal families, and two of these, ironically, were to lead to the births of Queen Mary and also the present Queen's husband, Prince Philip.

In 1835, His Royal Highness Prince Alexander of Württemberg, nephew of the Austrian Emperor, attended a ball at the Imperial Palace in Vienna, where he met the beautiful and gifted Countess Claudine Rhédey. The daughter of an ancient Hungarian family, she was not of royal birth, and the Prince married her morganatically on May 2, 1835. A few days later, the Emperor created her Countess Hohenstein. They had three children, the second of whom – Francis, Duke of Teck – married Queen Victoria's first cousin, HRH Princess Mary Adelaide of Cambridge, in 1866. *Their* eldest child, Queen Mary, was not born a Royal Highness, but merely a Serene Highness, as a result of her grandfather's *mésalliance*. Countess Claudine Rhédey, the Countess Hohenstein, had a tragic death. On October 1, 1841, she was present on horseback with her husband at a military review in Vienna. The horse bolted and threw her, and she was trampled to death by a squadron of cavalry. Queen Mary, who never knew her, erected a tablet to her grandmother's memory in the church at Erdö-Szent György in Roumania.

There were those who believed that her grandmother's morganatic status influenced Queen Mary's attitude towards Wallis Simpson. 'It is easy to understand why it was Queen Mary who most resented the Abdication,' wrote Lady Mosley. 'She was imbued with a sense of the importance of being royal, and she never recovered from having been a Serene Highness among Royal Highnesses.'[77]

In 1851, Prince Alexander of Hesse, brother of Grand Duke Louis III of Hesse, broke dynastic protocol by marrying a commoner, Countess Julia Hauke, the daughter of a Polish general. She was created first Countess, then Princess of Battenberg, after the village close to the Rhine where the Hesse family had a castle. Her husband, who was eventually forgiven by his elder brother and granted the title of His Serene Highness Prince Alexander of Battenberg, was the grandfather of Lord Mountbatten and the great-grandfather of Prince Philip.[78]

Probably the best known of all morganatic marriages took place in 1900 between the heir to the Austro-Hungarian throne, His Imperial Highness the Archduke Franz Ferdinand, and a commoner, Countess Sophie Chotek. The Emperor, Franz Joseph, created her Duchess Hohenberg, but Franz Ferdinand was forced to renounce the throne for his children by her, and on public occasions Sophie was made to walk behind the least important ladies of the royal blood and to sit at a distant end of the Imperial table. On June 28, 1914, Franz Ferdinand and Sophie were seated side by side in an open car in the Bosnian capital, Sarajevo, when they were both shot and killed by a nineteen-year-old assassin, Gabriel Princip. Even in death, Sophie was branded a second-class wife. Her coffin, devoid of the Imperial standard and royal emblems, was adorned only by a pair of court lady's gloves.

In October 1912, the brother of Tsar Nicholas II of Russia, His Imperial Highness the Grand Duke Michael Alexandrovitch, married his mistress, a twice-divorced commoner, Nathalie Cheremetevskaya, who had married first at sixteen, a merchant named Mamontov, and second, a Captain Wulfert of the Blue Cuirassier Guards. She and the Grand Duke already had a son, George, born two years before their marriage. Reluctantly the Tsar created his new sister-in-law Countess Brassova, and her son Count Brassov, but she was never received by Nicholas II, or by his wife or mother. Technically, Nathalie became Empress of Russia for a few hours on March 15, 1917, when Nicholas II abdicated for himself and his son, Tsarevitch Alexis. But Grand Duke Michael's reign as Tsar Michael II ended abruptly the following day when he was warned that his personal safety could not be guaranteed. He, too, abdicated and after 304 years, the Romanov dynasty came to an end. Michael was imprisoned and shot in Perm the following year, six days before Nicholas II and his family were allegedly shot at Ekaterinburg. Countess Brassova, however, survived her husband, the Russian Revolution, and her son, Count Brassov, who was killed in a car accident in 1931 at the age of twenty-one. She lived on in exile until her death in 1952.

In 1921, four years after the Russian Revolution, the Tsar's first cousin, His Imperial Highness the Grand Duke Andrew Vladimir-ovitch of Russia, married his mistress, Mathilde Kschessinska, the *prima ballerina assoluta* of the Imperial Ballet, who had also been the mistress of Nicholas II before his marriage, and later of his cousin, Grand Duke Serge Mikhailovitch. Mathilde's son, Vladimir ('Vova'), born in 1903, was officially fathered by Andrew, but was thought to be Serge's child. Kschessinska was never recognized as Grand Duchess Andrew, but was invariably addressed as Princess. Her son, granted the morganatic status of Prince Romanovsky-Krassinsky, was raised – by the present head of the Romanov family, the Grand Duke Vladimir Kyrilovitch – to the title of Prince Romanov. For thirty years, Kschessinska ran a ballet studio in Paris, where her pupils included Dame

Margot Fonteyn. She lived on to the age of ninety-nine, and until her
death in 1971, she continued to believe – as had her husband, Grand
Duke Andrew – that the mysterious claimant, Anna Anderson, later
Mrs John Manahan, who died on February 12, 1984, in Charlottes-
ville, Virginia, was the genuine Grand Duchess Anastasia, the youngest
daughter of Kschessinska's first royal lover, Tsar Nicholas II.

Only two morganatic marriages of note followed the Windsor
wedding in 1937. In 1941, King Leopold III of Belgium, then a
prisoner of the Germans at Laeken Palace outside Brussels, married as
his second wife Mademoiselle Mary Liliane Baels, a Flemish commoner and the daughter of a former cabinet minister. Since she was
not of royal birth, it was decided that the marriage was morganatic
and that she could not become Queen. She was granted the title,
Princess de Rethy, and her son and two daughters by the King were
not in the line of succession to the throne. Later, after Leopold's
abdication in 1951, her stepson, King Baudouin, created the Princess
de Rethy Her Royal Highness Princess Liliane of Belgium. Although
never popular in the country, she was treated with respect and
sympathy by both the Royal Family and the Belgian people at
Leopold's funeral in 1983.

In 1947, ex-King Carol II of Roumania, who had abdicated seven
years earlier in favour of his son,[79] married – as his third wife – the
notorious green-eyed, flame-haired Jewish divorcee who had been his
mistress for twenty-four years, Madame Elena Lupescu. Her influence
over Carol during his reign caused one Roumanian prime minister to
say in 1934: 'Through her meddling, thirteen governments and four
elections have followed in close succession. She is responsible for
almost every evil in this country.'[80] To the peasants 'a red-headed
witch lives at the palace and feeds off gold plates while we cannot find
straw for our children'.[81] The ex-King married her in Brazil when she
was believed to be on her death-bed. With dubious authority to do so –
since he was the former monarch of a kingdom that would shortly
cease to exist – Carol created her Princess Elena (Helen) of Hohenzollern. She made a miraculous recovery, and they held a second
wedding ceremony at home in Portugal. Six years later, in 1953,
Carol died from a heart attack, leaving her most of his personal
wealth, and also, allegedly, some part of the Roumanian crown
jewels. Lupescu outlived the King by twenty-four years, dying in
1977 at the age of eighty-one at her home in Estoril, where she had
lived in seclusion.

On December 7, 1976, forty years to the week of Edward VIII's abdication, a royal marriage took place that would certainly have been classified as morganatic had it been set back in time. On that day, in the chapel at Drottningholm Palace on the outskirts of Stockholm, His Royal Highness Prince Bertil of Sweden, uncle of King Carl XVI Gustaf, and formerly Regent Designate of the country, was at last permitted by his liberally minded nephew to marry a sixty-one-year-old divorcee and former Welsh dancer, Mrs Lilian Mary Craig, *née* Davies, daughter of a Swansea shopkeeper, who had shared the Prince's life for thirty-three years. Bertil had repeatedly been refused permission to marry her by his father, King Gustaf VI Adolf, who lived and reigned to the age of ninety-one. After the old King's death on September 15, 1973, the Swedish people had been touched by the sight of the softly pretty Lilian comforting Bertil at his father's State funeral.

The young King Carl Gustav himself married a German commoner, Silvia Renate Sommerlath, on June 19, 1976, and six months later was present with his new queen at Prince Bertil's wedding to Mrs Craig, who was permitted to share her husband's status fully, becoming Her Royal Highness Princess Lilian, Duchess of Halland.

Two years later, on June 30, 1978, the Queen of England's first cousin, His Royal Highness Prince Michael of Kent, married – at a civil ceremony in Vienna – an Austro-German Roman Catholic, Marie Christine von Reibnitz, who had divorced her first husband, the Old Etonian banker Tom Troubridge, son of a British admiral.

In circumstances that were debatable, to say the least, Mrs Troubridge had succeeded, with difficulty, in having her former marriage annulled by the Vatican. Pope Paul VI, however, refused permission for her to remarry in church owing to Prince Michael's public assertion that the children of the marriage would be brought up as Anglicans. Five years later, the Vatican relented, and on July 29, 1983, Prince and Princess Michael retook their marriage vows in Cardinal Basil Hume's private chapel at Archbishop House, Westminster.

Under the terms of the Act of Settlement of 1701, Prince Michael, by marriage to a Roman Catholic, automatically forfeited his rights as sixteenth in the order of succession to the British throne, and speculation was rife in 1978 – particularly among the gossip-loving Viennese, who dubbed her 'the second Mrs Simpson' – as to whether Prince Michael's wife would be acknowledged a Royal Highness and entitled to bows and curtseys.

In the event, the Austrian divorcee became Her Royal Highness, and a Princess, unlike the American divorcee, Wallis Simpson, who did not. Times had indeed changed, but too late for the Windsors. The Duke

had died six years earlier, and the Duchess, soon to be submerged in
the twilight of a long and tragic illness, received Prince and Princess
Michael in Paris shortly after their marriage, doubtless amused by the
official *volte face* which the passage of forty-one years had brought
about in the treatment of divorced commoners who marry British
princes.

When Stanley Baldwin told the House of Commons on December 4,
1936, that 'there is no such thing as what is called morganatic
marriage known to our law', he was either speaking from ignorance of
British royal history or deliberately, for obvious reasons of policy,
avoiding the various precedents.

Similarly, when the Duke of Windsor's principal apologist, Michael
Bloch, wrote of the Duchess of Windsor as having 'the unique privilege
for the wife of an Englishman of not sharing the dignity of her
husband's rank',[82] and Philip M. Thomas in *Burke's Peerage* maintained that she 'has suffered the indignity, unique in the annals of
British history, of being denied a social status and a status of precedence equal to that of her husband',[83] both were wrong. So, too, was
Patrick Montague-Smith, who wrote, as editor of *Debrett's Peerage*, 'I
know of no other case where such a restriction was applied.'[84]

The 'privilege', or 'indignity', was certainly not unique in the annals
of British history, for there had been several earlier examples of wives
of Englishmen who had been deprived of their husband's rank. There
were also enough precedents of morganatic marriage in the British
Royal Family for the custom to be 'known to our law'. In at least one of
these cases, the differing status between husband and wife had been
decided by a British sovereign personally.

Prior to 1923, when Elizabeth Bowes-Lyon was raised to the rank of
a British Princess, there had been seven examples of commoners
marrying British kings, or future kings, and receiving royal status.

Elizabeth Woodville, the queen of Edward IV, Anne Neville, the
queen of Richard III, Anne Boleyn, Jane Seymour, Catherine Howard
and Catherine Parr, queens of Henry VIII, and the Earl of Clarendon's
daughter, Anne Hyde, who became the first wife of Charles II's heir,
James, Duke of York – later James II – all began life as commoners.
Two of them were technically no longer commoners at the time of their
marriage. Lady Anne Neville, daughter of the Earl of Warwick, had
been married to Henry VI's heir, Edward Prince of Wales, before
becoming Richard III's consort. And Lady Anne Boleyn, daughter of
the Earl of Wiltshire and niece of the Duke of Norfolk, had been

created Marquess of Pembroke – a peerage in her own right – before being crowned as Henry VIII's second queen. The status of commoner, therefore, did not preclude a woman from royal, or even queenly rank.

But there were an equal number of examples of English wives who were not permitted to share their husband's royal status. On April 17, 1759, an Anglican clergyman, the Reverend James Wilmot, recorded having married George, Prince of Wales – eighteen months later he became King George III – to Hannah Lightfoot, the aptly-named daughter of a Wapping shoemaker.

Documents recording this marriage were produced in the Court of Probate and Divorce in 1866, and were found to be signed George P. and George Guelph, and witnessed by Lord Chatham and J. Dunning, who later became Solicitor-General and afterwards Lord Ashburton. The documents were hastily impounded by the Lord Chief Justice, who described them as 'treasonable'. His alarm is easily understood. If the documents were genuine – and handwriting experts were of the opinion that they were – the marriage, which took place thirteen years before the Royal Marriages Act came into force, was both canonically and legally valid.

If this were so, it would mean that George III's *official* marriage – to Charlotte of Mecklenburg-Strelitz – was bigamous; that his fifteen children by her were all illegitimate; that his sons, George IV and William IV, had no right to occupy the throne; neither had his granddaughter, Queen Victoria; and that, as a result, Edward VII, George V, Edward VIII, George VI and Elizabeth II were all usurpers.

The documents produced in the Court of Probate and Divorce in 1866 are now in the Royal Archives at Windsor. In 1910, the author, Mary Pendered, who made a careful analysis of the Hannah Lightfoot case, was refused permission to examine these documents 'in the interests of research'.[85] Popular rumour credited George III with fathering three children by Hannah Lightfoot. It seems possible, therefore, that there are living today descendants of this marriage with a better claim to the throne than the present Queen. Certainly Hannah Lightfoot, if wife she was, was never acknowledged as such, and George's marriage to her, if it took place, can only be described as morganatic.

If the marriage was a reality, and if it was childless, there was every reason for it to be officially suppressed. Acknowledgment of it would have meant that the succession to the throne would have excluded George's children by Queen Charlotte, and would have been vested ultimately in the person of the King's second brother, William Henry, Duke of Gloucester.

But Gloucester, also, had made an unsuitable marriage. In September 1766, at the age of twenty-three, he had secretly married the Dowager Countess of Waldegrave, eight years his senior, one of the four natural daughters of Sir Edward Walpole by a Durham milliner called Mrs Clements. The King only recognized the marriage with the utmost reluctance after the parties had sworn to it before three commissioners appointed to investigate the circumstances. There was nothing George III could do to prevent his unwanted and illegitimate sister-in-law from becoming Her Royal Highness the Duchess of Gloucester, but she was not recognized as such until the marriage was made public six years after it had taken place. By this time there were two children, both in the line of succession to the throne.

Four years after the Gloucester *mésalliance*, the King had even worse trouble with his third brother, Henry Frederick, Duke of Cumberland. There is evidence to indicate that in 1770, Cumberland contracted a secret morganatic marriage with Olive Wilmot, daughter of that same clergyman, the Reverend James Wilmot, who claimed to have married George III to Hannah Lightfoot eleven years earlier.

This marriage, if it took place, was never made public, and was conveniently ignored a year later, in 1771, when the Duke of Cumberland made a second – and possibly bigamous – marriage to a dashing young Derbyshire widow, Mrs Anne Horton, daughter of Lord Irnham. 'The new Princess of the Blood', recorded Horace Walpole, 'is a young widow of twenty-four, extremely pretty, not handsome, very well made, with the most amorous eyes in the world, and eyelashes a yard long, coquette beyond measure, artful as Cleopatra, and completely mistress of all her passions and projects. Indeed, eyelashes three-quarters of a yard shorter would have served to conquer such a head as she has turned.'[86]

Sir Nathaniel Wraxall reported that 'The King held her in great alienation',[87] as well he might. Confronted by two unwanted sisters-in-law, neither of royal blood and both of inappropriate antecedents for the eminence they had attained, and haunted possibly by the memory of his own clandestine marriage to Hannah Lightfoot, George III now took steps to prevent – as he hoped – further similar damage to his royal house.

On March 24, 1772, the Royal Marriages Bill became law, ruling that 'no descendant of the body of his late Majesty King George the

second ... shall be capable of contracting matrimony, without previous consent of his Majesty, his heirs or successors ... and that every
marriage or matrimonial contract, of any such descendant, without
such consent first had and obtained, shall be null and void, to all
intents and purposes whatsoever'.

Under the terms of this Act, the secret marriage, on December 15,
1785, of George III's eldest son, the Prince of Wales – later George IV –
with Maria Fitzherbert, became null and void. Since Mrs Fitzherbert
was a Roman Catholic, and honourably refused to abandon her
religion, the marriage was also invalidated by the Bill of Rights of 1689
and the Act of Settlement of 1701. In the eyes of the Christian church,
however, the Prince's marriage to Mrs Fitzherbert was canonically
valid, and she, too, therefore, must be regarded as a morganatic wife in
some senses.

The Royal Marriages Act by no means put an end to George III's
dynastic headaches. If the King had had troubles with his brothers,
they were nothing compared with the problems created by five of his
nine sons.

The Prince of Wales's covert but soon widely rumoured union with
Mrs Fitzherbert was only the beginning of the scandals. George III's
second son, Frederick, Duke of York, married Princess Frederica of
Prussia in 1790, but separated from her in less than a year. In 1803, the
Duke set up house with Mary Anne Clarke, who had risen from the
obscurity of Bowling Inn Alley, Chancery Lane, to become London's
leading *demi-mondaine*. In the end, she involved York in a serious
political scandal over her traffic in army commissions. She was the
great-great-grandmother of Dame Daphne du Maurier, who wrote a
novel – *Mary Anne* – about her life, and whose husband, Lt-General
Sir Frederick ('Boy') Browning, became, ironically, Comptroller of the
Household of Queen Elizabeth II, and Treasurer to her husband,
Prince Philip.

In 1790, George III's third son, the Duke of Clarence – later King
William IV – set up house at Bushey with the actress Mrs Jordan,[88]
celebrated for her portrayal of high-spirited hoydens and tomboys in
breeches. They lived together for more than twenty years, in the course
of which she bore the Duke ten illegitimate children. The relationship
would now be legally recognized as a Common Law marriage, and
although Dorothy Jordan herself received neither title nor status, her
eldest son was created Earl of Munster, and her other nine children all
bore the title of Lord and Lady, with the semi-royal surname, Fitz

Clarence, ranking as the younger sons and daughters of a marquess.

At the same time, also in 1790, George III's fourth son, Edward, Duke of Kent, set up home with a beautiful but mysterious Frenchwoman, Mademoiselle Julie de St Laurent, who was subsequently known as Madame de St Laurent. They lived together happily for almost twenty-eight years.

The scandalous private lives of two of the royal dukes were brought to an abrupt end on November 6, 1817, when Princess Charlotte, daughter of the heir to the throne, the Prince Regent, died in childbirth, together with her infant son.

Pressure from Parliament over the security of the future succession now forced the Duke of Clarence, who had separated from Mrs Jordan some years earlier, to marry Princess Adelaide of Saxe-Meiningen, by whom all his legitimate children died, either at birth or shortly afterwards. The Duke of Kent was similarly prised by expediency from his cosy *ménage* with Madame de St Laurent and plunged into matrimony with the widowed Princess Victoria of Leiningen.

The daughter of this marriage, who became Queen Victoria nineteen years later, was rumoured to have employed two masked men to steal from Quebec the marriage certificate certifying that her father had made Julie de St Laurent his morganatic wife. There were also supposed to be children of Julie's – a son, or sons – by the Duke of Kent, who were adopted by others at birth, and whom Queen Victoria allegedly supported financially.

The undoubted title holder in the morganatic marriage marathon was George III's sixth son, Augustus Frederick, Duke of Sussex. In 1792, at the age of nineteen, Prince Augustus met the fourth Earl of Dunmore's daughter, Lady Augusta ('Goosey') Murray, a sensuous beauty five years older than himself. They were married in Rome on April 4, 1793, by an Anglican clergyman called Gunn, but without witnesses. They returned to England and had a second marriage ceremony performed at St George's, Hanover Square. Just over nine months later, a son, Augustus, was born to them in Essex. When the news reached George III, he ordered the marriage to be annulled. This did not deter Augusta from joining her husband in Berlin, where they lived together for six years. In August 1801, a daughter, Emma Augusta, was born.

Prince Augustus was now offered the dukedom of Sussex and £12,000 a year provided that he would separate from his wife. He did so, allowing her £4,000 a year, but in 1806 had to bring an injunction to stop her from using the Royal Arms and calling herself Duchess of Sussex. In 1809, the Duke removed the two children – now called Augustus d'Este and Emma d'Este – from her custody. The son later became Colonel Sir Augustus d'Este, and Emma finally became Lady Truro and wife of the Lord Chancellor. The hapless morganatic wife, Lady Augusta Murray, died in 1830 under the title of Countess d'Ameland.

In the intervening years, the Duke of Sussex also fathered an illegitimate daughter by a Miss Tranter, whose parents owned an inn near Windsor Castle. The child, Lucy Beaufoy Tranter, was the great-grandmother of the actress, Dame Anna Neagle, whose most celebrated screen performance would be as the Duke of Sussex's niece, Queen Victoria.[89]

Unabashed by the hullabaloo created by his first marriage, the Duke of Sussex made a second morganatic match in 1831 by marrying Lady Cecilia Buggin, *née* Gore, daughter of the second Earl of Arran and widow of Sir George Buggin. In 1834, she dropped the surname Buggin and assumed her mother's maiden name, Underwood.

The marriage was recognized and validated in 1840 by Queen Victoria, who – in return for the Duke of Sussex, as eldest surviving son of George III, allowing Prince Albert to take precedence over him – created Lady Cecilia Underwood the Duchess of Inverness, but *not* a Royal Highness. At receptions, she would be left halfway down the room while her husband sat at the Queen's table. Victoria did once allow the Duchess to sit at her table, but only on the express condition that she took her place last, as the junior lady present.

The Duke of Sussex died in 1843. His second morganatic wife survived him by thirty years and went on living at Kensington Palace. Their tombstones in Kensal Green cemetery perpetuate the divergence in their rank: *In memory of H.R.H. AUGUSTUS FREDERICK, DUKE OF SUSSEX* and *In memory of CECILIA LETITIA, DUCH-ESS OF INVERNESS, Wife of H.R.H. Duke of Sussex.*

The one remaining example of morganatic marriage in the British Royal Family occurred only ninety years before the Windsor wedding.

On January 8, 1847, Queen Victoria's first cousin and Queen Mary's uncle, His Royal Highness Prince George of Cambridge, then twenty-seven, married a thirty-year-old dancer, Sarah Louisa Fair-brother, who had played Robin Hood in a pantomime at Drury Lane Theatre. They already had two sons, George William Adolphus, born in 1843, and Adolphus Augustus Frederick, born in 1846. A third son,

Augustus Charles Frederick, was born in 1847, six months after the marriage.

In 1850, Prince George became Duke of Cambridge on the death of his father, but his wife was never recognized as Duchess of Cambridge or became a Royal Highness. She was known simply as Mrs Fitz-George, and it was under that name that she died on January 12, 1890, at the age of seventy-four, after almost fifty years of happiness with her royal husband. On her oak coffin was inscribed: 'Louisa FitzGeorge, the beloved wife of H.R.H. the Duke of Cambridge'. Her eldest son, George FitzGeorge, became a colonel in the 20th Hussars. The second son became Rear-Admiral Sir Adolphus FitzGeorge KCVO. And the third became Colonel Sir Augustus FitzGeorge KCVO, of the 11th Hussars.

If Sir John Simon, Lord Hailsham and Sir Donald Somervell hoped to use the morganatic status of the Duchess of Inverness and Mrs FitzGeorge as precedents for their intended treatment of the Duchess of Windsor, they were again on insecure ground, for both marriages, though canonically valid, were technically illegal under the Royal Marriages Act.

But while the Duke of Sussex and the Duke of Cambridge, as subjects of the sovereign, in the line of succession to the throne, were both bound by the Royal Marriages Act, the Duke of Windsor, as a former sovereign, no longer in the line of succession, was not affected by it. Edward VIII's Declaration of Abdication Act, 1936, had stated that 'The Royal Marriages Act, 1772, shall not apply to his Majesty after his abdication.' There could be no question about the legality of the Duke of Windsor's intended marriage to Wallis Warfield, and George VI, therefore, had no genuine grounds for intervention by the use of the Royal Prerogative.

Grounds had to be found, however, but since the Duchess of Windsor, under Common Law, had every right to the status of Royal Highness, it is hardly surprising that the means of depriving her of it did not subsequently bear scrutiny by constitutional experts. In the event, Queen Victoria's Letters Patent of February 5, 1864 – stipulating that children of sovereigns 'shall have and at all times hold and enjoy the title, style and attribute of "Royal Highness"' – were conveniently ignored.

Although these and King George V's Letters Patent of November 30, 1917, made it quite clear that the Duke of Windsor had never lost the title of Royal Highness, the Crown's law officers decided to argue that by his abdication, Edward had forfeited royal rank. The Letters Patent which Simon, Hailsham and Somervell drew up for the formal creation of the dukedom of Windsor began 'by quite falsely representing the Letters Patent of 1917 as applying only to princes in lineal succession to the Crown, which of course the Duke of Windsor was not, and then upon this assumption, as deliberately fallacious as the preamble to the statutes of King Henry VIII, proceeded to grant to the Duke the qualification of Royal Highness and then went on to restrict this to him only and to provide that no wife of his should enjoy it'.[90]

The 'lineal' argument has been bought by several historians, even, surprisingly, Lady Donaldson, who observes, 'it is difficult to see what other meaning they (the 1917 Letters Patent) could have'.[91]

But there is nothing whatever in the Letters Patent of 1917 to support this argument, and the lie was finally given to it in 1978, when Prince Michael of Kent, having forfeited his place in the line of succession in order to marry a Roman Catholic, remained a Royal Highness, and was permitted to share that status with his divorced wife. Lady Donaldson now concedes: 'I thought the "lineal" view sound at the time but as you say it has been rather blown upon.'[92]

The obvious illegality of what has become known to constitutional historians as 'the depriving Act of 1937'[93] was expertly summarized by the editor of *Debrett's Peerage*, Patrick Montague-Smith, in three questions: '(1) Can one receive a title or style which one already has by birth and membership of the House of Windsor *without restriction* and yet subsequently, in May 1937, be restricted by Letters Patent to such a title or style for himself only? (2) If one accepts that the title or style of HRH emanates from the Sovereign following the abdication, *again without restriction*, can this legally be restricted at a subsequent date to himself only? (3) Is it legal to prevent a wife holding the same titles and styles permitted to her husband?'[94]

The specious arguments employed by Simon, Hailsham, and Somervell — that the Duke of Windsor had lost royal rank by abdicating; that as a concession to his former kingly status he was being recreated a Royal Highness; but that the title could not be extended to his wife or children — were merely camouflage of the actual truth. The Royal Family, and in particular the Queen and Queen Mary, held Wallis Simpson in abhorrence and did not wish her to become a Royal Highness. The decision to deprive her of that rank was a reflection of personal dislike, public unpopularity, and the desire for retribution.[95]

She was to be made the scapegoat for an act of renunciation she herself had not performed but which they believed she had induced.

In order to give protection to the King's action, and to make it appear that it had been forced upon him by circumstances, the matter of the title was quite unnecessarily referred to the Cabinet, which meant that it would also have to be referred to the Dominion governments – a shrewd move in the light of Wallis's fierce unpopularity at that time. Stanley Baldwin, who was retiring from the premiership, 'greatly disliked having to assume the leading responsibility for ratifying the Letters Patent'.[96] He refused to sign the telegrams to the Dominion premiers and got Simon to persuade his successor, Neville Chamberlain, to do so.

Predictably, when presented with the choice of whether Wallis should be raised to royal rank or not, most of the Dominion governments replied in the negative. The New Zealand prime minister, Michael Savage, on being told that she would be known as Her Grace the Duchess of Windsor, reportedly commented, 'And quite enough too!'[97]

Armed with this carefully extracted ammunition, the decision to exclude Wallis from royal status was finally ratified at a meeting of the British Cabinet on May 26, 1937 – the last at which Baldwin would preside. The minutes of that meeting, like all the other Cabinet meetings which dealt with the Abdication, are closed until the year 2037.

Two days later, the following announcement appeared in the London Gazette: 'Whitehall, May 28, 1937. The King has been pleased by Letters Patent under the Great Seal of the Realm bearing date the 27th day of May 1937, to declare that the Duke of Windsor shall, notwithstanding his Instrument of Abdication executed on the 10th day of December 1936, and His Majesty's Declaration of Abdication Act 1936, whereby effect was given to the said Instrument, be entitled to hold and enjoy for himself only the title style or attribute of Royal Highness so however that his wife and descendants if any shall not hold the said title style or attribute.'[98]

The same announcement appeared a day later in The Times, accompanied by a leading article which sounded dangerously like dictation from Buckingham Palace and presented the Court point of view impeccably: 'Their decision is in keeping with the tradition that a right to the title of Royal Highness and to the recognition accorded to it by custom, at home, throughout the Empire, and elsewhere abroad, is essentially the attribute of a potential successor to the Throne – the Duke of Windsor himself remaining a special exception to the rule. It also accords with such parallels as are to be found in other official practice and should relieve the ceremony which is to take place in France next week from some part of the burden of speculation and discussion that has settled upon it.'[99]

Sir Walter Monckton, now the only remaining mediator between George VI and the Duke of Windsor, was perfectly aware of the machinations that had resulted in the withholding of the HRH. 'If the King had been left to himself,' he noted significantly, 'I feel confident that he would not have assented to this course because he knew the effect it would have on his brother.'[100]

But the King had not been left to himself. Urged on by the Queen,[101] he had consented to what *Burke's Peerage* would later describe as 'the last act of triumph of an outraged and hypocritical Establishment . . . the most flagrant act of discrimination in the whole history of our dynasty'.[102]

Monckton was right to warn Sir John Simon that it 'would create an intense bitterness in the Duke that should not be underestimated'.[103] It is usually stated that the Duke did not receive the news until Monckton arrived at the Château de Candé on June 2, the day before the wedding. In fact, it had been published for all the world to see fully six days previously, and on May 28, Lord Beaverbrook had sent Brigadier Michael Wardell to Candé with an advance copy of the official announcement.[104]

Monckton, when he arrived, carried with him a personal letter from George VI, in which the King 'hoped that this painful action he had been forced to take would not be regarded as "an insult"'.[105] The hope was naturally disappointed. 'This cold blooded act', as the Duke described it later, appeared to him as the deadliest form of insult that could have been offered. 'I know Bertie,' he said, 'I know he couldn't have written this letter on his own.'[106] He believed it had been drafted by Sir John Simon. 'My brother just took a piece of paper that was handed to him and copied it. It was not an idea he'd have thought of himself . . . Without question, other influences were working on him – somebody close to him, perhaps . . .'[107] Once again, this was the clearest possible reference to his sister-in-law, Queen Elizabeth.

He immediately wrote to the King to say that he would fight the ruling. 'I hope that you and all of Wallis's friends and mine will recognize her after tomorrow as "Her Royal Highness" and that the ladies will curtsey to her,' he told Herman Rogers. And he instructed his equerry, Dudley Forwood: 'Notify the staff to address my wife as "Your Royal Highness". I expect you to do the same.'[108]

'The bitterness is there all right,' noted Lady Alexandra Metcalfe at Candé. 'He had an outburst to Fruity while dressing for dinner. The family he is through with . . . He intends to fight the HRH business as legally the King has no right to stop the courtesy title being assumed by his wife. Monckton and Allen agree but let's hope he does nothing. Wallis . . . said it didn't matter to her but she minds a great deal really and says Monckton has made her sign just Wallis on the documents today. She said that she realized there was no insult they hadn't tried to heap on her. She thanked me effusively twice for having come and said she thought it was sweet of me.'[109]

On Thursday, June 3, 1937, Queen Mary noted in her diary: 'Alas! the wedding day in France of David & Mrs Warfield . . . We all telegraphed to him.'[110]

A civil marriage by the Mayor of Monts was followed by a religious ceremony conducted by an Anglican clergyman, the Reverend R. Anderson Jardine, then Vicar of St Paul's Church, Darlington, who had been warned on the day previously in a telegram from the Bishop of Durham that he was 'without episcopal licence or consent to unite the Duke of Windsor and Mrs Simpson'. Jardine ignored the telegram and went ahead anyway. Like Charles Bedaux, however, he was to prove a distinct liability after the wedding. He lost no time in having cards printed with the words 'The Duke's Vicar', beneath his name. He offered himself for lecture tours and even had a Hollywood agent. In 1941, he was given the pastorate of a small Los Angeles church, which he promptly renamed 'Windsor Cathedral'.

At 12.14 p.m., therefore, in front of a renegade clergyman, with no member of his family in evidence, and in the presence of only sixteen people, the former King and Emperor who had ruled over millions of subjects less than six months earlier, married the woman for whom he had given up all the glittering prizes of his birthright.

Immediately afterwards, Walter Monckton began the controversy which would continue for years by giving the new Duchess of Windsor an unmistakable bow. 'For my part,' he wrote, 'I had never any doubt. I always told the Duke that I would treat his wife as his wife should be treated. Besides, I find that my head bows very easily.'[111]

In London, the BBC news bulletins dismissed the wedding in fifty-five words. In the House of Commons, the Prime Minister,

Neville Chamberlain, was asked: 'Has the Government already decided to send, or are they considering the sending of a message of
congratulation to the Duke of Windsor on his wedding?' Chamberlain
made no reply. The next day's Court Circular ignored the wedding
completely.

'We shook hands with them in the salon,' recorded Lady Alexandra
Metcalfe after the service. 'I realized I should have kissed her but I just
couldn't . . . If she occasionally showed a glimmer of softness, took his
arm, looked at him as though she loved him one would warm towards
her, but her attitude is so correct. The effect is of a woman unmoved by
the infatuated love of a younger man. Let's hope that she lets up in
private with him otherwise it must be grim . . . A very nice telegram
came from the King & Queen and one from Queen Mary . . . No one
will ever know to what extent Wallis was at the bottom of everything.
Baldwin is supposed to say that as a schemer & intriguer she is
unsurpassed. My opinion is that she must have hoped to be either
Queen or morganatic wife as if she had realized she would get neither
she would & could have stopped him putting forward the whole idea.
Nevertheless, although I loathe her for what she has done, I am unable
to dislike her when I see her.'[112]

That evening the Windsors left Candé to spend their honeymoon at
Schloss Wasserleonburg, the home of Count Paul Münster. There, in
the peace of the Austrian Tyrol, they had leisure to reflect on the
strength of the forces now so obviously ranged against them.

The Duke blamed several people for the withholding of royal status
from his wife. The Duchess blamed only one person. She believed that
this official stigma, like all the other slights she would experience, was
subtly inspired by the enmity of a clever and dangerous woman – her
new sister-in-law, Elizabeth, the Queen of England.[113]

8

'I WOULDN'T RECEIVE HER'

As THE DUKE OF WINDSOR and his officially non-royal bride began their honeymoon at Schloss Wasserleonburg, one of the new Duchess's most outspoken critics, Viscountess Astor, made a much-publicized arrival in New York. In response to questions from reporters on the subject of the former King, the redoubtable Nancy declared: 'Edward's position is tragic.' 'For Edward or for England?' asked a reporter. Lady Astor smiled enigmatically, gave no answer, and, in Compton Mackenzie's description, 'like a sibyl she retreated from exposition'.[1]

Within only weeks of the wedding, the Windsors were plunged into controversy on several fronts. Confusion was rife over the Duchess of Windsor's position in society. The two leading authorities, *Debrett's Peerage* and *Burke's Peerage* – normally in relative harmony on such matters – issued conflicting tables of precedence. *Debrett's* ranked the Duchess of Windsor eighth in Britain, after the Queen, Queen Mary, Princess Elizabeth, Princess Margaret, the Princess Royal, the Duchess of Gloucester and the Duchess of Kent – but ahead of two other royal ladies, Queen Mary's sister-in-law, Princess Alice, Countess of Athlone, and George V's niece, Princess Arthur of Connaught. By this ranking, *Debrett's* accorded Wallis the status of a royal duchess. *Burke's*, however, ranked her thirty-third in Britain, coming not merely after all the royal ladies, but after all the non-royal duchesses also. The Royal College of Arms, appealed to for clarification, commented tersely: 'Only the King is able to decide and state the exact position. The less said about this the better.'[2]

The Windsors were not helped by the element of vulgar exploitation that already surrounded them. In Baltimore, one of Wallis's childhood homes, 212 East Biddle Street, was opened as the Windsor Museum, 'A Shrine to Love'. For a dollar, tourists could view Wallis in wax in the act of curtseying to King George V and Queen Mary. For a further twenty-five cents they were invited to increase their sexual prowess by lying down in the magic bathtub in which she had reputedly bathed. Among the visitors was Loelia, Duchess of Westminster, who told author Hugo Vickers: 'We went off to this appalling little house in a very minor street, it might have been in a seaside town, a row of ghastly little houses and there it was . . . On the bannister was a plaque on which was written, "This is where Aunt Bessie kept an eye on Wallis and her beaux". Can you beat it? Well worth a dollar.'[3]

In London, the Duke of Windsor brought a successful libel action against the author Geoffrey Dennis, whose book, *Coronation Commentary*, 'repeated the rumour that the lady who is now the plaintiff's wife occupied before his marriage to her the position of his mistress'.

This generally unsavoury aura was in marked contrast to the performance of the new King and Queen, who had gained popularity rapidly in the first six months of their reign. The former Labour prime minister, Ramsay MacDonald, visiting them at Buckingham Palace, 'told the Queen that the King had "come on magnificently since his accession". She had been pleased. "And am I doing all right?" she asked. "Oh you . . .", Ramsay had answered with a sweep taking that all for granted.'[4]

Queen Elizabeth had taken over the former King's role of charismatic royal superstar, but not everyone was prepared to switch allegiance. Compton Mackenzie, a passionate Edward VIII man – he received his knighthood only after the reign of George VI had ended – commented: 'Much praise has been written of her present Majesty, and perhaps some of those who have been sickened by the rapidity with which adulation of his ex-Majesty has changed to disparagement will henceforth doubt the conviction of writers who extol the virtues and graces of royalty.'[5]

Chips Channon, the friend of Wallis Simpson, also had reservations about the new reign. 'The present King and Queen are popular, very, and increasingly so, but they have no message for the Labour Party who believe them, and rightly, I fear, to be but the puppets of a palace clique. Certainly they are too hemmed in by the territorial aristocracy, and have all the faults and virtues which Edward VIII lacked in this particular field.'[6]

The Windsors soon received a number of pointers to the totality of their exclusion from the life of the Royal Family. The Duke, as George V's eldest son, had produced £4,000 – half the total cost – for the St George's Chapel monument to his father, designed by Sir Edwin Lutyens. He was not even invited to its dedication, nor was it ever mentioned that he had contributed towards it.

In August 1937, while the Windsors were still on their honeymoon

at Wasserleonburg, the Duke and Duchess of Kent arrived to stay
with her brother-in-law and sister, Prince and Princess Paul, at the
Regent's hunting lodge just over the Yugoslav border. According
to Prince Paul's account, given later to the writer Alastair Forbes:
'The first thing George told us was "I must speak to David as I want
to pay him a visit. Unfortunately I have strong instructions from
Mama that Marina (being a foreigner by birth) shouldn't be the first
female member of the family to call on her", as the feeling against
the Duchess of Windsor in England was very strong at that time.
I immediately called David on the phone and George said, "I've just
arrived and may I come and see you with Paul?" David told him
to wait a moment and G. thought that he was consulting his wife.
After a few minutes he returned and asked, "Are you coming with
your wives?" Whereupon G. said that, as they had just arrived and
our mother-in-law was in the house, it wasn't convenient *at that
moment*. D's answer was "In that case, it's No" and put down the
receiver.'[7]

Princess Marina's mother – the mother-in-law referred to – was Her
Imperial and Royal Highness, the Grand Duchess Helen Vladimirovna
of Russia, Princess Nicholas of Greece, 'a formidable Romanov lady
who was certainly in agreement with the two English Queens and King
George VI that this was to be a visit without wives'.[8]

The argument used, that the Duchess of Kent was 'a foreigner by
birth', was again a thin disguise of the truth. The Duchess of Windsor
was equally 'a foreigner by birth'. Queen Mary, evidently supported
by Queen Elizabeth, had prevailed upon Marina not to call on her new
sister-in-law and the intention was transparently an act of social
ostracism to which any newly-married wife would naturally take
exception.

According to Walter Monckton's account, the Duke of Kent,
dismayed by his brother's curt refusal to receive Prince Paul and
himself without their wives, referred his difficulties to the King.
George VI, on Monckton's advice, directed both Kent *and* his wife to
call on the Windsors, but Princess Marina remained adamant in her
refusal to go.[9] Her decision was less an act of disobedience to the King
than one of conformity with the strong feelings of the Queen, Queen
Mary, and of her own mother who, being on the spot at the time,
naturally held sway.

In the end, the Duke of Kent and Prince Paul went to Wasserleonburg without their wives, but were received by the Duke of Windsor

only, who later said that when Kent 'showed up without Marina, the Duchess properly refused to see him, and I gave him a brotherly lecture he wouldn't soon forget'.[10]

As a direct consequence of this pointed family snub to Wallis, a coolness developed between Windsor and his once favourite brother. A Christmas present to the Duke of a gold box from the Duke of Kent was immediately returned with a note saying: 'The only box I have come to expect from my brothers is a box on the ear.'[11]

When, five years later, the Duke of Kent was killed on active service at the age of thirty-nine, there was no letter or message of sympathy from the Windsors to his widow. The Duchess of Windsor had been her sister-in-law for twenty-eight years when Princess Marina finally called on her – and then it was on the neutral territory of the London Clinic, with the object of seeing the Duke after an eye operation.

While the Windsors brooded over family slights at Wasserleonburg, the King and Queen returned to Balmoral for the first time since Elizabeth's icy confrontation there with Wallis the previous September. The mood this time was very different. 'The Ghillies Ball was held in an enormous Gothic hall. Here they danced ceaselessly throughout the night. The King and Queen jigged with great abandon. The Queen ducked under huge ghillies' arms in the various complications of the reels. Pipes squealed, people hooted and laughed . . . Even old Princess Marie Louise twinkled her toes by the hour.'[12]

After leaving Wasserleonburg, the Windsors took a suite at the Hotel Meurice in Paris, while they searched for a permanent home. It was now that the sinister influence of Charles Bedaux came disastrously into the picture.

In his farewell broadcast to the British nation nine months earlier, Edward had declared: 'I now quit altogether public affairs.' As a man renouncing the most exalted position in public life, it was the only undertaking he could suitably give, but it soon became apparent that he had thought better of it.

Monckton, who had visited the Windsors at Wasserleonburg, recognized that it was Wallis who was pushing the Duke into staging a comeback as a public figure. 'She, I think, was in some sense beating against the bars. She wanted him to eat his cake and have it. She could not easily reconcile herself to the fact that by marrying her he had become a less important person.'[13]

On September 3, Thomas Carter, the Duke's former Clerk, and now Chief Clerk Accountant of the Privy Purse, issued the following communiqué: 'In accordance with the Duke of Windsor's message to the world Press last June that he would release any information of interest regarding his plans or movements, His Royal Highness makes it known that he and the Duchess of Windsor are visiting Germany and the United States in the near future for the purpose of studying housing and working conditions in these two countries.'

The effect of this announcement in Whitehall and at Buckingham Palace was like a thunderclap. The Duke had asked neither advice nor permission of the Foreign Office. The King and Queen firmly supported Chamberlain's policy of appeasement, but they privately regarded the Fascist dictatorships with distaste and misgiving. For a member of the Royal Family, as distinct from a politician, to visit Germany at this point and give the appearance of approval of the Nazi régime seemed disastrously compromising to the monarchy.

Those of the King's advisers like Hardinge, Lascelles and Simon, who had always distrusted the Duke of Windsor, nodded knowingly and felt vindicated in their determination to isolate him from any sphere of influence. Others were quick to say that the planned visit substantiated the many earlier rumours of pro-German sympathies on the part of both Edward VIII and Mrs Simpson. Angriest of all was the Queen, who saw the announcement and the visit as a deliberately calculated attempt to undermine her husband and divert attention from the new King back to the old. Elizabeth blamed her brother-in-law less than his ambitious wife, who she believed was at the back of the plan.[14]

The Windsors' few remaining friends in London were aghast at the idea of the visit. Lord Beaverbrook flew to Paris in an attempt to dissuade them from going. He even offered to send his private plane back to London to fetch Churchill, the one person he felt might be able to convince them of the utter folly of the undertaking. But the Duke obstinately refused to consult Churchill or even to seek the advice of the Foreign Office. He knew both would tell him not to go.

The stated object of the German visit – 'studying housing and working conditions' – was the merest camouflage for a public relations exercise designed to put the former King and his consort back in the international spotlight and to enhance the business relations of Bedaux with his Nazi associates. The Windsors were the unsuspecting victims of crude manipulation.

But the Duchess's hopes of her husband once more being treated like a sovereign were swiftly dashed. On their arrival at the Friedrichstrasse Station in Berlin on October 11, the Windsors were met by the Third Secretary of the British Embassy, Geoffrey Harrison, who handed them a letter from the Chargé d'Affaires, Sir George Ogilvie-Forbes, explaining that the Ambassador, Sir Nevile Henderson, had rather unexpectedly left Berlin, and that he himself 'had been directed by the Foreign Office to take no official cognizance' of their visit.[15]

They were therefore not received at the British Embassy, and were almost exclusively in the hands of a notorious Nazi thug, Dr Robert Ley, *Gauleiter* of Cologne and head of the German Labour Front for twelve years, who ultimately hanged himself in order to escape trial as a war criminal at Nuremberg. This fat, aggressive alcoholic whizzed the Windsors about Berlin at breakneck speed in a huge open black Mercedes-Benz with an ear-piercing siren and a radio that constantly blared out German martial music, to which Ley kept time by rolling his head from side to side. The Duchess was so unnerved by these expeditions that the Duke was eventually forced to insist on more leisurely progress.

They met all the principal Nazi leaders: Dr Josef Goebbels, the Director of Propaganda; Heinrich Himmler, head of the Gestapo; and Rudolf Hess, Hitler's deputy. They were taken to have tea with Reichsmarschall Hermann Göring and his wife, Emmy, who, after observing the Duchess's style and appearance, 'could not help thinking that this woman would certainly have cut a good figure on the throne of England'.[16]

The writer Alastair Forbes, who made a careful study of the subject, had 'always been reluctant to believe that the Duke had spoken ill of his brother the King to Reichsmarschall Göring,' but in the light of subsequent evidence, he did believe it.[17]

'It also seems clear', Forbes added, 'that he [the Duke] never understood the nature of Hitler's policy of genocide and persecution of Jews and other minorities. To my own knowledge, shortly after the war he tactlessly came up to an Austrian who had left Hitler's Europe as a refugee and said in German that had he remained King there would have been no war. He was incorrigibly frivolous and quite unsuited to being the constitutional monarch of a country whose system he derided as "slipshod democracy".'[18]

For fourteen days the Windsors toured German cities and factories, greeted everywhere with the Nazi salute and the words, 'Heil Windsor!', to which the Duke responded, 'Heil Hitler!' On at least three occasions, Windsor was seen to give the full version of the Nazi salute, with extended arm upraised. Much was made of this after the war; possibly too much. It is now conveniently forgotten that in May 1938, six months *after* the Windsor visit, the England soccer team were photographed in Berlin, standing obediently in line and raising their arms high in the full Nazi salute. This was done at the insistence of the pro-appeasement British Ambassador, Sir Nevile Henderson, who, four months before he absented himself from Berlin during the Windsors' visit, had declared: 'Far too many people have an erroneous conception of what the National-Socialist regime really stands for. Otherwise they would lay less stress on Nazi dictatorship and much more emphasis on the great social experiment being tried out in this country.'[19]

An official of the Saxon State Chancery let slip that Berlin had ordered all local authorities to address the Duchess of Windsor as Her Royal Highness. She was accordingly received with bows and curtsies at a dinner given in the Windsors' honour at a Berlin restaurant by Wallis's flatterer from pre-Abdication days in London, Joachim von Ribbentrop, now German Foreign Minister. And she had a place card which proclaimed, *Ihre Königliche Hoheit die Herzogin von Windsor* – Her Royal Highness the Duchess of Windsor, at an elaborate dinner given at the Grand Hotel, Dresden, by the Duke's Nazi cousin, Charles Edward, Duke of Saxe-Coburg, who thus became the first European royalty to recognize Wallis's right to royal status.

Reports of all these deferential attentions to the Duchess were not slow in reaching London, where, on October 20, while the Windsors were still trapped in their Wagnerian nightmare, Freda Dudley Ward, the woman whose taste and discretion would have steered Edward away from this disastrous expedition, got married again quietly at Marylebone Register Office to the Marqués de Casa Maury.

On October 22, the Windsors travelled to Berchtesgaden to take afternoon tea with the Führer himself at his mountain retreat some seventy miles from Munich and overlooking Austria, which the Third Reich would so shortly gobble up. Hitler greeted them personally, and a photograph of the Führer bowing low over the Duchess of Windsor's hand, a huge swastika adorning his left sleeve, was wired onto the front pages of the world.

During tea, Wallis found it difficult to take her eyes off him. 'His face had a pasty pallor, and under his moustache his lips were fixed in a kind of mirthless grimace ... his eyes were truly extraordinary –

intense, unblinking, magnetic, burning with the same peculiar fire I had earlier seen in the eyes of Kemal Atatürk. Once or twice I felt those eyes turned in my direction. But when I tried to meet their gaze, the lids dropped, and I found myself confronted by a mask. I decided that Hitler did not care for women.'[20]

According to the Führer's interpreter, Dr Paul Schmidt, who was present at the meeting, the Duchess 'made a lasting impression on Hitler. "She would have made a good Queen," he said when they had gone.'[21]

The official German account of the Führer's conversation with the Duke of Windsor was mysteriously missing from the Nazi files captured by the British at the end of World War II, but Hitler seemed in no doubt as to the Duke's attitude to the Third Reich. 'I am certain that through him permanent friendly relations with England could have been achieved,' he told Albert Speer. 'If he had stayed, everything would have been different. His abdication was a severe loss for us.'[22]

The *New York Times* was in full agreement with this view, and, summing up the Windsors' German tour, considered that the Duke's 'gestures and remarks during the last two weeks have demonstrated adequately that the Abdication did rob Germany of a firm friend, if not indeed a devoted admirer, on the British throne. He has lent himself, perhaps unconsciously but easily, to National Socialist propaganda. There can be no doubt that his tour has strengthened the régime's hold on the working classes . . . The Duke is reported to have become very critical of English politics as he sees them and is reported as declaring that the British ministers of today and their possible successors are no match for the German or Italian dictators.'[23]

Charles Bedaux, who had kept a low profile during the German visit, now went ahead with preparations for a similar tour of the United States. But the poisonous publicity resulting from the Duke's apparent sympathy with fascism, combined with the hatred felt within the American labour movement for Bedaux and his system of speeding up work in factories, created sudden spontaneous combustion. In Wallis's home city, Baltimore, the local branch of the American Federation of Labour denounced Bedaux as 'the arch-enemy' of the workers, and vowed to boycott the receptions planned for the Duke and Duchess, 'whether emissaries of a dictatorship or uninformed sentimentalists'.

When the Windsors booked their passage to New York on the *Bremen*, a German liner, it was the final spark that caused an explosion of criticism. Such was the outcry that only three days after they returned to Paris from Germany, and a week before their scheduled departure for America, the duke felt obliged to call a press conference at which he expressed the 'considerable concern and embarrassment' felt by them both over 'mis-statements' in the press.[24]

From New York, the beleaguered Bedaux, overwhelmed by the uproar, cabled the Duke: 'Because of the mistaken attack upon me here, I am convinced that your proposed tour will be difficult under my auspices. I respectfully . . . implore you to relieve me completely of all duties in connection with it.'

On November 10, having relinquished all his business interests in the United States, Bedaux escaped by the service door of the Plaza Hotel in New York, took a train to Montreal, and from there fled to France. He was not to set foot on American soil again until he was flown to Miami under arrest in 1943 to be tried for treason. The Windsors, thoroughly chastened by the furore, abruptly cancelled their American tour and remained in their Paris hotel suite.

In Britain, the reaction to this fiasco, and to the German visit also, had been uniformly unfavourable. 'Who are the Duke's advisers?' asked the Labour politician, Herbert Morrison. 'I do not know. But either they are very bad ones or he will not take good advice. If the Duke wants to study social problems he had far better quietly read books and get advice in private rather than put his foot in it in this way . . . Although what he is going to do with this knowledge I do not know, for he cannot be permitted to re-enter public life – in this country at any rate . . . The choice before ex-kings is either to fade out of the public eye or to be a nuisance. It is a hard choice perhaps, for one of his temperament, but the Duke will be wise to fade.'[25]

The attitude of George VI and Queen Elizabeth to this avalanche of bad publicity was clearly revealed when Sir Ronald Lindsay, the British Ambassador to the United States, returned from London to Washington, where he had talks with Undersecretary of State Sumner Welles.

'The Ambassador said that before his departure from England he had been summoned to spend a few days with the King and Queen,' wrote Welles. '. . . they both felt that at this time when the new King was in a difficult situation and was trying to win the affection and confidence of his country people, without possessing the popular appeal which the Duke of Windsor possessed, it was singularly unfortunate that the Duke of Windsor was placing himself in a position where he would seem constantly to be courting the limelight. The Ambassador went on to say that he had found on the part of all the governing class in England a very vehement feeling of indignation against the course of the Duke of Windsor based in part on the resentment created by his relinquishment of his responsibilities and in even greater part due to the apparent unfairness of his present attitude with regard to his brother, the King. The Ambassador said that in Court circles and in the Foreign Office and on the part of the heads of political parties, this feeling bordered on the stage of hysteria. The Ambassador said rather significantly that there recently had been a widening of this sentiment of indignation because of the fact that the active supporters of the Duke of Windsor within England were those elements known to have inclinations towards fascist dictatorships and that the recent tour of Germany by the Duke of Windsor and his ostentatious reception by Hitler and his regime could only be construed as a willingness on the part of the Duke of Windsor to lend himself to these tendencies. The Ambassador expressed the personal opinion that the Duke of Windsor himself is probably not cognizant of the state of feeling in this regard and that it is being exploited without his knowledge . . . What the British desired he said was to prevent any action on the part of the authorities of the British Government which would permit the Duke of Windsor to appear in the light of a martyr . . .'[26]

But if the King and Queen felt aggrieved by recent events, so did the Windsors. Within less than a year of his departure from Britain, the Duke was already pressing to return to the country. This idea was unwelcome to his brother, his sister-in-law, and to the Government, and Windsor was indignant when hints were dropped that his annual income of £21,000 from the Privy Purse might be in jeopardy if he attempted to come to Britain without the King's consent.

'When I decided to give up the throne last December,' wrote the Duke to the Prime Minister, Neville Chamberlain, 'I realized that the only dignified and sensible course for me to follow, was to leave the country for a period, the length of which was naturally to be determined by a number of considerations. But I never intended, nor would I ever have agreed, to renounce my native land or my right to return to it – for all time.

'If my understanding of the present situation is correct, it is now proposed that my personal freedom in this respect be linked with a private family arrangement on financial matters which my brother, the present King, made with me the day before I abdicated, in such a way, that he would be permitted to break his private agreement with me if I were to exercise my right to visit my country, without first obtaining his approval under the advice of his ministers.

'I regard such a proposal as both unfair and intolerable, as it would amount to accepting payment for remaining in exile . . .

'It is hardly necessary for me to repeat to you my loyalty to my brother as King; nor as a patriotic Englishman could I countenance any disruptive action in others. But I cannot refrain from saying, with the frankness you would expect of me, that the treatment which has been meted out to my wife and myself since last December, has caused us acute pain . . .'[27]

The situation was now a vicious circle. The Windsors, with reason, felt themselves consigned to oblivion. 'The drawbridges are going up behind me,' the Duke had said to Wallis. 'I have taken you into a void.'[28] The feeling of hopelessness which this isolation created, caused them both to behave with a lack of circumspection. Since they were being treated so badly – as they saw it – what did further criticism matter? Whether they would have behaved any better had they been treated well, in their own estimation, is a matter for speculation.

Their first Christmas card as a married couple gave an unfortunate impression. Drawn by the French artist, Etienne Drian, it depicted the Duke as a small, boyish, vulnerably wistful figure seated in a chair. Perched on the arm of the chair, and towering over him with an aura of purposeful dominance, was the strong-faced, determined and elongated figure of the Duchess. The effect produced by the drawing was that of an unhappy boy in the custody of a large and autocratic nanny. The Christmas card was referred to among members of the Royal Family as 'David and the Giantess'.[29]

The Windsors spent that Christmas where Wallis had spent the previous one – with Katherine and Herman Rogers at the Villa Lou Viei in Cannes. On January 7, they were guests of honour at a dinner given at the Château de l'Horizon by the legendary Maxine Elliott, the American actress who had a theatre named after her in New York and had been the mistress of Edward VII. Churchill and Lloyd George were both present, and, speaking to the former of the Abdication, Miss Elliott observed, 'We did it better in my day.'[30]

The Duke was still determined to fight the King's ruling in withholding from Wallis the title of Royal Highness. He retained one of Britain's most eminent constitutional lawyers, Sir William Jowitt –

later the first Earl Jowitt and Lord Chancellor – to look into the legality of the Letters Patent of May 1937. In January 1938, Sir William came to Paris to discuss the whole vexed issue with the Duke, and later advised him by letter that in his view there was 'considerable question that the King's action in this regard was legally sound'.[31] This opinion increased the Windsors' growing sense of injustice and resentment.

In London, one newspaper painted a depressing picture of the dilapidation of Fort Belvedere after a year of standing empty, with the red flags rusting in the holes of the miniature golf course, dead leaves floating on the surface of the swimming pool, weeds growing apace between the flagstones of the terraces, a handful of darts lying forgotten on the window-sill, and the names of the flowers and shrubs obliterated by the weather from the wooden pegs.[32]

George VI had promised his brother the use of Fort Belvedere if he came back to live in Britain, but since the Queen and her supporters were determined that the Windsors should not return,[33] no one bothered to keep the Fort in a state of good repair.

All the time, George and Elizabeth continued to gain prestige. 'Starting at the top – the King and Queen are doing very well,' wrote Lord Dawson of Penn in March 1938. 'They are basing themselves on real work and merit and not on flairs.'[34]

In the public mind, there was already a definite rivalry between Elizabeth and her sister-in-law, Wallis Windsor. This was reflected in the hate mail the Duchess continued to receive. 'One typical example, found torn in half in a waste-paper basket by a servant, was a picture of the new Queen. Underneath was written: "Take a good look at this photo. Do you imagine you could possibly have taken the place of this lady?"'[35]

In May 1938, the Windsors took a lease on the Château de la Cröe at Cap d'Antibes, one of the two houses offered to them for their wedding a year earlier. They moved there for the summer, 'after being ordered by the British Embassy to leave Paris before the State Visit of the King and Queen',[36] which was due to begin on June 28. On June 23, however – the Duke of Windsor's forty-fourth birthday – Queen Elizabeth's mother, the Countess of Strathmore, died in London at the age of seventy-five, and the State Visit to France was postponed for three weeks.

Before it went ahead, Windsor received a letter from his mother, Queen Mary, which gave depressing confirmation of her changed attitude towards him, and of the probable attitude of the rest of the family: 'You ask me in your letter of the 23rd of June to write to you frankly about my true feelings with regard to you and the present position and this I will do now. You will remember how miserable I was when you informed me of your intended marriage and abdication and how I implored you not to do so for our sake and for the sake of the country. You did not seem able to take in any point of view but your own . . . I do not think you have ever realized the shock, which the attitude you took up caused your family and the whole Nation. It seemed inconceivable to those who had made such sacrifices during the war that you, as their King, refused a lesser sacrifice . . . My feelings for you as your Mother remain the same, and our being parted and the cause of it, grieve me beyond words. After all, all my life I have put my country before everything else, and I simply cannot change now.'[37]

The sadness of Lady Strathmore's death indirectly brought about Queen Elizabeth's first international triumph. The Queen did not wish to wear colours so soon after her mother's death, and it was clearly out of the question for her to wear only black throughout the first State Visit of the reign – and to Paris, of all cities, at the height of mid-summer.

'Is not white a royal prerogative of mourning, Your Majesty?' asked the Queen's designer, Norman Hartnell.[38] On receiving an answer in the affirmative, Hartnell, in the incredibly brief space of three weeks, transformed his royal rainbow into dazzling alabaster. Even the Queen's furs were snow or silver.

The effect of this luminous ensemble electrified Paris. Whether in the night-time splendour of the Elysée Palace, in a billowing crinoline of Valenciennes lace, sprinkled with silver; or at the Opera in a satin gown held by clusters of white camellias; or at a garden party on the lawns at Bagatelle in a sweeping picture hat of white osprey, Elizabeth captivated the French. In one moment, while watching the ballet by the lakeside on Ile Enchanté, she opened a parasol of transparent lace and tulle, and 'at a stroke . . . resuscitated the art of the parasol makers of Paris and London'.[39] 'Today France is a monarchy again', proclaimed the Paris headlines. 'We have taken the Queen to our hearts. She rules over two nations.' And the wife of the President, Madame Lebrun, told her royal guest: 'I wish to assure your Majesty that she has won the heart of the whole of Paris.'[40]

For the Duchess of Windsor, relegated to the Riviera, her sister-in-law's spectacular success was a bitter development. In the French capital where Wallis had chosen to make her home, and where, only six months earlier, she had been voted top of the list of the ten best-dressed women in the world, the lady she herself had dubbed 'the Dowdy Duchess' was now being hailed by the Paris press as 'the best-dressed Queen to visit the world's fashion centre'.

During the last engagement of the State Visit, at Villers-Bretonneux, where the King unveiled a memorial to the eleven thousand Australians who fell in France during World War I, the Queen walked forward spontaneously and scattered on the open ground an armful of red poppies picked in the neighbouring fields and handed to her that morning by a French schoolboy. Watching this incident on a newsreel film in Berlin, Adolf Hitler described Queen Elizabeth as 'the most dangerous woman in Europe'.[41] It was an assessment with which the Führer's recent guest, the Duchess of Windsor, was wholly in agreement.

It was already clear that the Duke intended to ignore George VI's ruling on the subject of the Duchess's status. In the summer of 1938, when Dina Wells Hood first visited the Windsors to be interviewed for the post of private secretary, she found the Duke alone. 'He rose to receive my curtsey and bade me be seated in an armchair opposite his own. "Her Royal Highness is out", he said, "but will be back at any moment".'[42]

Colin Davidson, however, who was the Duke's equerry and had been his friend since Osborne days, did not agree with his master over the question of the Duchess's status. 'Though he was devoted to both the Duke and the Duchess he consistently refused to address the Duchess as a royal personage,' recorded Miss Hood. 'He had touched on this point at one of our interviews in London. Though he admitted that regular members of the household must comply with the Duke's wishes, he himself felt strongly that HRH laid himself open to criticism by insisting on the royal title for his wife. He never called the Duchess anything but "Duchess", nor did he bow to her as he did to the Duke.'[43]

But even on the most public occasions, Windsor continued to invest his wife with the royal prefix specifically denied her by the British Court. At the beginning of August 1938, Harold Nicolson met them at a dinner party given by Somerset Maugham at the Villa Mauresque, his home on Cap Ferrat. ' "I am sorry we were a little late", said the Duke, "but Her Royal Highness couldn't drag herself away." He had said it. The three words fell into the circle like three stones into a pool.

Her (gasp) Royal (shudder) Highness (and not one eye dared to meet another).'[44]

Nicolson also dined with the Windsors at the Château de la Cröe. 'The Duchess cannot speak French or German and thus her signs to the servants become wild gestures, and as such noticeable. He sitting opposite is as gay as a cricket and does not seem to notice this ungainly business on the part of his *hausfrau*.'[45]

At the Maugham dinner, however, Nicolson had noted: '. . . it is pathetic the way he is sensitive about her. It was quite clear to me from what she said that she hopes to get back to England. When I asked her why she didn't get a house of her own somewhere, she said "One never knows what may happen. I don't want to spend all my life in exile." '[46]

At the end of that same month of August, the question of 'what may happen', and of the Windsors' possible return to Britain, caused the patient Walter Monckton to visit the King and Queen at Balmoral, where the Prime Minister, Neville Chamberlain, was also among the guests. As soon as the subject of the Windsors arose, the King promptly said that he thought it best for the Queen to participate in the discussion.[47] It was clearly Elizabeth's influence that would predominate on this issue.

' "The Prime Minister", noted Monckton, 'thought that the right course was for the Duke of Windsor to be treated as soon as possible as a younger brother of the King who could take some of the royal functions off his brother's hands. The King himself, though he was not anxious for the Duke to return as early as November 1938 (which was what the Duke wanted) was not fundamentally against the Prime Minister's view. But I think that the Queen felt quite plainly that it was undesirable to give the Duke any effective sphere of work. I felt then, as always, that she naturally thought that she must be on her guard because the Duke of Windsor, to whom the other brothers had always looked up, was an attractive, vital creature who might be the rallying point for any who might be critical of the new King who was less superficially endowed with the arts and graces that please.'[48]

After the King and the Prime Minister had gone off for a discussion about the worsening international situation with Germany, the Queen invited Monckton to walk with her in the grounds, and he became still more aware of Elizabeth's implacable opposition to the Windsors and to any question of their return to Britain. ' "The result of my visit", noted Monckton, "was to give me the difficult task of postponing the Duke's return from November into the New Year." '[49]

In September, the problem of the Windsors was relegated to the background by the international crisis over Germany's threatened invasion of Czechoslovakia, culminating in Chamberlain's third confrontation with Hitler in two weeks, and his hollow temporary triumph at the Munich Conference, from which the British premier believed he had brought back 'Peace with Honour'.

The Queen put a bold face on the crisis, and on September 27, at the launching of the Cunard liner named after her, the *Queen Elizabeth*, she delivered, in a clear and confident voice, a message from the King: 'He bids the people of this country to be of good cheer, in spite of the dark clouds hanging over them and, indeed, over the whole world. He knows well that, as ever before in critical times, they will keep cool heads and brave hearts.'

It was six weeks before the weary Chamberlain could return to the vexed problem of the Duke and Duchess of Windsor. The Prime Minister's next move was to sound out public opinion on a meeting between the Windsors and other members of the Royal Family. The chosen guinea pigs were the Duke and Duchess of Gloucester, who were returning from a safari in Kenya. It was decided that on their way back to England, they should stop off in Paris for one night to see the Windsors.

'It was Neville Chamberlain's idea, not ours', stresses Princess Alice, Duchess of Gloucester. 'The Government were still undecided whether to assign the Duke an official role or not, and before reaching a conclusion they wanted some guidance in the form of public reaction in England to news of our visit.'[50]

On November 11, therefore, the Gloucesters reached Marseilles at six in the morning, and flew on to Paris in the King's scarlet and silver plane, both wearing Flanders poppies, and standing up on board the plane to keep the two-minutes silence for Armistice Day.[51]

They arrived at the Hotel Meurice just after one o'clock in the afternoon, and a street violinist played the National Anthem as they were met by the British Ambassador and his wife, Sir Eric and Lady Phipps, and taken up to the Windsors' third-floor suite. There the Duchess of Gloucester kissed her American sister-in-law, the royal brothers exchanged friendly handshakes, and the four had a leisurely lunch consisting of oysters, Russian fish pie, chicken grill, Moroccan figs, and 1923 vintage Moselle.

In the evening, the Windsors took their guests to dine at Larue's Restaurant in the rue Royal, and the Duchess of Gloucester, who 'did not feel in the least chic, with the red dust of Kenya hardly out of my hair',[52] wore a simple blue dress in marked contrast to the elaborate purple creation worn by Wallis, who had diamond clips in her hair. Not for the first time, Wallis's personal style in dress failed to accord with the carefully understated image of a British royal lady.

The *Daily Mail*'s Paris correspondent, Harold G. Cardozo, felt, 'There was no doubt but that the Duke of Windsor was delighted at seeing his brother again and being able to discuss with him the details of his own possible future journey back to England to see his mother, Queen Mary, and other members of the Royal Family. It is expected here that the visit will be in time for the Christmas festivities at Sandringham.'[53]

This expectation, however, proved to be optimistic. The following day's Court Circular noted that 'the Duke and Duchess of Gloucester have arrived from abroad', but omitted to mention that they had visited the Windsors.[54] On November 14, the Gloucesters lunched with the King and Queen at Buckingham Palace but neither volunteered much 'about the meeting with David', beyond the fact that Wallis's splendid dress had made it rather awkward for the Duchess of Gloucester, who had taken no grand clothes with her on the safari.[55]

The Gloucester visit produced a thumbs-down for the Windsors. As Princess Alice recalled, 'some mention of the meeting did appear in the English papers and a lot of old ladies duly wrote furiously disapproving letters, which I found quite upsetting'.[56]

From the beginning of the Windsor marriage eighteen months earlier, controversy had raged among women in British society as to whether they should or should not curtsey to the Duchess of Windsor. Opinion was almost equally divided. Even some of Wallis's closest friends felt unable to pay her this courtesy. The Hon. Mrs Helen Fitzgerald did not curtsey. Lady Brownlow did not. Mrs Colin Buist did not. Kitty Miller, wife of the American impresario Gilbert Miller, said: 'I didn't – I don't think many Americans did.'[57]

One American, however – Mrs Martin Scanlon, wife of the United States air attaché in Paris – always curtsied. So did Mrs Euan Wallace, wife of the Parliamentary Secretary to the Board of Trade. So did the Hon. Mrs Brinsley Plunket, *née* Aileen Guinness. So did Lady Pierson Dixon. And so, later, did Sir Oswald Mosley's wife, formerly the Hon. Diana Mitford, daughter of Lord Redesdale. 'I always curtsied to the Duchess,' wrote Lady Mosley. 'The Duke wished it I am sure, and if I go to people's houses I should never be uncivil to my host. Apart from that, she was his legal wife, and in the opinion of Walter Monckton and William Jowitt she was in fact a royal highness. She was always called that by friends. English people bowed and curtsied, Americans seldom, other foreigners always. Lady Monckton for example always did (English).'[58]

Dina Wells Hood recalled: 'Among the Windsors' friends, there were of course many who decided the matter for themselves. Quite a number of the ladies dropped curtsies to the Duchess personally. Mrs Scanlon did so when she was staying in the house. When Grace Moore[59] met the Windsors on the Riviera she curtsied obviously and deliberately to the Duchess, to the point that the incident was reported and discussed in the local press. Even visitors from England occasionally made a point of paying this tribute to the Duchess. Lady Diana Cooper did so, and so did Lady Priscilla Willoughby when she and her husband, Sir John Aird, dined with the Windsors in Paris that summer during their honeymoon.'[60]

Diana Cooper, indeed, continued to curtsey, even when she became the wife of the British Ambassador in Paris, thereby inaugurating the custom by which Frenchwomen invariably curtsied to the Duchess of Windsor. Even she had occasional misgivings, however. On November 17, 1938, Chips Channon noted in his diary: 'Diana Cooper rang me early to ask all about the Buckingham Palace party to which they had not been invited. Was it, she wondered, because Duff had resigned, or because she had curtsied to the Duchess in Paris?'[61]

On the occasion in question – a cocktail party given by the Windsors at the Hotel Meurice – Lady Diana had been accompanied by Mrs Euan Wallace. Both had curtsied to the Duchess of Windsor. 'I did it to please the Duke', Mrs Wallace explained later, 'and not for any formal reason. I have been a great friend of the Duchess for a long time, and knew her when she was Mrs Simpson.'[62]

Lady Diana would always give a similar explanation of her reasons for curtseying to Wallis. 'To the ground – deeper than usual,' as she would describe it. 'It was all to please *him*.'[63]

One leading member of British society who was emphatically not in agreement with either lady was the Countess of Pembroke, a Paget by birth, sister of the sixth Marquess of Anglesey, and a staunch friend of Queen Elizabeth, who had often been her guest at Wilton House, Salisbury. At a shooting party given by the Euan Wallaces at Lavington Park in the first weekend of December 1938, 'Bee' Pembroke took Diana Cooper and Barbara Wallace to task in front of their husbands for the social misdemeanour of curtseying to the Duchess of Windsor.

'I asked them why they did this,' said Lady Pembroke, 'as the Duchess is not entitled to it. They told me they did so to please the Duke.

'I told them that personally nothing would induce me to curtsey to the Duchess, as it is not customary in this country to curtsey to any but royal personages. I am afraid my reply rather angered Mr Duff Cooper.'[64]

Her newspaper interview on the subject also angered the Duke of Windsor, who was stung into replying publicly: 'The Duchess and I are less interested in curtsies than courtesies. Lady Pembroke is, of course, an expert on both.'[65]

Compton Mackenzie now took up the cudgels in print: 'How far she is able to reconcile her respect for the technicalities of etiquette with the courtesy she owes as a great lady is a matter for Lady Pembroke's social conscience.

'What is intolerable is that the Duke of Windsor should be exposed to an implied insolence which by any strict interpretation of the laws of etiquette is justified.

'There are two remedies for the present state of affairs. The first and most obvious is to recognize formally that the Duchess of Windsor is HRH the Duchess of Windsor.

'The second is for the Duke of Windsor to renounce his royal rank. Such a step would affect the prestige of royalty, and the first remedy would be at once the more simple and the more popular.'[66]

But royal recognition of the Duchess was as far away as ever, and the Windsors solved the problem in their own fashion – by simply assuming the royal rank of which Wallis had been deprived.

When they moved into their first Paris house, 24 Boulevard Suchet, the Duchess was *Son Altesse Royale* to the servants, and all members of the Windsors' staff were instructed to address her as 'Your Royal Highness', to begin letters to her, 'Madam, may it please Your Royal Highness', and to end, 'I have the honour to be, Madam, Your Royal Highness's devoted and obedient servant'.[67]

The Windsors adopted the royal monogram, 'WE', formed from their initials, for their joint use. And Dina Wells Hood recalled their method of receiving guests at formal receptions at the house in the Boulevard Suchet: 'On reaching the top of the broad stairway each guest was announced by name and moved forward to meet the Duke and Duchess. The men bowed, the ladies curtsied. And as the ducal pair stood close together, the difficult issue of deciding whether or not the Duchess was entitled to this royal prerogative could happily be avoided.'[68]

Queen Elizabeth showed no signs of softening her attitude to her sister-in-law. When someone mentioned to her that the 'Duchess of Windsor had done much' for the Duke, 'stopped him drinking – no more pouches under his eyes', her reply was bitter. 'Yes,' she said, 'who has the lines under his eyes now?'[69]

And the Queen's lady-in-waiting, the Hon. Mrs John Little Gilmour – known as 'Tortor' – who had been a close friend for many years, was startled by Elizabeth's quick anger when she asked her whether the Duchess would accompany the Duke of Windsor if he came to England. 'No, certainly not; wouldn't receive her if she did,' said the Queen-Empress in a tone of blistering sharpness.

Mrs Gilmour, amazed by the royal vehemence she had unintentionally unleashed, ventured hesitantly, 'May I mention this?'

'Certainly,' said the Queen with an air of icy dismissal.[70]

I wouldn't receive her. One month after that vow was uttered by the first lady in the land, a Gallup Poll was taken in Britain to assess whether people would like the Duke and Duchess of Windsor to come back and live in the country. Rather surprisingly, in view of the reaction to the Gloucesters' visit to Paris two months earlier, the result was:

> Yes   – 61 per cent
> No   – 16 per cent
> Don't Know – 23 per cent

The figures were not pleasing to Buckingham Palace, or to the Prime Minister, who had by now recognized that the family obstacles to the Duke's return – principally those created by the resolute opposition and influence of the Queen – were insuperable. On February 22, 1939, Chamberlain wrote to the Duke in Paris to say that so far as the desired homecoming was concerned, 'the time was not yet ripe'.[71]

The Windsors, with their hopes of a constructive plan for the future once more frustrated, began to cast about for projects with which to fill the vacuum at the centre of their lives. They came up with another disastrous idea – again of the sort which Buckingham Palace and Whitehall saw as a calculated attempt to undermine the position of the new King.

With the shadow of war looming ever larger over Europe, the Duke

accepted an invitation from Fred Bate of the National Broadcasting
Company to broadcast an appeal for peace world-wide. The plan was
unfortunate for two reasons. It renewed the impression, already
conveyed by his tour of Germany, that Windsor, after abandoning his
responsibilities in public life, was striving to recapture the spotlight.
Secondly, the broadcast was for an American company, aimed principally at the United States, and made at the very moment when the King
and Queen were about to embark on a crucial State Visit to Canada
and America.

On May 6, George VI and Queen Elizabeth sailed from Portsmouth
on the *Empress of Australia*, and the following day the Windsors
travelled by car to Verdun, where the Duke recorded his broadcast. If
it was not a deliberate attempt to upstage his brother and sister-in-law
and the State Visit, it had all the appearance of being so.

On this occasion, even Windsor's staunch press ally, Lord Beaverbrook, added his voice to the general criticism. 'The decision of the
Duke of Windsor to broadcast to the United States today is to be
regretted', said a leading article in the *Daily Express*. 'The moment is
unhappily chosen. The King is on his way to America. Any word
spoken in the United States at present should come from him. It would
have been better for the Duke to wait. It is reported that the Duke will
make an appeal for peace in his broadcast. Such an appeal would have
been uttered more appropriately after the King's peace mission had
been brought to a conclusion.'[72]

In spite of this rebuke, and others, the broadcast went ahead,
although the BBC refused to relay it in Britain, as did Nazi Germany.

In the course of his appeal for peace, the Duke said: 'For two and a
half years I have deliberately kept out of public affairs and I still
propose to do so.' These words were received with a certain derision in
London, where many felt that self-effacement was the last virtue the
Duke had practised, and the last thing he sought in the future.

The effect of the broadcast on the King and Queen, as they sailed
towards America on a visit requiring the utmost tact and diplomacy,
can be readily imagined. It comes as no surprise to find Marie Belloc
Lowndes recording in her diary at this time: 'The King constantly talks
of his brother: it is as if he can't think of anything else; he seems
haunted by him.'[73]

Haunted was an apt word to describe George VI's sense of being
constantly pursued by this noisy and fractious royal ghost who refused
to fade with dignity into his chosen retirement.

For the Windsors, whose own projected tour of America had been abandoned in a storm of controversy, the triumph of the King and Queen's State Visit must have been galling.

In Canada, where they were received with acclamation, the Governor-General, Lord Tweedsmuir – better known as the novelist, John Buchan – thought the King 'a wonderful mixture . . . of shrewdness, kindliness and humour. As for the Queen, she has a perfect genius for the right kind of publicity . . . For example, when she laid the foundation stone at the new Judicative Buildings I heard the masons talking and realized that some of them were Scots, and she made me take her and the King up to them, and they spent at least ten minutes in Scottish reminiscences, in full view of 70,000 people, who went mad! Then at the unveiling of the War Memorial, where we had some 10,000 veterans, she asked me if it was not possible to get a little closer to them. I suggested that we went right down among them, if they were prepared to take the risk, which they gladly did. It was an amazing sight, for we were simply swallowed up. The faces of the Scotland Yard detectives were things I shall never forget! But the veterans made a perfect bodyguard. It was wonderful to see old fellows weeping, and crying "Ay, man, if Hitler could just see this". The American correspondents were simply staggered. They said that no American President would ever have dared to do that. It was a wonderful example of what true democracy means, and a people's king.'[74]

On June 9, 1939, George VI and Elizabeth arrived at Niagara Falls in the State of New York and became the first reigning King and Queen of England to enter the United States of America. Elizabeth Bowes-Lyon had come to the land where her ancestor, Colonel Augustine Warner, had settled almost three hundred years earlier. From Niagara Falls the Royal Train crossed Wallis Windsor's native Pennsylvania, travelling south-eastward into the Maryland of her Warfield childhood. And in Wallis's home city of Baltimore, where her own intended visit had been the subject of bitter criticism eighteen months earlier, the King and Queen made a brief stop at the State Capitol and received one of the biggest welcomes of the entire tour.

In Washington, named after Elizabeth's other American ancestor, the first President of the United States, three-quarters of a million people lined the streets for their procession to the White House. A negro servant dubbed Elizabeth 'that honeychile Mrs Queen', while a senator on Capitol Hill grasped the King's hand and exclaimed, 'My, you're a great Queen-picker'. One of the next day's headlines proclaimed, "THE BRITISH RE-TAKE WASHINGTON', and observers found that 'Elizabeth was the perfect Queen: eyes a snapping blue, chin tilted confidently . . . fingers raised in a greeting as girlish as it was regal. Her long-handled parasol seemed out of a story book.'[75]

In New York, the enthusiasm for the royal couple was even greater. An incredible four million spectators jammed the Manhattan sidewalks to watch them driving to the World's Fair, where crowds sang 'Rule Britannia!' and 'Land of Hope and Glory'. The diffident King and his 'spell-binding' Queen won over everyone from President and Mrs Roosevelt downwards. Elizabeth was nominated 'Woman of the Year' – 'because, arriving in an aloof and critical country, she completely conquered it and accomplished this conquest by being her natural self'.[76]

When the time came to say goodbye, and the Royal Train pulled slowly out of Hyde Park railroad station, the Roosevelts led the crowds thronging the banks of the Hudson River in singing 'Auld Lang Syne'. Anglo-American friendship had been reforged in a way that was to prove a vital factor in the grim years ahead.

The Queen herself would later say: 'That tour made us! I mean it made us, the King and I. It came at just the right time, particularly for us.'[77] No longer were George VI and Elizabeth the reluctant understudies of Edward VIII. They had achieved an international popularity in their own right. It showed in their behaviour. Arriving back in Britain on June 22, they received a tumultuous welcome on their drive through London. 'The King wore a happy schoolboy grin,' recorded Harold Nicolson. 'The Queen was superb. She really does manage to convey to each individual in the crowd that he or she have had a personal greeting. It is due, I think, to the brilliance of her eyes. But she is in truth one of the most amazing Queens since Cleopatra. We returned to the House with lumps in our throats.'[78]

But the sands of peace were now fast running. On August 22, the announcement of the Nazi–Soviet Pact made a European war inevitable and imminent. At the Château de la Cröe, the Windsors' house guests scattered in all directions, and forty-eight hours later only one – Fruity Metcalfe – remained.

The Duke persisted in his one-man overtures for peace. On August 29, as 'a citizen of the world', he sent a telegram to Hitler, urging him to desist, and another to King Victor Emmanuel III of Italy. Hitler replied, blaming the situation on England, and King Victor Emmanuel answered that Italy was remaining neutral.

At dawn on September 1, Germany invaded Poland, and a few hours later Walter Monckton managed to get through by telephone to the Château de la Cröe to say that the King was prepared to send his private aeroplane to fetch the Windsors on the following day. But what Alastair Forbes would later call the Windsors' 'galloping paranoia'[79] reasserted itself. In a further telephone conversation with Monckton, the Duke instructed him to enquire whether he and the Duchess were to be accommodated at Windsor or another of the royal residences.

Later they told Fruity Metcalfe: ' "We are *not* going – the plane is coming for you . . . tomorrow." I looked at them as if they really *were* mad – Then they started off – "I refuse to go *unless* we are invited to stay at Windsor Castle & the invitation and plane are sent personally by my brother etc." . . . Of course there never was a plane as I knew they'd never send it and of course Walter would have repeated all the rot talked on the phone. If Walter had any sense he shd *never* have repeated one word of this, as it was all temper . . .'[80]

The offer of a royal plane, as Metcalfe rightly assumed, had been abruptly withdrawn, and the former King was therefore still on French soil when Britain declared war on Germany on September 3.

Four days later, after a nightmarish air journey, an exhausted Walter Monckton arrived at Cap d'Antibes in a small, battered Leopard Moth, which looked 'as though the tyres were flat and the plane tied up with string'.[81]

Monckton's news was that the Duke's request for royal accommodation had been flatly refused, and that he and the Duchess would only be permitted to return at all provided he agreed to accept one of two minor posts: Deputy Regional Commissioner to Sir Wyndham Portal in Wales; or Liaison Officer with No. 1 British Military Mission to French GHQ under General Howard-Vyse. Windsor had little alternative but to agree, and undertook to return immediately by any means except air, on account of the Duchess's growing terror of flying.

On the following day, September 8, they set out across France with Fruity Metcalfe, and opinion seemed to be favourable to their return. In London, *The Times*, still edited by one of Windsor's former critics, Geoffrey Dawson, commented: 'No one could dream of the Duke's absence from England at a time in which absence would become intolerable exile, or suppose for a moment that anything would be lacking on the Government's part to speed the fulfilment of his dearest and most urgent wish.'[82]

The *New York Times* echoed this sentiment: 'Even in those quarters where his previous decisions were most sharply denounced it will be agreed that there is only one appropriate place for the Duke of Windsor, and that is with his own people.'[83]

The Windsors reached Cherbourg on September 12, and were met there by Lord Louis Mountbatten, commander of HMS *Kelly*, which was to carry them back to England. They were piped aboard and sailed at four in the afternoon. Towards ten o'clock that evening the *Kelly* nosed its way into a blacked-out Portsmouth Harbour, to the very same quay from which the former King had sailed almost three years earlier. As the *Kelly* came alongside, the jetty lights flashed on, revealing a red carpet and a guard of honour provided solely on the initiative of Winston Churchill as First Lord of the Admiralty. As the Windsors stepped back on to British soil, the guard presented arms and the band of the Royal Marines played the first six bars of the National Anthem.

No member of the Royal Family awaited them, no messenger, no message – not even a royal car. A request for one had been categorically refused by Buckingham Palace.

Only two people stood on the quayside to receive them: Lady Alexandra Metcalfe and Walter Monckton. The Windsors were saved from having to spend the night in a Southsea hotel by Churchill's order to the Commander-in-Chief at Portsmouth, Admiral Sir William James, to offer them hospitality for the night at Admiralty House. While the Admiral and Lady James were being 'very nice . . . almost desperately polite'[84] to her, the officially non-royal Duchess found herself wondering what she and her husband could expect from the country that had cold-shouldered them for three years.

'I wouldn't receive her,' her sister-in-law, the Queen, had declared only nine months earlier. It remained to be seen whether the circumstance of a world war would alter that trenchant resolve.

9

'A WOMAN'S JEALOUSY'

ON SEPTEMBER 12, 1939, the day on which the Duke and Duchess of Windsor returned to Britain after almost three years of exile, a London national newspaper, the *Daily Mirror*, carried a front-page photograph of the Queen of England. It showed Elizabeth being mobbed by delighted crowds during a surprise tour of South London's ARP defences. The relaxed and imperturbable queenly style was on full display, and, in Wallis Windsor's later acid phrase about her sister-in-law on a different occasion, 'her justly famous charm was highly evident'.[1]

The caption beneath the photograph read: 'Her gracious smile has always been infectious, always spontaneous. Today it's an *example* to us all. Now turn to pages 8 and 9, *and smile with them*.'[2]

But while Londoners at war and the newspaper reading public gained reassurance from the Queen's smile, there were two people in the country who signally failed to feel its warmth directed towards them: her brother-in-law and his wife. At Admiralty House, Portsmouth, on the morning after the Windsors' arrival, there was still no word from Buckingham Palace and no suggestion of welcome from any member of the Duke's family.

On the previous day, however, while the Windsors were still *en route* for England, there had been evidence of urgent royal conferences at the Palace.

Queen Mary, at the King's request, had left London directly war was declared, and had withdrawn − with a retinue of fifty-five servants − to Badminton House, the Gloucestershire estate of her nephew-in-law and niece, the Duke and Duchess of Beaufort, where she was to stay throughout the war.

But on the day of the Windsors' arrival, she suddenly returned to London, and was photographed driving, grim-faced and unsmiling, into Buckingham Palace. 'This is the first time Queen Mary has seen the King and Queen since the war started; she came up from the country, and was at the Palace for over an hour and a half.'[3]

The object of her visit was clearly a matter considered too confidential to be entrusted to the telephone. It seems certain that it must have concerned the imminent return of her eldest son and the wife Queen Mary had once dubbed 'an adventuress'. Possibly the old Queen feared that the King might be prevailed upon to receive Wallis, and drove to London to add her influence to that of Queen Elizabeth to ensure that this did not happen.

With the Palace's icy silence unbroken, the Windsors drove from Portsmouth to the Metcalfe's Sussex home, South Hartfield House, near the village of Coleman's Hatch in Ashdown Forest. There they were swiftly tracked down by newspaper reporters who had been informed, on telephoning Buckingham Palace, that officials of the King's household were unaware of the Duke and Duchess's return.[4] The silence continued and became almost tangible. 'I do think the family might have done something,' noted Lady Alexandra Metcalfe in her diary, 'he might not even exist . . .'[5]

When communication of a sort did at last come, it was impersonal and through the mouth of an intermediary, Walter Monckton, who was asked to inform the Duke that the King would receive him – but not the Duchess – for a brief meeting at Buckingham Palace on the afternoon of Thursday, September 14. Behind this development, the message was clear. The war made no difference. The King and Queen would still not receive the Duchess; neither would Queen Mary, the Princess Royal, Princess Marina, or any of the other royal ladies.

'So far as David's family or the Court were concerned', wrote Wallis later, 'I simply did not exist . . . Nothing was ever said. It was simply a case of our being confronted with a barrier of turned backs, rigid and immovable. For the first time I saw David's face set itself into a mask barely concealing his deep-smouldering anger.'[6]

The King received his brother after returning with the Queen from a tour of the London Docks. Elizabeth, although present at Buckingham Palace at the time, did not receive her brother-in-law and had made it abundantly clear that she had no wish to do so. On each of the Duke's subsequent visits to his brother, the Queen was conspicuous by her absence. The late Lord Plunket,[7] one of the Royal Family's favourite courtiers, 'used to say he could always tell when the ex-King was due to call on one of his London stopovers because of the sudden chill in the atmosphere – though nothing was said – and the way in which George VI's wife would "drive out" of Buckingham Palace'.[8]

The meeting between King and ex-King lasted an hour and went smoothly. 'There were no recriminations on either side,' noted George

VI in his diary.[9] On Monckton's advice, the Duke avoided contentious subjects, and Wallis – the most obvious of all – was not mentioned. Neither was the Queen.

Windsor told his brother that of the two war jobs offered, he preferred that of Deputy Regional Commissioner in Wales to the staff liaison post in France, since he doubted that he had sufficient knowledge of the changes in modern warfare to make a success of the latter. The King did not disagree. He said there was no hurry about making a decision. 'Let's see how things go,' he added finally. 'Meanwhile, I'll discuss your ideas with the Government.'[10]

The King wrote to the Prime Minister, Neville Chamberlain, on the same day: 'The whole tone of our meeting was a very friendly one. He seems very well & not a bit worried as to the effect he left on people's minds as to his behaviour in 1936. He has forgotten all about it.'[11]

But others had not forgotten. Before the day was over, George VI had been brought to realize the inconvenience of having his brother underfoot throughout a possibly protracted war. The Queen, in particular, was strongly opposed to the Duke's presence in Britain – partly because she feared he would divert attention and popularity from the King; but chiefly because it would mean having the Duchess on the scene as well, which none of the Royal Family wanted.

By the evening of September 14, the King had changed his mind and decided that there was now only one job to choose from. 'The conclusion reached by His Majesty', wrote Sir Alexander Hardinge to the Secretary of State for War, Leslie Hore-Belisha, 'is that His Royal Highness would be most suitably employed as a member of the Military Mission to France, of which General Howard-Vyse is the head.'[12]

The following day, after a friendly meeting at the Admiralty with Churchill, and a less friendly one at Downing Street with Chamberlain – who showed him a pile of letters 'from people who – well – don't want you back'[13] – the Duke saw Hore-Belisha at the War Office and discovered that the post in Wales for which he had expressed a preference had been abruptly withdrawn overnight by the King without explanation. Windsor was to be assigned to the British Military Mission at Vincennes, was to relinquish his Field-Marshal's baton for the temporary rank of Major-General, and was to report for duty as soon as possible.

The Duke then said that before leaving for France, he wanted to tour the military Commands in Britain and to take the Duchess with him.

Hore-Belisha foresaw immediate problems but said he would see what could be done.

On the following day, September 16, Hore-Belisha recorded in his diary: 'The King sent for me at 11 a.m. He was in a distressed state. He thought that if the Duchess went to the Commands, she might have a hostile reception, particularly in Scotland. He did not want the Duke to go to the Commands in England. He seemed very disturbed and walked up and down the room. He said the Duke had never had any discipline in his life.'[14]

The mention of Scotland was significant. Only three hours later, after lunching with his strong-minded Scottish queen, the King's attitude towards his brother suddenly hardened, and Hore-Belisha, to his astonishment, found himself summoned back to the Palace for the second time – on a Saturday afternoon. 'HM remarked that all his predecessors had succeeded to the throne after their predecessors had died. "Mine is not only alive, but very much so." He thought it better for the Duke to proceed to Paris at once.'[15]

Hore-Belisha returned to the War Office, where he had the embarrassing and delicate task of saying no to the Duke yet again. 'I explained that the troops were moving about, the secrecy involved, and that the Duke's presence would attract attention. It would create an excellent impression with the public, I said, if the Duke showed readiness to take up his appointment at once; that Howard-Vyse was impatiently waiting for him in Paris. The Duke appreciated all the arguments and expressed agreement . . .'[16]

Windsor asked if his brother, the Duke of Gloucester, was being paid for his war service, and was told that no member of the Royal Family ever accepted payment for service in the Army. The Duke then said that he would like the fact that he was not being paid to be announced in the press.[17] No announcement was made. The request was another unfortunate illustration of the ex-King's insatiable appetite for personal publicity and attention – even while his country was at war.

The Windsors remained in England for a further thirteen days while the problems of staff, uniforms and military instructions were resolved. Apart from his one brief interview with the King, no member of his family communicated with him, and Queen Mary expressed no desire to see him.

One afternoon, the Duke and Duchess made a sentimental journey to Fort Belvedere. Wallis recorded: 'The lawn was overgrown; the garden in which we had spent so many happy hours together had become a mass of weeds; and the house itself, shuttered, damp, and dark, was slowly decaying. It was a sad visit.'[18]

The loyal Lady Colefax, somewhat in eclipse since the Abdication, gave a luncheon for them in Lord North Street, at which the historian, G. M. Young, saw the Duke as 'A gentleman; a major in a not quite first class regiment, and not likely to go further than that; happily married to a devoted wife, not his equal but doing her best to live up to him.'[19]

Before their departure, Lady Alexandra Metcalfe recorded: 'Wallis said they realized there was no place ever for him in this country & she saw no reason ever to return. I didn't deny it or do any pressing. They are incapable of truly trusting anybody therefore one feels one's loyalty is misplaced. Their selfishness and self-concentration is terrifying. What I am finding it difficult to put into words is the reason for his only having so few friends. One is so perpetually disappointed.'[20]

On September 29, the Windsors, accompanied by Fruity Metcalfe, sailed from Portsmouth on the destroyer *Express*, and arrived that evening in Cherbourg, where they were met by a party of officers from the Howard-Vyse Mission. The Duchess temporarily took up residence in a Versailles hotel while the Duke proceeded to Mission Headquarters at Vincennes to report to his new commanding officer, Major-General Sir Richard Howard-Vyse.

'I see endless trouble ahead with the job in France', Lady Alexandra Metcalfe had predicted, 'as I don't think he will think it big enough.'[21] In this she was swiftly proved correct. The post of "liaison officer" in France was absurdly nebulous, carrying neither influence nor genuine responsibility. It had been invented for one purpose only: to get the former King out of England as fast as possible. Even the French Military Attaché in London, General Lelong, described the posting as 'a matter of pure expediency. They do not quite know what to do with this encumbering personage, especially in England . . .'[22]

Within one week of Windsor's arrival there was evidence of embarrassment. On October 6, when the Duke called at British GHQ near Arras to visit the British Commander-in-Chief, Lord Gort, the Duke of Gloucester, also a Major-General, and attached to Gort's staff with an equally nebulous post of 'Chief Liaison Officer', tried to avoid him by going to Lille for the day. In view of the family estrangement, Gloucester was 'rather concerned by the approach of the Duke of

Windsor to the British sector'.[23] It was only when Windsor asked
pointedly to see his brother that Gloucester reluctantly showed up.

Twelve days later, the Duke of Gloucester was involved in another
awkward incident concerning the Duke of Windsor. On October 18,
Windsor and Gloucester set out with Gort to tour the British Expedi-
tionary Force. On the boundary between the 1st and 2nd Divisions,
Gloucester wrote to the King, 'things began to go wrong'.[24] The
headquarters guard of the 2nd Coldstreams turned out and presented
arms as Lord Gort, General Sir John Dill, and the two royal brothers –
Windsor unconsciously walking ahead of Gloucester, who now out-
ranked him – went by. '. . . to my horror', Gloucester reported to the
King, 'I saw David taking the salute in spite of the C-in-C & Dill being
present'.[25]

Lord Gort was visibly annoyed and the tour 'turned into something
of a triumph for the Duke of Windsor and therefore, as Prince Henry
and the King obviously saw it, as something of a slight, if an unintentional one, to the King'.[26] Windsor's gesture in returning the salute
had been automatic and unintentional, but once again the impression
was unfortunately conveyed that the former King seemed disposed to
ignore the changes in rank and status brought about by his abdication.

Back at Mission Headquarters in Vincennes, the Duke received a
cold official reprimand for violating military etiquette by taking a
salute technically intended for the Commander-in-Chief and the Duke
of Gloucester. The Duchess considered this 'petty to say the least . . .
we had two wars to deal with – the big and still leisurely war, in which
everybody was caught up, and the little cold war with the Palace, in
which no quarter was given'.[27] In her view, her husband's talents were
being wasted, particularly his 'gift for dealing with troops – the gift of
the common touch and understanding . . . It seemed to me tragic that
this unique gift, humbly proffered, was never really called upon, out of
fear, I judged, that it might once more shine brightly, too brightly.'[28]

A month later, Fruity Metcalfe wrote to his wife: '. . . HRH appears
now to realize that he has no power here & is *not* to have any. It is a
bitter blow but he's taking it.'[29]

On December 4, the King went to France for a six-day tour of the
front, and the Duke of Windsor was advised to keep a low profile
during the royal visit. There was to be no meeting between the
brothers, and the Duchess wrote acidly to her aunt, Bessie Merryman:
'My brother-in-law arrives in France tomorrow, but competition still
exists in the English mind – so one must hide so there is no rivalry. All

very childish except that the biggest men take it seriously. Anyway the Duke can leave the front and spend those days with me so that the cheers are guaranteed.'[30]

On December 30, the Duchess pulled even fewer punches in a letter to Lady Colefax: 'Everything goes on the same here except that even though the Duke wears the uniform the same Palace vendetta goes on making the job difficult and nearly impossible. I have been able to get within the sound of gunfire through joining the French Red Cross automobile section. I need not add that the British had not asked me to help them – so time and money have gone to the French. We are both thoroughly disgusted and fed up in every way but are caught like rats in a trap until the war ends.'[31] Wallis was under no illusion about the source of the 'Palace vendetta' or the identity of the person who had sprung the trap in which she and the Duke felt caught. For every evil that befell them the Duchess blamed her sister-in-law, the Queen.

But Wallis was wailing in a wilderness. The first four months of war had immeasurably strengthened the position of both the King and the Queen. Elizabeth's air of calm assurance had won widespread admiration. And George VI, the hesitation in his speech growing gradually less as time went on, made a profound impact with his first wartime Christmas broadcast by speaking some lines from the poem, 'The Gate of the Year' by Marie Louise Haskins: 'I said to the man who stood at the Gate of the Year, "Give me a light that I may tread safely into the unknown." And he replied, "Go out into the darkness, and put your hand into the Hand of God. That shall be to you better than light, and safer than a known way." '[32]

Aware of the strength of the forces against her, a note of personal defeatism began to creep into Wallis's letters. 'How I long to leave this dying and quarrelsome old lady Europe and come to the New World,' she wrote to Aunt Bessie. And of the war, she added: 'What did it prove twenty years ago? Just a reason for this one. It seems so futile to me ... The Duke does not like his job, too inactive – besides a lot of pressure from the Palace which makes it impossible to do well. Even the war can't stop the family hatred of us.'[33]

The wider conflict served to underline the essential differences in character between the Duchess of Windsor and the Queen. While Wallis spoke of the 'Bore War' and its futility, Elizabeth spoke publicly of 'the proud privilege of serving our country in her hour of need. The call has come and from my heart I thank you ... for the way that you have answered it.'[34] The contrasting attitudes of the sisters-in-law to the crisis explain why Elizabeth was suited to be Queen and Wallis emphatically was not.

The Duke of Windsor made a further brief visit to London on January 21 to report to the Chief of the Imperial General Staff, General Sir Edmund Ironside. Although, on this occasion, the Duchess did not accompany him, the Royal Family, informed in advance of his presence in England, again made no attempt to communicate with him. Without any offer of alternative accommodation, the Duke stayed for three nights in Claridge's Hotel.

A week later, Fruity Metcalfe, having witnessed the reunion between the Windsors, noted: 'It was really delightful to see how pleased he and W. were to get together again. It is *very true* & deep stuff.'[35]

The Duchess was still complaining bitterly about the Duke's treatment by his family. 'The D's job is ridiculous and instead of using him where he might help the cause, due to jealousy which even the death of men can't temper he has a childish job . . .'[36] Several weeks later, she reported: 'We may have to go to London shortly for a few days and I think I will go this time just in case I have forgotten their bad manners. As the French are so well-mannered one might forget!'[37] But the projected visit never took place.

On May 10, 1940, the Germans invaded Holland, Luxembourg and Belgium and began their final assault upon France. On the same day, in London, Winston Churchill succeeded the discredited Neville Chamberlain as Prime Minister of Britain. If the Windsors felt they now had a friend and ally in the seat of power, who might be prepared to intervene in order to improve their own position, they were to be swiftly disappointed. Apart from the fact that Churchill was wholly preoccupied with attempts to shore up the beleaguered Allied cause, and most particularly the crumbling resistance of France, neither the King nor the Queen had favoured him as Chamberlain's successor. Both had preferred the Foreign Secretary, Lord Halifax, who was a personal friend of theirs, but Halifax had declined the premiership.

George VI and Queen Elizabeth regarded Churchill with strong reservations, partly as a result of his opposition to the Munich Pact, which they had supported, but chiefly on account of his championship of Edward VIII at the time of his abdication, and his known friendship with the Windsors subsequently. Less than a year previously, the King had told President Roosevelt that 'only in very exceptional circumstances would he consent to WSC's being made PM'.[38]

George VI's first letter to Churchill as Prime Minister warned him against the appointment of Lord Beaverbrook – another conspicuous supporter of the Duke of Windsor – as Minister of Aircraft Production.[39] Churchill managed to circumvent the royal disapproval in this instance, and Beaverbrook was appointed. But coming to power at last at the age of sixty-five, with an uphill battle of daunting magnitude before him, Churchill was heavily dependent upon the personal support of the King and Queen. While he might successfully disagree with them about a ministerial appointment, he was powerless to influence their decisions concerning members of their own family. In the case of the Windsors, therefore, his hands were now tied.

On May 14, the Germans pierced the French defences near Sedan. Two days later their Panzer divisions reached the Oise. That afternoon the Duke of Windsor burst into the house in Boulevard Suchet, gave his wife two hours to pack, and rushed her out of Paris and southward across a chaotic and panic-stricken France to Biarritz, where he installed her at the Hôtel du Palais. Returning to Paris, the Duke learned that his brother, the Duke of Gloucester, had been winched out of Boulogne on May 19 and flown back to the security of Buckingham Palace in advance of the retreating British Army.

On May 27, as the Germans turned from the coast towards Paris, Fruity Metcalfe, who had loyally remained with Windsor as an unpaid and unofficial ADC, parted from him in the evening in the normal way with the words, 'Good-night, Sir, see you tomorrow.' At 8.30 the following morning, Metcalfe telephoned as usual to the Boulevard Suchet for his daily instructions. He was answered by a servant. When he asked to be put through to the Duke, he received the reply, 'His Royal Highness left for Biarritz at 6.30 this morning.'[40]

Metcalfe was attached to no military mission and was on nobody's pay roll. After twenty years of devoted friendship, the best man at Windsor's wedding and his generous host in England the previous autumn had been abandoned without a word of thanks or warning to find his way home unaided. Metcalfe neither saw nor heard from the Duke for more than six years. When they did meet again, at Windsor's request, in 1946, neither apology nor explanation was forthcoming. The episode was never mentioned. It was a betrayal that Metcalfe's wife never forgot and never entirely forgave.[41]

Of the Duke of Windsor's hasty departure from the French capital, Churchill would later write – although he deleted the sentence from his

final text – 'Already there is a great deal of doubt as to the circumstances in which your Royal Highness left Paris.'[42]

If there was doubt as to the circumstances, there could be none as to
the reason. It was Wallis. After collecting her in Biarritz, the Duke
drove with her to the Château de la Cröe, which they reached on May
29. On the way, they learned that the Belgian king, Leopold III, had
surrendered to the Germans. 'This is the finish,' said the Duke, 'Europe
is lost.'[43]

In London, that same week, Queen Elizabeth was sounding a very
different note from her brother-in-law. While *Operation Dynamo* –
the heroic evacuation of 335,000 Allied troops from Dunkirk – was in
progress, a lady-in-waiting unwisely mentioned rumours of 'panic on
the beaches'. She was instantly made aware of the royal displeasure. 'I
don't believe it,' said the Queen angrily. 'Never say that of the great
British people.'[44]

On June 9, the French Government fled to Tours. Five days later the
Germans entered Paris, and at mid-day on June 19, the Windsors left
the Château de la Cröe and set out by road for the Spanish frontier,
which they crossed at Port Bou at seven o'clock on the evening of
Thursday, June 20. Exhausted by their gruelling and traumatic journey they spent the night in a hotel in Barcelona, and on the following
day the Duke sent a terse telegram to the Foreign Office for the
attention of Churchill: 'Having received no instructions have arrived
in Spain to avoid capture. Proceeding to Madrid. Edward.'[45]

On receipt of this, a Foreign Office memorandum was drafted which
concluded that 'the return of the Duke and Duchess to this country
might raise certain complications. On the other hand if he were to
remain in the Iberian Peninsula he might run a chance of being
captured by the Germans and another set of equally awkward complications would arise . . .'[46]

That same afternoon, the Foreign Secretary, Lord Halifax, drew the
attention of the War Cabinet 'to the fact that the Duke of Windsor was
reported to have arrived in Barcelona'. The Cabinet agreed 'that His
Majesty's Ambassador at Madrid should be instructed to get in touch
with the Duke, to offer him hospitality and assistance, and to ascertain
his wishes'.[47]

On the following day, Churchill telegraphed to the Duke in Madrid
that 'we should like Your Royal Highness to come home as soon as
possible'.[48] At the same time, the Foreign Office notified the British
Ambassador to Spain, Sir Samuel Hoare – an old friend of the Duke's –

that a flying-boat would be sent to Portugal to collect the Windsors, adding: 'Please invite Their Royal Highnesses to proceed to Lisbon.'[49]

This accidental elevation of the Duchess to temporary royal rank brought an immediate reaction from Buckingham Palace. On June 24, Sir Alexander Hardinge, as Principal Private Secretary, sent a written rebuke to the Foreign Office, indicating the King's 'extreme displeasure' that the Duke and Duchess had been referred to as 'Their Royal Highnesses'. 'This appellation was false and utterly impermissible. His Majesty's express wish . . . was that steps be taken to ensure that such an official error never occur again.'[50]

In the meantime, the Windsors had arrived in Madrid, where Hoare had arranged for them to stay at the Ritz Hotel. There he called on them on the evening of their arrival after they had dined in the hotel restaurant in full view of the German Ambassador. Spain was officially neutral, but since the defeat of the French – who had signed an armistice with the Germans on the day before – the Falangist régime had abandoned most appearances of neutrality. Eleven days earlier, Spain had announced that she was 'non-belligerent', as opposed to neutral, and the pro-Nazi faction in Madrid, led by Interior Minister, Ramón Serrano Suñer, was clamouring ceaselessly for entry into the war against the Allies.

The victorious German armies were now advancing towards the Pyrenees. If Spain joined the German cause or was invaded by the Germans, Britain would ultimately lose Gibraltar and control of the Straits, as well as entry into the Mediterranean and access to her vital oil supplies.

The Spanish dictator, Franco, a master of inaction, watched the situation impassively, declining to commit himself to any particular course, largely on account of his knowledge that Spain, only a year after the ending of the ruinous Civil War, lacked the resources for participation in an international conflict. Yet if he became convinced – as many were at this moment – that Britain was on the point of defeat, enforced peace, or being invaded, Franco would be compelled to join the Germans for the sake of survival.

This was the political background to the Windsors' arrival, and this the desperate situation against which their highly questionable behaviour must be judged. Madrid was a hotbed of diplomatic intrigue, with Nazi propagandists intent on persuading the Spanish Government that Britain was disunited, demoralised and virtually defeated. To the Germans, the arrival of the former King of England and his morganatic wife, both pointedly cold-shouldered by the British Government, the Court and the Royal Family, seemed like manna from heaven.

On June 23, the German Ambassador in Madrid, Baron Eberhard von Stohrer, telegraphed Foreign Minister Ribbentrop in Berlin: 'The Spanish Foreign Minister requests advice with regard to the treatment of the Duke and Duchess of Windsor who were to arrive in Madrid today, apparently in order to return to England by way of Lisbon. The Foreign Minister assumed . . . that we might perhaps be interested in detaining the Duke of Windsor here and possibly in establishing contact with him.'[51]

Ribbentrop replied: 'Is it possible in the first place to detain the Duke and Duchess of Windsor for a couple of weeks in Spain before they are granted an exit visa? It would be necessary at all events to be sure it did not appear in any way that the suggestion came from Germany.'[52]

To what extent the Windsors were aware of the dangers confronting them in this situation, or of the inferences that might be drawn from the ambiguities in their conduct, will never be known for certain. Yet it was at this critical moment for his country, when he and his wife were being closely scrutinized by German, Spanish and British agents, that the Duke chose to make a most unbecoming issue of his personal grievances. The next nine days in Madrid, and a subsequent month in Lisbon, demolished any remaining hope of the Windsors overcoming the barriers that had risen against them, and created deeply-held prejudices that were to hinder them both for the rest of their lives.

On his arrival in Madrid, the Duke received Churchill's telegram of June 22, requesting him 'to come home as soon as possible'. On June 24, he replied to it, demanding answers on two points. Would he be given a job in England? And would the Royal Family receive and recognize the Duchess?[53]

Churchill's answer side-stepped both issues. 'It will be better for Your Royal Highness to come to England as arranged, when everything can be considered.'[54] But Windsor would not yield without definite assurances on both points, and Churchill was powerless to give them. For the next forty-eight hours, while Britain fought for her very survival, telegrams rained back and forth between the harassed premier and the stubborn ex-sovereign over the settlement of a private family feud.

Twenty-six years later, the Duke attempted to justify his attitude, recalling that Churchill's 'personal advice to me was not to quibble about terms, but to come home and wait patiently while he "worked things out". But I could not in honour take this line. The year before, while we had been in England, the presence of the Duchess at my side had never been acknowledged, even perfunctorily. Before going back I wanted an assurance that simple courtesies would be forthcoming. Winston could not manage this. From a distance, what I insisted on may look to be of small value. But the perspectives of my life had changed, and the matter loomed mighty large for me.'[55]

The Duchess later also attempted to vindicate his attitude: '. . . in truth, all that he ever specifically asked for was a fairly simple thing: that I be received, just once, by the King, his brother, and the Queen, in order to erase by that single gesture of hospitality the stigma attaching to my never having been received since our marriage by the Royal Family, his family'.[56]

It is depressing to find that not even the passage of many years had enabled the Duke or the Duchess to see this episode in its true context. By digging their toes in and refusing to leave Madrid until assurances of recognition for the Duchess were forthcoming, the Windsors were guilty of a form of blackmail that, in a time of national crisis, bordered on something arguably worse. Although, to give them the benefit of the doubt, they may not have realized the urgency of the need to remove them from a potentially compromising situation, their stubborn procrastination was construed in London as a deliberate and disloyal use of their proximity to the Germans, and vulnerability to capture, as a means of bargaining to achieve their demands.

The moral issue apart, their strategy was lamentable. Pointing this petty personal pistol at the heads of their critics in a time of war merely hardened the opposition to them. It produced further outbursts of rage from the King, and a cold and obstinate contempt from the Queen. She, of all people, would not be forced into receiving anyone if she chose not to do so.[57]

'In the light of past experience,' the Duke telegraphed to Churchill on June 27, 'my wife and myself must not risk finding ourselves once more regarded by the British public as in a different status to other members of my family.'[58]

To this Churchill reacted sharply. 'Your Royal Highness has taken active military rank, and refusal to obey direct orders of competent military authority would create a serious situation. I hope it will not be necessary for such orders to be sent. I most strongly urge immediate compliance with wishes of the Government.'[59]

Churchill submitted this draft to Buckingham Palace, and Sir Alexander Hardinge replied: 'The King thinks that the Prime Minister's telegram would have a very salutary effect.' Hardinge added that he did not see how it was possible for the Duke 'as an ex-King to perform any useful service in this country' but that he might be given 'some appointment on Wavell's staff in Egypt'.[60]

In the meantime, Sir Samuel Hoare telegraphed from Madrid to say that the Duke had now dropped his first condition, about receiving an official post, 'and that it boiled down to both of them being received once only for quite a short meeting by the King and Queen, and notice of this fact appearing in the Court Circular'. All that was at issue, Hoare concluded, was a 'once only' audience of 'a quarter of an hour'.[61]

Churchill appreciated Hoare's reasoning but already knew the family situation to be hopeless. The King, and more especially the Queen, would not receive Wallis for one second, let alone a quarter of an hour.[62]

The Duke of Windsor did not see Churchill's ultimatum until after his departure from Madrid. Although he was still refusing to return to England without assurances about the Duchess, he had agreed to leave for Portugal. He was unable to do so immediately, however, owing to his brother, the Duke of Kent, being in Lisbon as the head of the British delegation to the celebrations commemorating the eight hundredth anniversary of Portuguese independence. The Anglophile Portuguese dictator, Dr Antonio de Salazar, had indicated that 'the presence of the Duke of Windsor at the same time as that of the Duke of Kent would be inconvenient and undesirable for several reasons . . .'[63]

On July 2, Kent departed from Lisbon and the Windsors set out from Madrid. They left behind them in the Spanish capital a damaging legacy of indiscretions with pacifist overtones. Their apologists in later years have always dismissed German accounts of these comments as fabrications. One source that can hardly be described as tainted, however, was the American Ambassador in Madrid, Alexander Weddell, who recorded: 'In a conversation last night . . . the Duke of Windsor declared that the most important thing now to be done was to end the war before thousands more were killed or maimed to save the faces of a few politicians . . . In the past ten years Germany had totally reorganized the order of its society in preparation for this war.

Countries which were unwilling to accept such a reorganization of society and its concomitant sacrifices should direct their policies accordingly and thereby avoid dangerous adventures. He stated that this applied not merely to Europe but to the United States also. The Duchess put the same thing somewhat more directly . . . declaring that France had lost because it was internally diseased and that a country which was not in condition to fight a war should never have declared war.'[64]

These disastrously ill-timed and unfeeling remarks found their way rapidly to London, where they appalled both King and Prime Minister, and outraged the Queen, a passionate Francophile, who, when France fell, had broadcast to French women in their own language as one who had 'always loved France so warmly'. The Queen told them: 'I share your suffering today and feel it . . . A nation defended by such men and loved by such women must sooner or later attain victory.'[65]

When the Windsors arrived in Lisbon on July 3, the British Ambassador, Sir Walford Selby, handed the Duke Churchill's stern telegram sent two days earlier. The Duke was devastated. The clear hint of possible court martial proceedings against him distressed him deeply. Four months later, this blow to his pride still rankled, and in the draft of a letter to Churchill he wrote, 'you threatened me with what amounted to arrest, thus descending to dictator methods in your treatment of your old friend and former King . . .'. In the draft, the Duke had originally written, 'gangster methods', but this had been changed – in the Duchess's handwriting – to 'dictator methods'.[66]

On the evening of the Windsors' arrival in Lisbon, Churchill was received in audience by the King at Buckingham Palace. Later that night, at Downing Street, Churchill told Beaverbrook that the Duke was to be offered an appointment as Governor and Commander-in-Chief of the Bahamas. 'Max, do you think he'll take it?' asked the Prime Minister. 'He'll find it a great relief,' replied Beaverbrook. 'Not half as much as his brother will,' added Churchill.[67]

Eleven days later, the Colonial Secretary, Lord Lloyd, dined with his friend, Sir Ronald Storrs, who noted: 'G [George Lloyd] told me that the Windsor appointment in the Bahamas is the King's own idea, to keep him at all costs out of England.'[68]

In order to explain the Bahamas appointment to the Dominion Governments, Lord Lloyd drafted a telegram to be sent by Churchill, which originally read: 'The activities of the Duke of Windsor on the Continent in recent months have been causing HM and myself grave uneasiness as his inclinations are well known to be pro-Nazi and he may become a centre of intrigue. We regard it as a real danger that he should move freely on the Continent. Even if he were willing to return to this country his presence here would be most embarrassing both to HM and to the Government.'[69]

Churchill regarded this as too drastic, and amended it in his own handwriting to read: 'The position of the Duke of Windsor on the Continent in recent months has been causing His Majesty and His Majesty's Government embarrassment, as, though his loyalties are unimpeachable, there is always a backwash of Nazi intrigue which seeks to make trouble about him. The Continent is now in enemy hands. There are personal and family difficulties about his return to this country.'[70]

The Duke's reaction to Churchill's telegram formally offering him the appointment was to observe that the Bahamas were 'one of the few parts of the Empire I missed on my travels. It's a small governorship and three thousand miles from the war.'[71] The point was not lost on the Duchess, who immediately christened the posting 'The St Helena of 1940.'[72] The Duke nevertheless cabled back to Churchill: 'I will accept appointment as Governor of the Bahamas as I am sure you have done your best for me in a difficult situation.'[73]

Lord Halifax, a firm friend of the Queen, wrote to Sir Samuel Hoare: 'I dare say it is quite a good plan that they should go to the Bahamas, but I am sorry for the Bahamas . . .'[74]

Public reaction to the news of the appointment was favourable, however, but disquieting rumours were already filtering through to London concerning the Duchess of Windsor's reported conversations and activities in Lisbon. 'As I told you once before,' wrote Sir Alexander Hardinge from Buckingham Palace to Churchill's aide, Eric Seal, at Downing Street, 'this is not the first time that this lady has come under suspicion for her anti-British activities and as long as we never forget the power that she can exert over him in her efforts to avenge herself on this country we shall be all right.'[75]

The day after Hardinge wrote this bitter indictment, the Queen met Harold Nicolson at a lunch party and spoke of 'personal patriotism. That is what keeps us going. I should die if I had to leave.' Nicolson expressed surprise to learn that Elizabeth was practising every day in the grounds of Buckingham Palace with a .303 rifle and a .38 revolver. 'Yes,' she said, 'I shall not go down like the others' – presumably a reference to the royal families of Belgium, Denmark and Luxembourg, who had become prisoners of the Germans. If Hitler invaded Britain, as many assumed he would, the Queen planned to go down fighting, with a gun in her hand. 'I cannot tell you how superb she was,' Nicolson wrote to his wife. 'I anticipated her charm. What astonished me is how the King is changed. He is now like his brother. He was so gay and she so calm. They did me all the good in the world . . . *We shall win*. I know that. I have no doubts at all.'[76]

Not everyone shared Nicolson's confidence. Following the fall of France, panic had set in among certain people in Britain. There was a dangerous defeatism in the air, and a surreptitious but steady exodus of wealthy socialites with homes or resources in the United States. Awareness of this certainly lay behind the Queen's stout patriotic pronouncements and Hardinge's contemptuous outburst concerning Wallis.

The American Ambassador in London, Joseph Kennedy, father of the future President, was making no secret of his belief that Britain was doomed. At an Embassy dinner party one evening, he told the Scottish-born beauty Mrs Charles Sweeny: 'This country is finished. It will be overrun by the Germans in a matter of weeks. All the roads will then be blocked with refugees, just as they are now in France. You and your children must get out. As the wife of an American you would be crazy to stay here.'

Margaret Sweeny – later the Duchess of Argyll – was disgusted. 'This country will never be finished', she told him, 'and I have no intention of leaving'.[77] She was as good as her word. She stayed put in the Dorchester Hotel throughout the Blitz, and her refusal to leave London influenced many of the waverers.

In Lisbon, the Windsors continued to display a total disregard for the fact that their movements were being carefully watched and their conversations reported back to London. Both persisted in expressing views that seemed anti-British. To her aunt, the Duchess complained of the Duke suffering 'one humiliation after another . . . Can you fancy a family continuing a feud when the very Empire is threatened and not putting every available man in a spot where he would be most useful? Could anything be so small and hideous? What will happen to a country which allows such behaviour?'[78]

On July 11, the German Ambassador in Lisbon, Baron Oswald von Hoyningen-Huene, reported to Berlin: '. . . the designation of the Duke as Governor of the Bahama Islands is intended to keep him far away from England, since his return would bring with it very strong encouragement to English friends of peace, so that his arrest at the instance of his opponents would certainly have to be expected. The Duke intends to postpone his departure for the Bahama Islands as long as possible, at least until the beginning of August, in hope of a turn of events favourable to him. He is convinced that if he had remained on the throne war would have been avoided, and he characterizes himself as a firm supporter of peaceful arrangement with Germany. The Duke definitely believes that continued severe bombings would make England ready for peace.'[79]

From Berlin, Ribbentrop sent a copy of Huene's report to the German Ambassador in Madrid, Baron von Stohrer, urging that the Windsors should be invited back to Spain on some plausible pretext, 'persuaded or forced to remain on Spanish soil', and 'informed at the appropriate time in Spain that Germany on her side wishes for peace with the British people, that the Churchill clique is standing in the way of this, and that it would be a good thing if the Duke were to hold himself in readiness for further developments. Germany is determined to force England to peace by every means of power and upon this happening would be prepared to accommodate any desire expressed by the Duke, especially with a view to the assumption of the English throne by the Duke and Duchess. If the Duke should have other plans, but be prepared to co-operate in the establishment of good relations between Germany and England, we would likewise be prepared to assure him and his wife of a subsistence which would permit him, either as a private citizen or in some other position, to lead a life suitable for a king.'[80]

Meanwhile trouble had arisen over the Windsors' travel plans. The Foreign Office was 'strongly opposed to allowing the Duke of Windsor to go to New York, which he apparently wishes to do, on his way to Nassau'.[81] The British Ambassador in Washington, Lord Lothian, was equally opposed, and felt that the publicity generated by a visit by the Windsors to New York 'will be of an icy character.'[82] On July 18, the Duke telegraphed angrily to Churchill: 'Have been messed about quite long enough and detect in Colonial Office attitude very same hands at work as in my last job. Strongly urge you to support arrangements I have made as otherwise will have to reconsider my position.'[83]

There was also 'trouble about two men-servants whom the Duke wishes to take with him and who are of military age ... Lord Lloyd expressed the hope that he would not press for these two men, and quoted the precedent of Lord Athlone who had agreed not to take men of military age to Canada.'[84]

The Duchess, furious at the order to avoid New York, protested by telegram at the 'obstacles' being put in her husband's way.[85]

By now, patience with the Windsors was wearing extremely thin. Lord Lloyd saw the King, 'whose line was "tell him to do what he is told".'[86]

Over the two servants, Sir Alan Lascelles and Sir Walter Monckton both agreed that 'HRH has to be treated as a petulant baby, and that there was a by no means remote possibility that he was prepared to face a break on this subject, and that he was unable to appreciate how ludicrous the affair would appear when made public'.[87] In the end, Churchill persuaded the War Office to release one of the two servants the Duke wanted in the Bahamas, but remained adamant about New York. On July 23, he cabled: 'His Majesty's Government cannot agree to Your Royal Highness landing in the United States at this juncture. This decision must be accepted. It should be possible to arrange, if necessary, for the Duchess either to proceed from Bermuda to New York for medical reasons, or, alternatively, it will always be easy for her to go there from Nassau by sea or land.'[88]

The Windsors grudgingly accepted this as final, but during their last week in Lisbon, there was evidence of further indiscretion on their part. Through Miguel Primo de Rivera, Marqués de Estella, a Spanish friend of the Duke, and with the help of the Windsors' host in Portugal, the banker Dr Ricardo de Espirito Santo e Silva, the Germans made indirect contact with the Duke and Duchess.

On July 25, Baron von Stohrer reported to Berlin from Madrid that Primo de Rivera had returned from Lisbon: 'He had two long conversations with the Duke of Windsor; at the last one the Duchess was present also. The Duke expressed himself very freely. In Portugal he felt almost like a prisoner. He was surrounded by agents, etc. Politically he was more and more distant from the King and the present English government. The Duke and Duchess have less fear of the King, who was a complete nincompoop ('reichlich töricht'), than of the shrewd Queen who was intriguing skilfully against the Duke and particularly against the Duchess. The Duke was considering making a public statement and thereby disavowing present English policy and breaking with his brother.'[89]

In a second account, Baron von Stohrer recorded that when Primo de Rivera 'gave the Duke the advice not to go to the Bahamas, but to return to Spain, since the Duke was likely yet to be called upon to play an important role in English policy and possibly to ascend the English throne, both the Duke and Duchess gave evidence of astonishment. Both appeared to be completely enmeshed in conventional ways of thinking, for they replied that according to the English constitution this would not be possible after the Abdication. When the confidential emissary then explained his expectation that the course of the war might bring about changes even in the English constitution, the Duchess especially became very pensive.'[90]

Since the man to whom they were speaking, Miguel Primo de Rivera, was the son of the former Spanish dictator and leader of the Madrid Falangists – the official Fascist Party of Spain – the Windsors must have been well aware that their attitudes and comments stood every chance of being reported to the Germans. What view can be taken of their chronic indiscretions in such circumstances?

Forty years later, the Windsors' ultimate apologist – their Paris attorney, Maître Suzanne Blum – was questioned about their alleged pro-German sympathies. The visit to Hitler in 1937? 'But *everybody* stayed with Hitler' replied Maître Blum. Contact with enemy agents during the war? 'The documents are forged,' she claimed. 'But the documents are published officially on behalf of the Foreign Office!' responded the interviewer, David Pryce-Jones. 'Foolishness,' exlaimed Maître Blum. 'Deception.'[91]

But whose deception is it? The accounts of the conversations with Primo de Rivera were among the German Foreign Office documents captured by the British in 1945. Were they forged by the Germans five years earlier in the expectation of losing the war so that a distorted impression of the Windsors might fall into British hands? Or does Maître Blum suggest they were forged by the British?

They were only too clearly not forged at all. One does not need to rely solely on German accounts for evidence of the Windsors' indiscretions in Madrid and Lisbon. That these were fully known in London at the time is attested by a letter which Churchill wrote to the Duke of Windsor on July 27: 'Even while you have been staying at Lisbon, conversations have been reported by telegraph through various channels which might have been used to your Royal Highness's disadvantage.'[92]

Assuming that Primo de Rivera's account is based on what the Windsors actually said, what of their allegations against 'the shrewd Queen'? *Was* Elizabeth 'intriguing skilfully against the Duke and particularly against the Duchess'? Lady Hardinge, one of the Queen's closest friends, denied this. 'I think that no one – excepting the Windsors – considered Queen Elizabeth to be the person who blocked the Duchess's path.' This was only 'what *they* thought'.[93]

Maître Blum's assistant, on the other hand, the British barrister and historian, Michael Bloch – who was given free access to the Windsors' archives – claims to have discovered evidence of Queen Elizabeth's intrigues against the Duke and Duchess, but declines to say what it is. 'The inside people with whom *I* had off-the-record conversations', he added, 'seemed to have little doubt that things would have been different for the Duke and Duchess of Windsor but for Queen Elizabeth's attitude.'[94]

On the day before they left Lisbon, the Duke wrote to Churchill: 'I naturally do not consider my appointment as one of first-class importance, nor would you expect me to. On the other hand, since it is evident that the King and Queen do not wish to bring our family differences to an end, without which I could not accept a post in Great Britain, it is at least a temporary solution to the problem of my employment in this time of war.'[95]

On the following day, August 1, at three o'clock in the afternoon, to the great relief of the British Government, the Windsors sailed from Lisbon on the American liner, SS *Excalibur*.

Their departure was not quite the end of the mischief that had surrounded them. On the day afterwards, August 2, the German Ambassador in Lisbon, Baron von Hoyningen-Huene, reported to Berlin that he had conferred with 'our confidant the Duke's host, the banker Ricardo Espirito Santo Silva . . . he visited me at my residence, where we discussed thoroughly possible further courses of action . . . The Duke paid tribute to the Führer's desire for peace, which was in complete agreement with his own point of view. He was firmly convinced that if he had been King it would never have come to war. To the appeal made to him to co-operate at a suitable time in the establishment of peace, he agreed gladly . . . He would remain in continuing communication with his previous host and had agreed with him upon a code word, upon receiving which he would immediately come back over. He insisted that this would be possible at any time, since he had forseen all eventualities and had already initiated the necessary arrangements.'[96]

On August 9, the Windsors arrived in Bermuda, where they stayed for six days. On August 15, the day they left for Nassau, Baron von

Hoyningen-Huene again wired Berlin from Lisbon: 'The confidant has just received a telegram from the Duke from Bermuda, asking him to send a communication as soon as action was advisable. Should any answer be made?'[97]

No reply to this telegram was found in the captured German documents. This is scarcely surprising. By the time it was sent, the Battle of Britain was raging in the skies above London, and on August 15, 180 of the Luftwaffe's fighters were shot down. Hitler at last recognized that Britain would never capitulate or enter into an arranged peace. A quisling King was no longer necessary. Eight days later the blitz on London began.

The behaviour of the Windsors in Madrid and Lisbon had seriously compromised them both, even in the eyes of erstwhile admirers such as Churchill. That summer, the Prime Minister discussed them with his predecessor, Lord Baldwin. Churchill admitted to Baldwin that he had been wrong about the Abdication and added that the prospect of Wallis Simpson as Queen 'was an eventuality too horrible to contemplate'.[98] He admitted the same thing to Lord Beaverbrook, when the latter mentioned the Abdication. 'Perhaps we were both wrong that time,' said Churchill.[99]

On his way to the Bahamas, the Duke of Windsor was comforted by only one thought. The wife of a British Governor had a settled status with which nothing could interfere. But already in Bermuda, the ambiguity of the Duchess's own status caused difficulty. The wife of the Governor of Bermuda 'endured the usual embarrassment of feeling unable to curtsey to the Duchess even though aware that it would make the Duke happy if she did',[100] and the Duke was incensed to discover that the Secretary of State for the Colonies, Lord Lloyd, had sent unsolicited instructions to Bermuda explaining how they were to be treated. The Duchess, he ruled, was to be addressed as 'Your Grace' and was not entitled to any form of curtsey. The Duke immediately overruled this, insisting that his wife was to be addressed as 'Duchess'.[101] 'I don't know,' he added, 'whether we will be able to stick it down in Nassau if this sort of thing is going on all the time.'[102]

There can be little doubt of the sense of horror felt by both the Windsors, although carefully concealed, on their arrival in Nassau on August 17, with the sweltering summer heat at its most intense, the land crabs scuttling creepily along the pavements, and the termite-riddled Government House judged by the Duke 'impossible to occupy . . . in its present condition and it will take at least two months to make it habitable'.[103] Small wonder that the Duke was alone in church on the following morning, and that the Duchess was conspicuous by her absence from the service.

Within one week, the Duke had proposed leaving the island to go to the ranch he owned in Canada while the repairs to Government House were carried out, and when this suggestion was vetoed by Lord Lloyd for its obvious unsuitability, the Windsors borrowed houses first from Mr and Mrs Frederick Sigrist and then from Sir Harry and Lady Oakes.

The Duchess caused some offence among the local colonial ladies by removing from the walls of Government House the portraits of the Duke's ancestors, Queen Victoria and George IV, and by flying in a New York decorator to match the new colour scheme to the shade of her powder puff.

Two days after their arrival, the Duke discovered a telegram sent from Buckingham Palace more than three weeks earlier by the Lord Chamberlain for the guidance of Government House officials: 'You are no doubt aware that a lady when presented to HRH the Duke of Windsor should make a half-curtsey. The Duchess of Windsor is not entitled to this. The Duke should be addressed as "Your Royal Highness" and the Duchess as "Your Grace". Ends.'[104]

At the Windsors' first social appearance in the Bahamas – at the exclusive Emerald Beach Club in Nassau – the acknowledged leader of local society, Lady Williams-Taylor, did not curtsey to the Duchess, and her husband, Sir Frederick, an elderly Canadian millionaire who was president of the club, pointedly omitted any reference to Wallis in his speech of welcome. On rising to reply, the Duke gave a crushing illustration of public royal displeasure. In the original text of the speech, he said, which had been submitted to him before dinner, the welcome had included the Duchess. The fact that she was not mentioned in the spoken version was doubtless due to the dim light at the speaker's table. He felt sure that this would never happen again. 'Emerald Beach guests said that while the Duke was having his say was the most magnificently embarrassing moment of their lives . . . Later the Duchess started to rise with the rest of the guests. "You don't have to stand up for me, darling," the Duke domestically advised her. "It's a pleasure to stand up for you, darling," she countered with double meaning.'[105]

While the Windsors were coping with their personal blitz, the King and Queen, in London, were dealing with the real one. On September

13, Buckingham Palace received a direct hit. Six bombs fell in all, one destroying the Chapel, another blowing in the windows of the room in which George VI and his wife were sitting. Had those windows been closed instead of open, both of them would have been horribly injured, if not killed, by flying glass. Queen Elizabeth's reaction to this became one of the clarion cries of British defiance. 'I'm almost comforted that we've been hit,' she wrote to a friend. 'It makes me feel I can look the blitzed East End in the face.'[106]

It was her unflinching example throughout the years of the war that won Elizabeth an unassailable place in the affections of the British people. Her behaviour also made a deep impression on Americans. It was one of Wallis Windsor's fellow countrywomen, a Chicago housewife called Mary Winter, who gave voice to this in a poem, 'Tribute to a Queen':

> Be it said to your renown
> That you wore your gayest gown,
> Your bravest smile, and stayed in town
> When London Bridge was falling down,
> My Fair Lady!

On one occasion, as the King and Queen walked among the ruins resulting from the German bombardment, a man called out 'Thank God for a good King', and George VI at once replied, 'Thank God for a good people.'[107] After one heavy air raid, the Queen knelt in the rubble to coax a terrified dog out of the hole in which he was cowering. On another occasion, she took a baby from a mother whose arm had been injured by falling debris and finished dressing the child herself. One eye-witness retained a vivid memory of a group of Cockney women crowding around the Queen and shouting to each other 'Ain't she lovely? Ain't she just *bloody* lovely!'[108]

When Elizabeth was asked tactfully whether she thought it was quite appropriate for her 'to wear her best dress' when visiting bomb-stricken areas, she replied simply, 'Of course. They would wear their best dresses if they were coming to see me.'[109] In answer to repeated agitation that Princess Elizabeth and Princess Margaret ought to be sent to safety in Canada, the Queen responded: 'The children won't leave without me, I won't leave without the King; and the King will never leave.'[110]

But Elizabeth's unfaltering smile was often the product of stern self-control. Behind it lay strain and emotion. 'I feel quite exhausted after seeing & hearing so much sadness, sorrow, heroism and magnificent spirit,' she wrote to Queen Mary. 'The destruction is so awful, & the people so *wonderful* – they *deserve* a better world.'[111]

In an air-raid shelter, Elizabeth took cover with President Roosevelt's personal representative, Harry Hopkins, who recorded: 'The Queen told me that she found it extremely difficult to find words to express her feeling towards the people of Britain in these days. She thought their actions were magnificent and that victory in the long run was sure, but that the one thing that counted was the morale and determination of the great mass of the British people.'[112]

In Nassau, meanwhile, the Duchess of Windsor was writing, less than a month after her arrival: 'I hate this place more each day.'[113] Three weeks later it had become 'this dump'.[114] In her next letter, she observed: 'One might as well be in London with all the bombs and excitement and not buried alive here.'[115] And a month after that: 'We both hate it and the locals are petty-minded, the visitors common and uninteresting.'[116]

At the beginning of October, when the American newspaper columnist, Adela Rogers St Johns, arrived in Nassau to write a series about the Windsors, it became clear that the Duchess was still heaping open derision on her sister-in-law, the Queen. Mrs St Johns told the Duke's Comptroller, Major Gray Phillips: 'In my first hour alone with the Duchess, in that office where you took me, I had quotes from her that would have rocked the British Empire . . . You must have heard her opinion of the present Queen of England – the "Dowdy Duchess". Her witty and amusing speculations about the family life of the Royal Family. She is not discreet, Major Phillips.'[117]

In the series that resulted from this week of interviews – *The Windsors' Own Love Story* – Wallis was quoted as saying: 'How can you expect me to wish him to stay here? . . . I, too, wish us to do our duty. But is there scope here for his great gifts, his inspiration, his long training? I am only a woman, but I am his wife, and I do not believe that in Nassau he is serving the Empire as importantly as he might.' The British Ambassador in Washington, Lord Lothian, was horrified to read these comments in print and reported them immediately to Whitehall, where the Windsors' stock sank still lower.

The King had already learned, without amusement, of Wallis's habit of crossing out the heading, Government House, on official stationery and substituting the word, 'Elba'. Of the Governor's residence itself,

Wallis told her aunt, 'we are going to dish this shack up so that at least one isn't ashamed of asking the local horrors here'.[118]

It was evident that the Duke of Windsor had begun to join his wife in denigration of the Queen, for he wrote of 'the mean and petty humiliations in which a now semi-Royal Family with the co-operation of the Government has indulged itself for the last four years'.[119]

At Windsor Castle on an evening in February 1941, Elizabeth was the recipient of a different sort of attack. As the Queen entered her bedroom, a man sprang out at her from behind a curtain and seized her round the ankles. 'For a moment,' she confessed later, 'my heart stood absolutely still', but she remained calm and said quietly, 'Tell me about it.' As the intruder – a half-crazed deserter whose family had all been killed in the raids – poured out his tale of misery, Elizabeth moved slowly across the room until she was within reach of the bell. She continued to listen to the man's account for ten minutes, and afterwards admitted that she had felt deeply sorry for him. As in the case of the Abdication, however, her sympathy was secondary to her absolute disapproval of any dereliction of duty. The man had deserted his post and let down his country. Nothing could ever excuse such an action and she berated the intruder in trenchant terms.

'During her lecture the word "parasite" cropped up from time to time. "And now I will ring the bell and have you turned over to the castle guard," she said finally. "I advise you to serve your punishment like a man, and then serve your country like one." '[120]

On March 27, the Windsors set out in the yacht, Rene, for a tour of the Out Islands of the Bahamas, stopping briefly at Crooked Island, Long Island, Cat Island and Abaco, 'each one worse than the last in dreariness', in the view of the Duchess, who believed that their imprisonment in this stagnant backwater was 'all because of a woman's jealousy and a country's fear his brother wouldn't shine if he was there!'.[121]

A woman's jealousy. There were, of course, no prizes for guessing who the woman was, but what sort of jealousy was it that Wallis attributed to her sister-in-law, the Queen?

Maître Blum's assistant, Michael Bloch, clearly believes, after having unrestricted access to the Windsors' personal archives, that it was not jealousy of the Duke but of the Duchess, for having married him. 'A story which I believe the Duke repeated to his friends, and which strikes me as not improbable, is that Lady Elizabeth Bowes-Lyon had been regarded as a possible bride for the Prince of Wales; that he had spurned the idea categorically; and that she consequently bore some kind of resentment against him.'[122]

This rumour had been around for many years in the context of backstairs second-hand gossip. There was even a grain of truth in part of it, in as much as King George V and Queen Mary had both said privately that Elizabeth was the sort of girl they wished the Prince of Wales would marry. She had never been regarded as a possible bride for him, however, since by the time the King and Queen came to know her at all well, she was already being courted by their *second* son.

The Dowager Lady Hardinge of Penshurst, one of the Queen Mother's lifelong friends, laughed merrily when I put the idea to her. 'That's really too absurd,' she said. 'She is one of my oldest and dearest friends, and I was with her a great deal at that stage of her life. What you have to understand is that Lady Elizabeth Bowes-Lyon had very exacting standards of fidelity even then. There were quite a number of people who wanted to marry her, including the son of one neighbouring family in Scotland. I will not give this man's name, but she was quite attached to him. During his courtship of her, however, it became known that he had flirtations on the side, and that was something she wouldn't put up with. The idea that she would *ever* have considered marriage with the Prince of Wales, who had already been involved with two married women, is simply out of the question. He would never have measured up to her standards in any way at all, morally, or in terms of character. Besides, if she had ever thought there was a serious prospect of her becoming Queen, I very much doubt if she would even have married the Duke of York, devoted as she was to him.'[123]

The Duke of Windsor continued to deplore the war and to express doubts over England's ability to win it. 'The outlook for the world gets blacker and blacker,' he wrote to his wife's aunt, 'and I can see no ending to it all let alone a victorious one. The whole of mankind is going to suffer bitterly for the folly of this conflict, and one can only thank God that one is not of those who are responsible for its prosecution.'[124]

A month later, on August 5, 1941, the German Ambassador in Lisbon, Baron von Hoyningen-Huene, sent a telegram to the Foreign Office in Berlin which confirmed that the Duke was still in contact with his Nazi-sympathizing host in Portugal, Dr Ricardo de Espirito Santo e Silva: 'The intermediary familiar to us from the reports at the time has received a letter from the Duke of Windsor confirming his opinion as recently stated in a published interview that Britain has virtually lost the war already and the USA would be better advised to promote peace, not war.'[125]

The interview referred to was presumably one with an American journalist, Fulton Oursler, of the influential magazine, *Liberty*,[126] which earned the Duke a rebuke from Churchill, who telegraphed that 'the language, whatever was meant, will certainly be interpreted as defeatist and pro-Nazi, and by implication approving of the isolationist aim to keep America out of the war . . . I must say it seems to me that the views attributed to your Royal Highness have been unfortunately expressed . . . I could wish, indeed, that your Royal Highness would seek advice before making public statements of this kind.'[127]

The Windsors had been permitted a brief visit to Miami the previous December in order for the Duchess to undergo a dental operation. Now they were at last given permission for an extended visit to the United States, provided it did not clash with the Duke of Kent's presence in Canada and Washington during the first week of September. 'That family of my husband's is always going to snub me', Wallis wrote to her aunt, 'so one has to face up to the fact, and face up to these humiliating situations which will forever give the American press a chance to belittle us . . . I do not mind having to wait until Kent has had his fling, but I do resent their attitude most heartily.'[128] Two weeks later she reported: '. . . we have been advised to stay in a hotel rather than in a private house or on Long Island . . . There seem to be too many jealousies awakened the other way . . . The world is funny – but not so funny as England's royal family . . .'[129]

Lord Halifax, who had become British Ambassador on the death of Lord Lothian the previous December, was absent from Washington when the Windsors arrived there on September 25, and the Chargé d'Affaires was not present at Union Station to greet them. The small group of minor officials from the British Embassy remained on the upper level of the station until the moment the train arrived, and only then came down to meet it. One Washington reporter found it 'a sad show to watch . . . British and American officials giving the brush-off to a man who, with all the weaknesses one may accuse him of, was still a king once . . .'[130] The Embassy provided morning cocktails, an occasion on which Edwina Mountbatten and Diana Cooper both curtsied to the Duchess, but Edwina d'Erlanger did not, on the grounds that Wallis was simply an American like herself.

On October 13, the Duchess at last got her triumphant homecoming to Baltimore, where she and the Duke drove with the Mayor through large, excited crowds to a civic reception, and four days later they were back in Washington for lunch with the British Ambassador and his wife.

Halifax, the friend of Queen Elizabeth, had only met the Duchess briefly once before. He now admitted to being 'impressed with her general dignity and behaviour and . . . adroit good manners' but he was 'still left puzzled as to how he could have found her charm so overwhelming as to give up kingship and emperorship for it . . . She conversed quite easily . . . and never said anything that had any east wind in it – again a mark of wisdom.'[131]

The Windsors were cordially received at the White House for lunch with the President and Mrs Roosevelt, but the British Press Service Report of their American visit reached a crushingly unfavourable conclusion: 'The general impression created was that of a rich and carefree couple, travelling with all the pre-war accoutrement of royalty, and with no thought either of the suffering of their own people or of the fact that the world is at war.'[132]

In December, the bombing of Pearl Harbor at last brought America into the conflict. On January 14, 1942, one of the Windsors' closest friends in the Bahamas, the Swedish millionaire industrialist Axel Wenner-Gren – in whose yacht, the *Southern Cross*, the Duke and Duchess had made their first brief visit to Miami in December 1940 – was placed on the American State Department's 'Proclaimed List of Blocked Nationals'.

President Roosevelt's personal emissary, Harry Hopkins, 'said that the Duke's entourage was very bad. Moreover HRH's recent yachting trip with a violently pro-Nazi Swede did not create a very good impression. It was the astounding success of the King and Queen's visit to the US which had made America give up its partizanship of the Windsors.'[133] After being told this by Hopkins, Churchill had warned the Duke of Windsor about Wenner-Gren: 'This gentleman is, according to the reports I have received, regarded as a pro-German international financier, with strong leanings towards appeasement, and suspected of being in communication with the enemy. Your Royal Highness may not, perhaps, realize the intensity of feeling in the United States about people of this kind and the offence which is given to the Administration when any countenance is given to them.'[134]

Wallis, meanwhile, continued to deride their posting – 'this double-zero job', as she described it to the Countess of Sefton.[135] Three months later, she wrote: 'I really do wish we could move somewhere inhabited at least by our own class. These awful people day in and day out — it is as though you associated with the shop owners of Washington'.[136] Nassau, to her, was 'this moron paradise'.[137]

The Windsors' reservations were not merely social. The Duke, regrettably, made no secret of his unbecoming prejudices in the matter of colour. He later admitted to his astonished cousin, Lord Mountbatten, that during his Governorship black men were not permitted to enter Government House by the front door. And when a liaison officer was needed by the American contractors building airfields in the Bahamas, the Duke vetoed the obvious candidate, Harry Clinton, declaring, 'We can't have a coloured man for this job. We must have a white man.' At his insistence the job was given to a white, Karl Claridge, and not long afterwards thousands of angry Bahamians rose up in Nassau's first riot.[138]

In April 1942, the Duchess decided 'to make one last try', without telling the Duke, 'to reach his mother and to heal the breach between them'.[139] Addressing her mother-in-law formally as 'Madam', the Duchess wrote: 'I hope you will forgive my intrusion upon your time as well as my boldness in addressing Your Majesty. My motive for the latter is a simple one. It has always been a source of sorrow and regret to me that I have been the cause of any separation that exists between mother and son and I can't help feeling that there must be moments perhaps, however fleeting they may be, when you wonder how David is. The Bishop of Nassau is leaving in a short time for England, having been appointed by the Archbishop of Canterbury, Dr Lang, as Secretary to the Society for the Propagation of the Gospel, an advancement over his post here. I thought if you wished to hear news of David you might send for him. His name is the Rt Reverend John Dauglish. He is a delightful man and has been of the greatest help to us here, not only through his understanding but his knowledge of local conditions on this tiny isle. He can tell you if all the things David gave up are replaced to him in another way and the little details of his daily life, his job etc., the story of his flight from France leaving all his possessions behind. The horrors of war and endless separations of families have in my mind stressed the importance of family ties. I hope that by the end of the summer, we will be nearer that victory for which we are all working so hard and for which England has so bravely lighted the way.'

The daughter-in-law Queen Mary would never know ended the

letter formally: 'I beg to remain Your Majesty's most humble and obedient servant, Wallis Windsor.'[140]

The Duchess later recorded: 'In due course I received from the Bishop a letter telling of his audience with Queen Mary. She had shown keen interest in David's work in the colony and had asked many questions. But when the Bishop had mentioned what I was doing with, I judge, some show of appreciation and approval, there was no response. He met a stone wall of disinterest. Eventually, however, some weeks later there did come a curiously oblique response. David read me a letter from his mother. In it was this sentence: "I send a kind message to your wife."

'David was astonished. "Now what do you suppose," he asked in genuine bewilderment, "has come over Mama?" I made no comment . . .'[141] The Duke only learned the truth thirteen years later when he read the draft of his wife's memoirs, in which the text of her letter to her mother-in-law was published for the first time.

In reality, Queen Mary was not quite as disinterested as she pretended. One of the old Queen's many wartime excursions from Badminton House was to visit Himley Hall, the Earl of Dudley's family home near Birmingham. Gradually, writes Lord Dudley's son, the present Earl, 'it became clear to my father that the purpose of the visit was to investigate the arrangements and lay out of the house party on the occasion when in 1936 the Duke of Windsor as King stayed with my father, together with Mrs Simpson, Mr Ernest Simpson and Mr Ernest Simpson's girlfriend, who went by the name of Buttercup . . .'[142]

Wallis shortly became convinced that Queen Elizabeth's friend, the Earl of Halifax, was using his position as British Ambassador in Washington to their detriment. 'I hear Halifax works continually against the Duke even to putting spokes in the wheels of things he tried to arrange for the Colony . . . Funny people – they better get on with the war and not be so small.'[143]

The Royal Family, meanwhile, suffered their own losses. On September 19, 1941, the Queen's nephew, the Hon. John Patrick Bowes-Lyon, the Master of Glamis, had been killed in action at the age of thirty-one, leading a detachment of the Scots Guards through a confused night action in the Halfaya Pass in Libya. Elizabeth's father, the Earl of Strathmore, then eighty-six, never fully recovered from his grandson's death, and died at Glamis Castle three years later.[144]

George VI was already beginning to show signs of the strain of

wartime sovereignty. The Prime Minister's wife, Clementine Churchill, noted, after one of her lunches for the King and Queen: 'The
King did not say much – He looked thin and rather tired . . .'[145]

Then, on August 25, 1942, the Duke of Kent was killed at the age of
thirty-nine when the Sunderland aircraft in which he was flying to a
tour of RAF establishments in Iceland crashed on a mountainside at
Morven in north-west Scotland. From Nassau, Wallis described it as
'a most tragic death . . . He was the one with the most charm left at the
job – and they made a couple more up with the advances of this world
– in spite of the "turn-coat" to us.'[146] Yet there was no word of sympathy for the widowed Princess Marina from either of the Windsors.

That winter, the Duke again resurrected the vexed issue of his wife's
HRH, requesting Churchill 'to submit to the King that he restore the
Duchess's royal rank at the coming New Year's (Honours), not only
as an act of justice and courtesy to his sister-in-law, but also as a
gesture in recognition of her two years public service in the Bahamas'.[147] Churchill took six weeks to reply and then telegraphed that
the King was 'not willing to take action in sense desired . . . I am sorry
not to have more agreeable news but I hope Your Royal Highness will
not attach undue importance to this point after the immense renunci-
ations you have made.'[148]

In the spring of 1943, the Duchess was alarmed by rumours that
Lord Halifax was to be succeeded as British Ambassador in Washington by the Queen's brother, the Hon. David Bowes-Lyon. 'I hear H.
may leave', she wrote to her aunt, 'and the brother of the lady who is
so kind to me may come in his place. Most uncomfortable forces I
fear.'[149]

Her fears were groundless. Bowes-Lyon was not a candidate for the
ambassadorship, but had been sent to Washington to take over the
political warfare and propaganda work of British Security Co-
ordination, much to the regret of the Canadian-born Secret Service
chief Sir William Stephenson (alias 'Intrepid'), who considered the
choice unfortunate.[150] Bowes-Lyon, described by Sir Robert Bruce
Lockhart as 'our worst cloak and dagger expert' and the 'only member
of (Royal) family who intrigues',[151] was considered by Brendan
Bracken, the Minister of Information, to have 'far exceeded his powers
and . . . traded on his social status to assume functions far beyond the
range (limited) of his ability.'[152] Lockhart credited him with 'two
assets; his royal connection and his charm. Both are wasting assets
because David has a poor mind and no knowledge of Europe. More-

over, he is full of suspicions and is quite incapable of "playing straight".[153] Sir John Wheeler-Bennett thought him 'a bad man' whose 'capacity for intrigue and untruthfulness has almost no limit'.[154]

It was perhaps inevitable that the Windsors should see the arrival of the Queen's intriguing brother as the latest move against them on the part of Elizabeth herself, whom they regarded as the arch-intriguer.

But the Queen was less preoccupied with the Windsors at this moment than with eventual victory. 'We look forward to the future battles', she wrote to Mrs Churchill, 'with the comfortable feeling that we've got the right man as Prime Minister, and the best and most civilized people in the world to fight those battles – tolerant & brave & humorous.'[155]

On May 19, 1943, Churchill addressed Congress, and the Windsors, who were in Washington, went to hear his speech from the diplomatic gallery. 'As the Duke descended to his seat in the front row,' noted Lord Moran, Churchill's physician, 'he got as much clapping as Winston, or more, by which we were surprised.'[156]

Churchill was annoyed. When the Duke had two long meetings with him in Washington, requesting a change of post, the premier was coolly non-committal. Of this, Lord Moran wrote: 'It is not Winston's habit to live with his mistakes. He is a very loyal servant of King George and is no longer . . . interested in the Duke.'[157]

During the same visit, the Duke called on the American Secretary of State and asked for the Duchess's letters to be exempt from censorship, just as his own were because of diplomatic status. The request was refused. Adolf Berle, co-ordinator of intelligence in Washington, noted: 'I believe that the Duchess of Windsor should emphatically be denied exemption from censorship. Quite aside from the shadowy reports about the activities of this family, it is to be recalled that both the Duke and Duchess of Windsor were in contact with Mr James Mooney of General Motors, who attempted to act as mediator of a negotiated peace in the early winter of 1940; that they have maintained correspondence with Bedaux, now in prison under charges of trading with the enemy and possibly of treasonous correspondence with the enemy; that they have been in constant contact with Axel Wenner-Gren, presently on our blacklist for suspicious activity, etc. The Duke of Windsor has been finding many excuses to attend to "private business" in the United States, which he is doing at present.'[158]

That summer, the Duke wrote to his brother, the King, 'in an attempt to bring you to your senses with regard to your attitude towards my wife and myself ... ever since I returned to England in 1939 to offer my services and you continued to persecute (me) and then frustrate my modest efforts to serve you and my country in war, I must frankly admit that I have become very bitter indeed. The whole world knows that we are not on speaking terms which is not surprising in view of the impression you have given via the FO and in general that my wife and I are to have different official treatment to other royal personages ...'[159]

The Duchess had never lost her unfortunate propensity for exhibiting brash frivolity in circumstances that demanded a more compassionate reaction. On July 8, 1943, when the millionaire baronet Sir Harry Oakes was found brutally murdered, his body burned and battered, at his Nassau mansion, Wallis's first comment was: 'Never a dull moment in the Bahamas.'[160]

The Duke's plea to Churchill for a change of post finally resulted in the offer of the Governorship of Bermuda – another island even smaller than the Bahamas and still more remote, with half the population, although with a better climate.

Ironically the post had first been offered to Queen Elizabeth's brother, David Bowes-Lyon, whose wife, Rachel, was asked by Churchill one evening at dinner in Washington, 'How would you like to live in Bermuda?' She had replied that she 'could not think of anything more ghastly'.[161] Bowes-Lyon turned it down and so did the Duke of Windsor. 'It was now clear beyond all question,' thought the Duchess, 'that David's family were determined to keep him relegated to the furthermost marches of the Empire.'[162]

Hitler had not yet abandoned his plans for the restoration of Edward to the throne from which he had abdicated. In the autumn of 1943, the Führer noted: 'England for the good of the world must remain unchanged in its present form. Consequently, after final victory, we must effect a reconciliation. Only the King must go – in his place the Duke of Windsor. With him we will make a permanent treaty of friendship instead of a peace treaty.'[163]

The Windsors were now becoming deeply disconsolate. Wallis's parting words to her aunt in her last letter of 1943 had an anguished ring to them. 'When will we be released from this life?'[164]

In the spring of 1944, her protests became more bitter. The Duke, she said, had been 'dumped here solely by family jealousy!'[165] And to a

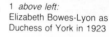

1 *above left:*
Elizabeth Bowes-Lyon as
Duchess of York in 1923

2 *above right:* Wallis Warfield
as Mrs Earl Winfield
Spencer Jr in 1920

3 The man who was
to be the cause of their
antipathy: Edward,
Prince of Wales, in 1921

4 *above left:* The Duke and Duchess of York. 'She was his will power, his all' wrote Chips Channon

5 A kiss for the Duchess of York from the Prince of Wales in 1927. Elizabeth was on friendly terms with her brother-in-law until Mrs Simpson entered his life

6 Edward and Wallis during the *Nahlin* cruise. The publicity resulting from their indiscreet behaviour undermined his popularity and prestige

7 The King and Mrs Simpson at Balmoral where the Duchess of York openly showed her disapproval and dislike of Wallis

8 *centre:* 'This is Windsor Castle. His Royal Highness Prince Edward.' On the night of his abdication, the ex-King broadcasts to the nation

9 *bottom:* December 10, 1936. The Duke of York returning home on the night before he became King. 'I feel like the proverbial "sheep being led to the slaughter" ' he wrote

10 May 12, 1937. The newly crowned
King-Emperor and Queen-Empress.
'Majesty had swathed the
"smiling Duchess" '

11 Smiles at the Château de Candé three
weeks later as Wallis becomes the Duchess
of Windsor, but no member of the Royal
Family attended the wedding

12 Hitler greets
the Windsors at
Berchtesgaden on
October 22, 1937.
Their visit to
Germany infuriated the
new King and Queen

13 Queen Elizabeth's
calm demeanour during
the Blitz won her a
permanent place
in the affections of
the British people

14 *left:* The Duke
of Windsor watches
with haunted eyes
as Prince Philip
kisses the
Queen Mother's hand
after King
George VI's funeral

15 A murmured confidence
between Wallis and her
constant companion,
Jimmy Donahue.
Their relationship threatened
the Windsor marriage
and provoked criticism
even from friends

16 The Windsors at play.
Their flamboyant lifestyle
was not admired by the
Queen Mother

17 *below:* The Duke's
eye operation at the
London Clinic in 1965
led to the first recognition
of the Duchess by the
British Sovereign since the
Windsor wedding in 1937

above left: June 7, 1967. The first meeting between the Queen Mother
and the Duchess of Windsor in more than thirty years as
sisters-in-law. Wallis pointedly omitted to curtsey

above right: A guest at Buckingham Palace for the first time since
her marriage, the widowed Duchess gazes sadly from the window
of the State Suite as the Queen rides out to attend the
Trooping the Colour ceremony

After years of bitterness and estrangement, the royal sisters-in-law
stand together at the Duke of Windsor's funeral on June 5, 1972

21 July 15, 1980. From the steps of St Paul's Cathedral,
the Queen Mother acknowledges the cheers of the London crowds
before a service of thanksgiving for her eightieth birthday

22 *above right:* The twilight's last gleaming.
Wallis in her eightieth year, shortly before illness
finally engulfed and imprisoned her

23 April 29, 1986. The moment of farewell. The Queen Mother watches
the Duchess of Windsor's coffin leaving St George's Chapel,
Windsor, on its final journey to the royal burial ground at Frogmore

friend she wrote: 'They only murdered Sir Harry Oakes once. They will *never* stop murdering the Duke of Windsor . . . It is his own family who are against him.'[166]

In the autumn, the Duke again pleaded with Churchill to intercede in the family feud. 'Were the King and Queen to behave normally to the Duchess and myself when we pass by England, and invite us merely to tea at one of their residences, a formality which as a matter of fact is prescribed by Court protocol in the case of Colonial Governors and their wives, it would avoid any division of feeling being manifested . . . It would never be a very happy meeting, but on the other hand it would be quite painless, and would have the merit of silencing, once and for all, those malicious circles who delight in keeping open an eight-year-old wound that should have been healed officially, if not privately, ages ago.' Surely, he added, the Prime Minister would agree that this short meeting would be 'the best cure for an evil situation'. Would Churchill not try to persuade the King and Queen 'to swallow "the Windsor pill" just once, however bitter they may think it is going to taste'?[167]

That Churchill did try to do precisely this is supported by the fact that he delayed for almost three months in replying. When he did so, however, the news was bad. The Prime Minister had pleaded with the King for one meeting. General de Gaulle had done the same. Princess Alice, Countess of Athlone, and the Duchess of Beaufort had both added their voices to the argument for reconciliation.[168] George VI had refused. Neither the Queen nor Queen Mary would alter their resolve not to receive the Duchess.

'I do not see any prospect of removing this difficulty', Churchill told the Duke. 'I have not concealed my regret that this should be so.'[169]

Faced with the utter hopelessness of this situation, Windsor decided to resign the Governorship of the Bahamas ten weeks before his term of office automatically expired. His resignation was announced on March 15, 1945, and on April 30, the day on which Hitler shot himself in his Berlin bunker, the Duke formally ceased to be Governor.

He and the Duchess sailed from Nassau on May 3, and five days later, on Victory in Europe day, as the King and Queen stood on either side of Churchill on the balcony of Buckingham Palace to acknowledge the wild jubilation of the London crowds, the Windsors relaxed in Palm Beach.

A week later they arrived in Washington, where Sir John Balfour recorded: 'On the third evening of his stay the Duke asked us to invite to dinner an elderly American friend of his – a railroad tycoon named Young. Both of them seemed oblivious to Nazi misdeeds and were at one in thinking that, had Hitler been differently handled, war with Germany might have been avoided in 1939.'[170]

It almost defies belief that in the month in which the concentration camps were thrown open, with the stench of mountains of rotting corpses, when the gas chambers were inspected, and the full extent of Nazi genocide of the Jews became known to a horrified world, the former King of England was still expressing the view that Hitler might have been 'differently handled'.

After the Windsors had returned to Paris to salvage their possessions in the Boulevard Suchet and at the Château de la Cröe, the Duke came to London alone. On October 5, Queen Mary noted in her diary: 'At four *David* arrived by plane from Paris on a visit to me – I had not seen him for nearly nine years! It was a great joy meeting him again, he looked very well – Bertie came to dinner to meet him.'[171] The Queen was again conspicuous by her absence from the family reunion.

On the Duke's return to Paris, the Duchess wrote to her aunt: 'The Duke's London visit passed off most pleasantly even though their attitude regarding me is the same and they prefer we do not live in GB as it would be too much competition for the brother – which seems weak. Also they do not want him to find work outside as the idea is you can't give a King a job. Wonderful people aren't they . . . What do you think of it all?'[172]

The Duke also wrote to the King: 'While I am frank to admit that I was sorry when your answer was in the affirmative to my question as to whether my taking up residence in Great Britain would be an embarrassment to you, I . . . am . . . prepared to put your feelings before my own in this matter. On the other hand, don't forget that I have suffered many unnecessary embarrassments from official sources uncomplainingly in the last nine years, but I have reason to believe from the spirit of your recent two long talks with me that it is now your desire that these should cease.'[173]

Almost a month later the King replied that he was 'very pleased' the Duke accepted he should not return to live in Britain; that there could be no question of official work for him in peacetime; but that everything would be done to assist any plans the Windsors might have to leave Europe permanently and settle in the United States.[174]

A number of factors dictated the King's attitude. In the autumn of 1945, George VI sent Owen Morshead, then librarian at Windsor

Castle, and Anthony Blunt, the art historian and former Cambridge lecturer, on a highly secret mission to Germany. Blunt was Queen Elizabeth's third cousin, being descended from her ancestor, George Smith, the Member of Parliament for Midhurst from 1800 to 1806. The destination of Blunt and Morshead was Schloss Friedrichshof, Kronberg, just north-west of Frankfurt, and they carried with them a personal letter from King George to the head of the Hesse royal family, Prince Philip, Landgrave of Hesse-Cassel.

The letter asked the Hesse family to hand over to Blunt and Morshead an archive of papers stored at Kronberg, and then in the possession of Prince Philip's twin brother, Prince Wolfgang. Some of these documents concerned the Duke of Windsor's dealings with the Germans. The King was worried these might fall into the hands of the Americans and end up being published, particularly since the castle was then being used as an American army club.

Blunt and Morshead managed to locate the papers in two packing cases in the castle attic, and, in spite of opposition from the WAC captain in charge of Kronberg, they succeeded in removing them to Windsor Castle. When the papers ultimately arrived at Whaddon Hall, near Bletchley, where the rest of the captured German archives were being sorted, there were indications that the British Government was anxious to examine the Windsor documents before their contents became too widely known.

Kenneth Duke, one of the British officers handling the Berlin archives, recalled that one Windsor file, dealing with the Duke's exchanges with Hitler's emissaries in Lisbon in 1940, 'was removed from the general collection by higher ups, but was later returned'.[175] Another of the British officers, Professor Donald Cameron Watt, later Professor of International History at the University of London, remembered: 'Among the four hundred tons of documents there was a section relating to the Duke of Windsor. Everything we thought should have been in this file was indeed there – with one exception . . . there was no account of the conversation with Hitler in 1937. There was simply no trace of this in the archive. Of course it is quite possible that the Windsor material had been sifted before it reached Whaddon Hall. The royal archivists have proper historians to advise them these days but at that time they were very secretive.'[176]

The King's decision not to give the Windsors any further official work may have resulted from the documentary evidence of the Duke's 'indiscretions' during the war.

Certainly the Royal Family's favour to Blunt and Morshead indicated intense gratitude for the success of their confidential mission. Blunt became Surveyor of the King's Pictures in 1945 (a post he retained for twenty years after Elizabeth II's accession); a Commander of the Royal Victorian Order in 1947; and a knight in 1956. Morshead also was knighted in 1958.

In 1964, when confronted by information passed on by the FBI, Blunt confessed to having been a Soviet spy during his wartime service in MI5. Astonishingly, he was permitted to retain his post as Surveyor of the Queen's Pictures in order not to alert the Russians to his unmasking. In 1979, however, his treachery was publicly conceded by the Prime Minister, Margaret Thatcher, in a statement to the House of Commons. Professor Blunt was stripped of his knighthood and died in disgrace in 1983.

There was one other factor in the King's hardened attitude towards the Windsors: a domestic one. It was hinted at during a television interview which Kenneth Harris filmed with the Duke and Duchess in 1969.

Harris: 'Why didn't you get a job, do you think?'

The Windsors both laughed and exchanged a meaningful look.

Duke: 'You'd have to ask ... [*there was a pause*]. *Most* of the people, I'm afraid, are underground now who prevented me. Oh, I don't know, it is hard to say.'[177]

The word '*most*' was strongly emphasized. One of the people the Windsors firmly believed had prevented them from ever being given another job was far from 'underground' in 1969.

She was very much alive, and residing in London at Clarence House, St James's Palace, under the exalted title of Her Majesty Queen Elizabeth The Queen Mother.

10

'THE WOMAN WHO KILLED
MY HUSBAND'

THE COMING OF PEACE FOUND George VI weary in spirit and exhausted in mind and body. At the age of only forty-nine he suddenly seemed an old man before his time. 'I feel burned out,' he admitted.[1]

The year of victory brought shadows also. The King was deeply affected by the sudden death, on April 12, 1945, of President Roosevelt. 'He was a very great man', he wrote in his diary, '& his loss will be felt the World over. He was a staunch friend of this country, & Winston will feel his loss most of all in his dealings with Stalin.'[2]

After overcoming his strong initial distrust, the King had come to rely increasingly on Churchill, and it was a further blow when the old warrior was resoundingly defeated at the General Election in July. George VI was ill at ease with Winston's successor as Prime Minister, Clement Attlee, whom, at first, he found 'completely mute'.[3]

On August 6, the atomic bomb was dropped on Hiroshima, and three days later a second on Nagasaki. Both acts were judged expedient for the ending of the war with Japan but caused private anguish to the King and Queen, who viewed with revulsion the resultant mass slaughter and disfigurement of women and children.

Queen Elizabeth also was tired, but her powers of resilience were greater than those of the King. Throughout the conflict she had been the only woman in Britain to know the full extent of the casualties, and she had few illusions about the problems facing the British in peacetime. As she observed later, 'times were almost worse at the end of the war, when the people were all tired; they had been through so much'.[4]

Five years in the Bahamas had changed the Windsors too. Meeting them again in Paris, in September 1945, for the first time in four years, Lady Diana Cooper recorded: 'The two poor little old things were almost pathetic. Fear, I suppose, of losing their youthful figures, or homesickness, has made them both Dachau-thin. She is much commoner and more confident, he much duller and sillier.'[5]

Both had hopes that the change in government in Britain might improve their personal fortunes and that Attlee's Labour cabinet might regard them more favourably than Churchill had done. During his stay at Marlborough House with Queen Mary in October, the Duke called on the new Foreign Secretary, Ernest Bevin, unaware that it was his brother, the King, who had insisted to Attlee that Bevin should go to the Foreign Office in preference to Hugh Dalton. The Duke's proposal to Bevin was that the post of 'ambassador-at-large' to the United States might be created for him. He would not necessarily operate from Washington, and he would not concern himself with orthodox diplomacy or impinge on the traditional activities of the official British Ambassador. Instead he would rove the country, promoting British trade and bringing Americans and visiting Britons together.

The Duke tried to enlist the King's support for this idea, but neither Bevin nor Attlee was any more enthusiastic about the Windsors than Churchill had been; if anything, less so. The couple's wartime indiscretions had disqualified them from serious consideration for any responsible position in the public sphere, and there remained the obstacle of the Queen's resolute opposition to them.

Elizabeth's dislike of them both was now compounded by her memory of how, in her view, they had tried to dictate personal terms at a time of desperate national crisis. Her attitude over this was uncompromising. As she remarked in one of her post-war speeches: 'Those who laid down their lives did not ask for conditions and guarantees. They offered everything and expected nothing.'[6]

As long as Elizabeth remained Queen, her brother-in-law's chances of re-employment were virtually nil. On January 27, 1946, Prime Minister Attlee confirmed to the House of Commons that no diplomatic or official position had been offered to the Duke of Windsor. And, it seemed clear, none would be.

The Windsors were back in limbo, and the Duke painfully lacked the inner resources of character necessary to carve a new life of any meaning for himself. 'He is so pitiful,' wrote Susan Mary Alsop from Paris to Marietta Tree. 'I never saw a man so bored. He said to me, "How do you manage to remain so cheerful in this ghastly place? . . . You know what my day was today? . . . I got up late and then I went with the Duchess and watched her buy a hat, and then on the way home I had the car drop me off in the Bois to watch some of your [American] soldiers playing football and then I had planned to take a walk, but it was so cold that I could hardly bear it. In fact I was afraid that I would be struck with cold in the way people are struck with heat so I came straight home . . . When I got home the Duchess was having her French lessons so I had no one to talk to . . ." I thought this description of a day was pretty sad from a man who used to be Edward VIII by the Grace of God of Great Britain, Ireland and the British Dominions beyond the Seas, King, Defender of the Faith and Emperor of India.'[7]

That spring, Noël Coward, who had never approved of the Windsors, recorded a softer impression of them at a small dinner given by the Duff Coopers at the British Embassy in Paris. 'Sat next to Wallis,' wrote Coward. 'She was very charming and rather touching. He loves her so much, and at long last I am beginning to believe that she loves him.'[8]

In London, other observers noted how completely the Queen's domestic influence held sway within her own family. The heir presumptive, Princess Elizabeth, was about to emerge from her teens, but was still clearly subject to her mother's authority. On one occasion, an elderly councillor offered the Princess a glass of sherry, which was accepted with alacrity, but 'at once' she heard her mother's 'quiet but firm voice behind her, "Oh! lemonade, I think, Elizabeth." '[9] Sometimes, however, the princesses rebelled mildly against their mother's inflexible pre-war standards of propriety. On one occasion the Queen was shocked to observe one of her elder daughter's ladies-in-waiting cycling across the quadrangle of Buckingham Palace in a headscarf. 'She can't come here like that,' said the Queen sharply. 'Oh, Mummy,' remonstrated Princess Elizabeth, 'these days girls simply don't have a hat.'[10]

In January 1946, Wallis headed the New York Dress Institute's list of the ten best-dressed women in the world for the first of three consecutive years. To her, Queen Elizabeth was still 'the Dowdy Duchess', and she continued to poke fun, both privately and publicly, at her sister-in-law's ornate style in fashion. Many people believed her biting comments about the Queen to be motivated by jealousy. Elizabeth held the highest rank in Europe, the glittering position Wallis had coveted. 'I felt sure the former Mrs Simpson was seeing her through green eyes,' wrote Adela Rogers St Johns later. 'Neither as Duchess of York nor wife of George VI nor mother of the present Queen Elizabeth would Elizabeth Bowes-Lyon ever make the best-dressed list, too true, her clothes belonged to *her*, the couturiers didn't dictate them.'[11]

In the autumn of 1946, the Windsors came to Britain together and stayed at the Earl and Countess of Dudley's home, Ednam Lodge, at Sunningdale. The problem of Wallis's status was still causing embarrassment socially, and when Loelia, Duchess of Westminster invited them over to Send Grove for cocktails, she briefed her guests beforehand: ' "Remember now, you've all got to curtsey to him but *not* to her." I'm frightfully flustered introducing people, that kind of thing. I shake hands warmly with him and sink to the floor with her. The other guests all glare at me.'[12]

Wallis had brought with her on the trip her entire collection of jewels. Lady Dudley – later Laura, Duchess of Marlborough – recalled that 'The Duchess's jewel case was no ordinary affair. It was a trunk in which she had many of HRH's fantastic collection of Fabergé boxes and a great many uncut emeralds which I believe belonged to Queen Alexandra. The Duchess liked jewels very much, though this is rather an understatement as she was continually having them re-set, mostly in Paris. One of these priceless baubles had only just reached her, a vast sapphire which she had had converted into a bird of paradise by Van Cleef and Arpels. But the butler's prudent suggestion that this trunkful of things scarcely to be found in an Aladdin's cave should be put in the strong-room was rejected by the Duchess. Her jewel case, she said, would remain, as it always did, under her maid's bed! On the afternoon of this disastrous day her maid, in preparation for her holiday, asked that this trunk of valuables should be put in the Duchess's bedroom temporarily, later to be put in the strong-room at the request of my maid, who did not fancy having such a treasure under her bed.'[13]

Between 6.30 and 7 o'clock on the evening of Wednesday, October 16, with the Windsors and the Dudleys both in London, and all the servants enjoying high tea downstairs, person or persons still unknown swung a white rope up to the bedroom of Lady Dudley's daughter in the front of Ednam Lodge, climbed up it and into the house, crossed the passage into the Duchess's bedroom, and there found the entire treasure trove sitting in front of the fireplace. The thieves – if that is what they were – made an uninterrupted and almost clean haul, leaving behind only the white rope still hanging from the window ledge, the heavy Fabergé gold boxes on a window-sill, and about eighteen odd earrings – none of which matched – scattered in one of the bunkers of Sunningdale golf course.

On returning to learn of this disaster, the Windsors' 'galloping paranoia' was once again reactivated, and this time not surprisingly. There was clearly something very odd about the circumstances. None of the Dudleys' guard dogs had barked. The detective guarding the entrance to the house had seen and heard nothing. The Duchess not unnaturally suspected an 'inside job', and it was now that Lady Dudley saw 'an unpleasant and to me unexpected side of her character . . . She wanted all the servants put through a kind of third degree, but I would have none of this, all of them except for one kitchen maid being old and devoted staff of long standing. By the following night the Duke was both demented with worry and near to tears. The Duchess started the next day with a grim face and wearing on her dress about the only jewel that remained to her. Just before we all went out for a little stroll she said, "David, put this brooch in a safe place." On our return he could not remember where he had put it! He thought the most likely place was the room he was using for sorting the papers he had fetched from Windsor. There ensued a frantic search, but to no avail.

'When it was time for bed the Duchess and Eric went upstairs; it had been a grim day. The Duke said he was going to continue the search although he looked grey with worry and exhaustion. I was desperately sorry for him, and anyhow I would have stayed to help him in his search, hoping at least to find this one remaining jewel to which the Duchess appeared so attached. We stayed up most of the night; he obviously feared to go up to bed empty-handed. I made endless cups of black coffee while the Duke went through his papers, which he seemed convinced was the likeliest place. At about 5 a.m. by some miracle we found it, under a china ornament. Never have I seen a man so relieved. He was still ashen in the face but he rushed upstairs.'[14]

Asked by the press about the jewellery she had been wearing on the night in question, the Duchess made a reply that became almost as famous as the robbery itself. 'A fool would know that with tweeds or other daytime clothes one wears gold, and that with evening clothes one wears platinum.'[15] This remark, uttered in a Britain ruled by rationing and aching under austerity, created a tidal wave of derision among struggling housewives and a shudder of horror in Court circles. Once again the Windsors seemed to be frivolous and flashy personalities without sensitivity to public opinion or concern for existing hardships.

The Scotland Yard investigation of the burglary continued for years, but not a single stone was recovered nor any genuine clue found as to the identity of the thieves. The Duchess's collection had been insured for £400,000. This was substantially less than the cost of replacing it. Eventually, however, the Duke's underwriters paid for all the lost pieces to be replaced, and reinsured the new collection for £800,000, on condition that at least half of it remained in the security of a bank vault at all times.

Some of the stolen jewels could never be replaced exactly, however, on account of their unique quality and value. Those which most defied substitution were the priceless uncut emeralds which Queen Alexandra had brought to England from Denmark at the time of her marriage in 1863. On her death in 1925, she had left these to her eldest grandson, the Prince of Wales, on the understanding that they would one day adorn the future Queen of England. Edward VIII had given them to Wallis Simpson in London, long before their marriage, and she had taken them with her when she left Fort Belvedere for France on December 3, 1936. After the Abdication, the British Royal Family had made no secret of their feelings that, since Edward's wife was not the King's consort, Queen Alexandra's emeralds ought to be returned to Britain to take their place among the Crown Jewels.

The Duchess, hyper-suspicious at the admittedly odd circumstances in which the robbery was performed, and also at the fact that no trace of the jewels was ever found anywhere in the world in the years that followed, several times expressed her conviction that they had been stolen by the British Secret Service, acting on the orders of the King and Queen, in order that the Royal Family might regain possession of the disputed emeralds. No evidence has ever come to light to support this suggestion, but there is no doubt that the Windsors themselves believed it to be possible.[16]

On January 31, 1947, the King, Queen Elizabeth and the two princesses sailed from Portsmouth for South Africa on what was to be the last overseas tour of George VI's reign. Their departure coincided with the worst British winter within living memory. Ice, snow, gales and fog paralysed the country. Roads were blocked and rail points frozen solid. Within four days, two million people had been thrown out of work by a chronic coal shortage. The Austin car factory closed down, leaving 15,000 workers jobless. More than two hundred cotton firms ceased production. Two thousand dockers went on strike in the London docks, and drastic power cuts left homes without electricity for up to five hours a day.

The King's temper, increasingly uncertain since the pressures of the war years, grew visibly worse with the news of this crisis. He felt it a betrayal to be in the sunshine of South Africa – even on official duty – while his people were shivering at home. 'I am very worried over the extra privations which all of you . . . are having to put up with in that ghastly cold weather with no light or fuel,' he wrote to Queen Mary. 'In many ways I wish I was with you having borne so many trials with them.'[17]

The Queen shortly informed her mother-in-law: 'This tour is being very strenuous as I feared it would be & doubly hard for Bertie who feels he should be at home. But there is very little he could do now, and even if he interrupted the tour & flew home, it would be very exhausting & possibly make it difficult to return here. We think of home all the time, & Bertie has offered to return but Mr Attlee thought that it would only make people feel that things were getting worse, & was not anxious for him to come back.'[18]

During the tour, the harassed King-Emperor several times showed irritation and temper in public. When he and the Queen-Empress opened the South African Parliament, he was heard to bark a series of impatient commands at his equerry, Group Captain Peter Townsend, who preceded the royal couple. 'For God's sake, stop!' yelled the King as 'Die Stem', the South African anthem, began to play. 'I froze to a standstill', recalled Townsend, 'but the anthem is a long one and, as it ended, the royal patience began to run out. "Go on, for God's sake!" I heard King George VI shout again.'[19]

As the Royal Family, in their open Daimler, drove through the mining towns of the Rand, the King's nerves were again on edge. 'He immediately took over the driving, from the back seat, uttering a series of cross and contradictory orders. Before long, the well-intentioned chauffeur was badly rattled. The Queen was trying to calm the King; the princesses were trying to make light of things, which got worse and worse until I thought to myself "If we go on like this there's going to be an accident."

'Then it happened – not an accident, but something which at that moment looked far more sinister. A black man, wiry and of medium build, shot out of the swarm of sweating, shouting Africans and sprinted with terrifying speed and purpose towards the royal Daimler. He clutched something in one hand and before the police could stop him had with the other grabbed hold of the car so tightly that the knuckles of his black hand showed white.'[20] While the King shouted at the chauffeur to accelerate, the Queen performed the remarkable feat of holding the man at bay with the point of her parasol in her right

hand, while she continued to wave regally to the crowds with her left.
In a moment or two the man lost his grip and fell into the road, where
he was seized by the police and dragged away. It was then discovered
that all he had in his hand was a ten shilling note he had wanted to
present to Princess Elizabeth for her twenty-first birthday due in a few
days. The King, when he learned this, was stricken with compunction.
'Find out how he is,' he told Townsend. 'I hope he was not too badly
hurt. I am sorry about today. I was very tired.'[21]

The Queen's charm and self-possession came to the rescue repeatedly. When George VI was reduced to frozen silence by a dour
old Afrikaner who announced that he could never forgive the English
for having conquered his country, Elizabeth smilingly responded,
'Oh, I understand that perfectly. We feel very much the same in
Scotland . . .'[22]

But the Queen's personal success could not disguise the ominous
decline that was now apparent in the King's health. He lost more than
a stone in weight during the tour. He was troubled by a cough which
persistently refused to clear up. He was suffering from severe cramp in
both legs, and he seemed permanently tired.

In Cape Town on April 21, her twenty-first birthday, Princess
Elizabeth, referring to the traditional motto of British royal heirs – 'Ich
Dien': 'I Serve' – made a moving broadcast containing a solemn vow of
self-dedication: 'I declare before you all that my whole life, whether it
be long or short, shall be devoted to your service . . .' This was an
expression of the central concept of monarchy: that the sovereign, and
the heir to the throne, will put duty before all other considerations. It
was the concept Edward VIII had denied so dramatically in 1936.

The King and Queen returned to Buckingham Palace on May 12, the
tenth anniversary of their Coronation, to find the Windsors once more
in London. Their arrival had again been marked by an ostentatious
display of luxury, with three army trucks and two jeeps depositing a
mountain of luggage in front of Claridge's.

On May 26, a family luncheon was given at the Palace in honour of
Queen Mary's eightieth birthday, but the Windsors, despite their
presence in London, were not invited to it. Two days later, Harold
Nicolson met them both at Lady Colefax's house. The Duke, he noted,
'has stopped calling his wife "Her Royal Highness". He calls her "the
Duchess". I notice also that people do not bow as they used to, and
treat him less as a royalty than they did when he had recently been
King.' The Duchess he found 'much improved. That taut, predatory

look has gone; she has softened. I have a talk with her alone. She says that they do not know where to live. They would like to live in England, but that is difficult. He retains his old love for Fort Belvedere. "We are tired of wandering," she says. "We are not as young as we were. We want to settle down and grow our own trees." He likes gardening, but it is no fun, gardening in other people's gardens. Where can they live? They are sick of islands (after Nassau), otherwise they might go to the Channel Islands. They are sick of France. He likes America, but that can never be a home. He wants a job to do. "You see," she says, "he was born to be a salesman. He would be an admirable representative of Rolls Royce. But an ex-King cannot start selling motor-cars." I feel really sorry for them. She was so simple and sincere.'[23]

The Duke called at 10 Downing Street and spent forty minutes there with the Prime Minister, leaving by the back entrance to avoid reporters. Again Attlee had to tell him that he had no job to offer him. Windsor also called on the new Lord Chancellor, Earl Jowitt, and reminded him of his earlier opinion, arrived at in 1938, concerning the questionable legality of the King's Letters Patent of May 1937, depriving the Duchess of the title of Royal Highness. Jowitt was at last in a position to rectify this injustice, but he was not disposed to do so now that he held the highest office in the British judiciary. The Duchess commented later: 'All that the Duke got from the Lord Chancellor was a fishy stare which he interpreted as an unfavourable legal ruling.'[24]

The Windsors returned to France on June 3, their tenth wedding anniversary. 'Ten years have passed, but not the romance,' said the Duke. 'It's gone on and on.' And the Duchess added pointedly: 'I'm afraid a great deal of wishful thinking went into the predictions that our marriage wouldn't last.'[25]

On July 9, Buckingham Palace announced the engagement of Princess Elizabeth to Lieutenant Philip Mountbatten, the son of Prince and Princess Andrew of Greece, and the nephew of Lord Mountbatten. When the invitation list of 2,200 guests was released in October, the names of the Duke and Duchess of Windsor were conspicuous by their absence. Princess Elizabeth's uncle and her American aunt-in-law were the only close relations of the bride and bridegroom not present at the wedding in Westminster Abbey on November 20. The guest list was the ultimate responsibility of the Queen.

At the party at Buckingham Palace on the evening of the wedding, Clementine Churchill noted 'Our Queen's dazzling & magnetic charm

... shimmering, gleaming & sparkling.'[26] The King's eyes followed his wife lovingly and a few days later he wrote to Princess Elizabeth during her honeymoon: 'I have watched you grow up all these years with pride under the skilful direction of Mummy, who as you know is the most marvellous person in the World in my eyes . . .'[27]

Some members of the Royal Family were beginning to feel that the continued ostracism of the Windsors was shabby and wrong. The Duke's nephew, the Earl of Harewood – whose divorce would later cause him to experience a similar estrangement from the family – wrote of him, 'all of us knew that he was condemned for putting private life above duty. But it was hard for the younger amongst us not to stand in amazement at the moral contradiction between the elevation of a code of duty on the one hand, and on the other the denial of central Christian virtues – forgiveness, understanding, family tenderness.'[28]

A further setback for the Windsors in the autumn of 1947 was the dismissal of Duff Cooper as British Ambassador in Paris. The Coopers had consistently invited the Windsors to Embassy functions, and Lady Diana's public curtsies to the Duchess had prompted most Frenchwomen to follow suit and show Wallis the respect due to royalty. The Coopers were succeeded by friends of the King and Queen, Sir Oliver and Lady Harvey, who strongly disapproved of the Windsors and flatly refused to invite them to the Embassy.

The fact that the Windsors had now virtually abandoned hope of ever receiving another official job or being reconciled with the Royal Family was indicated by the Duke's decision, in the summer of 1947, to begin work on his memoirs with an American ghostwriter, Colonel Charles J. V. Murphy, an editor with the *Time-Life* organisation. The news of this defiant departure from convention – British royalty did not, in those days, give interviews or write about their lives – caused further distress to the King and apprehension among his advisers. An initial series of three articles based on the forthcoming book began to run in *Life* on December 8, and five days later appeared in Britain. Noël Coward noted: 'Invitation from Ward Price on behalf of Rothermere and the *Sunday Dispatch* to write a thousand-word tribute to the King for his birthday on Sunday, in order to offset the bad taste of the *Sunday Express* in publishing the Duke of Windsor's memoirs on that day.'[29]

In spite of these irritations, Queen Elizabeth contrived to bring gaiety into the King's declining years. On April 7, 1948, after a visit to

Windsor Castle, Clementine Churchill wrote to her: '. . . I can truth-fully say that I have not enjoyed a week-end Party so much for what seems an immeasurable space of time.

'After "Clumps", which I had not played for forty years (or more) & then in a much more sedate fashion, I felt nearly forty years younger.

'It was moving and stimulating to feel the pulse of Life beating strongly in Your Majesty's family, delightful to see the wonderful treasures all in their places, and to feel "here firm though all be drifting".'[30]

At another post-war party at Sandringham, the Queen 'clapped her hands to summon one of her pages, and when he appeared she asked him to bring the box containing all the masks and dressing-up materials. At once, the party became *en fête*, inspired by the overflow-ing good spirts of their leader, and they danced to the gramophone till midnight. Later, upstairs, when the members of the houseparty were going to their respective rooms, a door opened suddenly and a surprising figure, complete with a man's bowler hat and twirling a furled umbrella, came down the corridor, singing the chorus from *Burlington Bertie*.'[31] It was the Queen.

On April 26, King George and Queen Elizabeth drove in an open landau through vast and cheering London crowds to a service of thanksgiving at St Paul's Cathedral to mark their Silver Wedding anniversary. The entire Royal Family was present – again with the exception of the Windsors, who were not invited. That afternoon, in brilliant sunshine, the King and Queen drove in an open car through twenty miles of London streets and were received everywhere with spontaneous affection. The couple who had begun their reign in uncertainty and apprehension had won overwhelming popularity. That both were moved and touched by it was apparent in their broadcasts to the nation that evening, when the King spoke falteringly of years 'full of difficulty, of anxiety, and often of sorrow. On me, in my endeavour to fulfil my appointed task, they have laid a heavy burden. I make no secret of the fact that there have been times when it would have been almost too heavy but for the strength and comfort which I have always found in my home.'[32]

The family snubs to the Windsors continued. A month after the Silver Wedding, Princess Elizabeth and her husband, the Duke of Edinburgh, visited France. They did not call on the Windsors, who were excluded from the British Embassy reception for them in Paris.

That autumn, the cramp in the King's legs grew progressively worse.

By August he was in 'discomfort most of the time'.[33] By October his left foot was numb all day and the pain kept him awake at night. On October 26, he and the Queen opened Parliament in full state for the first time since the war, and four days later the King underwent a searching medical examination. As a result, Professor Sir James Learmonth, a leading authority on vascular complaints, was called in, and his examination on November 12 confirmed that the King's condition was serious. There was evidence of early arteriosclerosis. There was a grave risk of gangrene developing, and considerable danger that the right leg might have to be amputated. The King forbade any word of the gravity of his illness to be given to Princess Elizabeth, whose first child, Prince Charles of Edinburgh, was born two days later, on November 14.

On November 23, the following statement was issued: 'The King is suffering from an obstruction to the circulation through the arteries of the legs, which has only recently become acute; the defective blood supply to the right foot causes anxiety. Complete rest has been advised and treatment to improve the circulation in the legs has been initiated and must be maintained for an immediate and prolonged period. Though his Majesty's general health, including the condition of his heart, gives no reason for concern, there is no doubt that the strain of the last twelve years has appreciably affected his resistance to physical fatigue.'[34]

There could have been no clearer admission, in medical terms, of the effect of the burden Edward VIII had bequeathed to his reluctant brother. The projected royal tour of Australia and New Zealand by the King and Queen was postponed indefinitely, and George VI resigned himself to a period of enforced invalidism.

Four months later, although encouraged by the improvement in his health, the royal doctors decided that the King's circulation could only be maintained by a right lumbar sympathectomy operation, which was performed at Buckingham Palace on March 12, 1949. Nine days later, Queen Mary told Harold Nicolson, ' "he is so ill, poor boy, so ill". This in such a sad voice.'[35]

On June 9, for the first time, the King drove in an open carriage to Horse Guards Parade to watch his Brigade of Guards troop the Colour, and remained seated throughout the ceremony. Princess Elizabeth took her father's place and rode at the head of the procession.

That summer, the Earl of Harewood – son of the King's sister, the

Princess Royal – startled the Royal Family by making known his wish to marry Marion Stein, the daughter of an Austrian Jewish musician. After some hesitation, the Princess Royal wrote to the King on her son's behalf, since Lord Harewood – under the terms of the Royal Marriages Act – needed the sovereign's consent in order to marry Miss Stein. George VI received his nephew, but refused to give his consent until approval had first been obtained from Queen Mary, who was 'in a great state, and she won't talk about it'.[36] To the old Queen, the idea of George V's grandson marrying an unknown Austrian jewess, whose father worked for the London music publishers, Boosey and Hawkes, must have seemed almost as shocking as her eldest son's marriage to a twice-divorced American commoner.

Marion Stein was a charming, intelligent woman and also an accomplished pianist. Queen Mary raised no permanent objection and the King's consent was given on July 18. The engagement was announced the following day, and the marriage took place without great ceremony on September 29 at St Mark's Church, North Audley Street, with a wedding anthem composed by the bride and bridegroom's mutual friend, Benjamin Britten.

The Duke of Windsor's impending memoirs were by no means the only source of literary aggravation for the Royal Family. The Queen was astounded to receive from her close friend, Nancy, Viscountess Astor, a pre-publication copy of a book called, *The Little Princesses*, about to come out in New York, and written by – of all people – the trusted royal governess, Marion Crawford, who had been in the family's employment for seventeen years.[37]

After 'Crawfie's' marriage in 1947 to Major George Buthlay, they had been given a 'grace and favour' home – Nottingham Cottage, Kensington Palace – a dinner service from Queen Mary, a coffee set from Princess Elizabeth, and table lamps from Princess Margaret. Mrs Buthlay had also been created a Commander of the Royal Victorian Order in 1949.

It has been suggested that Crawfie nursed a grudge against Queen Elizabeth for not having made her a *Dame* Commander of the Royal Victorian Order – 'a bit above her station' in the view of one courtier[38] – or for not appointing her a lady-in-waiting, and that the disappointed governess therefore embarked on a literary career out of pique.

The real reason was far more practical. Neither Crawfie nor her husband had much capital. He had retired from his job with Drum-

mond's Bank and both the Buthlays had only modest pensions on
which to live. Crawfie sold her reminiscences to Bruce and Beatrice
Gould, the most successful man-and-wife editorial team in the United
States, and then in charge of the Curtis Company monthly, *Ladies
Home Journal*, in which *The Little Princesses* began serialisation in
January 1950. The Goulds had had her story taken down as she talked,
and although there had been rumours that she 'had been assisted by a
distinguished literary figure' — said to be either Harold Nicolson or
Osbert Sitwell[39] — the text had in fact been arranged and polished by
an obscure woman's writer called Dorothy Black.

The London publishers, George Newnes, paid $90,000 (then about
£30,000) for the British serial rights, and *Woman's Own* added
500,000 extra sales to their circulation overnight through Crawfie's
nursery saga.

By today's standards, what she wrote was gushing and innocuous in
the extreme, but Queen Elizabeth, on receipt of Nancy Astor's advance copy, was aghast that anything should have been written at all.
The Queen wrote back to Lady Astor expressing her shock and
sadness, particularly since Marion Crawford had undertaken in writing not to publish anything about the princesses. She could only think
that her once much trusted governess must have gone off her head to
do such a thing.[40] Significant amendments were made — allegedly by
the Queen herself — to the American version of *The Little Princesses*
before its publication in Britain. Among the episodes most noticeably
amended was Wallis Simpson's uninvited visit to the Duke and
Duchess of York at Royal Lodge in April 1936.

Within a matter of weeks, the Buthlays were ordered to leave the
'grace and favour' cottage at Kensington Palace. They were now in
extreme *dis*favour. Crawfie went on to write four further royal
books.[41] She also became a regular columnist for *Woman's Own*, but
her career in journalism came to an abrupt and inglorious conclusion
in 1955, when — somewhat in advance of the actual events, in order to
meet the magazine's deadline — she elected to write about the ceremony of Trooping the Colour and Royal Ascot. 'The bearing and
dignity of the Queen . . . at the Horse Guards' Parade last week caused
admiration among the spectators . . .' she assured her readers, adding
that 'Ascot this year had an enthusiasm about it never seen before'.[42]
Alas for poor Crawfie, by the time this fervent prose appeared in print,
the Trooping had been cancelled owing to a rail strike, and Royal
Ascot had been postponed.

The Buthlays retired to a small house in the Aberdeenshire village of Bieldside. The Royal Family still drive past the gate on their way to Balmoral. Crawfie lives there today in her late seventies, but there are no royal visitors. Even after thirty-five years, her betrayal of confidence has been neither forgotten nor forgiven. Her name remains taboo in Palace circles, and mention of her in the presence of the Queen, the Queen Mother or Princess Margaret produces an icy silence. Crawfie has long since maintained a silence of her own. She had her entry removed from *Who's Who* in 1969. She gives no interviews and closes her front door in the faces of importunate reporters.

'"Do you regret what you did?"' the London gossip columnist, Peter Tory, asked her recently. 'The question was followed by a pause so long that in the end I enquired whether she was still on the line. Yes she was, she said, but really wished to make no further comment.'[43] She now even declines to answer letters personally, responding to written enquiries through an Aberdeen firm of solicitors.

George VI was still simmering with indignation over the royal governess's revelations when the Duke of Windsor's second autobiographical series – of four articles – began running in *Life* on May 22, 1950. The King gave way to one of his worst 'gnashes'. He felt himself to be haunted by fifth columnists on every side. How could he justifiably condemn a royal servant for a breach of confidence when his own brother was writing about private family matters for money?

The King began to look increasingly strained and haggard in public. At the Derby the following month, as the Royal Family drove in procession up the Epsom course, one spectator noticed that the King was heavily made up with rouge in an effort to disguise the alarming yellow pallor of his face.[44] His summer holiday in Scotland brought some respite to the weary monarch, and he was cheered by the news of the birth at Clarence House on August 15 of his second grandchild, Princess Anne, although he did not see the baby until mid-September, when she was brought to visit him at Balmoral.

The Windsors, in the meantime, although steadfastly ostracized by the Duke's family, continued to behave with all the *hauteur* of royalty. At a Paris dinner party given by the jewellery designer, the Duke di Verdura, in honour of ex-King Umberto of Italy, the deposed monarch arrived forty-five minutes late and, recorded Chips Channon, 'omitted to apologize to the Windsors who by that time were hungry and cross'. The Duchess, unimpressed by Umberto's recent regal status or by his manners, was stung into observing, 'At least we weren't kicked out –

we went of our own accord!' Channon added: 'King Beppo was not amused.'[45]

If the Windsors did not change, neither did Queen Elizabeth. Her attitude towards divorce continued to be inflexible even when it concerned her own family. On September 16, 1950, her Bowes-Lyon niece, Anne, Viscountess Anson – who had been the innocent party in her divorce action against her husband, Viscount Anson [46] – married Prince Georg of Denmark, son of Prince Axel of Denmark and the former Princess Margaretha of Sweden. In spite of being with the King at Balmoral, the Queen firmly declined to attend her niece's second marriage, held – according to the rites of the Danish Protestant Church – in Glamis Castle Chapel, in the presence of Prince and Princess Axel, Crown Prince Olav of Norway,[47] and other members of European royalty. The Archbishop of Canterbury, Dr Geoffrey Fisher, later explained that Queen Elizabeth 'didn't disapprove; but she wouldn't go. Didn't want to get muddled up in it, if you see what I mean. Of course, the papers made the most of it . . . marriage in Scotland of a divorced woman – the whole bag of tricks.'[48]

The Queen did, however, drive over from Balmoral with Princess Margaret to attend the family lunch at Glamis Castle which followed the marriage service, and which was presided over by her nephew, Timothy, the new sixteenth Earl of Strathmore, whose own unconventional marriage eight years later was to be a source of regret to his royal aunt. Elizabeth's intransigence over such matters within the Bowes-Lyon family made it doubtful that she would ever relax her opposition to her twice-divorced American sister-in-law.

That summer Wallis first encountered the man who would provoke the only serious rumours there would ever be about the durability of the Windsor marriage. He was a blond, blue-eyed, thirty-five-year-old homosexual exhibitionist called James Paul Donahue Jr – known to the gossip columns as Jimmy – who had inherited some $15,000,000 from his grandfather, the five-and-dime stores magnate Frank W. Woolworth.

From the days of her intimacy with John McMullen, Wallis had always had an affinity with homosexuals, and Donahue, a carefree hedonist, was among the most outrageously amusing she had ever met. Even the Duke, who had a suspiciously vehement aversion to men he called 'pansies', capitulated to Donahue's fey charm.[49] For a time, Jimmy and the Windsors were a threesome, but as Charles Murphy laboured heroically to coax the Duke into concentrating on his long-delayed book – now several years past its original deadline – the Duchess was increasingly to be seen escorted by Donahue alone. They dined out together all over Paris – at Maxim's, Monseigneur, L'Eléphant Blanc, Schéhérezade. They danced together, laughed together, sang duets together. So totally preoccupied with each other did they seem to be, that one guest of theirs, a Spanish Marquesa, put into words what many people in Paris and New York secretly believed: 'Why, they're in *love*!'[50]

In November, when the time came for the Windsors' annual two months in New York, the Duchess sailed alone, leaving the Duke behind in Paris to continue work with Murphy on the book. In the event, the progress made was negligible owing to Windsor's pathetic disorientation and abstraction in the absence of his wife. The problem was magnified by the Duchess being unavailable on almost every occasion her husband tried to telephone her, and by the rapidly mounting speculation on the part of the New York press concerning her now being seen almost constantly in the company of Donahue.

When the New York *Daily Mirror* columnist, Walter Winchell, announced boldly that 'The Duke and Duchess of Windsor are phfft!', the situation was considered sufficiently serious for the British Embassy to draw it to the attention of the King's private secretary – and the Duke's arch-critic – Sir Alan Lascelles.

Here, after thirteen years of marriage, was the situation – the scandal – the British Court had always envisaged; the very circumstances that had argued so strongly against the Duchess being made a Royal Highness. For the ailing King, the Windsors were a neverceasing source of agitation and anxiety, and it was at George VI's personal request that Walter Monckton now telephoned Charles Murphy in Paris to ask if the Duke was aware of what was being written in New York, and also to enquire if there was any truth in the rumours that the most famous marriage of the century was on the rocks.

The Duke *was* aware, owing to the arrival of a wad of American newspaper clippings. At seven o'clock one morning he telephoned Murphy to say that he was throwing up work on the book and sailing for New York. The excuse he gave was that Russia might enter the Korean War, thereby creating escalation into world conflict. If that occurred, his place was with the Duchess. Murphy was not deceived. He realized that the Duke was motivated by one thing only: fear of losing his wife to a man twenty years his junior. Faced with the abandonment of more than three years of work, Murphy made a lightning decision to accompany the Duke in the slim hope of salvaging the book.[51]

When the *Queen Elizabeth* docked in New York on December 6, the Duchess was waiting on the pier. So was an army of reporters and photographers. 'The Duke', said one account, 'thew his arms around the Duchess . . . seven times they kissed.'[52] They 'embraced for the benefit of the camera men . . . The couple denied published reports that they were estranged . . .'[53]

The marital crisis appeared to be over, but not before Wallis's liaison with Donahue had become a subject of scandal in the press and of concern at Buckingham Palace.

Two months later, the Duchess was hospitalized in New York for an operation, the nature of which was never disclosed. The Duke's distress was so evident that it penetrated even his mother's iron reserve on the subject of her unwanted daughter-in-law. 'I feel so sorry for your great anxiety about your wife', Queen Mary wrote to him, 'and am thankful that so far you are able to send a fair account so we must hope the improvement will continue. Do write me a short account of what has really happened.'[54]

The Duchess gradually recovered and, with the Duke's fears allayed, Murphy was at last able to finish the book, although the final chapters were completed with only spasmodic assistance from Windsor. *A King's Story* – even the title caused resentment in London – was launched in New York in April 1951. It was to earn the Duke close on one million dollars – over £300,000.

When the British edition was published that same year, the distortions it contained enraged many of the central participants in the ex-King's brief reign. Lady Hardinge, the wife of his former private secretary, wrote: '. . . while his family held its peace, he apparently found it necessary . . . to exchange a highly coloured and, in my view, one-sided account of his Abdication, for a large cheque'.[55]

With excruciatingly bad timing for which the Duke cannot be blamed personally – but for which Queen Elizabeth found it hard to forgive him – the British launching of the book coincided with the final collapse of the King's health. Public consciousness of this may have partially dictated the uniformly unfavourable quality of the reviews. The *Times Literary Supplement* critic observed that during the Abdication crisis, Stanley Baldwin had felt the struggle to be 'one between himself and Mrs Simpson through the person of the King;'[56]

and Wilson Harris in the *Spectator* spoke for many when he wrote that 'on the Duke's resolve to drag every detail of this old unhappy affair to light again when it had been well forgotten some judgment is called for. It must be unreservedly adverse.'[57]

Lady Donaldson has since added: 'Behind the scenes the book caused unrestrained anger and concern. Those who had taken part in the events the Duke described were often astonished to read a version of them which bore no relation to their own memories ... Many people would have liked to make some public protest. All were restrained from further publicity out of consideration for King George VI.'[58]

This consideration was now desperately needed. The King had been out of action most of the summer with a pesistent temperature, a troublesome cough, and what was believed to be catarrhal inflammation of the left lung. He was deeply tired and his nerves were ragged from seemingly endless health problems. When he and Queen Elizabeth attended Princess Alexandra's confirmation that summer in the little Victorian chapel in the grounds of Royal Lodge, the strain on both King and Queen was audible to the congregation. 'Just before the choirboys filed in and the service began, his voice was heard raised in lively argument with his Consort ... "They're off again," said Alexandra, with one of her inimitable grimaces. "Why can't they wait till I've been done?" '[59]

At Balmoral in August, the King developed a chill and sore throat. On September 8, at the insistence of his doctors, he travelled to London for further examinations and X-rays. The result of these was that a bronchoscopy was performed at Buckingham Palace on September 15 to remove tissue from the King's lung for examination. It was now discovered that he was suffering from a malignant growth and that the only possibility was an operation to remove the whole of the left lung. The King was told of the need for the operation but not of the reason for it. At Balmoral, however, the Queen demanded the truth from the royal doctors and was informed that her husband was suffering from cancer. She was also told that the lung operation would be extremely hazardous and that the danger of a fatal thrombosis either during or immediately following it was considerable.[60]

Queen Elizabeth received this news with outward calm and immediately returned to London. She gave no indication of her inner feelings but they may be gauged by the fact that – for one of only three occasions in her long life[61] – she avoided the public and ordered her chauffeur to drive into Buckingham Palace by a side entrance in Constitution Hill.

The Windsors were once again in London, and this critical time in George VI's life was aggravated by publicity in the British press concerning his brother's memoirs. It is small wonder that Elizabeth, in widowhood, felt unable to think of the Duke and Duchess of Windsor without anger and resentment. Yet one of the King's last acts before undergoing the operation was a gesture of affection to his brother. He gave instructions to the Master of the Household, written in his own hand, to deliver three brace of grouse to the house in Upper Brook Street where the Duke of Windsor and his wife were staying. 'I understand he is fond of grouse,' he said.[62]

The King's left lung was removed on the morning of Sunday September 23. Certain nerves of the larynx also had to be sacrificed, which involved the risk that he might not be able to speak again above a whisper.

Large crowds, waiting in anxious silence outside the Palace, watched the posting of a bulletin which stated: 'Whilst anxiety must remain for some days, His Majesty's immediate post-operative condition is satisfactory.'

The Queen, her two daughters, and the Duke of Edinburgh, drove to Lambeth Palace to pray for the King's recovery at a service held by the Archbishop of Canterbury. But in the medical world the odds against recovery were known to be heavy. Wilson Harris, the editor of the *Spectator*, asked Harold Nicolson to prepare an obituary of the King after meeting Churchill's doctor, Lord Moran, who 'had shaken his head gravely'[63] over the royal illness. And the former royal radiologist, Sir Harold Graham Hodgson, told a friend: 'The King is not likely to live more than eighteen months. The end will probably come suddenly. The operation was six months too late.'[64]

The Queen, who knew the whole truth, calmly went about her duties as senior Counsellor of State on behalf of the sovereign. When, after a six-day delay, Princess Elizabeth departed on October 7 with the Duke of Edinburgh for a long-arranged visit to Canada and the United States, she carried with her a sealed envelope to be opened in the event of her father's death. It contained her Accession documents.[65]

On October 25, at the General Election, the Conservatives were returned to power with the slim majority of seventeen seats over Attlee's Labour Party. The Windsors were still in London and the

Duke, although aware of the seriousness of the King's illness, called on Churchill to press once more for an official job. The Duchess was standing in the drawing-room of the house in Upper Brook Street when he returned from his visit to Downing Street. ' "Was it no?" she asked. He made a grimace, raised his right hand, and then turned it thumb down. She walked to the tall window, to stare broodingly into the fog. "I hate this place," she said, oblivious to the nearness of an American friend standing close by. "I shall hate it to my grave." '66

Again she blamed the person she believed responsible for the limbo in which they were confined: 'the Dowdy Duchess'; 'the shrewd Queen'; her sister-in-law, the unrelenting Elizabeth. Wallis raged perpetually against the enmity of this one woman. As Adela Rogers St Johns had discerned, 'Her bitterness, dark and real and terrible, against the waste of this man's gifts, was partly for herself. They had sat out St Helena as good soldiers – that wasn't her idea of a *life*. Now with years and years ahead of them, growing older years, what would they do with their lives, with the days? The world may be well lost for love but it isn't *lost*, really, it's still there to be lived in, still there with its leaden hours.'67

Churchill had no job to offer but he did at least order the British Ambassador in Paris, Sir Oliver Harvey, to repair the omission of the Windsors' names from the list of invitations to Embassy functions. Sir Oliver gave in under protest, but he and Lady Harvey made their feelings obvious by inviting only members of the Embassy staff to meet the Duke and Duchess.

'The Duchess walked round the circle in a frigid silence; then at last came to a face she knew and cried: "Lees, how lovely; that was fun at Chantilly last Sunday, wasn't it?" '68 This hardly endeared the visitors to the Ambassador and his lady. 'Chantilly', where the Windsors had recently met Lees Mayall, the First Secretary at the Embassy, was a reference to the Château de St Firmin, the home of the former British Ambassador and his wife, Duff and Diana Cooper, with whom the Harveys were then reluctantly engaged in a bitter rivalry that amounted to a feud.

On October 9, it had been announced that, owing to the King's illness, he and the Queen would not be able to undertake their planned tour of East Africa, Australia and New Zealand in the coming year, and that Princess Elizabeth and her husband would go in their place.

By November 14, the King was well enough to be photographed with his grandson, Prince Charles, on his third birthday, and on

December 4, he introduced Princess Elizabeth and the Duke of Edinburgh as members of the Privy Council. Six days later, he was
considered sufficiently recovered to revoke the mandate of the Counsellors of State. Until that time, Queen Elizabeth had carried out most
of the duties of the sovereign.

A troublesome cough forced the King to undergo a second bronchoscopy on December 13, and although the cough disappeared as a
result, a pronounced hoarseness remained, which was painfully apparent in his last Christmas broadcast, pre-recorded in easy stages on
December 21. When the familiar voice, with its usual slight hesitation,
came over the air waves into millions of homes on Christmas Day, the
King's listeners were moved by the effort and courage that audibly
went into every word he spoke.

On January 29, 1952, the King underwent a searching examination
at Buckingham Palace, where his doctors pronounced themselves
pleased with his progress.

On the evening of the following day, the Royal Family went to see
the musical, *South Pacific*, at Drury Lane Theatre, both as a celebration of the King's recovery and as a farewell to Princess Elizabeth and
the Duke of Edinburgh, who were leaving next day for their five-
month tour of East Africa, Australia and New Zealand.

The following morning, Thursday, January 31, George VI stood
hatless on the tarmac of Heathrow Airport to bid farewell to his
daughter and son-in-law as they left on the first stage of their long
journey. As he stood waving with the Queen and Princess Margaret,
his eyes straining for a last glimpse of his beloved Lilibet, the cameras
moved into close-up on the King's gaunt, hollowed-out features, his
hair blown into disorder by a bitter wind. Seven weeks earlier he had
celebrated his fifty-sixth birthday. That day he looked many years
older. On television and cinema screens across the country, a shocked
public saw the full extent of the change in their sovereign; the man
who, as Churchill would shortly say, 'walked with death as if death
were a companion, an acquaintance whom he recognized and did not
fear'.[69]

On the following day, the King, with the Queen and Princess
Margaret, returned to 'dear Sandringham', as his father had always
referred to it, and continued shooting with a small houseparty of
friends. On Tuesday, February 5, there were some twenty guns in the
party, including tenants, local police and visiting gamekeepers. 'The
Norfolk scene was set for the occasion, the wide arc of blue sky,

sunshine and long shadows, a crispness underfoot and the call of mating partridges ringing clearly across broad fields.'[70]

The bag for the day's shooting was 280 hares, four rabbits and two pigeons. At the end, 'the King sat waiting on the forward bank of the hedge, and . . . merrily chided his neighbour, one who had spent as much time with him at Sandringham as anyone, 'I bet I shoot any hares before they cross that hedge to you!"

'A great many hares came forward . . . Towards the end they seemed to see the King and darted through the hedge towards his neighbour. The first was bowled over by His Majesty on the crest of the bank. His friend looked across and was greeted by a gleeful grin. The second was far out in front when it made the hedge, but the King got it none the less. The third, and the last, was at full speed . . . but His Majesty killed it cleanly against the hedge. It was his last shot.'[71]

The King was in a contented mood and said to his friends, 'A good day's sport, gentlemen. I will expect you here at nine o'clock on Thursday.'[72] He returned to the house for tea and then went to visit Prince Charles and Princess Anne in their nursery.

While the King was out with the guns, the Queen and Princess Margaret sailed up the Norfolk Broads in a motor cruiser, *Sandra*, to have lunch with the artist, Edward Seago, at his riverside home at Ludham. In the afternoon they went with him to Barton Broad to take tea at Barton Hall. 'I got back to Sandringham rather late,' wrote Queen Elizabeth to Seago afterwards, 'and as I always did, rushed straight to the King's room to say that I was back and to see how he was. I found him so well, so gay and so interested in our lovely cruise on the river; and then I told him that you had sent the pictures back in my car and we went straight to the Hall where they had been set out. He was enchanted with them all, and we spent a very happy time looking at them together. We had such a truly gay dinner, with the King like his old self, and more picture looking after dinner.'[73]

Princess Margaret played the piano and sang for her father. The King did a crossword, then walked to the kennels to check the paw of his golden retriever, which had been injured by a thorn. He came back through the gardens. The family listened to the BBC radio news to hear about Princess Elizabeth and the Duke of Edinburgh relaxing at a game sanctuary called Treetops, by the Sagana River in Kenya.

At 10.30, George VI picked up a countryman's magazine, said 'I'll see you in the morning', and left the Queen sitting by the fireside. He went to the ground-floor room he had used as a bedroom ever since his illness began, in order to avoid climbing stairs. A cup of hot chocolate was brought to him and he read the magazine for an hour and a half until about midnight, when a watchman in the garden saw him fastening the latch of his bedroom window that had been recently repaired.[74] Then 'he fell asleep as every man and woman who strives to fear God and nothing else in the world may hope to do'.[75]

At 7.15 on the following morning – Wednesday, February 6, 1952 – the King's valet, James MacDonald, came to wake him for his morning bath and found him dead.[76] Sometime in the early hours, the coronary thrombosis that had so long threatened him, ended his life peacefully without sufficient pain to disturb his sleep.

At about the same time, Queen Elizabeth's maid, Gwen Suckling, brought her morning tea as usual. A few moments later a message came from the equerry on duty, Commander Sir Harold Campbell, asking to see Her Majesty urgently. The request, at such an early hour, was so unusual that the Queen must have guessed immediately that it was bad news. Sir Harold had known her for almost thirty years and now had the painful duty of telling her that the King was dead. She saw his hesitation and came to his assistance, making the task 'curiously easy'.[77]

She went to the King, and then, from his study, issued the orders for the day, as he would have done. She asked for a vigil to be kept at the door of her husband's room, adding: 'The King must not be left.'

Sir Harold Campbell wrote to his wife: 'I never knew a woman could be so brave.'[78] But a visit to the nursery was almost her undoing. Prince Charles, now unknowingly the heir to the throne, demanded to be told when Grandpa was coming back to play soldiers with him. The widowed Queen, moved beyond words, hugged her grandson to her and could not answer. The three-year-old Prince, puzzled that his nurses were in tears, said gently, 'Don't cry, Granny.'[79]

Queen Mary, at eighty-four, faced the sudden death of a third son with stoicism. At 9.30 that morning she was working in her sitting-room as usual when her Woman of the Bedchamber, Lady Cynthia Colville, asked to see her. The old Queen looked steadily at Lady Cynthia as she came into the room. 'Is it the King?' she asked calmly. Lady Cynthia told her. Later that day Lady Shaftesbury called at Marlborough House, and Queen Mary said, 'I suppose one must force oneself to go on to the end?' 'I am sure that Your Majesty will,' replied her visitor quietly.[80]

The new Queen, Elizabeth II, who had succeeded to the crown while asleep in a house built into the branches of a tree in an African forest, arrived back at Heathrow Airport from Entebbe at four o'clock on the afternoon of Thursday, February 7. As the black-clothed girl of twenty-five walked alone down the steps of the aircraft to where Churchill, Attlee and her other ministers stood waiting with their heads bowed, she said sadly, 'This is a very tragic homecoming.'

At 4.30, Queen Mary drove out of the gates of Marlborough House. 'Her old grannie and subject must be the first to kiss her hand,' she said.[81] And as the royal standard was broken over Clarence House, the old lady made her first curtsey of state to the sixth British sovereign she had known in her lifetime.

The proclamation of Elizabeth II was delayed for twenty-four hours due to strange and delicate circumstances. 'Very secret word reached the constitutional authorities'[82] that there was the remotest possibility that the Queen Mother might be pregnant since she had missed two menstrual cycles. It was almost certainly the start of the menopause, or possibly the result of emotional distress caused by the King's illness. Yet however unlikely it seemed that the elder Elizabeth could be pregnant at the age of fifty-one, the possibility could not be ruled out. Had a pregnancy been confirmed, the succession would have passed into abeyance, and Counsellors of State would have been appointed to rule the kingdom for nine months until the sex of the widowed Queen's child became known. If it were a boy, he would succeed to the throne, displacing the heir presumptive, Princess Elizabeth. It was quickly established that the Queen Mother was not pregnant, and the heralds assembled in a blaze of scarlet and gold at Temple Bar and on the ramparts of St James's Palace to proclaim that 'the high and mighty Princess Elizabeth Alexandra Mary is now, by the death of our late Sovereign of happy memory, become Queen Elizabeth the Second, by the grace of God Queen of this realm and of all Her other realms and territories, Head of the Commonwealth, Defender of the Faith, to whom her lieges do acknowledge all faith and constant obedience with hearty and humble affection'.[83]

The Duke and Duchess of Windsor had received the news of the King's death by telephone in their six-room apartment on the twenty-eighth floor of the Waldorf Towers in New York. On the evening of the following day, February 7, the Windsors held a press conference in the Verandah Grill on the sun deck of the Cunard liner, *Queen Mary*. Around them were impressionist decorations of acrobats, ballet dancers, a witch and her cauldron, and a cat. It was, one observer thought, 'the most macabre setting in which British Royalty can ever have appeared. For audience, there was a crowd of gum-chewing reporters, photographers and film cameramen.'[84]

The Duke, a black mourning band on one sleeve, read a prepared statement. 'This voyage, upon which I am embarking aboard the *Queen Mary* tonight', he began, 'is indeed sad – and it is all the sadder for me because I am undertaking it alone. The Duchess is remaining here to await my return.' The Duke had been bluntly informed by Buckingham Palace – even before his niece's return from Kenya – that there could be no question of Wallis accompanying him to the funeral. Neither the widowed Queen nor Queen Mary was prepared to tolerate her presence.

The Duchess, wearing a black sealskin bolero over a black costume, with a black fur cap perched on the side of her head, stood in silence behind the grand piano and uttered not a single word during the press conference. It was noted, however, that she 'repeatedly . . . glanced at [the Duke] in compassion'.[85]

The Duke continued: 'I am sailing for Great Britain for the funeral of a dear brother, and to comfort Her Majesty, my mother, in the overwhelming sorrow which has overtaken my family and the Commonwealth of British Nations . . . The late King and I were very close . . . King George VI steadily maintained the highest standards of constitutional monarchy. And these same attributes will, I am sure, descend to his daughter, the new Queen.'[86]

Throughout his statement, there was not a single reference to the person who might be expected to feel the King's loss most: his widow, the Duke's sister-in-law, Elizabeth.

When the *Queen Mary* docked at Southampton, however, on the afternoon of Wednesday, February 13, the Duke – with the Atlantic now separating him from the influence of the Duchess – made a significant insertion in his original statement: '. . . my brother drew strength in his heavy responsibilities from what I once described as "a matchless blessing – a happy home with his wife and children". So, as we mourn a much-loved Monarch, our hearts go out to the widowed Queen Mother and her two daughters in their grief.'[87]

From Southampton, the Duke drove to his mother's London home, Marlborough House, where he stayed throughout his visit. That afternoon he went to Buckingham Palace for tea with his sister-in-law, the Queen Mother, and his niece, the new sovereign. As the widowed Queen and her estranged brother-in-law confronted each other at last across the tea cups, the polite surface of the conversation masked fifteen years of bitterness and resentment on both sides.

That evening the Duke went with Queen Mary and his sister, the Princess Royal, to Westminster Hall, where the King's coffin lay in state. Mother, son and daughter stood for fourteen minutes before the purple-draped catafalque. The Duke, in homage to his dead brother, dropped to one knee as he entered and left the Hall.

Few monarchs had begun their reigns with such deep misgivings as George VI. Fewer still had ended them with such sincere respect, admiration and sympathy. The *Daily Mirror* editorial spoke for many when it said: 'This was by any standards, anywhere, a good man.'[88]

More than three hundred and five thousand of his subjects queued for long hours in bitterly cold weather to file slowly past his coffin, and many thousands more lined the streets on February 15 to pay their last respects to him. The feeling that existed everywhere was expressed several years later by his elder daughter: 'Much was asked of my father in personal sacrifice and endeavour, often in the face of illness; his courage in overcoming it endeared him to everybody. He shirked no task, however difficult, and to the end he never faltered in his duty to his peoples. Throughout all the strains of his public life he remained a man of warm and friendly sympathies – a man who by the simple qualities of loyalty, resolution and service won for himself such a place in the affection of all of us that when he died millions mourned for him as for a true and trusted friend . . .'[89]

As the King's funeral cortège moved slowly through the streets of London, the Duke of Windsor, in a line of four royal princes – with his brother, the Duke of Gloucester, his nephew, the Duke of Kent, and his nephew-in-law, the Duke of Edinburgh – walked behind the coffin, just as he had done, as King, sixteen years earlier at the funeral of his father. Chips Channon, watching the procession, noted: 'Windsor jaunty – what must have been his thoughts and regrets?'[90]

Queen Mary did not attend the funeral, but as the cortège passed Marlborough House, the Queen Mother, the new Queen, the Princess Royal and Princess Margaret were seen to lean forward in the closed Irish State Coach to catch a glimpse of her. Sitting at her window with Lady Airlie, the old Queen 'whispered in a broken voice, "Here *he* is", and I knew that her dry eyes were seeing beyond the coffin a little boy in a sailor suit. She was past weeping, wrapped in the ineffable solitude of grief. I could not speak to comfort her. My tears choked me. The words I wanted to say would not come. We held each other's hands in silence.'[91]

St George's Chapel, Windsor, where the King was buried, was surrounded by flowers. They came from rich and poor, the great and the humble, the famous and the unknown. One card read, 'In memory of our beloved King, from the street traders of Fulham'. Another bore the signature, Winston S. Churchill, and was inscribed, 'In loyal and affectionate memory of their august Sovereign King George VI, the royal founder of the George Cross, with humble duty from Her Majesty's Government'. The wreath was in the shape of the George Cross and bore the words at its centre, 'For Gallantry'.

On the King's coffin rested a wreath of white orchids, white lilies, and white carnations. On the card the widowed Queen had written in her clear and strong hand, 'For darling Bertie, from his always loving Elizabeth'.

At the end of the service, as George VI's coffin descended slowly into the vault of his ancestors, the Queen and her mother curtsied for the last time and walked from the Chapel. Outside, the Duke of Edinburgh 'took off his Naval cap and kissed the Queen Mother on the cheek. He kissed her hand and then, for a second, he turned full towards her and saluted her. As his car was drawing away, he again turned to salute her.'[92] Standing close by and watching his veiled sister-in-law with eyes that looked haunted by guilt, was the Duke of Windsor.

Two days after the funeral, Queen Elizabeth The Queen Mother – as she was now to be known – issued a moving message to the nation: 'I want to send this message of thanks to a multitude of people – to you who, from all parts of the world, have been giving me your sympathy and affection throughout these dark days.

'I want you to know how your concern for me has upheld me in my sorrow, and how proud you have made me by your wonderful tributes to my dear husband, a great and noble King.

'No man had a deeper sense than he of duty and of service, and no man was more full of compassion for his fellow men.

'He loved you all, every one of you, most truly. That, you know, was what he always tried to tell you in his yearly message at Christmas; that was the pledge that he took at the sacred moment of his Coronation fifteen years ago. Now I am left alone, to do what I can to honour that pledge without him.

'Throughout our married life we have tried, the King and I, to fulfil with all our hearts and all our strength the great task of service that was laid upon us.

'My only wish now is that I may be allowed to continue the work we sought to do together.

'I commend to you our dear daughter: give her your loyalty and devotion; in the great and lonely station to which she has been called she will need your protection and your love.

'God bless you all; and may He in His wisdom guide us safely to our true destiny of peace and good will. Elizabeth R.'[93]

The great task of service that was laid upon us. Was there some unconscious hint of reproach in those words? The burden had been unsought, and in the opinion of many, the effort of shouldering it had cost the King his life. Did Elizabeth blame her brother-in-law? Any woman widowed at the early age of fifty-one, having lost her husband at the age of fifty-six, might easily succumb to the temptation to apportion blame.

But as Elizabeth prepared to efface herself from public life and to confront the desolation of widowhood, there were indications that her bitterness was directed less towards the former King than to the woman for whom he had abdicated. For many weeks after the King's death, no one had the temerity to mention the Duchess of Windsor in his widow's presence. When at last her sister-in-law's name was spoken, there was a moment of silence. Then the Queen Mother answered in 'a short, sharp voice' her listener never forgot.

'Oh yes,' she said. 'The woman who killed my husband.'[94]

Don't stop now!!

11

WALLIS AND 'THE MONSTER
OF GLAMIS'

'OUR HEARTS GO OUT', said Winston Churchill, 'to that valiant woman with the famous blood of Scotland in her veins who sustained King George through all his toils and problems.'[1]

Elizabeth Bowes-Lyon, Britain's last Queen-Empress, had need of all her valour in the months following the King's death. Like widows before her and widows since, she had difficulty in grasping that the man with whom she had shared everything for almost thirty years had gone for ever from her life. 'One cannot yet believe that it has all happened', she admitted to Edward Seago, 'one feels rather dazed . . .'[2]

Outwardly it had always seemed to be the confident Queen who gave strength to the hesitant King. As Lady Cynthia Colville pointed out, 'few people realized how much she had relied on *him* – on his capacity for wise and detached judgement, for sound advice, and how lost she now felt without him . . . That was the measure of her greatness as a woman. She drew him out and made him a man so strong that she could lean upon him.'[3]

Now that her daughter reigned, Elizabeth had become the second lady in the realm. She retained the status of a queen. She was still referred to as Her Majesty and permitted to sign herself Elizabeth R. Every woman in the land, except the sovereign, was expected to curtsey to her, and every man to bow. Even the new Queen's husband kissed his mother-in-law's hand, and Prince Charles and Princess Anne were taught to bow and curtsey before racing into their grandmother's arms. But many of her prerogatives under the constitution had vanished with the King's life. It was no longer treason to plot her death as it had been when she was Queen Consort.

The title of Queen Mother – used by neither Queen Mary nor Queen Alexandra – had been adopted to distinguish her in the public mind from the new sovereign, who bore the same Christian name. In practice, however, the cumbersome appellation, Queen Elizabeth The

Queen Mother, was used only for official purposes. In the various royal households, Elizabeth II is referred to simply as The Queen, and her mother as Queen Elizabeth.

George VI's widow had few illusions about the changes wrought in her life by her husband's death. She had watched her imposing mother-in-law unwillingly relegated to a secondary position. She understood all too well the inexorable machinery of royal tradition. 'The King is dead. Long live the Queen.'

Cecil Beaton would shortly observe: 'I did not realize how life can be ruthless, even to queens. We all know what happened to Henry's six wives, and certainly today we have become a bit more civilized; but still human nature can be pretty base. Through a sad break of fortune Queen Elizabeth loses her husband at an early age, and from that very moment her position in life is changed completely. Although she is undoubtedly treated with great love, consideration and sympathy by her daughter who is now reigning monarch . . . nevertheless, no doubt unknown to the present Queen, her mother is suddenly given quite casual treatment by many at Buckingham Palace.'[4]

For some months the widowed Queen was subject to an intense and uncharacteristic depression. At Birkhall – which had now become her home again – members of her household tried in vain to persuade her to invite over friends who were staying with her daughter at Balmoral. 'Oh, no, they won't want to come' she would answer, sometimes adding sadly, 'No one understands . . .'[5]

Two people who did understand her utter desolation of spirit in those first months of widowhood were Commander Clare Vyner and his wife, the former Lady Doris Gordon-Lennox, sister of the Duke of Richmond and one of Elizabeth's lifelong friends. It was while she was staying with the Vyners at their remote Caithness home, The House of the Northern Gate, that the Queen Mother first saw the derelict sixteenth-century Highland fortress, Barrowgill Castle. Learning that this little stronghold of the old Earls of Caithness was threatened with demolition, and falling in love with its grey stone walls and the cannon still mounting guard in the drive, Elizabeth promptly bought Barrowgill and restored its original and more romantic name, the Castle of Mey.

The purchase of this retreat, standing on the northernmost tip of Scotland, fuelled rumours that the widowed Queen was planning to retire completely from public life. But if the Windsors, hearing this, began to hope that Elizabeth's days of power and influence were over, they were to be swiftly disillusioned by the attitude of the new Queen.

Elizabeth II had inherited much of her father's diffidence and reserve, and in spite of fifteen years of careful training for the throne, was scarcely more attracted to the duties of sovereignty than George VI had been. The very last thing the young Queen wanted was for her experienced and extrovert mother, whose gift for public relations and for dealing with all manner of people was unrivalled, to disappear from the scene. Within one month of the King's death, Elizabeth II sent her mother a new red leather despatch box bearing the words in gold lettering, H.M. Queen Elizabeth The Queen Mother. It was a gift which the young Queen intended as a symbol of her mother's usefulness to the new reign.

Elizabeth II also ordered that the Queen Mother was to receive from the Lord Mayor of London the same honours as those accorded to a Head of State. When meeting her, he was to wear his crimson and gold reception robe only used otherwise to greet the sovereign or the ruler of a foreign country.[6]

And when the new Regency Act of Elizabeth II's reign was drawn up, it contained special provision for the Queen Mother's continued eligibility to serve as a Counsellor of State in the sovereign's absence. Elizabeth was the first dowager queen in British history to do this, and during her daughter's absences from Britain she not only reverted to being first lady in the land in terms of precedence, but, as the senior Counsellor of State, received ministers, saw and signed State papers, and presided over meetings of the Privy Council. This status remains unchanged today.

Like Elizabeth II, the Prime Minister, Winston Churchill, was adamant about the need for the Queen Mother to retain an active role in public life. During her weeks of seclusion at Birkhall, when she seemed reluctant to receive visitors, Churchill, who had been staying at Balmoral, took the unconventional step of calling upon her uninvited. What was said by the old warrior to the royal widow is not yet known for certain, but it is believed to have verged on bluntness. From the day of the Prime Minister's visit, certainly, can be traced Elizabeth's intended re-emergence into active life.

Dame Edith Sitwell sent her a copy of her new anthology, *A Book of Flowers*, and the Queen Mother replied: '. . . I started to read it, sitting by the river, and it was a day when one felt engulfed by great black clouds of unhappiness and misery, and I found a sort of peace stealing round my heart as I read such lovely poems and heavenly words.

'I found a hope in George Herbert's poem, "Who could have thought my shrivel'd heart, could have recovered greenesse. It was gone quite underground," and I thought how small and selfish is sorrow. But it bangs one about until one is senseless, and I can never thank you enough for giving me such a delicious book wherein I found so much beauty and hope, quite suddenly one day by the river.'[7]

On May 13, 1952, she performed her first public engagement since the King's death. As Colonel-in-Chief of the Black Watch regiment, she flew to Scotland to inspect and address the 1st Battalion before its departure for the Korean battle front. It had taken that other 'Widow of Windsor', Queen Victoria, thirteen years to emerge, with Disraeli's sly persuasion, from her cocoon of mournful seclusion after Prince Albert's death. Elizabeth the Queen Mother was back on stage after only ninety-six days of widowhood.

This was bad news for the Windsors, who had been hoping strenuously that the new reign would bring about an improvement in their fortunes. Within less than three weeks of George VI's death, the Duke of Windsor had sought a private meeting with his niece, the Queen, to discuss the family situation.

On February 26, Chips Channon noted in his diary: 'Royalties poured in all day, No. 5[8] was a living Gotha ... I had to have a luncheon party, for no better reason than that the Queen and Prince Philip wanted to be alone with the Duke of Windsor.'[9]

The Duke's concerns were fivefold: money, domicile, a job, recognition of his wife by the new sovereign, and that most vexed issue of all: the Duchess's HRH.

Would the Windsors' £21,000 a year from the Privy Purse be continued now that the King was dead? Yes, but there was a flicker of doubt initially, and its continued payment seemed to be conditional upon acceptance of the answers to all the other points.

Would the Queen grant the Windsors tax-free status in Britain – which they already enjoyed in France – in order to allow them to return to live permanently at Fort Belvedere? Knowing her mother's implacable attitude, Elizabeth II was not in the least enthusiastic about having the Windsors in permanent residence in Britain, particularly in a Crown property on the edge of Windsor Great Park. Too many embarrassments could be envisaged. The Queen, realizing her uncle's marked lack of enthusiasm for paying British income tax, replied cautiously that she would consult the Government, but that only the sovereign was traditionally exempt from taxation. Even her mother

would now pay it, and it seemed most improbable that any other
member of the Royal Family could be granted exemption without
awkward questions arising. The ultimate official answer to the request
for tax exemption was a firm refusal, and this put an end to any
lingering ideas the Windsors still had about returning to live in Britain.
Very shortly, Fort Belvedere was sold, on a Crown lease, to the
Queen's first cousin, the Hon. Gerald Lascelles, who lived there until
1976, when he in turn sold the property to the Sultan of Dubai.

Would the Queen give the Windsors a worthwhile job? A Governor-
Generalship, an ambassadorship, or something of the sort? Elizabeth
II was non-committal. Again she considered carefully the problem of
her mother's disapproval. She consulted Churchill, who advised
against it.

Finally the Duke came to the more personal matters. Would his
niece receive the Duchess, and put right a fifteen-year-old injustice by
recognizing her as a Royal Highness? Again the Queen was politely
non-committal. On these points she was influenced less by her
mother's views, and those of Queen Mary, than by her deep devotion
to her father and her strong sense of duty to his memory. For her to
receive the Duchess of Windsor would, she knew, be contrary to her
father's wishes. And to confer royal rank on Wallis would be to admit
publicly that George VI's Letters Patent of May 1937 were illegal and
unconstitutional. This was something she would never do.

The final obstacle to all of Windsor's hopes and ambitions was the
fact that his arch-critic, Sir Alan Lascelles, was remaining on as
Principal Private Secretary for the first year of the new reign. With
Lascelles as her chief adviser, and her mother as senior Counsellor of
State, Elizabeth II was most unlikely to incline a favourable ear to any
request from the Windsors.

With his income intact, but otherwise empty-handed, the disconsolate Duke returned to Paris to report yet another failure to his wife.
That autumn, the Windsors, accepting at last that neither a job nor a
return to Britain was forthcoming, bought the first and last home they
ever owned as a married couple: a seventeenth-century French mill, Le
Moulin de la Tuilerie, near the village of Gif-sur-Yvette, on the
northern slope of the valley of the Chevreuse, some forty-five minutes'
drive from Paris. The previous owner had been the French painter,
Etienne Drian, who had drawn the unfortunate study of the Windsors
which was reproduced on their first Christmas card in 1937.

The following spring, the French Government offered the Windsors

– at the nominal rent of £25 a year – the lease of 4 Route du Champ d'Entraînement, an imposing mansion standing in its own two-acre grounds on the Neuilly side of the Bois de Boulogne. The property of the City of Paris, it had been occupied for a year after the liberation by the interim President of France, General Charles de Gaulle. It was in this house that the Windsors were to live for the rest of their lives.

Jimmy Donahue was still very much on the scene and his growing intimacy with the Duchess had become an established society talking-point. He was seated next to her at the Windsors' table in the grand ballroom at the Waldorf-Astoria in New York on January 5, 1953, when 1,200 socialites paid £9 a head to attend The Duchess of Windsor Ball, organized by the bulky high-priestess of international party-givers, Elsa Maxwell, in aid of wounded American ex-servicemen. For the first half of the evening, Donahue and the Duchess 'had their heads together, and were buried deep in conversation that made now one and then the other gurgle with laughter . . . The Duke across the table . . . listened in desultory fashion to the gales of laughter, and seemed preoccupied . . .'[10]

After dinner, there was a dramatic roll of drums, and the curtains parted to reveal the Duchess of Windsor in a $1,200 white taffeta and coral Paris dress – one of three that she wore during the course of the evening. To the strains of a special composition entitled, 'The Windsor Waltz', she led a parade of society models on to the dance floor. The reaction to this in British royal circles was again unfavourable. It was considered undignified, vulgar, and unbecoming behaviour on the part of a woman of fifty-six who was married to the former King of England.

The occasion also marked the beginning of a much-discussed feud between the Duchess and Elsa Maxwell, who publicly took Wallis to task in print for being 'so completely engrossed in herself and in her pursuit of pleasure that she neither knows nor cares what others are thinking or feeling'.[11] The Duchess retaliated by privately referring to Miss Maxwell, a supposed lesbian, as 'the old oaken bucket in the Well of Loneliness'.[12]

Elsa, on her side, was 'shrewd enough to keep telegrams and such despatched by her erstwhile friend. Among the many thus preserved for posterity, are messages requesting Miss Maxwell to invite 'the third man' to such and such a party. The third man being, of course, ten-cent-store heir Jimmy Donahue.'[13]

The Windsors were still in New York in March 1953, when word

reached them that the eighty-five-year-old Queen Mary was rapidly
failing in health. The Duke's sister, the Princess Royal, who had been
in the Caribbean, paused in New York for one night between planes to
collect her brother, and it was only then that she met for the first time
the woman who had been her sister-in-law for sixteen years. The
Princess Royal's impression of the Duchess of Windsor was apparently
not unfavourable. 'She told me afterwards that she had found her
charming,' recorded her son, the Earl of Harewood.[14]

Since Queen Mary had steadfastly refused to receive her eldest son's
wife, it was obviously inappropriate for Wallis to accompany her
husband to his mother's deathbed. The Duke therefore travelled alone
with his sister to London and stayed at his former home, York House,
with the Duke and Duchess of Gloucester. He and his sister-in-law, the
Queen Mother, were both at the bedside when Queen Mary died
peacefully at 10.20 on the evening of March 24, and her personal
standard, flying above Marlborough House, was lowered for the last
time.

That the Duke of Windsor had loved his mother deeply cannot be
doubted. He once admitted that she was the only thing about England
he had ever missed.[15] In spite of this, however, he could never bring
himself to forgive her for her determined ostracism of his wife. From
London, immediately after her death, he wrote to the Duchess in New
York: 'I somehow feel that the fluids in her veins must always have
been as icy-cold as they now are in death.'[16]

Just as there had been no place for Wallis at Queen Mary's
deathbed, so there could be none at her funeral, even though there was
ample time for her to reach London – either by sea or air – in the seven
days before it took place. The Duke therefore attended alone, 'looking
nervous and fidgety . . . obviously very unhappy'.[17]

The Duchess could scarcely be expected to feel deep regret over the
death of the mother-in-law who had never wanted to know her, but
once again there was a certain sense of propriety lacking in Wallis's
public behaviour. On the evening of March 31 – the day on which
Queen Mary's funeral had taken place in London – New Yorkers were
astonished to see the Duchess of Windsor and Jimmy Donahue dining
and dancing together at a Manhattan nightclub. The incident was
rapidly reported to the young Queen and to her mother, and it served
to harden still further the existing view that Wallis was unacceptable
as a member of the Royal Family.[18]

As long as Queen Mary had lived, the suspicion had existed that the opposition to the Windsors might emanate from her alone, or might at least have continued out of deference to her known views. That possibility was now eliminated. Queen Mary was dead, and acceptance of the Windsors at Court could no longer offend her. Yet the barrier – 'the family-designed asbestos curtain', as Wallis had called it – remained.[19] During the Duke's stay in London for his mother's funeral, he was informed that he and the Duchess would not receive invitations to the Coronation on June 2.

The Queen Mother, who had decided to follow Queen Mary's departure from precedent by attending her daughter's crowning,[20] had made it clear to everyone concerned that the Duchess of Windsor's presence in the Royal gallery – to be occupied by herself, Princess Margaret and the other royal ladies – was not merely unwelcome but out of the question.[21] This would mean relegating Wallis to the back row of the seats occupied by the twenty-seven non-royal duchesses, among whom she technically ranked last of all. Since this, or the Duke's attendance without her, would be an obvious source of criticism, it was decided to invite neither of them, on the grounds that the Duke, as a former sovereign, albeit an uncrowned one, could not properly attend and witness the coronation of one of his successors on the throne. It was a specious argument, for there was no existing precedent concerning an abdicated uncrowned monarch, and the Windsors were bound to view the decision as the latest in a long line of petty humiliations.

The widowed Queen finally left Buckingham Palace and moved into Clarence House on May 18, only fifteen days before the Coronation. Some of the higher-up Palace officials 'couldn't think why the Queen Mother stayed on here so long – not that she will relish the move to Clarence House for there won't be the number of servants there that she's accustomed to'.[22]

Once installed in her new home, only a few hundred yards from the Palace, Elizabeth sent for a spiritualist medium, Lilian Bailey, who conducted a seance for her in an attempt to communicate with the dead King. It was apparently successful, for afterwards, in a gesture of gratitude, the Queen Mother 'unpinned her brooch and fastened it to Miss Bailey's lapel'.[23] As far as it is known, this was the Queen Mother's only recourse to spiritualism, and, in view of her lifelong adherence to orthodox Christianity, it seems that some particular dilemma must have impelled her.

Opinion at the new court was not unanimously in favour of

continuing the ostracism of the Windsors. Both Queen Mary's sister-in-law and her niece, Princess Alice, Countess of Athlone and the Duchess of Beaufort, had strongly urged reconciliation. The Queen Mother, responding to the pressures around her, may have wondered at this point, with Queen Mary no longer on the scene, if she was justified in maintaining an unrelenting attitude towards her brother-in-law and his wife. If the spirit of George VI expressed any views on this dilemma, they must have been adverse, for another fourteen years were to pass before the Duchess of Windsor would meet his widow.

On June 2, the Queen Mother received an affectionate and moving reception from the London crowds as she drove in her own procession to Westminster Abbey to see her daughter crowned. One columnist, Anne Edwards, though that 'the star of the day – apart from the Queen – was a woman . . . glittering from top to toe, diamonds everywhere, a two-foot hem of solid gold on her open dress – the Queen Mother playing second lead as beautifully as she played first. On she came up the aisle with a bow here to Prince Bernhard, a bow there to the row of ambassadors, and up those tricky steps with no looking down like the Duke of Gloucester – no half turn to check on her train like the Duchess of Kent, no hesitation at the top like Princess Margaret, no nervous nods of her head like Princess Mary. She is the only woman I ever saw who can always slow up naturally for a camera.'[24]

The Windsors, watching the Coronation on television at the Paris home of the American hostess, Margaret Biddle, had a less flattering reaction. As the cameras moved into close-up on the widowed Queen, wearing the diamond circlet of her crown, her purple, gold and ermine-edged train carried by four pages, Wallis was heard to remark to her husband, 'Oh look, here comes the Dowdy Duchess'. The Duke almost dutifully responded, 'Here comes the Blimp'.[25]

Three months later, in August, the Windsors were cruising around the Gulf of Genoa aboard Jimmy Donahue's yacht. The now almost permanent *ménage à trois* had resurrected rumours about the ex-King's allegedly ambivalent sexuality. The Duke was thought by some to be almost as attracted to Donahue as the Duchess was. A week after the trio's departure from Portofino, Noël Coward arrived there and had an outspoken discussion with Truman Capote on the Windsor-Donahue triangle. 'I like Jimmy,' Coward told him. 'He's an insane camp, but fun. And I like the duchess; she's the fag hag to end all – but that's what makes her likable. The duke, however, well, he pretends not to hate me. He does, though. Because I'm queer and he's queer but, unlike him, I don't pretend not to be. Anyway, the fag hag must be enjoying it. Here she's got a royal queen to sleep with and a rich one to hump.'[26]

In November, Elizabeth II and Prince Philip flew off on a six-month tour of the Commonwealth, leaving the Queen Mother as first lady of the kingdom in their absence. No sooner had the Queen departed than the Windsors arrived in London, accompanied by thirty-five pieces of luggage – a collection described by the Duchess's secretary as 'just an ordinary wardrobe for a week's stay'.[27]

Together they made their first visit to a London theatre since the Duke's abdication seventeen years earlier. At the Winter Garden Theatre, where they saw Agatha Christie's thriller, *Witness for the Prosecution*, the impresario, Sir Peter Saunders, had been asked to keep their arrival a secret, and not to have photographers present until they left. In order to reach their box, however, they had to walk through the stalls, and within seconds everyone in the theatre knew they were there. As they entered their box, the entire audience rose and applauded. The Windsors, looking surprised and also moved, walked to the front of the box to acknowledge the ovation. As they left the theatre at the end of the play, cheering crowds surrounded their car. 'Certainly, in my mind,' commented Sir Peter Saunders, 'there was no doubt about the feeling of the people of England towards this couple.'[28]

From the theatre, the Windsors drove to Quaglino's Restaurant, where they had first dined together twenty years earlier when the Duke, as Prince of Wales, had given a dinner party for Wallis's thirty-seventh birthday. The news of their enthusiastic reception at the theatre was prominently reported the following morning, with photographs of a beaming Duchess confidently preceding her husband into their car.

In the Mall, the Queen Mother's personal standard – the Royal Arms of Great Britain, impaled with the blue lions and the black archers' bows of the Earls of Strathmore – flew crisply in the December wind to show that the acting first lady in the land was in residence at her London home. But no word of welcome came to the Windsors from Elizabeth during their stay, nor was there an invitation to call at Clarence House.

Coronation Year ended with the Duke and Duchess in New York, celebrating New Year's Eve at the El Morocco nightclub, where they were photographed with paper crowns on their heads. Both the picture

and the headgear seemed sadly symbolic. The Windsors, their lives
bereft of all serious purpose, had become tinsel figures. Moving
aimlessly from party to party, nightclub to nightclub, resort to resort,
they were eternal nomads; human flotsam, permanently adrift, heading for nowhere.

In the autumn of 1954, the Duchess of Windsor suffered a further
reverse in her feud with her sister-in-law. The Queen Mother, visiting
Wallis's native America for the first time since the King's death,
achieved an astonishing personal triumph.

Elizabeth herself had had misgivings about the visit, the principal
object of which was for her to accept the proceeds of the King George
VI Fund, launched in the United States by Lewis Douglas, the former
American Ambassador in London. The Queen Mother felt that her
success with Americans during the State Visit of 1939 had resulted
from the King's personal popularity, and from her position as his wife.
She now tended to agree with the view bluntly expressed in some
circles that 'no American is going to be very interested in the middle-
aged widow of a King'.[29]

In the event, this opinion could scarcely have been more mistaken.
She arrived in New York on October 26 in the *Queen Elizabeth* – the
liner she herself had named and launched in 1938 during the Munich
crisis – to be greeted by enthusiastic crowds and an editorial in the
New York Times which stated: 'Of all the many reasons for welcoming Queen Elizabeth, the Queen Mother, the pleasantest is that she is
so nice . . .'[30]

Daily she stopped the traffic, and excited crowds jammed the
sidewalks to greet 'Ma Queen', 'Mama Liz', 'The royal lady with the
peaches-and-cream complexion and twinkling orbs.'[31] Down in Har-
lem, a small wide-eyed Negro boy demanded, 'Hey, ain't you the
Queen Mom?' This sobriquet, much repeated, and later anglicized in
Canada, was to pass into British folklore for ever.

When she went to see the hit Broadway musical, *The Pajama Game*,
the packed audience rose as she entered and remained standing and
applauding for so long that she was forced to rise from her seat and
turn, almost in tears, to acknowledge the ovation.

Most Americans who were asked by reporters to explain their
enthusiasm for the fifty-four-year-old royal widow gave, as the prim-
ary reason, Elizabeth's example during the war. This factor was also
stressed in the citation for the honorary Doctor of Laws degree
bestowed on her by Columbia University, in which she was described

as 'a noble Queen, whose quiet and constant courage in time of great stress sustained a nation and inspired a world'.

As if all this were not galling enough for the American sister-in-law rejected by the British as a consort for their King, the Queen Mother continued her triumphal progress into Wallis Windsor's home territory of Maryland and Virginia. In the latter State she was greeted as 'our Virginian cousin', and on November 11 – Armistice Day – the girl who had gone from a house in Bruton Street to marry her prince, knelt at prayer in Bruton Church, in the pew used by her great ancestor, George Washington, the first American president.

After four years of rumour and innuendo, Jimmy Donahue had finally faded from the lives of the Windsors, allegedly following a fit of pique during which he kicked the Duchess on the shin in their hotel suite in Baden-Baden.[32] The court jester accepted his banishment willingly and made no effort to repair his royal friendship. Apart from a $100,000 gift in 1960 to the Metropolitan Opera, Donahue's name disappeared from the newspaper columns – until December 6, 1966, when his mother found him dead in bed from 'acute alcoholic and barbiturate intoxication' at her New York apartment at 834 Fifth Avenue. He was fifty-one.

If scandal had ended for the Windsors, it was about to begin for the Queen Mother. She returned from her American triumph to a potentially explosive family crisis. Her younger daughter, Princess Margaret, had been in love for two years with a divorced man sixteen years her senior.

Group Captain Peter Townsend, a much-decorated Battle of Britain fighter ace, had become the late King's equerry in 1944, and Deputy Master of the Royal Household in 1950. After fathering two sons, he had divorced his wife, Rosemary Pawle, in 1951, and the following year the widowed Queen Mother appointed him Comptroller of her new household.

In the summer of 1953, only a few weeks before the Coronation, the Princess and the courtier admitted their love for each other. Tommy Lascelles, the Queen's private secretary – and the Duke of Windsor's sternest critic – rounded on the unfortunate Townsend. 'You must be either mad or bad,' he told him.[33]

In Paris, Wallis Windsor heard the news with undisguised glee. 'So now it's happened to her own daughter,' she commented to her friend, Kitty Miller. And with the widest of smiles she added, 'It must be simply *terrible* for her.'[34]

Wallis was not far wrong. Although sympathetic to Margaret, Elizabeth had found the news devastating. When she came to tell her own household about it, she broke down in front of them for the first time within the memory of any of them. Even the intransigent Lascelles was shaken. 'The Queen Mother wept when I talked to her,' he told Sir John Colville. 'I have never seen her shed tears before.'[35]

Elizabeth's distress is easily understood. Here was her own daughter proposing to marry a divorced person – the very thing for which she and the King had outlawed the Windsors for fifteen years. She liked Townsend enormously and the King had been fond of him. Townsend was the innocent party in his divorce, but then so had Wallis Simpson been in both of hers.

The Queen Mother knew instinctively not only that the Queen, as Head of the Church of England, could never sanction her sister's marriage to a divorced man, but that the Government – even in the more enlightened fifties – would not do so either. If Margaret persisted in her desire to marry Townsend, it would mean relinquishing her royal status, her place in the line of succession to the throne, and her income – £6,000 a year from public funds and a further £15,000 from the Civil List upon marriage. She would be abandoning her public duty in favour of private happiness – the misdeed for which the Duke of Windsor remained condemned by the Royal Family.

The Queen Mother's assessment of the situation was swiftly proved correct. Churchill was sympathetic to Margaret and Townsend, just as he had been to Edward VIII and Wallis Simpson, but his Cabinet unanimously decided that he must advise the Queen against the marriage. Townsend was packed off to Brussels as air attaché, and Princess Margaret was asked to wait until her twenty-fifth birthday, when, if she was still of the same mind, she could marry Townsend without the Queen's consent under the Royal Marriages Act.

On August 21, 1955, Margaret arrived at the age of royal independence. Amid mounting press speculation, and after a separation of two years, Townsend flew back to Britain on October 12, and on the following day was received by the Queen Mother and Princess Margaret at Clarence House. For the next nineteen days, the situation was permanent front page news and reminiscent of the week leading up to the Abdication.

Elizabeth II remained sympathetic to her sister, hoping that some compromise could be found to ensure her happiness without creating a constitutional crisis.

The Queen Mother was outwardly sympathetic, treating both Margaret and Townsend with understanding and kindness. Inwardly, however, her attitude had hardened. She was altogether more inflexible on the issue than the Queen. As Townsend himself had once discerned, 'beneath her graciousness, her gaiety and her unfailing thoughtfulness for others she possessed a steely will'.[36] That strength now quietly manifested itself. Her criterion was the simplest possible. The King would never have approved of the proposed marriage and therefore neither could she.

It transpired that Princess Margaret was unwilling to relinquish royal status, her public duties and her income. Therefore, even without the need for the Queen's consent, she would still require the Government's agreement. On October 18, the Cabinet met under the new Prime Minister, Sir Anthony Eden. The Lord President of the Council, the fifth Marquess of Salisbury – significantly one of the Queen Mother's oldest and closest friends – vehemently opposed the marriage on religious grounds. Salisbury added an ultimatum. If the Cabinet gave its consent, he would resign immediately.

Three days later, on October 21, the Queen, in the presence of the Queen Mother and Princess Margaret, unveiled a statue of George VI in the Mall. Elizabeth II's words on that occasion were seen by many as a reminder to her sister of what the King would have expected of her: 'Much was asked of my father in personal sacrifice and endeavour . . . He shirked no task, however difficult, and to the end he never faltered in his duty to his peoples.'

During some stages of the crisis, the strain began to affect even the Queen Mother's customary imperturbability. Her familiar smile was noticeably absent on several public occasions, and twice she avoided the probing scrutiny of the press cameras by having the windows of her car blacked out. This action, so uncharacteristic of her, and never adopted before or since, was the measure of Elizabeth's anxiety, tension and, occasionally, anger over the Townsend affair.

Even when Princess Margaret had decided finally against the marriage, the Queen Mother still urged her daughter – as Queen Mary before her had urged Edward VIII – against making a public statement.[37] In this respect, however, Margaret proved as resolute as her uncle had been in 1936. Disregarding her mother's counsel, she ended the crisis at 7.21 on the evening of October 31, when she announced that, 'mindful of the Church's teaching that Christian

marriage is indissoluble, and conscious of my duty to the Commonwealth', she had decided not to marry Townsend.[38]

For the Windsors, the result was a disappointment. Had Margaret
stepped down from her position in order to marry a divorced man, it
would have been hailed in a popular sense as the triumph of love over
duty, and – to some extent – as a vindication of the Duke's decision in
1936. As it was, the Queen Mother's views and values had prevailed.
Princess Margaret's affirmation of her 'duty to the Commonwealth'
and her acceptance of the doctrine 'that Christian marriage is indissoluble' was regarded by many as implied criticism of the Windsors
and all they stood for. Time and circumstances were to erode Margaret's attitude and, ultimately, to render her sacrifice pointless, but
that could not be forseen in 1955.

The Windsors believed that Margaret's decision had been forced
upon her by her mother, her mother's friends – like Lord Salisbury –
and the diehard section of the Court. Wallis's reaction to the news was
to acquire a fourth pug to join Disraeli, Trooper and Davey Crockett.
She at once named the newcomer after Princess Margaret's discarded
suitor but, like his namesake, the dog failed to stay the course in royal
circles. ' "We did have a fourth, called Peter Townsend," the Duchess
explained with her least nice grin, "but we gave the Group Captain
away." '39

While the Townsend crisis had been running its course, Wallis had
been engaged on the task of writing her memoirs – or, rather, allowing
someone else to write them. It was a process that went far from
smoothly. Having first retained the services of the American journalist,
Charles J. V. Murphy, the *Time-Life* editor who had guided the Duke's
memories into print, Wallis became irritated by his scepticism over her
version of various events, and by his habit of interrupting her regularly
with the words, 'Oh, come, *come* Duchess.'40

In a fit of exasperation, she fired Murphy from the project. His
replacement as ghostwriter was Cleveland Amory, an American society
chronicler best known later as the editor of *Celebrity Register*. He,
too, was fired by Wallis after disagreements over certain aspects,
notably her treatment by the British Royal Family.41 A third ghostwriter, Kennett L. Rawson, briefly entered the fray but, in the end,
the Duke had to approach Charles Murphy, cap in hand, and beg him
to return to the project in order to meet the deadline and save the
contract.

The book that finally resulted from all this – *The Heart has its*

Reasons – was launched in New York on February 20, 1956, and served to widen still further the rift between the Windsors and the Royal Family. Its publication in Britain reopened the Abdication controversy and goaded Lord Hardinge of Penshurst into publishing in full, in *The Times*, his famous letter to Edward VIII of November 13, 1936, together with his own version of the facts, which differed substantially from the Duchess's. Elizabeth II was affronted by the barely concealed malevolence of Wallis's remarks concerning the Queen Mother, particularly the acid observation, 'Her justly famous charm was highly evident.'[42]

The Duchess's ghostwriter, Charles Murphy, a man of independent spirit, had remained unimpressed by Wallis's habitual abuse of her sister-in-law. 'My own judgment of the Queen Mother,' he wrote in 1983, 'is that she is an admirable woman and a very proper Queen.'[43]

At this time, the Queen Mother also was engaged in recounting the past. She was assisting John Wheeler-Bennett with the official life of King George VI. Like Wallis, Elizabeth was not above adding a touch of cosmetic surgery to recent history. Wheeler-Bennett had been recommended by George V's biographer, Harold Nicolson. 'But from the start Wheeler-Bennett's task proved a more difficult one than Harold's. He had to compete with one of the best royal biographies ever written, and with a widowed Queen Mother who was less complaisant than Queen Mary had been. When he had finished the book Wheeler-Bennett sensed that the Queen Mother was not pleased with the dominant role he had assigned to her.'[44]

Again like Wallis, Elizabeth did not wish to appear as a strong woman dominating an uncertain husband. Unlike Wallis, however, Elizabeth did not allow her implacable hostility towards the Windsors to be expressed or reflected in any form in Wheeler-Bennett's book, even though the author himself became almost uncomfortably well aware of her attitude during his many conversations with her. 'In my talks with Sir John Wheeler-Bennett,' remembered the Irish historian, Harford Montgomery Hyde, 'he made it quite clear that Queen Elizabeth disliked both her brother-in-law and his wife.'[45]

The acrimony between the two women reached its highest point in the mid-fifties. Any bad news about Elizabeth was good news to Wallis. When, in the Grand National on March 24, 1956, the Queen Mother's horse, Devon Loch, collapsed only fifty yards from the winning post while six lengths ahead of the field, the Duchess was jubilant.

'The Queen Mother never turned a hair,' recorded Harold Nicolson. ' "I must go down," she said, "and comfort those poor people."
So down she went, dried the jockey's tears, patted Peter Cazalet on the
shoulder and insisted on seeing the stable-lads, who were also in tears.
"It was the most perfect display of dignity that I have ever witnessed,"
said [the Duke of] Devonshire.'[46]

Wallis was unimpressed. She regarded Elizabeth as the complete
actress, adept at making 'the most perfect display' out of any situation.
It delighted her to see one of racing's most glittering prizes snatched
from her sister-in-law's grasp in the last few yards.

'That poor, poor animal,' murmured Wallis, in mock commisera-
tion. 'To make all that effort and then to do a belly-flop. How
devastating!'

'No, no, darling' interposed the Duke. 'You've got it wrong. It's his
owner who has the belly-flop.' And he roared with laughter at his
schoolboy joke.[47]

In spite of her insistence that it did not matter to her, the withheld
HRH continued to rankle with the Duchess. In 1957, when Sir Walter
Monckton was created a Viscount, she accused him bitterly, 'You got
yourself a title, but you didn't get *me* one!' Monckton, who had done
so much for the Windsors, and who had been instrumental in persuading the French Government to allow them to live in France without
paying taxes, was so incensed by the remark that he left their house
immediately with his wife.[48]

In April 1957, Elizabeth II and Prince Philip made a State Visit to
France. The Windsors, who had been in the United States, were due
back in Paris at this time, but since there was no question of their
presence at any of the functions attended by the Queen, or of her
calling on them at home, they extended their stay in New York until
her departure.

The Windsors were in Paris two months later, when the Queen
Mother, accompanied by the Duke of Gloucester, came to France to
unveil the Dunkirk Memorial on June 29. A family reunion would
have been easy to arrange during this visit, and it need not have
attracted publicity, but to Elizabeth it was still unthinkable. Wallis had
become the Duchess of Windsor twenty years ago that month, yet as
sisters-in-law she and Elizabeth had never once met and it began to
look as if they never would.

A month later, at the end of July, Series D, Volume X of the captured
German Documents on Foreign Policy was published in London by the

British Foreign Office. This section contained the documents relating to the Windsors' stay in Spain and Portugal during the summer of 1940, and the Duke had been informed in advance of the coming publication.

Lady Donaldson has told us: 'It was no secret to the Duke's advisers and those closest to him that, during the period which elapsed between his receiving this information and the publication of the documents he was an exceedingly unhappy and worried man.'[49]

The Foreign Office – possibly in an effort to avoid embarrassment for the rest of the Royal Family, as much as for the Duke – issued a statement that seemed to be both a disclaimer and an apologia. It stressed that the Duke had been 'subjected to heavy pressure', had 'never wavered in his loyalty to the British cause', and that the 'German records are necessarily a much-tainted source'.

In his own statement, issued simultaneously, the Duke maintained: 'These communications comprise in part complete fabrications and in part gross distortions of the truth.' This was an elaborate and perhaps necessary exercise in face-saving for the Queen of England's uncle. It is, however, difficult to be convinced by it. The views attributed to the Windsors by the alleged German sources are all too consistent with the views attributed to them by disinterested non-German sources, such as Alexander Weddell, the United States Ambassador in Madrid.

It is hard to see what point there would have been in the German ambassadors in Madrid and Lisbon misleading their own Foreign Ministry over the Windsors' attitudes to Britain and the war. And if – as the Windsors' Paris attorney, Maître Suzanne Blum, was eventually to claim – the compromising documents are all forged, it is even harder to explain why the Germans would have bothered to do this in 1940, when they had every expectation of winning the war, and no reason to suppose that the documents would ever pass out of German possession.

In the Duke of Windsor's lifetime, his reputation was protected. The Foreign Office statement, and his own, was reported at face value by the British Press in 1957, and no doubts were expressed about his loyalty to Britain.

For the Royal Family, however – and particularly for the Queen Mother – the publication of the German documents must have resurrected bitter memories of the alarm and anxiety the Windsors had caused during the war years and especially at the most critical point of the struggle.

Even after the war, the Duke and Duchess had continued to show an extraordinary lack of circumspection over their choice of friends, and the dangers of being misunderstood on account of the company they kept. In view of the Windsors' rumoured pro-German and Fascist sympathies, it seemed doubly unfortunate that among their closest friends and most constant guests in post-war Paris were Sir Oswald and Lady Mosley.

Sir Oswald, founder of the British Union of Fascists, was one of those who believed that Wallis Simpson would have made an excellent Queen of England. He later derided 'the stiff absurdity of the English ruling class when they rejected any form of marriage with an American of beauty, intelligence, charm and character'.[50]

Mosley and his wife – formerly the Hon. Diana Mitford – had been friends of Hitler, whom they continued to admire and defend for the rest of their lives. Both had been arrested on Churchill's orders in June 1940 and imprisoned under Regulation 18B, which permitted the Government to detain indefinitely without trial any members of any organization if 'the persons in control of the organization have or have had associations with persons concerned in the government of, or sympathies with the system of government of, any Power with which his Majesty is at war'. Conditions in Holloway Prison were not luxurious in 1940, and Lady Mosley was soon asking for hotwater bottles at the height of summer. More than forty years later, she remained bitterly indignant over the treatment of her husband and herself by Churchill,[51] of whose wife, Clementine, the Mitfords were cousins.

By flaunting their friendship with the Mosleys, the Windsors invited further disapproval from the British Establishment and from the Royal Family. They also created an awkward situation at the British Embassy in Paris. No member of the Embassy could be invited to the Windsors' house when either Sir Oswald or Lady Mosley was present. In fact, between 1954 and 1960, during Sir Gladwyn Jebb's tenure as British Ambassador in Paris,[52] it was a written rule that if any member of the Embassy staff found themselves in the same room as the Mosleys, they were to make an excuse and leave immediately.

The Mosleys were not the only close friends of the Windsors to sympathize with the Third Reich. Their favourite Palm Beach host, the American railroad tycoon Robert R. Young, firmly believed that Hitler should have been appeased and war with Germany avoided.

This friendship came to an abrupt end in January 1958, when Mr Young, depressed by the financial decline of his New York Central Railroad, went into his billiard room in Palm Beach and shot himself through the head.

On December 28, 1957,[53] Queen Mary's official biographer, James Pope-Hennessy, arrived at the Windsors' country home, Le Moulin de la Tuilerie, to gather the Duke's memories of his mother. He found there 'every conceivable luxury and creature-comfort . . . a perfection of sybaritic living. It is, of course, intensely American, but I would think consciously aimed. The Queen Mother at Clarence House is leading a lodging-house existence compared to this.'[54]

Pope-Hennessy found the Duchess of Windsor 'one of the very oddest women I have ever seen . . . I should say she was on the whole a stupid woman, with a small petty brain, immense goodwill (une femme de bonne volonté) and a stern power of concentration.' He was 'tempted to classify her simply as An American Woman par excellence, were it not for the suspicion that she is not a woman at all. She is, to look at, phenomenal. She is flat and angular, and could have been designed for a medieval playing-card. The shoulders are small and high; the head very, very large, almost monumental; the expression is either anticipatory (signalling to one, "I know this is going to be loads of fun, don't yew?") or appreciative – the great giglamp smile, the wide, wide open eyes, which are so very large and pale and veined, the painted lips and the cannibal teeth. There is one further facial contortion, reserved for speaking of the Queen Mother, which is very unpleasant to behold, and seemed to me akin to frenzy.'[55]

Pope-Hennessy quickly realized that the subject of her sister-in-law was a burning irritant to the Duchess.

'Duchess: "I suppose you've had to see everybody about yah book?"'

'J.P-H.: "Oh yes, I have had a lot of interviews. The Duke's sister has been very helpful, and the Queen Mother."'

'Duchess: "I don't think she was very close though."'

'J.P-H.: "The Queen Mother?"'

'Duchess (in a slightly steely tone): "Why yes, I don't think the Queen Mother would know much about Queen Mary."'

'J.P-H.: "Well, of course, she doesn't remember as far back as the Duke would."'

'Duchess: "Y'know, there are only three real royalties in the world today. The Dook, his brother Gloucester and his sister."'[56]

Wallis went on to tell Pope-Hennessy about a maid she had recently employed, who had previously been with the Queen Mother for five years. There seemed to be a faint suggestion that the woman became a saboteur in the Duchess's wardrobe. '. . . I had to get rid of her: I had a Balenciaga dress with a crinoline. Well, Irene ironed that crinoline so that you couldn't see what it was by the time she'd finished. I took it back but even Mr Balenciaga himself couldn't decide just *what* she had done to that crinoline. And she just *burned up* five more of my dresses. Well, that surprised me, because I thought that, after all those years with the Queen Mother, if she hadn't learnt to iron a crinoline, what *had* she learned?'[57]

After dinner on his last evening with the Windsors, Pope-Hennessy sat 'in a corner with the Duchess and we discussed Them and England, and it was then she looked so very fierce when saying how badly they had been treated and kept referring back to the Queen Mother'.[58]

By this point, the Windsors were in the habit of abusing Elizabeth to anyone who cared to listen. The Duke, his former affection for his sister-in-law long forgotten, was heard to refer to her as 'that fat Scotch cook',[59] and sometimes as 'the Loch Ness Monster'.[60] Wallis's repertoire of derision now extended beyond her original epithet, 'the Dowdy Duchess'. Elizabeth had become 'that fourteen-carat beauty' and, more often, 'the monster of Glamis'.[61]

The Duchess's use of the Glamis legend to ridicule her sister-in-law served as a reminder that Elizabeth was capable of showing as much sternness and inflexibility towards her own family, the Bowes-Lyons, as she had to the Windsors.

On June 18, 1958, in the Chapel at Glamis Castle, the Queen Mother's nephew, Timothy Bowes-Lyon, the sixteenth Earl of Strathmore, who was then forty, married an Irish nursing sister of thirty-five, Mary Bridget Brennan. No member of the Royal Family or of the Strathmore family was present at the ceremony. The only witnesses were a St Andrews dentist and his wife, a Mr and Mrs Lockhart White. The castle chaplain, Canon Harry Rorison, had declined to conduct the service because he did not regard the marriage as 'suitable'. This was a view with which the Queen Mother and the rest of Lord Strathmore's family fully concurred.

Mary Brennan, one of the ten children of a merchant from Clonaslee in the Irish Republic, was of working-class background and completely unknown in society. She was also a Roman Catholic, but, after considerable hesitation, she reluctantly agreed to a Protestant marriage service, which was performed by the Rector of St John's Episcopal Church, Forfar.

Timothy Strathmore, a second son – his elder brother was killed on active service in 1941 – had been a family problem ever since his schooldays at Stowe, where he had shown a healthy but inconvenient interest in the housemaids. Succeeding to the earldom in 1949 as a bachelor of thirty-one, he made an unsatisfactory head of the Strathmore family. He was an alcoholic and also an epileptic. He met his future wife in one of the clinics where he went periodically to 'dry out', and where she was a member of the nursing staff.

At the time of the marriage, the Earl's bride volunteered the information that her father, Peter Brennan, was dead. She may have been under that impression, but in fact he was very much alive, and shortly afterwards turned up, extensively interviewed, behind the bar of a club in Leicester, where he was working as a steward.

No people are more conservative or more class-conscious than the Scots, and in the county of Angus the unfortunate first impression was that the flamboyant Irish nurse would make an unlikely Countess of Strathmore, an inappropriate *châtelaine* for Glamis, and an unsuitable wife for the Queen of England's first cousin. Neither the Queen Mother nor her daughters made any move to meet the bride, and during the first weeks of the marriage few of the neighbouring landed families in Scotland called at Glamis to pay their respect to the new Countess.

On December 8, 1959, a daughter, Lady Caroline Frances Bowes-Lyon, was born at a London nursing home. Three weeks later, on New Year's Day 1960, the child died at Glamis from bronchopneumonia. In certain Scottish drawing-rooms, there was less interest in the tragedy of the baby's death than the fact that Lady Strathmore had allegedly brought her child north in a third-class sleeping compartment.

British society is not noted for its sympathy in misfortune, and the bereaved Countess was still not accepted socially or received by the Royal Family. In October 1961, when the Queen Mother visited Glamis for the first time since her nephew's marriage, Lady Strathmore was undergoing treatment in a Dundee nursing home. The Queen Mother did not return to Glamis when the Countess was in residence, although she frequently visited another nephew, Lord Elphinstone, at nearby Drumkilbo.

Lady Strathmore gradually became haunted by the sadnesses in her life: her baby's tragic death; a feeling of guilt over the renunciation of her Catholic faith; the obvious lack of acceptance of her by her husband's family; and, perhaps most of all, the gloomy and oppressive atmosphere of Glamis itself. Lord Strathmore had several times had the castle exorcised in an attempt to quieten its resident ghosts.

During the next few years, the unfortunate Countess changed from the healthy, outgoing woman who had nursed others, into a nervous invalid who suffered from constant headaches and seemed to have developed a kind of death wish. 'She came to believe that she was suffering from an incurable illness,' explained the Glamis factor, James Kemp.[62] On September 8, 1967, the maid who took Lady Strathmore's breakfast to her bedroom at Glamis found her dead in bed from a massive self-administered overdose of the barbiturate, Seconal. She was forty-five.

No inquests are held in Scotland, and it was never publicly stated that Lady Strathmore had taken her own life. A post mortem, carried out on the orders of the Procurator Fiscal's office in Forfar, revealed that there was nothing wrong with the dead woman physically beyond the acute barbiturate poisoning from which she died. The case was reported to the Crown Counsel in Edinburgh as a suicide.

Lady Strathmore's will confirmed the morbid dread she had developed from her unhappy life at Glamis. The first clause stated: 'I desire my body to be buried but before this is done I wish my main artery to be severed by the Doctor attending me just before my death.'

Three days after her body was discovered, the Countess's funeral took place at the private burial ground at Glamis.[63] The Royal Family was in residence at Balmoral, less than fifty miles away, but no member or representative attended. Among the flowers, however, was a wreath from the Queen Mother for the niece-in-law she had neither known nor accepted.

For the remaining five years of Lord Strathmore's life, he became a virtual recluse, seen by hardly anyone. He died at Glamis, on the stroke of midnight on September 13, 1972, from the effects of a coronary thrombosis and epilepsy. He was fifty-four. He was succeeded as seventeenth Earl by his first cousin, Fergus Bowes-Lyon, who had an eminently respectable wife – a McCorquodale, from the same family into which Barbara Cartland had married twice – and three children, the second of whom was called Elizabeth after her royal great-aunt.

With an acceptable family living in the castle again, including a new Lady Elizabeth Bowes-Lyon, the Queen Mother returned to Glamis during the Perth Races in September 1977, and spent her first night within the castle walls for almost twenty years.

It is valid to compare Elizabeth's studious aloofness towards the Irish nurse with her determined ostracism of the American divorcee who was her sister-in-law. Mary Brennan had had no previous husbands and nothing was known against her other than the accident of humble birth. Yet she provoked an obvious distaste and disapproval in her husband's aunt which caused her to be ignored by the Queen Mother during nine years of marriage as completely as Wallis Simpson had been ignored for more than twenty.

Was there a common factor? On the surface there was little resemblance between the unsophisticated Irish girl and the wisecracking American socialite. The only arguable link was that both women aspired to marriage with men of a status far removed from their own; men who were regarded by their families as vulnerable and therefore dependent upon the women concerned. Both marriages were judged 'unsuitable', and the wives were condemned ultimately for ambition: the offence – as some saw it – of elevating themselves socially by taking advantage of male inadequacy. It was the reaction Queen Mary had crystallized into two words when she branded Wallis Simpson 'an adventuress'.

Did the tragic saga of the unacceptable Countess of Strathmore throw any light on the complex character of the Queen Mother? The Duchess of Windsor certainly thought so. To Wallis, it merely confirmed what she believed she had discovered many years earlier: that behind Elizabeth's famous smile, her celebrated charm and the adored public image was a coldly obstinate woman of narrow and snobbish principles, fiercely unforgiving, and formidable in her opposition to any who failed to accord with her inflexible personal standards.[64]

In April 1959, accompanied by Princess Margaret, the Queen Mother visited Rome and was received in private audience by Pope John XXIII. At one point during the visit, an Italian woman carrying a small child seized Elizabeth by the arm and shouted for 'bread and work'. The demonstrator was swiftly arrested by the Italian police, but the Queen Mother's infallible gift for public relations came to the rescue. She at once sent a handwritten message to the Mayor of Rome: 'I hope nothing will happen to that poor woman. Elizabeth R.' The distraught mother was released without charges being brought against her.

Elizabeth and her daughter returned to London via Paris, where they lunched with President de Gaulle at the Elysée Palace. Once again, the Queen Mother had passed through the French capital without meeting her brother-in-law and his wife.

As the years advanced, the things that remained important to Wallis began to lose importance for Elizabeth. The Duchess resorted to discreet facial surgery to help preserve her still youthful appearance. The Queen Mother preferred to let time tell its own story. One set of photographs by Cecil Beaton, which had been tactfully retouched, were returned to him from Clarence House with the gentle comment: 'Her Majesty does not wish it to be thought that life has left her entirely unscathed.'[65]

On February 19, 1960, Elizabeth II gave birth to her third child, Prince Andrew. One week later, the Queen Mother announced the engagement of Princess Margaret to the photographer, Antony Armstrong-Jones, the son of divorced parents.

Approached by journalists for his reaction to the news, the Duke of Windsor commented briefly: 'I do not know the gentleman but I wish my niece and her betrothed every happiness.'

Invitations, embossed with the words, 'The Lord Chamberlain to Queen Elizabeth The Queen Mother is commanded by Her Majesty to invite . . .', began to go out from Clarence House to several thousand people. When the guest list was complete, however, it was found that the Queen Mother's Lord Chamberlain had not been commanded by Her Majesty to invite the Duke and Duchess of Windsor, the uncle and aunt-in-law of the bride. Once again they were pointedly excluded from a family occasion, and now, with George VI and Queen Mary no longer on the scene, there was only one person who could reasonably be suspected of responsibility for the omission.

The wedding took place in Westminster Abbey on May 6, and the Windsors watched it on television. To Wallis, the principal interest appeared to be the presence in the Abbey of Tony Armstrong-Jones's divorced mother, the Countess of Rosse, together with his divorced stepmother, the former actress Carol Coombe, and his father's third wife, a BOAC air hostess, Jennifer Unite, who was only one year older than the bridegroom.

Two divorces were apparently no longer a barrier to presence on royal occasions, and the Duchess of Windsor observed acidly, 'Well at least they can't say I haven't kept up with the Joneses.'[66]

Four days after her daughter's wedding, the Queen Mother left London for Rhodesia and Nyasaland, to open the Kariba Dam on the

Zambesi river. During the tour, newspapers all over the world published a story, first headlined in the New York *Daily News*, that Elizabeth was planning to marry again. The 'prospective bridegroom' was identified as the Treasurer of her household and her lifelong friend, Sir Arthur Penn, who, at seventy-four, was fifteen years her senior.

This was one of the few occasions in her public career when Elizabeth reacted angrily to the press. Colin Black, the press officer for the royal tour, was ordered in no uncertain terms to issue a categorical denial: '... her Majesty stated that a report in an American newspaper that she and Sir Arthur Penn were contemplating marriage was "complete and absolute nonsense". These were her Majesty's last words. In fact, her Majesty used a stronger word.'

This was an effective way of scotching rumours, for the original story died in a new blaze of speculation as to what the 'stronger word' might have been. Only seven months later, at Christmas, Sir Arthur Penn became seriously ill, and the Queen Mother went repeatedly to see him in hospital. He died on December 30, the day before he was due to retire from her service.

No one, not even the Windsors, had believed that Elizabeth would marry again. Ex-Queen Victoria Eugenia of Spain – 'cousin Ena' – dismissed the story as 'a piece of false news so patently absurd ... George VI's widow is keen above all to remain as she is: a respected, honoured and highly popular Queen Mother. It is quite out of the question that she could even entertain the idea of re-marrying, whoever the prospective partner.'[67]

The family snubs to the Windsors continued. On June 8, 1961, the Duke of Kent – Prince Eddie, son of the Duke of Windsor's favourite brother – married Katharine Worsley at York Minster. Again the Windsors were not invited, and the young couple went off to spend their honeymoon at the Queen Mother's Deeside home, Birkhall.

On November 3, Princess Margaret's first child, Viscount Linley, was born at Clarence House, his father having reluctantly accepted the earldom of Snowdon the previous month. When the baby was christened at Buckingham Palace on December 19, with David as his first name, there was speculation in some sections of the press that he had been called after the Duke of Windsor – a welcome, if belated, tribute to the former King. This notion was instantly demolished by press officers at both Buckingham Palace and Clarence House. Princess Margaret's son, they emphasized, had certainly not been named after the Duke of Windsor, but after the Queen Mother's favourite brother, the Hon. Sir David Bowes-Lyon, who had died three months earlier at the age of fifty-nine from a coronary thrombosis while staying with Elizabeth at Birkhall.[68]

In her sixties, the Queen Mother continued to carry out a crowded programme of public engagements both at home and overseas. She had no time for idleness, and once told her daughters, 'The work you do is the rent you pay for the room you occupy on earth'.[69]

In Elizabeth's view – seldom expressed except in private, and then only to close and trusted friends – the Windsors paid no rent. Instead of feeling martyred because there was neither job nor place for them in the country the Duke had abandoned, why did they not find their own sphere of work? They were not poor. They paid no taxes. They had the status and resources to do almost anything – endow a hospital, found a charity, work for international human rights. Instead they were photographed – aged sixty-seven and sixty-five respectively – dancing the Twist in a Paris nightclub. In Elizabeth's eyes, her brother-in-law and his wife were a pampered, idle couple, with a frivolous and shallow lifestyle, who did nothing to justify the deference and privileges they still expected.[70]

On April 24, 1963, there was another royal wedding in Westminster Abbey when Princess Alexandra of Kent married the Hon. Angus Ogilvy. The Duke of Windsor wanted very much to see his favourite brother's daughter married, particularly since the bridegroom was the nephew of his former equerry and once closest friend, Bruce Ogilvy. Yet again, however, there was no invitation for the Windsors. Even if the bride's mother, Princess Marina, had been prepared to ask them, there would still have been complications, for Angus Ogilvy's father, the Earl of Airlie, was the Queen Mother's Lord Chamberlain. Like the Duke and Duchess of Kent before them, it was to Elizabeth's Scottish home, Birkhall, that Princess Alexandra and her husband went for their honeymoon.

This time the snub had gone beyond the mere absence of an invitation. In the approved souvenir programme for Alexandra's wedding, published by permission of Princess Marina, the Duchess of Windsor was the only member of the family whose name was omitted from the genealogical table of British royalty. George VI, the Duke of Gloucester, the Duke of Kent and the Princess Royal all had the names of their marriage partners clearly stated, together with the year in which they were married. Even Marion Stein and Angela Dowding, the non-royal wives of the Earl of Harewood and the Hon. Gerald Lascelles, were included. But under Edward, Duke of Windsor were the words, '(formerly King Edward VIII)'. There was no reference to his wife or to the fact that he had ever married.[71]

In the following December, the Duchess of Windsor gave a rare interview to her fellow Baltimorean, Susan Barnes, later the wife of the Labour cabinet minister, Anthony Crosland.

After pointing out that the Duke 'is so popular with the British public', the Duchess added, with a significance that came via omission, 'On the other hand, the people who are there now do a wonderful – you can't call it a *job*. What *do* you call it?'

Susan Barnes asked Wallis if she thought she would ever be accorded the title of Royal Highness. ' "Never!" said the Duchess, swinging her crossed leg impatiently. "I don't mind. There are a great many things I have had to learn not to give any importance to . . . I don't know, but I think the refusal to give me equal rank with my husband may have been done to make things difficult for us. It *is* difficult – because people are puzzled about what to do with me. At parties. At any time. They don't understand being married to Mr Smith and being called Mrs Jones. And I know it hurts my husband . . . I know that he has been hurt very deeply . . . I don't mind for myself. I've lived without this title for twenty-five years. And I'm still married to this man!" '[72]

At the beginning of February 1964, the royal sisters-in-law were both in hospital in London at the same time – the Queen Mother in King Edward VII's Hospital for Officers to have her appendix removed; the Duchess of Windsor in the London Clinic for another facial operation. Only one street separated the two hospitals, but neither flowers nor messages passed between the long-estranged women. On June 23, however, when the Duke celebrated his seventieth birthday, he received a telegram of congratulations from his niece, the Queen. This may have been less a personal gesture on Elizabeth II's part than an indication that her advisers, bearing in mind the advancing age of the Windsors, and also the mounting press criticism of their treatment by the Royal Family, had decided that it was now expedient to effect a limited reconciliation – at least in a public sense.

In the following December, when the Duke entered the Methodist Hospital in Houston, Texas, to have an aneurism removed from his abdominal aorta by the celebrated heart surgeon, Dr Michael

DeBakey, he found his room bright with flowers sent by the Queen, Princess Margaret, and his sister, the Princess Royal. The operation was a success, and on the last day of 1964, the Windsors flew to New York, sailing back to France at the end of January.

The Duke's doctors now decided that he needed a further operation to repair the detached retina of his left eye. On medical advice it was agreed that this surgery would be best performed at the London Clinic. In the last week of February 1965, therefore, the Windsors once again arrived in London. There was no reason for them to suppose that this visit would be any different from all the others as far as the attitude of the Royal Family was concerned.

Certainly no one imagined that the problem of the Duke's impaired vision would be the means of ending almost thirty years of Establishment myopia towards the Windsors; still less that it would bring about the first official recognition of the Duchess by the British sovereign.

12

THE DUCHESS BECOMES
PERSONA GRATA

WHEN THE DUKE AND DUCHESS of Windsor arrived at the London Clinic on February 23, 1965, their arch enemy, the Queen Mother, was away on an official visit to Jamaica. Prince Philip was also on an overseas tour, and the Queen herself was confined to Buckingham Palace with a severe chill.

The Windsors, therefore, at once became the royal focal point of press interest. Their advancing age, the Duke's impaired vision, and his forthcoming operation combined to create a new sympathy for the exiled couple and a certain popular indignation on their behalf. When, the media now demanded to know, would the Royal Family relent in their cold-blooded ostracism of 'a blind old man and the woman who had been his wife for nearly thirty years?'.[1]

Elizabeth II's advisers, who were far more attuned to the expediencies of public relations than those of George VI had been, realized at once that the Court was now being criticized on humanitarian grounds, and with apparent justification. Sir Michael Adeane, the Queen's astute private secretary,[2] felt that the time had certainly arrived for some gesture on the sovereign's part towards the Windsors. In addition to this, Walter Monckton's widow, Biddy – the Dowager Viscountess Monckton of Brenchley[3] – passed a personal message to Buckingham Palace to say that the Duke of Windsor would be much cheered and also touched if his niece, the Queen, could find time to visit him while he was in the London Clinic.[4]

Elizabeth II hesitated. She recognized the wisdom of the advice tendered to her, and personally had nothing against the idea of visiting her uncle in the clinic, or even of a long-delayed meeting with the Duchess. But with the Queen Mother still out of the country, the Queen wished to do nothing that might be construed as going behind her mother's back.[5]

On February 27, the Queen Mother returned from Jamaica, where she had lunched at Firefly, the home of Noël Coward, who recorded:

'She has infinite grace of mind, charm, humour and deep-down kindness, in addition to which she looks enchanting. She puts everyone at ease immediately without condescension or apparent effort . . . It was all tremendous fun, without a moment of strain, and she left behind her five gibbering worshippers.'[6]

For all the 'deep-down kindness', however, Elizabeth II, knowing the family history, must have approached with trepidation the delicate task of raising the Windsor dilemma with her mother. It will be many years before we are allowed to know how she did so and what was said between them, but the two-week pause that now ensued before the Queen took any action in the matter clearly indicates that her mother was consulted.

After fifteen years as Queen of England, and a further thirteen as Queen Mother, Elizabeth had an intelligent awareness that what was desirable and what was expedient could not always be reconciled. While she had no intention of revising her personal estimate of the Windsors, or of changing her own attitude towards them, she readily agreed with her daughter's advisers that a public thaw was indicated.[7]

There was also, perhaps, at this time, something of a private thaw in the sterner aspects of Elizabeth's character. In a recent interview with Dorothy Laird, for an authorized biography to be published the following year, written with 'the gracious permission and assistance' of the Queen Mother, Elizabeth had said, '. . . as one grows older, one becomes more and more tolerant, and finds that nearly everyone is, in some degree, nice. The only regret one has as one grows older is that things do not matter so strongly.'[8]

It seems possible, therefore, that Elizabeth II may have found, to her surprise, that the long vendetta between her mother and the Windsors – on the Queen Mother's side, at least – had lost some of its acrimony, and that, instead of registering outraged objections to her daughter's proposed gesture, Elizabeth was able to view it with equanimity. Perhaps she may have felt that even if her husband had lived – George VI would have been sixty-nine then – a *rapprochement* might have been deemed acceptable by that point.

This seems to have been her thinking, for to the Windsors' great surprise, among the flowers that now poured into the Duke's private suite in the London Clinic was one particularly beautiful arrangement 'to David', and signed, in his sister-in-law's clear and upright hand, simply 'Elizabeth'.[9]

Reassured by her mother's attitude, Elizabeth II now acted on the advice given to her. At 6.40 on the evening of Monday, March 15 – by which time the Duke had undergone three operations on his left eye – the Queen's maroon-coloured Rolls Royce drew up outside the front entrance of the London Clinic in Devonshire Place.

The Queen, accompanied – significantly – by her Principal Private Secretary, Sir Michael Adeane, and her bodyguard, Detective Inspector Albert Perkins, entered the Clinic to be received by the chairman of the governors, Sir Aynsley Bridgland, and the Matron, Miss Joan Lewis. The Duke's doctors and surgeons – Sir Stewart Duke-Elder, Mr James R. Hudson and Mr Lorimer Fison – were then presented, and the Queen and Adeane went to the Windsors' three-room suite on the fourth floor, where she was greeted by the Duchess with a deep curtsey. It was their first meeting for twenty-nine years, since Wallis Simpson's uninvited visit to Royal Lodge in the Spring of 1936, when the ten-year-old Princess Elizabeth had asked her governess, 'Who is she?'

The seventy-year-old Duke, clad in pyjamas and dressing gown, his left eye heavily bandaged, sat in an armchair in the sitting-room, with the Queen and the Duchess sitting on either side of him. The meeting lasted twenty-five minutes and the presence of Adeane was a key factor. Not only did the Principal Private Secretary's attendance add weight to the subsequent view that the encounter was an 'official recognition' of the Duchess of Windsor by the sovereign, but Sir Michael was also there to advise on another matter.

Through Lady Monckton, the Queen had already got wind of the fact that the Duke had an important request to make. In 1957, he had bought a large plot in Green Mount Cemetery, Baltimore, where many of Wallis's Warfield and Montague relations are buried. But now that he was seventy and almost certainly in the last decade of his life, the Duke felt unhappy at the idea of his mortal remains being consigned to foreign soil. He wanted his body to return home to be buried at Windsor with the rest of his family. Would the Queen permit him to lie in the private royal burial ground at Frogmore, near his favourite brother, the Duke of Kent? Would she allow Wallis to be buried beside him, and might they both have private funeral services in St George's Chapel, Windsor?[10]

The far-sighted Adeane at once envisaged the unsuitable publicity liable to result from a former King of England, exiled in life, being exiled also in death, and particularly from a quasi-royal funeral in the United States. In view of the growing sympathy for the Windsors on the part of both press and public, it seemed wholly desirable for the Duke, at the end of his life, to be brought back into the British fold.

The Queen, privately, felt less enthusiasm for the idea of her twice-divorced American aunt-in-law resting in perpetuity in close proximity to Queen Victoria,[11] or for the prospect of having to attend her funeral service in St George's Chapel, a place traditionally associated with British royalty, but she saw how much it meant to her uncle, and she received his request with kindly attention and promised to give it her careful consideration.[12]

At the Duke's suggestion, his two Irish nurses, Catherine Cronin and Ita Riordan, were brought to be presented to his niece, and at 7.15, the Queen left the London Clinic, smiling broadly, and commenting to the Matron, 'I have enjoyed my visit.'[13]

The following morning's London newspapers gave the royal reconciliation front-page headline coverage, and the general reaction was summed up by the *Daily Express* editorial, which stated that the Queen's gesture to the Windsors 'will be warmly approved by the nation'.[14] Speculation was rife over what had been discussed between Elizabeth II and her uncle's wife. One cartoon showed the Duchess of Windsor observing acidly to the Duke, '. . . and what she didn't seem to realize was that without me she wouldn't have *been* Queen'.[15]

But in reality, the Windsors, heartened by the gradual prising open of royal doors after almost thirty years in the wilderness, were at last learning the art of circumspection. 'The Queen is so good-looking today and dresses so beautifully'[16] was Wallis's only authenticated comment on the woman whose mother she had branded 'the Dowdy Duchess' and an international fashion disaster.

Two days after the Queen, there was another royal visitor. At six o'clock on the evening of Wednesday, March 17, the Duke's sister, Mary, the Princess Royal, arrived at the London Clinic, carrying a bouquet of flowers. She stayed for forty-five minutes, meeting her sister-in-law, the Duchess, for only the second time in twenty-eight years. As she left, apparently in perfect health and spirits, no one could have guessed that it was also to be Princess Mary's last meeting with her brother.

In the wake of the Queen and the Princess Royal, Princess Marina also visited the London Clinic to see the Duke and at long last came face to face with the sister-in-law she had refused to call on during the Windsors' honeymoon at Schloss Wasserleonburg in the summer of 1937. With the Duke and Duchess of Gloucester – both only recently recovered from a serious car accident[17] – now in Australia, the Queen Mother was the only notable absentee from the family gatherings at the London Clinic, although her flowers were by the Duke's bedside as a token of her goodwill.

If Elizabeth was displeased by the much-publicized family attention being belatedly shown to her brother-in-law and his wife, she gave no sign of it. The Exchange Telegraph Company had rigged up 'The Blower' – a racecourse commentary service – for her at Clarence House, allowing the royal dowager to receive the same information on betting odds, form, jockey changes and weights that was relayed to betting shops throughout Britain. And on the afternoon of Friday, March 19, the Queen Mother was in her gayest mood at Sandown Park, where she watched her horse, Antiar, romp home in the Beech Open Chase, taking her total of winners for that season to twenty-four, the same as her previous best tally in Britain in the season of 1961–1962. She ended the season with twenty-seven winners.

That same afternoon, while Elizabeth was happily acknowledging the applause of racegoers in the unsaddling enclosure at Sandown, the Duke of Windsor, in a tweed coat, the bandages over his left eye now removed in favour of dark glasses, was being gingerly helped down the steps of the London Clinic by the Duchess and a nurse, and into his Rolls Royce. At Claridge's he was lifted into a wheelchair and taken up to his sixth-floor suite. A London Clinic spokesman explained, 'He has been ordered by doctors not to move around too much in case he joggles the eye.'[18]

After the weekend, the Queen paid a second visit to her uncle and aunt-in-law. This time, accompanied by her Assistant Private Secretary, Sir Edward Ford, she had tea with the Windsors in their Claridge's suite, and brought the answer to the Duke's request. Yes, the Duke, on his death, might certainly be interred in the private royal burial ground at Frogmore, and the Duchess, at her own death, would be welcome to lie beside him. And yes, both of them might have private funeral services at St George's Chapel.[19] It was the first time in many years that the Windsors had not heard the word, 'no', from the Duke's family. Touched and reassured, the Duke now gave orders for his plot in Green Mount Cemetery, Baltimore, to be sold.

A few days later, on Sunday, March 28, the Windsors received a telephone call at Claridge's to inform them that the Duke's sixty-seven-year-old sister, the Princess Royal – who had visited them in the London Clinic only eleven days earlier – had collapsed and died from a coronary thrombosis at 3.15 that afternoon in the grounds of her Yorkshire home, Harewood House. She had been strolling after lunch with her elder son, the Earl of Harewood, and her grandsons, James and Jeremy Lascelles, when she stumbled and said, 'I feel dizzy . . .' Lord Harewood helped her to a seat and asked her what was wrong. 'She said rather faintly, "I don't really know." I supported her while the boys ran off to get a car to take her home. There was no apparent crisis and I had no idea that in the quarter of an hour which intervened before the car came, she had died quite peacefully in my arms.'[20]

It was at once announced that the Windsors would not attend the funeral at Harewood the following Thursday. 'Doctors have advised the Duke . . . not to make the long journey to Leeds while he is still convalescing from his eye operations.'[21] They would, however, head the congregation at the London memorial service held on the same day. Yet again, therefore, Wallis avoided coming face to face with her sister-in-law, Elizabeth. When the Queen, Prince Philip, the Queen Mother, Princess Margaret and Lord Snowdon joined the Harewood family at the funeral on April 1, the only reminder of the Windsors was a wreath of white carnations with a black-edged official Buckingham Palace card attached to it, inscribed with the words: 'In loving memory from David and Wallis.'[22]

While the Queen Mother, visibly moved, was bidding farewell to the late King's sister at Harewood, the Windsors were arriving at Westminster Abbey to lead 2,500 mourners, including the former Prime Minister, Earl Attlee, and Lady Churchill, Sir Winston's widow, at a memorial service. They entered by a side door in order to avoid the danger from flashlights or jostling by the crowds outside, and the Duchess, beautifully dressed in an elaborate fur-trimmed black coat, confidently preceded the Duke, who was still wearing dark glasses, and guided him carefully into the Abbey.

'In a spontaneous gesture of respect, the crowded congregation rose to its feet as the Windsors entered . . . After the service, the Duke thanked the dignitaries who had taken part. Then, with the Duchess gently helping him, he climbed back into their car.'[23]

A month later, the Windsors were in the headlines again, this time as a result of the London premiere on May 3 of A King's Story, Jack Le Vien's film based on the Duke's memoirs. Several of the surviving participants in their lives were at the premiere, including Lady Churchill,[24] Sir John and Lady Aird, the Dowager Viscountess Monckton of Brenchley and Lady Alexandra Metcalfe. The Windsors themselves were not present. They were back in Paris and the Duke's doctors had forbidden him to travel to London for the occasion. 'The Duchess and I are very disappointed,' he commented.[25]

Le Vien's film cleverly juxtaposed flickering old newsreels of the golden-haired Prince of Wales alongside contemporary colour interviews with the ageing couple in the garden of their Paris home. Even the Queen Mother made a brief appearance in the proceedings, emerging gracefully from a royal limousine as the Duchess of York, and looking anything but dowdy.

The film was favourably received by the London critics. Cecil Wilson, in the *Daily Mail*, summed up the general reaction when he wrote: 'However you viewed the Abdication at the time, it still stirs the heart to see the ex-King sitting at his desk re-enacting in old age his farewell broadcast to the nation between shots of his early idolatry.

'Even more stirring is the final garden glimpse of this Romeo and Juliet turned Darby and Joan walking into the distance arm in arm to the closing words of the broadcast.'[26]

Later that month, after consultation with Buckingham Palace, Princess Alexandra and her husband, the Hon. Angus Ogilvy, who were on a brief holiday in Paris, called on the Windsors at the house in the Bois de Boulogne – the first of a series of visits made by younger members of the Royal Family when passing through the French capital.[27]

With the limited recognition and acceptance of her as the Duke's wife, Wallis's inveterate bitterness towards the Royal Family began to give way at last to a careful policy of 'forgive and forget'. 'Life is short for us all,' wrote Godfrey Winn after a weekend with the Windsors at Le Moulin de la Tuilerie, 'and what was it that the Duchess had also said to me? Why, how it was the very core of her own personal philosophy never to harbour old scores, or dwell on past grievances, however just, but to think always of tomorrow, instead of yesterday. As she had put it into words so vividly: "That keeps the lethal poison out of one's own veins." '[28]

There was still occasional evidence, however, that the 'lethal poison' had not been entirely banished when it came to the subject of her sister-in-law, Elizabeth.

On the evening of Tuesday, December 6, 1966, the Queen Mother attended a reception in London given by the Women's Voluntary Service. As she moved among the guests, she was her usual smiling and composed self, and no one present suspected that the sixty-six-year-old royal widow was in acute physical discomfort.

Later that evening she entered King Edward VII's Hospital for Officers for an examination, and on the following Saturday, December 10 – by a supreme irony the thirtieth anniversary of the Abdication which made her Queen of England – Clarence House issued this bulletin: 'Queen Elizabeth the Queen Mother this morning underwent an abdominal operation for the relief of partial obstruction. Her condition immediately after the operation is satisfactory.' The bulletin was signed by six doctors, of whom two – Sir Ralph Marnham and Sir Arthur Porritt – were noted specialists in proctology, the study and treatment of disorders of the rectum.

The news that her sister-in-law had undergone a serious operation for the removal of an obstruction in the bowel produced a cryptic comment from the Duchess of Windsor. 'It must be all those chocolates.'[29] This was presumably an allusion to a recently published story that the Queen Mother was 'adored by some of the more respectable poets' because she liked to sit up in bed reading poetry aloud and popping chocolates into her mouth in between stanzas, 'with true eighteenth-century gusto'.[30]

The Queen Mother spent Christmas in the hospital, and when she eventually emerged three weeks after the operation, she looked pale and thin, having lost more than a stone in weight. The public had been reassured about her condition by statements that tests for malignancy had proved negative. Within the medical profession, however, it was widely rumoured that the surgeons had discovered cancer, but had managed to halt its progress by performing a colostomy operation. Those who believed this pointed to the Queen Mother's lengthy period of convalescence. For twelve weeks she remained completely out of public view, not even venturing on to a racecourse until March 3, when she saw her horse, Makaldar, win the Eastleigh Handicap Hurdle at Newbury. She undertook no official public engagements until a further six weeks after that, making four and a half months of inactivity in all.

It is not unusual in operations for bowel obstruction for a temporary colostomy to be performed. In the Queen Mother's case, however, rumours of a permanent colostomy have persisted. As recently as 1979, the pseudonymous Helen Cathcart, an author acknowledging the Queen Mother's 'great helpfulness in according me hitherto unpublished information on certain details', wrote of the major surgery performed in 1966: 'If Queen Elizabeth suffered a phase of post-operative depression, not uncharacteristic after a colostomy, she adapted readily to the need henceforth of a consistently regulated life . . .'[31]

The Countess of Longford disagreed with Helen Cathcart. The newspaper columnist, Jean Rook, who interviewed the Countess, wrote: 'Myths settle on Royals like dust on their statues. The greatest, claims Lady Longford, is that the Queen Mum's "quite serious operation" years ago left her with a colostomy. "That was a tale put out by the Americans, and it's not true," she said.'[32]

In her subsequent biography,[33] however, Lady Longford, far from repudiating the rumour, dismisses the 'serious operation' in seven lines, merely noting that 'The first time she reappeared next year on the receiving line at a Buckingham Palace party she looked small and wan.'[34] Why did Lady Longford not deny the rumour in her book? 'I was told emphatically by Clarence House that the Queen Mother had not had a colostomy but they did not wish me to discuss it and suggested a serious abdominal operation was enough. I think they felt that the very use of the word "colostomy" would make the usual rapid reader take it for granted she had had one.'[35]

Helen Cathcart, subsequently challenged on *her* use of the word 'colostomy', reacted defensively: 'Dear, dear, I certainly did *not* state *unequivocally* . . . The sentence begins with an *If* . . . I cannot quite agree with Lady Longford, however . . .'[36]

On January 3, 1967, a week after the Queen Mother left hospital, the Royal Family's disapproval of the Duchess of Windsor was brought to mind again by the headline news that the Queen's first cousin, the Earl of Harewood, was being sued for divorce by the Countess, the former Marion Stein, on the grounds of his adultery with an attractive Australian, Patricia Tuckwell, formerly a violinist with the Sydney Symphony Orchestra, and the sister of one of the world's leading French horn players, Barry Tuckwell. Miss Tuckwell had a grown-up son, Michael, by her first marriage to an Australian photographer, Athol Shmith, and for a time – under the name of Bambi Shmith – she had been a well-known fashion model in Melbourne. She had met Lord Harewood in Milan in January 1959, and in September 1965, he had left his wife and the family home in Orme Square, Bayswater, to share a house with Miss Tuckwell in Hamilton Terrace, St John's Wood, where a son, Mark, had earlier been born to them on July 5, 1964.

Lord Harewood's mother, the Princess Royal, had strongly dis-approved of the situation. She had known about the child, who had been born nine months before her death, but Lord Harewood 'had the impression she would have done anything rather than raise the subject herself. We in fact talked about him only once, and she received what I had to say in total silence and made no comment of any kind, except to ask on the subject of a divorce: "What will people say?" '[37]

Elizabeth II also disapproved of the situation and had had a series of talks with both Lord and Lady Harewood, urging them to remain together for the sake of outward appearances.[38] The Queen was aware of the potential scandal developing, for Buckingham Palace press officers knew that several London newspapers had reporters per-manently stationed in Hamilton Terrace, watching the house Lord Harewood was sharing with Miss Tuckwell and their baby son.

When the divorce action was finally set down in the lists, Lord Harewood, against his wife's wishes, issued an unprecedentedly frank public statement through his London solicitors: 'We have recently, on Lord Harewood's behalf, accepted service of divorce proceedings, whereby Lady Harewood petitions for divorce on the grounds of her husband's adultery with Miss Patricia Tuckwell. Lord Harewood will not defend these proceedings and he and Miss Tuckwell would wish to marry if and when they are legally free to do so.

'Lord Harewood has lived separately from Lady Harewood for the last sixteen months at his house in St John's Wood, London. A son, Mark, was born there to Miss Tuckwell in July 1964, of whom Lord Harewood is the father.'[39]

The last divorce within the British Royal Family – between Queen Victoria's granddaughter, Princess Marie Louise of Schleswig-Holstein and her husband, Prince Aribert of Anhalt – had taken place in December 1900, almost seventy years earlier, and had then been instantly defused by Victoria's indignation against her grandson-in-law: 'Tell my granddaughter to come home to me. V.R.', the old Queen had wired protectively.[40]

Even in the scandal-attuned 1960s, the explicit frankness of Lord Harewood's admissions created such an impact in terms of sensational publicity that a whole era of royal conventions and attitudes seemed to have ended. The once burning issue of Wallis Simpson's two relatively discreet divorces now faded into a muted historical perspective.

Awareness of this almost certainly played some part in the Queen's decision that summer to invite the Duchess of Windsor to be present for the first time with other members of the Royal Family at a public occasion. The event, by the greatest irony of all, was to be the unveiling of a plaque in memory of Queen Mary, who had consistently refused to receive her American daughter-in-law. Once again, Elizabeth II's gesture was not entirely the spontaneous act of reconciliation it was later made to appear. There can be no doubt that the Queen would have consulted her mother about a decision that would involve the elder Elizabeth in her first confrontation in thirty years with the sister-in-law she had studiously excluded from her life.

The Queen Mother must have recognized – just as the Queen's advisers did – that however unwelcome the prospect might be, there was not a great deal of choice in the matter. The Duke of Windsor was now most unlikely to attend without the Duchess, and any com-memoration of Queen Mary in the absence of her eldest son – one of her only two surviving children – would be bound to attract criticism. Further family discord, in the year of the Harewood scandal, was something the Royal Family could scarcely afford. The Queen's decision was therefore automatic, and she told Lord Mountbatten, 'I'm asking Uncle David to come. Of course, he must bring his wife.'[41]

By now, however, the Windsors themselves were possibly becoming aware of the decreasing options available to the Royal Family in the long-running estrangement, and were no longer very interested in belated public gestures of welcome. It had been the Queen's original intention to hold the unveiling ceremony on Friday, May 26 – the actual centenary of Queen Mary's birth – but the Duke and Duchess, who were in New York, regretfully replied that they would be unable to be present on that date owing to long-standing social engagements. Only a short while previously, this reply would have been accepted with relief, but not now. The Queen, realizing the importance of their presence, reluctantly postponed the occasion until Wednesday, June 7.

On the afternoon of Monday, June 5, the Windsors arrived at Southampton on the liner, *United States*, on which they had celebrated their thirtieth wedding anniversary two days earlier. As the ship docked, the royal couple could be seen waving from the deck rail, the Duchess dressed in a summery blue and white striped coat, the Duke wearing a blue cornflower in his button-hole. As they came hand in hand down the gangplank to be greeted by Lord Mountbatten, a crowd of Southampton dockers raised a loud cheer, and several of them yelled, 'Good old Teddy.'[42]

Asked if he was surprised to receive an official invitation to the unveiling, the Duke replied firmly: 'Not at all. It is only natural that her eldest son should be invited to this purely private family ceremony, and that the Duchess should be with me. The Duchess and I would like to express a sincere hope that the very private nature of our visit will be respected.'[43] Asked if they might make their home in England again, he replied simply, 'No.'[44] Would the invitation inaugurate a new and better relationship with the Palace? 'I don't think so', said the Duke, adding 'The Duchess has seen the Queen and other members of the Royal Family and we are looking forward to seeing them again.'[45]

Only once did the former King betray any sign of irritation. A television newsreel interviewer asked about 'disagreements with the Royal Family'. The Duke did not even allow the question to be completed. 'We know nothing at all about them,' he interrupted dismissively.[46] As he said this, an expression of regret was clearly visible on the Duchess's face, but she said nothing. The most touching moment for the assembled reporters was when the Duke was asked where and how he would like to spend the remaining years of his life. Turning towards the Duchess and smiling, he answered, 'Together.'[47]

From Southampton, the Windsors were taken by Lord Mountbatten to stay that night at his Romsey home, Broadlands, where the Queen and Prince Philip had spent the first part of their honeymoon. There the Duke and Duchess planted a tree to commemorate their visit, and received an address of welcome from the Mayor of Romsey, who mistakenly called the Duchess 'Your Royal Highness' and hastily corrected himself: 'I *beg* your pardon! Your Grace –.'[48]

The following morning's Court Circular made no mention of their arrival in Britain, but a crowd had assembled outside Claridge's to watch them go in. 'As they did so, someone in the crowd called out, "Welcome home, Sir", and the Duke raised his trilby in acknowledgement.'[49]

The Windsors lunched that day at the Duke's former home, York House, St James's Palace, with his brother and sister-in-law, the Duke and Duchess of Gloucester. The Duke of Windsor had been known to poke fun in a mild way at his only surviving brother, as in one exchange with the actress, Lilli Palmer:

'Pause. "Do you know my brother Gloucester?"'

'"No, Sir, I've never had the pleasure."'

' "Pleasure!" he said, rolling his eyes heavenward.'[50]

The flippancy of this, like other conversational gambits in his later years, belied the Duke of Windsor's true feelings. He had heard the reports of Gloucester's declining health – his impaired circulation, increasing deafness and failing memory – with genuine sympathy and concern, and in February of that year he had written to his brother from Paris: 'I'm afraid it's this wretched business of growing older for which there are absolutely no compensations.'[51] A month after that, when the Gloucesters paused in New York on their way back to England from Jamaica, the Duke of Windsor took the trouble to go out to Kennedy Airport in order to see them during their wait between planes.[52]

On the surface, however, brotherly diffidence prevailed. On June 6, when the Windsors arrived at York House for lunch, the Duke rushed past his brother and sister-in-law in order to greet the Duke of Gloucester's valet, Alfred Amos, who had been a junior footman in the ex-King's household, and whose father had been Head Keeper to King George V at Sandringham.[53] It was a simple family luncheon, with only the Gloucesters and the Windsors present, and Alfred Amos remembered with pride that 'the Duke of Windsor was most enamoured by the crème caramel and asked how it was made'.[54]

The following morning, a large crowd gathered outside Claridge's to watch the Windsors leaving for St James's Palace, where the Royal Family – with the exception of the Queen, Prince Philip and the Queen Mother – were to assemble prior to the unveiling. The royal cars would have less than one hundred yards to drive, and Hugo Vickers, one of the most scrupulous observers of British royalty, notes: 'There were no formal processions that day in case there were unseemly demonstrations of loyalty to the Duke (of Windsor).'[55]

As it was, the Windsors noticeably received the loudest cheer of the day when their car drew up outside Marlborough House, and the Duchess's chic Parisian elegance earned the admiration of fashion writers, one of whom considered that she 'looked charming and younger than her years in a deep blue shantung coat and a white fur scarf with matching straw pillbox'.[56] The Duke, on the other hand, 'looked as strained as ever. He nodded briskly to several people and shook Lord Harewood and Mr Gerald Lascelles by the hand.'[57]

Harewood, now heading for the same totality of royal disfavour that Windsor himself had once known, had been relegated to the second row of guests and was attending alone. His estranged countess

– their divorce would become final in one month's time – was not present, although the Queen had lunched with her only five days earlier at Benjamin Britten's Suffolk home before opening the Snape Maltings Concert Hall, the new headquarters of the Aldeburgh Arts Festival.[58] Next to Lord Harewood stood his younger brother, the Hon. Gerald Lascelles, and his wife – a former actress, Angela Dowding – who were then occupying the Duke of Windsor's much-cherished old home, Fort Belvedere. Ten years later, this marriage also would collapse, and Gerald Lascelles, like his brother, would share a house with another woman while waiting for his divorce to come through.

The Windsors were followed to their places in the front row by the Duke and Duchess of Gloucester, the former using a black walking stick to support him. The entire Royal Family was now assembled and awaiting the arrival of the Queen Mother, then of the Queen and her husband. The only absentees from the unveiling were Princess Margaret who, when the unveiling date was changed, was unable to rearrange an engagement to presenting a new standard at an RAF station in Wittering; Princess Alexandra, who was away in Canada, and Prince William of Gloucester, who was in Nigeria.

There was a perceptible pause, and all present – the official guests, the watching crowds numbering more than five thousand, and, most of all, the press – were conscious that the stage was set for an historic encounter between two women who had been bitter enemies for a third of a century; sisters-in-law who had never met once since becoming related to each other by marriage. The band of the Coldstream Guards had now stopped playing and an expectant hush had settled over the scene in the Mall. The Duke of Windsor fiddled nervously with his tie. There was an almost tangible aura of tension. Then the silence was broken suddenly by a burst of applause and renewed cheering as the Queen Mother's maroon Rolls Royce came slowly into view.

Elizabeth, a vivid figure in pale lilac, stepped from the car with apparent serenity, smiling, composed, and gesturing in familiar fashion to the spectators. Betraying no sign of nervousness or strain, she walked slowly but surely towards the waiting guests, and the Duchess of Gloucester, Princess Marina, the Duchess of Kent, Mrs Gerald Lascelles, and every woman present – except one – curtsied to her. She went directly to the brother-in-law she had last met fourteen years earlier at Queen Mary's funeral, and the Duke of Windsor –

smiling and courtly – bowed to kiss his sister-in-law's hand. Elizabeth averted her head slightly and the Duke placed a further kiss on her left cheek.

The Duchess of Windsor, a bright but inscrutable smile on her face, had turned slightly towards her sister-in-law and appeared to be surveying with interest her very elaborate millinery. According to one source, she 'concentrated on counting the berries on the Queen Mother's hat wondering if she would get any recognition without wanting to seem that she was staring'.[59]

In the meantime there had been a ripple of astonishment among the courtiers present that the Queen Mother and the Duke of Windsor had kissed each other. Afterwards Elizabeth was reported as saying, 'I felt so sorry for him.'[60]

The Queen Mother then turned to the Duchess of Windsor and extended her hand. The Duchess took it but stood her ground and did not curtsey. Later, when her friend, Kitty Miller, expressed surprise at so pointed and public an omission, Wallis answered: 'She stopped people from curtseying to me. Why should I curtsey to her?'[61]

Elizabeth gave no sign of noticing the intended snub. 'How nice to see you,' she began – the only one of her comments that floated within earshot of spectators.[62] She continued to talk to the Duchess for several minutes, moving her head from side to side in an animated way, and the Duchess was seen to reply, although her responses appeared to be brief, verging on the monosyllabic. The conversation between the two protagonists was curtailed by the arrival of the Queen and Prince Philip, and the Queen Mother moved to her position on the other side of the Gloucesters.

Elizabeth II, dressed in a tangerine-coloured coat and hat, had an unusually severe expression on her face, which may have been the product of nerves connected with the momentous encounter she knew to have taken place a moment or two before her arrival. As she walked past her uncle and aunt-in-law, giving the Windsors a rather perfunctory nod, the Duke bowed his head deeply and the Duchess bobbed a brief but unmistakable curtsey. In that moment, the Queen Mother glanced across the Gloucesters and noted Wallis's deference to the Queen. The sisters-in-law exchanged a look. On Wallis's part it seemed to say, 'I will curtsey to your daughter, but I will *never* curtsey to you.'

What was it Wallis had said in her interview with Susan Barnes three years earlier? '. . .the people who are there *now* . . .' Yes, she would acknowledge them. This queen had been only a child when the campaign against her had started. *She* was not responsible for the long years of ostracism. But curtsey to that other queen who, in her eyes, had slighted, humiliated and intrigued against her? Never.

The Duchess must have found it difficult to enter wholeheartedly into the Bishop of London's short service of thanksgiving 'for the life and example of Thy servant Queen Mary'. One of the central threads in that 'life and example' had been the utter rejection of Wallis Simpson and everything she stood for. As the prayers ended, the Queen walked across to the wall and parted the blue curtains covering the plaque – a head of Queen Mary in bronze – deemed by many of those who still remembered her to be hideously ugly and a most unworthy memorial.

After the service, the Queen and her mother moved slowly among the guests, and the Queen Mother was seen to say something quick and light to the Windsors, causing them both to smile broadly. As she said goodbye to the Duke, he once more went through the complicated procedure of kissing her hand and cheek. The Duchess merely shook hands and again did not curtsey.

'I do hope we meet again,' the Queen Mother is reported to have told her sister-in-law. But Wallis evidently believed that the time for polite small talk had gone.

'When?' she asked pointedly. The Queen Mother smiled and moved away.[63]

The Queen, possibly displeased to note that her mother had not received from the Duchess the deference due to her rank, again looked stern as she shook hands with the Windsors in her turn. Once more the Duchess curtsied, but the Queen's acknowledgement appeared to verge on brusqueness.

The Queen, Prince Philip, the Queen Mother and the Duchess of Gloucester departed for Epsom to attend the Derby. Would the Windsors be joining them there in the royal box? They would not. 'The Queen hasn't invited them,' confirmed a spokesman for the Duke. Buckingham Palace echoed coolly: 'No arrangements have been made for the Duke to join the Queen at the races.'[64]

Instead the Windsors were driven to Kensington Palace, where Princess Marina, generously dismissing their failure to send her any word of sympathy when her husband was killed twenty-five years earlier,[65] gave a small private family lunch party for them. It was attended by the Duke and Duchess of Kent and also by Prince Michael, but no one outside the Kent family was invited to meet the former King and his morganatic wife.[66]

That afternoon, the Windsors returned to Paris, travelling – as a special concession from the sovereign – in an Andover of the Queen's Flight. The following morning, the Court Circular, in entries under Buckingham Palace, Clarence House, St James's Palace, Kensington Palace and Coppins, recorded the presence at the unveiling of the Queen, Prince Philip, the Queen Mother, the Duke and Duchess of Gloucester, Princess Marina, the Duke and Duchess of Kent and Prince Michael of Kent. Of the Windsors there was no mention whatever.[67] The Duchess, for the first time in thirty years of marriage, had publicly taken her place with her husband's family, and was therefore now presumed to be Persona Grata. But to officialdom and the compilers of the Court Circular, the former King and his wife remained non persons.

The unveiling had certainly broken the family ice, however, at least as far as the younger generation was concerned. Later during 1967, Prince Michael of Kent visited his uncle and aunt several times, both at the town house in the Bois de Boulogne and at Le Moulin de la Tuilerie. The Duke and Duchess of Kent also called on a number of occasions, as did Prince William of Gloucester. All four of them addressed the Duchess as 'Aunt Wallis', and the woman Queen Mary had called 'an adventuress' and George VI had referred to as 'Mrs —', must have felt a limited measure of acceptance at last.

In the autumn of 1967, the bible of the Establishment, *Burke's Peerage*, came out solidly in favour of the Duchess of Windsor's right to the title of Royal Highness, urging that 'steps should be taken without further delay to right this the most flagrant act of discrimination in the whole history of our dynasty. To do so does not require an Act of Parliament for the matter is solely within the Royal Prerogative, and all that is necessary is the issue of Letters Patent revoking those of 27th May 1937'.[68]

But Elizabeth II would never repudiate her father's decision, particularly in the lifetime of her mother, who would certainly disapprove of such a step. However just the arguments in her favour might be, Wallis would never be officially recognized as a Royal Highness.

Now fully recovered from the effects of her serious operation, the sovereign's mother had resumed a full programme of engagements with all her characteristic flair and humour. After his somewhat rowdy installation as Rector of Dundee University, the actor, Peter Ustinov, noted: '. . .I shall always cherish the resilient grace of the Queen Mother during my inauguration, when we were pelted with toilet rolls by the students, which she picked up as though someone had mailed them to the wrong address.'[69]

The summer of 1968 brought a deep sadness to the Royal Family. On July 17, Princess Marina entered the National Hospital for Nervous Diseases for an investigation of a muscular weakness in her left leg. It was discovered that she was suffering from an inoperable brain tumour. On August 26, she went into a coma, and at 11.45 on the morning of Tuesday, August 27, she died 'peacefully in her sleep' at Kensington Palace at the age of sixty-one. 'She was beautiful up to the last,' said her sister-in-law, the Queen Mother.[70]

The funeral took place at St George's Chapel, Windsor, on the following Friday, August 30. The Duke and Duchess of Windsor were both invited to attend, but the Duke came alone, travelling on a scheduled Air France flight.[71] There was speculation that the Duchess's absence from her sister-in-law's funeral might be due to her well-known fear of flying, but Hugo Vickers discounts this: 'I know for certain that the Duchess didn't come to Princess Marina's funeral out of tact – it was after all a time of great grief.'[72]

During the service, the Duke of Windsor sat in the second row of the Garter Stalls, next to his nephew Prince Richard of Gloucester.[73] If he chanced to study the following day's Court Circular, the former King Edward VIII must have reflected how low he had fallen in the table of royal precedence. Of the eighteen family mourners listed, the Duke of Windsor ranked last. One member of the family did even worse. The Earl of Harewood, now in complete disfavour, was not seated with the Royal mourners, and attended the funeral alone, without his second wife, who had not been invited.

The Duke of Windsor and his sister-in-law, the Queen Mother, were among those who followed Princess Marina's coffin to its final resting place next to the Duke of Kent's grave in the private royal burial ground at Frogmore. It was on that day that the Duke chose the site of the graves for himself and his Duchess, a few yards from those of his favourite brother and Princess Marina, and beneath the shade of a wide-spreading plane tree.[74]

After the funeral, the Duke had a conversation with his great-niece, Princess Anne. 'I know you ride very well,' he told her, 'and I'm so glad that you enjoy riding as much as I did. But why don't you ever go foxhunting?'

The Princess replied in two words. 'Blood sports.'[75]

Princess Marina's funeral was the last occasion on which the Queen Mother would meet her brother-in-law. When the Duke left Windsor Castle on that August afternoon in 1968 to drive to Heathrow Airport to catch his flight back to Paris, Elizabeth, without realizing it, bade her final farewell to the golden-haired prince who had stood beside Bertie at her wedding forty-five years before. As the years had passed since the King's death, and age and infirmity had taken its toll of the Duke, Elizabeth's anger had lessened in intensity. When she spoke of David now, it was with an air of sadness and regret. 'He was such fun,' she would sometimes say,[76] almost as if he were no longer alive. And indeed, for Elizabeth, the charming brother-in-law she first remembered had ceased to exist on the day Wallis Simpson's stranglehold had begun. Under Wallis's influence, he had become 'something quite different, something apart. It was as if he had crossed an alien frontier. He never again thought for himself or had a mind of his own.'[77]

Whether that was true or not, there could be no doubting the Duke's happiness in his subjugation. In October 1969, the Windsors recorded a long interview with the British journalist, Kenneth Harris, at the house in the Bois de Boulogne. When it was screened in Britain by BBC Television on January 13, 1970, the viewing audience for the series – entitled 'Tuesday Documentary' – rose from the customary average of four million to over eleven million.

Addressing the Duchess as 'Ma'am', Harris asked if she had any regrets. 'Oh, about certain things, yes. I wish it could have been different . . . naturally we've had some hard times, but who hasn't? You just have to learn to live with that.'[78]

When she added, 'We have been very happy', the century's most discussed lovers – then aged seventy-five and seventy-three – joined hands. Frances Donaldson later summed up the effect of that moment: 'The camera, we are told, cannot lie. Afterwards it seemed to many people that the most important thing the interview had revealed was that Fruity Metcalfe had been right all those years ago when he said that what bound these two people together was "*very true* and deep stuff".'[79]

At the end of the interview, Harris asked the Duke if *he* had any regrets about not having remained king. There was a pause, and for the last time the camera moved into close-up on 'the wistful old face' that 'seemed not even to be the shell of the once brilliantly smiling Prince of Wales'.[80] Then he answered: 'No. I would like to have, but I was going to do it under my own conditions. So I do not have any regrets. But I take a great interest in my country – my country which is Britain – your land and mine. I wish it well.'[81]

On April 4, 1970, President and Mrs Richard Nixon gave a dinner in honour of the Windsors at the White House, with an elaborate menu that included *Le Saumon Froid Windsor* and *Le Soufflé Duchesse*. Few among the one hundred and six guests could have failed to be moved as the Duke, looking frail and leaning on a black cane, replied to the President's champagne toast with the words: 'I have had the good fortune to have had a wonderful American girl consent to marry me and have thirty years of loving care and devotion and companionship – something I have cherished above all else.'

On October 3, 1970, the heir to the throne, Prince Charles – who had been invested as Prince of Wales at Caernarvon Castle fifteen months earlier – was shooting near Paris with the British Ambassador to France, Sir Christopher Soames,[82] and his son, Nicholas. Their route back to the British Embassy took them through the Bois de Boulogne, and Charles, reminded of his exiled great-uncle and aunt's nearby home, asked Sir Christopher to arrange a visit.

Soames was hesitant. Although he and his wife, Mary – Winston Churchill's youngest daughter – were on cordial terms with the Windsors, he was aware of the Queen Mother's attitude towards them, and felt, for this reason, that the Queen might have reservations about the heir to the throne calling on the Duke and Duchess at home. Charles was adamant, however, and after a certain amount of telephoning, the Ambassador, his son and the Prince went to the house in the Bois de Boulogne after dinner that evening.

They found the Windsors' drawing-room 'full of appallingly vulgar Americans',[83] and after greeting the Duchess politely as 'Aunt Wallis', Charles retired with the Duke to a corner of the room, where they talked together for more than an hour about matters of mutual interest, including their respective investitures at Caernarvon. For the Duke, it was the last but one contact with his family, and the only brief opportunity he would ever have of getting to know the young man who would one day occupy the throne he had vacated. When the time came for Charles to leave, the former Prince of Wales and his successor 'parted rather emotionally'.[84]

On June 3, 1971, the Windsors celebrated their thirty-fourth and last wedding anniversary, and the Duchess, sixteen days short of her seventy-fifth birthday, cut a last defiant dash, appearing in a floor-length slit skirt over brown floral crepe hot pants designed by Givenchy. But the party – their long years of pre-eminence in the playground of the world – had almost flickered out.

Wallis had never smoked, firmly regarding it as a dirty and dangerous habit. For years she had urged the Duke to cut down on his smoking. To please her he had tried. He began smoking half-cigarettes in a holder.

In the late summer of 1971, however, his voice became increasingly hoarse. Sometimes it shrank to a whisper. In due course, his doctors located the cause – a small tumour in his throat.

On November 17, a biopsy was performed. The growth was found to be both malignant and inoperable. Daily cobalt therapy was prescribed, but the doctors knew that at the Duke's age – seventy-seven – it was now only a question of time.

Time's up !!.

13

'I KNOW HOW YOU FEEL'

NEITHER THE DUKE OF WINDSOR nor his wife was told that he was suffering from inoperable cancer of the throat. French medical ethics preclude such disclosures, particularly in the case of the elderly.

The tumour was at the left base of his neck, and on November 30, 1971, the Duke began a course of daily cobalt treatments in the slim hope of shrinking the growth and sending it into remission. At best, however, such a policy could only extend his life marginally. The deep-ray treatment rapidly exhausted him, and when, on December 15, wearing dark glasses and a red carnation in the button-hole of his dinner jacket, he accompanied the Duchess to a gala evening at the Lido nightclub, even hardened Paris press photographers were shocked by his obvious frailty and shrunken appearance.

In the London newspapers on that same day, the Duke's sister-in-law, the Queen Mother, was the subject of the first overt criticism she had received in almost half a century in public life. On the previous afternoon, the House of Commons had debated the Select Committee's report on the 1972 Civil List, with recommendations of increased allowances for members of the Royal Family, including a rise for Princess Margaret from £15,000 to £35,000, and for the Queen Mother from £70,000 to £95,000.[1]

The anti-monarchist Labour Member of Parliament, Willie Hamilton, described Princess Margaret as 'this expensive kept woman' and the Queen Mother as her 'old mum', adding: 'It is obscene that this House should be spending its time giving an old lady like that £95,000 . . . We say she always has a pleasant smile on her face. My God, if my wife had that pay she would never stop laughing.'

These remarks, described by the left-wing *Daily Mirror* as 'a little *lèse-majesté* towards Queen Elizabeth, the Queen Mother',[2] provoked the pro-monarchist Conservative, Norman St John-Stevas, into quoting one of the standard conventions contained in Erskine May's textbook of parliamentary procedure: 'disrespectful use of Her Majesty's name would normally give offence outside of Parliament; and it is only consistent with decency, that a member of the legislature should not be permitted openly to use such language in his place in Parliament'. St John-Stevas then asked: 'Does not that rule, by analogy, apply to the former Queen of this country, and to the Queen's sister?'[3]

While the Royal Family suffered in public, the Windsors suffered in private. Early in 1972, the Duchess wrote to Lady Sefton – 'Dearest Foxie' – 'We are not well. I have a flood of nerves and the Duke is having X-ray for his throat . . . I too from worry have a painful time with my old friend the ulcer . . . There is nothing to be said for growing old.'[4] On January 12, the cobalt therapy came to an end. It had failed to reduce the tumour and had weakened the Duke to such an extent that it was considered dangerous to continue. The doctors decided to allow the cancer to take its natural course.

At the end of February, the Duke was operated on for a double hernia at the American Hospital in Paris. The operation itself was minor and successful, but under the anaesthetic, his surgeon, Dr Jean Thin, and the specialists, re-examined the throat tumour and found, as they had feared, that it was not in remission. The Duke's forty-year-old Irish nurse, Oonagh Shanley, was told that now 'the only hope was to make his few remaining months as comfortable as possible . . . He has no idea of this, nor has the Duchess. At their ages . . . it would be needlessly distressing.'[5]

The decision not to tell the Duchess that her husband was dying was largely dictated by the state of her own health, which had been causing concern for several years. Eighteen months earlier, Cecil Beaton had noted: 'She seems to have suddenly aged, to have become a little old woman. Her figure and legs are as trim as ever, and she is as energetic as she always was, putting servants and things to rights. But Wallis had the sad, haunted eyes of the ill. In hospital they had found that she had something wrong with her liver and that condition made her very depressed. When she got up to fetch something, she said: "Don't look at me. I haven't even had the coiffeur come out to do my hair," and her hair did appear somewhat straggly. This again gave her a rather pathetic look. She loves rich food and drink but she is now on a strict diet and must not drink any alcohol.

'Wallis tottered to a sofa against the light in a small overcrowded drawing-room. Masses of royal souvenirs, gold boxes, sealing wax, stamps and seals; small pictures, a great array of flowers in obelisk-shaped baskets. These had been sent up from the Mill, which will be sold now the Duke is not able to bend down for his gardening . . .

"Well, you see, we're old! It's awful how many years have gone by and one doesn't have them back!"

'. . . The Duchess leaning forward on tiny legs, looked rather blind, and when an enormous bouquet of white flowers and plants arrived, she did not seem able to see it. She leant myopically towards it and asked, "What's that? A tuberose? An arum lily?" The man corrected her – "An auratum" – "Ah yes, will you tell them how beautifully they have done them." I watched her try to open the card . . . "Who is it from?" asked the Duke. "Don't be so full of curiosity," said his wife trying to read without glasses . . . The two old people, very bent, but full of spirit and still both dandies, stood at the door as I went off . . .'[6]

The decline in Wallis's health was not only physical. Arteriosclerosis, first diagnosed three years earlier, had begun to interfere with the supply of blood to her brain, causing sudden personality changes and disconcerting lapses of memory. During 1969, the Duke occasionally telephoned friends late in the afternoon and confessed, with evident agitation and embarrassment: 'Our secretary has gone home and the Duchess can't seem to recall just where we are dining tonight. By any chance, do you happen to know?'[7] And in 1970, he confided to his friend, the iron and steel magnate, Winston Guest: 'I'm afraid the Duchess is losing her mind . . .'[8]

Forty-eight hours after the hernia operation, the Duke had recovered sufficiently for the Duchess to visit him twice a day in the American Hospital. Although the hospital was in Neuilly, only a few moments' drive from the Windsors' house, the Duke nevertheless fretted over the inconvenience to Wallis of having to make even that short journey to see him.

By the fifth night he had become openly restless and told Nurse Shanley: 'I'm not going to be separated from the Duchess for one more night. If I go home tomorrow, will you come with me, to look after me?'[9] Oonagh Shanley agreed, believing that the Duke's desire to go home was due solely to his concern for his wife. But a remark made later that day to the president of the American Hospital, Perry H. Culley, an old friend of the Windsors, suggests that the Duke was possibly not as much in ignorance of the truth about his condition as the doctors had supposed. 'I want to die in my own bed,' he said.[10]

The following afternoon, Nurse Shanley drove with the Duke and Duchess along the Bois de Boulogne and through the imposing latticed iron gates of 4 Route du Champ d'Entraînement. In the huge marble reception hall, all twenty-five members of the Windsors' staff stood waiting in their royal livery to welcome the Duke home. A glass and gilt lift took him to his bedroom on the first floor, where he was immediately put to bed beneath the scarlet, blue and gold tapestry bearing his own personal standard. He had exactly three months more of life left to him.

Next morning, remembered Nurse Shanley, 'He began his day with the question he was to ask every morning until his death: "Is the Duchess awake yet?" If she was he would tell his black and white pug, Diamond, who slept on his bed, "Come on Diamond, move." Then he'd emerge from his bathroom shaved, brushed, and smelling of talc . . . Then, in his dressing gown, he'd go to his wife's bedroom.'[11]

Throughout their marriage, Wallis had been by far the less demonstrative of the two, and there had been times – particularly during the Donahue years – when the Duke's unceasing infatuation and almost dog-like devotion had seemed to bore and irritate her. During the last months of his life, however, the small group of close friends still encouraged to call at the house noticed that her personality had softened and that her manner towards him had grown gentler and more loving.

To one friend with whom she had been discussing ex-King Umberto of Italy, Wallis commented: 'Kings haven't much of a part to play nowadays; it's not Umberto's fault if he's forgotten.' Then, looking towards her own ex-King, who was sitting out of earshot, she added: '*He* will·be spoken of for a long time to come – because of *me*!'[12]

Although she never once put the possibility into words, her staff believed that inwardly the Duchess had steeled herself to face and accept the fact that the Duke was dying. When, several weeks later, Oonagh Shanley was summoned back to the house to resume her nursing duties, she found him 'thinner, weaker, his voice hoarse'. The Duchess told her: 'I've arranged for hot drinks and sandwiches to be left in your room every night, in case . . .' Her voice, very low and quiet, trailed off unhappily without completing the sentence.[13] That evening during dinner, Wallis confided to the Irish nurse: 'I have this lasting sense of loss that we could never have a child. Above everything we both wanted one but, you see, I had to have a hysterectomy only twelve months after we married.'[14]

This explanation was a new variation on a long-existing theme. Wallis had got used to being asked why the century's most publicized love affair had never produced a child. Sometimes she would answer with one of her characteristic epigrams: 'Because David isn't heir-conditioned.' At others she would say that having married two weeks short of her forty-first birthday, she and the Duke felt it a little late in the day to start a family.

The 'hysterectomy' version seems dubious to say the least, although it was rumoured that this is what she may have had done in New York in February 1951, when the Duke's 'great anxiety' about her condition caused even Queen Mary to abandon her prejudices sufficiently to enquire after the health of her unacknowledged daughter-in-law. There are those who maintain that a hysterectomy *was* performed at that time because the Duchess's doctors had discovered a malignancy in her womb. But in February 1951, Wallis was almost fifty-five, and any question of her bearing a child was long since past.

It is difficult to accept that she could have had a hysterectomy, or any other major operation, performed twelve months after the wedding – that is to say, in the summer of 1938 – without the fact becoming public knowledge. At that time the Windsors were still under intense scrutiny by the world press, and during that summer they were much occupied moving all their possessions into the Château de la Cröe. Had the Duchess of Windsor – voted earlier that year the world's best-dressed woman – entered a hospital or a clinic on the Riviera, the fact would certainly have been detected, as were her later facial operations in London, in spite of the precaution she invariably took in entering the hospital under an alias. The Château itself was not in a sufficiently organized state in 1938 for an operation to have been performed there privately, and when they were not at La Cröe, the Windsors were in Paris, occupying a hotel suite at the Meurice, and all their movements – like the meeting with the Gloucesters that November – were carefully watched and faithfully chronicled by the French press.

The account of an early hysterectomy has the air of a protective device. Wallis may have wished to scotch speculation that the Duke, with his rumoured sexual deficiencies, was either impotent or unable to father a child. Alternatively she may have been shielding herself. In eight years of married life with each of her two previous husbands, both highly sexed men, she conceived no child, although Spencer and Simpson fathered children by other wives. There is the obvious possibility that Wallis may have been unable to bear children even if the Duke had been capable of fathering them.

By April, six weeks after his hernia operation, the Duke's coughing spasms had grown worse and his periodic fevers more frequent. His weight had begun to drop rapidly and he now weighed less than seven stone. The Dowager Lady Monckton, who called to see him, was shocked by his sudden deterioration, and on her return to London, she went directly to Buckingham Palace to inform the Queen's private secretary, Sir Martin Charteris.[15]

Biddy Monckton's news caused intense concern to Charteris. On May 15, the Queen and Prince Philip were scheduled to begin a State Visit to France, which was regarded by the British Government as being of the utmost importance concerning Britain's desired entry into the European Economic Community. If the Duke of Windsor died before May 15, the visit would have to be cancelled. Worse still, if he died during the six days it was in progress, it would have to be curtailed. The British Ambassador in Paris, Sir Christopher Soames, discreetly approached Dr Jean Thin to ask if the Duke was likely to live until May 20, the day on which the Queen would leave France.[16] Thin was doubtful in view of his patient's now rapid decline. From the end of April, daily bulletins were telephoned from Paris to Buckingham Palace. In the meantime, it was arranged that the Queen, Prince Philip and Prince Charles would pay a brief call on the Windsors on May 18.

At the beginning of May, the Duke began to suffer slight haemorrhages of the throat. On each occasion this happened, he insisted that the Duchess should not be told. On May 10, he had his first cardiac arrest and almost died. 'We had to work very quickly to save him,' recalled Nurse Shanley. 'He knew it, but next morning his first question was, "You haven't told Wallis?"

' "No, Sir."

' "How many days before my family comes?"

' "Eight days, Sir. You'll be feeling better by then."

' "I'm determined to . . ." '[17]

On Monday, May 15, the Queen and Prince Philip arrived at Orly Airport to be greeted by President Pompidou. That evening they attended an elaborate state banquet at the Grand Trianon. The Queen, wearing an orchid-mauve satin dress and magnificent jewels, told the President, 'We drive on different sides of the road but we are both going the same way.'

Behind the urbane diplomatic façade, however, there was intense anxiety among the Queen's entourage over the Duke of Windsor's failing strength. But Elizabeth II had inherited something of her mother's imperviousness to anything unpleasant. The Queen preferred not to confront the imminence of her uncle's death. When a reporter asked Sir Martin Charteris whether Her Majesty realized how gravely ill the Duke was, he replied sardonically: 'You know he's dying. I know he's dying. But *we* don't know he's dying.'[18]

On the morning of Thursday, May 18, the Duke was so weak that he was given a blood transfusion to produce the necessary strength for him to receive the royal visitors. Then, at noon, Dr Thin and Nurse Shanley began the long task of getting the patient ready for his last meeting with his family. It took almost four hours. The Duke was adamant that his niece should not see him in bed wearing pyjamas, and insisted, against his doctor's advice, on getting up and being properly dressed to receive her. He also demanded that the array of tubes now employed to keep him alive be removed from view, with the exception of one intravenous drip which could not be dispensed with, but which Dr Thin managed to keep covered.

At four o'clock, the royal party, who had spent the earlier part of the afternoon watching the races at Longchamp, arrived at 4 Route du Champ d'Entraînement. The Duchess of Windsor, waiting alone on the steps in a short-sleeved Dior afternoon dress of dark blue crêpe, curtsied deeply to the Queen, then to Prince Philip, and finally to Prince Charles.

Wallis led the royal visitors into the drawing-room where she poured china tea for them. The atmosphere was informal and relaxed. It was the first and last occasion that the Duchess would receive the British sovereign in her own home, and although one of her guests once commented that Wallis 'evidently hates tea, and looks very out of place pouring it out',[19] she acted the role of hostess with poise and dignity. The Queen avoided any reference to the gravity of the Duke's condition, and the Duchess, in spite of her anxiety, did not mention it beyond apologizing for the fact that he was not strong enough to come downstairs to receive them, but was greatly looking forward to seeing them in the sitting-room adjoining his bedroom on the first floor.

After fifteen minutes in the drawing-room, the Duchess first took the Queen upstairs alone to see the Duke. She found him sitting in a wheelchair, dressed in a smart blue blazer that hung loosely on his emaciated body. He now weighed only a little more than six stone.

Dr Thin and Nurse Shanley were both in the room, and the latter recalled: 'As Her Majesty came in the Duke stood up, a great effort for him, said, "My dear," made her a slight bow, and kissed her on both cheeks.'[20]

Seeing that the strain of rising to greet her had drained him, the

Queen gently insisted that he must sit down again immediately. She also sat and asked him how he felt. 'Not so bad,' he answered gamely, and for a fleeting moment the ghost of the old Prince Charming smile crossed the gaunt and wizened face.

Prince Philip then came in and shook his uncle-in-law warmly by the hand. The Duke, at this moment, appeared overcome by weakness and falteringly apologized for being unable to rise to greet him. Nurse Shanley noted: 'As the Duchess brought Prince Charles in [the Duke's] face lit up and he started asking him about the Navy . . . but, after a few minutes, I saw the Duke's throat convulse, and he began coughing.

'He motioned me to wheel him away, the Royal Family stood up and I had the feeling that this was his way of avoiding any formal goodbyes. It had all been brief, immensely cordial, and very important to him, but he had no reserves of strength left.'[21]

The Queen, with her husband and son, went downstairs with the Duchess, and spent a few moments more in conversation with her before leaving. Even at this moment of sadness, the royal schedule had to be considered. The visit had lasted half an hour, and the Queen was due to leave in order to dress for a ball in Paris that evening. As the Duchess and her royal guests emerged from the house, the Queen on her left, Prince Philip on her right, Prince Charles on his mother's left, they paused for a few moments to allow the waiting press photographers to record an obviously historic occasion in the annals of the House of Windsor. Wallis, her thin arms at her sides, glanced down, appearing momentarily overcome, perhaps aware that this long-delayed royal visit to her home had come too late to mean very much to her or her husband. The Queen smiled at her encouragingly, and Prince Philip seemed to be trying to relieve the occasion of some of its poignancy with some brisk and cheerful banter.

As the royal guests shook hands and said goodbye, the Duchess again sank into a deep curtsey to all three in turn. As on their arrival, Wallis performed faultlessly correct court curtseys, very different in style from her perfunctory bobs at the unveiling ceremony five years earlier. Perhaps she felt that the long and bitter chapter of her dealings with the Royal Family, so often marked by discourtesy on both sides, should end with a public display of good manners. The Duchess remained standing on the steps as the royal car moved off. She watched it drive out of the gates and then turned and slowly re-entered the house.

The State Visit came to an end two days later and the Queen left

France on May 20. The following Thursday, May 25 – exactly one week after the Queen's visit to the house – was the first morning the Duke did not attempt to leave his bed. 'During that evening,' noted Nurse Shanley, 'his temperature soared and he was on an intravenous drip. In spite of a sedative, he lay with his eyes open, semi-delirious and muttering . . . his eyes brimmed with tears . . . he said something about ". . . England . . . not away . . ." and then "the waste . . . the waste".'[22]

At three in the morning, the Duke at last drifted into sleep. It was then that Nurse Shanley, who had settled herself into an armchair for the night's vigil, was alarmed by 'a sickening thud and crash that suddenly shattered the silence. It came from the bathroom and as I leapt up and went in there it happened again, this time followed by a rasping croak, and I realized that some night creature was hitting against the window . . .

'It was now about 3.45 a.m. I'd been monitoring the Duke, not at all sure he would live much longer, so I woke the Duchess's maid, Giselle, in case I needed assistance while I telephoned the doctor.

'"What on earth are those birds making that horrible noise?" I asked her and she said, "Oh, it's the *corbeaux*" (which I translated as crows) "though I've *never* heard them in the night before." Then she added, "But then, they're the Royal birds, aren't they?"

'She said it matter-of-factly but I glanced at her in astonishment. I suddenly realized she meant the huge, shiny black ravens I'd often seen in the garden and then all the ominous legends, learned in childhood, came to my thoughts. The fatal ravens consecrated to the Danish war God, the ravens in *Macbeth* croaking their warning of Royal death.

'It doesn't do for a night nurse to allow herself to become imaginative nor, even today, do I think I was. I simply looked at the Royal Coat of Arms pinned to the wall above the bed, and the face of the man who'd once been a king, and thought "Some things don't change. The ravens have come for him." Even if I'd had no medical training, because of those ravens I'd still have known the end was near.'[23]

By the following morning, Friday, May 26, even the Duchess was left in no doubt that her husband was sinking fast. At her urgent summons, their American physician, Dr Arthur J. Antenucci, flew immediately from New York to Paris. On arriving at the Duke's bedside, however, he realized at once that there was nothing to be done – except to wait for the inevitable. Even the Duke's private secretary, John Utter, now gave up stonewalling with the press and started to concede to reporters that his master was 'not in very good shape'.[24]

On the Saturday, May 27, the last full day of the Duke's life, the Duchess was with him almost constantly. The intense strain on Wallis had become apparent to all around her, and she visibly struggled to maintain her composure and self-control as the Duke, his voice now only a feeble whisper, valiantly strove to comfort and reassure her. At 8.30 that evening, only six hours before he died, he roused himself from semi-consciousness to tell her that he didn't feel 'too bad'.[25]

When his wife left the room for a moment, however, the Duke asked Oonagh Shanley, 'Am I dying?' The nurse, well accustomed to that question from patients *in extremis*, answered briskly, 'You're quite intelligent enough to decide that for yourself.'[26]

The Duchess, sensing that the end was very near, wanted to stay up all night, but not even in dying would the Duke consent to the smallest inconvenience to the woman he had loved devotedly for almost forty years. 'No, darling,' he told her, 'I shall soon be asleep, get some rest, please.'[27]

Soon after Wallis left the room, the Duke again lapsed into semi-consciousness. Until eleven o'clock that night, the Duke's valet, Sidney Johnson, a handsome Bahamian Negro who had entered the Windsors' service in Nassau thirty-two years earlier as a fifteen-year-old trainee, sat with Oonagh Shanley, keeping vigil by his master's beside. Sidney and Nurse Shanley were both Catholics, and together they began to pray, reciting the words of the Act of Contrition. 'I don't think the Duke heard the words,' recalled Nurse Shanley, 'but I'm sure he sensed they were prayers because his lips moved as though he was praying too.'[28]

The end came suddenly and peacefully, without consciousness or struggle, and with insufficient time or warning to fetch the Duchess. Nurse Shanley was monitoring the Duke's pulse and recorded, 'as he slept, his blood pressure fell to nothing and my hand was on his wrist as his heart stopped. It was 2.20 a.m. on Sunday, May 28, 1972.'[29] A month before his seventy-eighth birthday and six days short of their thirty-fifth wedding anniversary, the world's most famous love story had ended.

In a few minutes Nurse Shanley went to fetch the Duchess. She came at once. 'At his bedside she said "My David", and kissed his forehead. Then cupping her hands gently round his face she said again, "My David – you look so lovely." Her quietness was much sadder than tears. Giselle and I both cried for her, we couldn't help it.'[30] After a few moments, Wallis was led back to her room, and Dr Antenucci, who was still in the house, was summoned to administer a sedative. Sidney Johnson, who had been devoted to the Duke, insisted on maintaining a solitary vigil by his master's body for the remainder of the night.

The news was immediately telephoned to Buckingham Palace by John Utter, and a brief official statement was issued shortly after 6 a.m.: 'It is announced with deep regret that His Royal Highness the Duke of Windsor has died at his home in Paris at 02.25 today, Sunday, May 28, 1972.'

The Queen, who was at Windsor Castle, was woken in the early hours and informed of her uncle's death. She at once telephoned the news to the Queen Mother, who was at Royal Lodge, and also to the Duchess of Gloucester, the wife of the Duke of Windsor's only surviving – and now paralyzed – brother. Flags on all public buildings throughout Britain were immediately lowered, and London woke that Sunday morning to the tolling of the Great Bell of St Paul's Cathedral, informing his one-time subjects of the passing of the uncrowned king who had reigned over them for 326 days.

Tributes at once began to pour in from all over the world. President Nixon, who was on a visit to Moscow, issued a statement from the Kremlin: 'He was a man of noble spirit and high ideals, for whom millions of Americans felt a deep respect and affection.' The French Foreign Minister, Maurice Schumann, who had been present at the Windsors' wedding as a young reporter, felt that the Duke 'must be thanked for having, in an implacable age, safeguarded a sort of rift in the clouds for the rights of the heart'. The *Daily Mail* commented in its editorial: 'We cherish the memory of that most charming and most English of Englishmen whose love for a woman lost him his crown . . . but not the affection of his people.'[31] And *The Guardian*'s editorial considered that the Duke 'was most fortunate in a long life in marrying a woman of admirable warmth and character.'[32]

The Queen sent a personal telegram to the Duchess: 'I am so grieved to hear of the death of my uncle. Philip joins me in sending you our heartfelt sympathy. I know that my people will always remember him with gratitude and great affection and that his services to them in peace and war will never be forgotten. I am so glad that I was able to see him in Paris ten days ago. Elizabeth R.'

From Royal Lodge, the Queen Mother also telegraphed a message to the Duchess. Its text was not released for publication, but it was signed informally, 'Elizabeth'. The omission of the customary 'R' for

Regina seemed to indicate that the Queen Mother's sympathy came, for the first time, as a sister-in-law rather than as a queen.

Elizabeth II ordered nine days of court mourning. The Duke's wishes, made known in 1965 during his niece's visit to the London Clinic, were to be honoured in every respect. The Royal Air Force would fly his body home to Britain. He would lie in state for two days in St George's Chapel, Windsor. Then, after a private funeral service, he would be buried at Frogmore, and the Duchess would one day lie beside him.

After half a day of telephone discussions between Sir Martin Charteris at Windsor and John Utter in Paris, the Lord Chamberlain, Lord Maclean, announced: 'The Duchess of Windsor has accepted the Queen's invitation to stay at Buckingham Palace.' Questioned on the reasons for this belated courtesy after so many years of using a hotel suite at Claridge's, the Palace press office answered, 'for this occasion, and for obvious human reasons, protocol has been waived.'[33] *The Guardian* commented: 'The Queen has apparently decided that, with the passing of a generation since the abdication, it would be wrong to pursue the subtle ostracism which the Royal Family has hitherto practised.'[34]

Not everyone was impressed by the gesture, or the taste revealed by admitting the Duchess as a grieving widow to the place from which she had been consistently excluded during thirty-five years of marriage. Leslie Pine, the former editor of *Burke's Peerage*, commented: 'I welcome it. But the invitation should have been extended to both of them before the Duke's death.'[35] And *The Sun*, speculating that the Duke's request to be buried at Windsor was made with his wife's position in mind, added: 'It is as if the Duke, in a final gesture of loyalty to the woman he loved and of defiance to the Palace, were saying: You did not recognize her in my lifetime. Now I am dead, you must.'[36] Such recognition as there was, however, was largely dictated by circumstances. 'How ironic it is,' said the London *Evening News*, 'that the first occasion since the abdication on which she will have been welcomed to the palace will be for her husband's burial. Would this visit not be an appropriate time for her to be accorded the courtesy title of Her Royal Highness on which the Duke had set his heart?'[37]

But those who felt that the Queen's invitation to the Duchess might presage the granting of the long-denied HRH, were firmly disabused by the Palace press office. The Duchess, they declared unequivocally, could receive no royal title. The rank of Royal Highness was reserved

solely for those in the line of succession to the throne. This was an
argument which the Queen herself would openly repudiate only six
years later, when her first cousin, Prince Michael of Kent, was
permitted to remain a Royal Highness after forfeiting his place in the
succession by marrying a Roman Catholic, and when royal status was
also conferred upon his divorced wife. The continuing obstacle to the
granting of royal rank to the Duchess of Windsor was the Queen's
reluctance to reverse her father's decision, and her fear of offending
her mother, whose attitude to the matter remained unchanged. There
was one other reservation, much discussed among courtiers.[38] Now
that the Duchess was a widow, how would she behave? Would she
remarry? Would another Jimmy Donahue appear on the scene? Even
now, on the verge of her seventy-sixth birthday, the Royal Family
retained its long-established wariness of Wallis's character.

In Paris, meanwhile, the full impact of what she had lost began to
affect the Duke's widow. 'The Duchess is slightly unwell and has not
been able to receive visitors,' John Utter announced on the day
following the Duke's death. Of the many friends who called at the
house to offer sympathy, only two – King Umberto and Maurice
Schumann – were received personally. Schumann, who stayed only
five minutes, told reporters as he left, 'She is not feeling well.'

After the long weeks of strain and anxiety, Wallis had suffered a sort
of nervous collapse. She was mentally confused and deeply depressed.
Dr Antenucci at once foresaw that she would not be well enough in
time to accompany the Duke's body when it was flown to England
forty-eight hours later. He also felt, in view of her condition, that it
was advisable to minimize the amount of time she would spend with
members of the Royal Family, and the ordeal which this would
inevitably impose. Plans were therefore reshaped, and it was agreed
that the Duchess would travel to London separately on the following
Friday, giving her an extra forty-eight hours in which to rest and
recover her strength.

On the morning of Wednesday, May 31, Wallis, a frail and forlorn
figure dressed in black, stood on the steps of 4 Route du Champ
d'Entraînement, surrounded by members of her household staff, as the
Duke's coffin of English oak, draped in the Royal standard, left for Le
Bourget airport in a nine-car cortège which included the British
Ambassador, Sir Christopher Soames, and the French Secretary of
State, Jacques Baumel. From Le Bourget, a Royal Air Force VC 10 jet
flew the body to the RAF airfield at Benson in Oxfordshire, where the

Duke and Duchess of Kent, members of the British Government, and the French Ambassador, Geoffroy de Courcel, waited to receive it. As the coffin, bearing a single magnificent wreath – a cross of red and white gladioli and carnations, tied with blue ribbon, 'from Wallis' – was carried from the plane, a Royal Guard of Honour from the Queen's Colour Squadron of the RAF presented arms, and the Central Band played the first six bars of the National Anthem.

The coffin, guarded by RAF officers, rested overnight in the Royal Air Force Chapel at Benson. At seven o'clock on the following morning, it was taken by road to Windsor Castle. One enterprising cameraman photographed the ex-King's hearse being driven past the crowned and sceptred statue of his great-grandmother, the Queen-Empress Victoria. As the Duke's coffin entered the King Henry VIII Gate of the Castle, the Union Jack on the Round Tower was lowered. All other flags in the town were already flying at half-mast. For the next twenty-four hours, the Duke's body rested in the Albert Memorial Chapel, before being moved to St George's Chapel for the public Lying-in-State to begin.

In Paris, meanwhile, every effort was being made to prepare and fortify the disoriented Duchess for the ordeal ahead of her. Her friend, the Paris couturier, Hubert de Givenchy, had rushed through some mourning dresses for her, and his tailors accomplished the remarkable feat of making a black coat for her in a single night.

On the morning of Friday, June 2, as a queue of more than ten thousand people, stretching for more than a mile around the walls of Windsor Castle, began to file slowly and silently past the ex-King's coffin, the Duchess of Windsor, accompanied by Grace, Countess of Dudley,[39] the British Ambassador's wife, Lady Soames, John Utter, Dr Antenucci, and Brigadier Douglas Greenacre – Equerry to the Queen, and formerly to the Duke of Windsor when Prince of Wales – left Paris in an aircraft of The Queen's Flight. Lady Soames later remembered that 'although she was obviously deeply distressed, the Duchess, during the flight and the time I was with her, was extremely calm.'[40]

Her arrival in England brought Wallis the first recognition she had received in the Court Circular during thirty-five years of marriage to the former sovereign: 'Buckingham Palace, June 2. By command of The Queen, Admiral of the Fleet the Earl Mountbatten of Burma was present at Heathrow Airport-London this morning and, on behalf of Her Majesty, greeted the Duchess of Windsor upon arrival in this country in an aircraft of The Queen's Flight.'[41] The Court Circular had recognized her at last, but as a widow, not as a royal wife. Even now it seemed to some observers that Wallis was still the victim of subtle Establishment discrimination. Had she accompanied the coffin two days earlier, she would have shared in the royal honours accorded to her dead husband and been greeted by the Duke and Duchess of Kent, both Royal Highnesses. Instead, arriving alone, she was met by Lord Mountbatten, Queen Victoria's great-grandson, but nevertheless non-royal in status, and descended on his father's side from a morganatic marriage.

As the tiny black-clad widow came alone down the steps of the plane, nervously glancing beneath her and cautiously gripping the rail with her right hand, television cameras brought the watching millions a poignant metamorphosis. The alluring American who had once detonated Britain's greatest constitutional crisis – 'This fascinating woman . . . the most fatale of femmes. The serpent of old Potomac'[42] – had ceased to be the scarlet creature of legend and had become a fragile elderly figure already haunted by the spectre of ill-health.

Among the reception party to greet her was the Queen's lady-in-waiting, the Hon. Mary Morrison, known at the Palace as 'Mossy'. Miss Morrison shook hands politely but did not curtsey. The Duchess, ignoring this, thanked each member of the air crew. When she came to the waiting Rolls Royce, Wallis found that Mountbatten, instead of giving her precedence, had unchivalrously climbed into the car ahead of her. Her face, caught in a television close-up, reflected surprise and a certain distaste at this boorish discourtesy to a widow four years his senior.

The Queen, however, had been more considerate. On her orders all cross-traffic along the Duchess's route into London was blocked off until her four-car procession had passed, in order to spare her the distress of being stared at while the cars were held up at intersections. As the royal Rolls Royce, flanked by police outriders, slowed down to enter the gates of Buckingham Palace – where she had last been invited as Wallis Simpson in 1936 during the brief reign of Edward VIII – the Duchess gave a valiant smile and wave to the waiting cameramen. Their photographs showed her looking pale and drawn, but exquisitely elegant in her black Parisian coat, a half-veil across her face, a single black bow crowning her immaculately coiffeured upswept hair. If age had caught up with Wallis, it had not robbed her of style.

Described by Palace officials on her arrival as 'unwell, tired and distressed', she was at once escorted to the State Suite on the first floor, overlooking the Mall, which is customarily reserved for visiting Heads of State. Lady Dudley, John Utter, Dr Antenucci and her French maid, Giselle, accompanied her.

Shortly afterwards the Duchess lunched with the Queen and Princess Anne in the Queen's private apartments, and Elizabeth II explained that the following morning's traditional ceremony of Trooping the Colour would begin with a lament in remembrance of the Duke of Windsor.

Surprisingly, it had been the Queen's wish that the Duchess should attend the ceremony and should drive with other members of the Royal Family from the Palace to Horse Guards Parade. The royal procession which precedes the Queen to the Trooping is always led by the Queen Mother, riding regally in an open barouche, and there was speculation among courtiers that the Duchess of Windsor would occupy the place of honour beside her sister-in-law in the carriage, and would stand with her on the balcony overlooking the parade ground. It would have been the most public and effective means of proclaiming reconciliation between the two women. But for Wallis, so long regarded by the Royal Family as an ambitious woman, these proposed gestures of public recognition had come too late. She had no desire to be put on display as a bereaved widow or to receive the sympathetic applause of the crowds lining the Mall. Had the invitation come when her husband was alive, it would have meant something. Now it seemed pointless. Tactfully pleading ill-health and exhaustion as her excuse, the Duchess asked the Queen if she might remain in her suite and watch the ceremony on television. Later that day it was announced from Clarence House that the Queen Mother had cancelled her traditional carriage procession to Horse Guards Parade, 'out of respect for the Duke of Windsor'.

On Saturday, June 3 – the thirty-fifth anniversary of the Windsors' wedding – the Queen rode out on horseback from Buckingham Palace at the head of the parade, a black arm-band adorning her scarlet tunic. Photographers training telephoto lenses on the windows of the State Suite saw the Duchess of Windsor pull aside the curtains and look down on the scene below. The deep black of her mourning was relieved by a double strand of magnificent large pearls from which hung one huge pearl pendant. Her cheeks were hollowed, her mouth taut, her eyes haunted. The photograph that resulted was Sophoclean in its sadness.

On the television in her suite, Wallis watched the Queen arrive at Horse Guards Parade and pause to salute her mother on the balcony above. There was a roll of drums followed by a minute's silence and a further roll of drums. Then the lament, 'The Flowers of the Forest', was played by the pipers of the Scots and Irish Guards.

Immediately after the Trooping, the Queen and the rest of the Royal Family left for Windsor and it had been expected that the Duchess would join them there for the weekend, but instead she chose to remain at Buckingham Palace. Taking her place, however briefly, in the family circle – the family that had so long rejected her – must have seemed a sort of mockery now that she was alone. She felt unequal to the strain of it. Lady Dudley remained with her, and Biddy Monckton came to the Palace to tell her how impressive the Duke's Lying-in-State was, and recommended that she should go herself. Almost sixty thousand people had filed past the Duke's coffin, and that afternoon the Queen, Prince Philip and Princess Anne had visited the chapel while the public were still being admitted and had stood for six minutes in front of the catafalque with their heads bowed in silent prayer.

That evening, after the Lying-in-State was closed to the public, Lord Mountbatten came to the Palace to take the Duchess to Windsor. Prince Charles escorted her into St George's Chapel, and for eight minutes she stood silently in front of her husband's coffin on the dark blue, gold-edged catafalque, guarded at all four corners by a member of the Household Cavalry with plumed head bowed and sword reversed. To Prince Charles and Mountbatten, the Duchess was heard to say several times, 'Thirty-five years . . . thirty-five years . . .',[43] and her body began to sway with emotion. Prince Charles gently took her arm and led her from the Chapel. She was driven back to Buckingham Palace where she spent the following day resting quietly in her suite.

On Monday, June 5 – the day of the funeral – the *Daily Mail* published a leading article with photographs of the Queen Mother and the Duchess of Windsor facing each other. The headline read: 'Today history brings them together – Two women who, surprisingly, have so much in common'. The author, Vincent Mulchrone, wrote: 'The memories behind their black veils will remain their own . . . They are sisters-in-law long estranged. They have lived curiously parallel lives, but in different dimensions, different styles . . . In the ordinary way, their links would have been of the closest. As it is they are practically strangers, and it may be too late to make friends . . . The Duchess may have forgiven. She will certainly not have forgotten. That is what will add an extra touch of tragedy when the two women kneel before the one-time King today.'[44]

Impeccably stylish in her new Givenchy black coat, with a plain black pillbox hat crowning her dark hair, and an almost waist-length veil through which pearl-studded earrings glinted, Wallis left Buckingham Palace soon after ten o'clock that morning, accompanied by Lady Dudley, Brigadier Greenacre and John Utter. It was her last departure from the seat of British royalty. She would never enter the Palace again.

Shortly before eleven o'clock, she arrived at Windsor Castle and was taken to the Dean's Room in St George's Chapel, where members of the Royal Family were assembling. The Duke of Windsor's nephew, the Earl of Harewood, who had now succeeded his uncle as Britain's number one royal outcast, had not been invited. Thinking that an invitation might have gone astray in the post, Harewood actually telephoned the Lord Chamberlain's office and was informed, with some embarrassment: 'You are not on the list.' One columnist commented: 'The charitable theory of oversight is unconvincing since the earl's younger brother, Gerald Lascelles, was invited and attended . . . That, as a divorced person, he should be barred from the funeral of an uncle who married at such deliberate cost a divorced person, is a ludicrous persistence of Abdication attitudes, bordering on the unbelievable. Yet no other official explanation is offered.'[45]

The Duke's only surviving brother, Prince Henry, the Duke of Gloucester, was also not present. A long series of strokes had deprived him of speech, hearing and mobility. No one had told him of his eldest brother's death, but from his wheelchair he watched the funeral on television at Barnwell Manor, and the tears he shed seemed to indicate that he understood what had happened.[46]

During her three days at the Palace, Wallis had been visibly confused. The combined effect of the arteriosclerosis and Dr Antenucci's sedatives had caused her mind to wander, and on several occasions she had startled the Queen, Prince Philip and their children by referring to the dead Duke as if he were still alive and was expected to join them momentarily. Now, although she had already met all the members of the Royal Family who greeted her in the Dean's Room, she seemed at moments bewildered and apprehensive, as if she neither knew where she was nor with whom.

The Queen Mother, her habitual unpunctuality still in evidence in her seventy-second year, was several minutes late arriving from Royal Lodge. As she entered, she went immediately to where the Duchess was standing and shook her hand sympathetically. The two sisters-in-law were the only women present wearing veils.

The castle's great curfew bell, which had been tolling mournfully for an hour, at last fell silent as the funeral service began. The royal party sat in the raised stalls on the south side of the choir, the Queen nearest to the catafalque, the Duchess on her left, with only Prince Philip intervening between the widow and her sister-in-law, the Queen Mother. The Duke of Windsor's first cousin, King Olav of Norway, sat on the Queen Mother's left. The Duchess sat with her head bowed and did not look up as her husband's coffin was carried into the chapel by eight scarlet-coated guardsmen of the Prince of Wales's Company, 1st Battalion, Welsh Guards. The coffin, still draped in the former King's personal standard, bore a single superb cross of white Easter lilies chosen and assembled for the Duchess by the gardener at Windsor Castle.

As the hymns and prayers began, Wallis again looked lost and the Queen was several times seen to help her find the place in her hymn-book. From a vantage point nearby, Dr Antenucci kept a close watch on his patient in case she broke down or collapsed during the service. On the whole, however, she bore up well, and one observer noted: 'The only sign of the strain on the Duchess of Windsor was the way she gripped the back of the stall in front of her when standing for the hymns.'[47] Another writer recorded: 'She did not weep, but fidgeted, twisted her rings, and on at least two occasions her face broke into a sudden smile that was more like a grimace.'[48]

One verse of *The King of Love My Shepherd is* seemed strangely appropriate to the errant Prince they were mourning:

> *Perverse and foolish oft I stray'd,*
> *But yet in love he sought me,*
> *And on His Shoulder gently laid,*
> *And home, rejoicing, brought me.*

After Garter King of Arms, Sir Anthony Wagner, had proclaimed the styles and titles of the man who was 'sometime the most high, most mighty, and most excellent monarch, King Edward the Eighth, Emperor of India, Defender of the Faith', the Archbishop of Canterbury, Dr Michael Ramsey, gave the blessing, and four trumpeters of the Household Cavalry sounded the Last Post and Reveille. As the final trumpet notes died away, the Queen rose from her stall and 'motioned gently to the Duchess'.[49] The Queen, walking with the Dean of Windsor, led the procession out of the chapel. The Duchess, supported by Prince Philip, paused for several moments by the altar and bowed her head deeply to the coffin. Behind her, escorted by King Olav, walked the Queen Mother, who also inclined her head to the coffin.

As the Royal Family emerged from St George's Chapel into the scrutiny of press and television cameras, the Queen Mother, walking for the first time behind the woman who had once been anathema to her, was seen to have a gentle smile on her face. The Duchess still seemed very disoriented. At one moment she plucked at the elbow of the Queen in front of her, and Elizabeth II turned abruptly with a hint of surprise in her expression. Wallis leaned towards her as if seeking guidance on some point.

A minute or two later, the Queen Mother moved forward from where she had been standing beside King Olav and took the bemused widow gently by the arm. As if to distract Wallis from the sadness of the occasion, Elizabeth gestured in the direction of the hundreds of floral tributes massed around the walls of St George's Chapel. The Duchess, looking strained and distressed, glanced towards the flowers and could be seen, through the thick folds of her veil, to be answering the Queen Mother. In that moment, as the sisters-in-law briefly stood side by side, the bitter enmity that had persisted between them for so long seemed to fade. They ceased to be queen and queen-*manquée*, and became simply two elderly women, both widows, one trying to help the other.

Leaving the Duke's body in St George's Chapel to be guarded by the Household Cavalry, the Royal Family and their guests returned to the Castle for luncheon. While cocktails and sherry were being served, the Queen Mother guided the Duchess to a settee and talked with her quietly, employing all the 'justly famous charm' on which Wallis had once acidly commented. But the effect of Dr Antenucci's sedatives was wearing off, and the Duchess was now visibly struggling to contain her emotions.[50]

At luncheon, Wallis sat at the second of five tables, between Prince Philip and Lord Mountbatten. The Queen and the Queen Mother presided over adjoining tables. Guests noted that the Duchess ate hardly anything and spoke very little during the meal. After lunch she drove with the Queen and Prince Philip to Frogmore for the Duke's burial. To general surprise, the Queen Mother also attended the committal service. At 2.25, the Duke of Windsor's coffin was lowered into the grave on the site he himself had chosen – beneath a wide-spreading plane tree, and surrounded by hawthorns, rhododendrons, wild azaleas and flowering cherries. It was close to the garden where he had played as a child.

When the mourners returned to the Castle, the Duchess's disorientation seemed to have increased. She told the Prime Minister, Edward Heath: 'You must come to Paris to see us. The Duke and I would love to have you.'[51] She asked Princess Margaret if she was 'having a good time', and more than once said, 'Where is the Duke?' The Queen Mother, watching all this with an expression of great compassion on her face, again took her sister-in-law's arm and gently guided her to a chair. 'I know how you feel,' she said quietly. 'I've been through it myself.'[52]

Many of those who had known the Windsors in earlier days – Lady Diana Cooper, Sir Cecil Beaton, Mary, Duchess of Buccleuch, Lady Monckton, Lady Alexandra Metcalfe and others – were present at the funeral, but few of them were allowed anywhere near the widow. People were discreetly kept at a distance by courtiers in an attempt to prevent Wallis's confused ramblings from becoming public knowledge.

At 3.15, forty minutes after the Duke's body had been lowered into the ground, the Duchess, accompanied by Lady Dudley, Brigadier Greenacre, Dr Antenucci, John Utter, and her maid, Giselle, walked towards three waiting cars. The Queen, the Queen Mother, and every member of the Royal Family came to the entrance of the private apartments to see her off. Buckingham Palace, explaining her very early departure, announced: 'It is the Duchess's wish that she would like to return home at this time. The last few days have been a massive strain for her and her wishes are quite understandable.'[53]

Throughout her four days in Britain, Wallis had imposed herself on the Royal Family to the smallest extent possible. She had politely declined to attend the Trooping the Colour ceremony. She had opted out of the family weekend at Windsor, and she was now relieving them of her presence at the earliest opportunity. She had shown throughout a dignified reticence of which they had never thought her capable.

Much was made subsequently of the fact that no member of the Royal Family accompanied her to the airport, but in reality she received the highest honours, being escorted to Heathrow by the most important official in the Queen's household, the Lord Chamberlain,

Lord Maclean. Also in attendance on her at the airport were the Queen's lady-in-waiting, the Hon. Mary Morrison, and – ironically – Lieutenant-Colonel John Johnston, the son-in-law of the Duke of Windsor's arch-critic, Alec Hardinge. Brigadier Douglas Greenacre, the Queen's Equerry, was to accompany Wallis on the return flight to Paris.

On the tarmac at Heathrow, Miss Morrison, who seemed to dwarf the Duchess, shook hands with her unbendingly and again there was the significant omission of a curtsey. It was the final official reminder of Wallis's enduring morganatic status. 'Chips' Maclean, the new Lord Chamberlain, stood with his right hand on the rail of the steps leading up to the aircraft of the Queen's Flight. His head was fractionally inclined forward in what could have been construed as a bow.

The Duchess, her frail form fleetingly silhouetted against the light by her dramatic black clothes, mounted the ten steps with surprising swiftness. Press and television cameramen trained their lenses on her receding back in the hope that she might turn one last time to wave goodbye, but she did not turn. The tiny, purposeful figure disappeared into the plane. The steps were wheeled away, the doors were closed, and at four o'clock the aircraft, with the emblem of the British crown glinting in gold on its side, rose into the clouds.

While Wallis's departure was in progress, at Westminster both Houses of Parliament were debating a Motion 'That an Humble Address be presented to Her Majesty on the death of His Royal Highness the Duke of Windsor, expressing the deep sympathy which this House extends to Her Majesty and to all members of his family on their grievous loss, and recording grateful remembrance of his devoted service to his country and to the British Empire.'[54]

Moving the Motion in the House of Commons, the Prime Minister, Edward Heath, ended by paying tribute to 'the wife for whose love King Edward was content to give up his patrimony and who has repaid his devotion with an equal loyalty, companionship, and love. His death is, above all, her loss, and to her the House will wish to extend its profound sympathy.'[55]

The Democratic Unionist member for North Antrim, the Reverend Ian Paisley, at once intervened on a point of order: 'Surely, today, when this matter is brought before the House, specific mention should have been made in the Motion of the person who will miss the Duke most.'[56] The Speaker replied: 'That is not a matter of order for the Chair.'[57]

The Opposition Leader, Harold Wilson, also paid tribute to the Duke's 'gracious lady, the Duchess of Windsor . . . We all welcome the fact that she has felt able to be in Britain to hear and sense the feelings of our people, and we are all appreciative of the dignity she has shown, not only in these tragic days but over all the years. We hope that she will feel free at any time to come among and freely communicate with the people whom her husband, Prince of Wales, King, and Duke, lived to serve.'[58]

The Liberal leader, Jeremy Thorpe, added: 'I would have hoped that it might have been possible to mention his widow by name in the Motion which we shall pass, for not only does our sympathy go out to his family but in particular it goes out to his widow whose sadness has been shared by many in this country and whose composure and dignity have won our deep respect.'[59]

Predictably, however, the anti-monarchist Member of Parliament, Willie Hamilton, was not impressed by the proceedings, and said: 'There are many people who are sick and tired by the hypocrisy, humbug and cant in which we have engaged and which we have seen successive people in what we call the Establishment engage in during the last seven days. It is simply not good enough for us now to salve our consciences by paying these tributes after the man is dead.

'Every speaker has paid tribute to the late Duke's widow. No woman could have behaved with more dignity and grace in face of the humiliations and indignities piled on her by the Government, the House and by our Governments over the last thirty-six years. We can sympathize today, but we should examine our consciences about the last thirty-six years.'[60]

The Labour Member for Romford, Dick Leonard, then rose to ask if it would 'be in order to move an Amendment including the name of the Duchess of Windsor before the reference to the Royal Family?'.[61] The Speaker replied: 'I think that that is a matter for me to decide. I have already had notice of a manuscript Amendment from the Hon. Member for Cornwall, North (Mr Pardoe), to insert in Motion, after the second reference to "Her Majesty", the words "to Her Grace the Duchess of Windsor". I think that it would be in accordance with the wishes of the House if I allowed that Amendment to be moved. Perhaps the Hon. Member will move it formally.'[62]

The Amendment was moved and the words, 'Her Grace the Duchess of Windsor', were formally inserted in the Humble Address presented to the Queen. Even in the House of Lords, where Lord Byers praised 'the way in which the late King George VI and the present Queen Mother responded to the challenge'[63] of the Abdication, tributes were paid to the Duchess, and Lord Shackleton expressed the hope that the Lord Privy Seal, Earl Jellicoe, would 'consider sending a special message to the Duchess of Windsor, the widow of a Member of this House, expressing our personal sympathies, our affection and our gratitude to her for her devotion and for giving so much of her life to her man'.[64]

The wheel had come full circle. The American divorcee whom George V had contemptuously referred to as 'that woman', whom Queen Mary had called 'an adventuress', and George VI had dismissed as 'Mrs. —', or 'She', had at last received the recognition and the tributes of the British Parliament.

At 5.20 that afternoon, the Duchess's plane landed at Villacourlay Airport. She drove home to the great empty rooms of the house in the Bois de Boulogne. Upstairs, on the table in her dressing room, the first thing she saw was her husband's own personal tribute to her, written in his clear, boyish hand on framed royal stationery:

> *My friend, with thee to live alone*
> *Methinks were better than to own*
> *A crown, a sceptre, and a throne.*

The following morning's Court Circular was more prosaic and accorded Wallis her last official recognition in life. Her attendance at her husband's funeral was recorded in six words. 'The Duchess of Windsor was present.' Later in the entry came the further information: 'By command of The Queen, the Lord Maclean (Lord Chamberlain) was present at Heathrow Airport, London, this afternoon upon the departure of the Duchess of Windsor for France.'[65]

For the Royal Family and the British Court, a long and uncomfortable chapter in its history had been brought to a close with suitable propriety and superficial politeness. Between the Duchess of Windsor and her sister-in-law, the Queen Mother, however, there remained a strange and touching epilogue to be played out.

14

'IN FRIENDSHIP'

FOR THE FIRST TIME IN thirty-five years, Wallis was alone with her splendour. The staff at the house in the Bois de Boulogne still wore the royal livery. They still bowed and curtsied to her and continued to address her as 'Votre Altesse Royale'. John Utter, as always, called her 'Ma'am', and his deputy, Johanna Schütz, went on informing Dior by telephone that 'Son Altesse Royale veut visiter vos salons cet après-midi.' No one sat in the Duchess's presence without permission. Her stationery still bore the emblem of a crown above her personal monogram, and in letters written on her behalf, the word 'her' was given a capital H. The royal portraits, ornaments and coats of arms remained in their accustomed positions in the large, imposing rooms of the Neuilly mansion, but the man for whom she had created that gilded substitute kingdom was gone.

'Her Royal Highness' had lost more than a husband. She had lost her leading man, the co-star of her personal extravaganza, the entire raison d'être for her style of living. The Prince was dead. The royal fairy-tale was over. The leading lady was left on stage surrounded by her props and all the tinsel of make-believe, but the curtain had fallen, the audience had departed. What remained to be acted out seemed only a hollow charade without point or substance.

Like Elizabeth Bowes-Lyon when she ceased to be Queen of England, Wallis, always outwardly the dominant partner in her marriage, lost much of her poise and confidence in the first weeks of widowhood. Efforts were made to reassure her. From Buckingham Palace, Prince Charles wrote to his great-aunt in terms of warmth and sympathy. It was, she told friends, 'a *beautiful* letter',[1] offering his help and support whenever it might be needed.

But if midnight had struck and Prince Charming was lost to her, this quasi-royal Cinderella had scarcely reverted to rags. In response to her evident anxiety over money and the future, Lord Mountbatten presently informed her that the Duke's capital, to which she was sole heir, could not be less than two million pounds, and that most estimates put it at four million, with her jewels and the Duke's many royal heirlooms worth a further three million. Meanwhile the French Foreign Minister, Maurice Schumann, called on her to say that his Government would not be imposing death duties on the ex-King's estate, that the Duchess would continue to remain immune from taxation, as in the Duke's lifetime, and that she was welcome to stay on as tenant of the Neuilly house for the rest of her life if she chose.

Even these assurances did not entirely banish the spectre of penury from Wallis's mind. Soon after the Duke's death, her Paris staff was reduced from twenty-five to fourteen, and the Moulin de la Tuilerie, which had been on the market for two years without finding a buyer, was advertised in the *Wall Street Journal*. It was finally sold in June 1973 for £320,000 to a Swiss millionaire, Edmond Antar.

In all other respects, however, Wallis continued to behave as if her husband were still alive. On Mountbatten's advice, she returned the Duke's Garter robes, uniforms, orders and decorations to the Queen, but his rooms in the house remained exactly as he had last used them. Every night the Duchess would visit the Duke's rooms before going to her own, would check that all the lights were on, that her husband's favourite photographs of her were in their usual places, and finally, on turning to leave, would call out, 'Good night, David.'[2]

In spite of Prince Charles's concern for her, the Royal Family made no further move to include Wallis in their activities. On July 8, six weeks after the Duke of Windsor's death, Prince Richard of Gloucester married a Danish secretary, Birgitte van Deurs. The wedding was a low-key affair, held at Barnwell in order to make it possible for the bridegroom's paralysed father, the seventy-two-year-old Duke of Gloucester, to be present in his wheelchair at the reception. Although on friendly terms with her sister-in-law, Alice, the Duchess of Gloucester, Wallis was not invited to the wedding, possibly because the Queen Mother was attending as the principal royal guest.[3]

Wallis no longer cared enough to take offence at being excluded from royal occasions, and her sadness was genuine when, only seven weeks later, on August 28, the Gloucesters' elder son, Prince William, who had visited the Windsors in Paris, was killed as his Piper Cherokee plane crashed in flames at the Goodyear International Air Trophy Race at Halfpenny Green Airport, near Wolverhampton. The charred body of the thirty-year-old Prince was identifiable only by a ring he had been wearing. It was thirty years, almost to the day, that the Duke of Windsor's favourite brother, Prince George, Duke of Kent, had died in an air accident. Wallis was not invited to attend Prince William's funeral at St George's Chapel, Windsor, on September 2, but the royal wreaths included a large spray of white lilies which bore a card with the words, 'With love from the Duchess of Windsor.'[4]

In spite of continuing apprehension as to how she might behave as a widow, Wallis was careful to do nothing that might offend or embarrass the Royal Family. An offer for her to appear on Bob Hope's television show was politely but firmly declined.

That summer her faithful friend, Grace Dudley, joined her for a quiet three-week stay in Biarritz where, chaperoned by Aunt Bessie, she had spent her first overseas holiday with the Prince of Wales in August 1934. When, four months after the Duke's death, she began to re-emerge into the social life of Paris, it was at private dinner parties where her escort was usually a twenty-six-year-old Parisian, Claude Roland. As a 'walker' for the seventy-six-year-old Duchess, Roland was a sensible choice. Anyone nearer her own age might have invited gossip and possible speculation in the press.

In September, in the 1972 edition of Debrett's Peerage, the editor, Patrick Montague-Smith, expressed considerable doubt – as Burke's Peerage had done in 1967 – regarding the validity of the Letters Patent of May 1937 depriving the Duchess of Windsor of the title of Royal Highness. 'It is doubtful', he wrote, 'how knowledgeable the British and Commonwealth Ministers of the Crown were on constitutional and legal issues; whether they consulted eminent authorities for advice before the May statement was issued; or if they did do so, whether they took the advice which was offered.'[5]

Montague-Smith, an acknowledged expert on such matters, came to the clear conclusion that the 1937 ruling was in error. But even in old age and widowhood, Wallis continued to be the object of deep prejudice and resentment in Britain. Montague-Smith was disconcerted to find himself the recipient of angry letters of protest, to the point where he felt obliged to clarify matters publicly. 'My intention in referring to the style of HRH in the Preface of the new Debrett was to investigate its history by a series of questions, and not to come to the aid of the Duchess of Windsor, however chivalrous this would have been. I have always regarded the Abdication as necessary.'[6] Later he commented: 'All my correspondents . . . assumed that I was a defender of the Duke and Duchess of Windsor. Five . . . congratulated me in defending the Duke and Duchess, and the remainder criticized me for being a partisan in an unworthy cause.'[7]

The long antipathy between the Duchess of Windsor and her

sister-in-law, the Queen Mother, was publicly resurrected that autumn when Royce Ryton's play, *Crown Matrimonial*, opened in London at the Theatre Royal, Haymarket, on October 19, starring Wendy Hiller as Queen Mary, Peter Barkworth as Edward VIII, and Andrew Ray as the Duke of York.

Wallis Simpson, although much discussed during the action, did not actually appear in the play, but the Queen Mother, as Duchess of York, did – the first occasion on which Elizabeth had been portrayed on stage or screen.[8] The actress chosen to play her, Amanda Reiss, although rather slimmer than Elizabeth had been at thirty-six, achieved a remarkable similarity, recreating the famous dark fringe and what Wallis remembered as 'the beauty of her complexion and the almost startling blueness of her eyes'.[9]

The author had put into Elizabeth's mouth some trenchant comments about Wallis: 'I don't think . . . that I shall ever be able to hear the words "Mrs Simpson" without a shudder'. And in an exchange between Edward VIII and his sister-in-law, the King remarks: 'You married Bertie because you loved him and I trust you have stayed married for the same reason.' Elizabeth replies: 'I waited some time, months if not years before I was certain, and being certain I then made vows which to me mean a great deal. I would never have made them if I hadn't meant to keep them. All married people make these vows of their own free will. No one forces us to do so. Wallis Simpson has made them twice and broken them twice.' Later in the conversation, Elizabeth tells the King: 'Everything has to be sacrificed to your vanity, the country, Bertie, your mother, me, the throne, everything and everyone, so that you can be happy in your private life. You are mesmerized by your own legend.' And the King replies: 'Don't forget you have a legend too. The perfect wife and mother. I hope it's not making you smug.'[10]

Audience reaction appeared to indicate that the British theatre-going public were firmly on Elizabeth's side in her views about Wallis. Although Amanda Reiss was not a star, and her role in the play occupied only one tense scene in the second Act, her entrance, dressed in a fur-trimmed powder-blue evening gown, was invariably greeted by an ovation and shouts of affectionate recognition. At one performance an elderly man bellowed, 'Here she comes, God bless her', as if it were the Queen Mother herself walking onto the stage, and the audience erupted in loyal and enthusiastic applause which held up the play for several minutes. Other actresses who played the role of the

Duchess of York were later to encounter similar reactions. Such was Elizabeth's popularity, and Wallis's evident lack of it, only five months after the Duke of Windsor's death.

The Queen Mother did not visit the Theatre Royal, Haymarket, to see the play during its long London run. In 1974, however, Amanda Reiss recreated the role of Elizabeth in a British television production of *Crown Matrimonial*, which starred Greer Garson as Queen Mary, and the Queen Mother watched it with interest in the privacy of her own home.[11] Miss Reiss had evidently done her homework on Elizabeth's voice and did her utmost to recreate the 'justly famous charm' and what Lord David Cecil remembered as the 'tones of drowsy melting sweetness that seemed to caress the words they uttered'.[12] The Queen Mother was amused by the portrayal of her earlier self. It triggered her natural talent for mimicry. Princess Margaret was later to say: 'I shall never forget her imitation of the actress imitating her.'[13] Was Elizabeth possibly reminded of that moment forty years earlier that had begun the long feud between the sisters-in-law: overhearing Wallis Simpson's exaggerated imitation of her in the drawing-room at Fort Belvedere?

If the British continued to disapprove of the Duchess of Windsor, public opinion in her adopted country, France, proved kinder. An American television film, *The Woman I Love*, starring Richard Chamberlain as Edward VIII and Faye Dunaway as Wallis Simpson, was shown on French television, followed by a discussion in which the French Foreign Minister, Maurice Schumann, the British historian, Professor Hugh Thomas, and Lord Tennyson, a resident of Paris, took part. Members of the public were invited to telephone the studio with questions or comments, and the views expressed were overwhelmingly in favour of the Duchess and openly critical of the Royal Family's treatment of her.[14] This continued unchanged. The Palace's policy towards Wallis had reverted to its former pattern. She was conspicuous by her absence from the celebrations in November to mark the Silver Wedding anniversary of the Queen and Prince Philip, having received no invitation to the Westminster Abbey service of thanksgiving, to the Guildhall luncheon that followed it, or to any of the more private family festivities.

In Paris, Wallis made faltering efforts to recapture the sparkle of the social life that had been all-important to her when the Duke was alive. But the old *élan* had disappeared. In its place there was now uncertainty, mental confusion and physical infirmity. Emerging from a party at

Maxim's she suddenly tottered and was caught only just in time by the doorman before she pitched head-first into the gutter.[15]

On December 14, 1972, Margaret, Duchess of Argyll gave a glittering party in London at the Dorchester Hotel to celebrate the eightieth birthday on the following day of the oil billionaire, J. Paul Getty. Margaret Argyll had known Wallis for almost forty years, and although she disapproved of the Abdication, she felt deeply sympathetic to her in the isolation of widowhood. She had also had her own experience, after the Argyll divorce case in 1963, of the weather-vane antics of a certain section of society. Margaret offered Wallis the place of honour at the dinner, which was attended by guests who flew in from all over the world including King Umberto, Lady Diana Cooper, the American Ambassador, Walter Annenberg, Patricia Cox, President Nixon's daughter and many other friends of Getty's. It was an occasion Wallis would have jumped at in the old days. Now a journey to London seemed an impossible ordeal. 'I just don't feel up to it,' she told Margaret Argyll. Later in her letter, she bemoaned the passing of 'what used to be known as "Gay Paree." '[16] The world was changing and it seemed to be leaving her behind stranded.

Part of her reluctance to come to London stemmed from the Royal Family's continuing coolness. There were indications, small but significant, that Elizabeth II retained stronger reservations concerning the Duchess of Windsor than her mother now did. The Queen's Christmas card to the Windsors jointly during her uncle's lifetime had invariably been signed, 'Fondest love Lilibet'. In her first Christmas card to the Duchess as a widow, she reverted to the formal relationship between sovereign and subject, signing herself, 'Elizabeth R'. The Queen Mother's 1972 Christmas card to Wallis, on the other hand, was signed merely, 'Elizabeth', while that from the Duke and Duchess of Kent came 'With love and affectionate greetings Eddie and Katharine'.[17] The Queen had not forgotten the intense anxiety the Windsors had caused her father, nor the public discourtesy the Duchess had shown to her mother at the unveiling of the plaque to Queen Mary.

Shortly after Christmas 1972 there began the long series of mishaps that were to impair Wallis's health permanently. As she walked across her Paris drawing-room with a cane, a small rug slipped beneath her and she crashed to the floor, hurting herself badly. A few days later, she found it painful to walk, and when at last the doctors took X-rays, it was discovered that she had broken her hip.

At the American Hospital, the nurses found their patient 'very senile'. She required constant supervision. 'She was very confused. She would ask the same question forty times and still not seem to understand the answer. We attached a button to her nightdress to turn off the light, but she just couldn't find it, as hard as she tried. They had to put sideboards on her bed because she kept trying to climb out at night. I remember her saying once that if it wasn't for her, Elizabeth wouldn't have been queen.'[18]

After her hip had been set, Wallis asked one of the nurses, 'Can you do the Charleston?'

'No, Ma'am. I never learned.'

'You should. It's easy and it's fun. Watch!'[19] Before the nurse could stop her, she got out of bed and began to dance, causing her hip to break again. The hip-joint was replaced with a part-plastic, part-silver substitute, and although she was able to walk normally, her movements never recovered their accustomed ease and grace.

Before she entered the American Hospital, Lord Mountbatten had called to see the Duchess, at her own request, to discuss the possibility of establishing a Duke of Windsor Foundation in memory of her husband. Wallis had been initially enthusiastic and had asked Mountbatten if he thought Prince Charles would agree to become involved in the project. Mountbatten said he thought Charles would be delighted to become Chairman of the Foundation, and that other surviving friends of the Duke – like Commander Colin Buist – could be asked to sit on the board. The income from the Foundation would then be used to help organizations or individuals the Duchess felt the Duke would have liked to support. Wallis promised to clear the idea with her French lawyer and then to give instructions to Sir Godfrey Morley, Senior Partner of the Duke's London solicitors, Allen & Overy, for her will to be redrawn.

That was in the autumn of 1972. In January 1973, Sir Godfrey, far from receiving the promised instructions, was curtly informed by letter that the Duke of Windsor Foundation had been abandoned; that the Duchess no longer required Allen & Overy to act for her; and that in future her French attorney, Maître Suzanne Blum, would be in sole charge of her affairs. Among Wallis's friends it was rumoured that Maître Blum had raised the disquieting possibility that the setting up of such a foundation, and the use of its income in Britain, might cause the French Government to revise its pledge not to impose death duties on the Duke's estate. Godfrey Morley felt the decision was more personally motivated on Blum's part. 'I had a feeling that she wanted to end the British connection – *any* connection with Britain.'[20]

Privately Maître Blum was thought to distrust Mountbatten's attempted influence on the Duchess. Mountbatten had never liked Wallis, but since the Duke's death he had been 'persistently on the telephone to her'.[21] There were some who felt his new interest verged on the acquisitive. He would wander through the Neuilly house, picking up the Duke's royal mementoes, and saying how much he would like to have this or that. Maître Blum's natural desire was to ensure that her client, no longer in full physical or mental health, was not exploited. It would have been natural to suspect advice that the Duke's money, now the Duchess's, should be used to benefit Britain, a country that had treated them both for many years as outcasts. Maître Blum was sole executrix of the Duke's will, and from this point onwards her influence over the Duchess's life became absolute.

Suzanne Blum was only two years and five months Wallis's junior,[22] but she looked and seemed at least twenty years younger than her age. Jewish, the daughter of a French businessman, and a distant cousin of the late French premier, Léon Blum, who had been imprisoned by the Nazis, she had been in practice at the Paris Bar since 1922. One of her first briefs was to defend the Hollywood film studio, Warner Brothers, against an action brought by the composer, Igor Stravinsky, for misuse of his music. Stravinsky was demanding 300,000 francs. With Blum against him, all he got was one franc. Subsequently, in between acting for Charlie Chaplin, Walt Disney, Twentieth Century-Fox, Rita Hayworth and Metro-Goldwyn-Mayer, she penned successful detective stories under the pseudonym of L. S. Karen.

She was first introduced to the Windsors in 1937 by the United States Ambassador in Paris, William C. Bullitt. She met them again after the war through a mutual friend, the American hostess, Mrs Margaret Biddle. The connection was fostered by the fact that Blum's first husband, Maître Paul Weill, was the Paris representative of the Duke's London solicitors, Allen & Overy. She became the Windsors' French attorney in 1946. When her first husband died, Maître Blum was already in her mid-sixties, but she discreetly remarried. Her second husband was General Georges Spillmann, a noted Arabic scholar and a Grand Officer of the Légion d'honneur, of which she herself became a Commander.

From their elegant Left Bank apartment in the rue de Varenne,

Suzanne Blum surveyed French society with a critical eye. In her late seventies, one observer found her 'a woman of incisive manner and sharp brains. Diminutive, she still dominates by her presence. Her face is unlined, her complexion excellent and her features bear evidence of her once having been a considerable beauty – and she manages to look elegant, even in her lawyer's robes'.[23] This was the formidable personality who henceforth would control all that remained of Wallis's crumbling life.

On May 29, 1973, Buckingham Palace announced the engagement of Princess Anne to Lieutenant Mark Phillips.[24] An international wire service promptly tracked down the Duchess of Windsor to a borrowed house – the Villa Roserie at Cap Ferrat – where she was holidaying with her staff and some friends. Unusually, she agreed to give a telephone interview on her reaction to the news. What she said made it clear that the Royal Family had not informed her in advance of the announcement. 'Oh, how wonderful. I have been reading all the rumours in the papers, but you cannot believe everything you read. This is wonderful. I have never met the young man, but of course I know Princess Anne very well.' She wished the couple 'all the happiness in the world.'[25]

Six weeks later, on July 11,[26] Wallis made what was to be her final visit to Britain and her first and last excursion to her husband's grave. Elizabeth II sent an aircraft of the Queen's Flight to bring her from Paris, and in strict privacy she was met at Heathrow Airport by the Duke of Kent and Lord Mountbatten, who entertained her to luncheon at Windsor Castle. There was no meeting with the Queen, who was in Scotland, or with her sister-in-law, the Queen Mother.

After luncheon, the Duke of Kent and Mountbatten drove her to Frogmore to visit her husband's grave, now covered by a plain white stone of Portland marble. The Duke and Mountbatten moved tactfully to one side as Wallis looked down at the words:

H.R.H. The Prince Edward
Albert Christian George
Andrew Patrick David
Duke of Windsor
Born 23rd June 1894
Died 28th May 1972
King Edward VIII
20th January–11th December 1936

The eight-line inscription was all that now remained of thirty-five years of her life. She looked around her at the wild azaleas, the hawthorns and the flowering cherries. It was a fragrant and peaceful spot, shaded by the great plane tree overhead. The British people would never see their former King's last resting place, or hers that would be beside it. Although Frogmore Gardens are opened for two days a year under the National Gardens Scheme, the public is never admitted to the royal burial ground, which is screened from view by a hedge. Wallis laid her flowers against the white marble stone and turned away. She was driven back to Heathrow and boarded the royal plane for the return journey to Paris. Her visit had lasted four hours. Without a word of publicity or the smallest ceremony, the woman who had once divided the nation and for whom the King of England had relinquished his throne left British soil for the last time in her life.

On August 9, accompanied by Grace Dudley and 'Foxie' Sefton, Wallis arrived at the Hôtel du Palais in Biarritz. Her physical frailty was increasing all the time, and the holiday was marred when she tripped against a raised marble hearthstone and sustained another bad fall, cracking five ribs in the process.

That summer, *France-Dimanche*, a newspaper renowned for its vivid imagination concerning royalty, delighted Windsor *cognoscenti* by announcing that the Duchess was to marry John Utter. Both of them denied it as a matter of course, but they need hardly have bothered. Far from aspiring to become her fourth husband, Utter was finding his late master's widow increasingly difficult to deal with. Although devoted to the Duke, he had never liked Wallis, or she him. Since the Duke's death, he had found her temper less predictable than ever and their relationship had steadily deteriorated.[27]

By the end of September, it was clear that the Royal Family did not intend to invite the Duchess to Princess Anne's wedding on November 14. Confirming the absence of an invitation, John Utter began by alleging: 'And there is no reason why we should expect one.'[28] To the British press, however, there seemed every reason, and by the end of October, urged to say why he thought she had not been asked, Utter was forced to admit: 'Can't think of any particular reason why not.'[29] He added that in spite of not being invited, Wallis still planned to send her great-niece a wedding present. The American wire service, United Press International, opportunistically offered to send the Duchess to the wedding to cover it for them exclusively. Her reply to this suggestion was a dignified refusal.

It is not hard to guess at the reasons for the omission. As far as the British Court was concerned, the public reconciliation at the Duke's funeral was no more than the tidying-away of loose ends. It had never been the intention to draw the Duchess permanently into British public life. Even if she were to be invited, the problems of protocol were formidable. Where were they to put her? If she sat with her sister-in-law, the Duchess of Gloucester, might it not be said that she was being accorded royal treatment, in contradiction of the ruling of 1937? If, on the other hand, they gave her *placement* according to her officially non-royal status, were they not liable to be accused of unkindness to an elderly widow? The simplest solution seemed to be not to invite her at all. As far as the Queen and her family were concerned, honour had already been done and seen to be done in the case of Wallis. Her precarious and unpredictable mental state, reported by Mountbatten and others, did not encourage them to invite her to further public occasions. She was not the only member of the family to be omitted from the guest list. The divorced Earl of Harewood and his second wife were similarly excluded from Westminster Abbey.

The snub did not appear to bother Wallis unduly. If the Duke had been alive, she would have minded for him. Now that she was alone, it somehow seemed unimportant. Two weeks before the royal wedding, she went on the town with something approaching her old gaiety. Having at last discarded the precautionary walking stick, she took to the dance floor with her old friend, Baron de Cabrol and, aged seventy-seven, performed the latest craze to hit Paris, The Slag.

She was seen dining out again at Maxim's, and when, in November, she gave a dinner party at the Neuilly house and introduced some twenty guests without a moment's hesitation, close friends like Lady Sefton began to hope that the ominous decline had been halted.[30] A few weeks later, she attended the Duc de Rochefoucauld's lavish birthday party for more than a hundred friends at his house on the avenue Montaigne, and waved her arms in the air in order to demonstrate flamenco to the other guests. 'I remember dancing flamenco in Madrid' she said. 'What a fabulous dance.'[31]

The new British Ambassador in Paris, Sir Edward Tomkins, and his wife, Gillian, treated Wallis with particular kindness and several times invited her to Embassy functions as the guest of honour. She always arrived last, left first, and was seated on the Ambassador's right at dinner, but the Foreign Office instructions regarding her official treatment remained unchanged.

At the first of these Embassy occasions in 1974, Margaret Duchess of Argyll was among the guests. In the 1950s, during her marriage to the eleventh Duke of Argyll, Margaret had remained seated when the Duchess of Windsor had walked over to her table at Maxim's. In the case of acknowledged royalty, it would have been customary to rise, but according to the official ruling, the Duchess of Argyll then ranked the higher of the two. Now that Wallis was a widow, however, and in declining health, Margaret was sympathetically disposed to show her every possible consideration.

As the Ambassador led the Duchess of Windsor into the room, Margaret Argyll turned to Lady Tomkins and whispered: 'Do we curtsey? I will if you do.'

'No,' replied the Ambassador's wife. 'We've been told not to.'[32] Wallis, the morganatic wife, was now a morganatic widow. One guest in the room, however – a former ambassadress, no less – ignored the Foreign Office ruling with her usual blithe independence. Lady Diana Cooper had always curtsied to the Duchess of Windsor in the Duke's lifetime, 'to please *him*'. Now, at the age of eighty-two, she sketched out an arthritic curtsey to Wallis as a widow, and her gesture made British officialdom look more than usually petty.[33]

The Duchess's next appearance at a British Embassy dinner un-happily revealed that the apparent improvement in her mental condi-tion had been only temporary. Received as always by Sir Edward Tomkins, whom she had known for almost twenty years, and seated at dinner in the place of honour on his right, she astounded the plump Ambassador by loudly demanding of the man on her own right, 'Who's that fat man on my left?'[34] On another occasion, escorted as usual by the patient John Utter, she enquired of an astonished fellow guest who Utter was. When told that he was her own secretary, she denied all knowledge of him and claimed never to have seen him before in her life.[35]

On April 9, 1974, Wallis arrived in New York on board the Italian liner, *Rafaello*, for what was to be her last visit to her native America. She went as usual to the Waldorf Towers, but instead of using suite 28A, which she had always occupied with the Duke, she now took a smaller one on the fortieth floor.

On May 7, only a few days before Wallis ended her month's stay, Princess Margaret and the Earl of Snowdon arrived at the Waldorf Towers during their tour of the United States and Canada. They were due to attend a performance by the Royal Ballet that evening, and were asked by reporters in the lobby if they were aware that Wallis was staying in the same hotel. The news took them by surprise. Lord Snowdon recalled: 'I well remember, with the greatest pleasure, the honour of meeting the Duchess of Windsor . . . we discovered she was in the hotel and just rang up to see how she was, and asked if she would like us to come up to see her.'[36]

Wallis, predictably, said she would love to see her niece and nephew-in-law, and the Snowdons duly 'popped up' to the fortieth floor for a fifteen-minute visit. As Princess Margaret's private secretary points out, 'it was a perfectly natural action that the Princess and her husband should call upon her uncle's widow. It was a private occasion, and Her Royal Highness did not have any of her Household in attendance.'[37]

The 'private occasion', however, came to be photographed, and the pictures of Princess Margaret and her American aunt appeared in newspapers all over the world. Asked if this had been at the Duchess's instigation or that of her niece, the Princess's private secretary further confirmed: 'It was Princess Margaret's suggestion that photographers should be allowed into the Duchess of Windsor's sitting room in New York to take a photograph of the occasion.'[38]

Margaret evidently regarded it as expedient that her encounter with Wallis should be known and recorded and seems to have felt no apprehension that the publicity might displease her mother or her sister in London. Two days later, Wallis left New York for the last time to return to Paris, and the Snowdons also departed – for Minneapolis and Winnipeg. Neither of them ever saw her again, although they did send her new photographs of themselves and their children, Viscount Linley and Lady Sarah Armstrong-Jones. Wallis's mental deterioration had also been apparent in New York, and she left behind her at the Waldorf Towers an uncharacteristic legacy of resentful gossip concerning her abusive insults to the hotel staff.[39]

On June 10, soon after her return to Paris, Wallis's last surviving brother-in-law, Prince Henry, the Duke of Gloucester, died at Barnwell Manor at the age of seventy-four. Wallis, Princess Alice Duchess of Gloucester, the Queen Mother and Princess Alice Countess of Athlone, were now the only four survivors of the family generation that had been involved in the Abdication. Like the Duke of Windsor, Harry Gloucester had a private funeral in St George's Chapel, and was buried at Frogmore. Once again, the Duchess of Windsor was not included in this family occasion.

On June 19, Wallis was officially seventy-eight, but she resurrected earlier doubts about her age and birth by suddenly asking a friend, 'Do you know that I'm really eighty-one?'[40] It seems certain that this remark was a further product of her mental decline. If it had been the truth, it would have meant that Wallis was born more than two years before her parents' marriage, and that would have been a circumstance unlikely to escape detection or to be forgotten in the small world of Baltimore. In spite of the absence of documentary corroboration, the official date of birth has been confirmed and accepted by contemporaries who knew her from earliest childhood.[41]

That autumn, Frances Donaldson's biography, *Edward VIII*, was published in London. A scholarly work, it presented a uniformly unfavourable assessment of the Duke of Windsor and a less than flattering impression of the Duchess. Elizabeth II had made no move to propose an official biography of the Duke, which was the usual practice in the case of a former sovereign. The historian, A. J. P. Taylor, explained this omission by claiming that 'the Royal Family consider Edward VIII's reign to be a non-event, and he has been completedly expunged'.[42] But the Donaldson book had all the scope of an official biography, and although the author significantly failed to list her personal sources, it was apparent from the text that she had received help from members of the Royal Family, co-operation from the Windsor archivist, and copious information from courtiers hostile to the former King. Lady Hardinge's assistance was particularly evident. Frances Donaldson, in fact, appeared to have spoken to almost everyone, except the Windsors themselves, who had been given no opportunity to balance the picture, although the Duke had been alive for more than two years of the author's work on the book. Lady Donaldson later explained this by saying, 'if I had seen them I would have been expected to write the story from their point of view'.[43]

Wallis, whose powers of concentration were now minimal, never read the Donaldson biography, but Maître Blum did and was outraged. She claimed 'it would take a 400-page book to refute',[44] and immediately complained to the publishers, Weidenfeld and Nicolson, on behalf of her client. To friends of the Windsors, the book seemed the final attempt of the British Establishment to blacken the dead Duke without allowing their hands to be seen in the exercise. The television rights of *Edward VIII* were immediately snapped up by an enterprising New Zealand-born freelance producer, Andrew Brown, with consequences that were to create even worse divisions between the Duchess of Windsor's advisers and the British Royal Family.

If Lady Donaldson's book failed to find favour in the eyes of Maître Blum, however, it was evidently acceptable to the Queen Mother. Three years later, the author produced a further, though infinitely less probing, royal biography, *King George VI and Queen Elizabeth*,[45] written with obvious assistance from Clarence House. Both King and Consort emerged from the text in glowing terms, and the book received unusual marks of royal approval. The Queen Mother was photographed at her writing desk with Lady Donaldson's tribute clearly visible in a prominent position in the forefront of the camera.

The following April, the British fashion writer, Prudence Glynn – in private life Lady Windlesham – went to the house in the Bois de Boulogne for a rare interview with the Duchess. This afforded one small piece of evidence that the Queen Mother had not been totally expunged from her sister-in-law's life. In 'a small, immensely comfortable sitting room', beside photographs of the Duke of Windsor, the visitor noticed 'one of George VI and Queen Elizabeth in Coronation robes with their crowns so far forward they look like candle snuffers'. There was one other curious fact: 'all the time I was with her I knew she reminded me of someone. It is something about the brow and eyes. It was only as the car shot across the Place de la Concorde that I realized that the Duchess has grown to have a strong look of the ladies of the Royal House of Windsor.'[46]

On August 4, 1975, the Queen gave a dinner party for eighty people in the Throne Room at Buckingham Palace to celebrate her mother's seventy-fifth birthday. Wallis, predictably, was not included in the family festivities. The newspapers were full of tributes to the Queen Mother, one of which noted: 'The one subject on which she has been obliquely criticized is that of her attitude to the Duke of Windsor and his wife, who was never allowed the title of Royal Highness. But it is only recently that official documents have revealed the extreme or even fascist tendencies in the Duke. The vindication is therefore hers.'[47]

Not everyone was bowled over by the 'justly famous charm'. That autumn, the anti-royalist Member of Parliament, Willie Hamilton, in his book on the monarchy, commented: 'If a personal public image is the thing to cultivate today, then the Queen Mother is among the best of gardeners. The words drip like honey from the printing presses of the land, with never a stray hornet to be seen with a sting in its tail . . . It is not surprising that a very prominent, right-wing ex-Labour

Cabinet Minister once described the Queen Mother as the most reactionary member of the Royal Family. She makes no speeches of any consequence. She gets through her public relations by pleasing facial exercises, or by purposely chatting to "the lads in the back row" and taking a drop of the hard stuff, her native Scotch whisky. Yet, behind the matey tipple and the ever-ready smile, there lurks the mind of a shrewd businesswoman . . .'[48]

In October, Lord Brownlow, who had escorted Wallis on her historic flight across France in 1936, and who had lost his position at court as a direct consequence, was seriously ill in the Harley Street Clinic. His third wife, Leila,[49] was bitter about Wallis: 'My husband won't have anything to do with the Duchess. They have not spoken since the funeral. We sent masses of flowers but received no acknowledgment from her whatsoever. Quite apart from this, she never rewarded my husband with a single memento of the Duke. However small, it would have reminded him of his old friend. This was very unkind of her. My husband was wonderful to the Duke for years.'[50]

In Paris, Johanna Schütz countered: 'It is very sad, but they must understand that the Duchess was very ill after the death of her husband and wrote no personal thank-you letters to anybody – except to the Queen. With regard to the mementoes, the Duchess decided that none should be given away until her death. No one got anything. Not Lord Brownlow, not anybody. I am most grateful to you for telling me about this. I am sure the Duchess will be in touch with them.'[51]

Miss Schütz duly passed on the message, but Wallis did not respond. Perry Brownlow, shaken by his abrupt dismissal as a Lord-in-Waiting, had been one of those who failed to show up at the Windsors' wedding, and Lady Alexandra Metcalfe had recorded that the Duke 'took Perry's back out the worst'.[52] Wallis had never forgotten, and Brownlow went to his grave without any word of comfort or gratitude from the woman he had once championed.

That autumn it emerged that the Duchess of Windsor had received no invitation to the following year's bicentennial celebrations in the United States. The Queen and the French President had both been invited to Washington, but the Baltimore girl who was America's only direct link with the British Royal Family was allotted no place by her own countrymen.

It hardly seemed to matter now, for Wallis's days of travelling were at an end. She was eating less and less, with the result that her weight had dropped to only a little more than six stone. Her only form of sustenance was a silver mug of iced vodka.[53] The continuous intake of alcohol combined with an almost complete absence of food caused a gastric ulcer to perforate, and on November 13 she suffered a serious stomach haemorrhage, and was rushed to the American Hospital for blood transfusions. The official bulletin mentioned treatment 'for physical exhaustion and long spells of weakness'. The haemorrhage was the final turning point in the breakdown of her health. As her friend, Lady Mosley, commented, 'from then on [she] was never quite well again. At times she seemed to be on the point of recovery, but it always eluded her, and her many friends could do little to help.'[54]

In December, she left the hospital and returned home to be looked after by nurses, but the future looked bleak. 'I fear that her days of entertaining and being entertained are over,' commented John Utter.[55]

Utter's own days in Wallis's employment were over too. As her life continued to narrow in scope, the need for his services disappeared. At the end of 1975, feeling unable to cope further with her deteriorating mental condition, he retired into private life in Paris, with neither pension nor severance pay for his years of service to the Windsors.[56] In retirement, Utter, who had always been loyal and discreet, gave evidence of a certain bitterness. In one interview, he said of his erstwhile employers: 'Their life was essentially a life of entertainment. It was really empty as far as I could judge, but it was what they enjoyed ... They were wretched personalities. They were completely egocentric ... sometimes the sound of their drunken bickering was unbearable. She was a dominating woman, no question of that ... he was certainly sincerely in love with her.'[57]

But the 'dominating woman' had lost her grip on life. In February 1976, she was back in the American Hospital being treated for 'a recurrent spell of weakness', and her health was said to be 'giving rise to serious concern among her friends'.[58]

In the meantime, divorce – the crime for which Wallis had so long been penalized – entered the Royal Family from three different directions. Prince Michael of Kent was on close terms with the estranged wife of his former Eton contemporary, Tom Troubridge, and a divorce was in progress. Gerald Lascelles had emulated his elder brother, the Earl of Harewood, by separating from his wife and setting up home with a former actress whom he had known for twenty years. A divorce would also follow in this case. And on March 19, 1976, Buckingham Palace at last gave in to persistent rumours and announced that Princess Margaret and the Earl of Snowdon 'have mutually agreed to live apart'. It was added that there were 'no plans for divorce proceedings', but a divorce eventually followed two years later.

The Queen Mother was said to be 'particularly distressed' by the news and it is easy to understand why. The crisis that had been narrowly avoided twenty years earlier had come to pass after all, and Elizabeth's own daughter was now in the same category as the sister-in-law she had felt unable to receive. That spring, the Queen Mother went to France on a tour of the Burgundy vineyards, but there was no move to call on the Duchess of Windsor in Paris.

Weakness now kept Wallis almost permanently confined to the house, but a fine, sunny morning in May encouraged her nurses to carry her *chaise longue* out onto the terrace. Two photographers with telephoto lenses had concealed themselves in the shrubbery and managed to photograph the Duchess being lifted by a uniformed nurse. The pathetic pictures of the emaciated, helpless woman with her sad and lifeless eyes were shown on French television and published in *France Soir*. Maître Blum immediately sued for invasion of privacy and damages of 80,000 francs were awarded.

After the haemorrhage, Wallis was forbidden further alcohol, but efforts to build up her weight and strength proved unavailing. One of her friends, Kitty Miller, believed that 'it has a lot to do with her loneliness. She won't eat, you see. She's got so thin she looks like a skeleton . . . I think she feels there is nothing to live for.'[59]

On June 19, the Duchess was officially eighty years old. There was a telegram of congratulations from the Queen, and a large mail resulting from a birthday tribute published the previous weekend in the *Sunday Express*.[60] The author, Michael Thornton, encountered the same public reaction as the editor of *Debrett's Peerage*, Patrick Montague-Smith, four years earlier. He received a large number of angry and abusive letters. Almost the only polite one came from Johanna Schütz, the Duchess's social secretary in Paris. Referring to her employer as 'Her Royal Highness', Miss Schütz wrote to Thornton: 'Your article in the London *Sunday Express* induced hundreds of unknown admirers to send their wishes and all these kind messages brought some cheer in Her sad face.'[61]

The ever-loyal Lady Monckton visited Wallis that summer and found her in terror of attack, possibly as a result of hallucinations. 'I'm frightened!' she told her. 'They've been here again! They've moved my things! It's the second time they've hijacked me.'[62] Biddy Monckton looked around the room and saw that everything was in its usual place. Nothing had been moved since the Duke's death.

In the drawer beside her bed Wallis kept the Duke's automatic pistol. It was always loaded and ready to use in case an intruder managed to invade her fortress. Outside, a former paratroop sergeant, supplied by the City of Paris, guarded the house, a sub-machine gun slung across his chest. A French police patrol car remained on permanent duty in the vicinity, and the electrical alarm fence around the house, linked to the nearest police station, was kept in constant working order. These precautions, and the Duchess's fears, may have resulted from rumours that the Baader Meinhof gang, or an extreme left-wing group affiliated to them, were planning to kidnap her and then raise a huge sum in ransom from the British Royal Family. Wallis remained a realist, even in ill-health. She took the threat of abduction seriously but ridiculed the notion of any ransom. 'As if *they* would pay one cent to get me back,' she scoffed. 'They'd probably pay them to keep me.'[63]

In July, Clarence House announced that the Queen Mother would make a three-day official visit to Paris in October. She would stay with the new British Ambassador and his wife, Sir Nicholas and Lady Henderson,[64] at the palatial British Embassy one hundred yards from the French President's residence, the Elysée Palace.

In view of the worsening condition of the Duchess's health, the news triggered immediate speculation in the British press, and the London gossip columnist, Peter McKay, devoted a long leading article to the forty-year-old antipathy between the sisters-in-law. It appeared under the questioning headline: 'WILL THE QUEEN MOTHER VISIT WALLIS WINDSOR?'[65]

Seventeen days later, one of McKay's Fleet Street rivals, Nigel Dempster, claimed that 'A touching reunion is on the cards . . .', and quoted an unnamed 'friend' as saying, 'They are both old ladies now and it is not improbable that they will meet . . . The Duchess is in very fragile health.' Clarence House cautiously conceded to Dempster that 'Her Majesty's agenda is very full, but we do not know what she will be doing in her spare time.'[66]

Silence now descended while discreet negotiations, prompted by the unwanted press publicity, opened between the Queen Mother's private secretary Sir Martin Gilliat at Clarence House and Johanna Schütz in Paris. After some hesitation on both sides, a teatime visit to the Duchess's house was finally pencilled in to the royal schedule for the Queen Mother's second day in Paris – Tuesday, October 26.[67]

In the meantime, Elizabeth had taken a party of friends to her Deeside home, Birkhall, where her energy, at the age of seventy-six, appeared devastating. 'Those who have been invited to join her there did not spend an idle holiday. A recent house-guest, who has returned exhausted to London, says the Queen Mother refuses to let friends dawdle inside the house, even when the rain is pouring down. Fishing expeditions are organized on the nearby River Dee, led by the Queen Mother.'[68]

On Monday, October 25, still in the highest spirits, Elizabeth and her entourage arrived at the British Embassy in Paris, where the Ambassador and Lady Henderson served a special pie, composed of quails stuffed with apples and raisins and laced with cognac and madeira, in her honour.

On the following morning, wearing a green silk dress and matching hat, and greeted by a fanfare from the State Trumpeters of the Household Cavalry, the Queen Mother, 'switching with equal felicity from one language to another',[69] opened the new British Cultural Centre in Paris. She was accompanied by the French Minister of Education, M. René Haby.

At four o'clock that afternoon, Elizabeth was to be driven in the British Ambassador's car to the house in the Bois de Boulogne for her first meeting with Wallis in more than four years, and the first visit which she had ever made to any of the Windsors' homes. The Queen Mother's staff were already bracing themselves for what was expected to be a tense encounter, when a telephone message came to the British Embassy from Johanna Schütz. It was very much regretted that, owing to the Duchess's continuing ill-health, 'it would now not be possible for Her Royal Highness to receive Her Majesty that afternoon'.[70]

Elizabeth listened to the message in silence, without apparent dismay. But for one factor, the last-minute cancellation might have been suspected as a deliberate snub – that Wallis did not *want* to receive the sister-in-law who had so long refused to receive her.

The factor which caused the Queen Mother to know that the circumstances were genuine, was the experience of Lord Mountbatten, who was also in Paris that week to accept an award by Vicomte Bernard de la Giraudiere on behalf of the champagne house of Laurent Perrier. Mountbatten had telephoned the Neuilly residence asking to see Wallis, and had been asked to come at four o'clock on Wednesday, October 27, the day following Elizabeth's proposed visit. But on the morning of October 26, while the Queen Mother was opening the British Cultural Centre, Mountbatten received a telephone call from Johanna Schütz with an imperious message from Wallis, which the secretary imparted with obvious reluctance. The Duchess, she said, wished him to know that she resented his presumption in arranging to bring with him to the house her own doctor, Jean Thin. Mountbatten, who had never met or spoken to Thin in his life, was flabbergasted. He at once called the doctor to seek elucidation. Shortly afterwards, Dr Thin called back. The Duchess, he explained, was 'suffering from hallucinations. I suggest that you not try to see her. It would be a – an unpleasant experience.'[71]

The Queen Mother, digesting all this information, was silent for some moments. Then, in a quiet and calm voice, she issued very precise instructions to her staff.

That afternoon, in place of the royal visitor, a secretary from the British Embassy delivered to the Neuilly house a magnificent bouquet of two dozen large roses: one dozen white, one dozen deep red. There was some surprise over the choice of colours, for red and white flowers are sometimes regarded as unlucky, and some hospitals will not accept them.

But in the language of flowers – of which Elizabeth and Bertie had been delighted students in the early days of their marriage – red and white roses together stand for 'unity'.[72]

Forty years after her anger at Churchill's mischievous discourse on the red rose of Lancaster and the white rose of York, Elizabeth had chosen those very emblems to bring to a close a battle that had raged even longer than the Wars of the Roses.

The Queen Mother's bouquet to the Duchess of Windsor was symbolic. It signified that after four decades of bitterness and hostility, the feud between them had ended in an honourable peace.

When the roses were brought to the Duchess's bedside, she opened the card attached to them. Written on it, in her sister-in-law's distinctive hand, were three words.

'In friendship, Elizabeth.'[73]

Would you believe this ??

15

A NATION'S GRATITUDE

THE FEUD BETWEEN THE ROYAL sisters-in-law came to an end on that October afternoon in 1976 when the Duchess of Windsor received the Queen Mother's roses and read the short and moving message that accompanied them. The years that followed provided an epilogue to the drama – one that tragically emphasized the extraordinary divergence in the destinies of the two women. For while Wallis sank deeper and deeper into the twilight of illness, isolation and oblivion, Elizabeth, in her eighties, basked in the refulgence of an astonishing Indian Summer, becoming arguably the most popular personality in the British Commonwealth.

In 1977, Elizabeth II celebrated her Silver Jubilee of twenty-five years on the British throne. In that year of national rejoicing, even the divorced Earl of Harewood and his second wife were given a qualified welcome into the family fold. It could hardly be otherwise with the Queen's own sister separated from her husband and then involved in a much publicized liaison with Roddy Llewellyn, a bisexual youth seventeen years her junior. The Harewoods were not invited to the Silver Jubilee Thanksgiving Service at St Paul's Cathedral on June 7, but they were asked to the Silver Jubilee dinner in Leeds on July 13, where the Queen was seen to greet her cousin George with a smile and to shake hands with the second Lady Harewood. The sovereign did not, however, stay at Harewood House as in former days, but slept on board the royal train. The reconciliation was only partial.

On May 4, both Houses of Parliament had presented loyal addresses to Elizabeth II in Westminster Hall. Prior to the Queen's arrival with Prince Philip, her mother had led members of the Royal Family to their places. As the Queen Mother entered, the assembled Lords and Commons rose to receive her, and she responded in inimitable style by inclining her head regally to both sides of the Hall.

At the Guildhall luncheon that followed the Jubilee service on June 7, the Lord Mayor of London, Sir Robin Gillett, spoke of the Queen as being 'blessed with a mother whose place in the hearts of the people has seldom, if ever, been equalled in our long history', and the Queen Mother, dressed in glowing peach, looked visibly moved as the applause crashed out around her.

During one of her public appearances in Jubilee year, the elder Elizabeth was informed breathlessly by a six-year-old boy: 'Ma'am, I've also met your daughter. Do you know, she's the *Queen*!' The Queen Mother looked enchanted. 'Yes, I know,' she replied. 'Isn't it *exciting*?'[1]

With the Harewoods publicly forgiven, and the spectre of divorce hovering over other members of the Royal Family, many people expressed the hope that the Duchess of Windsor would at least be invited to take part in the Jubilee celebrations, even if it proved impossible for her to accept because of her health. But no invitation was sent to Wallis. Her secretary, Johanna Schütz, reported: 'The Duchess is following everything as best she can. She is not too well. On the days she is unable to read I do it for her and we follow things together.' Lady Mosley, Wallis's only remaining English visitor, added: 'The Duchess spends her days on a *chaise longue*. I try to see her once a month, but apart from that she sees only a few Americans. It's very sad.'[2]

Relations between the Duchess of Windsor and Buckingham Palace were not improved by the news that Walter Monckton's son, the second Viscount Monckton of Brenchley, had handed over to the Queen, for safe keeping in the Royal Archives, his father's entire dossier of confidential letters and memoranda written by Edward VIII during the Abdication crisis, and also in subsequent years. Wallis and Maître Blum were both affronted by this revelation and felt that the wishes of the Duke of Windsor's widow should have been consulted before the Queen accepted the dossier. 'The papers were handed over a few weeks ago and will now remain in the Royal Archives,' said Lord Monckton. 'My sister, Lady Goulding,[3] and I felt the documents belonged with the Royal Family. I do not wish to disclose the nature or content of the papers. At no time did I contemplate selling them at auction or making them available to the public.'[4]

Three days after this announcement, Sir Robin Mackworth-Young, the Royal Librarian at Windsor Castle, flew to Paris aboard one of the Queen's personal Dart Herald aircraft and drove to the Duchess of Windsor's house. There he handed a file of documents to Johanna Schütz, who later said: 'It contained personal papers which the

Duchess sent for safe keeping to Windsor Castle soon after the Duke's death. They have now been returned.'[5]

In the following May, however, one of the royal archivists was given permission to go to the house in the Bois de Boulogne, where he spent several days sorting and removing from the Duke's study all papers 'relevant to the Royal Archives' at Windsor. The papers taken 'filled several boxes', and their collection 'was organized in secret through the British Embassy in Paris, which arranged to return them to Britain through the diplomatic bag'. A Buckingham Palace spokesman subsequently said: 'We can confirm that under a purely personal arrangement between the Queen and the Duchess, the Duke's papers have been taken into the Royal Archives.'[6]

The timing of this activity is of particular significance. In May 1978, as a result of intensive press publicity, public interest was mounting in *Edward and Mrs Simpson*, the £1-million seven-part television series produced by Andrew Brown – who owned the rights to Frances Donaldson's *Edward VIII* – and then being filmed by Thames Television at their Teddington studios, with Edward Fox as the King and Cynthia Harris as Wallis, supported by such illustrious performers as Dame Peggy Ashcroft as Queen Mary, Jessie Matthews as Aunt Bessie Merryman, and Elsie Randolph as Lady Colefax.

It was already clear that the saga of the uncrowned King and the American divorcee would once again capture the public imagination when it reached British television screens the following November, and Elizabeth II, aware of the Duchess's disintegrating health, was clearly anxious about leaving her uncle's personal papers in the Neuilly house, particularly since they included private correspondence from the Royal Family, as well as material concerning the Queen's father, King George VI, and also her mother, Queen Elizabeth. It was essential that these documents should be recovered and not allowed to fall into the wrong hands – certainly not in the Queen Mother's lifetime.

It remains to be seen precisely what the 'purely personal arrangement between the Queen and the Duchess' was, but some courtiers believe it concerned the ultimate recognition of Wallis – possibly posthumously – as a Royal Highness, thereby enabling her funeral, although strictly private, to take place with suitable ceremony.

Meanwhile, in the autumn of 1977, the Royal Family had been under further attack by Labour politicians in the House of Commons as a result of increases in the Civil List allowances, the Queen Mother's annual figure rising by £15,000 to £155,000. The Labour left-winger, Douglas Hoyle, described the Queen Mother and Princess Margaret as 'hangers-on', and added, of the former, 'she has a vast fortune. Anyway, if they fall on hard times they have still got State benefits behind them.' A Conservative right-winger, John Stokes, replied that the Queen Mother 'has given a lifetime of service to the country and is universally beloved. I am apalled anyone should dream of criticizing what she has been given.'[7]

Six days later, on November 15, 1977, Elizabeth became a great-grandmother, when Princess Anne gave birth to her first child, Peter Mark Andrew Phillips. The Queen Mother told reporters waiting outside Clarence House, 'This is one of the happiest days of my life. It's wonderful news, isn't it?'[8] Willie Hamilton did not think so. 'How charming,' he commented. 'Another one for the payroll.'[9]

During 1978, the year that would close with the screening of *Edward and Mrs Simpson*, the once taboo subject of divorce began to assume an entirely new significance for the British Royal Family. In February, it was revealed that the Queen's first cousin, Prince Michael of Kent, a Royal Highness in the direct line of succession to the throne, was planning to marry a thirty-three-year-old Austro-German Roman Catholic divorcee, Mrs Marie Christine Troubridge, whom he had known well for two years.

Born Baroness Marie Christine von Reibnitz at Carlsbad, Bohemia (now Czechoslovakia) on January 15, 1945, of aristocratic parents – Baron Gunther von Reibnitz and the former Countess Szapary – who subsequently divorced, she came to London in 1965 and began work as a secretary. On September 14, 1971, at Chelsea Old Church, she married an admiral's son, Tom Troubridge, a merchant banker who had been Prince Michael's contemporary at Eton. They separated in 1974, and in May 1977 divorce proceedings began between them 'by mutual consent. No one will be named in the action.'[10] Later that summer, Prince Michael and Mrs Troubridge holidayed together in Sardinia and on a Mediterranean yachting cruise.

In February 1978, Prince Michael and Mrs Troubridge visited the Archbishop of Canterbury, Dr Donald Coggan, at Lambeth Palace. Their engagement was delayed, and in May 1978, Mrs Troubridge's former marriage was annulled by the Vatican on grounds that were never disclosed. The development puzzled friends who believed that the Troubridges had certainly lived together as man and wife. The following month she reverted to her maiden name, under which her engagement to Prince Michael was announced. By the terms of the Act of Settlement of 1701, the Prince automatically forfeited his place in the order of succession to the throne by marrying a Roman Catholic. In addition to this, as a result of incautious comments that their children would be brought up as Anglicans, Pope Paul VI refused the former Mrs Troubridge dispensation to marry in church. Prince Charles commented that such decisions caused 'needless distress' and was rebuked by the Vatican for 'sheer impertinence'.[11] Prince Michael and his fiancée were married on June 30 in a civil ceremony at Vienna Town Hall, with the Duke of Kent, Princess Anne and Lord Mountbatten among the guests.[12]

Meanwhile, in spite of the new Princess Michael's previous marriage and divorce, and in spite of the fact that her husband was no longer in the line of succession to the throne, it was announced that she would become a Royal Highness – in complete contradiction of the arguments that had been employed in 1937 to justify the Duchess of Windsor's exclusion from that rank. The Queen's decision on this point caused criticism on the grounds of inconsistency. One newspaper reader commented: 'I understand that Prince Michael's future wife will be known as Her Royal Highness. This news puzzles and intrigues me; I have always believed the reason that the Duchess of Windsor could not be granted this title was because of her previous status. Has Buckingham Palace decided to change the rules or is having one's marriage annulled after six years not the same as being divorced?'[13]

In her moments of lucidity, Wallis must have asked herself the same question. What was the difference between the American divorcee and the Austro-German divorcee, beyond the passing of forty years? The situation must have amused Wallis, for when she heard that Prince and Princess Michael were in Paris shortly after their wedding, she asked to see them, and they made a brief visit to the Neuilly house,[14] where the divorcee who was 'Her Royal Highness' only within her own domain, met the divorcee who had become officially royal. As far as is known, Prince and Princess Michael were the last members of the British Royal Family who saw the Duchess of Windsor before she became unable to receive visitors.

In the meantime, Princess Margaret's latest visit to the Caribbean island of Mustique in the company of Roddy Llewellyn, who was now pursuing a singing career, brought harsh criticism.[15] On her return, Princess Margaret was admitted to King Edward VII's Hospital, where she was found to be suffering from alcoholic hepatitis, the only cure for which was total abstinence from alcohol for a year. In the previous August, it had also been alleged[16] that Margaret was suffering from porphyria, the illness – resulting from an imbalance in the metabolism – that is now believed to have been the cause of the psychological disorders suffered by King George III. The allegation was denied by Kensington Palace, where a spokesman had insisted that she was 'in splendid health'.[17]

On May 10, while she was still in hospital, it was announced that Princess Margaret and Lord Snowdon were to be divorced. Two weeks later, on May 24, their eighteen-year-old marriage was dissolved and a decree nisi was granted in proceedings lasting less than two minutes.[18]

A third divorce situation in the Royal Family occurred in August, when another first cousin of the Queen, the Hon. Gerald Lascelles, had his twenty-six-year marriage to the actress, Angela Dowding, ended with a 'quickie' decree nisi in the London Divorce Court. He subsequently married a second actress, Elizabeth Colvin, née Collingwood, the fifty-four-year-old daughter of a brigadier, by whom she already had a son, Martin, born in 1962. The events of 1978 began to make Wallis Simpson's marital record look almost staid.

On August 4, the Queen Mother's seventy-eighth birthday, Prince Charles paid tribute to his grandmother in his preface to a new book.[19] Writing of 'the sparkling, fascinating lady to whom this book is devoted', he said, '. . . ever since I can remember my grandmother has been the most wonderful example of fun, laughter, warmth, infinite security and, above all else, exquisite taste in so many things. For me, she has always been one of those extraordinarily rare people whose touch can turn everything to gold – whether it be putting people at their ease, turning something dull into something amusing, bringing happiness and comfort to people by her presence or making any house she lives in a unique haven of cosiness and character. She belongs to that priceless brand of human beings whose greatest gift is to enhance life for others through her own effervescent enthusiasm for life. She has been doing that for very nearly seventy-eight years, through war and peace, through change and uncertainty – an inspiration and a figure of love and affection for young and old alike. You have only to look at the pictures in this book to see what an impact she has made on her century.'[20]

Charles's affectionate assessment prompted the reflection that while Elizabeth had the good fortune to have a large and admiring family around her to pay tribute to her qualities, the old lady of eighty-two in the Bois de Boulogne had had no one since her husband died. When, shortly, someone did speak publicly in her defence, it was a lawyer, a woman almost as old as she herself. Since Wallis's days of accepting invitations were long past, Johanna Schütz had been released from her post as social secretary in April. With her departure, Suzanne Blum became, and remained, the sole spokeswoman for the Duchess.

In May 1978, Verity Lambert, the Director of Drama at Thames Television, flew to Paris to meet Maître Blum, not to ask for help, but merely to inform her, as a matter of courtesy, that the novelist, Simon Raven, was to be the scriptwriter for all seven episodes of *Edward and Mrs Simpson*, and that Edward Fox and Cynthia Harris were to play the King and Wallis.

Miss Lambert recalled: 'She took up her stance from the beginning and wasn't going to move. She had read Frances Donaldson's book and disliked it, but she admitted that the Duchess hadn't read it. She had an axe to grind, commenting on what she hadn't seen, indeed on what hadn't yet been written. We felt there was no point having the scripts read by people who were already predisposed to think it a bad idea to have the series made at all. I don't feel we libelled the Duchess. I don't feel we have infringed her privacy either.'[21]

Again as a matter of courtesy, Thames also informed Buckingham Palace, although no royal locations or facilities were sought, since Fort Belvedere – the principal setting used – was no longer Crown property, but in the private ownership of the Sultan of Dubai. It was stated by one court correspondent that 'members of the Royal Family, including the Queen and the Queen Mother, regard the projected series with great distaste',[22] but there is no evidence for this, and Buckingham Palace, far from discouraging Thames, gave their costume department the correct tartan for the Prince of Wales's kilt, with permission to use it. Moreover, during the first week of September, the Duke of Kent actually visited the *Edward and Mrs Simpson* set at the Teddington studios during the filming of the final episode depicting the Abdication itself. That did not suggest Royal disapproval of the series, in spite of the fact that both the Queen's parents were portrayed in it.

While Maître Blum continued to insist on sight of the scripts, and Thames Television continued to refuse, Wallis herself remained in complete ignorance of the series and of the dispute surrounding it. Soon after the visit of Prince and Princess Michael in July, a final twilight had engulfed her. She had not left the house, or even come downstairs, for more than a year. For a time her world consisted of a few painful steps between her bed and her sofa, but soon even that was impossible. She became paralysed from the waist down and her bed held her prisoner.

On November 7, the day before the first episode of *Edward and Mrs Simpson* was screened on British television, it was reported: 'Her health is such that even if the programme were shown in France, she wouldn't be able to watch it. She is not capable now of much coherent speech. She cannot read newspapers and has been bedridden for six months. In fact, she has no interest now in the outside world.'[23]

The first episode of the series took the story up to the spring of 1934, when Wallis supplanted Thelma Furness in the Prince's affections. Four days after it was shown, the Duchess found a distinguished and influential champion in John (now Sir John) Junor, the editor of the *Sunday Express*. At the head of his trenchant weekly column, Junor wrote: 'It is just as well that the Duchess of Windsor is old and frail and lives in France and was unable to see ITV's cruel portrayal of her love affair with the man who was once briefly our King.

'Was she really such an unattractive, scheming bitch as depicted on the box? Did she really make trite, banal conversation in a voice that sounded like a nail being drawn across a slate?

'Not as I remember her. I met her only once. As a young man at a time when she was already middle-aged. I sat next to her at a private dinner party in the South of France.

'I came away from that dinner enchanted by her warmth and her charm and the quality of her mind. I also began to understand why the man across the table had given up his throne for her. She was very far removed from the lady of last week for whom no man in his senses would have given up a bag of potato crisps.

'It may be that my judgment of the Duchess was wrong. But even if it were, could they not at least have waited until she was dead before enriching themselves by lampooning her so viciously?'[24]

Thames Television protested at this reaction. 'We certainly don't set out to make the Duchess look like a scheming bitch' a spokesman insisted.[25] The second episode, ending with the accession of Edward to the throne, was screened on November 15, and five days later, without having seen either episode, Maître Blum issued a statement denouncing the series as 'largely and essentially a fable based on an incorrect or distorted interpretation of the facts'. She spoke of a 'wave of calumnies' and added that an historian holding private papers of the Duke's might publish them soon, including 'the complete correspondence in

1936' between the Duke and the Duchess, which 'will make known everything that was said' between them at a time when 'they were linked only by friendship'.[26]

The London columnist, Jean Rook, was not sympathetic in her reaction to this: 'Wallis Simpson was no palpitating Pennsylvanian maiden. She was twice-married, forty-one, and she knew what she wanted.

'She "killed off" Edward's other ladyfriends. She upset his entire family, even the present Queen Mum. She blazed her importance to the Prince – who paid for her jewels – by publicly "dripping with emeralds" the size of pods, let alone peas.

'If she didn't fling herself at his crown, she queened it round Europe. And whether he was pulled by his infatuation for her, or pushed by Baldwin, she lost Edward VIII his throne.

'So it's a bit late now for Her Grace to behave like a startled doe, unwillingly chased up Whitehall and down the Mall.

'The Duchess should accept her place in Royal history. Dark but spacious. And she doesn't come off too badly, even on telly, as the all-time femme fatale.'[27]

A week later, with controversy growing – 'We could never have bought such publicity,' commented Verity Lambert – Maître Blum went further. Speaking from her country home in Niort in western France, and describing the series as 'this dreadful thing, I can't tell you how upset the Duchess is',[28] she stated: 'People will be amazed to discover how seriously they have been fooled. Mrs Simpson, the Duchess of Windsor, has been portrayed as a cheap adventuress, determined to get hold of the Duke of Windsor, determined to marry the King and destroy the King. The reverse is true. She was the reluctant partner. What has particularly distressed her – and myself – has been the allegation that she was Edward's mistress. This was quite untrue. The King did not want a mistress, and if he had, no doubt he would not have abdicated. He wanted a wife and the support of this one woman for the rest of his life.'[29]

Lady Alexandra Metcalfe described the interpretation of Edward VIII as 'unjust and unfair',[30] and Lady Diana Cooper, who, at the age of eighty-six, had acted as an adviser on the series, felt that Cynthia Harris was 'all wrong . . . she played Wallis as an ingénue – all soft and innocent and helpless. She tried to do it in a southern accent, which was a mistake. Wallis had a sort of drawl, but it was a drawl that came out fast if you see what I mean. And Wallis wasn't soft. Wallis was *hard*.'[31]

Lady Donaldson, who had been the historical adviser on the series, and whose husband was then Minister for the Arts, commented: 'I don't know what they are talking about. If they could tell me precisely the scenes which they find offensive then I could perhaps make the appropriate reply.' As for the possibility that the King and Wallis might have slept together before their marriage, Frances Donaldson added: 'There was no intention to suggest this anywhere in the script and I cannot think of any scene which could have given rise to this suggestion. I have no evidence that they were sleeping together. On the other hand, I have no evidence to suggest that they were not.'[32]

Interest focussed on the letters allegedly written between the King and Wallis before the abdication and before their marriage. Maître Blum said that the Duke of Windsor had given them to a friend who was an historian with the intention that they should be published after both he and the Duchess were dead. However, in the series 'such a bad image is given of the Duchess that it could not be left unanswered'. The historian had decided to act on the Duke's behalf 'because he would have liked the truth to be known'.[33] The Duchess, she said, had no part in the friend's decision to publish some of her letters prior to her death, but she had given her permission. The letters – several dozen – could be ready for publication within a year. Maître Blum had verified them as authentic.

'I have known the Duchess for thirty-two years,' said Maître Blum. 'I respect and admire her and am totally appalled at the way she has been so harshly treated. She does not deserve it and I intend to prove that she has been viciously maligned. The letters will tell the whole story.'[34]

Three months after her criticisms, Maître Blum admitted to the journalist, David Pryce-Jones, that far from being distressed by the television series, the Duchess had remained completely unaware of it, and therefore presumably could never have been asked to give permission for the publication of her letters.

Pryce-Jones also made the point: '. . . shouldn't we recognize that she [Wallis] was a mature, twice-married woman by the time she met him [the King]? Had she played the virgin, and obliged him to quit his throne in order to go to bed with her, she would have been a monster – while the Duke's sexuality would also have been called into question.'[35]

Maître Blum could see 'nothing but vultures crowding around the garbage cans', but Pryce-Jones concluded that 'It is she, not Thames

Television, who wishes the world to credit a fable.' Edward VIII, he felt, emerged from the series almost precisely as his sister-in-law, the Queen Mother, saw him: 'A perpetual adolescent schoolboy, a chinless wonder, a twit – who in the world does he resemble more than P. G. Wodehouse's Bertie Wooster? And Bertie is the great archetype of the British national character in the twentieth century. Bertie never did a hand's turn except use money he had not earned to play golf and run after a besotting girl. Just so Edward VIII. And if the King of England cannot be bothered to do his job, why should anyone else? He was perhaps the first and certainly the most notable dropout. No *moral* struggle at all. And let someone else pay for it.'[36]

There were shortly indications that the uproar over *Edward and Mrs Simpson*, coupled with the Palace's limited assistance to Thames Television and their refusal to become involved in the dispute, may have led to the Duke of Windsor's papers being reclaimed from the Royal Archives. The following summer, Buckingham Palace was said to 'categorically deny they hold any of the Duchess's papers', and Maître Blum was reported to be 'very concerned about the number of the Duchess's personal documents which have disappeared from her home since the Duke's death. She claims they later turned up in the Royal Archives in Windsor'.[37] A close friend of the Duke's who had lunched with Maître Blum at the Ritz in Paris, stated: 'Maître Blum told me that there are many papers still missing. She says she has an amazing file of correspondence with regard to her attempts to get the documents back to the Duchess . . . They disappeared from the Bois de Boulogne house just after the Duke died. There have been suggestions that they were stolen from the house.'[38]

In the meantime, the Duchess was back in the American Hospital, where she underwent an emergency operation on February 23, 1979, for the removal of an intestinal blockage. The Queen, who was then in the Middle East, was informed of the operation. A week later, Wallis was said to be making a 'remarkable recovery . . . hospital authorities said she was gaining strength rapidly. She is now once again eating solid food without problems.' Maître Blum added: 'Despite being very frail for some time, she has proved to have a very strong constitution. She is in no danger at the moment.'[39]

In May, however, she was back in the hospital with a bacterial infection, and she was still there on August 1, when the Queen Mother arrived in the Royal Yacht *Britannia* at Dover, where her two youngest grandchildren, Prince Edward and Lady Sarah Armstrong-Jones, watched her being installed as the first woman Lord Warden of the Cinque Ports. The Archbishop of Canterbury, Dr Donald Coggan, described Elizabeth as 'universally loved and respected – one who this nation and Commonwealth owe more than they can ever repay'. Admiral Judge Gerald Darling added: 'I doubt whether there has ever been a Lord Warden held in such high esteem for her unfailing charm and graciousness to all persons whether great or small.'[40]

On August 27, Lord Mountbatten was murdered by the IRA when a bomb planted on his converted fishing boat exploded half a mile off the west coast of Ireland. The Queen, who was at Balmoral, at once drove to her mother's home, Birkhall, to break the news to her personally. In the American Hospital in Paris, where the Duchess of Windsor was still receiving treatment, it was decided not to tell her of Mountbatten's death.

On September 14, Wallis at last left the hospital after four months as a patient there. As she was helped into her car, a shawl draped around her shoulders, the cameras were trained on the white, now almost skull-like face. The eyes registered an expression of fear and bewilderment, and the lips were parted in a tentative attempt at a smile. As the car moved away, she raised her right hand falteringly in a pathetic and gallant wave for the photographers.

In February 1980, the Liberal Member of Parliament, Cyril Smith, asked the Prime Minister, Margaret Thatcher, to declare the Queen Mother's eightieth birthday in the following August a national holiday: 'She has made a tremendous contribution to the life of the nation. We should take advantage of this occasion to show our love and thanks.' The *Daily Mail* agreed. 'She is much more than everyone's lovable old granny. She is a woman of greatness whose wholly beneficial influence upon our history ought to be acknowledged, and acknowleged now, in her presence, by the nation acting in community.'[41] Clarence House commented: 'The nation loves her dearly and undoubtedly she would be pleased to see people celebrating her birthday'.

As the great day approached, and Britain was gripped by royal birthday fever, more and more stories were recounted of Elizabeth's continuing stamina and humour. 'Suddenly at half past eleven at night,' said Lady Margaret Colville, 'her eyes will light up and she will dance a reel. She has fantastic energy.'[42]

A visitor to Clarence House sat with her on a sofa to talk. At that moment, a piece of cucumber from his sandwich fell into his tea. The Queen Mother was delighted. 'I'll turn round for fifteen seconds and come back to you,' she said.[43]

On July 15, 1980, a Service of Thanksgiving was held in St Paul's Cathedral for 'the first eighty years' of Elizabeth's life. For the only time in British history, at Elizabeth II's command, a queen dowager was given precedence over the reigning sovereign. The Queen Mother's carriage arrived at St Paul's last and left first.

As she emerged from Buckingham Palace with her grandson, Prince Charles, at her side, her State Landau accompanied by a Sovereign's Escort of the Household Cavalry, the cheers were so overwhelming that at moments she looked close to tears. On arrival at St Paul's where the Queen stood waiting for her, 'she turned on the steps . . . and in the wind the loose chiffon shoulders of her lilac dress flew free like a cape . . . the Wonder Woman of the Royal set'.[44] She raised her right arm high in the air in a regal salute to the huge London crowds, and a roar went up that seemed to shake St Paul's to its foundations. It was the gesture of a great star acknowledging her faithful public. 'The years fell away like a cloak and she was twenty again. She walked into the great cathedral, and the impact was tremendous. A blare of trumpets sounded a spine-tingling anthem. Then silence. And 2,700 heads turned in unison to greet her.'[45]

Elizabeth seemed to have achieved the zenith of her popularity, and the new Archbishop of Canterbury, Dr Robert Runcie, paid tribute to her with the words of Elizabeth I's 'Golden Speech' to her last Parliament: 'Though God hath raised me high, yet this I count the glory of my crown, that I have reigned with your loves.'

Afterwards, surrounded by her entire family, the tiny, vivid figure of the last Queen-Empress stood at the centre of the Buckingham Palace balcony, looking down at the vast crowd below her as they sang, 'For She's a Jolly Good Fellow'.

While Elizabeth acknowleged the acclaim of the British people, Wallis lay alone in the silent, empty house in the Bois de Boulogne, 'her face . . . like the Greek mask of tragedy, her mouth a square, her dark and penetrating blue eyes staring out of the window'.[46]

On August 4, the day of the Queen Mother's eightieth birthday, crowds of children pressed flowers and gifts into her hands outside Clarence House, and Mr Speaker, 'on behalf of the faithful Commons', acknowleged 'the debt we owe you for the loving care with which you have nurtured a Royal Family whom the whole world admires. As Queen Mother you have become the Nation's Mother, who is not merely honoured and respected, but who is deeply loved. You must be conscious of that love wherever you go. It is as strong and deep in the House of Commons as anywhere else in the land.'

In a gracious reply to both Houses of Parliament, Elizabeth said: 'My Lords, and Members of the House of Commons: I thank you for your messages of congratulations on my eightieth birthday, and I am deeply touched by the very kind sentiments that you have expressed. Eight decades is certainly a considerable span.

'During this time a great deal of history has unfolded and in many ways our lives have been transformed. New discoveries, new inventions, new outlooks, continually challenge the established order. But I am happy to feel that there is one constant factor: the good sense, loyalty and patriotism of the people of our land.

'During the war, The King and I, on our visits round the country, were sustained and inspired by the steadfastness, courage and compassion shown by our people. It is encouraging to find today that, in our schools and universities and among the younger generation these same qualities live on.

'I feel deeply grateful to have been given the opportunity to serve our beloved country in some small way and, through the years, in peace and war, I have been always helped and uplifted by the love of my family, the loyalty and understanding of our people, and by my faith in Almighty God.

'Once again, may I thank you all, from my heart, for your very kind messages on my birthday. Elizabeth Regina.'[47]

That summer was a sort of triumphal progress for the widowed Queen. She was in rollicking spirits on almost every occasion. Arriving for a private lunch party at the Eaton Square penthouse of the American-born musical comedy star, Dorothy Dickson, Elizabeth entered the drawing-room singing, 'Dancing time is just when the music is playing, When the stars are shimmying up in the sky . . .'.[48] It was a Jerome Kern song she and Bertie had heard Miss Dickson sing in *The Cabaret Girl* almost sixty years earlier, during their courtship.

On November 11, ablaze with rubies and diamonds, the Queen Mother arrived at 10 Downing Street to dine with the Prime Minister and the entire Cabinet, and in her traditional Christmas Day broadcast, Elizabeth II paid tribute to her mother as 'a person who has given selfless service to the people of this country and of the Commonwealth'.[49]

With the death in January 1981, at the age of ninety-seven, of Queen Victoria's last surviving granddaughter, Princess Alice, Countess of Athlone, Wallis, in her eighty-fifth year, became the oldest living member of the Queen's family. Her physical condition remained unchanged. Permanently bedridden and cared for by a team of nurses from the American Hospital, the wasted figure at the centre of the large bed slumbered through the days. Occasionally she flickered into moments of awareness, and the vivid blue eyes would scan the room, sometimes coming to rest on the flowers the Queen still sent once a month from the gardens at Windsor.[50]

'There is nothing to be said for growing old,' Wallis had written to Lady Sefton, and not even the Queen Mother entirely escaped the mishaps of age. In June she stumbled on a step at Royal Ascot and gashed her shin. The accident resulted in a small ulcer which became infected and caused a high temperature only days before Prince Charles's wedding to Lady Diana Spencer, the granddaughter of her lifelong friend and Woman of the Bedchamber, Ruth, Lady Fermoy.

Courtiers held their breath, but when July 29 came, the bridegroom's resilient grandmother was in her place at St Paul's, adorned in a beguiling shade of eau-de-nil, her left leg discreetly bandaged, to watch the wedding of the girl who would one day follow her as Britain's next Queen Consort. Afterwards, on the Palace balcony, when the bride and bridegroom had gone inside, the crowd began to call for the Queen Mother. As she stepped out alone to a great roar of approval, it seemed difficult to believe that this dynamic, seemingly indestructible little figure had first stood on that same balcony almost sixty years earlier as a bridesmaid to Princess Mary.

The following spring it was announced that Elizabeth was to make her first visit to Paris for six years to meet President Mitterrand and to open a new wing of a British hospital. Once again Clarence House was asked if the Queen Mother would be calling on the Duchess of Windsor. 'I don't think the Duchess would be well enough for a visit,' replied Major John Griffin. 'It is not planned at the moment'.[51]

Kenneth Rose, who had received generous help from the Queen Mother with his biography of her father-in-law, King George V, at once commented: '. . . spiteful tongues are saying that she will snub the Duchess of Windsor by ignoring her existence. The Duchess, as it happens, is in no state to be snubbed. For several years now she has lived in a twilight world of her own. But that is beside the point. Any

whispers of a continuing feud between the two sisters-in-law under-
rate the Queen Mother's generosity of heart.'[52]

Elizabeth arrived in Paris on May 11, and, says Sir Martin Gilliat,
'enquiries were made on arrival as to the Duchess of Windsor's
condition and flowers were sent to the Duchess' on that same day,[53]
Tragically, Wallis was now beyond being able to understand her
sister-in-law's sympathetic concern or even to appreciate the flowers.

On June 11, Elizabeth was returning to Portsmouth in the Royal
Yacht *Britannia* at the end of a series of official engagements as Lord
Warden of the Cinque Ports. On that same day, the Cunard liner,
Queen Elizabeth 2, was arriving back at Southampton from the
Falklands war with survivors from HMS *Antelope*, *Ardent* and
Coventry. The returning heroes thronged the decks of the *QE2* as it
steamed slowly past the Royal Yacht, and there on the Veranda Deck
of *Britannia* stood the familiar, pastel-clad little figure, taking the
salute in her inimitable way with her right arm raised aloft in cheerful
greeting. All hats were doffed and three rousing cheers drifted across
the waters of the Solent. It was a moving moment. For the fighting
men, some of them badly burned, that welcoming wave was their first
sight of home.

Eight days later, Wallis unknowingly arrived at her eighty-sixth
birthday, but for her the day was no different from any other day. No
visitors called at the house, not even Maître Blum, who explained: 'I
seldom go. I send flowers instead. The tragedy is that, although the
Duchess is barely conscious, she is not unwell in herself. In fact, she has
fewer drugs than I do . . . It is pathetic. She only occasionally utters a
word. Nobody visits her now, apart from me. She has no living
relation in America taking an interest in her.'[54]

Two days after this sad anniversary, the new Princess of Wales
gave birth to a 7 lb son at St Mary's Hospital, Paddington. 'Even if
God saves the Queen Mum until she's 100,' wrote Jean Rook, 'hers
must be the first State passing he'll have to face. They're not likely
to burden him with the death or life of his great-great, but *not* so
great aunt Wallis Windsor, even if she did indirectly hand him a
throne.'[55]

On August 4, Elizabeth's eighty-second birthday, Prince William of
Wales was christened in the Music Room at Buckingham Palace. As
the Queen Mother held her great-grandson in her arms, she must have
reflected with a certain pride that she had lived to see the British
throne, that had seemed so vulnerable when she and her husband

had ascended it, secure for two generations ahead in the male line.

Maître Blum, meanwhile, continued her efforts to rehabilitate the Windsors in the eyes of historians. Using her guardianship of the incapacitated Duchess as requisite authority, since her client was in no condition to be consulted on the matter, the eighty-three-year-old French advocate gave her assistant, the British barrister, Michael Bloch, access to the Windsors' archives in order to produce a book called *The Duke of Windsor's War*, designed to refute criticism of the former King's wartime activities. Dedicated 'To Maître Suzanne Blum, guide, pupil master, and friend', the book accorded the Duchess the title of Royal Highness, which she was officially denied, and can only be classified as scholarly hagiography. Everything of an inconvenient nature is omitted, and the Windsors emerge from the text as persecuted martyrs who in no way merited the cold shoulder presented to them by the Duke's country.

Evidence that this line of argument, however skilfully presented, was not convincing to contemporary historians, came a week before publication when Michael Bloch took part in a television programme concerning his book and the Duke of Windsor's reputation in general.[56] Dr David Cannadine, a history don at Christ's College, Cambridge, far from accepting Bloch's view of the ex-King's wartime conduct, 'believed that the Duke was not only an embarrassment but possibly an unacceptable risk to a Britain committed to total war. "The Duke's views on Germany," he said, "were very similar to those of Oswald Mosley – and no one would suggest that Mosley should be regarded as a non-risk man in the second world war." '[57]

Indeed, it seemed to many people deeply ironical that the Jewish Maître Blum, whose relations were imprisoned by the Nazis, and who despised any Frenchman who had sympathized with the German invaders of her country, should be the one to champion so fiercely the anti-Semitic Duke of Windsor, who would talk about 'little kike lawyers',[58] and who was frequently heard by Lady Diana Cooper to ask, 'What can you expect from these Jews?'[59]

To the end of his life he admired Germany, loved to speak the German language, and frequently protested – even when the concentration camps were disgorging their mountains of corpses – 'I never thought Hitler was such a bad chap.'[60]

On the evening of Sunday, November 21, the Queen Mother was presiding over a dinner party for fourteen at Royal Lodge when a fish bone became caught in her throat. Seated on her right was Hugh

Cavendish, the forty-one-year-old kinsman of the Duke of Devonshire, who had been invited to the dinner with his wife Grania, by
Princess Margaret, who was sitting on her mother's left. 'She was in
great discomfort' remembered Cavendish, 'and I had to persuade her
to stop being polite and trying to make conversation, before I gave her
a slap on the back.'[61]

Dr John Clayton, the Queen Mother's Windsor physician, was
urgently summoned to Royal Lodge, but all attempts to dislodge the
offending obstacle proved unsuccessful, and at 1.30 in the morning,
Elizabeth was driven in her own car to King Edward VII's Hospital for
Officers, where the fish bone was removed under a general anaesthetic.

'For a split second a whole choked nation held the breath for which
the Queen Mum was fighting,' wrote Jean Rook. 'This morning we
breathe again.'[62] Clarence House commented calmly: 'We understand
she will soon be back with us.'

At the hospital a bemused spokesman admitted, 'For a woman of
her age, her constitution is quite remarkable. After coming round from
the anaesthetic she was bubbling and cheerful for the rest of her stay.'
The following Sunday, Sir John Junor commented: 'When the Queen
Mother left King Edward VII's Hospital, she must, at the age of
eighty-two, and after a general anaesthetic, have been feeling far from
brilliant. One would never have guessed it. Everything she did was
absolutely in character. There was the warm friendly farewell word of
thanks for her nurse. The serene smile for the onlookers and photographers. Even a readiness to answer reporters' questions. Isn't it quite
extraordinary how she never, ever puts a foot wrong?'[63]

In April 1983, Elizabeth arrived at the sixtieth anniversary of her
marriage and entry into British public life. The 'justly famous charm'
went on display in Railton Road, Brixton, which not long before had
been the scene of savage race riots. Now the cheerful figure in pale blue
stood happily in the rain and swayed contentedly to a steel band's
lilting reggae while black and white hands reached out in unison to
greet her. Amid the fragrant aroma of cannabis, a pot-smoking
Rastafarian hailed the visit as 'a great breakthrough for harmonious
relations between all colours and creeds'.[64]

On June 19, while her sister-in-law, Wallis, spent another comatose
birthday – her eighty-seventh – in the seclusion of her Neuilly bedroom, Elizabeth flew to Ulster in defiance of IRA bomb threats. There
were six separate bomb scares during her visit, but she 'never wavered
during a day that would have sapped the stamina of someone half her

eighty-two years. The temperature was up in the seventies yet the Queen Mother seemed the coolest person around.'[65]

The beginning of July found Elizabeth in Oslo, acting as temporary consort to the widowed King Olav of Norway at the celebrations to mark his eightieth birthday.[66] The Norwegians cheered the couple through the streets of the city, and as the King and the Queen Mother entered the royal box at the Oslo concert house for the King's birthday gala, she was seen to be blinking back tears as the entire audience turned towards her while the choir sang *God Save The Queen*.

Two weeks later, at a Buckingham Palace garden party on a day of intense heat, with the temperature hovering around 88°F, the wily old royal stager, faced with the competition of the young Princess of Wales and the fashion-conscious Princess Michael of Kent, 'outshone them all, strolling under a white parasol clad in blue chiffon that billowed like a three-masted schooner in the Roaring Forties and created a cooling draught all of its own. That, as they say, is class.'[67]

Watching her in November, at the age of eighty-three, going through the traditional ceremony of planting poppy crosses in the Field of Remembrance at St Margaret's, Westminster, Jon Akass noted: 'She is as old as the century and the weariness and sadness shows. And in that attempted, tight-lipped smile, so does the courage ... She is held in affection even by those most churlish of her countrymen who remain unbeguiled by Princess Diana and are unable to laugh at the Duke of Edinburgh's jokes. She is going to be a difficult act to follow because she does not act. Her mannerisms, her style, her sometimes merry aplomb, are her own. She is the original.'[68]

As she approached her eighty-fourth birthday, the royal great-grandmother made visits to Germany and France, and her engagement diary had foreign tours pencilled in for more than two years ahead. 'She does not enjoy idleness,' explained a Clarence House aide, 'and takes the view that as long as she is fit and well, she loves to be doing things. Any idea of foreign travel is attractive to her.'[69]

Elizabeth confided to Councillor William Payne, the Mayor of Southwark, who is an arthritic, that she too suffered severe pain as a result of arthritis in her right hand – the one she uses to perform her celebrated half-wave, half-gesture to the watching crowds.[70] The handicap is well disguised. In 1984, she was photographed expertly wielding a cue for a lively game of pool in Jersey, and shaking a pair of maracas in rhythmic accompaniment to a South London reggae band. No contrast could be more poignant or more terrible than that between the royal sisters-in-law: Elizabeth, the idolized public figure, smiling and confident, continuing indefatigably on her royal way; and Wallis, that tragic ghost of a woman, the prisoner of her darkened room, incontinent, paralysed, incapable of speech or movement, now 'simply a body with a heart that beats'.[71] It had become a fairy-tale in reverse. The prince had departed and his princess had fallen into a sleep from which there would be no awakening.

The splendid house in the Bois de Boulogne was closed and shuttered. The main gate was rusted and padlocked. The gold crown that once surmounted it had long ago toppled to the ground. It had never been replaced. Burglar alarms were everywhere. The garden looked neglected and the wooden fence surrounding it leaned at a precarious angle. Above the terrace, which had once echoed to the laughter of summer lunch parties, the canvas sun-shades were weather-stained.

The staff, which had numbered twenty-five in the Duke's lifetime, now consisted of six people: Georges Sanègre, the faithful French butler, who still answered the telephone on the rare occasions that it rang; Ofélia, his Italian-born wife, who was the housekeeper; Gregory Martin, the gardener-cum-chauffeur, who would never drive his mistress again, but still collected groceries and medical supplies; the Duchess's Portuguese maids, Maria and Vittoria; and her Hungarian nurse, Madame Elvire Gozin.

Every morning Georges Sanègre would enter the Duchess's bedroom and draw back the curtains. 'Good morning, Your Royal Highness,' he would say, bowing his head to the silent, unanswering figure propped up against the pillows. He would bring in the day's mail and read some of the letters aloud to her. If friends had sent flowers, Ofélia would arrange them beautifully and Georges would carry the vase upstairs to show his mistress. She never spoke, but at moments the ghost of a smile seemed to hover in her watchful eyes and at the corners of her mouth.

A team of nurses from the American Hospital in Paris was on duty two at a time in three shifts around the clock. Each morning they lifted the emaciated, lifeless figure from her bed into a raised chair, where tea and a creamy cereal would be fed to her through a tube. Her once immaculately styled dark hair was now completely white and would be gently combed back into a ponytail. Make-up and her favourite perfume would be applied and a mirror held up in front of the unchanging and expressionless face.

No bracelets adorned the almost skeletal wrists. The fabulous jewels that had dazzled society now lay in a bank vault. Even her wedding ring was gone. Owing to encroaching arthritis, her doctor, Jean Thin, had ordered it to be gently cut from her finger.

After breakfast, Wallis's chair would be placed by the tall French windows of her bedroom, and there she would sit each day, staring out unseeingly at the trees and the flowers in her garden. Sometimes, for a fleeting moment, the still beautiful blue eyes would come alive with the gleam of memory. Sometimes they would fill with tears, which would be gently wiped away by her nurses.

One of the last people allowed to see her said sadly: 'Nothing in her eyes betrays that she has recognized you . . . she just sits hunched up in her chair and her hands flop down in front of her after you lift them to greet her.'[72]

Now even her closest friends were politely discouraged from coming to the house. The sight of people she knew, but with whom she could no longer communicate, caused Wallis such distress of mind that her blood pressure would soar dangerously. Even Lady Mosley, who continued to call regularly, was no longer allowed to see her and was asked to leave her flowers downstairs. One British well-wisher, who also brought flowers, was received with the usual exquisite courtesy by Georges Sanègre, who murmured softly, 'There is nothing left here except the spirit of a very dear lady.'

With her brain starved by arteriosclerosis and her body crippled by arthritis, there was no knowing how much longer the eighty-nine-year-old Duchess could survive. Yet her heart continued to beat with amazing strength, and longevity was in her blood. Her aunt, Bessie Merryman, had lived to be one hundred years old.[73] And the Queen Mother, although the last survivor – by nineteen years – of her parents' ten children, also had long life in her family. Her father lived to the age of eighty-nine.[74] Which sister-in-law would outlive the other?

Echoes of their long feud still lingered. At Clarence House, Sir Martin Gilliat assured the British journalist, Dick Barton: 'Queen Elizabeth would always see the Duchess of Windsor if the Duchess were well enough. The Queen Mother always enquires about her.'[75] But Wallis's days of receiving were over. For Elizabeth to see the woman she ostracized for so long in such a condition would have been a harrowing experience.

Each year, towards the end of her life, Wallis, through immobility, succumbed to pneumonia. Only expert nursing enabled her to survive. The last attack, far more severe than the others, came in April 1986. The British Embassy in Paris was at once alerted and Buckingham Palace was informed. With the chilling sense of expediency usual in such matters, orders were given for the royal burial ground at Frogmore to be tidied up in case the Duchess's illness should prove fatal. Behind the scenes, however, intense anxiety prevailed among courtiers and diplomats that the Duchess might die just before Elizabeth II's sixtieth birthday celebrations on April 21, or the crucial three-day Spanish State visit to London by King Juan Carlos I and Queen Sofia, scheduled to begin on April 22.

In the event, the Duchess appeared to rally. The Queen's birthday celebrations went ahead without any announcement of her aunt's illness, and on the following day, the King and Queen of Spain arrived at Windsor to a 21-gun salute. That afternoon they visited the Queen Mother at Royal Lodge and were entertained to tea in the same room where – fifty years before, to the very month – Wallis Simpson had made her uninvited visit to the Duke and Duchess of York.

In Paris, on the evening of Wednesday April 23, Wallis's condition suddenly deteriorated. Elvire Gozin, who had nursed her devotedly for ten years, sat up with her and kept vigil throughout the night.

The following morning, when Dr Thin arrived at the house in the Bois, he saw at once that the end was imminent and summoned the Very Reverend James R. Leo, the American Dean of the Episcopalian Cathedral in Paris, who had known the Duchess for twenty years and had visited her regularly throughout her long illness.

The Dean administered the last rites and read aloud from the eighth chapter of The Epistle of Paul the Apostle to the Romans: '. . . neither death, nor life, nor angels, nor principalities, nor powers, nor things present, nor things to come, nor height, nor depth, nor any other creature, shall be able to separate us from the love of God . . .'

James Leo took the dying woman's hand and asked her, 'You are looking forward to going home, aren't you my dear?' He felt a slight but unmistakable pressure from the hand that lay in his. A moment or two later, with the Dean, Dr Thin and Georges Sanègre at her bedside, Wallis slipped peacefully away. It was just before 11 a.m. (10 a.m. British time) on Thursday April 24, 1986. Two months short of her ninetieth birthday, the poor prisoner was at last released from a captivity she had endured for ten years.

Buckingham Palace announced the news 'with deep regret', which was modified in the following morning's Court Circular to: 'The Queen has learned with regret of the death of the Duchess of Windsor'. Elizabeth II ordered family mourning – as opposed to full Court mourning – from noon on the following day, after the departure of the King and Queen of Spain. Flags would be lowered only on the day of the funeral. Qualified though these arrangements were, they were without precedent in the case of a person officially deemed not to be royal.

On the evening of her death, the King and Queen of Spain entertained the British Royal Family at a banquet at the Spanish Embassy in London. The Queen, the Princess of Wales, Princess Anne, Princess Margaret, the young Duchess of Gloucester and Princess Alexandra all attended wearing brilliant colours and dazzling jewels. No sign of mourning, not even a black arm band, was visible on the part of any of the royal guests, male or female. Buckingham Palace stated that it would have been 'totally inappropriate' to interrupt a State visit.

The Queen Mother, who had been invited to the banquet, did not attend. Neither, significantly, did Wallis's other surviving sister-in-law, Princess Alice, Duchess of Gloucester. Pressed for the reason, a Clarence House spokesman said that the Queen Mother had had 'a private engagement', but declined to say what it was. Private engagements are seldom undertaken by the Royal Family during a State visit, and undoubtedly Elizabeth had felt unable to appear in public at a festive occasion on the evening of her sister-in-law's death.

But family mourning – which usually means that the Royal Family can accept only official and not social engagements – did not prevent the Queen Mother from attending Sandown races two days later to watch her grand-daughter, Princess Anne, competing in the National Hunt 'Bumper' Stakes on a horse called Well Wisher.

On Sunday, April 27, by command of the Queen, a Royal Air Force VC-10 flew to Paris to bring the Duchess of Windsor back to Britain. On board was the Lord Chamberlain, the Earl of Airlie, who was to accompany her body.

Wallis's six faithful servants wept openly as her coffin of dark English oak, devoid of a Royal standard, but bearing a magnificent wreath of white lilies, was carried from the house in the Bois de Boulogne by six Royal Air Force pallbearers. The Lord Chamberlain, the British Ambassador to France, Sir John Fretwell, the French Secretary of State for Foreign Affairs, Didier Bariani, and representatives of the City of Paris were among the official mourners lining the drive.

At Orly Airport, the French President's Household Cavalry, the Garde Republicaine, presented arms in a royal salute as the coffin was put on board the VC-10. But if France had recognized the Duchess's royal status, Britain had not. On instructions from Buckingham Palace, the plaque on the coffin was inscribed simply: 'Wallis, Duchess of Windsor, 1896–1986'. To the very last, the rank of Royal Highness had been denied her.

Wallis's nephew-in-law and the Queen's most senior ranking cousin, the Duke of Gloucester, stood with the Lord Privy Seal, John Biffen, on the tarmac at RAF Benson in Oxfordshire where the plane touched down. As the coffin was carried to the hearse, the Duke removed his top hat and all military personnel saluted.

The hearse drove slowly to Windsor Castle, and as it entered the King Henry VIII Gate, the Union Jack on the Round Tower was lowered and a detachment of the Irish Guards presented arms and gave a bugle salute. The woman who had been an official outcast for fifty years had returned with honour to the land that had rejected her.

The coffin was placed in the Albert Memorial Chapel, where her husband had also rested before his funeral, and on the following day, the Queen and other members of the Royal Family came to pay their respects. The Queen Mother was at Royal Lodge, but she did not visit the chapel. Her press secretary, Major John Griffin, explained tersely: 'She will pay her respects at the funeral.'

On the following day, Tuesday April 29, flags on all public buildings in Britain were lowered, and at 3.30 that afternoon, seventeen members of the Royal Family, led by the Queen, Prince Philip and the Queen Mother, assembled in St George's Chapel, Windsor, for the funeral service. The only notable absentee was Princess Margaret, who was said by one source to have 'an unbreakable engagement' – although none was announced for her in the following day's Court Circular – and by another source to have had 'an altercation' with the rest of the family over the 'sheer hypocrisy' involved in the arrangements.

The Prime Minister, Margaret Thatcher, was there with her husband. So too were the leaders of the other political parties, five former British Ambassadors to France, and the dead woman's few remaining friends – Lady Alexandra Metcalfe, now the last survivor of the Windsor wedding, Lady Mosley, Grace Countess of Dudley, Baron Guy de Rothschild and Laura Duchess of Marlborough.

There was a wreath from 10 Downing Street, inscribed, 'With deep sorrow from Her Majesty's Ministers', and another which said simply, 'Reunited at last with your beloved David'. The Queen Mother had sent a wreath of salmon-pink flowers, but it was not on the coffin, which was adorned only by a magnificent arrangement of white lilies and spring flowers from the Queen.

The service, conducted by the Dean of Windsor, must have been one of the briefest and most impersonal ever held. It lasted only twenty-four minutes. There was no Address, and the dead woman's name was not mentioned once. The Archbishop of Canterbury pronounced the blessing and eight scarlet-coated Welsh Guardsmen lifted the coffin from the purple-draped catafalque and, to the strains of *Nimrod*, carried it slowly, shoulder-high, from the chapel.

The seventeen royal mourners followed behind it, all but one of them gazing impassively ahead. The exception was the Queen Mother, walking, it was noticed, rather unsteadily, and turning her head from side to side to look into the faces of the congregation. She alone, of all the family, showed emotion. As she passed within three feet of one observer, he saw her lips tremble.

At the Great West Door, the Royal Family stood to pay their last respects. As the coffin passed her, the Queen Mother turned to look at it, and the cameras caught an expression that seemed impossible to define – a strange mixture of obstinacy, regret and memory. Elizabeth's own final departure would be very different from this private service, so devoid of pomp. As the last Queen-Empress, she would receive a State Funeral. Beneath her own crown, with the Koh-i-Noor diamond at its centre, she would pass through crowded London streets lined with troops to rest beneath a sculptured effigy of herself, and beside her beloved Bertie in his own Memorial Chapel. Elizabeth, in death, would take her place with the other Kings and Queens of England. Wallis, the queen who never was, was at this moment making her final journey to a humbler resting place.

Elizabeth II had decided that her mother, then only three months short of her eighty-sixth birthday, should not be exposed to the ordeal of her sister-in-law's burial. Only the Queen, Prince Philip, the Prince and Princess of Wales, Dr Thin, Grace Countess of Dudley, and the six Paris servants were to follow the Duchess to the graveside

The Queen Mother stood motionless at the top of the chapel steps as the coffin was lifted gently into the hearse. Her eyes followed the *cortège* as it moved slowly off towards Frogmore, to that wide-spreading plane tree beneath which Wallis would at last rejoin her David. She continued to watch until the cars disappeared into the distance. Elizabeth had seen the last of her.

In the meantime, the long-awaited love letters that Maître Blum had held aloft like the Sword of Damocles for seven years, had been edited by her amaneuensis, Michael Bloch, and had begun newspaper serialisation prior to publication in book form. The overwhelming reaction was total incredulity that Maître Blum and Mr Bloch should have deluded themselves into believing it was in the interests of their client to reveal them.

In reality, the correspondence, all of it embarrassingly trite, demolished what little remained of the Duke of Windsor's reputation and, far from rehabilitating the Duchess, showed her to have been scheming, shallow and self-interested.

Godfrey Talbot, the noted royal author and broadcaster, found the letters 'really quite boring . . . dull and repetitive. They tell us nothing. The facts of history have not been added to one bit . . .'[76]

Dr Peter Hildebrand, chief psychologist at the Tavistock Clinic in London, thought the letters revealed Wallis as 'an adventuress and social climber' and Edward as 'an infatuated schoolboy' whose 'passion and single-mindedness are adolescent, the language and the underlying feelings those of a spoiled child'.[77]

Dr Tony Whitehead, a consultant psychiatrist, felt after reading them not only that Edward could never have been a satisfactory king, but that 'he would have had difficulty running a sweet-shop'.[78]

And even that erstwhile admirer of the Windsors, Sir John Junor, was sadly disillusioned: '. . . by their boring banality the only thing they do prove is, and to me it comes as quite a shock, that she and King Edward VIII were utterly feather-brained, gadflies on the face of society'.[79]

In her will, the Duchess left the bulk of her estimated £1 million estate to medical research, the largest beneficiary being the Pasteur Institute in Paris. With the exception of individual pieces of jewellery believed to have been left to the Duchess of Kent and Princess Alexandra, the Royal Family did not benefit.

With the imminence of the fiftieth anniversary of the Abdication in December 1986, newspapers continued to feature the long feud between the royal sisters-in-law and to allege enduring enmity and a lack of forgiveness on the part of the survivor. But there can be no doubt of the sincerity of the Queen Mother's sympathy for the stricken Duchess in her tragic last years. Elizabeth had had cause to reflect on the possible injustice of those long years of ostracism and exile for the Windsors. As time had passed and royal conventions had changed, Wallis's behaviour had come to seem more and more dignified. In age, Elizabeth Bowes-Lyon must have found it possible to accept finally that it had been her destiny to become Queen of England, and that it had been equally Wallis Simpson's destiny to be the catalyst in the removal of a disastrously unsuitable monarch from the throne. As Lady Mosley logically pointed out: 'It was a paradox that the very people who said Edward VIII would have been an unsatisfactory king should have been those who pretended they couldn't ever forgive him for leaving. One would have imagined they would be so pleased and relieved.'[80]

Those with vision were certainly indebted to Wallis Simpson. Winston Churchill predicted: 'One day a grateful Commonwealth will erect her statue'.[81] Noël Coward's attitude was that 'a statue should be erected to Mrs Simpson in every town in England for the blessing she had bestowed upon the country'.[82] Even Queen Mary's niece, Mary, Duchess of Beaufort, agreed. '*I* always think that Mrs Simpson should have a public monument put up to her in this country.'[83] And Lady Diana Cooper was in no doubt either. 'We were lucky to get George VI and Elizabeth – they were by far the better loved in the end . . . Yes, in the end it was a blessing that Wallis came along and took him away.'[84]

It seems probable that Elizabeth herself had come to recognize the truth of this some years before she sent her symbolic roses and her moving message of friendship to the sick and lonely woman in the Bois de Boulogne.

In 1968, the Queen Mother visited the National Portrait Gallery for a private tour of an exhibition of Cecil Beaton's photographs. In her usual lively way, she enthused over Beaton's stylish work. 'Oh, I remember that sitting [her own]. It was really the end of an epoch. And Gertrude Lawrence – she was unlike anyone – she was quite unique. I'm glad you've given her a whole group to herself. Dear Rex Whistler – what a talent he had – so spontaneous. What a loss! Oh, and the frieze. Yes, I remember that Hesse diadem. That's one of the best of Marina. She was beautiful up to the last. And look at Marie Louise – what a character!'

Then she came to a photograph of her brother-in-law and his wife. There was a long pause while she studied the Windsors carefully. When she spoke at last, it was evident that the resentment Elizabeth had felt for so many years had finally faded.

'They're so happy, and really a great deal of good came out of it. We have much to be thankful for.'[85]

She had forgiven them.

Dear Brenda,

if after your due consideration you feel that I would enjoy this please pass it on.

Yours very truly,

Jayce

APPENDICES

Notes on the Chapters
Bibliography
Author's Acknowledgements
Index

NOTES ON THE CHAPTERS

Folios in brackets refer to notes of explanation rather than simple source notes.

Full details of the books and sources cited may be found in the Bibliography. In those few instances where a source is given as Private Information, it is because my informant has requested confidentiality and has asked not to be identified.

1. A MEETING AFTER THIRTY YEARS

1. Queen Mary's diary, December 9, 1936, quoted in James Pope-Hennessy, *Queen Mary*, p. 579.
2. J. Bryan III and Charles J. V. Murphy, *The Windsor Story*, p. 220.
3. William Hickey column, *Daily Express*, London, June 6, 1967.
4. Queen Mary to the Duke of Windsor in 1942, quoted by the Duchess of Windsor, *The Heart has its Reasons*, p. 356.
5. Queen Mary to the Duke of Windsor, February 27, 1951, quoted in James Pope-Hennessy, *Queen Mary*, p. 614.
6. Adela Rogers St Johns, *The Honeycomb*, pp. 439, 527.
7. The Duchess of Windsor, *The Heart has its Reasons*, p. 225.
8. Ibid, p. 225.
9. Helen Hardinge, *Loyal to Three Kings*, pp. 102–103.
10. Queen Mary's phrase, quoted in James Pope-Hennessy, *Queen Mary*, p. 574.
11. Sir Robert Bruce Lockhart, December 11, 1938, *Diaries, 1915–1938*, pp. 413–414.
12. In a letter to her aunt, Mrs Bessie Merryman, written from Cascais,

July 15, 1940, quoted in Michael Bloch, *The Duke of Windsor's War*, p. 94.
13. The Duchess of Windsor to Mrs Bessie Merryman, March 31, 1941, quoted in Michael Bloch, *The Duke of Windsor's War*, pp. 189–190.
14. Michael Bloch in a letter to Michael Thornton from Lisbon, May 25, 1983.
15. Anthony Holden, 'The Girl from Glamis who saved the Throne', *Sunday Express*, London, April 10, 1983.
16. James Pope-Hennessy, *A Lonely Business*, p. 211.
17. Ibid, p. 211.
18. *The Times*, London, June 8, 1967.
19. Diana Mosley, *The Duchess of Windsor*, p. 191.
20. Leonard M. Harris, *Long to Reign Over Us?*, pp. 118–119.
21. Private Information.
22. The Duchess of Windsor, *The Heart has its Reasons*, p. 225.
[23] The *Daily Mail*, London, June 8, 1967, reported that 'The Duchess of Windsor bowed slightly from the waist' to the Queen. Frances

Donaldson, in her *Edward VIII*, p. 404, says, 'On television that evening it could be seen that she merely bowed.' Both accounts are mistaken. Newsreel coverage shows quite clearly that the Duchess curtsied to the Queen, but not to the Queen Mother. Lady Donaldson, like J. Bryan III and Charles J. V. Murphy in *The Windsor Story* (p. 531), also puts the occasion in 1966, a year too early.

24. John Redfern, *Daily Express*, London, June 8, 1967.

2. ELIZABETH OF GLAMIS AND BESSIEWALLIS OF BALTIMORE

1. J. C. C. Davidson (the 1st Viscount Davidson), *Memoirs of a Conservative*, p. 110.
2. Quoted in Keith Middlemas, *The Life and Times of George VI*, p. 68.
3. Mabell, Countess of Airlie, *Thatched with Gold*, p. 201.
4. James Lees-Milne, *Harold Nicolson, 1930–1968*, p. 268.
5. 'My Husband Has Been Deeply Hurt, says the Duchess', by Susan Barnes, *Sunday Express*, London, December 8, 1963.
6. Mabell, Countess of Airlie, *Thatched with Gold*, p. 203.
7. Prince Charles's foreword in Godfrey Talbot's *The Country Life Book of Queen Elizabeth The Queen Mother*, p. 7.
8. Diana Mosley, *The Duchess of Windsor*, p. 153.
9. Ibid, p. 169.
10. Kenneth Harris, *Kenneth Harris Talking To*, p. 126.
11. Dorothy Laird, *Queen Elizabeth The Queen Mother*, p. 21.
12. William Hickey column, *Daily Express*, London, October 7, 1981.
13. David Pryce-Jones, 'TV Tale of Two Windsors', *The New York Times Magazine*, March 18, 1979.
14. Ralph G. Martin, *The Woman He Loved*, p. 11.
15. Edna Woolman Chase and Ilka Chase, *Always in Vogue*, p. 240.
16. William Somerset Maugham to Barbara Back, May 16, 1929.
17. Noël Coward's diary, December 6, 1964, quoted in *The Noël Coward Diaries*, p. 582.
18. Ibid, p. 582.

19. *See* Nigel Dempster's column, *The Daily Mail*, London, February 2, 1983. *See also* Craig Brown and Lesley Cunliffe, *The Book of Royal Lists*, p. 239.
20. David Pryce-Jones, 'TV Tale of Two Windsors', *New York Times Magazine*, March 18, 1979.
21. Told to Michael Thornton, quoted in 'The Royal Birthday For Which No Flags Will Fly', *Sunday Express*, London, June 13, 1976.
[22] Other sources state that Peter Montague arrived at Tidewater, Virginia, in 1643, but the earlier date is confirmed by William R. Marye, genealogist of the Maryland Society, and Francis Culver, librarian of the Maryland Historical Society of Baltimore, in their detailed account of the Duchess of Windsor's ancestry, in *Southern Spectator*, Baltimore, March 1937.
[23] David Sinclair in *Queen and Country*, p. 132, also p. 239, states that Warner settled in Virginia in 1628, when he would have been seventeen years old. Hector Bolitho, in 'The Queen's American Ancestors', *Past and Future*, London, December 1958, gives 1650 as the date of arrival, and took his information from tombstones in the family graveyard at Warner Hall.
24. The Duchess of Windsor, *The Heart has its Reasons*, p. 180.
25. See Ralph G. Martin, *The Woman He Loved*, p. 16.
26. The Duchess of Windsor, *The Heart has its Reasons*, p. 243.
27. Ibid, p. 243.

28. *Times Literary Supplement*, London, November 1, 1974.

29. *Sunday Times Weekly Review*, London, December 16, 1979.

30. *Times Literary Supplement*, London, November 1, 1974.

31. See Ralph G. Martin, *The Woman He Loved*, p. 15.

32. The Duchess of Windsor, *The Heart has its Reasons*, p. 18.

[33] This fact was noted in the Baltimore *Evening Sun* on July 2, 1942, following the seven-hour fire which destroyed three buildings of the Monterey Inn, Blue Ridge Summit, Pennsylvania, including Square Cottage, identified as the Duchess of Windsor's birthplace and General Robert E. Lee's one-time headquarters.

34. Marion Crawford, *The Little Princesses* (British edition), pp. 33–34.

[35] Cockayne's *Complete Peerage* gives the date as October 18, 1821, three days earlier.

[36] In 1969, the late sixteenth Earl of Strathmore told Michael Thornton, during a visit to Glamis, that the secret room had led off the present Charter Room, and showed him where it had been, adding that it had long since been 'bricked up'.

37. James Wentworth Day, *The Queen Mother's Family Story*, p. 133.

38. Ibid, p. 136.

39. Ibid, p. 134.

[40] The Hon. Violet Hyacinth Bowes-Lyon died on October 17, 1893.

[41] Ralph G. Martin, *The Woman He Loved*, p. 17. Alice's elder sister, Bessie Montague, was born five years before her, on August 19, 1864. She married, in 1894, D. Buchanan Merryman, who died in 1898. They had no children.

[42] The Duchess of Windsor, *The Heart has its Reasons*, p. 17. Stephen Birmingham in *Duchess*, p. 3, duplicates this error, as does Frances Donaldson in *Edward VIII*, p. 144, by saying that their 'child was born a year later'.

[43] Nellie W. Jones, *A School for Bishops*, p. 37. Ralph G. Martin in *The Woman He Loved*, p. 18, mistakenly says that the marriage took place at the church, rather than in the rectory. J. Bryan III and Charles J. V. Murphy in *The Windsor Story*, p. 4, state that it took place in Blue Ridge Summit, where Wallis was born. The Duchess of Windsor in *The Heart has its Reasons*, p. 20, sets the occasion 'according to one story in a church in Washington, according to another in a church in Baltimore'.

[44] The Duchess of Windsor, *The Heart has its Reasons*, p. 17. Diana Mosley, *The Duchess of Windsor*, p. 12, says, 'the birth was a little premature'.

45. Related by Wallis's cousin, Elizabeth Gordon Biddle Gordon, in *Days of Now and Then*, p. 71.

46. William Hickey column, *Daily Express*, London, June 23, 1976.

47. Private Information.

48. The Duchess of Windsor, *The Heart has its Reasons*, p. 130.

49. Baltimore *American*, June 21, 1896.

50. Baltimore *News*, July 6, 1896.

51. Baltimore *American*, July 5, 1896.

52. Baltimore *News*, September 28, 1896.

53. The Duchess of Windsor, *The Heart has its Reasons*, p. 19.

54. Baltimore *News*, November 16, 1896.

[55] The thirteenth Earl of Strathmore and his wife kept a flat there from 1899 until 1904, when the Earl died. The block was subsequently partly demolished in 1922 at which stage the name, Belgrave Mansions, ceased to be used. The site today is 23–33 Grosvenor Gardens, now occupied by Barclays Bank PLC, the Belgravia Cigarette Co., and Lloyds Bank PLC.

56. *Forfar Herald*, August 10, 1900.

[57] It is frequently stated, even by Robert Lacey in *Majesty*, p. 24, that

the Queen Mother was born Lady Elizabeth Bowes-Lyon. In fact she did not acquire the courtesy title of 'Lady' until her father succeeded to the earldom of Strathmore on February 16, 1904, when she was three and a half years old. Until that time she bore the prefix, The Honourable, before her Christian name.

[58] In an article in *The Evening News Magazine*, London, July 4, 1980, Helen Cathcart wrote: '. . . it remains a domestic secret whether the Queen Mother was in truth born at the family flat near Victoria Station – or in an ambulance on the way to the maternity home'. The *Daily Express* journalist Celia Brayfield, in a letter to Michael Thornton of August 10, 1983, states that Robin Esser, editor of the feature section, 'Express on Saturday', was informed by Helen Cathcart that the Queen Mother had personally told her that she was born in the ambulance.

Helen Cathcart herself is a well-known mystery. The author of some seventeen books on the British royal family, including two on the Queen Mother, five on Queen Elizabeth II, and biographies of Princess Alexandra, Lord Snowdon, the Duchess of Kent, Princess Anne, Princess Margaret and Prince Charles, Miss Cathcart has biographical entries in several reference books and writes on embossed notepaper, 'from Helen Cathcart'. In fact there is no such person. The name is a pseudonym for a freelance author, Harold A. Albert, born in 1920, and formerly (1940–1945) with the Ministry of Information. Ironically, it was a member of the Queen Mother's own staff at Clarence House who ultimately blew Mr Albert's cover, saying (to Lady Olga Maitland, *Sunday Express*, London, September 23, 1979), 'Oh, but we've known for years that Helen Cathcart is Harold Albert.' In *The*

Queen Mother Herself, p. ix, Helen Cathcart acknowledges the Queen Mother's 'great helpfulness in according me hitherto unpublished information . . .' But the same Clarence House spokesman told Lady Olga: 'As far as I know Mr Albert has never met the Queen Mother.'

59. *Forfar Herald*, August 24, 1900.

[60] Lord Glamis had taken forty-eight days – six days beyond the limit – to register Elizabeth's birth. In 1893, he had also been fined, taking even longer – fifty-four days – to register the birth of his son, the Hon. Michael Bowes-Lyon. When his youngest child, the Hon. David Bowes-Lyon, was born on May 2, 1902, Lord Glamis appears not to have registered the birth at all. There is no record of it in England, Wales or Scotland under Lyon or Bowes-Lyon. Sir David's widow, the Hon. Lady Bowes-Lyon, told the author, in a letter of July 18, 1983, that she believed her husband was born in London.

H. Montgomery Hyde, in a letter to the author of July 19, 1983, adds: 'Although registration of births was legally compulsory . . . many aristocrats disregarded this formality. For instance, Lord Queensberry did not register his third son's (Lord Alfred Douglas's) birth, nor did Alfred Douglas register the birth of his son Raymond, but notices of both births appeared in *The Times*.'

61. Helen Cathcart to Michael Thornton, undated letter, received on June 22, 1983.

[62] One recent book, *George and Elizabeth*, by David Duff, states that she was born at 20 St James's Square, London SW1. This is manifestly impossible, since this 1774 Robert Adam house, a protected building, was occupied in 1900, and for five years afterwards, by the Dowager Lady Williams-Wynn. Elizabeth's father did not lease it until 1906. It is now the head-

quarters of the Distillers Company, whose directors, headed by their Chairman, the late Sir Alex Mc-Donald, entertained the Queen Mother to lunch in 1975, when she recognized many of the features of the interior as being unchanged from her childhood.

63. Dorothy Laird, *Queen Elizabeth The Queen Mother*, published in 1966.

64. Dorothy Laird's letter to Michael Thornton, June 22, 1983.

[65] *Sunday Times*, London, May 25, 1980. Elizabeth was in fact twenty-two when she married.

66. The Rev. Dendle French's letter to Michael Thornton, July 27, 1983.

67. Mrs D. R. Murphy's letter to Michael Thornton, June 15, 1982.

68. Helen Cathcart to Michael Thornton, undated letter, received in August 1983.

69. Dorothy Laird, *Queen Elizabeth The Queen Mother*, p. 23.

70. Roger Elliot's letter to Michael Thornton, July 5, 1983.

3. THE GIRL WHO MIGHT HAVE BEEN QUEEN

1. The Duchess of Windsor, *The Heart has its Reasons*, p. 13.

2. Helen Cathcart, *The Queen Mother*, p. 22.

3. Elizabeth Gordon Biddle Gordon, *Days of Now and Then*, p. 71.

4. Geoffrey Bocca, *She Might Have Been Queen*, p. 18.

5. Cleveland Amory, *Who Killed Society?*, p. 235.

6. Ibid, p. 235.

7. The Duchess of Windsor, *The Heart has its Reasons*, p. 21.

8. Ibid, p. 21.

9. Ibid, p. 23.

10. Ibid, p. 23.

11. Dr Charles F. Bove, *A Paris Surgeon's Story*, p. 168.

12. Ibid, p. 168.

13. The Duchess of Windsor, *The Heart has its Reasons*, p. 243.

[14] Streatlam Castle was sold in 1922 and subsequently demolished.

[15] If he did, and if Macbeth's castle was supposed to be Glamis, Shakespeare was tampering with history. In reality, Duncan I did not die at Glamis, but at Pitgaveny, near Elgin.

16. Sir Walter Scott, *Letters on Demonology and Witchcraft*, p. 398.

[17] James Wentworth Day, *The Queen Mother's Family Story*, p. 141. In fact, Malcolm II only died in the castle from the wounds his murderers inflicted on him on Hunter's Hill.

[18] The name of the hostess is correctly stated by Jennifer Ellis in *Elizabeth the Queen Mother*, p. 15. Most biographers duplicate the original error of Lady Cynthia Asquith in *The Duchess of York*, p. 82, and *Queen Elizabeth*, p. 70, in stating that the party was given by the Countess of Leicester. John W. Wheeler-Bennett, in *King George VI: His Life and Reign*, p. 148, mis-spells the location as Montague House.

[19] Montagu House, built originally by one of the Dukes of Montagu, was rebuilt by his descendant, the fifth Duke of Buccleuch, and completed in 1864. It was demolished early in the 1930s to make way for government offices.

[20] This incident was first related in the 1920s. Sir John Wheeler-Bennett includes it in his official life of King George VI, p. 148, which was read and approved by the Queen Mother before its publication in 1958.

[21] For an explanation of the kinship between the dukes of Montagu, the

dukes of Manchester and the dukes of Buccleuch, see Brian Masters, *The Dukes*, pp. 395–397.

22. The Duchess of Windsor, *The Heart has its Reasons*, p. 13.

23. Ralph G. Martin, *The Woman He Loved*, p. 11.

24. The Duchess of Windsor, *The Heart has its Reasons*, p. 30.

25. Dorothy Laird, *Queen Elizabeth The Queen Mother*, p. 20.

26. Ibid, p. 33.

27. Robert Lacey, *Majesty*, p. 44.

28. Lady Cynthia Asquith, *The Duchess of York*, p. 71, and *Queen Elizabeth*, p. 59.

29. Joan Woollcombe, 'Sixty Years On', *The Times*, London, August 3, 1970.

30. Lady Cynthia Asquith, *Queen Elizabeth*, pp. 49–51.

[31] Ronald Gorell Barnes, third Baron Gorell, was born on April 16, 1884. An author and barrister, he was on the editorial staff of *The Times*, 1910–1915, and became President of the Royal Literary Fund. He died on May 2, 1963.

32. Lady Cynthia Asquith, *Queen Elizabeth*, p. 74.

33. Ibid, pp. 68–69.

34. James Wentworth Day, *The Queen Mother's Family Story*, p. 87.

35. Jennifer Ellis, *Elizabeth The Queen Mother*, p. 22.

36. New York *Evening Journal*, February 6, 1937.

37. Cleveland Amory, *Who Killed Society?*, p. 235.

38. Geoffrey Bocca, *She Might Have Been Queen*, p. 21. Also *Sunday People*, London, April 29, 1973.

39. Oldfields Centennial Diary.

40. The Duchess of Windsor, *The Heart has its Reasons*, p. 50.

41. *Much Ado About Nothing*, Act II, Scene III. Wallis's quotation noted in the *New York Times*, June 3, 1937.

42. Framed document in the files of Oldfields School, reproduced in Ralph G. Martin, *The Woman He Loved*, p. 32.

43. London Coliseum programme, week commencing Monday, August 3, 1914.

[44] Her third brother, Alec – the Hon. Alexander Francis Bowes-Lyon – had died unmarried on October 19, 1911, at the age of twenty-four. The youngest brother, David, was twelve when war was declared and was therefore too young for military service.

45. Iles Brody, *Gone with the Windsors*, p. 65.

46. The Duchess of Windsor, *The Heart has its Reasons*, p. 53.

[47] Lady Mary Bowes-Lyon had married the 16th Baron Elphinstone on July 14, 1910, and Lady Rose Bowes-Lyon would marry the Hon. William Leveson-Gower on May 24, 1916. He would succeed his elder brother on July 21, 1939, as the fourth Earl Granville.

48. Lady Cynthia Asquith, *Queen Elizabeth*, p. 83.

49. Dorothy Laird, *Queen Elizabeth The Queen Mother*, pp. 26–27.

50. The Duchess of Windsor, *The Heart has its Reasons*, p. 59.

[51] Some sources – see David Sinclair, *Queen and Country*, p. 43 – mistakenly put the Glamis Castle fire in December 1916.

52. *Evening Telegraph and Post*, Dundee, September 18, 1916.

53. Lady Cynthia Asquith, *The Duchess of York*, p. 131.

[54] *Baltimore News*, September 16, 1916. J. Bryan III and Charles J. V. Murphy, *The Windsor Story*, p. 13, give the date of the engagement announcement as September 19.

55. The Duchess of Windsor, *The Heart has its Reasons*, p. 64.

[56] The marriage took place on April 9, 1919. The Hon. Luke White succeeded his father as the fourth Baron Annaly on December 15, 1922. Lady Annaly, who remained one of the Queen Mother's closest

friends for thirty-six years, died on May 9, 1955

57. Elizabeth Longford *The Queen Mother*, p. 17.

58. Mabell, Countess of Airlie, *Thatched with Gold*, p. 166.

59. Helen Hardinge, *Loyal to Three Kings*, p. 28.

60. *See* Margaret Saville. *H.M. Queen Elizabeth The Queen Mother*, p. 26, also Anon, *King George and Queen Elizabeth*, p. 73.

[61] The Duchess of Windsor, *The Heart has its Reasons*, p. 130. J. Bryan III and Charles J. V. Murphy, *The Windsor Story*, p. 64, state that the clairvoyant was 'the celebrated New York astrologer Evangeline Adams', but in fact it was, says the Duchess (p. 129), 'the favourite pupil of the famous Evangeline Adams'.

62. The Duchess of Windsor, *The Heart has its Reasons*, p. 85.

63. *See* J. Bryan III and Charles J. V. Murphy, *The Windsor Story*, p. 67.

64. *Hansard, The Parliamentary Debates*, House of Commons, Fourth Series, Vol. XXVI, June 28, 1894.

65. Count Louis Hamon, *Cheiro's World Predictions*. pp. 69–70; 72.

[66] Viscountess Coke, born Marion Gertrude Trefusis on August 3, 1882, was a granddaughter of the nineteenth Baron Clinton and also of the fifth Duke of Buccleuch. She married, on December 2, 1905, the Hon. Thomas William Coke, becoming Viscountess Coke in 1909, and the Countess of Leicester in 1941, when her husband succeeded his father as fourth Earl. Her elder son, Thomas, born in 1908, became fifth Earl in 1949 and died in 1976. Her younger son, the Hon. David Coke, born on December 4, 1915, and named after the Prince of Wales, was killed on air operations in Libya in 1941. She herself died on November 23, 1955.

67. The Prince of Wales to Viscountess Coke, March 18, 1915. Letter now in possession of her daughter, Lady Silvia Combe.

68. The Prince of Wales to Viscountess Coke, March 14, 1917. Combe Papers.

69. Ibid, May 27, 1917. Combe Papers.

70. King George V's diary, July 17, 1917.

71. Kenneth Rose, *King George V*, p. 309.

72. Ibid, p. 308.

73. Helen Hardinge, *Loyal to Three Kings*, p. 66.

74. Brian Masters, *The Dukes*, p. 339.

75. The fourth Earl of Dudley's letter to Michael Thornton, May 26, 1983.

76. 'J.M.B.', *The Times*, London, July 25, 1930.

77. Ibid. The same story was told to the author on May 29, 1972, by Lady Victor Paget, who confirmed that the Prince of Wales was present when this incident occurred.

78. Lady Cynthia Asquith, March 2, 1918, in *Diaries 1915–18*, pp. 416–417.

[79] Lady Victor Paget was born the Hon. Bridget Colebrooke on January 29, 1892, younger daughter of the first and last Baron Colebrooke. She married on March 29, 1922, Lord Victor Paget, brother of the sixth Marquess of Anglesey. They were divorced in 1932. She died on January 27, 1975.

[80] Lady Victor Paget confirmed to the author on May 29, 1972, that at one time she had been the mistress of the Prince of Wales. She also told others this. *See* Hugo Vickers, 'Are You Being Sirred?', *Tatler*, London, Volume 276, Number 6, July 1981.

81. The author's interview with Lady Victor Paget, May 29, 1972.

82. Ibid.

[83] He succeeded his father as third Earl of Dudley in 1932. He died in 1969.

84. Rosemary, Viscountess Ednam, to Millicent, Duchess of Sutherland, March 9, 1919. Letter in the possession of the fourth Earl of Dudley.

[85] William Humble David Ward, fourth Earl of Dudley, born January 5, 1920.

[86] The Hon. John Jeremy Ward, born May 7, 1922, died December 9, 1929, and the Hon. Peter Alistair Ward, born February 8, 1926.

87. Denis Stuart, *Dear Duchess*, p. 167.

88. Frances Donaldson, *Edward VIII*, pp. 57–58.

[89] Freda was born Winifred May Birkin on July 28, 1894. She married on July 9, 1913, the Rt Hon. William Dudley Ward. They had two daughters: the actress, Penelope Dudley Ward, born 1914, who married first, in 1939, Fay Compton's son, Anthony Pelissier, and second, in 1948, the film director, Sir Carol Reed; and Angela, born 1916, who married in 1935, Major-General Sir Robert Laycock. Freda and Ward were divorced in 1931. She married secondly, on October 20, 1937, the Marques de Casa Maury (Peter de Casa Maury), from whom she was divorced in 1954. She died in London on March 16, 1983, at the age of eighty-eight – not eighty-six, as reported by the *Daily Mail* on the following day.

90. Lady Cynthia Asquith, March 12, 1918, *Diaries, 1915–18*, p. 421.

91. King George V to Count Albert Mensdorff, October 31, 1935, Mensdorff Papers, State Archives, Vienna.

[92] Suggestions that they may have been partners at a junior dance at Osborne in 1913 rest on unconvincing evidence.

[93] James Stuart (the first Viscount Stuart of Findhorn), *Within the Fringe*, p. 57. Lord Stuart places this conversation at the first ever Royal Air Force Ball, held at the Ritz in the summer of 1921, but in this he is clearly mistaken, for the Duke of York had visited Glamis Castle in September 1920, and had already proposed to Lady Elizabeth by the summer of 1921. It is probable that

Lord Stuart confused the two occasions and that the incident occurred at the Farquhar ball.

94. Mabell, Countess of Airlie, *Thatched with Gold*, p. 166.

95. Ibid, p. 167.

96. Ibid, p. 167.

97. John W. Wheeler-Bennett, *King George VI: His Life and Reign*, p. 150.

98. Mabell, Countess of Airlie, *Thatched with Gold*, p. 167.

99. Ibid, p. 167.

100. Ibid, p. 167.

101. Ibid, p. 167.

102. John W. Wheeler-Bennett, *King George VI: His Life and Reign*, p. 148.

103. Helen Hardinge, *Loyal to Three Kings*, p. 28.

104. Robert Lacey, *Majesty*, p. 45.

105. J. C. C. Davidson, *Memoirs of a Conservative*, pp. 109–110.

106. James A. Frere, *The British Monarchy at Home*, p. 99. For a variant of this story, see Alastair Forbes, 'Few Airs But Many Graces', *Observer Magazine*, London, June 22, 1980.

107. *Daily News*, London, January 5, 1923.

108. *The Star*, London, January 5, 1923.

109. Diary of Sir Henry Channon, January 5, 1923.

110. *The Star*, London, January 6, 1923.

111. Lady Cynthia Asquith, *The Duchess of York*, p. 36.

[112] Group Captain Sir Louis Greig, born on November 17, 1880, was a Scot and a graduate of Glasgow University. He met Prince Albert in 1909 at the junior Royal Naval College at Osborne where Greig, then a Surgeon-Lieutenant in the Royal Navy, was the assistant medical officer. Greig, who had played International Rugby football for Scotland, subsequently served with the Prince on HMS *Malaya* in 1917, and accompanied him as equerry when he transferred to the Royal Air Force and at Cambridge University. When the Prince was

created Duke of York in 1920, Greig became Comptroller of his Household, remaining in the post until 1924, when he was appointed Gentleman Usher in ordinary to King George V. He partnered the Duke of York in the doubles championship at Wimbledon in 1926, and later became Chairman of the All England Lawn Tennis Club. He was knighted in 1932 and died on March 1, 1953.

113. Diaries of King George V and Queen Mary, January 15, 1923.

114. The Duke of York to Queen Mary, January 16, 1923.

115. Diary of Sir Henry Channon, January 16, 1923.

116. Harry Cozens-Hardy, *The Glorious Years*, p. 13.

117. James Pope-Hennessy, *Queen Mary*, p. 529.

118. John W. Wheeler-Bennett, *King George VI: His Life and Reign*, p. 151.

119. Ibid, p. 151.

120. Helen Hardinge, *Loyal to Three Kings*, p. 40.

121. James Pope-Hennessy, *Queen Mary*, p. 529.

122. King George V to the Duke of York, September 20, 1923.

123. Dorothy Laird, *Queen Elizabeth The Queen Mother*, p. 68.

124. James A. Frere, *The British Monarchy At Home*, pp. 119–120.

125. The Duchess of Windsor, *The Heart has its Reasons*, p. 98.

126. Ibid, p. 90.

127. Ibid, p. 91.

128. Ibid, p. 125.

129. *Time* magazine, New York, October 5, 1936.

130. Cleveland Amory, *Who Killed Society?*, p. 238.

131. The Duchess of Windsor, *The Heart has its Reasons*, pp. 145–146.

[132] Thelma and Gloria Morgan were born on August 23, 1904. Gloria married, in 1923, Reginald Claypoole Vanderbilt, who died in 1925. Their daughter, Gloria Laura Vanderbilt, born on February 20, 1924, became the subject of a long and celebrated custody trial in the United States, *The Matter of Vanderbilt*, in 1934. Thelma married first, in 1921, James Vail ('Junior') Converse Jr, from whom she was divorced. In 1926, she married Marmaduke, first Viscount Furness, from whom she was divorced in 1933. Their son, William Anthony Furness, born on March 31, 1929, succeeded his father as second Viscount in 1940. Gloria Morgan Vanderbilt died in 1965, and Thelma, Viscountess Furness in 1970.

133. J. Bryan III and Charles J. V. Murphy, *The Windsor Story*, p. 63.

[134] Gloria Vanderbilt and Thelma, Lady Furness, *Double Exposure*, pp. 265–266. Frances Donaldson, in *Edward VIII*, p. 137, mistakenly sets this safari two years earlier on the Prince's previous visit to East Africa in 1928, at which time he had not yet met Lady Furness.

[135] Consuelo Morgan was two years older than the twins, having been born in 1902.

136. Gloria Vanderbilt and Thelma, Lady Furness, *Double Exposure*, p. 274.

[137] There have been several versions of Wallis Simpson's first social meeting with the Prince of Wales. The Duke of Windsor, in *A King's Story*, p. 254, sets it in the winter of 1931 at Melton Mowbray. Thelma Furness in *Double Exposure*, p. 274, puts it at 21 Grosvenor Square 'in the latter part of 1930, or early in 1931'. The Duchess of Windsor's account, however, in *The Heart has its Reasons*, p. 165, is the only one which fits the available facts.

138. The Duchess of Windsor, *The Heart has its Reasons*, p. 169.

4. 'THAT WOMAN'

1. The Duke of Windsor, *A King's Story*, pp. 254–255.
2. The Duchess of Windsor, *The Heart has its Reasons*, p. 171.
3. Gloria Vanderbilt and Thelma, Lady Furness, *Double Exposure*, pp. 274–275.
4. The Duchess of Windsor, *The Heart has its Reasons*, p. 171.
5. Ibid, p. 173.
6. Ibid, p. 174.
7. The Duke of Windsor, *A King's Story*, p. 255.
8. The Duchess of Windsor, *The Heart has its Reasons*, p. 175.
9. Ibid, p. 175.
10. Ibid, p. 176.
11. The Duke of Windsor, *A King's Story*, p. 235.
12. Lady Diana Cooper, *The Light of Common Day*, pp. 161–162.
13. The Duchess of Windsor, *The Heart has its Reasons*, p. 184.
14. Ibid, pp. 190–191.
15. Gloria Vanderbilt and Thelma, Lady Furness, *Double Exposure*, p. 291.
16. Ibid, p. 291.
17. The Duchess of Windsor, *The Heart has its Reasons*, p. 193.
18. Gloria Vanderbilt and Thelma, Lady Furness, *Double Exposure*, p. 295.
19. Ibid, p. 296.
20. Ibid, p. 296.
21. Ibid, p. 297.
22. The Duchess of Windsor, *The Heart has its Reasons*, p. 194.
23. Gloria Vanderbilt and Thelma, Lady Furness, *Double Exposure*, p. 298.
24. Ibid, p. 298.
25. J. Bryan III and Charles J. V. Murphy, *The Windsor Story*, p. 165.
26. Frances Donaldson, *Edward VIII*, p. 159.
27. Peter Tory, *Daily Mirror*, London, March 21, 1983.
28. J. Bryan III and Charles J. V. Murphy, *The Windsor Story*, p. 56.
29. Ibid, p. 59.
30. Count Louis Hamon, *Cheiro's World Predictions*, p. 73.
31. Cole Lesley, *The Life of Noël Coward*, pp. 187–188.
32. The Duke of Windsor, *A King's Story*, p. 182.
33. Philip Ziegler, *Diana Cooper*, pp. 174–175.
34. David Duff, *Mother of the Queen*, p. 138.
35. John W. Wheeler-Bennett, *King George VI: His Life and Reign*, pp. 155–156.
36. Laura, Duchess of Marlborough, *Laughter from a Cloud*, p. 36.
37. Lady Diana Cooper, *The Light of Common Day*, p. 73.
38. Virginia Woolf's diary, December 15, 1929, quoted by Margaret Forster in 'Eighty Memorable Years', *The Sunday Times Magazine*, London, August 3, 1980.
[39] The Crown Prince of Norway succeeded his father, King Haakon VII, as King Olav V on September 21, 1957. Crown Princess Märtha had died three years earlier on April 5, 1954. Their son, Crown Prince Harald, born on February 21, 1937, is the heir to the throne of Norway.
40. Harold Nicolson's book, published in London by Constable in 1927.
41. James Lees-Milne, *Harold Nicolson, 1886–1929*, p. 365.
42. Harold Nicolson to Vita Sackville-West, April 8, 1929, quoted in James Lees-Milne, *Harold Nicolson, 1886–1929*, p. 365.
43. James Lees-Milne, *Harold Nicolson, 1886–1929*, p. 365.
44. Marion Crawford, *The Little Princesses* (British edition), p. 9.
45. Dermot Morrah, *The Work of the Queen*, pp. 16–17. *See also* Kingsley Martin, *The Crown and the Establishment*, p. 161.
46. J. Bryan III and Charles J. V. Murphy, *The Windsor Story*, p. 104.
47. Sir Henry Channon, *Chips: The*

Diaries of Sir Henry Channon, pp. 51–52.

48. Helen Hardinge, *Loyal to Three Kings*, p. 54.

49. Gloria Vanderbilt and Thelma Lady Furness, *Double Exposure*, p. 282.

50. Ibid, see pp. 312–313.

[51] Prince George, Duke of Kent, born on December 20, 1902, was not in fact the youngest son of George V and Queen Mary. Prince John, born on July 12, 1905, was subject to fits of epilepsy, and lived in seclusion at Sandringham, where he died suddenly on January 18, 1919, at the age of thirteen, following an epileptic attack.

52. Marie Belloc Lowndes, January 20, 1937, *Diaries and Letters of Marie Belloc Lowndes, 1911–1947*, pp. 141–142.

53. Helen Hardinge, *Loyal to Three Kings*, p. 56.

54. The Duchess of Windsor, *The Heart has its Reasons*, p. 205.

55. Prince Christopher of Greece, *Memoirs of H.R.H. Prince Christopher of Greece*, p. 162.

56. Mabell, Countess of Airlie, *Thatched with Gold*, p. 200.

57. Ibid, p. 200.

58. The Duchess of Windsor, *The Heart has its Reasons*, p. 205.

59. Ibid, p. 225.

60. Helen Hardinge, *Loyal to Three Kings*, p. 55.

61. The Dowager Lady Hardinge of Penshurst to Michael Thornton, December 17, 1974.

62. Adela Rogers St Johns, *The Honeycomb*, pp. 439, 527.

[63] Mrs Hogg, formerly Ella Hallam, married Brigadier Oliver Hogg in 1919. They had one son. She died in 1968 and the Brigadier in 1979.

64. Private Information. Letters to the author of May 30 and June 12, 1983.

65. Ibid.

66. Peter Townsend, *Time and Chance*, p. 123.

67. Private Information.

68. Elizabeth Longford, *Elizabeth R*, p. 302.

69. Diana Mosley, *The Duchess of Windsor*, p. 127.

70. The Duchess of Windsor, *The Heart has its Reasons*, p. 211.

71. Sir Henry Channon, April 5, 1935, *Chips: The Diaries of Sir Henry Channon*, pp. 29–30.

72. John W. Wheeler-Bennett, *King George VI: His Life and Reign*, p. 156.

73. Helen Hardinge, *Loyal to Three Kings*, pp. 56–57.

74. The Duchess of Windsor, *The Heart has its Reasons*, p. 216.

75. Kenneth Rose, *King George V*, pp. 391–392.

76. Count Albert Mensdorff, October 31, 1935, Mensdorff Papers, State Archives, Vienna.

77. Ibid.

78. Sir Henry Channon, May 31, 1935, *Chips: The Diaries of Sir Henry Channon*, p. 35.

79. Ralph G. Martin, *The Woman He Loved*, p. 149.

80. Edna Woolman Chase and Ilka Chase, *Always in Vogue*, p. 241.

81. J. G. Lockhart, *Cosmo Gordon Lang*, p. 396.

82. Mabell, Countess of Airlie, *Thatched with Gold*, p. 197.

83. Sir Henry Channon, October 7, 1935, *Chips: The Diaries of Sir Henry Channon*, p. 43.

84. Ronald Tree, *When the Moon was High*, p. 65.

85. Cecil Beaton, *Self Portrait with Friends*, p. 47.

86. Margaret, Duchess of Argyll, *Forget Not*, p. 87.

87. King George V's diary, November 6, 1935.

88. Princess Alice, Duchess of Gloucester, *The Memoirs of Princess Alice, Duchess of Gloucester*, p. 110.

89. King George V to the Duchess of Gloucester, January 14, 1936.

90. Marie Belloc Lowndes, January 20, 1937, *Diaries and Letters of*

Marie Belloc Lowndes, 1911–1947, p. 145.

91. Ibid, pp. 145–146, entry for January 20, 1937.

92. Ibid, p. 143, entry for January 20, 1937.

[93] She had been invited, with the Prince of Wales, to an important dinner at the German Embassy in London on July 10, 1935, and Hitler's special envoy, Joachim von Ribbentrop, had also made strenuous efforts to cultivate a friendship with her.

94. The Duchess of Windsor, *The Heart has its Reasons*, p. 218.

95. Harold Nicolson, January 13, 1936, *Diaries and Letters 1930–39*, p. 238.

[96] Mabell, Countess of Airlie, *Thatched with Gold*, p. 197. 'Lilibet' was the Royal Family's name for Princess Elizabeth. Lady Algernon Gordon-Lennox, formerly Blanche Maynard, married in 1886, the second son of the sixth Duke of Richmond. Lord Algernon had died in 1921. She died in 1945.

97. Keith Middlemas and John Barnes, *Baldwin: A Biography*, p. 976.

98. James Pope-Hennessy, *A Lonely Business*, p. 214.

[99] In her memoirs, Princess Alice, Duchess of Gloucester, p. 109, mistakenly says that it was the death of the King's youngest sister, Queen

Maud of Norway, that plunged the Court into mourning at this time. In fact, Queen Maud survived to attend the Coronation of King George VI and Queen Elizabeth, and did not die until November 20, 1938.

100. The Duke of Windsor, *A King's Story*, p. 261.

101. Edna Woolman Chase and Ilka Chase, *Always in Vogue*, p. 240.

[102] Marie Belloc Lowndes, January 20, 1937, *Diaries and Letters of Marie Belloc Lowndes, 1911–1947*, p. 146. Lord Charles Montagu (1860–1939) was the second son of the seventh Duke of Manchester, brother of the eighth Duke, and uncle of the ninth Duke. By a strange coincidence, he was also a kinsman of Wallis Simpson.

103. James Lees-Milne, *Harold Nicolson, 1930–1968*, pp. 86–87.

104. Ibid, pp. 86–87.

105. Sir Henry Channon, January 22, 1936, *Chips: The Diaries of Sir Henry Channon*, p. 54.

[106] George V's only daughter, Princess Mary, Countess of Harewood, had been created the Princess Royal in 1931, after the death of her aunt, Princess Louise, Duchess of Fife, who had previously held the title.

107. Ralph G. Martin, *The Woman He Loved*, p. 468.

5. MRS SIMPSON DROPS IN AT ROYAL LODGE

1. The Duchess of York to Lord Dawson of Penn, March 9, 1936, quoted in Francis Watson, *Dawson of Penn*, p. 285.

2. Ibid.

3. Sir Henry Channon, February 12, 1936, *Chips: The Diaries of Sir Henry Channon*, p. 58.

4. Lady Diana Cooper, *The Light of Common Day*, p. 163.

5. Ibid, p. 163.

6. Philip Ziegler, *Diana Cooper*, p. 176.

7. Princess Alice, Duchess of Gloucester, *The Memoirs of Princess Alice, Duchess of Gloucester*, p. 113.

8. Mabell, Countess of Airlie, *Thatched with Gold*, p. 198.

9. Helen Hardinge, *Loyal to Three Kings*, pp. 84–85.

10. The Duke of Windsor, *A King's Story*, p. 292.

[11] William Pleydell-Bouverie, seventh Earl of Radnor, born 1895, died 1968.

12. Helen Hardinge, *Loyal to Three Kings*, p. 55.

13. Ibid, pp. 54–55.

14. Cecil Beaton, *Self-Portrait with Friends*, p. 47.

15. Helen Hardinge, *Loyal to Three Kings*, p. 54.

16. Ibid, p. 85.

17. Hardinge Papers, quoted in Frances Donaldson, *Edward VIII*, p. 184.

18. Helen Hardinge, *Loyal to Three Kings*, p. 89.

19. Ibid, p. 89.

20. Ibid, p. 89.

21. Ibid, p. 89.

22. Ibid, p. 90.

23. Ibid, p. 90.

24. Ibid, p. 91.

25. Anita Leslie, *Mrs. Fitzherbert*, p. 100.

26. Joanna Richardson, *The Disastrous Marriage*, p. 228.

27. Anita Leslie, *Mrs. Fitzherbert*, p. 234.

28. Helen Hardinge, *Loyal to Three Kings*, p. 91.

29. Ibid, p. 92.

30. Ibid, p. 93.

31. Ibid, p. 93.

32. Harold Nicolson, April 2, 1936, *Diaries and Letters, 1930–39*, p. 255.

33. The Duchess of Windsor, *The Heart has its Reasons*, p. 224.

34. Ibid, p. 225.

35. Ibid, p. 225.

36. Ibid, p. 225.

37. Marion Crawford, *The Little Princesses* (American edition), p. 72.

38. Ibid, p. 72.

39. Ibid, p. 72.

[40] Ibid, p. 72. In *Elizabeth R*, p. 57, Lady Longford states: 'Princess Margaret says the question was never asked.' But in a letter of May 25, 1983, written to Michael Thornton on behalf of Princess Margaret, Lord Napier and Ettrick admits: 'Her Royal Highness can-not herself remember the occasion . . . at Royal Lodge in April 1936.' The Princess, therefore, who was four months short of her sixth birthday at the time, cannot possibly know whether the question was asked or not.

41. Marion Crawford, *The Little Princesses* (American edition), p. 73.

42. The Duchess of Windsor, *The Heart has its Reasons*, p. 225.

43. Ibid, p. 225.

44. Marion Crawford, *The Little Princesses* (American edition), p. 73.

45. Sir Henry Channon, May 10, 1936, *Chips: The Diaries of Sir Henry Channon*, p. 60.

46. Monckton Papers, quoted in Frances Donaldson, *Edward VIII*, p. 208.

47. The Duchess of Windsor, *The Heart has its Reasons*, pp. 225–226.

48. Helen Hardinge, *Loyal to Three Kings*, p. 97.

49. Keith Middlemas and John Barnes, *Baldwin: A Biography*, p. 981.

50. Ibid, p. 980.

51. J. C. C. Davidson, *Memoirs of a Conservative*, p. 413.

52. G. M. Young, *Stanley Baldwin*, p. 233.

53. Helen Hardinge, *Loyal to Three Kings*, p. 97.

54. The Duchess of Windsor, *The Heart has its Reasons*, p. 226.

55. *The Times* and *Daily Telegraph*, London, May 28, 1936.

56. Helen Hardinge, *Loyal to Three Kings*, pp. 97–98.

57. Mabell, Countess of Airlie, *Thatched with Gold*, p. 198.

58. The Duchess of Windsor, *The Heart has its Reasons*, p. 223.

59. James A. Frere, *The British Monarchy At Home*, pp. 108–109.

60. The diary of Martin F. Scanlon, May 31, 1936, quoted in J. Bryan III and Charles J. V. Murphy, *The Windsor Story*, p. 141.

61. Harold Nicolson's diary, July 13, 1936, quoted in James Lees-Milne,

Harold Nicolson, 1930–1968, pp. 77–78.

62. James Lees-Milne, *Harold Nicolson, 1930–1968*, pp. 86–87.

63. Sir Henry Channon, July 7, 1936, *Chips: The Diaries of Sir Henry Channon*, p. 69.

[64] The Hon. Thomas Coke became the fifth Earl of Leicester in 1949. He died in 1976.

65. Helen Hardinge, *Loyal to Three Kings*, p. 102.

66. Lord Templewood, *Nine Troubled Years*, p. 216.

67. The Duchess of Windsor, *The Heart has its Reasons*, p. 227.

68. Lady Diana Cooper to Michael Thornton, undated letter, received in August 1983.

69. Helen Hardinge, *Loyal to Three Kings*, p. 102.

70. The Dowager Lady Hardinge to Michael Thornton, June 14, 1976.

71. Helen Hardinge, *Loyal to Three Kings*, p. 103.

72. The Dowager Lady Hardinge to Michael Thornton, June 14, 1976.

73. *The Times* and *Daily Telegraph*, London, July 10, 1936.

[74] Nancy Witcher Langhorne had been born in 1879, the daughter of Chiswell Dabney Langhorne of Mirador, Greenwood, Virginia. She married first, Robert Gould Shaw whom she divorced, and second, on

May 3, 1906, the Hon. Waldorf Astor, who succeeded his father as the second Viscount Astor on October 18, 1919. Six weeks later, on November 28, 1919, Viscountess Astor was elected Britain's first woman Member of Parliament – for the Sutton Division of Plymouth. She remained an MP until 1945. Her husband died in 1952, and their eldest son, William Waldorf Astor, succeeded as third Viscount. She died on May 2, 1964.

75. Harold Nicolson, May 28, 1936, *Diaries and Letters, 1930–39*, pp. 261–262.

76. *See* Chapter 2, note 31.

77. Sir Henry Channon, July 20, 1936, *Chips: The Diaries of Sir Henry Channon*, p. 72.

78. Sir Robert Bruce Lockhart, July 27, 1936, *The Diaries of Sir Robert Bruce Lockhart, 1915–1938*, p. 350.

79. Sir Henry Channon, July 27, 1936, *Chips: The Diaries of Sir Henry Channon*, p. 73.

80. Ann Morrow, *The Queen*, p. 19.

81. *Cavalcade*, London, August 15, 1936.

82. Janet Flanner of the *New Yorker*, quoted in Geoffrey Bocca, *She Might Have Been Queen*, p. 61.

83. Geoffrey Bocca, *She Might Have Been Queen*, p. 64.

6. THE DUCHESS OF YORK REJECTS QUEEN WALLIS

[1] An American friend of Wallis Simpson, 'Foxie' Gwynne – so called because of her red hair – had been born Josephine Armstrong, daughter of George Nathan Armstrong of Glenns, Virginia. Divorced from her first husband, Erskine Gwynne, she met the seventh Earl of Sefton on the *Nahlin* cruise in 1936, and they were married on December 9, 1941.

2. The Duchess of Windsor, *The Heart*

has its Reasons, p. 230.

3. Lady Diana Cooper, *The Light of Common Day*, p. 178.

4. Lady Diana Cooper to Robert Lacey, 'The King and Mrs Simpson', *Radio Times*, London, December 3–10, 1976.

5. Lady Diana Cooper, *The Light of Common Day*, p. 184.

6. Philip Ziegler, *Diana Cooper*, p. 177.

7. Ibid, pp. 177–178.

8. The Duchess of Windsor, *The Heart has its Reasons*, pp. 238–239.

9. Ibid, p. 232.

10. The Duke of Windsor, *A King's Story*, p. 311.

11. The Duchess of Windsor, *The Heart has its Reasons*, pp. 238–239.

12. J. G. Lockhart, *Cosmo Gordon Lang*, p. 397.

13. Helen Hardinge, *Loyal to Three Kings*, p. 112.

14. J. G. Lockhart, *Cosmo Gordon Lang*, p. 397.

15. *Evening Express*, Aberdeen, September 19, 1936.

16. *Evening Express*, Aberdeen, September 23, 1936.

[17] Frances Donaldson in *Edward VIII*, p. 215, says: '... the King himself was seen openly arriving at Ballater Station to meet Mrs. Simpson ...'. The 1978 Thames Television series, *Edward and Mrs. Simpson*, based on Lady Donaldson's book, repeated this error. J. Bryan III and Charles J. V. Murphy, *The Windsor Story*, p. 196, also state: '... he was spotted on the platform at Ballater ...'

18. *Evening Express*, Aberdeen, September 21, 1936.

19. Marie Belloc Lowndes, January 20, 1937, *Diaries and Letters of Marie Belloc Lowndes, 1911–1947*, p. 148.

20. *Evening Express*, Aberdeen, September 23, 1936.

21. Sir Henry Channon, November 11, 1936, *Chips: The Diaries of Sir Henry Channon*, p. 79.

22. Private Information.

23. *The Times* and *Daily Telegraph*, London, September 24, 1936.

24. Marie Belloc Lowndes, January 20, 1937, *Diaries and Letters of Marie Belloc Lowndes, 1911–1947*, p. 148.

25. Mary, Duchess of Buccleuch's letter to Michael Thornton, June 3, 1983.

26. Helen Hardinge, *Loyal to Three Kings*, p. 114.

27. Ibid, p. 114.

[28] Born on December 25, 1936.

29. Mary, Duchess of Buccleuch's letter to Michael Thornton, June 3, 1983.

30. Private Information.

31. Keith Middlemas and John Barnes, *Baldwin: A Biography*, p. 982.

32. Peter Townsend, *Time and Chance*, p. 145.

33. Elizabeth Longford, *The Queen Mother*, p. 169.

[34] All the descriptions and quotations in this paragraph and the preceding one are from Private Information, given to the author in confidence by a descendant of one of those present in the room at Balmoral Castle on September 26, 1936, and taken from notes made shortly after the incident. In 1936 it was – and still remains – the convention that royalty is received only by their official host or hostess, and that all others present wait to be acknowledged. Already, prior to this occasion, Wallis had caused anger by receiving the King's guests on his behalf. As Frances Donaldson observes in *Edward VIII*, pp. 189–190: 'One of the odd things about Fort Belvedere was that it seems to have been accepted ever since the days of Lady Furness that one of the women of the party should act as hostess. This was a convention not often observed in bachelor households in England except in a slightly embarrassed and half-hearted way by whoever knew the host best, and even then only in relation to such matters as the whereabouts of the lavatory, and her observance of it led Mrs Simpson to give a certain amount of offence. When she apologised to members of the King's Household, or other people who had been his friends for years, for not being present to welcome them, and then warmly pressed them to a drink, what was intended as a courtesy was often resented as an insolent show of power.'

35. Robert Sencourt, *The Reign of Edward the Eighth*, p. 100.
36. Diary of the Dowager Lady Hardinge of Penshurst, September 27, 1936.
37. *The Times* and *Daily Telegraph*, London, September 28, 1936.
38. The Duke of York to Queen Mary, October 13, 1936.
39. Marie Belloc Lowndes to Mrs King Patterson, November 26, 1936, *Diaries and Letters of Marie Belloc Lowndes, 1911–1947*, p. 152.
40. Harold Nicolson to Vita Sackville-West, October 6, 1936, quoted in James Lees-Milne, *Harold Nicolson, 1930–1968*, p. 78.
41. Helen Hardinge, *Loyal to Three Kings*, p. 116.
42. Ibid, p. 117.
43. The Duke of Windsor, *A King's Story*, pp. 317–318.
44. *Daily Mirror*, New York, October 26, 1936.
45. Marie Belloc Lowndes, January 20, 1937, *Diaries and Letters of Marie Belloc Lowndes, 1911–1947*, p. 150.
[46] Lady Longford, in *The Queen Mother*, p. 49, mistakenly says: 'Mrs Simpson obtained a divorce, the grounds being Ernest Simpson's adultery with a married woman named Mary Kirk Raffray. As this lady subsequently divorced her husband and became Simpson's third wife, the case may have been justified.' Mary Kirk Raffray, Wallis's school friend at Oldfields, was not cited in the Simpson divorce. She did figure briefly, unnamed, in that a letter written by her to Ernest in April 1936, but addressed in error to Wallis, was mentioned – but not read – in evidence. This was not in any sense the basis of the decree nisi, which was granted on the grounds of Ernest Simpson's adultery with Mrs E.H. ('Buttercup') Kennedy at the Hotel de Paris, Bray, on the night of July 28, 1936.

Mary Kirk Raffray became the third Mrs Simpson in 1937, and a son, Ernest Henry Child Kirk Simpson, was born to them on October 27, 1939. Mary died from cancer in 1942. Simpson married for the fourth time in 1948 – to a divorcee, Mrs Avril Leveson-Gower – and died in London on November 30, 1958.

47. Helen Hardinge, *Loyal to Three Kings*, p. 127.
48. Sir Donald Somervell quoted in H. Montgomery Hyde, *Baldwin, The Unexpected Prime Minister*, p. 570.
49. Marie Belloc Lowndes, January 20, 1937, *Diaries and Letters of Marie Belloc Lowndes, 1911–1947*, p. 149.
50. Peter Underwood, *No Common Task*, pp. 77–78.
51. Private Information. Letter of June 12, 1983, to the author.
52. Harold Nicolson, October 28, 1936, *Diaries and Letters, 1930–39*, pp. 276–277.
53. Cecil Beaton, *Self Portrait with Friends*, p. 48.
54. Helen Hardinge, *Loyal to Three Kings*, p. 131.
55. Sir Henry Channon, November 7, 1936, *Chips: The Diaries of Sir Henry Channon*, p. 76.
56. The Duke of York to Queen Mary, November 6, 1936.
57. Sir Henry Channon, November 7, 1936, *Chips: The Diaries of Sir Henry Channon*, p. 77.
58. Helen Hardinge, *Loyal to Three Kings*, p. 55.
59. Sir Henry Channon, November 7, 1936, *Chips: The Diaries of Sir Henry Channon*, p. 77.
60. Sir Robert Bruce Lockhart, November 13, 1936, *The Diaries of Sir Robert Bruce Lockhart, 1915–1938*, p. 357.
61. Helen Hardinge, *Loyal to Three Kings*, p. 133.
62. The Duchess of Windsor, *The Heart has its Reasons*, p. 246.

63. Cole Lesley, *The Life of Noël Coward*, p. 187.

64. Sir Henry Channon, November 13, 1936, *Chips: The Diaries of Sir Henry Channon*, p. 80.

65. Ibid, p. 80.

66. Lord Beaverbrook, *The Abdication of King Edward VIII*, pp. 34–35.

67. *Hansard, The Parliamentary Debates*, House of Commons, Fifth Series, 1936–7, Vol. 318, December 10, 1936.

68. Keith Middlemas and John Barnes, *Baldwin: A Biography*, p. 995.

69. John W. Wheeler-Bennett, *King George VI: His Life and Reign*, p. 281.

70. Princess Alice, Duchess of Gloucester, *The Memoirs of Princess Alice, Duchess of Gloucester*, p. 114.

71. J. Bryan III and Charles J. V. Murphy, *The Windsor Story*, p. 220.

72. James Pope-Hennessy, *Queen Mary*, p. 574.

73. Ibid, p. 576.

74. Sir Henry Channon, November 17, 1936, *Chips: The Diaries of Sir Henry Channon*, pp. 80–81.

75. Harold Nicolson, November 18, 1936, *Diaries and Letters 1930–39*, p. 279.

76. Sir Henry Channon, August 1, 1939, *Chips: The Diaries of Sir Henry Channon*, p. 206.

77. Ibid, p. 84, November 22, 1936.

78. John W. Wheeler-Bennett, *King George VI: His Life and Reign*, p. 283.

79. Sir Henry Channon, November 26, 1936, *Chips: The Diaries of Sir Henry Channon*, pp. 85–86.

[80] Marie Belloc Lowndes to her daughter, Elizabeth, Countess of Iddesleigh, Easter Monday, 1938, *Diaries and Letters of Marie Belloc Lowndes, 1911–1947*, p. 161. Lady Longford, in *The Queen Mother*, p. 53, describes Hannah Gubbay as 'the sister of Sir Philip Sassoon', rather than his cousin.

81. Helen Hardinge, *Loyal to Three Kings*, p. 149.

82. Iain Macleod, *Neville Chamberlain*, p. 197.

83. Marie Belloc Lowndes, January 20, 1937, *Diaries and Letters of Marie Belloc Lowndes, 1911–1947*, p. 152. See also Helen Hardinge, *Loyal to Three Kings*, p. 159, and Frances Donaldson, *Edward VIII*, p. 265.

84. Sir Henry Channon, November 29, 1936, *Chips: The Diaries of Sir Henry Channon*, p. 87.

85. Ibid, p. 87, entry for November 30, 1936.

86. Harold Nicolson, November 30, 1936, *Diaries and Letters, 1930–39*, p. 280.

87. Ibid, p. 280, entry for November 30, 1936.

88. John W. Wheeler-Bennett, *King George VI: His Life and Reign*, pp. 283–284.

89. *The Scotsman*, Edinburgh, December 2, 1936.

90. Ibid.

91. Sir Henry Channon, December 1, 1936, *Chips: The Diaries of Sir Henry Channon*, p. 88.

92. J. Bryan III and Charles J. V. Murphy, *The Windsor Story*, p. 285.

[93] James Pope-Hennessy, *Queen Mary*, p. 577. King Carol II of Roumania, as Crown Prince, had left his wife, Princess Helen of Greece, renounced his rights of succession to the throne, and gone into exile in 1925 with his mistress, Madame Lupescu. In 1930 he returned to Roumania and displaced his son, Michael, as King. He was forced into abdication in 1940 and again went into exile with Madame Lupescu, whom he subsequently married.

94. Helen Hardinge, *Loyal to Three Kings*, p. 159.

95. Blanche Dugdale, December 3, 1936, *Baffy, The Diaries of Blanche Dugdale, 1936–1947*, p. 32.

96. *Time* magazine, New York, November 7, 1936.

97. John W. Wheeler-Bennett, *King*

George VI: His Life and Reign, p. 285.

98. Ibid, p. 285.

99. Ibid, p. 285.

100. *See* Dermot Morrah, *Princess Elizabeth, Duchess of Edinburgh*, p. 62, and the same author's *The Work of the Queen*, p. 10.

[101] For details of the Duke of Kent's drug addiction and cure, *see* J. Bryan III and Charles J. V. Murphy, *The Windsor Story*, pp. 101–102. The Duke of Windsor, in *A King's Story*, p. 239, describes Kent as 'somewhat Bohemian by inclination', and the Duchess of Windsor, in *The Heart has its Reasons*, p. 204, adds, 'he had sowed his share of wild oats; but the Prince of Wales had taken him in hand, drawing him back once again into the accepted pattern'. One of Kent's earliest sexual relationships had been in 1926, at the age of twenty-three, with the diminutive but dynamic negro entertainer, Florence Mills, then thirty-one, who had been brought to England by Charles B. Cochran to star in his revue, *Blackbirds*, at the London Pavilion. Kent's taste for coloured ladies persisted even after his marriage to Princess Marina. The distinguished British diplomat, Sir Thomas Preston, sixth Baronet – who had been British Consul in Ekaterinburg at the time of the alleged murder of Tsar Nicholas II and the Russian Imperial Family – told the author that he had once, during a visit to Africa, called on the Duke of Kent unexpectedly and 'found him in bed with a black woman'.

That Kent was bisexual was widely known in London society in the 1930s, and references to this are even to be found in the diaries of that decade. On April 28, 1932, Sir Robert Bruce Lockhart noted (*Diaries, 1915–1938*, p. 215): 'In the afternoon Randolph Churchill came to see me. He tells me there has been a scandal about Prince George – letters to a young man in Paris. A large sum had to be paid for their recovery.' And on July 15, 1933, Lockhart recorded (*Diaries, 1915–1938*, p. 263) that the Kaiser's grandson, Prince Louis Ferdinand of Prussia, 'liked Prince George, said he was artistic and effeminate and used a strong perfume . . .'

Prince George first met Noël Coward in 1923, when Coward was twenty-three and the Prince was twenty. They became close friends. On August 26, 1942, the day after the Duke of Kent's death, Coward wrote: 'I shall miss him most horribly . . . I feel absolutely miserable . . . In memoriam I say, "Thank you for your friendship for me over all these years and I shall never forget you."' On August 29, 1942, after the funeral, he wrote: 'I tried hard not to cry, but it was useless . . . when the coffin passed with flowers from the garden at Coppins and Prince George's cap on it I was finished. I then gave up all pretence and just stood with the tears splashing down my face. . . The thought that I shall never see him again is terribly painful.' (*The Noël Coward Diaries*, p. 17.)

One of Coward's biographers, Sheridan Morley, recently alleged (*The Mail on Sunday*, December 30, 1984): 'It is well known that Noël was bisexual.' If this is well known, it is only to Mr. Morley. Dame Rebecca West spoke of Coward's sexual life as being 'untainted by pretence', and on Coward's own unvarying admission, he never had a sexual relationship with a woman in his life. As his secretary and friend for thirty-seven years, Cole Lesley, correctly stated (in *The Life of Noël Coward*, p. 93): 'He was homosexual.' At a small drinks party in his suite at the Savoy Hotel, London, on December 10, 1969, Coward told the author, in the presence of Cole

Lesley, Merle Oberon and other friends, that his relationship with the Duke of Kent had at one time been sexual: 'We had a little dalliance,' he said. 'It didn't last long. We were both very young at the time. He was absolutely enchanting and I never stopped loving him.' Sheridan Morley recently claimed that Coward himself had denied having a sexual relationship with the Duke. 'I had heard a rumour and asked him. He said there was no truth in it whatsoever', (*Sunday People*, December 30, 1984). But Morley is strongly contradicted by one of Coward's closest friends for more than twenty years, Charles Russell, who began by stage-managing the playwright's wartime tours and ultimately became Coward's New York representative. Mr Russell told the author in January 1985: 'Noël used to refer constantly to his affair with the Duke of Kent. He seemed rather proud of it and at times was almost a bore on the subject.'

102. H. Montgomery Hyde, *Baldwin: The Unexpected Prime Minister*, p. 415.

103. The Duchess of Windsor, *The Heart has its Reasons*, p. 270.

104. Sir Edward Peacock's Notes, quoted in Frances Donaldson, *Edward VIII*, p. 279.

105. The Duchess of Windsor, *The Heart has its Reasons*, pp. 273–274.

106. Sir Edward Peacock's Notes, quoted in Frances Donaldson, *Edward VIII*, p. 285.

107. Sir Henry Channon, December 8, 1936, *Chips: The Diaries of Sir Henry Channon*, p. 97.

108. Stanley Baldwin to his niece, Monica Baldwin, quoted in Frances Donaldson, *Edward VIII*, p. 250.

109. Ibid, quoted in Frances Donaldson, *Edward VIII*, p. 302.

110. Helen Hardinge, *Loyal to Three Kings*, p. 184.

111. Loelia, Lady Lindsay of Dowhill (Loelia, Duchess of Westminster), *Cocktails and Laughter*, p. 73.

112. James A. Frere, *The British Monarchy At Home*, p. 114.

113. Helen Cathcart, *The Queen Mother Herself*, p. 119.

114. Sir Henry Channon, December 10, 1936, *Chips: The Diaries of Sir Henry Channon*, p. 99.

115. James Lees-Milne, *Harold Nicolson, 1930–1968*, p. 86.

116. Blanche Dugdale, December 11, 1936, *Baffy: The Diaries of Blanche Dugdale, 1936–1947*, p. 34.

117. Harold Nicolson to Vita Sackville-West, December 15, 1936, quoted in James Lees-Milne, *Harold Nicolson, 1930–1968*, pp. 86–87.

118. Elizabeth Longford, *Elizabeth R*, p. 286.

119. The Duke of Windsor, *A King's Story*, p. 413.

120. Ibid, p. 414.

121. Compton Mackenzie, *The Windsor Tapestry*, p. 524.

122. John W. Wheeler-Bennett, *King George VI: His Life and Reign*, p. 298.

[123] Ibid, p. 298. Although Windsor had never been used previously as a royal or non-royal title, it had been the name of the British reigning dynasty since 1917, when George V, disturbed by malicious rumours that cast doubt on the loyalty of himself and his German wife to the Allied cause in World War I, decided to relinquish the name of Guelph, the patronymic of the House of Hanover, and Wettin, that of the Prince Consort, and to abandon all 'German degrees, styles, dignities, letters, honours and appellations'. When the King proclaimed his dynasty the House of Windsor — the name had been suggested by his Private Secretary, the first Baron Stamfordham — the Kaiser responded by letting it be known that he would be delighted to attend a performance of that well-known

opera, 'The Merry Wives of Saxe-Coburg-Gotha'.

124. James A. Frere, *The British Monarchy At Home*, p. 113.

125. John W. Wheeler-Bennett, *King George VI: His Life and Reign*, pp. 288–289.

7. THE QUEEN-EMPRESS AND THE NON-ROYAL DUCHESS

1. John W. Wheeler-Bennett, *King George VI: His Life and Reign*, p. 286.

2. Harold Nicolson, March 21, 1949, *Diaries and Letters, 1945–62*, p. 167.

3. Arthur Groom, *The Authentic Pictorial Record of King George VI*, p. 7.

4. Sir Henry Channon, December 5, 1936, *Chips: The Diaries of Sir Henry Channon*, p. 93.

5. Queen Elizabeth to Archbishop Lang, December 12, 1936, quoted in J. G. Lockhart, *Cosmo Gordon Lang*, p. 407.

[6] An unpublished privately-circulated satirical poem which began: 'Where are the friends of yesterday/That fawned on him,/That flattered her? . . .'

7. J. G. Lockhart, *Cosmo Gordon Lang*, p. 405.

8. Blanche Dugdale, December 15, 1936, *Baffy: The Diaries of Blanche Dugdale, 1936–1947*, p. 34.

9. Queen Mary to Prince Paul of Yugoslavia, written during Christmas 1936, and quoted by Alastair Forbes, *Times Literary Supplement*, London, January 4, 1980.

10. J. Bryan III and Charles J. V. Murphy, *The Windsor Story*, p. 287.

11. Mabell, Countess of Airlie, *Thatched with Gold*, p. 200.

12. Lady Bertha Dawkins to her daughter, March 27, 1937, quoted in James Pope-Hennessy, *Queen Mary*, p. 582.

13. Sir Henry Channon, May 12, 1937, *Chips: The Diaries of Sir Henry Channon*, p. 125.

14. Edna Woolman Chase and Ilka Chase, *Always in Vogue*, p. 246.

15. Ibid, pp. 244, 246.

16. Sir Henry Channon, December 8, 1936, *Chips: The Diaries of Sir Henry Channon*, p. 97.

17. Ibid, p. 116. Entry for February 26, 1937.

18. Hector Bolitho, *King Edward VIII: His Life and Reign*, p. 237.

19. Ibid, p. 237.

20. Ibid, p. 267.

21. Ibid, p. 260.

22. Ibid, p. 284.

23. Compton Mackenzie, *The Windsor Tapestry*, p. 151.

24. Ibid, p. 149.

25. Ibid, p. 153.

26. To Michael Thornton, at 31 Drummond Place, Edinburgh, in an interview conducted in the presence of Brodrick Haldane, shortly before Sir Compton Mackenzie's death on November 30, 1972, at the age of eighty-nine.

27. Hector Bolitho to Michael Thornton, at 1 St Nicholas Road, Brighton, January 1, 1961.

28. The 4th Earl of Dudley's letter to Michael Thornton of May 26, 1983.

29. Sir Henry Channon, December 22, 1936, *Chips: The Diaries of Sir Henry Channon*, pp. 103–104.

30. Ibid, p. 104, entry for December 22, 1936.

31. Frances Donaldson, *Edward VIII*, pp. 314, 316–317. Lady Donaldson, also in *Edward VIII*, p. 292, puts the Duke of Windsor's yearly income at £60,000, a figure duplicated by Lady Longford in *Eliza-*

beth R, p. 76. Michael Bloch, however, who has had access to the Windsors' own archives, states, in *Operation Willi*, p. 39, that the Duke's annual allowance was only £21,000.

32. Major Edward Metcalfe to Lady Alexandra Metcalfe, January 21, 1937, quoted in Frances Donaldson, *Edward VIII*, pp. 310–311.

33. Monckton Papers, quoted in Frances Donaldson, *Edward VIII*, p. 317.

34. Ibid.

35. The Dowager Lady Hardinge of Penshurst to Michael Thornton, July 23, 1974.

36. Private information.

37. The Duke of Windsor, *Sunday News*, New York, December 11, 1966.

38. Ibid.

39. Ibid.

[40] Monckton Papers, quoted in Frances Donaldson, *Edward VIII*, p. 316. In normal circumstances, a royal bridegroom does not have a best man, but instead two 'supporters', who are usually male relations of royal or noble rank.

41. Frances Stevenson, *Lloyd George: A Diary*, p. 327.

42. Major Edward Metcalfe to Lady Alexandra Metcalfe, January 24, 1937, quoted in Frances Donaldson, *Edward VIII*, p. 311.

43. Major Edward Metcalfe to Lady Alexandra Metcalfe, February 14, 1937, quoted in Frances Donaldson, *Edward VIII*, p. 314.

44. J. Bryan III and Charles J. V. Murphy, *The Windsor Story*, p. 319.

45. Harold Nicolson, March 17, 1937, *Diaries and Letters 1930–1939*, p. 298.

46. Philip Ziegler, *Diana Cooper*, p. 179.

47. Diana Cooper, *The Light of Common Day*, pp. 190, 193.

48. Ibid, p. 193.

49. Philip Ziegler, *Diana Cooper*, p. 180.

50. Sir Robert Bruce Lockhart, May 14, 1937, *The Diaries of Sir Robert Bruce Lockhart, 1915–1938*, p. 372.

51. Stephen Birmingham, *Duchess*. p. 178.

52. The Duchess of Windsor, *The Heart has its Reasons*, p. 295.

53. Ibid, pp. 296–297.

54. Mary Soames, *Clementine Churchill*, p. 274.

55. Lord Louis Mountbatten to King Edward VIII. December 7, 1936.

56. Michael Bloch, *The Duke of Windsor's War*, p. 18.

57. The Dowager Lady Hardinge of Penshurst to Michael Thornton, July 23, 1974.

58. *See* Michael Bloch, *The Duke of Windsor's War*, p. 338.

59. J. Bryan III and Charles J. V. Murphy, *The Windsor Story*, p. 341.

60. The Dowager Lady Hardinge of Penshurst to Michael Thornton, July 23, 1974.

61. H. Montgomery Hyde's letter to *The Times*, London, September 20, 1972.

62. The Dowager Lady Hardinge of Penshurst to Michael Thornton, July 23, 1974.

63. Marie Belloc Lowndes, January 28, 1937, *Diaries and Letters of Marie Belloc Lowndes, 1911–1947*, p. 155.

64. Stanley Baldwin to his niece, Monica Baldwin, quoted in Frances Donaldson, *Edward VIII*, p. 323.

[65] None of the nine previous monarchs who had vacated the British throne, either temporarily or permanently, had done so willingly. Edward II was forced to renounce the throne in 1327 in favour of his son, Edward III, and was subsequently murdered. Richard II was deposed in 1399 by his cousin, Henry of Bolingbroke, who became Henry IV. Richard also was murdered. Henry VI was deposed by force in 1461, and again in 1471, when he was murdered in the

Tower of London. His successor, the Yorkist usurper, Edward IV, briefly fled the country in 1470, but regained the throne ten months later. In 1483, his twelve-year-old son, Edward V, was deprived of the throne by his uncle, Richard III, and imprisoned with his younger brother, Richard Duke of York, in the Tower of London, where both disappeared – presumably murdered. In 1485, Richard III was killed at the Battle of Bosworth by the army of the invading claimant to the throne, Henry VII. In July 1553, Lady Jane Grey was proclaimed Queen Regnant but dethroned after a nine-day reign by the rightful heir to the crown, Mary I, who imprisoned and later executed her. Charles I was imprisoned in 1647 and subsequently deposed, tried and executed by Parliament. And the Roman Catholic James II, threatened by the invasion of his Dutch Protestant son-in-law, William of Orange, subsequently William III, fled his kingdom on December 11, 1688. Exactly 248 years later to the same day, Edward VIII ceased to be King, and left Windsor after making his farewell broadcast to the nation.

66. John W. Wheeler-Bennett, *King George VI: His Life and Reign*, pp. 294–295.

67. Ibid, p. 288.

68. Philip M. Thomas, 'The Duchess of Windsor – Her Position Reappraised', 104th edition of *Burke's Peerage*, 1967, pp. xxi–xxiii.

69. Ibid.

[70] In two recent instances, European monarchs have retained both the title of King and the prefix, His Majesty, after ceasing to reign. Carol II of Roumania, after abdicating in 1940 in favour of his son, King Michael I, continued to be known as His Majesty King Carol until his death in 1953. And Leopold III of Belgium, who abdi-

cated in 1951 in favour of his son, King Baudouin I, continued to be known as His Majesty King Leopold of the Belgians. Queen Wilhelmina, on the other hand, was known simply as Her Royal Highness Princess Wilhelmina of the Netherlands after her abdication in 1948, and her daughter, Queen Juliana, has been similarly known as Her Royal Highness Princess Juliana of the Netherlands since her abdication in 1980 in favour of her daughter, Queen Beatrix.

71. Elizabeth Longford, *The Queen Mother* (1981), p. 67, and *Elizabeth R* (1983), p. 76.

72. Elizabeth Longford, *Elizabeth R*, p. 76.

73. The Countess of Longford's letter to Michael Thornton, June 20, 1983.

74. Private information.

75. *See* Compton Mackenzie, *The Windsor Tapestry*, pp. 454–455.

76. *Wharton's Law Lexicon*.

77. Diana Mosley, *The Duchess of Windsor*, pp. 217–218.

[78] His Serene Highness Prince Louis of Battenberg, an Admiral in the British Navy, was requested by his cousin, King George V, to anglicize his name in 1917, in order to escape the taint of German connections during the war against the Kaiser. He therefore assumed the surname, Mountbatten, and was created first Marquess of Milford Haven. His younger son, Prince Louis of Battenberg, became Lord Louis Mountbatten, and was created the first Earl Mountbatten of Burma on October 28, 1947.

[79] King Michael I of Roumania, who was also forced off his throne and into exile by the Communists at the end of 1947.

80. Augustus Tilley, 'Madame Lupescu, royal mistress and courtesan in Pompadour style', *Daily Telegraph*, London, July 1, 1977.

81. Ibid.

82. Michael Bloch, *The Duke of Windsor's War*, p. 6.

83. Philip M. Thomas, *Burke's Peerage*, 1967, pp. xxi–xxiii.

84. Patrick Montague-Smith, 'The Title of H.R.H.', *Debrett's Peerage*, 1972, pp. 13–15.

85. Compton Mackenzie, *The Windsor Tapestry*, p. 254.

86. Ibid, p. 255.

87. Ibid, p. 256.

[88] Born in 1761, her real name was Dorothea Bland. Mrs Jordan was the name she used for stage appearances, although she never married. She lived with the Duke of Clarence until 1811. She made her final appearance on the stage in 1814, and died in Paris in 1816.

89. *See* Dame Anna Neagle, *There's Always Tomorrow*, pp. 28–31.

90. Philip M. Thomas, *Burke's Peerage*, 1967, pp. xxi–xxiii.

91. Frances Donaldson, *King George VI and Queen Elizabeth*, p. 64.

92. Lady Donaldson of Kingsbridge's letter to Michael Thornton, undated, received in August 1983.

93. Philip M. Thomas, *Burke's Peerage*, 1967, pp. xxi–xxiii.

94. Patrick Montague-Smith, 'The Title of H.R.H.', *Debrett's Peerage*, 1972, pp. 13–15.

95. *See* Sir Henry Channon, May 12, 1937, *Chips: The Diaries of Sir Henry Channon*, p. 125, for the attitude of Queen Mary and the Court towards Wallis, and Sir Robert Bruce Lockhart, December 11, 1938, *The Diaries of Sir Robert Bruce Lockhart 1915–1938*, pp. 413–414, for the hostility of Queen Elizabeth. It is difficult to see the decision to deprive the Duchess of Windsor of the title of Royal Highness as anything other than an act of retribution, or to disagree with the conclusion of Philip M. Thomas in *Burke's Peerage* 1967, pp. xxi–xxiii (*see* note 102).

96. H. Montgomery Hyde's letter to *The Times*, London, September 20, 1972.

97. H. Montgomery Hyde, *Baldwin: The Unexpected Prime Minister*, p. 518.

98. *London Gazette*, May 28, 1937.

99. *The Times*, London, May 29, 1937.

100. Lord Birkenhead, *Walter Monckton*, p. 166.

101. Private information.

102. Philip M. Thomas, *Burke's Peerage*, 1967, pp. xxi–xxiii.

103. Lord Birkenhead, *Walter Monckton*, p. 166.

104. *See* Geoffrey Bocca, *She Might Have Been Queen*, p. 158.

105. Frances Donaldson, *Edward VIII*, p. 322.

106. The Duchess of Windsor, *The Heart has its Reasons*, p. 298.

107. J. Bryan III and Charles J. V. Murphy, *The Windsor Story*, p. 343.

108. Ibid, p. 342.

109. Lady Alexandra Metcalfe's diary for June 3, 1937, quoted in Frances Donaldson, *Edward VIII*, pp. 324–325.

110. James Pope-Hennessy, *Queen Mary*, p. 586.

111. Lord Birkenhead, *Walter Monckton*, p. 156.

112. Lady Alexandra Metcalfe's diary for June 3 and June 4, 1937, quoted in Frances Donaldson, *Edward VIII*, pp. 325–326.

113. Mrs Gilbert Miller told the author on June 14, 1976, that the Duchess of Windsor regularly expressed her belief to friends that it was Queen Elizabeth alone who had been responsible for the withholding of the H.R.H. *See also* J. Bryan III and Charles J. V. Murphy, *The Windsor Story*, p. 555, who quote the Duchess as saying of the Queen Mother in 1972: '*She* is the one who kept the King from giving me the title that David wanted for me!'

8. 'I WOULDN'T RECEIVE HER'

1. Compton Mackenzie, *The Windsor Tapestry*, p. 416.
2. Stephen Birmingham, *Duchess*, p. 187.
3. Loelia Lindsay and Hugo Vickers, *Cocktails and Laughter*, p. 10.
4. Harold Nicolson, May 27, 1937, *Diaries and Letters 1930–39*, p. 301.
5. Compton Mackenzie, *The Windsor Tapestry*, p. 167.
6. Keith Middlemas, *The Life and Times of George VI*, p. 98.
7. Alastair Forbes, *Times Literary Supplement*, London, January 4, 1980.
8. Alastair Forbes, *Times Literary Supplement*, London, November 1, 1974.
9. Monckton Papers, quoted in Frances Donaldson, *Edward VIII*, p. 328.
10. J. Bryan III and Charles J. V. Murphy, *The Windsor Story*, p. 354.
11. Ibid, p. 354.
12. Cecil Beaton, *Self Portrait with Friends*, p. 60.
13. Monckton Papers, quoted in Frances Donaldson, *Edward VIII*, p. 327.
14. The Dowager Lady Hardinge of Penshurst told the author, on July 23, 1974, that Queen Elizabeth believed that the initiative for the German visit had come from the Duchess of Windsor rather than the Duke.
15. The Duchess of Windsor, *The Heart has its Reasons*, p. 303.
16. Emmy Göring, *My Life with Göring*, pp. 88–89.
17. Alastair Forbes, *Times Literary Supplement*, London, November 1, 1974.
18. Ibid.
19. Sir Nevile Henderson's speech of June 1, 1937, as guest of honour at the dinner of the German-English Society in Berlin, in the presence of Heinrich Himmler, head of the Gestapo.
20. The Duchess of Windsor, *The Heart has its Reasons*, p. 308.
21. Paul Schmidt, *Hitler's Interpreter*, p. 75.
22. Albert Speer, *Inside the Third Reich*, p. 72.
23. *New York Times*, October 23, 1937.
24. *New York Herald Tribune*, October 28, 1937.
25. *Forward* magazine, London, November 13, 1937.
26. Department of State memorandum of conversations, November 2, 1937, confidential file, National Archives, Washington D.C., FW 033.4111. This is the only official documentation that has come to light in which the King and Queen express their resentment at the Duke of Windsor's activities. Usually George VI and his consort maintained a careful silence on the subject of the Windsors. There is doubtless further documentation in the Royal Archives at Windsor, but it seems unlikely that this will be released for publication in the lifetime of Queen Elizabeth II.
27. The Duke of Windsor to Neville Chamberlain, December 22, 1937, quoted in Michael Bloch, *The Duke of Windsor's War*, pp. 7–8.
28. The Duchess of Windsor, *The Heart has its Reasons*, p. 289.
29. Private Information.
30. Andrew Barrow, *Gossip, A History of High Society from 1920 to 1970*, p. 92.
31. The Duchess of Windsor, *The Heart has its Reasons*, p. 298.
32. *Sunday Dispatch*, London, January 16, 1938.
33. Private information. There is also strong confirmation of Queen Elizabeth's opposition to the possibility of the Windsors' return to England in the Monckton Papers

and in Lord Birkenhead, *Walter Monckton*, p. 169.

34. Francis Watson, *Dawson of Penn*, p. 301.

35. John Scott, 'The Amazing Duchess', *Sunday People*, London, May 6, 1973.

36. Michael Bloch, *The Duke of Windsor's War*, p. 3.

37. Queen Mary to the Duke of Windsor, July 5, 1938, quoted in James Pope-Hennessy, *Queen Mary*, p. 575.

38. Norman Hartnell, *Silver and Gold*, p. 96.

39. Ibid, p. 97.

40. Dorothy Laird, *Queen Elizabeth The Queen Mother*, p. 190.

41. David Duff, *George and Elizabeth*, p. 141.

42. Dina Wells Hood, *Working for the Windsors*, p. 31.

43. Ibid, p. 53.

44. Harold Nicolson, August 5, 1938, *Diaries and Letters, 1930–39*, p. 352.

45 James Lees-Milne, *Harold Nicolson, 1930–1968*, pp. 107–108.

46. Harold Nicolson, August 5, 1938, *Diaries and Letters, 1930–39*, p. 352.

47. Monckton Papers. *See also* J. Bryan III and Charles J. V. Murphy, *The Windsor Story*, p. 386.

48. Lord Birkenhead, *Walter Monckton*, p. 169.

49. Ibid, p. 170.

50. Princess Alice, Duchess of Gloucester, *The Memoirs of Princess Alice, Duchess of Gloucester*, p. 117.

51. *Daily Mail*, London, November 12, 1938.

52. Princes Alice, Duchess of Gloucester, *The Memoirs of Princess Alice, Duchess of Gloucester*, p. 117.

53. *Daily Mail*, London, November 12, 1938.

54. *The Times* and *Daily Telegraph*, London, November 12, 1938.

55. King George VI to Queen Mary, November 14, 1938, quoted in Noble Frankland, *Prince Henry, Duke of Gloucester*, p. 137.

56. Princess Alice, Duchess of Gloucester, *The Memoirs of Princess Alice, Duchess of Gloucester*, p. 117.

57. *Daily Express*, London, February 14, 1979.

58. Lady Mosley's letter to Michael Thornton, May 14, 1983.

[59] The American opera singer and Hollywood film star, born in 1901, and killed on January 26, 1947, in an air crash in Copenhagen.

60. Dina Wells Hood, *Working for the Windsors*, p. 96.

61. Sir Henry Channon, November 17, 1938, *Chips: The Diaries of Sir Henry Channon*, p. 178.

62. *Sunday Dispatch*, London, December 11, 1938.

63. *Daily Express*, London, February 14, 1979.

64. *Sunday Dispatch*, London, December 11, 1938.

65. *Evening Standard*, London, December 12, 1938.

66. *Sunday Dispatch*, London, December 18, 1938.

67. John Utter to the author, June 5, 1976. *See also* Frances Donaldson, *Edward VIII*, p. 335.

68. Dina Wells Hood, *Working for the Windsors*, p. 96.

69. Sir Robert Bruce Lockhart, December 10, 1938, *The Diaries of Sir Robert Bruce Lockhart, 1915–1938*, p. 413.

70. Ibid, pp. 413–414, entry for December 11, 1938.

71. Michael Bloch, *The Duke of Windsor's War*, p. 8.

72. *Daily Express*, London, May 8, 1939.

73. Marie Belloc Lowndes, June 1, 1939, *Diaries and Letters of Marie Belloc Lowndes, 1911–1947*, p. 178.

74. John W. Wheeler-Bennett, *King George VI: His Life and Reign*, p. 380.

75. *Time* magazine, New York, June 19, 1939.

76. Trevor Hall, *The Queen Mother and Her Family*, p. 101.
77 Helen Cathcart, *The Queen Mother*, p. 160.
78. Harold Nicolson, June 23, 1939, *Diaries and Letters, 1930–39*, p. 405.
79. Alastair Forbes, *Times Literary Supplement*, London, January 4, 1980.
80. Major Edward Metcalfe to Lady

Alexandra Metcalfe, September 3, 1939, quoted in Frances Donaldson, *Edward VIII*, pp. 346–347.
81. Lord Birkenhead, *Walter Monckton*, p. 171.
82. *The Times*, London, September 9, 1939.
83. *New York Times*, September 15, 1939.
84. The Duchess of Windsor, *The Heart has its Reasons*, p. 324.

9. 'A WOMAN'S JEALOUSY'

1. The Duchess of Windsor, *The Heart has its Reasons*, p. 225.
2. *Daily Mirror*, London, September 12, 1939.
3. *Daily Mirror*, London, September 13, 1939.
4. Ibid.
5. Lady Alexandra Metcalfe's diary, September 25, 1939, quoted in Frances Donaldson, *Edward VIII*, p. 349.
6. The Duchess of Windsor, *The Heart has its Reasons*, pp. 324–325.
[7] Patrick Terence William Span Plunket, seventh Baron Plunket, born in 1923. He succeeded to the barony at the age of fourteen in 1938, when both his parents died in a horrifying air accident. He became equerry to George VI in 1948, and Deputy Master of the Household to Elizabeth II in 1954. He died in 1975.
8. Robert Lacey, *Majesty*, p. 123.
9. John W. Wheeler-Bennett, *King George VI: His Life and Reign*, p. 417.
10. The Duchess of Windsor, *The Heart has its Reasons*, p. 324.
11. King George VI to Neville Chamberlain, September 14, 1939.
12. John W. Wheeler-Bennett, *King George VI: His Life and Reign*, p. 417.
13. The Duke of Windsor, *Daily News*, New York, December 13, 1966.
14. R. J. Minney (Editor), *The Private Papers of Hore-Belisha*, p. 238.
15. Ibid, p. 238.

16. Ibid, p. 239.
17. Ibid, p. 239.
18. The Duchess of Windsor, *The Heart has its Reasons*, p. 325.
19. Geoffrey Madan, *Geoffrey Madan's Notebooks*, p. 81.
20. Lady Alexandra Metcalfe's diary, September 25, 1939, quoted in Frances Donaldson, *Edward VIII*, p. 349.
21. Ibid.
22. General Lelong to General Maurice Gamelin, September 19, 1939, Despatch 492/S, French Military Archives, Vincennes, 7/N/2817, translated by Michael Bloch in *The Duke of Windsor's War*, p. 29.
23. Noble Frankland, *Prince Henry, Duke of Gloucester*, p. 142.
24. The Duke of Gloucester to King George VI, October 19, 1939, quoted in Noble Frankland, *Prince Henry, Duke of Gloucester*, p. 143.
25. Ibid.
26. Noble Frankland, *Prince Henry, Duke of Gloucester*, p. 143.
27. The Duchess of Windsor, *The Heart has its Reasons*, p. 329.
28. Ibid, p. 329.
29. Major Edward Metcalfe to Lady Alexandra Metcalfe, November 20, 1939, quoted in Frances Donaldson, *Edward VIII*, p. 356.
30. The Duchess of Windsor to Mrs Bessie Merryman, December 3, 1939, quoted in Michael Bloch, *The Duke of Windsor's War*, pp. 45–46.
31. The Duchess of Windsor to Lady

Colefax, December 30, 1939. Colefax Papers.

[32] 'The Gate of the Year' was part of a collection of verse by Marie Louise Haskins published privately in 1908 under the title, *The Desert*. Miss Haskins, a lecturer at the London School of Economics, died in 1957 at the age of eighty-one.

33. The Duchess of Windsor to Mrs Bessie Merryman, January 21, 1940, quoted in Michael Bloch, *The Duke of Windsor's War*, pp. 52–53.

34. HM The Queen's Message to the Women of the Empire, broadcast from Buckingham Palace on November 11, 1939, and recorded by HMV Records, RC 3138.

35. Major Edward Metcalfe to Lady Alexandra Metcalfe, February 1, 1940, quoted in Frances Donaldson, *Edward VIII*, p. 356.

36. The Duchess of Windsor to Mrs Bessie Merryman, April 1940, quoted in Michael Bloch, *The Duke of Windsor's War*, p. 62.

37. The Duchess of Windsor to Mrs Bessie Merryman, May 6, 1940, quoted in Michael Bloch, *The Duke of Windsor's War*, p. 63.

38. Sir Robert Bruce Lockhart, April 29, 1955, *The Diaries of Sir Robert Bruce Lockhart, 1939–1965*, p. 748.

39. King George VI to Winston Churchill, May 10, 1940, quoted in Martin Gilbert, *Finest Hour*, p. 316.

40. Frances Donaldson, *Edward VIII*, p. 357.

41. J. Bryan III and Charles J. V. Murphy, *The Windsor Story*, p. 420.

42. Minute of June 28, 1940: Churchill papers, 20/9, quoted in Martin Gilbert, *Finest Hour*, p. 613.

43. Michael Bloch, *The Duke of Windsor's War*, p. 68.

44. Elizabeth Longford, *The Queen Mother*, p. 79.

45. Public Records Office, Kew, FO 800/326/187.

46. Public Records Office, FO 800/326/184.

47. War Cabinet Conclusions 174/40, June 21, 1940.

48. Public Records Office, FO 800/326/190.

49. Public Records Office, FO 800/326/191.

50. Michael Bloch, *The Duke of Windsor's War*, p. 75, and Public Records Office, FO 800/326/195.

51. German Documents on Foreign Policy, Series D, Vol. X, B15/B002531.

52. Ibid, 136/74207.

53. Michael Bloch, *The Duke of Windsor's War*, p. 83.

54. Public Records Office, FO 800/326/197–8.

55. The Duke of Windsor, *Daily News*, New York, December 13, 1966.

56. The Duchess of Windsor, *The Heart has its Reasons*, p. 341.

57. Private information.

58. Sir Samuel Hoare (Madrid) No. 437, sent 9.30 p.m., June 27, 1940, received 4.30 a.m., June 28, 1940: Churchill Papers, 20/9.

59. Telegram No. 458, 'Secret and Personal', July 1, 1940: Churchill Papers, 20/9, quoted in Martin Gilbert, *Finest Hour*, p. 698.

60. Sir Alexander Hardinge to Winston Churchill, June 28, 1940: Churchill Paper, 20/9.

61. Sir Samuel Hoare (Madrid) No. 440, sent 6.45 p.m., June 28, 1940, received 3.30 a.m., June 29, 1940: Churchill Papers, 20/9.

62. Private information.

63. Michael Bloch, *The Duke of Windsor's War*, p. 82.

64. Foreign Relations of the United States 1940, Vol. III, 1939/4357, p. 41.

65. HM The Queen's broadcast to the Women of France, June 14, 1940.

66. The Duke of Windsor to Winston Churchill, undated draft, October 1940, quoted in Michael Bloch, *The Duke of Windsor's War*, p. 93.

67. Sir John Colville's diary, July 3, 1940: Colville Papers, quoted in Martin Gilbert, *Finest Hour*, p. 699.
68. Sir Ronald Storrs' diary, July 14, 1940: Storrs papers, Library of Pembroke College, Cambridge, quoted by Michael Bloch in *The Duke of Windsor's War*, p. 97.
69. 'Most Secret and Personal', 'Decypher Yourself', draft telegram, July 3, 1940: Churchill Papers, 20/9.
70. Telegram of July 4, 1940: Churchill Papers, 20/14.
71. The Duchess of Windsor, *The Heart has its Reasons*, p. 342.
72. In a letter to her aunt, Mrs Bessie Merryman, postmarked Cascais, July 15, 1940.
73. Lisbon Telegram No. 369, 'Most Immediate', 6.21 p.m., July 4, 1940: Churchill Papers, 20/9.
74. Lord Halifax to Sir Samuel Hoare, July 8, 1940: Templewood Papers, XIII/20.
75. Sir Alexander Hardinge to Eric Seal, July 9, 1940: Churchill Papers, 20/9.
76. Harold Nicolson to Vita Sackville-West, July 10, 1940, quoted in Harold Nicolson, *Diaries and Letters, 1939–45*, p. 100.
77. Margaret, Duchess of Argyll, *Forget Not*, p. 97.
78. The Duchess of Windsor to Mrs Bessie Merryman, undated letter postmarked July 15, 1940, from Cascais.
79. German Documents on Foreign Policy, Series D, Vol. X, B15/B002549-51.
80. Ibid, B15/B002549-51.
81. Eric Seal to Winston Churchill, July 16, 1940: Churchill Papers, 20/9.
82. Washington telegram No. 1373, 'Immediate', 'Personal', July 17, 1940: Churchill Papers 20/9.
83. Public Records Office, FO 371/24249/149.
84. John Peck to Winston Churchill, July 20, 1940, quoted in Martin Gilbert, *Finest Hour*, p. 703.
85. Martin Gilbert, *Finest Hour*, p. 703.
86. Ibid, p. 703.

87. John Peck to Winston Churchill, minute of July 20, 1940: Churchill Papers 20/9.
88. Winston Churchill to the Duke of Windsor, Foreign Office Telegram No. 478, 'Secret', July 23, 1940: Churchill Papers, 20/9.
89. German Documents on Foreign Policy, Series D, Vol. X, B15/B002582-3.
90. Ibid, B15/B002588.
91. David Pryce-Jones, 'TV Tale of Two Windsors', *The New York Times Magazine*, March 18, 1979.
92. Winston Churchill to the Duke of Windsor, 'Secret', July 27, 1940: Churchill Papers, 20/9.
93. The Dowager Lady Hardinge of Penshurst to Michael Thornton, July 23, 1974.
94. Michael Bloch to Michael Thornton, May 25, 1983.
95. The Duke of Windsor to Winston Churchill, July 31, 1940: Churchill Papers, 20/9.
96. German Documents on Foreign Policy, Series D, Vol. X, B15/B002632-3.
97. Ibid, B15/B002641-2.
98. Keith Middlemas and John Barnes, *Baldwin: A Biography*, p. 1016.
99. Lord Beaverbrook, *The Abdication of King Edward VIII*, p. 109.
100. Frances Donaldson, *Edward VIII*, p. 379.
[101] Ibid, p. 379. A non-royal duchess is addressed as 'Your Grace' only by servants and tradespeople. Socially, the correct form of address is simply 'Duchess'. The Duke of Windsor's intervention here, however, may have been more on grounds of policy than correctness. If the Duchess of Windsor had been addressed as 'Your Grace', it would have been an admission that she was indeed not a Royal Highness. The Duke's insistence on the use of 'Duchess' as a form of address, left open the burning issue of the H.R.H.
102. Frances Donaldson, *Edward VIII*, p. 379.

103. Public Records Office, FO 371/24249/192.

104. Lord Chamberlain to Sir Charles Dundas, Telegram 134, 'Secret and Personal', July 24, 1940.

105. Geoffrey Bocca, *She Might Have Been Queen*, p. 207.

106. Godfrey Talbot, *The Country Life Book of Queen Elizabeth The Queen Mother*, p. 64.

107. John W. Wheeler-Bennett, *King George VI: His Life and Reign*, p. 467.

108. Ibid, p. 467.

109. Kenneth Harris, 'A Royal lady loved for her human gifts', *The Observer*, London, August 3, 1980.

110. Dermot Morrah, *The Work of the Queen*, p. 22.

111. Queen Elizabeth to Queen Mary, October 19, 1940.

112. Robert E. Sherwood, *Roosevelt and Hopkins*, p. 252.

113. The Duchess of Windsor to Mrs Bessie Merryman, September 16, 1940.

114. Ibid, October 7, 1940.

115. Ibid, October 25, 1940.

116. Ibid, November 21, 1940.

117. Adela Rogers St Johns, *The Honeycomb*, p. 527.

118. The Duchess of Windsor to Mrs Bessie Merryman, September 16, 1940, quoted by Michael Bloch in *The Duke of Windsor's War*, p. 142.

119. The Duke of Windsor to Winston Churchill, undated typewritten draft, probably written in October 1940, quoted in Michael Bloch, *The Duke of Windsor's War*, p. 147.

120. Geoffrey Wakeford, *Thirty Years A Queen*, p. 188.

121. The Duchess of Windsor to Mrs Bessie Merryman, March 31, 1941.

122. Michael Bloch to Michael Thornton, May 25, 1983.

123. The Dowager Lady Hardinge of Penshurst in conversation with Michael Thornton, July 25, 1974.

124. The Duke of Windsor to Mrs Bessie Merryman, July 7, 1941.

125. German Documents on Foreign Policy, No. 1862, Vol. V, 8, 108869.

126. The interview with Fulton Oursler was published in *Liberty* on March 22, 1941, and in the *Sunday Dispatch*, London, on March 16, 1941.

127. Winston Churchill to the Duke of Windsor, 'Private and Personal', March 17, 1941: Churchill Papers 20/49.

128. The Duchess of Windsor to Mrs Bessie Merryman, July 23, 1941.

129. Ibid, August 6, 1941.

130. Igor Cassini, *Washington Times Herald*, September 26, 1941.

131. Lord Halifax's diary, October 17, 1941: Garrowby papers, quoted by Michael Bloch in *The Duke of Windsor's War*, p. 217.

132. British Press Service Report, 789/1941, November 24, 1941.

133. Martin Gilbert, *Finest Hour*, p. 984.

134. Winston Churchill to the Duke of Windsor, 'Private and Personal', March 17, 1941: Churchill Papers, 20/49.

135. Michael Bloch, *The Duke of Windsor's War*, pp. 234–235.

136. The Duchess of Windsor to Mrs Bessie Merryman, March 30, 1942.

137. Ibid, April 13, 1942.

138. Sir Etienne Dupuch, *Tribune Story*, p. 88.

139. The Duchess of Windsor, *The Heart has its Reasons*, p. 355.

140. Ibid, p. 356.

141. Ibid, p. 356.

142. The fourth Earl of Dudley to Michael Thornton, May 26, 1983.

143. The Duchess of Windsor to Mrs Bessie Merryman, July 16, 1942.

[144] The fourteenth Earl of Strathmore and Kinghorne died on November 7, 1944, at the age of eighty-nine.

145. Clementine Churchill, November 2, 1941, quoted in Mary Soames, *Clementine Churchill*, p. 309.

146. The Duchess of Windsor to Mrs Bessie Merryman, August 29, 1942.

147. The Duke of Windsor to Winston Churchill, November 10, 1942.

148. Winston Churchill to the Duke of Windsor, December 22, 1942, quoted by Michael Bloch in *The Duke of Windsor's War*, p. 282.

149. The Duchess of Windsor to Mrs Bessie Merryman, March 18, 1943.

150. *See* H. Montgomery Hyde, *The Quiet Canadian*, pp. 170–171.

151. Sir Robert Bruce Lockhart, entries for August 11, 1944; and January 27, 1942, *The Diaries of Sir Robert Bruce Lockhart, 1939–1965*, pp. 137, 338.

152. Ibid, p. 164, entry for May 14, 1942.

153. Ibid, p. 241, entry for June 19, 1943.

154. Ibid, pp. 241, 364, entries for June 19, 1943; and November 3, 1944.

155. Queen Elizabeth to Mrs Winston Churchill, May 15, 1943.

156. Lord Moran, *Winston Churchill, The Struggle for Survival*, p. 97.

157. Ibid, p.97.

158. National Archives, Washington DC, 811. 711/4039, June 18, 1943.

159. The Duke of Windsor to King George VI, June 2, 1943, pencilled draft reproduced in Michael Bloch, *The Duke of Windsor's War*, pp. 296–297.

160. Michael Bloch, *The Duke of Windsor's War*, p. 303.

161. Sir Robert Bruce Lockhart, May 31, 1943, *The Diaries of Sir Robert Bruce Lockhart, 1939–1965*, p. 239.

162. The Duchess of Windsor, *The Heart has its Reasons*, p. 355.

163. Dr Johannes von Müllern-Schönhausen Collection, Vienna, 220–24, quoted in John Toland, *Adolf Hitler*, p. 771.

164. Michael Bloch, *The Duke of Windsor's War*, p. 327.

165. Ibid, p. 334.

166. Ibid, p. 335.

167. The Duke of Windsor to Winston Churchill, October 3, 1944.

168. Michael Bloch, *The Duke of Windsor's War*, p. 338.

169. Winston Churchill to the Duke of Windsor, December 31, 1944, quoted by Michael Bloch in *The Duke of Windsor's War*, p. 348.

170. Sir John Balfour, *Encounters with the Windsors*, quoted in Frances Donaldson, *Edward VIII*, p. 377.

171. James Pope-Hennessy, *Queen Mary*, p. 614.

172. The Duchess of Windsor to Mrs Bessie Merryman, October 22, 1945.

173. The Duke of Windsor to King George VI, October 18, 1945.

174. King George VI to the Duke of Windsor, November 10, 1945. *See* Michael Bloch, *The Duke of Windsor's War*, p. 365.

175. *Sunday Times*, London, November 25, 1979.

176. Ibid.

177. *Kenneth Harris Talking To*, p. 130.

10. 'THE WOMAN WHO KILLED MY HUSBAND'

1. John W. Wheeler-Bennett, *King George VI: His Life and Reign*, p.654.

2. King George VI's diary, April 13, 1945.

3. King George VI to the Duke of Gloucester, January 21, 1946.

4. Dorothy Laird, *Queen Elizabeth The Queen Mother*, p. 17.

5. Philip Ziegler, *Diana Cooper*, p. 242.

6. Dorothy Laird, *Queen Elizabeth The Queen Mother*, p. 238.

7. Susan Mary Alsop, *To Marietta from Paris, 1945–1960*, p. 55.

8. Noël Coward, March 25, 1946, *The Noël Coward Diaries*, p. 54.

9. James A. Frere, *The British Monarchy At Home*, p. 123.

10. Craig Brown and Lesley Cunliffe, *The Book of Royal Lists*, p. 114.

11. Adela Rogers St Johns, *The Honeycomb*, p. 439.

·12. Loelia Lindsay and Hugo Vickers, *Cocktails and Laughter*, p. 10.

13. Laura Duchess of Marlborough, *Laughter from a Cloud*, pp. 104–105.

14. Ibid, pp. 101, 105–106.

15. *Evening Standard*, London, October 17, 1946.
16. Private information.
17. King George VI to Queen Mary, March 3, 1947.
18. Queen Elizabeth to Queen Mary, March 9, 1947.
19. Peter Townsend, *The Last Emperor*, p. 217.
20. Ibid (paperback edition), p. 272.
21. Ibid (paperback edition), p. 272.
22. Jennifer Ellis, *Elizabeth The Queen Mother*, p. 100.
23. Harold Nicolson, May 28, 1947, *Diaries and Letters, 1945–62*, pp. 98–99.
24. J. Bryan III and Charles J. V. Murphy, *The Windsor Story*, p. 383.
25. Inez Robb, *Daily Mirror*, New York, December 8, 1946.
26. Mary Soames, *Clementine Churchill*, p. 405.
27. John W. Wheeler-Bennett, *King George VI: His Life and Reign*, p. 755.
28. The Earl of Harewood, *The Tongs and the Bones: The Memoirs of Lord Harewood*, p. 17.
29. Noël Coward, December 10, 1947, *The Noël Coward Diaries*, p. 97.
30. Mary Soames, *Clementine Churchill*, p. 426.
31. Godfrey Winn, 'Her Ever Gracious Majesty', *Woman* Magazine, London, August 8, 1970.
32. King George VI's broadcast to the nation, April 26, 1948, recorded by HMV Records, RB 9654.
33. King George VI's journal, quoted in John W. Wheeler-Bennett, *King George VI: His Life and Reign*, p. 762.
34. John W. Wheeler-Bennett, *King George VI: His Life and Reign*, p. 765.
35. Harold Nicolson, March 21, 1949, *Diaries and Letters, 1945–62*, p. 167.
36. The Earl of Harewood, *The Tongs and the Bones: The Memoirs of Lord Harewood*, p. 103.
[37] Marion Crawford was born in Ayr-shire, on June 5, 1909. She married Major George Main Buthlay at Dunfermline Abbey on September 16, 1947.
38. Elizabeth Longford, *Elizabeth R*, p. 117.
39. Ibid, p. 117.
40. Queen Elizabeth's letter to Viscountess Astor is in the Astor archives at Reading University. See also Peter Tory, *Daily Mirror*, London, February 24, 1983.
41. Marion Crawford, *The Queen Mother* (Queen Mary), 1951; *Queen Elizabeth II*, 1952; *Princess Margaret*, 1953; and *Happy and Glorious*, 1953.
42. *Woman's Own*, London, June 16, 1955.
43. Peter Tory, *Daily Mirror*, London, February 24, 1983.
44. Eye-witness account of Mrs Renée Tovey, given to the author in April 1984.
45. Sir Henry Channon, December 3, 1950, *Chips: The Diaries of Sir Henry Channon*, p. 451.
[46] Anne Ferelith Fenella Bowes-Lyon married Viscount Anson on April 28, 1938, and divorced him in 1948. Their son (Thomas) Patrick John Anson, became the fifth Earl of Lichfield in 1960, and a well-known photographer. Their daughter, Lady Elizabeth Anson, became noted as a successful organizer of large parties and married another photographer, Sir Geoffrey Shakerley, sixth baronet, in 1972. Princess Georg of Denmark died in 1980.
[47] He became King Olav V of Norway in 1957.
48. James Pope-Hennessy, *A Lonely Business*, pp. 241–242.
49. J. Bryan III and Charles J. V. Murphy, *The Windsor Story*, p. 469.
50. Ibid, p. 470.
51. Ibid, pp. 473–474.
52. Louis Sobol, *Journal-American*, New York, December 7, 195· .

53. *New York Times*, December 7, 1950.
54. Queen Mary to the Duke of Windsor, February 27, 1951, quoted in James Pope-Hennessy, *Queen Mary*, p. 614.
55. Helen Hardinge, *Loyal to Three Kings*, p. 177.
56. *Times Literary Supplement*, London, September 28, 1951.
57. *Spectator*, London, September 28, 1951.
58. Frances Donaldson, *Edward VIII*, p. 399.
59. Helen Cathcart, *Princess Alexandra*, p. 79.
60. Private information. *See also* Elizabeth Longford, *The Queen Mother*, p. 117.
[61] The other occasions were in December 1936, when, as Duchess of York, she cancelled all public engagements during the week leading up to Edward VIII's abdication; and in October 1955 when, at the height of the crisis concerning Princess Margaret and Group Captain Peter Townsend, the Queen Mother avoided being photographed by having the windows of her car darkened as she drove in and out of Clarence House.
62. John W. Wheeler-Bennett, *King George VI: His Life and Reign*, p. 789.
63. Harold Nicolson, September 23, 1951, *Diaries and Letters, 1945–62*, p. 209.
64. John Gordon, *Sunday Express*, London, February 6, 1972.
65. Elizabeth Longford, *Elizabeth R.*, p. 132.
66. J. Bryan III and Charles J. V. Murphy, *The Windsor Story*, p. 459.
67. Adela Rogers St Johns, *The Honeycomb*, p. 539.
68. Philip Ziegler, *Diana Cooper*, p. 262.
69. Winston Churchill's broadcast on the death of King George VI, February 7, 1952.
70. Aubrey Buxton, *The King in His Country*, p. 138.
71. Ibid, p. 138.
72. A. J. P. Taylor, *Sunday Express*, London, September 29, 1957.
73. Queen Elizabeth The Queen Mother to Edward Seago, February 1952, quoted in Jean Goodman, *Edward Seago: The Other Side of the Canvas*, p. 213.
74. John W. Wheeler-Bennett, *King George VI: His Life and Reign*, p. 803.
75. Winston Churchill's broadcast, February 7, 1952.
76. *Daily Mirror*, London, February 7, 1952.
77. Helen Cathcart, *The Queen Mother*, p. 200.
78. Dorothy Laird, *Queen Elizabeth The Queen Mother*, p. 267.
79. Anthony Holden, *Charles, Prince of Wales*, p. 61.
80. James Pope-Hennessy, *Queen Mary*, p. 619.
81. Ibid, p. 619.
82. Peregrine Worsthorne, 'Women and right to the throne', *Sunday Telegraph*, London, January 10, 1982. See also Peter Tory, 'Drama of Queen Mother and a royal heir', *Daily Mirror*, London, January 11, 1982; and Patrick Montague-Smith, 'Heirs apparent and heirs presumptive', *Sunday Telegraph*, London, January 17, 1982.
83. Proclamation of the Accession of HM Queen Elizabeth II by Garter Principal King of Arms, Sir George Bellew, at St James's Palace, February 8, 1952: *Fifty Years of Royal Broadcasts, 1924–1974*, BBC Records, REJ 187.
84. Kenneth Hord, *Daily Mirror*, London, February 8, 1952.
85. Ibid.
86. *New York Times*, February 8, 1952.
87. *Southern Daily Echo*, Southampton, February 13, 1952.
88. *Daily Mirror*, London, February 7, 1952.
89. Queen Elizabeth II's speech at the

unveiling of King George VI's Memorial in the Mall, October 21, 1955.

90. Sir Henry Channon, February 15, 1952, *Chips, The Diaries of Sir Henry Channon*, p. 465.

91. Mabell, Countess of Airlie, *Thatched with Gold*, p. 235.

92. *Daily Mirror*, London, February 16, 1952.

93. HM Queen Elizabeth The Queen Mother's message to the nation, February 17, 1952.

94. Private Information. *See also* Anthony Holden, 'The Girl from Glamis who saved the Throne', *Sunday Express*, London, April 10, 1983.

11. WALLIS AND 'THE MONSTER OF GLAMIS'

1. Winston Churchill's broadcast to the nation, February 7, 1952.

2. Queen Elizabeth The Queen Mother to Edward Seago, quoted in Jean Goodman, *Edward Seago: The Other Side of the Canvas*, p. 213.

3. Lady Cynthia Colville, *A Crowded Life*, p. 132.

4. Cecil Beaton, *Self Portrait with Friends*, p. 249.

5. Elizabeth Longford, *The Queen Mother*, p. 140.

6. Dorothy Laird, *How the Queen Reigns*, p. 224.

7. Queen Elizabeth The Queen Mother to Dame Edith Sitwell, September 15, 1952, quoted in Victoria Glendinning, *Edith Sitwell: A Unicorn among Lions*, p. 299.

8. Sir Henry Channon's London house in Belgrave Square.

9. Sir Henry Channon, February 26, 1952, *Chips: The Diaries of Sir Henry Channon*, p. 465.

10. Geoffrey Bocca, *She Might Have Been Queen*, p. 11.

11. *American Weekly*, December 18, 1955.

12. Stephen Birmingham, *Duchess*, p. 253.

13. Mary Van Rensselaer Thayer, *Washington Post*, March 2, 1956.

14. The Earl of Harewood, *The Tongs and the Bones: The Memoirs of Lord Harewood*, p. 18.

15. To the actress, Lilli Palmer. *See* her autobiography, *Change Lobsters and Dance*, p. 207.

16. The Duke of Windsor to the Duchess of Windsor, March 1953, quoted in Michael Bloch, *The Duke of Windsor's War*, p. 241.

17. Sir Henry Channon, March 29, 1953, *Chips: The Diaries of Sir Henry Channon*, p. 473.

18. Private information.

19. Helen Cathcart, *The Queen Mother*, p. 129.

[20] Prior to Queen Mary's attendance at the Coronation of King George VI and Queen Elizabeth in 1937, it had been the accepted tradition for a British dowager queen to remain absent from the crowning of her husband's successor.

21. Private Information.

22. Cecil Beaton, *Self Portrait with Friends*, p. 249.

23. Lady Olga Maitland, *Sunday Express*, London, October 2, 1983.

24. *Daily Express*, London, June 3, 1953.

25. Private information. See also Ralph G. Martin, *The Woman He Loved*, p. 468.

[26] Truman Capote, 'Indelible Exits and Entrances', *Esquire*, New York, Volume 99, No. 3, March 1983. Capote mistakenly places the incident in 1952, but Coward's own diaries prove that it took place at the end of August 1953.

27. Andrew Barrow, *Gossip, 1920–1970*, p. 176.

28. Peter Saunders, *The Mousetrap Man*, p. 144.

29. Dorothy Laird, *Queen Elizabeth The Queen Mother*, p. 278.

30. *New York Times*, October 26, 1954.

31. Charles Ventura, *New York World-Telegram*.

32. J. Bryan III and Charles J. V. Murphy, *The Windsor Story*, p. 483.

33. Peter Townsend, *Time and Chance*, p. 198.

34. Mrs Gilbert Miller to the author, June 14, 1976.

35. Elizabeth Longford, *Elizabeth R*, p. 152.

36. Peter Townsend, *Time and Chance*, p. 194.

37. Private information.

[38] Group Captain Peter Townsend returned to Brussels to his post as air attaché, which he left in 1956 in order to take up a writing career. He met Princess Margaret again on March 26, 1958, when the Queen Mother invited him to Clarence House, and in May of the same year he was invited to lunch at Royal Lodge. On December 21, 1959, he married Marie Luce Jamagne, a twenty-year-old Belgian tobacco heiress. They have a son and two daughters.

39. James Pope-Hennessy, *A Lonely Business*, p. 213.

40. J. Bryan III and Charles J. V. Murphy, *The Windsor Story*, p. 517.

41. Stephen Birmingham, *Duchess*, p. 249.

42. The Duchess of Windsor, *The Heart has its Reasons*, p. 225.

43. Charles J. V. Murphy's letter to Michael Thornton, June 14, 1983.

44. James Lees-Milne, *Harold Nicolson, 1930–1968*, p. 268.

45. H. Montgomery Hyde's letter to Michael Thornton, July 19, 1983.

46. Harold Nicolson, March 28, 1956, *Diaries and Letters, 1945–62*, p. 299.

47. Mrs Gilbert Miller to Michael Thornton, June 14, 1976.

48. J. Bryan III and Charles J. V. Murphy, *The Windsor Story*, p. 519.

49. Frances Donaldson, *Edward VIII*, p. 401.

50. Sir Oswald Mosley, *My Life*, p. 374.

51. *See* chapter 17 of Diana Mosley's autobiography, *A Life of Contrasts* (Hamish Hamilton, London, 1977).

[52] He later became Lord Gladwyn.

[53] James Pope-Hennessy's posthumous self-portrait, *A Lonely Life*, p. 209, mistakenly gives the date as 1958.

54. James Pope-Hennessy, *A Lonely Life*, pp. 210–211.

55. Ibid, p. 211.

56. Ibid, p. 216.

57. Ibid, p. 217.

58. Ibid, p. 223.

59. J. Bryan III and Charles J. V. Murphy, *The Windsor Story*, p. 407.

60. Mrs Gilbert Miller to Michael Thornton, June 14, 1976.

61. J. Bryan III and Charles J. V. Murphy, *The Windsor Story*, p. 407. Also J. Bryan III's letter to Michael Thornton, May 18, 1983.

62. To Michael Thornton at Glamis Castle during a visit in November 1969.

[63] The funeral took place on September 11, 1967.

64. Mrs Gilbert Miller told the author on June 14, 1976, that this was the Duchess of Windsor's reaction to the Strathmore tragedy and also her private assessment of the Queen Mother's character.

65. Betty Spencer Shew, *Queen Elizabeth The Queen Mother*, p. 15.

66. Mrs Gilbert Miller to Michael Thornton, June 14, 1976.

67. *News of the World*, London, October 1, 1961.

[68] The Hon. Sir David Bowes-Lyon died on September 13, 1961.

69. Private information. This is a favourite philosophy of the Queen Mother. *See* David Sinclair, *Queen and Country*, p. 236, and Ann Morrow, *The Queen Mother*, p. 191.

70. Private information.

71. *The Wedding of Her Royal High-ness Princess Alexandra of Kent and The Honourable Angus Ogilvy, Approved Souvenir Programme*, p. 31.

72. Susan Barnes, 'My Husband Has Been Deeply Hurt, Says The Duch-ess', *Sunday Express*, London, December 8, 1983.

12. THE DUCHESS BECOMES PERSONA GRATA

1. Helen Cathcart, *The Queen Mother*, p. 129.

[2] Sir Michael Adeane was Principal Private Secretary for twenty years, retiring in 1972, when he was created Lord Adeane, a life peer. He was succeeded by Sir Martin Charteris, now Lord Charteris and Provost of Eton.

[3] Walter Monckton, the first Vis-count Monckton of Brenchley, had died on January 9, 1965.

4. J. Bryan III and Charles J. V. Mur-phy, *The Windsor Story*, p. 528.

5. Private information.

6. Noël Coward, February 28, 1965, *The Noël Coward Diaries*, p. 593.

7. Private information.

8. Dorothy Laird, *Queen Elizabeth The Queen Mother*, p. 17.

9. Confirmed by Sir Martin Gilliat in his letter to Michael Thornton of May 23, 1983.

10. Private information.

[11] Queen Victoria's body lies in the Royal Mausoleum at Frogmore, which she had had built in 1864 as a last resting place for her dead husband, Prince Albert, and, ultimately, for herself.

12. Private information.

13. *Daily Express*, London, March 16, 1965.

14. Ibid.

15. *The Observer*, London, March 21, 1965.

16. Godfrey Winn, *Woman*, London, October 29, 1966.

[17] On January 30, 1965, the Glouces-ters were driving back to Barnwell Manor, their Northamptonshire home, from Buckingham Palace, where they had attended the Queen's lunch party following the funeral of Sir Winston Churchill. The Duke, although warned to give up driving by his doctors because of circulatory problems, insisted on taking the wheel of his Rolls Royce. Not far from home, with the Duch-ess dozing in the front seat beside him and their chauffeur, William Prater, in the back, the Duke lost control of the Rolls, which swerved off the road, crossed a footpath and a four-foot ditch, crashed through a thorn hedge, somersaulted three times and ended upside down in a cabbage field. The Duke, thrown clear, was virtually unscathed. Pra-ter had rib damage, and the Duchess had a broken arm, a broken nose, a cracked knee and deep facial wounds. Following close behind was a bus carrying a team of Mans-field miners who belonged to the St John's Ambulance Brigade. They administered first-aid until the ambulance arrived to take the Gloucesters and Prater to Bedford Hospital, where fifty-seven stitches were inserted in the Duchess's face. When the Duke later tried to visit his wife's bedside, she was too angry to see him. (Craig Brown and Lesley Cunliffe, *The Book of Royal Lists*, pp. 77–78.)

This accident is usually regarded as the start of the long illness that led to a series of strokes which para-lysed the Duke of Gloucester, de-prived him of the power of speech, and relegated him to a wheelchair until his death on June 10, 1974.

18. *Daily Mail*, London, March 20, 1965.

19. Private information. *See also* J. Bryan III and Charles J. V. Murphy, *The Windsor Story*, p. 553.

20. The Earl of Harewood, *The Tongs and the Bones: The Memoirs of Lord Harewood*, p. 295.

21. *Daily Express*, London, March 30, 1965.

22. *The Times*, London, April 2, 1965.

23. *Daily Express*, London, April 2, 1965.

[24] She was created Baroness Spencer-Churchill, a life peeress, two weeks later, on May 17, 1965.

25. *Daily Express*, London, May 4, 1965.

26. *Daily Mail*, London, May 4, 1965.

[27] The visit by Princess Alexandra and the Hon. Angus Ogilvy took place in May 1965, as confirmed by the Princess's private secretary, Miss Mona Mitchell, in her letter to Michael Thornton of July 12, 1983.

28. Godfrey Winn, *Woman*, London, October 29, 1966.

29. Mrs Gilbert Miller to Michael Thornton, June 14, 1976.

30. Andrew Duncan, *The Reality of Monarchy*, p. 87.

31. Helen Cathcart, *The Queen Mother Herself*, p. 220. On the subject of 'Miss Cathcart's' real identity, *see* chapter 2, note 58.

32. Jean Rook, *Daily Express*, London, July 16, 1980.

33. Elizabeth Longford, *The Queen Mother*, published in 1981.

34. Ibid, p. 157.

35. The Countess of Longford's letter to Michael Thornton, June 20, 1983.

36. Helen Cathcart to Michael Thornton, undated letter, received on June 22, 1983.

37. The Earl of Harewood, *The Tongs and the Bones: The Memoirs of Lord Harewood*, p. 295.

38. Private information.

[39] The Earl of Harewood, *The Tongs and the Bones: The Memoirs of Lord Harewood*, p. 220. Lady Harewood received a decree nisi in April, which became absolute early in July 1967. On July 28, the Queen, under the Royal Marriages Act of 1772, gave her consent to her cousin's re-marriage, and on July 31, 1967, Patricia Tuckwell became the new Countess of Harewood in a civil ceremony before a judge in New Canaan, Connecticut. Marion, Countess of Harewood, married secondly, on March 14, 1973, Jeremy Thorpe, leader of the Liberal Party until his much-publicized resignation on May 10, 1976.

40. Princess Marie Louise, *My Memories of Six Reigns*, p. 112.

41. J. Bryan III and Charles J. V. Murphy, *The Windsor Story*, p. 531.

42. *Daily Telegraph*, London, June 6, 1967.

43. Ibid.

44. Ibid.

45. *Daily Mail*, London, June 6, 1967.

46. BBC and ITV news bulletins, London, June 5, 1967.

47. *Daily Mirror*, London, June 6, 1967.

48. J. Bryan III and Charles J. V. Murphy, *The Windsor Story*, p. 532.

49. *Daily Express*, London, June 6, 1967.

50. Lilli Palmer, *Change Lobsters and Dance*, pp. 207–208.

51. The Duke of Windsor to the Duke of Gloucester, February 7, 1967.

[52] That was on March 9, 1967. Noble Frankland in *Prince Henry, Duke of Gloucester*, p. 292, mistakenly says that this was the last meeting between the brothers, but in fact there were two further meetings – on June 6, 1967, at the York House luncheon, and on the following day, at the unveiling of Queen Mary's plaque. Princess Alice, Duchess of Gloucester, in her *Memoirs*, p. 191, repeats Dr Frankland's error.

53. Letters to Michael Thornton from Hugo Vickers, May 13, 1983, and from Lt-Colonel Sir Simon Bland, May 26, 1983.

54. Lt-Colonel Sir Simon Bland to

Michael Thornton, June 27, 1983.

55. Hugo Vickers to Michael Thornton, May 13, 1983.

56. *Evening Standard*, London, June 7, 1967.

57. *The Guardian*, London, June 8, 1967.

58. *Daily Express*, London, June 3, 1967.

59. John Ellison, 'Wallis Windsor, Duchess in Exile', *Daily Express*, London, February 13, 1979.

60. Hugo Vickers to Michael Thornton, June 14, 1983.

61. Mrs Gilbert Miller to Michael Thornton, June 14, 1976.

62. John Ellison, *Daily Express*, London, February 13, 1979.

63. Ibid. The same exchange was also recounted to the author by Mrs Gilbert Miller on June 14, 1976.

64. *Daily Sketch*, London, June 7, 1967.

65. On the Windsors' failure to send any message of sympathy to Princess Marina, *see* Alastair Forbes, *Times Literary Supplement*, London, November 1, 1974, and January 4, 1980; also J. Bryan III and Charles J. V. Murphy, *The Windsor Story*, p. 447.

[66] Miss Alison Dixon, Private Secretary to Prince and Princess Michael of Kent, writes, in her letter to Michael Thornton of May 26, 1983: 'I have looked at Princess Marina's Visitors Book and the only two signatures for that date (June 7, 1967) are those of the Duke and Duchess of Windsor, which means any other guests present were members of the Kent family or they would have signed the book'.

67. *The Times* and *Daily Telegraph*, London, June 8, 1967.

68. Philip M. Thomas, 'The Duchess of Windsor – Her Position Reappraised', pp. xxi–xxiii, 104th edition of *Burke's Peerage*, 1967.

69. Peter Ustinov, *Dear Me*, p. 243.

70. Cecil Beaton, *Self Portrait with Friends*, p. 397.

71. The Duchess's inclusion in the invitation, and the Duke's flight, were confirmed by John Haslam, the Queen's Assistant Press Secretary, in his letter to the author of June 27, 1983.

72. Hugo Vickers to Michael Thornton, June 14, 1983.

[73] Who became the present Duke of Gloucester on his father's death on June 10, 1974.

74. J. Bryan III and Charles J. V. Murphy, *The Windsor Story*, p. 555, for a description of the plane tree, and Buckingham Palace letters to the author of May 25, 1983, from Michael Shea, and June 27, 1983, from John Haslam, confirming the proximity to the graves of the Duke of Kent and Princess Marina, plus the fact that the Duke of Windsor chose the site himself.

75. *Kenneth Harris talking to*, p. 139.

76. Frances Donaldson, *King George VI and Queen Elizabeth*, p. 34.

77. Sir John Aird's opinion, given to J. Bryan III and Charles J. V. Murphy, *The Windsor Story*, p. 318.

78. *Kenneth Harris Talking to*, p. 132.

79. Frances Donaldson, *Edward VIII*, p. 406.

80. Ibid, p. 405.

81. *Kenneth Harris Talking to*, p. 141.

[82] Now Lord Soames.

83. Anthony Holden, *Charles, Prince of Wales*, p. 32.

84. Ibid, p. 33.

13. 'I KNOW HOW YOU FEEL'

[1] The House of Commons debate was on December 14, 1971. Lady Longford, in *Elizabeth R*, p. 282, mistakenly places this event in the late 1970s, 'when the Queen Mother was approaching eighty', and quotes a sum of £92,000 instead of £95,000.

2. *Daily Mirror*, London, December 16, 1971.

3. Willie Hamilton, MP, *My Queen and I*, p. 60.

4. Quoted by Diana Mosley in *The Duchess of Windsor*, p. 201.

5. Joan Reeder, 'The end of a King's Story', *Woman*, London, July 5, 1980.

6. Cecil Beaton, *Self Portrait with Friends*, pp. 405–407.

7. J. Bryan III and Charles J. V. Murphy, *The Windsor Story*, p. 565.

8. Ibid, p. 565.

9. Joan Reeder, 'The end of a King's Story', *Woman*, London, July 5, 1980.

10. *See also* J. Bryan III and Charles J. V. Murphy, *The Windsor Story*, p. 546.

11. Joan Reeder, 'The end of a King's Story', *Woman*, London, July 5, 1980.

12. Diana Mosley, *The Duchess of Windsor*, p. 219.

13. Joan Reeder, 'The end of a King's Story', *Woman*, London, July 5, 1980.

14. Ibid.

15. J. Bryan III and Charles J. V. Murphy, *The Windsor Story*, p. 547.

16. Ibid, p. 547.

17. Joan Reeder, 'The end of a King's Story', *Woman*, London, July 5, 1980.

18. Sam White, *Evening Standard*, London, May 30, 1972.

19. James Pope-Hennessy, *A Lonely Business*, p. 215.

20. Joan Reeder, 'The end of a King's Story', *Woman*, London, July 5, 1980.

21. Ibid.

22. Ibid.

23. Ibid.

24. Andrew Barrow, *International Gossip, A History of High Society 1970–1980*, p. 64.

25. Joan Reeder, 'The end of a King's Story', *Woman*, London, July 5, 1980.

26. J. Bryan III and Charles J. V. Murphy, *The Windsor Story*, p. 548.

27. Joan Reeder, 'The end of a King's Story', *Woman*, London, July 5, 1980.

28. Ibid.

[29] Ibid. The official Buckingham Palace statement gave the time of the Duke's death as five minutes later than Nurse Shanley recorded it, possibly to accord with the added statement that the Duchess was at the bedside when her husband died. In fact she was not, although J. Bryan III and Charles J. V. Murphy in *The Windsor Story*, p. 548, claim that 'He died in his wife's arms at one twenty-three on Sunday morning.'

30. Joan Reeder, 'The end of a King's Story', *Woman*, London, July 5, 1980.

31. *Daily Mail*, London, May 29, 1972.

32. *The Guardian*, London, May 29, 1972.

33. *Daily Express*, London, May 29, 1972.

34. *The Guardian*, London, May 29, 1972.

35. *Daily Mail*, London, May 29, 1972.

36. *The Sun*, London, May 29, 1972.

37. *Evening News*, London, May 29, 1972.

38. Private information.

[39] The third wife and widow of the Duke of Windsor's close friend, the third Earl of Dudley, who had died in 1969. Born Grace Maria Kolin in Yugoslavia, she had formerly been the wife of Prince Stanislas Radziwill before marrying Lord Dudley in 1961.

40. Lady Soames's letter to Michael Thornton of July 13, 1983.

41. *The Times* and *Daily Telegraph*, London, June 3, 1972.

42. Jean Rook, *Daily Express*, London, May 31, 1972.

43. *Sunday Express*, London, June 4, 1972.

44. Vincent Mulchrone, *Daily Mail*, London, June 5, 1972.

45. Atticus, *The Sunday Times*, London, June 11, 1972.
46. *See* Noble Frankland, *Prince Henry, Duke of Gloucester*, p. 294.
47. Vincent Mulchrone, *Daily Mail*, London, June 6, 1972.
48. Stephen Birmingham, *Duchess*, p. 263.
49. Vincent Mulchrone, *Daily Mail*, London, June 6, 1972.
50. Private information.
51. Stephen Birmingham, *Duchess*, p. 263.
52. J. Bryan III and Charles J. V. Murphy, *The Windsor Story*, p. 555.
53. *Daily Mail*, London, June 5, 1972.
54. *Hansard, The Parliamentary Debates*, House of Commons, Fifth Series – Volume 838, Session 1971–72, 5th June–16th June, 1972, p. 37.
55. Ibid, p. 41.
56. Ibid, p. 41.
57. Ibid, p. 41.
58. Ibid, pp. 42–43.
59. Ibid, p. 44.
60. Ibid, p. 47.
61. Ibid, pp. 48–49.
62. Ibid, p. 49.
63. *Hansard, The Parliamentary Debates*, Fifth Series – Volume CCCXXXI, House of Lords, Seventh Volume of Session, 5th June–16 June, 1972, p. 7.
64. Ibid, p. 6.
65. *The Times* and *Daily Telegraph*, London, June 6, 1972.

14. 'IN FRIENDSHIP'

1. J. Bryan III and Charles J. V. Murphy, *The Windsor Story*, p. 568.
2. Ibid, p. 563. *Also* Charles Murphy, *Time* Magazine, New York, November 19, 1973.
[3] Prince Charles, Princess Margaret, Princess Alice, Countess of Athlone and Prince Michael of Kent were also present. The Queen and Prince Philip did not attend.
4. *News of the World*, London, September 3, 1972.
5. Patrick Montague-Smith, 'The Title of H.R.H.', *Debrett's Peerage, Baronetage, Knightage and Companionage*, 1972, pp. 13–15.
6. Letter to *The Times*, London, September 25, 1972.
7. Patrick Montague-Smith to Michael Thornton, May 17, 1983.
[8] In October 1973, after *Crown Matrimonial* had been running in London for a year, Phyllis Calvert took over the role of Queen Mary and John Fraser that of King Edward VIII. In 1974, when Miss Calvert took the play on a tour of the British provinces, Marcia Ashton played the Duchess of York. On October 2,
1973, the play opened at the Helen Hayes Theatre, New York – it was a short-lived failure – and Ruth Hunt played the Duchess of York, with Eileen Herlie as Queen Mary. In the British television production of *Crown Matrimonial* in 1974, starring Greer Garson as Queen Mary and Peter Barkworth as Edward VIII, Amanda Reiss again played the Duchess of York, as she did in the 1978 Thames Television series, *Edward and Mrs. Simpson*, with Edward Fox as Edward VIII, Cynthia Harris as Wallis Simpson, Dame Peggy Ashcroft as Queen Mary, and Andrew Ray as the Duke of York.

In January and February 1978, Jennifer Wilson portrayed the Queen Mother in Peter Clapham's *Most Gracious Lady*, 'an entertainment in words and music about the Queens of England from Elizabeth I to Elizabeth II', which toured the British provinces with Dame Anna Neagle as the star. On June 26, 1978, a second stage play about the Abdication, *The Woman I Love*, by

Dan Sutherland, opened at the Churchill Theatre, Bromley, Kent, with Martin Jarvis as Edward VIII, Holly Palance as Wallis Simpson, Ellen Pollock as Queen Mary, and Robert Beatty as Lord Beaverbrook. It was not presented in the West End.

On November 21, 1981, at the Palace Theatre, London, Gwen Nelson played the Queen Mother in *Her Royal Highness?*, a comedy by Royce Ryton (author of *Crown Matrimonial*) and Ray Cooney about the romance of Lady Diana Spencer and Prince Charles. It was savaged by the London critics and closed swiftly. In 1982, Gladys Crosbie appeared (silently) as the Queen Mother in Lindsay Anderson's satirical film, *Britannia Hospital*.

In the same year, Olivia de Havilland played the Queen Mother in *Charles and Diana, a Royal Love Story*, one of two American television films on the same saga. Miss de Havilland was a surprising choice, having brown eyes, and was unable to wear the blue-tinted contact lenses designed to make her look more authentic. In the rival television film, *Charles and Diana*, also made in 1982, the Queen Mother was played by Mona Washbourne. In 1983, John Standing (in private life Sir John Leon, fourth baronet) was cast as the Duke of Windsor and Barbara Parkins as the Duchess of Windsor in the film, *To Catch A King*, based on the alleged plot to kidnap the Windsors in Portugal in 1940.

9. The Duchess of Windsor, *The Heart has its Reasons*, p. 225.

10. *Crown Matrimonial* by Royce Ryton, Act Two, Scene Two, unpublished play script from the presenting London management, Michael Codron Ltd, pp. 2.2.7, 2.2.14, 2.2.17.

11. Private information.

12. Lady Cynthia Asquith, *The Duchess of York*, p. 80.

13. Elizabeth Longford, *Elizabeth R*, p. 302.

14. See Diana Mosley, *The Duchess of Windsor*, p. 209. Lady Mosley mistakenly calls the film, *The Woman He Loved*, which was the title of a book by Ralph G. Martin.

15. John Ellison, 'Wallis Windsor, Duchess in Exile', *Daily Express*, London, February 17, 1979.

16. The Duchess of Windsor to Margaret, Duchess of Argyll. Letter shown to the author.

17. Hugo Vickers, 'Are you being Sirred?', *Tatler*, London, Volume 276, Number 6, July 1981. Mr Vickers was shown the Christmas cards at the Duchess's house on March 9, 1973, by her deputy secretary, Miss Johanna Schütz, who had retained them after they had been discarded by the Duchess.

18. Ralph G. Martin, *The Woman He Loved*, pp. 496–497.

19. J. Bryan III and Charles J. V. Murphy, *The Windsor Story*, p. 566.

20. Ibid, p. 560.

21. Told by Maître Blum to David Pryce-Jones, 'TV Tale of Two Windsors', *New York Times Magazine*, March 18, 1979.

[22] Suzanne Blum was born on November 24, 1898. The title, Maître, is the standard designation for all members of the French legal profession, regardless of sex.

23. Sam White, *Evening Standard*, London, October 8, 1976.

[24] He was promoted to Captain three months later.

25. UPI report, *The Times*, London, May 30, 1973.

[26] J. Bryan III and Charles J. V. Murphy in *The Windsor Story*, p. 562, mistakenly give the date as June 23, the anniversary of the Duke's birthday. They also add that the Duchess 'had tea with the Queen', an impossibility, since Elizabeth II was in Scotland on July 11.

27. Stephen Birmingham, *Duchess*, pp. 267–268.

28. *Daily Express*, London, October 6, 1973.

29. *Evening News*, London, October 31, 1973.

30. J. Bryan III and Charles J. V. Murphy, *The Windsor Story*, pp. 565–566.

31. Andrew Barrow, *International Gossip*, p. 107.

32. Private information. *See also Sunday Express*, London, June 13, 1976, and *Daily Express*, London, March 3, 1978.

33. Private information.

34. J. Bryan III and Charles J. V. Murphy, *The Windsor Story*, p. 566.

35. Ibid, p. 566.

[36] The Earl of Snowdon's letter to Michael Thornton, June 1, 1983. Lord Snowdon had met the Duchess several times before – at the Duke's funeral in 1972, and some years before that in Venice with his uncle, Oliver Messel.

37. Lord Napier and Ettrick's letter to Michael Thornton, May 17, 1983.

38. Lord Napier and Ettrick's letter to Michael Thornton, May 25, 1983.

39. Stephen Birmingham, *Duchess*, p. 267.

40. Ibid, pp. 270–271.

[41] The Register and Recorder at Chambersburg Courthouse in Pennsylvania has no record of Bessiewallis Warfield's birth at Blue Ridge Summit on June 19, 1896, but registration was not compulsory at that time. Iles Brody, in *Gone With The Windsors*, p. 61, claims possession of two letters from contemporaries which allege that Wallis was actually born in 1890, five years before her parents' marriage, but Brody admits that jealousy on the part of both correspondents cannot be ruled out. There is no evidence – except rumour – to support an earlier date, and much to support the official date. The details of. Wallis's schooling and her

appearance at the time of her debutante season in 1914–15 all point to her having been born in 1896.

42. 'Town Talk', *Sunday Express*, London, September 7, 1975.

43. Lady Donaldson of Kingsbridge to Michael Thornton, undated letter, received in August 1983.

44. David Pryce-Jones, 'TV Tale of Two Windsors', *New York Times Magazine*, March 18, 1979.

45. Weidenfeld and Nicolson, London, 1977.

46. Prudence Glynn, *The Times*, London, April 15, 1975.

47. Nicholas de Jongh, *The Guardian*, London, August 4, 1975.

48. Willie Hamilton, *My Queen and I*, pp. 175–176.

[49] The widow of the second Baron Manton, she had married Lord Brownlow in 1969.

50. *Daily Express*, London, October 22, 1975.

51. Ibid.

52. Frances Donaldson, *Edward VIII*, p. 324.

53. J. Bryan III and Charles J. V. Murphy, *The Windsor Story*, p. 567.

54. Diana Mosley, *The Duchess of Windsor*, p. 209.

55. Andrew Barrow, *International Gossip*, p. 164.

56. J. Bryan III and Charles J. V. Murphy, *The Windsor Story*, p. 549.

[57] David Pryce-Jones, 'TV Tale of Two Windsors', *New York Times Magazine*, March 18, 1979. John Utter died in September 1980.

58. Nigel Dempster, *Daily Mail*, London, February 12, 1976.

59. Michael Thornton, 'The Royal Birthday for Which No Flags Will Fly', *Sunday Express*, London, June 13, 1976.

60. Ibid.

61. Johanna Schütz to Michael Thornton, July 1, 1976.

62. J. Bryan III and Charles J. V. Murphy, *The Windsor Story*, p. 566.

63. Mrs Gilbert Miller to Michael Thornton, June 14, 1976.

[64] Who had succeeded Sir Edward and Lady Tomkins in 1975.

65. *Sunday Express*, London, August 8, 1976.

66. *Daily Mail*, London, August 25, 1976.

67. The date and time of the scheduled visit is confirmed by Sir Martin Gilliat in his letter to Michael Thornton of May 23, 1983.

68. Peter McKay, *Sunday Express*, London, October 17, 1976.

69. *The Times*, London, October 27, 1976.

70. Private information.

71. J. Bryan III and Charles J. V. Murphy, *The Windsor Story*, pp. 568 –569.

72. Anna Christian Burke, *The Language of Flowers*, p. 50.

73. Private information. *See also* Mervyn Pamment, *Sunday People*, London, November 7, 1976.

15. A NATION'S GRATITUDE

1. Godfrey Talbot, *The Country Life Book of Queen Elizabeth The Queen Mother*, p. 164.

2. *Daily Express*, London, May 16, 1977.

[3] Walter Monckton's only daughter, Valerie, the wife of Sir (William) Basil Goulding, third baronet.

4. *Daily Mail*, London, July 20, 1977.

5. *Daily Express*, London, July 23, 1977.

6. Charles Laurence, *Sunday Telegraph*, London, March 4, 1979.

7. *Daily Telegraph*, London, November 10, 1977.

8. *Daily Express*, London, November 16, 1977.

9. Andrew Barrow, *International Gossip*, p. 215.

10. Nigel Dempster, *Daily Mail*, London, February 7, 1978.

11. Anthony Holden, *Charles, Prince of Wales*, pp. 245, 247.

[12] Five years later, on July 29, 1983, the Vatican, under a new Pope, John Paul II, relented, and Prince and Princess Michael retook their wedding vows in a 15-minute service in Cardinal Basil Hume's private chapel at Archbishop House, Westminster.

13. Tom Langmaid, *The Observer*, London, June 11, 1978.

14. Confirmed by Miss Alison Dixon, private secretary to Prince and Princess Michael of Kent, in her letter to the author of May 26, 1983.

15. Compton Miller, *Evening News*, London, March 14, 1978.

16. By James Brough, author of a book entitled, *Margaret: The Tragic Princess* (1978), pp. 236–249.

17. *Sunday Express*, London, August 28, 1977.

[18] On December 15, 1978, Lord Snowdon married again at Kensington Register Office to his close companion for more than two years, Mrs Lucy Lindsay-Hogg.

19. Godfrey Talbot, *The Country Life Book of Queen Elizabeth The Queen Mother*.

20. Ibid, p. 7.

21. David Pryce-Jones, 'TV Tale of Two Windsors', *New York Times Magazine*, March 18, 1979.

22. Audrey Whiting, *Sunday Mirror*, London, June 18, 1978.

23. *Evening News*, London, November 7, 1978.

24. *Sunday Express*, London, November 12, 1978.

25. *Daily Express*, London, November 22, 1978.

26. David Pryce-Jones, 'TV Tale of Two Windsors', *New York Times Magazine*, March 18, 1979.

27. *Daily Express*, London, November 22, 1978.

28. *Daily Mail*, London, November 27, 1978.

29. *The Times*, London, November 27, 1978.
30. *Sunday Times*, London, November 26, 1978.
31. Stephen Birmingham, *Duchess*, p. 273.
32. *Daily Mail*, London, November 27, 1978.
33. Ibid.
34. *Daily Express*, London, December 2, 1978.
35. *New York Times Magazine*, March 18, 1979.
36. Ibid.
37. Lady Olga Maitland, *Sunday Express*, London, June 24, 1979.
38. Ibid.
39. *Sunday Telegraph*, London, March 4, 1979.
40. *Daily Telegraph*, London, August 2, 1979.
41. Peter Greig, *Daily Mail*, London, February 14, 1980.
42. William Wolff, *Evening News*, London, February 18, 1980.
43. Ibid.
44. *Daily Mail*, London, July 16, 1980.
45. *Daily Express*, London, July 16, 1980.
46. Diana Mosley, *The Duchess of Windsor*, p. 211.
47. Queen Elizabeth The Queen Mother's reply to Addresses of Congratulations from the House of Lords and the House of Commons, August 5, 1980.
48. Private information.
49. HM The Queen's Christmas broadcast, December 25, 1980.
50. Private information.
51. *Daily Mirror*, London, April 29, 1982.
52. *Sunday Telegraph*, London, May 2, 1982.
53. Sir Martin Gilliat's letter to Michael Thornton, May 23, 1983.
54. Lady Olga Maitland, *Sunday Express*, London, June 20, 1982.
55. *Daily Express*, London, June 23, 1982.
56. *Timewatch*, BBC-2, September 29, 1982.
57. Herbert Kretzmer, *Daily Mail*,

London, September 30, 1982.
58. Stephen Birmingham, *Duchess*, p. 247
59. Ibid, p. 273.
60. Nigel Dempster, *Daily Mail*, London, November 24, 1982.
61. Private information.
62. *Daily Express*, London, November 24, 1982.
63. *Sunday Express*, London, November 28, 1982.
64. *Daily Mirror*, London, April 21, 1983.
65. *Daily Express*, London, June 21, 1983.
[66] On July 2, 1983.
67. Alan Hamilton, *The Times*, London, July 14, 1983.
68. *Daily Express*, London, November 11, 1983.
69. *Daily Express*, London, March 26, 1984.
70. William Payne's letter to Michael Thornton, March 7, 1984.
71. Lady Mosley's letter to Michael Thornton, May 14, 1983.
72. Brian Vine, *Daily Mail*, London, January 18, 1985.
[73] She died on November 28, 1964, three months after her one hundredth birthday.
[74] Her last sister, Rose, Countess Granville, died on November 17, 1967.
75. Dick Barton's letter to Michael Thornton, March 22, 1984.
76. Daily Express, London, April 29, 1986.
77. Daily Express, London, May 5, 1986.
78. Ibid.
79. Sunday Express, London, May 4, 1986.
80. Lady Mosley's letter to Michael Thornton, May 14, 1983.
81. J. Bryan III and Charles J. V. Murphy, *The Windsor Story*, p. 569.
82. Cole Lesley, *The Life of Noël Coward*, p. 187.
83. James Pope-Hennessy, *A Lonely Business*, p. 234.
84. Stephen Birmingham, *Duchess*, p. 273.
85. Cecil Beaton, *Self Portrait with Friends*, p. 397.

BIBLIOGRAPHY

Queen Elizabeth the Queen Mother

ANONYMOUS, *King George and Queen Elizabeth*, Allied Newspapers, London, 1937.

ANONYMOUS, *Our King and Queen and the Royal Princesses*, Odhams, London, 1937.

ANONYMOUS, *The Coronation of King George VI and Queen Elizabeth*, Odhams, London, 1937.

ANONYMOUS, *The Coronation of Their Majesties King George VI and Queen Elizabeth. Official Souvenir Programme*, Odhams, London, 1937.

ANONYMOUS, *Their Majesties' Silver Wedding*, Pitkins, London, 1948.

ANONYMOUS, *The King and Queen with their People*, John Murray, London, 1941.

ANONYMOUS, *The Queen Mother*, Purnell Books, Maidenhead, Berkshire, 1980.

ANONYMOUS, *The Queen Mother: Tribute to a Royal Lady*, Harmsworth, London, 1980.

ANONYMOUS, *The Royal Family in Wartime*, Odhams, London, 1945.

ASQUITH, Lady Cynthia, *Queen Elizabeth: Her Intimate and Authentic Life*, Hutchinson, London, 1937.

The Duchess of York, Hutchinson, London, 1928.

The Family Life of Her Majesty Queen Elizabeth, Hutchinson, London, 1937.

The Married Life of Her Royal Highness The Duchess of York, Hutchinson, London, 1933.

The Queen, Hutchinson, London, 1937.

BAXTER, Beverley, *Destiny Called Them*, Oxford University Press, London, 1939.

BECKLES, Gordon, *Coronation Souvenir Book*, Daily Express, London, 1937.

BIRCH, Margaret, *Her Majesty Queen Elizabeth The Queen Mother*, IPC Magazines, London, 1973.

BIRT, Catherine, *Her Majesty Queen Elizabeth The Queen Mother*, Pitkins, London, 1952.

BOLITHO, Hector, *Their Majesties*, Max Parrish, London, 1951.

'The Queen's American Ancestors', pp. 7–10, *Past and Future*, London, December 1958.

BOORMAN, Henry R. P., *Merry America: Their Majesties' Tour of Canada, the United States of America and Newfoundland, 1939*, Kent Messenger, Maidstone, 1939.

CARNEGIE, Robert K., *And the People Cheered: An Account of the Visit of the King and Queen to Canada, 1939*, Legionary Library, Ottawa, 1940.

CATHCART, Helen, *The Queen Mother*, W. H. Allen, London, 1965.
The Queen Mother Herself, W. H. Allen, London, 1979; Hamlyn Paperbacks, London, 1980.

CHATWYN, Alys, *H.R.H. The Duchess of York*, W. Collins Sons & Co., London, 1928.

COOK, Elsie T., *Royal Cavalcade: The Coronation Book of King George VI and Queen Elizabeth*, Ward Lock, London and Melbourne, 1937.

CURLING, Bill, *Royal Champion: The Story of Steeplechasing's First Lady*, Michael Joseph, London, 1980.

DARBYSHIRE, Taylor, *The Royal Tour of the Duke and Duchess of York*, Edward Arnold, London, 1927.

DAY, James Wentworth, *The Queen Mother's Family Story*, Robert Hale, London, 1967.

DONALDSON, Frances [Lady Donaldson of Kingsbridge], *King George VI and Queen Elizabeth*, Weidenfeld and Nicolson, London, 1977.

DUFF, David, *Elizabeth of Glamis*, Frederick Muller, London, 1973; Magnum Books, London, 1977, 1980.
George and Elizabeth: A Royal Marriage, Collins, London, 1983.
Mother of the Queen, Frederick Muller, London, 1965.

ELLIS, Jennifer, *Elizabeth, The Queen Mother*, Hutchinson, London, 1953.

FIFE, Charles W. D., *King George VI and Queen Elizabeth*, Rankin Bros, London, 1937.

FRANCIS, Dick, *The Sport of Queens*, Michael Joseph, London, 1974.

HALL, Angus, *The Queen Mother: 75 Glorious Years*, Phoebus/BPC Publishing, London, 1975.

HALL, Trevor, *The Queen Mother And Her Family*, Colour Library Books, Guildford, 1983.

HARDY, Charles, *John Bowes and the Bowes Museum*, Frank Graham, Newcastle-Upon-Tyne, 1970.

HERBERT, Ivor, *The Queen Mother's Horses*, Pelham Books, London, 1967.

KEAY, Douglas, *Queen Elizabeth The Queen Mother*, IPC Magazines, London, 1980.

LANE, Peter, *The Queen Mother*, Robert Hale, London, 1979.

LAIRD, Dorothy, *Queen Elizabeth The Queen Mother*, Hodder and Stoughton, London, 1966; Coronet Books, London, 1975.

LANG, Mrs Andrew, *The Book of Princes and Princesses*, Longmans, Green and Co., London, 1908.

LASCELLES, Gertrude [The Hon. Mrs Francis Lascelles], *Our Duke and Duchess*, Hutchinson, London, 1932.

LIVERSIDGE, Douglas, *The Queen Mother*, Arthur Barker, London, 1977; 1980.

LONGFORD, Elizabeth, Countess of, *The Queen Mother*, Weidenfeld and Nicolson, London, 1981; Granada Publishing, London, 1981.

LUCAS, Ian F. M., *The Royal Embassy: The Duke and Duchess's Tour of Australasia*, Methuen, London, 1927.

MORRAH, Dermot, *The Royal Family in Africa*, Hutchinson, London, 1947.

MORRISON, Ian A., *H.M. Queen Elizabeth The Queen Mother*, Ladybird Books, Loughborough, 1982.

MORROW, Ann, *The Queen Mother*, Granada, London, 1984.

MURRAY, G. M. (Preface), *The Coronation of King George VI and Queen Elizabeth*, Crouch & Co., London, 1937.

NICKOLLS, L. A., *The First Family*, Macdonald & Co., London, 1950.

PATIENCE, Sally, *The Queen Mother*, Lutterworth Press, Guildford, 1977.

REED, Freddie, *The Queen Mother and Her Family: A Personal Tribute*, W. H. Allen, London, 1979.

ROGERS, Malcolm, *The Queen Mother: A Celebration*, National Portrait Gallery, London, 1980.

SAVILLE, Margaret, *H.M. Queen Elizabeth The Queen Mother*, Pitkins, London, 1953.

SHEW, Betty Spencer, *Queen Elizabeth The Queen Mother*, Hodder and Stoughton, London, 1955.

SHEWELL-COOPER, W. E., *The Royal Gardeners: King George VI and his Queen*, Cassell, London, 1952.

SINCLAIR, David, *Queen and Country: The Life of Elizabeth the Queen Mother*, J. M. Dent, London, 1979; Fontana Paperbacks, 1980.

TALBOT, Godfrey, *The Country Life Book of Queen Elizabeth The Queen Mother*, Country Life Books, London, 1978.

Queen Elizabeth The Queen Mother, Jarrold & Sons, Norwich, 1973.

VARIOUS, *The Queen's Book of The Red Cross*, Hodder and Stoughton, London, 1939.

WAKEFORD, Geoffrey, *Thirty Years A Queen*, Robert Hale, London, 1968.

WULFF, Louis, *Silver Wedding*, Sampson Low, Marston & Co., London, 1948.

The Duchess of Windsor

AMORY, Cleveland, *Who Killed Society?*, Harper, New York, 1960.

BALFOUR, Sir John, *Encounters with the Windsors*, unpublished private account, undated.

BIRMINGHAM, Stephen, *Duchess: The Story of Wallis Warfield Windsor*, Macmillan, London, 1981.

BOCCA, Geoffrey, *She Might Have Been Queen*, Express Books, London, 1955; originally published as *The Woman Who Would Be Queen*, Rhinehart, New York, 1954.

BRODY, Iles, *Gone with the Windsors*, Winston Publishers, Philadelphia, 1953.

BROOKMAN, Laura Lou, *see* WILSON, Edwina H.

BRYAN, J. III, and MURPHY, Charles J. V., *The Windsor Story*, Granada, London, 1979.

COOKE, Anne Kirk, and LIGHTFOOT, Elizabeth, *The Other Mrs. Simpson: Postscript to the Love Story of the Century*, Vantage Press Inc., New York, 1977.

GARRETT, Richard, *Mrs. Simpson*, Arthur Barker, London, 1979.

HOOD, Dina Wells, *Working for the Windsors*, Allan Wingate, London, 1957.

MARTIN, Ralph G., *The Woman He Loved*, W. H. Allen, London, 1974.

MONTAGUE-SMITH, Patrick, 'The Title of H.R.H.', *Debrett's Peerage, Baronetage, Knightage and Companionage*, 170th year, edited by Patrick Montague-Smith, Kelly's Directories, Kingston-Upon-Thames, 1972.

MOSLEY, Diana [The Hon. Lady Mosley], *The Duchess of Windsor*, Sidgwick and Jackson, London, 1980.

ST JOHNS, Adela Rogers, *The Honeycomb*, Doubleday and Company, Inc., Garden City, New York, 1969.

THOMAS, Philip M., 'The Duchess of Windsor – Her Position Reappraised', 104th edition, *Burke's Peerage, Baronetage and Knightage*, edited by Peter Townend, Burke's Peerage Limited, London, 1967.

WILSON Edwina H. (pseudonym of Laura Lou BROOKMAN), *Her Name Was Wallis Warfield*, E. P. Dutton & Co. Inc., New York, 1936.

WINDSOR, The Duchess of, *Some Favourite Southern Recipes*, Charles Scribner's Sons, New York, 1942.

The Heart has its Reasons, Michael Joseph, London, 1956.

King Edward VIII – The Duke of Windsor

ALLEN, Peter, *The Crown and the Swastika*, Robert Hale, London, 1983.

ARBELLOT DE VACQUER, Simon, *Edouard VIII, Roi Moderne*, Denöel et Steele, Paris, 1936.

BEAVERBROOK, Lord, *The Abdication of King Edward VIII*, edited by A. J. P. Taylor, Hamish Hamilton, London, 1966.

BIRCH, Neville Hamilton, and BRAMSON, Alan, *Captains and Kings*, Pitman, London, 1972.

BLOCH, Michael, *The Duke of Windsor's War*, Weidenfeld and Nicolson, London, 1982.

Operation Willi, Weidenfeld and Nicolson, London, 1984.

BOLITHO, Hector, *King Edward VIII: His Life and Reign*, Eyre and Spottiswoode, London, 1937.

With the Prince in New Zealand, Edwin Sayes, Auckland, 1920.

BROAD, Lewis, *The Abdication: Twenty-Five Years After*, Frederick Muller, London, 1961.

CHASE, Edna Woolman, and CHASE, Ilka, *Always in Vogue*, Victor Gollancz, London, 1954.

COOKE, Alistair, 'Edward VIII, The Golden Boy', in *Six Men*, The Bodley Head, London, 1977.

CURTIES, Henry, *A Forgotten Prince of Wales*, Everett & Co., London, 1912.

DENNIS, Geoffrey, *Coronation Commentary*, William Heinemann, London, 1937.

DONALDSON, Frances [Lady Donaldson of Kingsbridge], *Edward VIII*, Weidenfeld and Nicolson, London, 1974.

DUPUCH, Etienne, 'Governorship of the Duke of Windsor', in *Bahamas Handbook*, Nassau, 1960.

GRAHAM, Evelyn, *Edward P., a New and Intimate Life Story of H.R.H. The Prince of Wales*, Ward, Lock & Co., London and Melbourne, 1929.

HANSARD, *The Parliamentary Debates*, Fifth Series, Volume CCCXXXI, House of Lords, seventh volume of Session, and House of Commons, Fifth Series, Volume 838, Her Majesty's Stationery Office, London, 1972.

HARRIS, Kenneth, *Kenneth Harris Talking To*, Weidenfeld and Nicolson, London, 1971.

HIBBERT, Christopher, *Edward: The Uncrowned King*, Macdonald, London, 1972.

INGLIS, Brian, *Abdication*, Hodder and Stoughton, London, 1966.

KINROSS, Lord (3rd Baron), *The Windsor Years*, William Collins & Sons, London, 1967.

LEEDS, Stanton B., *Cards the Windsors Hold*, J. B. Lippincott Co., Philadelphia and New York, 1937.

LEGGE, Edward, *Our Prince*, Eveleigh Nash, London, 1921.

MACKENZIE, Compton, *The Windsor Tapestry*, Rich and Cowan, London, 1938.

MAINE, Basil, *Edward VIII: Duke of Windsor*, Hutchinson, London, 1937.

MERRIS, V. A., *Eduard, Herzog von Windsor*, Höger-Verlag, Vienna, 1937.

MOORE, Harras, *The Prince of Wales and His Bride*, Digby Burnand & Co., London, 1921.

OWEN, Frank, and THOMPSON, R. J. T., *His Was The Kingdom*, Arthur Barker, London, 1937.

PARKHURST, Genevieve, *A King in the Making*, G. P. Putnam's Sons, New York and London, 1925.

PYE, Michael, *The King Over The Water*, Hutchinson, London, 1981.

RAVEN, Simon, *Edward and Mrs. Simpson*, television drama series in seven episodes, produced by Andrew Brown and directed by Waris Hussein, unpublished scripts, Thames Television, London, 1978.

RYTON, Royce, *Crown Matrimonial*, a play in two acts, directed by Peter Dews. Unpublished play script, Michael Codron Ltd, London, 1972.

SENCOURT, Robert, *The Reign of Edward the Eighth*, Anthony Gibbs and Phillips, London, 1962.

TOWNSEND, W. and L., *The Biography of H.R.H. The Prince of Wales*, Albert E. Marriott & Son, London, 1929.

VERNEY, Frank E., *H.R.H. – A Character Study of the Prince of Wales*, Hodder and Stoughton, London, 1926.

WELLS, Warren Bradley, *Why Edward Went*, R. M. McBride & Co., New York, 1937.

WHITE, J. Lincoln, *The Abdication of Edward VIII*, G. Routledge and Sons, London, 1937.

WINDSOR, HRH The Duke of, *A Family Album*, Cassell, London, 1960.
A King's Story, Cassell, London, 1951.
The Crown and the People, 1902–1953, Cassell, London, 1953.
Windsor Revisited, Houghton Mifflin, Boston, 1960.
Series of six articles, *Daily News*, New York, December 11–16, 1966.

King George VI

BEAL, Erica, *King-Emperor: The Life of King George VI*, Collins, London, 1941.

BOLITHO, Hector, *George VI*, Eyre and Spottiswoode, London, 1937.

BROAD, Lewis, *Crowning the King*, Hutchinson, London, 1937.

BUXTON, Aubrey, *The King in his Country*, Longmans, Green & Co., London, 1955.

DARBYSHIRE, Taylor (Edited), *In the Words of the King: Selected Speeches of George VI*, Hutchinson, London, 1938.
King George VI: An Intimate and Authentic Life, Hutchinson, London, 1937.
The Duke of York, Hutchinson, London, 1929.

FIFE, Charles W. D., *King George VI and his Empire*, Rankin Bros, London, 1937.

FULFORD, Roger, *His Most Excellent Majesty George the Sixth*, Pitkins, London, 1952.

GORDON, Keith V., *The King in Peace and War*, John Lane, London, 1940.

GORMAN, Major J. T., *George VI: King and Emperor*, W. & B. Foyle, London, 1937.

GREATOREX, Clifford, *King George VI, The People's Sovereign*, RTS-Lutterworth Press, London, 1939.

GROOM, Arthur, *The Authentic Pictorial Record of King George VI*, Pitkins, London, 1952.

HYDE, Robert R., *The Camp Book*, Ernest Benn, London, 1930.

INDUSTRIAL WELFARE SOCIETY, *King George VI and Industry: A Tribute*, Industrial Welfare Society, London, 1952.

JUDD, Denis, *King George VI 1895–1952*, Michael Joseph, London, 1982.

MEE, Arthur, *Salute the King*, Hodder and Stoughton, London, 1937.

MIDDLEMAS, Keith, *The Life and Times of George VI*, Weidenfeld and Nicolson, London, 1974.

MOFFATT, James, *King George Was My Shipmate*, Stanley Paul & Co., London, 1940.

PANETH, P., *King George VI and His People*, Alliance Press, London, 1944.

PUDNEY, John, *His Majesty King George VI*, Hutchinson, London, 1952.

STUART, Dorothy Margaret, *King George the Sixth*, George G. Harrap & Co., London, 1937.

THOMPSON, G. M., *The Life and Times of King George VI*, Odhams Press, London, 1952.

TOWNSEND, Peter, *The Last Emperor: King George VI and his Reign*, Weidenfeld and Nicolson, London, 1975; Panther, London, 1978.

VARIOUS, *Crown and Empire: The Coronation of King George VI*, The Times Publishing Company, London, 1937.

WHEELER-BENNETT, John W., *King George VI: His Life and Reign*, Macmillan, London, 1958.

The Royal Family

ALICE, HRH Princess, Countess of Athlone, *For My Grandchildren*, Evans Brothers, London, 1966.

ALICE, HRH Princess, Duchess of Gloucester, *The Memoirs of Princess Alice, Duchess of Gloucester*, Collins, London, 1983.

BROUGH, James, *Margaret: The Tragic Princess*, W. H. Allen, London, 1978.

BROWN, Craig, and CUNLIFFE, Lesley, *The Book of Royal Lists*, Routledge & Kegan Paul, London, 1982.

CATHCART, Helen, *Her Majesty*, W. H. Allen, London, 1962.
Princess Alexandra, W. H. Allen, London, 1967.

Royal Lodge, Windsor, W. H. Allen, London, 1966.

Sandringham: The Story of a Royal Home, W. H. Allen, London, 1964.

CHRISTOPHER, HRH Prince, of Greece, *Memoirs of H.R.H. Prince Christopher of Greece*, Hurst and Blackett, London, 1938.

CRAWFORD, Marion, *Princess Margaret*, George Newnes, London, 1953.
The Little Princesses, Cassell, London, 1950; Harcourt, Brace and Company, New York, 1950.

DEMPSTER, Nigel, *H.R.H. The Princess Margaret: A Life Unfulfilled*, Quartet Books, London, 1981.

DUNCAN, Andrew, *The Reality of Monarchy*, Heinemann, London, 1970.

ELLIOT, Roger, *Astrology and the Royal Family*, Pan Books, London, 1977.

FISHER, Graham and Heather, *Prince Andrew*, W. H. Allen, London, 1981.

FRANKLAND, Noble, *Prince Henry, Duke of Gloucester*, Weidenfeld and Nicolson, London, 1980.

FRASER, Lady Antonia (Edited), *The Lives of the Kings and Queens of England*, Weidenfeld and Nicolson, London, 1975.

FRERE, James A., *The British Monarchy At Home*, Anthony Gibbs & Phillips, London, 1963.

GORE, John, *King George V: A Personal Memoir*, John Murray, London, 1941.

HAMILTON, Willie, MP, *My Queen and I*, Quartet Books, London, 1975.

HARDINGE, Helen [The Dowager Lady Hardinge of Penshurst], *Loyal to Three Kings*, William Kimber, London, 1967.

HAREWOOD, The Earl of, *The Tongs and the Bones: The Memoirs of Lord Harewood*, Weidenfeld and Nicolson, London, 1981.

HARRIS, Leonard M., *Long to Reign Over Us?*, William Kimber, London, 1966.

HIBBERT, Christopher, *The Court at Windsor*, Longmans, London, 1964.

HOLDEN, Anthony, *Charles, Prince of Wales*, Weidenfeld and Nicolson, London, 1979.

HOUGH, Richard, *Edwina, Countess Mountbatten of Burma*, Weidenfeld and Nicolson, London, 1983.

LACEY, Robert, *Majesty: Elizabeth II and the House of Windsor*, Hutchinson, London, 1977.

LAIRD, Dorothy, *How The Queen Reigns*, Hodder and Stoughton, London, 1959.

LONGFORD, Elizabeth, Countess of, *Elizabeth R*, Weidenfeld and Nicolson, London, 1983.
The Royal House of Windsor, Weidenfeld and Nicolson, London, 1974.
Victoria R.I., Weidenfeld and Nicolson, London, 1964.

MARIE LOUISE, HH Princess, *My Memories of Six Reigns*, Evans Brothers, London, 1956.

MARTIN, Kingsley, *The Crown and the Establishment*, Hutchinson, London, 1962.

MORRAH, Dermot, *Princess Elizabeth, Duchess of Edinburgh*, Odhams, London, 1950.
The Royal Family, Odhams Press, London, 1950.
The Work of The Queen, William Kimber, London, 1958.

MORROW, Ann, *The Queen*, Granada, London, 1983.

NICOLSON, Harold, *King George V*, Constable, London, 1952; Pan Books, London, 1967.

POPE-HENNESSY, James, *Queen Mary, 1867–1953*, George Allen and Unwin, London, 1959.

RING, Anne, *The Story of Princess Elizabeth*, John Murray, London, 1930.

ROSE, Kenneth, *King George V*, Weidenfeld and Nicolson, London, 1983.

TOWNSEND, Peter, *Time and Chance*, Collins, London, 1978.

Other Works

AIRLIE, Mabell, Countess of, *Thatched with Gold*, Edited by Jennifer Ellis, Hutchinson, London, 1962.

ALSOP, Susan Mary, *To Marietta from Paris, 1945–1960*, Weidenfeld and Nicolson, London, 1976.

ARGYLL, Margaret Duchess of, *Forget Not*, W. H. Allen, London, 1975.

ASQUITH, Lady Cynthia, *Diaries 1915–18*, Hutchinson, London, 1968.

ATHOLL, Katharine Duchess of, *Working Partnership*, Arthur Barker, London, 1958.

BARROW, Andrew, *Gossip: A History of High Society from 1920 to 1970*, Hamish Hamilton, London, 1978.
International Gossip: A History of High Society, 1970–1980, Hamish Hamilton, London, 1983.

BEATON, Cecil, *Self Portrait with Friends: The Selected Diaries of Sir Cecil Beaton, 1926–1974*, edited by Richard Buckle, Weidenfeld and Nicolson, London, 1979.

BIRKENHEAD, 2nd Earl of, *Lord Halifax*, Hamish Hamilton, London, 1965.
Walter Monckton, Weidenfeld and Nicolson, London, 1969.

BOVE, Dr Charles F., *A Paris Surgeon's Story*, Little, Brown and Company, Boston, 1956.

BURKE, Anna Christian, *The Language of Flowers*, Compiled and Edited by Mrs L. Burke, Hugh Evelyn, London, 1963.

CHANNON, Sir Henry, *Chips: The Diaries of Sir Henry Channon*, edited by Robert Rhodes James, Weidenfeld and Nicolson, London, 1967.

COLVILLE, Lady Cynthia, *A Crowded Life*, Evans Brothers, London, 1963.

COOPER, Lady Diana, *The Light of Common Day*, Rupert Hart-Davis, London, 1959.

COZENS-HARDY, H. T., *The Glorious Years*, Robert Hale, London, 1953.

COWARD, Sir Noël, *The Noël Coward Diaries*, edited by Graham Payn and Sheridan Morley, Weidenfeld and Nicolson, London, 1982.

DAVIDSON, J. C. C., *Memoirs of a Conservative*, edited by R. V. R. James, Weidenfeld and Nicolson, London, 1969.

DUGDALE, Blanche, *Baffy: The Diaries of Blanche Dugdale 1936–1947*, edited by N. A. Rose, Valentine, Mitchell, London, 1973.

DUPUCH, Sir Etienne, *Tribune Story*, Ernest Benn, Tonbridge, 1967.

GILBERT, Martin, *Finest Hour: Winston Churchill 1939–41*, Heinemann, London, 1983.

GLENDINNING, Victoria, *Edith Sitwell: A Unicorn Among Lions*, Weidenfeld and Nicolson, London, 1981.

GOLDSMITH, Barbara, *Little Gloria . . . Happy At Last*, Macmillan, London, 1980.

GOODMAN, Jean, *Edward Seago: The Other Side of the Canvas*, Collins, London, 1978.

GORDON, Elizabeth Gordon Biddle, *Days of Now and Then*, Dorrance and Co., Philadelphia, 1945.

GÖRING, Emmy, *My Life with Göring*, David Bruce and Watson, London, 1972.

HAMON, Count Louis, *Cheiro's World Predictions*, London Publishing Co., London, 1927.

HARRISON, Tom, *Living Through the Blitz*, Collins, London, 1976.

HARTNELL, Norman, *Silver and Gold*, Odhams, London, 1955.

HYDE, H. Montgomery, *Baldwin: The Unexpected Prime Minister*, Hart-Davis, MacGibbon, London, 1973.
The Quiet Canadian, Hamish Hamilton, London, 1962.

JONES, Nellie W., *A School for Bishops: A history of the Church of St. Michael and All Angels, Baltimore*, Sowers Printing Co., Lebanon, Pennsylvania, 1952.

JUNE [Mrs Edward Hillman, formerly Lady Inverclyde], *The Glass Ladder*, Heinemann, London, 1960.

LEES-MILNE, James, *Harold Nicolson, 1886–1929*, Chatto and Windus, London, 1980.
Harold Nicolson, 1930–1968, Chatto and Windus, London, 1981.

LESLEY, Cole, *The Life of Noël Coward*, Jonathan Cape, London, 1976.

LESLIE, Anita, *Mrs. Fitzherbert*, Hutchinson, London, 1960.

LINDSAY OF DOWHILL, Loelia, Lady [Loelia, Duchess of Westminster], *Cocktails and Laughter*, edited by Hugo Vickers, Hamish Hamilton, London, 1983.

LOCKHART, J. G., *Cosmo Gordon Lang*, Hodder and Stoughton, London, 1949.

LOCKHART, Sir Robert Bruce, *The Diaries of Sir Robert Bruce Lockhart, 1915–1938*, edited by Kenneth Young, Macmillan, London, 1973.
  The Diaries of Sir Robert Bruce Lockhart, 1939–1965, edited by Kenneth Young, Macmillan, London, 1980.

LOWNDES, Marie Belloc, *Diaries and Letters of Marie Belloc Lowndes, 1911–1947*, edited by Susan Lowndes, Chatto and Windus, London, 1971.

MACLEOD, Iain, *Neville Chamberlain*, Frederick Muller, London, 1961.

MADAN, Geoffrey, *Geoffrey Madan's Notebooks*, Oxford University Press, London, 1981.

MARLBOROUGH, Laura Duchess of, *Laughter from a Cloud*, Weidenfeld and Nicolson, London, 1980.

MASTERS, Brian, *The Dukes*, Blond and Briggs, London, 1975.

MIDDLEMAS, Keith, and BARNES, John, *Baldwin: A Biography*, Weidenfeld and Nicolson, London, 1969.

MINNEY, R. J. (Edited), *The Private Papers of Hore-Belisha*, Collins, London, 1960.

MORAN, Lord, *Winston Churchill, The Struggle for Survival*, Constable, London, 1966.

MOSLEY, Diana [The Hon. Lady Mosley], *A Life of Contrasts*, Hamish Hamilton, London, 1977.

MOSLEY, Sir Oswald, *My Life*, Thomas Nelson & Sons, London, 1968.

NEAGLE, Dame Anna, *There's Always Tomorrow*, W. H. Allen, London, 1974; Futura, London, 1979.

NICOLSON, Harold, *Diaries and Letters 1930–1939*, edited by Nigel Nicolson, Collins, London, 1966.
  Diaries and Letters 1939–1945, edited by Nigel Nicolson, Collins, London, 1967.
  Diaries and Letters 1945–1962, edited by Nigel Nicolson, Collins, London, 1968.

PALMER, Lilli, *Change Lobsters and Dance*, W. H. Allen, London, 1976.

PICKSTON, Margaret, *The Language of Flowers*, Michael Joseph, London, 1968.

POPE-HENNESSY, James, *A Lonely Business: A Self-Portrait of James Pope-Hennessy*, edited by Peter Quennell, Weidenfeld and Nicolson, London, 1981.

RICHARDSON, Joanna, *The Disastrous Marriage*, Jonathan Cape, London, 1960.

SAUNDERS, Peter, *The Mousetrap Man*, Collins, London, 1972.

SCHMIDT, Paul, *Hitler's Interpreter*, Edited by R. H. C. Steed, Heinemann, London, 1951.

SCOTT, Sir Walter, *Letters on Demonology and Witchcraft*, John Murray, London, 1830.

SHERWOOD, Robert E., *Roosevelt and Hopkins*, Harper, New York, 1948.

SHIRER, William L., *The Rise and Fall of the Third Reich*, Secker and Warburg, London, 1970.

SLATER, Leonard, *Aly, a biography*, W. H. Allen, London, 1966.

SOAMES, Mary, Lady, *Clementine Churchill*, Cassell, London, 1979.

SPEER, Albert, *Inside the Third Reich*, Weidenfeld and Nicolson, London, 1970.

STEVENSON, Frances, *Lloyd George: A Diary*, edited by A. J. P. Taylor, Hutchinson, London, 1971.

STUART, Denis, *Dear Duchess: Millicent, Duchess of Sutherland, 1867–1955*, Victor Gollancz, London, 1982.

STUART, James [1st Viscount Stuart of Findhorn], *Within the Fringe*, The Bodley Head, London, 1967.

TEMPLEWOOD, Lord, *Nine Troubled Years*, Collins, London, 1954.

THORNTON, Michael, *Jessie Matthews*, Hart-Davis, MacGibbon, London, 1974; Mayflower Books, St Albans, 1975.

TOLAND, John, *Adolf Hitler*, Doubleday & Co. Inc., New York, 1976.

TREE, Ronald, *When The Moon Was High: Memoirs of Peace and War, 1897–1942*, Macmillan, London, 1975.

UNDERWOOD, Peter, *No Common Task*, Harrap, London, 1983.

USTINOV, Peter, *Dear Me*, William Heinemann, London, 1977; Penguin Books, London, 1978.

VANDERBILT, Gloria, and FURNESS, Thelma Viscountess, *Double Exposure*, Frederick Muller, London, 1959.

VICKERS, Hugo (Edited), *Cocktails and Laughter, The Albums of Loelia Lindsay*, Hamish Hamilton, London, 1983.

WATSON, Francis, *Dawson of Penn*, Chatto and Windus, London, 1950.

WHEELER-BENNETT, John W., *Special Relationships: America in Peace and War*, Macmillan Press, London, 1975.

YOUNG, G. M., *Stanley Baldwin*, Rupert Hart-Davis, London, 1952.

ZIEGLER, Philip, *Diana Cooper*, Hamish Hamilton, London, 1981.

ACKNOWLEDGEMENTS

A work spanning more than eighty years of documentation could scarcely be written, as this has been, on a small island in the Mediterranean, without a large amount of goodwill, kindness and patient assistance on the part of many people.

I am grateful to the members of the Royal Family, and in particular to Her Majesty Queen Elizabeth The Queen Mother, for allowing my questions to be answered so fully in spite of their awareness that the subject matter of this book might not be to their liking.

My thanks go in full measure to the following representatives who, over the years, have replied to me on behalf of The Queen, Queen Elizabeth The Queen Mother, the Duchess of Windsor, Princess Anne, Princess Margaret, Princess Alice, Duchess of Gloucester, the Duke and Duchess of Kent, Prince and Princess Michael of Kent, and Princess Alexandra: Mr Ronald Allison, Mr Michael Shea, Mr John Haslam, Lt.-Colonel Sir Martin Gilliat, Mrs D. R. Murphy (formerly Miss Lucy Gosling), the late Mr John Utter, Miss Johanna Schütz, Lord Napier and Ettrick, Lt.-Colonel Sir Simon Bland, Lt.-Commander Sir Richard Buckley, Miss Alison Dixon, and Miss Mona Mitchell.

To five people I owe a special debt of gratitude: to the Earl of Dudley, for allowing me to see and use a letter written by his mother, the late Viscountess Ednam, to his grandmother, Millicent Duchess of Sutherland; to the Hon. Julian Hardinge, for kindly consulting on my behalf unpublished entries in the diaries of his grandmother, the late Dowager Lady Hardinge of Penshurst; to Mr Hugo Vickers, who generously took time off from the major task of writing the official biography of Sir Cecil Beaton in order to reply to a long series of letters and questions; to Mrs Colin Wheeler, of Fleet in Hampshire, whose kindness in tape recording broadcasts and television programmes has proved invaluable; and to Mr Dick Barton, who has repeatedly interrupted his own career in journalism in order to make telephone calls, resolve uncertainties and obtain photocopies on my behalf.

My thanks also go to the following people for replying to my letters and questions: Mr Harold A. Albert, the Reverend Keith Angus (Minister of Crathie), Margaret Duchess of Argyll, Mr Philip Attenborough, Lord Blake, Mr Michael Bloch, Mr Mark Bonham Carter, the Hon. Lady Bowes-Lyon, Mr Simon Bowes-Lyon, Miss Celia Brayfield, Professor Michael Brock (Warden of Nuffield College, Oxford), Mr Hugo Brunner, Mr Joseph Bryan III, Mary Duchess of Buccleuch, Mr J. R. Cater, Miss Helen Cathcart, Mr Michael Codron, Mr Michael Colefax, Mrs Norman Colville, Miss Mary Cooling, Lady Diana Cooper, the late Sir Noël Coward, Miss Marion Crawford (Mrs George Buthlay), Mrs Susan Crosland, Mr Jeremy Deedes, Lady Donaldson of Kingsbridge, Mr John Ellison, Mr Alastair Forbes, the Reverend Dendle French (Vicar of St Paul's Walden), Mr Roger Elliot, Mr Brodrick Haldane, the late Dowager Lady Hardinge of Penshurst, Lord Hardinge of Penshurst, Dr Harford Montgomery Hyde, Mr Brian Inglis, Mr A. L. Ingram (Procurator Fiscal, Forfar), Miss Dorothy Laird, Mr Peter Lane, Mr Jack Le Vien, Mr Douglas Liversidge, Lady Lloyd, the Countess of Longford, Viscount Margesson, Laura Duchess of Marlborough, the late Mrs Gilbert Miller, Mr Patrick Montague-Smith, Mr Hugh Montgomery-Massingberd, Miss Ann Morrow, the Hon. Lady Mosley, the late Earl Mountbatten of Burma, Colonel Charles J. V. Murphy, Mr Patrick Nicholson, Mr Peter Ord (Glamis Castle Estate Office), the Earl of Oxford and Asquith, the late Lady Victor Paget, Mr Nicholas Paget, Mr William Payne, Sir Ronald Preston, Mr Peter Quennell, the Countess of Rosebery, Mr Charles Russell, Mr Terence St John, the Earl of Snowdon, Lady Soames, Mr Godfrey Talbot, Sir Edward Tomkins, Mrs Renée Tovey, Mr Peter Townend, Lord Wigram, the Countess of Willingdon, Mrs Melisande M. Woodside, and Mr Philip Ziegler.

I have received extensive help and documentation from the librarians, staff and archivists of many organisations. Among these I would particularly like to thank the staff of the British Library Reading Room, Bibliographical Information Service, and Newspaper Library at Colindale; Denise Drummond and the staff of the City of Westminster Central Reference Library; Miss M. J. Swarbrick, Chief Archivist at the City of Westminster Archives Department; Ann Duce at the City of Westminster Marylebone Library; Irene F. Pollock, Keeper of Enquiry Services at the City of London Guildhall Library; the Librarian in charge of the Edinburgh Room at the City of Edinburgh Central Library; the staff of the Theatre Museum

(Enthoven Collection) at the Victoria and Albert Museum; Mr A. E. B. Owen, Senior Under-Librarian at Cambridge University Library; Mrs Joan Auld, Archivist at the University Library, Dundee; Mr D. J. Butler, County Archivist, Durham County Council; Mrs Elizabeth Conran, Curator of The Bowes Museum; Joanne C. Fehlner at the Library of Congress, Washington D.C.; Mr Wesley L. Wilson in the Maryland Department of the Enoch Pratt Free Library, Baltimore, for particular helpfulness concerning the Duchess of Windsor and her family; Margaret and Leonard Halsey-Barrett at the New English Language Library in Mahón, Menorca; Mr W. W. Ellis, Property Records Manager of The Grosvenor Estate; Kathleen A. Bursley of Harcourt Brace Jovanovich Inc.; Mr T. H. Kelly, Librarian of Associated Newspapers Group; Mr J. Bland, Deputy Librarian of Express Newspapers; Mr D. Ash, Librarian of the *Daily Telegraph*; Mr C. P. Wilson, Chief Librarian of *The Times*; Mr James Bishop, Editor of the *Illustrated London News*; and the librarians of *The Observer*, the *New York Times*, *Time* Magazine, New York, and *Woman* (IPC Magazines, London).

I am grateful to the picture librarians of all the photographic agencies consulted, and in particular to Hazel Jones at Syndication International, Liz Moore at the *Illustrated London News*, Paul Matthews at The Photo Source (Keystone Press, Central Press and Fox Photos), Leon Meyer at The Associated Press, Terry Norman at London Express News and Feature Services, and David Spark at Westminster Press.

Jenny Dereham, my expert editor at Michael Joseph, transformed the usually gruelling task of editing the manuscript into a civilized combination of light-heartedness and razor-sharp professionalism; while Dinah Wiener, my accomplished agent at Curtis Brown, maintained throughout a serene aura of confidence, never once wavering in her support or her belief in this project.

Among the personal friends whose help and encouragement has enabled me to complete this book, I want to thank especially Marja-Liisa and Christopher Clark; Elizabeth Taaffe; and, in Menorca, Jane Gray and Terence Hazzard, for so kindly taking and transmitting countless telephone messages; and for their patience and understanding in putting up with my uncertain temper for more than a year, Denise Cheer, Anders Nordenhall, and Nicolau Pons.

The greatest debt of all I have left until last. My sister, Jean Thornton Wheeler, has assisted me from the first day of work on this book until today, the last. She typed the entire manuscript, gave constructive and sometimes penetrating criticisms of each chapter, made many telephone calls on my behalf, visited libraries, undertook research, carried books, cooked all the meals, kept visitors from the door, frequently sustained flagging spirits, and generally put up with complete chaos in her life for more than a year. Never before, surely, has any person made so great a contribution to a published work without actually writing it. To her, my love and gratitude.

MICHAEL THORNTON,
Menorca, 1985.

INDEX